Southeast Asia over Three Generations
Essays Presented to Benedict R. O'G. Anderson

James T. Siegel & Audrey R. Kahin, Editors

Southeast Asia over Three Generations
Essays Presented to Benedict R. O'G. Anderson

Southeast Asia Program Publications
Southeast Asia Program
Cornell University
Ithaca, New York
2003

Editorial Board
  Benedict R. O'G. Anderson
  Tamara Loos
  Stanley O'Connor
  Keith Taylor
  Andrew Willford

Cornell Southeast Asia Program Publications
640 Stewart Avenue, Ithaca, NY 14850-3857

Studies on Southeast Asia No. 36

© 2003 Cornell Southeast Asia Program.

All rights reserved. Except for brief quotations in a review, no part of this book may be reproduced or utilized in any form or by any means, electronic or mechanical, including photocopying and recording, or by any information storage or retrieval system, without permission in writing from the Cornell Southeast Asia Program.

Printed in the United States of America

ISBN 0-87727-735-4

Cover art: from *Lunettes et Télescopes*, by André Danjon and André Couder (Paris: Editions de la Revue D'Optique Théorique et Instrumentale, 1935), p. 667.

TABLE OF CONTENTS

Introduction
   James T. Siegel and Audrey R. Kahin   7

The Construction of National Heroes and/or Heroines
   Charnvit Kasetsiri   13

Laughing at Leviathan: John Furnivall, Dutch New Guinea, and the Ridiculousness of Colonial Rule
   Danilyn Rutherford   27

A New Regime of Order:
The Origin of Modern Surveillance Politics in Indonesia
   Takashi Shiraishi   47

The Specter of Coincidence
   John Pemberton   75

Images of Colonial Cities in Early Indonesian Novels
   Tsuyoshi Kato   91

Hải Vân, *The Storm*, and Vietnamese Communism in the Inter-war Imagination
   Peter Zinoman   125

Move Over, Madonna: Luang Wichit Wathakan's *Huang Rak Haew Luk*
   Thak Chaloemtiarana   145

Foreignness and Vengeance: On Rizal's *El Filibusterismo*
   Vicente L. Rafael   165

The Question of Foreigners: Bai Ren's *Nanyang Piaoliuji* and the Re/making of Chinese and Philippine Nationness
   Caroline S. Hau   189

The Marginalization of the Indians in Malaysia:
Contesting Explanations and the Search for Alternatives
   Francis Loh Kok Wah   223

De-Othering Jek Communists: Rewriting Thai History
from the Viewpoint of the Ethno-Ideological Other
    Kasian Tejapira   245

Pag-ibig, Pagtatalik at Pakikibaka:
Love and Sex inside the Communist Party of the Philippines
    Patricio N. Abinales   263

The Dialectics of "EDSA Dos": Urban Space,
Collective Memory, and the Spectacle of Compromise
    Eva-Lotta E. Hedman   283

Pilkades: Democracy, Village Elections, and Protest in Indonesia
    Douglas Kammen   303

When Soldiers Kill Civilians:
Burma's Crackdown in 1988 in Comparative Perspective
    Mary P. Callahan   331

Other Schools, Other Pilgrimages, Other Dreams:
The Making and Unmaking of *Jihad* in Southeast Asia
    John T. Sidel   347

Interkom in Indonesia: Not Quite an Imagined Community
    Joshua Barker   383

Contributors   397

Introduction

Ben Anderson introduces *The Spectre of Comparisons* with an anecdote about himself, Sukarno, and a diplomat whom he does not identify. Sukarno is speaking, and Ben is translating for the diplomat. Sukarno speaks of Hitler and the Third Reich. The Third Reich is not the result of mass murder and world war. It is, in Sukarno's language, a nationalist paradise. Hitler, for his part, is neither a murderer, nor an anti-Semite, nor a fascist. The Third Reich becomes a nationalist paradise. The diplomat does not believe what Sukarno is saying. "Are you sure that's really what he's saying?"

Ben is sure. I think I might have doubted my linguistic capacity in that circumstance, but Ben is a true polyglot, and he is not in the habit of denying much. It is what Sukarno is saying. Ben tries to explain how it would be reasonable to say such a thing. But the diplomat returns to his embassy, furious and convinced that Sukarno "was a demented and dangerous mountebank."

No matter how diplomatic the man was, he could not find what Sukarno said reasonable. Ben himself had difficulty. "I felt a kind of vertigo." But the vertigo comes not merely from the outrageousness of Sukarno's thought. It came from understanding Sukarno's reasonableness once one understood that Sukarno saw Europe through "an inverted telescope." The possibility of another reason, one bearing on the most serious matters, questions of life and death, one says without exaggeration, moved Ben outside his normal, European perspective. But this same perspective, shaped in the first place by his excellent command of languages and the assurance that gives him to take things in at the first level, made him persist. Ben here is the translator, faithful to what he heard. As a translator he could take things in that he would have to reject as someone judging their contents. It is a stance toward the foreign that allows it every possibility to speak for itself. Beyond translation, however, is explication. He tells the diplomat how, as a leftist and a nationalist, Sukarno could think such a thing. It is the moment when he becomes dizzy. Hitler is no longer who he was. "It was going to be difficult from now on to think of 'my' Hitler in the old way."

Which does not mean that he condones Hitler. But it does mean that he is able to hold opposing forms of the reasonable in his mind. And, once more, to enjoy doing so.

I imagine this moment as the point of departure for the efforts that led to the extraordinary essays later collected in *Language and Power*. Essays such as "The Languages of Indonesian Politics" could not have been written unless unwonted and even unwanted thoughts were allowed a place. And they could not have been written unless there was an urge to reflect Indonesia to an unspecified world—a world, that is, which would listen not because it heard what it knew, but which was forced to listen by the power of language. Ben thus from the beginning of his career reflected Indonesia to the world, one says. But the visual metaphor is inadequate since this reflection begins with hearing. Listening to what was said,

Ben could find a reasonableness that would surprise not only him, but also, in my opinion, Sukarno and the other Indonesians whom he heard.

On numerous occasions (but not numerous enough) with Ben and students we had in common, I have seen the process at work. A student would present something. Ben would listen and find in it something that was there, but whose import the student had not yet seen. This, to my mind, was teaching as miracle. It always worked. As a result, his students, talented as they were before they encountered him, found qualities in themselves that they had not suspected. It is this achievement that we want to celebrate at the moment of his retirement.

Without, however, neglecting to emphasize Ben Anderson's early work. It has been forty years since some of the first essays were written. It is not surprising that viewpoints have changed. In political studies, more even than in history and perhaps as much as in anthropology—to mention the fields to which these essays belong—there is process of replacement rather than addition of studies. But these essays have lasted beyond their political half-life. Instead of disappearing, they continue to be suggestive. One cannot classify these studies or say what their central points are. Rather, they open up a world. Rereading them, one recognizes truths, even though in some cases the conditions of those truths have changed radically. The old debate between Harry Benda and Herb Feith came down to a question of whether the Javanese past endures. The answer, though not at all the resolution, can be found in these essays of Ben where one can still see the forces at work which he described nearly a half century ago. One can say the same about *Java in a Time of Revolution,* the book form of Ben's thesis. There is a guiding idea here, and, in my opinion, its significance has been far from exhausted. That the Indonesian revolution was incomplete, that a social revolution never was accomplished, has had effects that are not always on the surface. The New Order maintained itself on the basis of fears that are the remnants of revolutionary incompletion. The killings of 1965-66, and the present stasis of the Indonesian polity, cannot, in my opinion, be understood without reference to the haunting of the revolution whose origin was first delineated in *Java in a Time of Revolution*. I will not speak of Ben's work on nationalism that followed. It has received much attention, just as it deserves. Put alongside the early work, one expects that even when the interest in nationalism wanes, we will still turn to *Imagined Communities* for the richness of its insights and the elegance of its presentation.

Given the strength of his work, one cannot say that Ben's days of teaching have ended with his retirement from Cornell. No one who has read his work can easily put him out of mind, even when, and perhaps especially when, one cannot reduce what one has read to a few summary sentences. What follows from the exposure to such teaching, whether that means simply reading his work or having him as a thesis director, is necessarily various and unpredictable. As his colleague, however, I can testify to its strength. Many theses, not to mention much other work, would have been written in quite different ways were it not for Ben's interventions. It has always been difficult to predict what sort of comments he would make. He comprehended a student's point of view and amplified it. Ben's pedagogic talent allowed the student to speak. His influence has been enormous, but its mark is often invisible. One should not look to the essays that follow for the development of Ben's ideas, though in some essays one can find it. It is our pride, however, to present these pieces for their quality, which, we are convinced, would not be so high had their authors not worked with Ben, because once one has been "reflected back to oneself," one consolidates this vision and then applies it. This does not happen without affection and love. One has to want to listen, and one has to want to be seen in the eyes of the other. Ben stimulated these feelings in others as he displayed them himself. The effects endure as these pieces testify. They are meant to indicate our indebtedness to him.

We solicited articles that show the authors have in mind, but probably in the back of their minds, Ben's regard. We want to concentrate on Southeast Asia as opposed to the theoretical study of nationalism. The latter has received so much attention that Ben's enormous contribution to Southeast Asian studies risks being obscured. We therefore asked contributors to write about particular countries of Southeast Asia. To find the contributors, we went through whatever lists were available to us. It later became apparent that we had missed some names. Furthermore, letters sent to some persons known to us were returned marked "address unknown" months later, when it was too late for the persons to contribute. We apologize to these people. We thank all who contributed. And we note that others wanted to, but could not because of the very short space of time we gave them.

Three generations of researchers appear in this volume. "Generation," in this context, implies modifications of subject matter and of method as younger scholars modify what they have learned from their seniors. But here one cannot discern a common approach or a common subject, or even a development of such over time. Is there then a genealogy? A genealogy comes into being when there is imperative responsiveness. One has to acknowledge one's indebtedness to or one's responsibility for someone else. In questions of scholarship and writing it is, of course, hard to measure indebtedness. Commonality of content is not a measure. But the volume attests to a mutual responsiveness between Ben and his students which once pertained and which continues. Is it, was it, imperative? I cannot say. But one can say that Ben allowed his students great freedom in their subjects and their approaches. The diversity of both in the papers included here show that. They testify as well to the existence of a genealogy which goes unformalized and is all the better for that. Compared to the kinship that governs families, and some scholarly genealogies, the kinship Ben established with his students generated fewer complexes and offered more freedom, which has allowed the talents of these scholars to produce such a variety of interesting and important papers. One expects this to continue in the fourth and fifth generations and beyond, when, inevitably, the influence of Ben might become less apparent. Nonetheless, I am sure it will still be strongly at work, inflecting and reinflecting Southeast Asia and beyond.

James T. Siegel

Bringing the present volume to publication has been a challenge. In drawing the essays together we have always been conscious of Ben's ideas and standards as an editor, for in his editing, to an almost equal degree as in his writing and teaching, he has made an enormous contribution to scholarship on Southeast Asia, particularly on Indonesia. The notable example is the journal *Indonesia*, which he has edited or co-edited for over thirty-five years. It was his brainchild, sprung from conversations with Claire Holt in the early 1960s and largely following the model of the journal *Djawa*, published by the Java Institute in the interwar years. Since its first issue, in April 1966, Ben has shaped and guided its development, making it a meeting place for the network of Indonesia specialists not only in the United States but throughout the world. It is perhaps worth quoting from his own characterization of the journal after its first 25 years:

> ...the halfbreed spirit of *Indonesia* has vigorously lived on. In the leisurely, *liefhebberij* way of *Djawa*, it has continued to publish articles much longer than those usually tolerated by disciplinary journals. The assumption continues to be that readers who know and love their Indonesia are not bored or made restless by Indonesian detail. . . . *Indonesia* has regularly featured controversial "theoretical" essays, debating the nature of Indonesian society and history, as well as current politics and policies; and it has offered analyses of military and civilian leadership groups. It has also carried on the one thing that *Djawa* and the *China Quarterly* had in common—the translation of important vernacular texts—literary, historical, political—to help Indonesian voices speak in their own accents to the outside world.[1]

In some ways this volume has followed *Indonesia* in its eclecticism, expanding the focus from Indonesia to most of the other countries of Southeast Asia as Ben himself has expanded his own focus of interest and research. As with *Indonesia*, imposing an order on the essays has been in many ways arbitrary, for here too the authors have drawn on the myriad aspects of Ben's thoughts and influences, so that topics and themes frequently overlap.

In the opening essay Charnvit Kasetsiri uses Ben's concept of the "imagined community" of a nation as a background to narrating the current efforts in Indonesia to create national heroes to fit within the current national context. At the same time he points up the similarities and differences between the creation of such heroes in Indonesia and Thailand and the interrelationships and overlapping of issues and problems among the peoples of Southeast Asia's archipelagic zone that now provides the core of the largely ineffective ASEAN community.

The subsequent group of essays concentrates on the colonial experience in the Netherlands East Indies. Danilyn Rutherford applies Furnivall's depiction of the ridiculous aspects of British colonialism in Burma as portrayed in *Fashioning of Leviathan* (frequently used by Ben in his classes) to point up similar ludicrous examples in the Dutch expansion into Western New Guinea. At the same time she shows that "absurdity is no stranger to the violent exercise of colonial power," and that this absurdity has contributed to the territory's checkered history during its

---

[1] *Indonesia* 50 (October 1990): 3.

transformation from the Dutch "West New Guinea" through Indonesia's Irian Jaya to its current anomalous status as "Papua."

Takashi Shiraishi focuses on the development of the intelligence services in the Netherlands East Indies—showing that as the Dutch constructed a system of surveillance that was both ubiquitous and obvious they more firmly established a fantasy of subversion, learning little of political value. John Pemberton's discussion of the ghostly qualities revealed by the camera among the 'modern' machines in the sugar factory in Tjolomadoe in Central Java highlights the anomalies of colonial rule. Moving between the ghost inhabiting one of the machines and the ghostly implications of photography, he shows the permeability of the boundaries between the traditional and the modern. Closing the section, Tsuyoshi Kato discusses six Indonesian novels from the early part of the last century. He portrays the struggle of young people seeking independence and identity in the modern cities which are still penetrated and controlled by the agencies of the Dutch colonial state. His essay also provides a bridge to the following contributions which focus on specific novels.

These essays, by Peter Zinoman, Thak Chaoemtiarana, Vicente Rafael and Caroline Hau, reflect Ben's perception of Southeast Asian novels as fields for analyzing the region's history and politics. Peter Zinoman's treatment of Hải Vân (in Vũ Trọng Phụng's *The Storm*) whose background and activities mirror those of Ho Chi Minh, sheds light on late colonial Vietnamese attitudes towards the Indochinese Communist Party and its prime leader. (At the same time its central figure echoes the other outstanding maverick nationalist Communist of the period—Indonesia's Tan Malaka, with whom Ben has always been fascinated.) Thak Chaloemtiarana shifts the focus to Thailand and to *Huanga Rak Haew Luk* by Luang Wichi Wathakan "the architect of Thai nationalism." This novel embraces not only nationalism and modernity, but also issues of gender. Militant feminism appears in the figure of the heroine, who in interacting with members of other nations embodies the energy of emerging Thai nationalism.

While also basing his essay on a single novel, *El Filibusterismo* by the Philippine national hero, José Rizal, Vicente Rafael moves into a consideration of the place of the alien in the national imagination and how this foreignness translates into a nationalism that is specifically Filipino. Here the Castilian language fulfils the role of keeping the foreign in circulation available for use or misuse by either nationalists or colonialists. The boundary that marks the foreign is itself put into question.

The question of foreignness in Philippine society is also the theme of Caroline Hau's essay, this time the overlapping Chinese/Filipino consciousness. Here a consideration of Bai Ren's *Nanyang Piaoliuji* provides the basis for showing how the alienness of Chinese in the Philippines stimulates a double nationalism, Chinese and Filipino. The "hidden history of the Chinese Left in the Philippines and its role in the making of national communities in both China and the Philippines" offers a nuanced view of the possibilities for redefining nationness. In an almost paradoxical way, Hau demonstrates that one can participate in the nationalism of the other and develop one's own nationalism as a result.

The position of the alien, either ethnic or ideological, and its incorporation into the national consciousness is also a preoccupation of the next three essays, where Francis Loh Kok Wah considers the marginalization of the Indian community in Malaysia, Kasian Tejapara examines the role of language in combating the marginalization of the dual elements of Chineseness and Communism in Thai cultural politics, and Patricio Abinales deals with the arguably alien element of communism and its domestication in the Philippines. Abinales' analysis of the 1977 document "On Marriage," put out by the Communist Party of the Philippines, shows the party's struggle to adjust principles of communism to bring them into line with the reality of sexual relations among the younger married and unmarried cadre. Failing in this attempt, it imposes strictures more in accord with the reactionary structures of the Catholic Church.

The last group of essays deals with some of the fundamental questions confronting the countries of contemporary Southeast Asia. Eva Lotte Hedman considers the geographical context of the massive demonstrations in 1986 and 2001 that helped overthrow two Philippine presidents and how the changes in "people power" over fifteen years were reflected in their EDSA location; Doug Kammen examines the place of village level elections in the age of post-Suharto "*reformasi*"; Mary Callahan contrasts the character and experiences of the armies of Burma and Indonesia and how these have affected the responses of each when faced with threats from civilian reformers to their dominant role in the political life of their country; and John Sidel examines the role of "jihad" in the thinking and actions of Islamic movements in the Philippines and Indonesia, considering their background and history as well as their ties to trans-national Islamic institutions and networks and how these have influenced their current character.

Finally, Joshua Barker, in discussing the "interkom," the set of cables connecting houses over various distances, shows us a version of Indonesian dreaming about sociality. The cables, strung up by the users, not by a company or the state, show a desire for sociality not altogether different from that discussed by Tsuyoshi Kato in an earlier Indonesia. There is a dreamy side to its use as a means for chatting, sometimes with neighbors, but sometimes with others known only through their voices. There is, says Barker, "not quite an imagined community, but not quite a face-to-face community either. Perhaps we could call it voice to voice." It is one where it is safe to imagine something a little way beyond the village or the neighborhood to which it is always safe to return. The political implications of such a form of communication are presently only latent. But here is a new technological form of communication linked to old social forms in such a way that it hints at another form of political activity, one different from but comparable to nationalism as Ben understood it.

Audrey R. Kahin

THE CONSTRUCTION OF NATIONAL HEROES AND/OR HEROINES

Charnvit Kasetsiri

If we utilize Professor Benedict Anderson's theory that nations are "imagined communities" and "cultural artifacts," then we will realize that nations are the products of historical developments, and not at all age-old, "natural" phenomena which will persist till the end of time. Accordingly, national heroes and heroines, which are inseparable components of "nation-ness," must also be seen as "cultural artifacts." They have to be constructed, they have to be invented, they have to be processed; most crucially, there have to be "projects" to bring them into existence. Generally speaking, this work of construction is in the hands of ruling classes, which then "spread" them down for the consumption of the middle and lower classes, according to particular temporal and geographic circumstances.

FROM SINGAPORE TO RIAU

Toward the end of October (October 23-25) 1999, I happened to be invited, along with two old friends, Dr. Taufik Abdullah, a historian from Jakarta, and Dr. Cheah Boon Kheng, a historian from Penang, to participate in a national-level seminar on the topic of Indonesian *pahlawan nasional* (national heroes); and on this occasion we were lucky enough to observe close up a very interesting project for the creation of a new such hero.

We took the ferry from Singapore to the industrial park on the island of Batam, about thirty kilometers away. In less than half an hour, we set foot on Indonesian soil to receive a warm welcome from our host, the Deputy Governor of Riau.

Riau (was then) one of Indonesia's twenty-seven provinces—East Timor was not yet free. Although Indonesia's *propinsi* (provinces) are given that name (rather like the Thai *jangwad*), their huge size and large populations make them more truly comparable to the federal states of Malaysia. A provincial governor is thus an important man, with powers resembling those of cabinet ministers. (Another good parallel might be the status of *"khweng"* heads in Laos, whose authority is much greater than that of *jangwad* governors in Thailand, where power is highly centralized in the Ministry of the Interior.) Furthermore, in Indonesia, provincial governors are political figures, appointed directly by the President. In the Suharto era, most of these governorships were given to army officers, rather like the situation in Thailand under the Sarit-Thanom-Praphat oligarchy.

Under the Indonesian system of territorial administration, there are three levels below the governor: first the *kabupaten*, headed by a *bupati* (formally corresponding to Thailand's *ampheu*), then the *kecamatan* (sub-district), and finally the *desa* (village). The resemblance to Thailand's territorial administrative hierarchy is rather striking, and it is interesting to investigate why this should be so. We should recall that when King Chulalongkorn instituted his administrative reforms (dividing the realm into *monthon, thesaphiban, muang, tambon,* and *muban*), the Thai were heavily influenced by the examples of the huge neighboring British and Dutch colonies. The odd thing is that most Thai scholars still think that King Chulalongkorn got his reform ideas from Europe; yet the truth of the matter is that his models were drawn from what he learned from his visits to Singapore, Java, and India (which in those days included Burma).

At first sight, Indonesia's system of territorial administration looks quite democratic. Candidates for governor and *bupati* are elected by electoral bodies at their respective levels; their names are then passed up to the Ministry of the Interior for review; while the final selection and appointment are the President's prerogative. Village heads, however, are directly elected by the villagers themselves. But in practice, the system works like the administrative systems of all undemocratic states (including Thailand), which under a thin "democratic" veneer operate in a highly authoritarian and/or feudal manner (in the style of "national" *phu di*, who gussy themselves up in the products of Rolex, Gucci, Louis Vitton, and Information Technology: they look very "globalized," but underneath they are basically even more provincial than real provincials).

From Batam, which is really just a stone's throw from Singapore's Sentosa Island Park, we took an ordinary speedboat, owned by an Indonesian businessman. Making a big noise as it bumped across the little waves, it took us through narrow channels between islets big and small, passing dozens of smaller vessels plying their way back and forth, to the "mainland" of Sumatra. Though Riau's territory includes more than three thousand tiny islands, its population numbers a mere four million or so. Most of its land area is comprised of the flat delta of the great Indragiri River, which flows down from high mountains to the west, and broadens out into a muddy flood, full of torn-off branches of samae and mangrove trees. The landscape is very much like the Gulf of Siam delta of the Chao Phraya and other nearby rivers in the old days, before economic development in the 1960s destroyed the natural resources and the natural environment of Chonburi and Cha Cheung Sao down to Samut Prakan, Samut Sakhon, and Samut Songkhram.

Riau is still a central point for the haze or smog caused by systematic deforestation and the burning of residual tree stumps, branches, and secondary growth on a colossal scale, which in every dry season creates a dense blanket of black smoke. The vast land area affected by this deforestation and massive burning, extending from Sumatra to Borneo, has created a problem for which no effective solution has yet been found. The huge murky haze regularly spreads from Sumatra across to Malaysia, and sometimes extends its outer perimeter as far north as Surat Thani, causing, quite unnecessarily, an uncountable number of victims of respiratory ailments.

The odd thing is that ASEAN has been utterly incapable of creating the cooperation necessary to tackle this problem, even though it affects directly such members as Indonesia, Singapore, Malaysia, Brunei, and Thailand. ASEAN thus gives the impression of being nothing more than a small group of leaders who hold meeting after meeting, play golf, and guard their status as perfectly impotent "paper tigers." The armies, navies, and air forces which these countries' mass media always claim are "super-fantastic" never put in even one day's work to control the spread of the black haze. The national leaders' mindset is such that they can not see that this smog is the true enemy of their respective nation-states (far more so than the leftwingers/communists condemned in the past, and the NGOs condemned today).

What is even more depressing is that these ASEAN leaders generally put the blame for the smog on Indonesia's small farmers and peasants, instead of focusing on the giant palm-oil, pineapple, and tobacco plantations which are the real culprits behind the massive deforestation, using buzz-saws and bulldozers to level the soil for their agribusinesses. But blaming the "little people" seems to be a general aspect of the mentality of these high-level gentlemen; one can see exactly the same mentality in the way our own high officials regularly blame and scold the hill tribes for destroying forests and watersheds.

Ordinary people in Singapore and Malaysia who have suffered the serious health problems caused by the smog say that their governments do not dare to take any serious measures because they don't want to embarrass (i.e. are scared to death of) Indonesia. So they keep mum in accordance with the policy of "constructive engagement," and never dream of uttering the slightest public criticism. Indonesia, in turn, acts as if it were the Big Brother of Malaysia and Singapore, in exactly the same way that the Thai always like to think of themselves as the Big Brother of "Baby Brother" Laos (or Cambodia).

The sea lanes along which we passed in the speedboat seemed like grand boulevards connecting the huge, scattered terrain of Southeast Asia's archipelagic zone. For hundreds, even thousands of years, these waters have proved no obstacle for travelers. Those peoples who in our time have become citizens of Malaysia, Indonesia, the Philippines, and Oceania (as far even as Hawaii) have throughout the ages used these sea lanes to travel, to trade, and to migrate to new homes. One can see why the Indonesian expression for "mother country" is so appropriate: *tanah air* means "land/water" fused to become one.

This intimate connection between "land/water" in the past spread the use of the Malay language all over these regions (and in modern times made it the national language of Malaysia, Indonesia, and Brunei), turning it into the lingua franca for trade and communications. We should not forget that in the old days Ayutthaya itself used the Malay language to communicate with states to its south. We even have clear evidence that in its dealings with the (Dutch) United East India Company's headquarters in Batavia (today Jakarta), the kings of Ayutthaya used the same language. It was only during the reign of King Taksin that the state switched to the Chinese language and the Chinese writing system. The new lingua franca continued to be used far into the era of the Jakkri dynasty, when it was eventually replaced by English and "American."

The sea channels we followed were in earlier times used by the famous "sea robbers" whom we Thai call, borrowing from Malay, *jon salat*. In fact, the Malay word *"selat"* simply means "narrow channel." The peoples who lived on the little islands skirting these channels in the old days were called *orang selat* ("channel people" in Malay), and by no means all of them were robbers or pirates. The Thai also used to call these people the *chao le,* or sea people, while the Westerners tended to use the term "sea gypsies." Many of the local names for these little islands (*pulau* in Malay) and hamlets (*kampung*) are humorous allusions to the channels. The captain of our speedboat pointed to a hamlet on an island up ahead and told us its odd name, which can be translated as "dancing widow."

Just at this moment, the Deputy Governor broke in with the typical loud voice of a "big shot" to say, "This is the route used by smugglers between Singapore and Riau," then burst into laughter as if this were the most normal thing in the world. Indeed, as we proceeded on our way, we passed many little boats piled high with bananas and coconuts. What may have lain hidden underneath the produce we didn't know and had no need to find out.

Our express boat, with its deafening roar, sailed on for about another hour, till we could see ahead the dim outline of the huge island of Sumatra. The sea was quite calm and the waves very small, but our boat's keel bumped and jumped continuously because its two-hundred horsepower engine was racing at top speed. Finally we turned into the mouth of a big river and disembarked at Guntung, which is the name both of the pier and of the small local sub-district. Most of the inhabitants grow coconuts for the market. Here we were given a "big shot" welcome by Sia Tae, a Teochiu businessman and the owner of our speedboat. We learned that although he had officially adopted an Indonesian name, he still cherished his clan name, which, funnily enough, was also the clan name of the King of Thonburi and Bangkok.

Sia Tae welcomed us in his air-conditioned reception room, which was full of pictures of important people, including former President Suharto and Madame Tien Suharto. The local officials, army officers, police, and civil administrators had been invited to join in receiving our group and were all ready and waiting. Everything was very "official," but the atmosphere was quite relaxed in the manner typical of social gatherings between the holders of political power in a bureaucratic polity and the holders of economic/financial power represented by transnational businessmen. Sia Tae was busy signing a contract for the planned rehabilitation and upgrading of the coconut farms of the farmers in the province of Riau. At this point we understood that the Deputy Governor had come with us not merely for the "national hero construction project" but for an "economic development project," to say nothing of image-building public relations, with newsmen and video cameras all over the place.

After a lunch where we were given shrimp from one of Sia Tae's farms, we were taken for a tour to admire a factory for producing and crating palm oil and coconut cream. This factory of Sia Tae's had been built more than thirty years earlier; indeed if we include the time of Aa Tia (his father), who also ran the plantation and sold palm and coconut products, the business was more than half a century old. Most of the product is exported to Singapore. The total area covered by Sia Tae's plantation and factory is really huge, bigger indeed than the entire island of Singapore, and must have involved no little destruction of forests and waterside mangroves.

When no one was watching us, Professor Cheah and I asked Sia Tae in a roundabout way whether he wasn't worried about the situation in Indonesia, since anti-Chinese feeling that erupted in the riots of 1998 surely continued to smolder.

But Sia Tae said he wasn't worried at all. Probably he could not say much more than that under the circumstances; we were in a crowd of military officers, police, and Ministry of the Interior bureaucrats. We did, however, gather that Sia Tae owns houses and condominiums in Jakarta, Singapore, and other places. We felt sure that if there were real trouble, he could cross to Singapore in his speedboat without any difficulty. Nation-state borders evidently have little importance for "globalized" businessmen like Sia Tae. For all their other differences, big Chinese entrepreneurs and national-level politicians in Indonesia have one thing in common: they are prepared to flee the country at a moment's notice, with condominiums and deposits in foreign banks long set by against a rainy day.

We traveled on against the current for another two hours before turning into a canal leading off from the big river. On the banks we could see monkeys digging crabs out of their holes. Never in my life have I seen such vast, densely packed coconut plantations as those stretched out along the whole length of the canal. I realized then just how big the island of Sumatra really is. The total area is more than 400,000 square kilometers, not much less than the whole of Thailand's 500,000. There was no room for doubt that the smog from Sumatra's forest fires could block out the sun over half of Southeast Asia.

Finally, we reached our destination, the district capital of Tembilahan on the banks of the Indragiri River. Here again we witnessed a striking example of the power of the state bureaucracy. By the pier the *bupati*, in a bemedaled safari suit, accompanied by his staff, was awaiting us, while servants obsequiously rushed up to take our bags. We then set off in a long motorcade, with motorcyclists in front, all lamps ablaze, to warn ordinary people to get out of the way. Not a whit different from the motorcades of princes, and both awesome and exciting.

The *bupati*'s residence was also no less grand and vast than those of princes. The reception hall was floored with marble and fitted out with huge carpets, French-style furniture, hanging chandeliers, and the kind of garish, touristy paintings of which nouveaux rich persons all over Southeast Asia are so typically fond. Dr. Taufik turned to me and explained that this *bupati*'s residence was a bit special. Riau is a very rich province, and its customs duties bring in the kind of money that makes this type of glamorous "palace" possible. In addition, the rising movement for *"reformasi"* has sucked a lot of power away from the center in Jakarta. The central government still has authority in the realm of foreign policy, but with regard to international relations each province largely goes its own way. This trend is particularly clear in the field of economics. Thus Riau has been able comfortably to construct an "economic triangle" with Malaysia and Singapore, without going through Jakarta at all.

All of this made me reflect on the movement for "reform" which has been rising in various countries in Southeast Asia. One shouldn't forget that well before the collapse of the socialist economies in the socialist countries towards the end of the 1980s, we were hearing about Gorbachev's policies of *perestroika* and *glasnost*, about *Đổi Mới* in Vietnam, and "New Thinking" in Laos. Or, still more definitively, the movement for political reform in Thailand which brought us the present so-called "People's Constitution" in the period between the last days in power of General Chaovalit Yongjaiyut and Chuan Leekphai's return to power (1997). Nor should one overlook the "reform" movement in Malaysia, which drove Prime Minister Mahathir bin Mohamad to accuse his Deputy Prime Minister Anwar Ibrahim (who had been his closest protégé for the previous ten years) of "secretly practicing homosexual sex." Otherwise the reform movement would probably have led to Mahathir's downfall, parallel to the downfalls of Suharto and General Chaovalit.

That evening there was a formal dinner with a "culture show" in the typical style of the bureaucratic polity. The occasion came to an end with each of the attending "big shots" stepping up in turn to sing one or two of his favorite songs, no matter whether he sang like a lark or a crow, and no matter whether he pleased or annoyed the other guests. You could see that power-holders in Indonesia and Thailand are exactly alike in their abilities and their dogged persistence in the field of song. One is hard put to decide whether this is something peculiar to Thailand or Indonesia, or whether it is more likely part of a new trans-Southeast Asian bureaucratic culture.

THE CONSTRUCTION OF A "NATIONAL HERO": THE CASE OF TENGKU SULONG

The seminar was scheduled for two full days. Half of the first day was consumed by the official opening ceremonies. The deputy governor (the governor was away on official business in Hong Kong), the *bupati*, the military officers, the police, the civilian bureaucrats, and the academics, both male and female, were dressed in sarongs and "national dress": batik shirts sagging under the weight of medals. No surprise, then, that after the ceremonies were over the "big shots" (who probably had important duties to carry out) almost all disappeared. Only a few quietly crept back into the seminar room, having replaced their "national dress" with ordinary clothes. Almost all of the people who stayed on were academics—and schoolchildren ("specially invited" and mostly fast asleep), who took their turns speaking in an orderly manner. It was at this juncture that I became an eyewitness of the process by which a "national hero is constructed."

The topic of the seminar was the question of whether or not Tengku Sulong deserved to be nominated as a "national hero." The Indonesian state has set up a step-by-step procedure for determining whether So-and-so deserves the honor of being raised to the official status of "national hero/ine." The process starts at the provincial level, with the governor, who sends the nomination up to the Minister of Social Affairs, who sets up a committee to study the matter. If the committee approves the candidate, his/her name goes to the President, who makes the official appointment.

In the present case of Riau's Tengku Sulong, the governor's office had to create a three-stage process; our seminar belonged to the first stage, Broadly speaking, these stages could be summarized as: l. Excavation and Restoration; 2. Reproduction and Dissemination; and 3. Nomination and Recognition.

Well, who was Tengku Sulong? Put perhaps oversimply, he was the feudal lord of the Sultanate of Riau (the title Tengku refers to this position) in the middle of the nineteenth century, and he fought the Dutch to the death (including his own). The question, however, was whether he was sufficiently well known and deserving to be honored as a national-level hero. At first glance, he seemed to fit perfectly into the ranks of those heroes who "with a brave heart fought to preserve the land of Indonesia for his descendants, even to the point of sacrificing his own life." Accordingly, it was only fitting that all his fellow Indonesians rise to their feet to say: "Let him not have died in vain! Let us love our country more than life, as our ancestors (and heroes) did before us!"

But here we should step back a little and take a wider look. The Indonesian nation-state has so far constructed more than one hundred "national hero/ines." But birth of this "program" was quite simple and almost accidental: no big ceremonies and no step-by-step bureaucratic procedures were involved. Prof. Taufik Abdullah explained to us that in the late 1950s, when President Sukarno, "The Leader of the Nation," was still in power, it happened that the family of Abdul Muis (1886-1959) had fallen on hard times after Muis's death. A man of the same generation as Phraya Phahon and Phraya Songsuradet, the Thai revolutionaries of 1932, Muis had the reputation of being an outstanding nationalist; he had once been the Deputy Leader of Indonesia's first major nationalist organization, the Sarekat Islam.

Muis was a Minangkabau from West Sumatra. In his time, the members of the Minangkabau elite were unusually well educated. The province produced many intellectuals who were pioneers in promoting the nationalist movement. In most respects, Muis was quite typical of this group, but he had one additional talent: he was a writer. In this regard, his work resembled that of his pioneering Thai contemporary Mom Chao Akatdamkeung Raphiphat. For example, his pioneering novel *Salah Asuhan* (Wrong upbringing) depicted the problems faced by a young man who was born and came to adulthood in the midst of the deepening conflicts between his own ancient and conservative Minangkabau culture and the modernizing Western culture of the Dutch colonialists. The protagonist of the novel experiences conflicts in his tortured relations with a white woman and with his Minangkabau wife which look very similar to those we find in Akatdamkeung's *Lakhon Heang Chiwit* (Play of life) and *Phiw Khaaw, Phiw Leuang* (White skin, yellow skin), suggesting that such problems were typical of all Western-educated elites in Southeast Asia at that time, no matter whether they lived in colonized countries or not (the cases of Chao Fa Jakraphong and the family of Mom Manee seem closely related to the above).

In the case of Muis, the ad hoc purpose of his elevation to National Hero was simply to provide financial benefits for his needy family. Muis was the first person to be elevated to this position, but thereafter the construction of national heroes and heroines gradually became an important matter of state. The pace of construction increased markedly under the rule of General Suharto, along with a proliferation of regulations and ceremonies. Indeed, more and more the creation of national heroes/heroines became a "matter of state" exploited for the benefit of Suharto's own *kaki tangan* (clique). For example, when, a few years ago, Madame Tien, who was notorious as the "back door" of the Suharto regime, died, she was immediately proposed by one of Suharto's cabinet ministers as a "national heroine."

Here was yet another instance of the evils of Indonesian society which have come to be known by the initials KKN, which stand for the English-derived words *Korupsi, Kolusi,* and *Nepotisma*. These words have been repeated so often in recent years that no one really remembers their foreign origins, in just the same way that Reform has become completely Indonesianized as *Reformasi*.

For these reasons, the image of National Hero/ine has become politically problematic. The institution has been sharply criticized as a creature of the Jakarta elite and of the island of Java, and as ignoring the "outer" regions and provinces, such as Sumatra, Kalimantan, and Sulawesi (compare Bangkok and Thailand's "outer" regions). Thus one big reason why Riau was now putting forward its own candidate for National Hero was a strong reaction against the indifference of the Center. Indeed this was a general phenomenon in the twilight of Suharto's regime (Suharto was a man so thoroughly Javanese that his domestic image was more that of a King of Java than of a President of the Indonesian nation).

The lieutenant-general representing the security forces (i.e. the army), who chaired the provincial candidacy subcommittee and sat with us, told me that these days the screening of candidates requires a lot of hard work. The subcommittee has to deal with demands and proposals pouring in from all quarters of the compass, and this means meetings every week. The construction of National Heroes/Heroines in Indonesia has evidently become a matter of extraordinary importance.

Seen from this angle, Indonesia seems very different from Thailand. Although the two countries' heroines and heroes resemble one another in that they have to have participated in military struggles to defend "the nation" against external enemies (we Thai mostly use the Burmese for this purpose; as Thailand was never directly colonized, we don't designate the Westerners as our perpetual enemies, but instead utilize our age-old neighbors for that purpose). Yet those Thai who get promoted as official national heroes and heroines rarely have any other occupation, for instance as learned people/philosophers, or as intellectuals and writers; Sunthorn Phu is the obvious exception. Most of them have been military leaders and monarchs (such as all the official Great Kings), or people closely associated with the military or the monarchy, such as deputies or representatives. Good examples are Siharatdecho, Chaokhun Phichai Dabhak, Thao Suranari, Thao Thepsatri, Thao Srisunthon, etc. etc. Our national heroes are very few in number compared to those of the Indonesians, and the process whereby they are appointed is not nearly as elaborate and complicated. Participation in their construction is limited to a handful of top power-holders and office-holders in Bangkok.

I remember very well how in 1982, during the two-hundredth anniversary celebrations for Krung Rattanakosin (Bangkok), officials at the center were required to elevate Phra Phutthayotfa Julalok, the founder of the dynasty, to the rank of Great King (*maharat*). I myself received a circular from Professor Rong Syamanond, in the name of the Commission for Revising History, which was directly attached to the Prime Minister's Office, containing data on Rama I's activities and asking each recipient for his or her view as to whether the title of Great King was appropriate for this candidate. It was understood that once the Commission had received the responses to its questionnaire, it would then hold a meeting proposing the official announcement planned all along. The simplicity of the procedure, and the very few people involved, make a sharp contrast with Indonesia's hugely complex net of vertical and horizontal interactions.

Once the opening ceremonies were over, the seminar itself began with a keynote speech by my old friend Dr. Taufik which offered us a broad overview of the problems involved in the creation of national heroines and heroes. Taufik told us that from the start he had never really been in favor of this kind of endeavor, because there are always serious historical questions about who genuinely merits the honor; the official definitions of national hero/ine are confused and overlap chaotically; and the process of decision-making and decision-implementing is in Indonesia completely top down, i.e. is in the hands of the President. Thus the honorees are typically Javanese, and, if not political leaders, have to have a background of battlefield resistance to the Dutch. This in turns means one-sidedness at the national level, and habitual neglect of and lack of interest in the outer regions.

Dr. Taufik elaborated this point further by saying that if the serious intent was to include heroes and heroines in a national family album, the inclusion should be comprehensive and even-handed, and the decision-making should come from the bottom up, i.e. from the regions. If things worked this way, a person from Aceh or from any other region outside Java would find, on opening the album, figures from his or her home province and not merely heroes from the capital city of Jakarta, or from Java (which have long been the centers of power in the archipelago). Dr. Taufik's recommendations that the process be made more comprehensive and more fair in its emphasis on regions and localities struck me as well worth seriously considering as it relates to the case of Thailand too.

To summarize Dr. Taufik's argument: the proper aim of any program for constructing national heroes and heroines should be the unity and integrity of the nation. This is why I have stated that "history" and "ideology (nationalism)" cannot walk happily hand in hand; nationalist ideology tends to marginalize real history, by altering it, distorting it, adding to it and subtracting from it, to construct something quite novel. These distortions have become so serious that the younger generation of scholars has felt it necessary to stand up and "rescue history from the nation." Still more urgent today is a redefinition of the nation such that we can ask: what really is a nation? And (since practice is often far removed from theory) to whom does the nation belong?

Our consideration of Tengku Sulong's candidacy did not go as smoothly as might have been expected, since in fact a strenuous dispute arose in the course of that first day. Prof. Dr. Ibrahim Alfian, a senior historian from Yogyakarta's Gadjah Mada University, began the "excavation and restoration" of Tengku Sulong by stating that he had fought against the Dutch to the point of sacrificing his own life; that he had built a walled fortress fitted out with large cannons to battle the colonialist army and naval forces; and that he died the model death of a nineteenth-century national hero. In brief, he showed all the necessary qualifications for being elevated to national hero.

But at this point, the National Archivist and former professor of history at the University of Ujung Pandang in Makassar (Sulawesi), a tall young man with the short name of Mukhlis, tossed a big bomb into the midst of our seminar. He said that in searching through the relevant documents in the National Archives he had discovered that Tengku Sulong's "war of resistance to the Dutch" was an insignificant affair, crushed in less than a month by a small Dutch force commanded by a lowly First Lieutenant.

Furthermore, it transpired that in the war the actual conflicting parties were competing local elites. In other words, the fighting was really closer to a civil war than a battle "for the nation" or "to save the nation" in the contemporary sense. What Tengku Sulong fought to defend was his sultanate and his personal interests, not the interests of the Indonesian nation-state, or of the Indonesian people.

Accordingly, some of his rivals allied themselves with the Dutch, who exploited these local conflicts and jealousies to intervene and finally conquer Riau with the greatest of ease.

As I sat there listening, I couldn't help thinking of some of our own would-be "national heroines": for example, the cases of Phra Maha Thammaracha or Phra Suphankalya, for both of whom certain state officials and private civic groups have struggled to construct a "national image." The historical reality is that these people were participants in the politics and the warfare of the dynastic, not the national, state. The behavior, the beliefs, the traditions, and the customs of the figures involved belong to "the old feudal/sakdina world, not the modern world of the nation-state." This is why texts cited in the chronicles remark that Phra Suphankalya was criticized for being "more concerned about her husband than her relatives/clan." But the letter *"yorying"* in *yat* (family) was easily bent into *"chorchang"* in *chat* (nation) at the insistence of nationalist ideology to allow her to be imagined as a national heroine.

This instance then led me to reflect more widely on a whole series of cases: for example, the "story/legend" of Phra Ruang, Nai Khongkhrao sending tribute to the Old Khmer (Khom) was reimagined/reinvented to make Phra Ruang a king, and a part of the "history" of the "Thai People" in the "Age of Sukhothai." The process of "excavation and restoration" began with Rama VI's verse stage-play "Phra Ruang," which concluded with these rousing official-nationalist appeals: "I ask only that we Thai never allow ourselves to fall into ruin! For this great task be united in race, united in spirit. Help one another single mindedly to cherish and preserve our race and our religion, to the end of time. Long Live the Thai! Chaiyo!"

This style of imagination eventually ended by becoming what historians like Craig Reynolds have called "a plot of history that has turned Sukhothai into Thailand's first royal capital." And this plot has firmed up into an endless flood of things that can be adduced to exemplify an ageless "Thainess" or "Thai Nation," such as Thai orthography, Loi Krathong, Nang Nopphamat, Suphasit-Traiphum Phra Ruang, etc. etc.

To conclude: the question "Will Tengku Sulong end up a National Hero?" was evidently not a substantive question at all. In the framework of a project of national hero construction, our seminar was foreordained to wind up with an official recommendation by our good bureaucrat colleagues, to be forwarded up to higher authorities for further consideration, and then further forwarding still higher up to the highest authority of all: the President. But what president will have the courage to reject the powerful appeal of nationalism? In the present era of *"reformasi,"* when the institutions of the central government have been so seriously weakened, the people in power at the center are unlikely to have any intention of defying the strong political current from below and from the periphery. Seen from this angle, there is something nice about Indonesia having so many different kinds of national heroes and heroines; and if there is politics in Tengku Sulong's becoming a national hero, well that is perfectly fine too.

CONCLUDING REMARK

National heroes and heroines are the products of the imaginary of nationalism, and came into historical being at the same time as the nation. Both "nation" and "nationalism" are among the most interesting phenomena in the modern world of the past two centuries. Some scholars have even gone so far as to term nationalism a "new religion" which, even if it has no Founder or Prophet, has given people all over the world faith and inspiration.

Nationalism arose first in the "New World" of the Americas. This New World was also the original source and model for the nation-state: the USA already had its national revolution in 1776, and the states of Latin America followed not long after. The influence of this new "-ism" crossed back over the Atlantic to the Old World and eventually engendered many new nations and states while destroying dynastic states in the era that began with the Revolution of 1789 (that created the French nation-state). At the start of the twentieth century, nationalism spread into Asia. Together with the collapse of colonialism in the course of World War II, this Asian nationalism brought into being a large number of new nation-states, from East Asia down through Southeast Asia, and over to South Asia.

One can say therefore that the building of nation-states all over the world has been a vast and long process going back more than two hundred years, and further, that this process shows no sign of ending (the recent collapse of the Soviet Union also led to the emergence of a dozen new nation-states; but note also the cases of East Timor, Tibet, and Taiwan, where nationalist imaginings are still being suppressed and unfulfilled).

In brief, nationalism gave birth to a new form of state (the nation-state) superseding the older dynastic and theocratic states. Today this form of state is generally accepted as the most modern and most legitimate form of state in existence. Such states start as "imagined communities" which have to assemble a common "will" in their imaginations, and then build it in the visible form of the nation-state (with national heroines and heroes appended).

If we ask the question why all this work of construction is necessary, the answer is that the nation-state does not come into being naturally or automatically. As I have stressed earlier, it requires "imagining" in order to be born, and even after its birth, it requires constant movement, constant activity, and constant "production" to stay alive. Furthermore, to this basic production must be added other, additional components which, once determined on as "the uniqueness" of the nation, have to be constructed and disseminated in various forms: e.g. prints. Historical works must be created with a clear "plot," i.e. a lengthy, continuous account of the nation's development in a straight line from the past to the present. In turn, the key themes of these works must be crammed into classroom textbooks, particularly at the behest of the political authorities, who always want to be sure that the nation's young people have these themes fixed firmly in their heads.

Other parallel activities are also necessary, including the construction of national heroines and heroes (who are taken as representing the essence of the national character), the fixing/determination of a "national language," the raising of national monuments and the manufacturing of historical theme-parks, the creation of stories and legends (in the form of historical plays, patriotic songs, and so forth), and even the invention of various symbolic forms which manifest the nation or are insistently marked by it—e.g. flags, clothing styles, foods, flowers, animals, and so on. From all the above we can see that imagining the nation and building the nation are gigantic projects whose completion always lies beyond the horizon.

Among our Southeast Asian neighbors, the ideology of nationalism was the unintended consequence of colonialism itself. The colonialists brought it with them from Europe and America, and, without realizing this, implanted it in the imaginations of a new generation of native leaders. For these young leaders were the products of the schools and educational systems established by the colonial rulers, which obviously were profoundly influenced by educational systems in the West itself. Eventually nationalism in our region developed into movements of resistance, hostile to colonialism and determined to destroy it.

Southeast Asian nationalism developed in very different forms and ways, however, ranging from the armed revolutions in Indonesia and Vietnam which fought to prevent the return of the Dutch and French colonialists after the Japanese Occupation, to the peaceful negotiations and compromises with the British and American colonialists through which Malaysia and the Philippines became independent. One also finds hybrid forms like the Thai, where the dynastic state, challenged by new circumstances and new ways of thinking, dressed itself up in the costume of the nation-state, producing an "official nationalism" which continues to play an important role up to the present.

For a certain period, nationalism's prestige and legitimacy declined severely, especially in the eyes of Europeans, because of its extremist expression in Germany under Hitler, in Italy under Mussolini, and in Japan under Hirohito and Tojo. In Thailand too, nationalism lost much of the legitimacy it had enjoyed during World War II under the leadership of Field Marshal Phibunsongkhram and Luang Wijit Wathakan; the Thai intelligentsia in particular became highly critical of the government. Yet "official" Thai nationalism of the type invented by Rama VI, with the monarch as its high center (note the slogan Nation, Religion, and Monarch, and the national tricolor flag, in which blue, white, and red were turned into five stripes), was altered and adapted over and over again by Field Marshal Phibun and Luang Wijit Wathakan according to their own nationalist ideas, replacing the Monarch with "the Thai race" as its central axis. (Although the country's name was changed from Siam to Thailand, the old tricolor remained unchanged.) Subsequently, this nationalism was refurbished and remodeled under the slogan "For the Nation and the Throne" under the military regime of Sarit-Thanom-Praphat; and from the Prem era on it was again adapted in a hybrid manner till it achieved its present highly wrought form.

Over the past two decades, the emergence of the mirage of a globalized world dominated by transnational conglomerates and information technology has encouraged the clichéd idea that national borders have lost their significance, that we live in a single "global village," and that nationalism is reaching its historical end. Mankind is said to face now the "end of history," and even the "end of ideology."

Nonetheless, the decline of the socialist economies, the disintegration of the Soviet Union, the wars between the socialist states of China, Vietnam, and Cambodia, the bursting of the economic and currency bubbles in Southeast Asia, the racial strife in the Balkan peninsula (especially in the former Yugoslavia), the cases of East Timor and Aceh, and China's difficulties with Tibet and Taiwan (closer to home, we could also mention our own Pattani), show us very clearly that the power of nationalism will remain with us for a very long time.

It is going to be very difficult to "escape from the nation and nationalism." In our present circumstances, the most plausible and feasible way out lies in creating new concepts which will help us make nation and nationalism genuinely shared projects and imaginations encompassing us all, not merely rhetorical and sham tropes, as in the past. The nation must truly become the common property of all groups and strata. It must become a comfortable and attractive home for us all. And it must form a place where equality and dignity are the shared interests of everyone. If these goals can be achieved, "nation and nationalism" will have a bright future and cease being merely a rhetorical device to protect the interests and privileges of particular individuals, cliques, groups, or institutions, as has been the case for far too long.

Laughing at Leviathan: John Furnivall, Dutch New Guinea, and the Ridiculousness of Colonial Rule

Danilyn Rutherford

One step above the sublime, makes the ridiculous.
                Thomas Paine, 1795[1]

... strictly speaking, we do not know what we are laughing about.
                Sigmund Freud, 1905[2]

Colonialism has rarely been called "ridiculous." Exploitative, yes; violent, of course; but rarely has it been presented as the butt of a joke. Yet if we believe John Furnivall, every study of the spread of colonial rule should bring precisely this quality to light. Furnivall begins *The Fashioning of Leviathan*, his 1939 study of the first decades of British colonialism in Burma, by reflecting upon why so little has been written about the birth of empires. Even Hobbes avoided the topic. Hobbes referred to "that great *Leviathan* called a Commonwealth or State" as "but an Artificial Man."[3] But when it came to describing Leviathan's birth, Hobbes recast the creature as a "Mortall God" and described the event in mythical terms. According to Furnivall,

> Hobbes is driven to myth because Leviathan has this at least in common with the immortal gods—that we know little or nothing of his childhood. This is not strange, for no god is quite immune to ridicule, and children cannot help being ridiculous at times: if Aphrodite had caught cold, when rising from the

---

[1] Thomas Paine, *Age of Reason*, quoted in *The Compact Oxford English Dictionary*, Second Edition (Oxford: Oxford University Press, 1991), p. 1590.

[2] Sigmund Freud, *Jokes and their Relation to the Unconscious*, trans. James Strachey (New York: W.W. Norton, 1960), p. 102.

[3] See John S. Furnivall, *The Fashioning of Leviathan*, reprinted from *The Burma Research Society's Journal* 29, Part 1 (Rangoon: Zabu Meitswe Pitaka Press, 1939), p. 3.

foam on her first birthday, she was already big enough to use her pocket-handkerchief without being told to do so by her nurse. A god must feel secure in his divinity to let himself be laughed at, and Leviathan is not sufficiently at home in heaven to allow it.[4]

John Furnivall understood very well the inherently ridiculous nature of the colonial state on the frontiers of empire. Ben Anderson, who introduced Furnivall's texts to budding scholars of Southeast Asia, did so for good reason. *The Fashioning of Leviathan* is a comic masterpiece, as well as an insightful foray into the violent underpinnings of modern colonial power. In this essay, I relate these two aspects of Furnivall's study, showing how laughter and insight go hand in hand. I apply the lessons implicit in Furnivall's humor to the imperial frontier that long persisted in western New Guinea, in the eastern hinterlands of the Netherlands Indies, an area that now comprises the Indonesian province of Papua (formerly Irian Jaya). I show how phenomena that some might call "mestizo"—but that Furnivall called "ridiculous"—were an unintended effect of colonial intervention—and an incitement to bring the territory under greater control.

My argument takes Furnivall at his word: I approach the comedy that pervades *The Fashioning of Leviathan* as a means of diagnosing a central feature of colonial practice. In excavating the ridiculous from the archives of British imperialism, Furnivall does more than make fun of colonialism; he reveals an aspect of the colonial situation that both dogged the apparatus and stimulated its growth. As such, Furnivall's method enables us to build on the findings of more recent scholars, who have called into question conventional explanations of European imperialism. Consider Elsbeth Locher-Scholten's analysis of Dutch efforts to consolidate colonial rule within the Netherlands Indies' boundaries at the turn of the twentieth century. This endeavor did not in any simple sense result from the "economic interests of the metropole," "international competition," or the need to create a "diversion from internal problems."[5] At the same time, its impetus did not come from the "periphery"—that is, the colony—alone. A new set of global imperatives, including "the expanding demands of economic privileges (tariffs and mineral exploitation) and the task of the modern western state to provide for the safety of European entrepreneurs, missionaries, and civil servants," created the context for colonial expansion.[6] Paying heed to the interests and anxieties of the colonial administrators who called for increased intervention in areas under their jurisdiction, Locher-Scholten shows how a concern for "the prestige of our nation among foreigners" in this increasingly fraught setting was a key factor in the launching of "pacification" campaigns. These campaigns began when local officials felt that their authority had been called into question, generally through the resistance of indigenous rulers to official incursions. "Ethical imperialism," as Locher-Scholten dubs the phenomenon, giving new meaning to a favorite Dutch watchword of the time, had enormous effects. Twentieth-century state formation "resulted in foreign domination in many details of personal life, a process of

---

[4] Ibid.
[5] Elsbeth Locher-Scholten, "Dutch Expansion in the Indonesian Archipelago Around 1900 and the Imperialism Debate," *Journal of Southeast Asian Studies* 25,1 (March 1994): 91-111. See p. 93.
[6] Ibid., p. 111.

westernization which in turn led to the forceful reaction of nationalism and at last to Indonesian national independence."[7] Yet the potential for laughter lay at its origins. The intervention of local officials sparked a reaction that led Dutch authorities to worry about their regime's reputation in the eyes of the natives, no doubt, but also from the perspective of an imagined global audience. "Ethical imperialism" began, in other words, with officialdom's fear of appearing ridiculous: the opposite, one might argue, of having prestige.

In this essay, I suggest that Dutch New Guinea is a particularly good place to explore what we might learn from laughing at Leviathan. Above, I repeated part of Locher-Scholten's citation of an 1892 statement from the head of civil administration in Batavia. The full sentence reads: "The prestige of our nation among foreigners does not allow us to leave the population of Irian Jaya [sic] in their miserable and depraved condition."[8] From a distance, it was easy to blame the irregularities of colonial practice in New Guinea on the "depravity" of its Papuan inhabitants. Up close, in the North Moluccan town of Ternate, where officials responsible for administering the territory in the nineteenth century were based, intervention in New Guinea brought to the foreground vicissitudes that every colonial project to some degree shares. Called upon to create an impression of colonial sovereignty, at the lowest possible cost, these officials dreaded that others would discover the absurd nature of their claims. In the conclusion, I reflect on the implications of this aspect of western New Guinea's colonial history for the Netherlands' post-war decision to retain the territory as a separate colony when the rest of the Indies gained independence. But before turning to this history, let us first consider Furnivall's insights on the logic and limits of modern colonial power.

HOBBES IN BURMA

The Fashioning of Leviathan focuses on a species of "Mortall God" for which, as Furnivall notes, the "searching light of truth" was likely to be particularly "embarrassing."[9] The study provides a "step by step" account of

> the incorporation in the Indian Empire of newly conquered territory; the building up of a local administrative organization; the gradual adjustment and adaptation of this local organization to the mechanism of the central government; and, finally, the assimilation of the new province within the general imperial system, so that it could no longer be distinguished from the rest of India except by such accidents of geography as its peoples and product.[10]

Furnivall constructs this narrative on the basis of letters written between 1825 and 1843 by Mr. Maingy and Mr. Blondell, the first two commissioners of the occupied

---

[7] Ibid.

[8] Ibid. p. 107. See also Director Binnenlandsch Bestuur to the Governor-General 6-2-1892, Historische nota in Algemeene Rijksarchief (hereafter ARA), Col., vb. 8-12-1897, no. 33.

[9] "If there are sceptics, and especially if Leviathan himself be uneasy about his birth certificate and the social status of his parents, the searching light of truth may be embarrassing." Furnivall, *The Fashioning of Leviathan*, p. 3. Furnivall clearly has the colonial state in mind here.

[10] Ibid., pp. 3-4.

zone of Tenasserim, the earliest outpost of what later became British Burma. At the time the letters were written, Tenasserim's future was far from certain. This narrow belt of coastal forest, accessible only by boat, had been won from the Thai by King Alaungp'aya of Burma some fifty years before the British assumed control. Viewed from the metropole, the occupation was but one variable in the British attempt to determine what sort of presence in the region would best serve the Empire's interests. The commissioners thus faced a challenge: to make the territory pay, they needed investment, to get investment they needed a commitment from the Empire, to get a commitment from the Empire, they needed to make the territory pay. They had to do all this while instituting a political order entirely different in form and ideology from the polity that had come before.

The magnitude of this task becomes clear when we compare Furnivall's portrayal of the first commissioner's arrival in Tenasserim with the following description of his Burmese predecessor's eighteenth-century campaign to capture the south. Robert Taylor writes:

> [King Alaungp'aya's] initial power came from his army, a force unparalleled in recent times, and grew as he developed a more complete array of hegemonic devices, including symbolic regalia and the means to manipulate ethnic identity. The momentum of his victories and the legends that swept around the new king provided him with an aura of supernatural power. By chain letters and sponsored ballads, he sowed fear among the population ahead of his armies, thereby weakening the will of his opponents and creating massive defections. In promising release from slavery, he won over additional groups of men.[11]

Enter Mr. Maingy on September 9, 1825, with four clerks, three translators, and a pair of servants. Shipwrecked on his first attempt, the new commissioner finally made it to the port town of Mergui and posted his own "chain letter," which proclaimed his intention to provide Mergui's inhabitants with a "civil and political administration on the most liberal and equitable principles."

> Rest assured that your wives and children shall be defended against all foreign and domestic enemies. That life and property shall enjoy every liberty and protection, and that your religion shall be respected and your Priests and religious edifices secured from every insult and injury. Proper measures shall immediately be adopted for administering justice to you according to your own established laws, so far as they do not militate against the principles of humanity and natural equity. In respect to revenue and all other subjects your own customs and local usages shall be taken into consideration, but the most free and unrestricted internal and external commerce will be established and promoted.[12]

---

[11] See David P. Chandler, William R. Roff, John R. W. Smail, David Joel Steinberg, Robert H. Taylor, Alexander Woodside, and David K. Wyatt, *In Search of Southeast Asia: A Modern History*, revised edition, ed. David Joel Steinberg (Honolulu: University of Hawaii Press, 1985), p. 101.

[12] Furnivall, *The Fashioning of Leviathan*, pp. 5-6.

The new commissioner closed by promising that at "all hours and places" "even the poorest inhabitants" would be welcome to see him "on business."[13] Mr. Maingy did keep an elephant and seemed to have a sense of personal dignity, but he was hardly the stuff of ballads. One can hardly imagine a greater contrast between the commissioner's sporting efforts to legitimate his rule and the majestic aura his predecessor maintained.

Mr. Maingy fashioned his Leviathan, in good Hobbesian style, "by Art according to the rules of common sense."[14] His goal was to create a secure and lawful environment in which "liberal principles" (and commerce) could thrive. In Furnivall's chapter headings, one finds the colonial state stripped down to its essentials: jails and policing, road building and revenue, foreign policy. But as Ben Anderson pointed out so aptly to his students, the question that propels Furnivall's inquiry is not how the inhabitants of Tenasserim were incorporated into the British Empire, but how someone like Mr. Maingy could think himself capable of such a feat. The answer lies in the internal workings of the colonial bureaucracy.

By basing his analysis solely on the commissioners' official correspondence, Furnivall establishes the degree to which the apparatus sustained the confidence of Mr. Maingy and his successor, Mr. Blondell, and controlled their fate. Mr. Maingy's letters ended up in "the Secret and Political Department of the Government of India where, apparently they were regarded as so inviolably secret that for some years they were filed unread."[15] Mr. Blondell, by contrast, had to answer to bureaucrats in Calcutta who were beginning to develop an institutional memory with regard to Tenasserim. Furnivall registers the ebb and flow of bureaucratic supervision by populating the study with multiple "Leviathans." On the one hand, the reader is invited to witness Leviathan's birth on Burmese soil; on the other, Leviathan is always already present in the form of Calcutta's meddling hand in the region's affairs. Although Furnivall associates "common sense" with the rationality of a system "geared for profit and productivity," Leviathan's guiding principles turn out to be equally multifarious. There is local common sense, residing in the commissioners' expeditious responses to Tenasserim's limitations and opportunities. There is common sense in Calcutta and presumably in England, serving different sets of utilitarian needs. What counts as common sense changes what counts as what Furnivall calls "human decency." As "Leviathan Indicus" assumes control of Tenasserim, those who fashioned the local system with a "velvet glove" become the human grit in the machine. This is why Mr. Blondell, who instituted the "compassionate" policy of taxing tribal communities at six times the going rate, can end the book as a "conservative" and "nationalist."[16] However ironically, Furnivall anticipates Ben Anderson's argument that nationalism is a product of the administrative pilgrimages offered by the colonial state.[17]

Make no mistake: however serious Furnivall's conclusions might be, *The Fashioning of Leviathan* is incredibly funny. There are two ways of accounting for

---

[13] Ibid., p. 6.

[14] Ibid., p. 136; see also ibid., p. 76. "[Leviathan's] machinery is regulated by the laws of common sense, and he will grind out bread so long as he can go on grinding at a profit."

[15] Ibid., p. 19.

[16] Ibid., p. 134.

[17] See Benedict Anderson, *Imagined Communities: Reflections on the Origin and Spread of Nationalism* (New York: Verso, 1991), pp. 53-56.

this feature of the text. On the one hand, Furnivall deploys comedy for a classical purpose: to demean an exalted institution. *The Fashioning of Leviathan* anticipates themes from Furnivall's monumental studies of colonialism, *Netherlands India* and *Colonial Policy and Practice*.[18] In these decidedly less humorous works, Furnivall elaborates a critique of colonial society, calling it "plural," i.e. inhabited by ethnic and racial groups that only meet in the market. In a population utterly lacking the "common will" that Furnivall viewed as integrating functioning democracies, the "survival of the cheapest" is the rule that prevails. In *The Fashioning of Leviathan*, Furnivall notes, in a similar vein, that colonialism's "common sense" is often at odds with the "claims of life."[19] Obliquely, by taking up Hobbes's moniker to describe the colonial state, Furnivall calls attention to what he regards such a regime as missing—the "sense in common" or "common will" that is arguably a key element of Hobbes's understanding of the basis and outcome of the social contract.[20] For Furnivall, who views the precolonial order as one where people were "fast bound to honesty by the ties of social life," it is the colonial system that inaugurates a life that is "nasty, brutish and short."[21]

On the other hand, the study plays on a potential for comedy that is intrinsic to the materials Furnivall cites. Take, for instance, Furnivall's account of the importation of convict labor from the subcontinent.

> The Commissioner recognized that the jails were not very secure. But they were not meant to be very secure. He regarded the convicts as so much cheap labour imported to make roads; if he had to spend money in housing the labourers he might as well employ more expensive local labour on the roads. But the people in India who supplied the convicts looked at matters in a different light; when they were asked to supply convicts for Tenasserim, they thought it a providential opportunity to get rid of their hard cases. At that time the Government of India was engaged on rooting out the thugs, that strange caste of professional murderers. So it happened that among one batch of convicts sent to labour on the roads there were twenty-five who had been "guilty of Thuggee and Murder,—part of a desperate gang of Thugs which had lately been broken up in Central India" and "whose safe custody was an object of paramount importance." Nasty fellows to build roads with, these, or to keep in confinement in a wooden bungalow with a thatched roof. It was hardly playing the game to send convicts of that type to a well-meaning officer who had quite

---

[18] See John S. Furnivall, *Netherlands India: A Study in the Plural Economy* (Cambridge: Cambridge University Press, 1944); John S. Furnivall, *Colonial Policy and Practice* (New York: New York University Press, 1948, reprinted 1956). In 1939, when *The Fashioning of Leviathan* was published, Furnivall was part way through his second career, as a bookstore owner with close ties to the Burmese nationalist movement. His first career had been as a colonial official, serving in the south of Burma, where the study was set.

[19] Moreover, whatever "Leviathan cannot comprehend he instinctively regards as dangerous and puts forth all his strength to crush." Furnivall, *The Fashioning of Leviathan*, p. 136.

[20] See Richard Tuck's introduction to Thomas Hobbes, *Leviathan*, ed. Richard Tuck (Cambridge: Cambridge University Press, 1991), pp. i–lxxiv. The inhabitants of the plural society lack precisely what Hobbes's Leviathan inaugurates, according to Tuck's reading: a public language that enables them to express and reconcile their opposing intentions, so they will not be driven to violence by uncertainty and fear.

[21] See Furnivall, *The Fashioning of Leviathan*, p. 45.

enough trouble in building up his own little corner of the Empire. Mr. Maingy protested vigorously, but in vain. He asked for convicts and kept on asking; Thugs were convicts, so they sent him Thugs, and kept on sending. It is not surprising then to read of murders by Thug convicts who "not only confessed the murder, but gloried in the act and vied with each other in shouldering the guilt." Even that did not convince the authorities in India that thugs should not be exported to Tenasserim. For, many years later, a young missionary, destined to become famous as an educational pioneer in Burma, was sent to the hospital in Moulmain, seriously ill. But he found the hospital more dangerous than his disease. Left alone under the charge of a convict hospital assistant, apparently quiet and well mannered, he was alarmed by a sudden change in the man's demeanour. All was quiet in the hospital, and the convict was performing the usual duties of a sick nurse, when suddenly a ferocious glare lighted up his eyes and he sprang at the sick man's throat. Fortunately, for lack of practice, his hands had lost their cunning, and the noise of the struggle attracted help; the assailant was overpowered and, presumably, discharged from his duties in the hospital. He was a thug; one of the men sent in the early days to labour on the roads, and after all these years his lust for murder was not yet quenched. The missionary lived to educate Prince Thibaw, and to see his pupil massacre his relatives on a scale that would have done credit to the most devout of thugs. Still, it was rather a slur on the medical profession to appoint a professional murderer as a hospital assistant.[22]

The judicial system provides fodder for similar stories. In an attempt to respect his native subjects' own sense of justice, Mr. Maingy appointed a jury of local notables to render decisions, which included sentencing a man accused of rape to be paraded through town with his face blackened, despite the fact that they had just acquitted him.[23] Mr. Maingy found the courts to be quite efficient—no lawyers were allowed, so cases sailed quickly through the system—even though there was room for improvement. "There might have been even less crime, if people understood what the English regarded as offenses."[24] Furnivall does not relate these details solely to amuse his readers. Rather, in detailing the absurd outcome of decisions that must have seemed reasonable at the time, these anecdotes illustrate the forces that led to Calcutta's intrusion into local affairs. In more neutral terms, one could describe Mr. Maingy's "ridiculous" policies as an effect of the "mestizo" qualities of the situation in Tenasserim.[25] After all, Mr. Maingy did try to draw on Burmese "law and order" in establishing his regime. Still, in suggesting a smooth confection of ingredients, the term does not quite capture Mr. Maingy's predicament. Mr. Maingy was compelled to envision the world he created from the perspective of distant others who shared his commitment to "humanity" and "natural equity." Yet this world took shape through his interactions with colonial "subjects" who no doubt interpreted his behavior in very different terms.

This scenario, in which one comes to perceive a situation from multiple perspectives, all at once, is essential to the comic, if we can trust Freud's

---

[22] Ibid., pp. 37-38.
[23] Ibid., p. 19.
[24] Ibid., p. 30.
[25] See Jean Taylor, *The Social World of Batavia* (Madison: University of Wisconsin Press, 1984).

formulations. The comic, like jokes and humor, derives from the "economy of expenditure" that results when one contrasts what one witnesses to more proper or predictable ways of acting. In the difference between the energy it takes to meet conventional expectations and that exposed by the comic figure one observes, emerges the "quota" that one "laughs off."[26] A common form of comedy takes as its object the "naïve," a person who devotes more effort to physical activities (e.g., walking or gesturing in an exaggerated way) and less to mental activities (e.g., reasoning with little regard for logic) than the observer imagines him or herself expending in a similar situation. But another form, more relevant for our purposes, entails a process of degradation, through which an esteemed person or institution is put into a comic situation or frame.

One way to render such persons or institutions ridiculous is to make them "tally with something familiar and inferior, on imagining which there is a complete absence of any expenditure upon abstraction."[27] Furnivall's comparison of that abstraction *par excellence*, the colonial state, to a runny-nosed child, a devouring monster, and an out-of-control machine certainly fits within Freud's formulations. But another and potentially more potent component of *The Fashioning of Leviathan*'s comic vision lies in the nature of the materials on which Furnivall drew. The writings of European colonial officials, like Mr. Maingy, provide a fertile field for the "Janus-faced" experience of the comic. On the one hand, these officials had to present their actions as meeting the standards of a colonial regime whose objectives were framed in terms of abstract values. On the other hand, they had to appeal to local interlocutors, to elicit, at the very least, a simulacrum of consent. The fact that officials sought this consent against the backdrop of the threat of force did not resolve the interpretive dilemma faced by the state's agents; if anything, it made it even more difficult to gauge when the "natives" were making a mockery of one's rule. Colonial encounters brought to the forefront what Freud describes as key sources of pleasure in "innocent" jokes: the "illogic" that comes into focus when different forms of rationality come into contact, a fixation on the "acoustic images" of alien words. No doubt, this potential pleasure would have been a source of discomfort for officers responsible for reforming native ways.

In *The Fashioning of Leviathan*, Furnivall uses laughter not only as a weapon, but also as a lens to bring into focus aspects of the colonial situation that might otherwise have remained obscure. It is no accident that this work is comic, whereas *Netherlands India* and *Colonial Policy and Practice* are not. In fact, the earlier and the later works are not as similar as one might think. Where Furnivall's account of the "plural society" provides a portrait of what one might call the horizontal dimension of the colonial system—as epitomized in the market, where groups maintain their distance, even as they interact—*The Fashioning of Leviathan* focuses on the vertical dimension.[28] The colonial official, unlike the colonial capitalist, cannot take difference for granted, for what is at stake is the validation

---

[26] See Freud, *Jokes and their Relation to the Unconscious*, p. 149. See also Ibid., p. 234: "It is a necessary condition for generating the comic that we should be obliged, simultaneously or in rapid succession, to apply to one and the same act of ideation two different ideational methods, between which the 'comparison' is then made and the comic difference emerges."

[27] Ibid., pp. 210-11. Freud notes that this procedure allows the observer "to have an idea of [the institution] as though it were something common place, in whose presence I need not pull myself together but may, to use the military formula, 'stand easy.'" Ibid., p. 201.

[28] I would like to thank Jim Siegel for suggesting this contrast.

of inequality. As Homi Bhabha and others have noted, modern colonial discourse is inherently unstable.[29] The colonial project is justified by the racist presumption that the colonizers are inherently more civilized and rational than those they colonize. But it is also justified by a vision of progress in which this disjuncture, however gradually, is bridged. The ridiculous emerges at moments like those described in *The Fashioning of Leviathan*, when officials come face to face with the estrangement that is a necessary component of the civilizing mission. The colonial market, at least as Furnivall describes it, does not stimulate this kind of self-consciousness; even the power of currency to erode differences, so stressed by Marx and others, fails to threaten colonial boundaries.[30] Furnivall was clearly mistaken in presuming the existence of ethnic and racial identities that were as much the outcome of colonial practice as its object. But his formulations do open an interesting angle on the complexities of colonial consciousness. To complicate matters even further, one could argue that the ridiculous arises when the "vertical" meets the "horizontal." On the one side, we have colonial officials anxiously seeking an indication of the "natives'" recognition of their authority. On the other side, we may well have "natives" using their interactions with the state's agents to appropriate something of value from across a linguistic and cultural divide.

Furnivall is not the only writer to have found comedy at the heart of state power.[31] But *The Fashioning of Leviathan* provides a distinctive perspective on the colonial situation. To arrive at this perspective, one must move beyond Furnivall's understated wit, which follows the conventions of a particular brand of British humor, to scrutinize those aspects of colonial rule that provided this sensibility with such fertile ground.[32] Approached in this fashion, Furnivall's study demonstrates why it is possible to read colonial reports against the grain, as more than simply an expression of metropolitan ideologies. In the fodder for ridicule that lurks in these reports, one finds evidence of a range of alternative points of view. In the remainder of this essay, I explore the comparative

---

[29] See Homi Bhabha, "The Other Question," *Screen* 24,6 (November/December 1983): 18-36. It seems to me that this account of the "ridiculous" provides us with one way of thinking about what Bhabha describes as the threat underlying the fetishistic production (and reproduction) of the colonial stereotype.

[30] See Karl Marx, *Capital*, ed. Frederick Engels, trans. Samuel Moore and Edward Aveling (New York: International Publishers, 1967), vol. 1, p. 132. See also Georg Simmel, *The Philosophy of Money*, second edition, trans. Tom Bottomore and David Frisby (London and New York: Routledge, 1978); Paul Bohannon, "Some Principles of Exchange and Investment among the Tiv," *American Anthropologist* 57 (1955): 60-70.

[31] See, e.g., Slavoj Zizek, "The Obscene Object of Postmodernity," in *Looking Awry: An Introduction to Jacques Lacan through Popular Culture* (Cambridge, MA: MIT Press, 1993), p. 146. In a commentary on Kafka, Zizek points to the phantasmatic underpinnings of bureaucratic authority. "In so far as the law is not grounded in truth, it is impregnated in enjoyment," Zizek writes, on the basis of Kafka's account of the "obscene, nauseous phenomena" pervading the legal system described in *The Trial*. See also Achille Mbembe, *On the Postcolony* (Berkeley: University of California Press, 2001), p. 133. Mbembe refers to obscenity (and jokes that refer to it) as "one modality of power in the postcolony," as well as "one of the arenas in which subordinates reaffirm or subvert that power." Significantly, Mbembe distinguishes between colonial and postcolonial violence, the former being linked, if not fully reducible, to "an overriding concern for profits and productivity." What Mbembe calls the "aesthetics of vulgarity" has a greater role to play in the postcolony, with its rulers' obsession for majesty and pomp. Ibid., p. 113

[32] Sandra Macpherson, David Levin, and Jacqueline Goldsby helped me clarify this point.

implications of this interpretation of Furnivall's study by examining the fashioning of colonial authority in a part of the Netherlands Indies where Leviathan's "infancy" was extended. The anecdotes that follow may not be as funny as those that Furnivall recounts, but they prove equally revealing. In coastal New Guinea, as in Tenasserim, colonial expansion turned on the fact that Leviathan just could not take a joke.

ABSTINENCE AND DISPLAY

Western New Guinea became part of the Netherlands Indies early in the nineteenth century.[33] In 1828 and 1848, the Netherlands Indies government drafted secret documents asserting sovereignty over areas of western New Guinea supposedly ruled by the North Moluccan sultanate of Tidore. These documents were kept secret for the simple reason that their publication would have exposed the degree to which Tidore's sphere of influence had been inflated to suit Dutch needs. While there is no doubt that the Tidoran sultans sporadically received tribute from the "Papuan islands," the polity's authority was most tangible in the Raja Ampats, in the waters west of the Bird's Head peninsula.[34] Yet the colonial government used Tidore's dealings in the region as the basis for its claim to New Guinea's entire western half, which was made public in 1865.[35] If indirect rule always rested on more or less fictitious foundations, when it came to New Guinea, Dutch officials were acutely aware of the fragile underpinnings of their right to rule.

New Guinea was scarcely the only section of the colony where Dutch authority existed more or less only on paper. Before the period of "ethical imperialism" described by Locher-Scholten, the Indies government "abstained" from direct

---

[33] On the history of colonial governance in western New Guinea, see A. Haga, *Nederlandsch Nieuw-Guinea en de Papoesche eilanden: Historische bijdrage*, 2 vols. (Batavia: Bruining/'S-Gravenhage: Nijhoff, 1884); F. C. Kamma, "De verhouding tussen Tidore en de Papoese eilanden in legende en historie," *Indonesië* 1 (1947-48): 361-70, 536-59; *Indonesië* 2 (1948-49): 177-88, 256-75; *Dit Wonderlijk Werk*, vol. 1 (Oegstgeest: Raad voor de Zending der Ned. Hervormde Kerk, 1976), vol. 2 (Oegstgeest: Raad voor de Zending der Ned. Hervormde Kerk, 1977); Paul W. van der Veur, *The Search for New Guinea's Boundaries* (Canberra: ANU Press, 1966); I. F. M. Salim, *Vijftien Jaar Boven Digoel: Concentratiekamp in Nieuw Guinea, Bakermat van Indonesische Onafhankelijkheid* (Amsterdam: Uitgeverij Contact, 1973); Rogier Smeele, "De Expansie van het Nederlandse Gezag en de Intensiviering van de Bestuursbemoeienis op Nederlands Nieuw-Guinea 1898-1942" (Doctoral Thesis, Institute of History, Utrecht University, 1988); Elke Beekman, "Driekleur en Kruisbanier, De Utrechtsche Zendingsvereeniging op Nederlands Nieuw-Guinea 1859-1919" (Doctoral Thesis, Erasmus University, 1989); Jan van Baal, *Ontglipt Verleden*, 2 vols. (Franeker: van Wijnen, 1989).

[34] Leonard Andaya stresses the role of Tidore in New Guinea. See Leonard Andaya, *The World of Maluku: Indonesia in the Early Modern Period* (Honolulu: University of Hawaii Press, 1993). But see Pamela Swadling, *Plumes from Paradise* (Boroko, PNG: Papua New Guinea National Museum/Robert Brown, 1996), pp. 109-10. Swadling argues that in the period before 1660, when the Dutch made their first formal treaty with Tidore, the North Moluccan Sultan of Bacan was the one who had "real influence" in the Raja Ampats.

[35] No sooner did the Dutch expand Tidoran rule than they created a mechanism for dissolving it, in contracts that contained a clause stipulating that the Netherlands Indies government could assume direct governance of the region at any time. See Swadling, *Plumes from Paradise*, p. 119.

involvement in much of the so-called "Outer Islands."[36] What was peculiar about western New Guinea was not simply its size, not simply its isolation, but also the fact that it abutted the holdings of other colonial powers. This was also the case in Borneo, yet in New Guinea, the threat posed by foreign intervention—or even just foreign attention—seemed much more palpable.[37] It was not until the 1870s that England and Germany officially set the boundaries of their own colonies on the eastern half of the island. There was little actual saber rattling, merely a vague anxiety on the part of the Dutch that outsiders might mistake the territory for unclaimed land.

During the nineteenth century, to assuage this fear, the government pursued what Rogier Smeele has called a policy of display: through limited concrete measures, the Netherlands Indies government attempted to create the impression of colonial occupation in New Guinea.[38] Fort du Bos, founded in southwestern New Guinea in 1828, proved short-lived; disease and attacks by hostile locals decimated the small garrison of Dutch and native soldiers. Undertaken in response to rumors that the Australians were contemplating establishing a similar post, the experiment was the last of its kind for years to come. Instead of establishing settlements, the Indies government dispatched war ships to erect and maintain escutcheons at intervals along New Guinea's coasts. Accompanied by the Tidoran war fleet, or *hongi*, the crews built or repaired bases for the metal shields, which were embossed with the Dutch coat-of-arms. Meanwhile, their commanders confirmed the appointment of local headmen, leaders who had received their Tidoran titles from various sources, ranging from the Sultan and his vassals, to European ship captains, to Papuan relatives and trade friends, who passed along such signs of investiture as gifts.[39] Each headman received a suit of clothing and a flag, which he was instructed to trot out whenever a foreign ship anchored near the village. The Dutchmen also distributed gifts of beads and knives to the natives, before loading up with food and water for the voyage to the next site.

While the erection of escutcheons left sporadic evidence of Dutch sovereignty in the territory, it did not solve what Dutch administrators referred to as the problem of peace and order—the government's failure to establish a monopoly over the legitimate use of violence. Given his responsibility for European security in New Guinea, the Dutch Resident of Ternate was not pleased when Protestant missionaries approached him in the mid-1850s with plans to establish a post in Doreh Bay, a popular harbor on the northeastern tip of the Bird's Head.[40] Yet the

---

[36] For much of the century, the administration concentrated its interests and investment on the "inner island" of Java, which a system of forced cultivation transformed into one of the most profitable pieces of colonial real estate in the world. Dutch activities in the outer islands were overshadowed by a long and costly war in Aceh, a polity at the northwestern tip of Sumatra near the strategic Strait of Malacca. See J. van Goor, ed., *Imperialisme in de Marge: De Afronding van Nederlands-Indie* (Utrecht: HES, 1986).

[37] Part of this anxiety could be due to the fact that in the 1780s and 1790s, the Bird's Head peninsula had sheltered the English supporters of a rebellious claimant to the Tidoran throne. See Andaya, *The World of Maluku*, pp. 220-38.

[38] See Smeele, "De Expansie van het Nederlandse Gezag."

[39] See R. F. Ellen, "Conundrums about Panjandrums: On the Use of Titles in the Relations of Political Subordination in the Moluccas and along the Papuan Coast," *Indonesia* 41 (April 1986): 47-62.

[40] See Kamma, *Dit Wonderlijk Werk*, vol. 1, p. 50.

Resident soon found a use for the evangelists, who were well apprised of regional happenings, since they supported themselves by trading with the Papuans. The administration gave the "brothers" a monthly stipend for rescuing foreign shipwreck victims, whom the natives tended to kill. Eventually, the missionaries became a thorn in the government's side, with their grisly accounts of Papuan raiding and immorality, which usually ended with a plea for the administration to apply a firmer hand. In the meantime, by preventing the scandal that would have resulted from the death of foreign nationals, the missionaries helped keep the Residents' superiors off their backs.

After the Berlin Conference of 1885, which made effective occupation a condition for the holding of colonial possessions, the stakes in New Guinea rose. As we have seen, when in 1895 the Estates General in the Hague finally agreed to allocate funds for the placement of colonial administrators and police in New Guinea, lawmakers justified the measure not only in terms of the plight of the "deeply sunken" population, but also of the Netherlands' reputation in the colonial world.[41] In the south, attacks by Tugeri tribesmen had led to complaints by the British, who had demanded that the Dutch either control their Papuan subjects or move the border so that the British could curb the raids themselves. In the north, spurred by a new fashion in ladies' hats, a "feather boom" had brought scores of Malay and European traders and hunters to New Guinea, where, with their modern rifles, they had exacerbated the region's security problems by starting a small arms race among the various tribes. Between 1898 and 1901, the government founded permanent posts at Manokwari, Fak-Fak, and Merauke.[42] But the government's accomplishments never lived up to the expectations of optimistic observers, who cherished hopes that New Guinea would not only cover the cost of its own administration, but actually turn a profit for the Dutch. Despite the introduction of a head tax and corvée labor in limited parts of the territory, the Netherlands continued to follow a policy of display, albeit by different means.

One could argue that the policy of display continued into the 1950s, when the Netherlands retained this final fragment of the colony after the rest of the Indies gained independence.[43] But to understand the impetus behind the Netherlands' costly post-war project in New Guinea, one must attend to a prior series of colonial moments. To borrow Locher-Scholten's terms, the Dutch authorities were "pulled into the periphery" in coastal New Guinea not simply by the "resistance" of their Papuan subjects, but also by the unexpected effects of their interventions. In the writings of officers charged with governing the territory, one detects a heightened awareness of the prospect of surveillance, not simply by their own superiors, not simply by other Europeans, but also by the Papuans, who turned their encounters with authority to their own peculiar ends.

---

[41] See Locher-Scholten, "Dutch Expansion in the Indonesian Archipelago," p. 107. See also Smeele, "De Expansie van het Nederlandse Gezag."

[42] With the exception of three years in the 1920s, when New Guinea was governed as a separate residency, the territory remained divided between administrative units based on Ternate and Ambon.

[43] In this time of rapid decolonization, Dutch officials were keenly aware of the publicity value of the social welfare programs they undertook on behalf of the "primitive" Papuans. Administratively and philosophically, the "ethical project" in the Indies as a whole provided a model for the mission in New Guinea. See van Baal, *Ontglipt Verleden*, vol. 2, p. 169.

VISIONS OF THE RIDICULOUS

The best place to find the ridiculous in colonial documents concerning New Guinea is neither at the end nor at the beginning of an account. Dutch officials who described their forays into the territory, not surprisingly, incorporated particular agendas into their reports. One wrote of the Papuans' "sweet, timid" nature, as part of a diatribe against the depredations of the Tidoran war fleet. "Under a civilized government, they would surely quickly attach themselves to the same and could demonstrate great service," G. F. de Bruyn Kops concluded, in an effort to convince his superiors of the value of introducing direct Dutch rule. Some decades later, van der Crab ended a description of a similar journey with harsh words on the Papuans' "disposition"—which was "in a word, bad"—to support his argument against greater investment in this god-forsaken land.[44] But in the middle of these reports—and often in the middle of particular paragraphs or even sentences—one finds an indication of these same officers' awareness of imagined observers, above and beyond the official audience for which these texts were penned.

Take, for example, de Bruyn Kops's description of the pleasure with which one group of Papuans greeted the erection of an escutcheon in 1848. The natives

> ... took it with joy that the pole was a sign that the Dutch government had taken the place under its protection, because they hoped through this to remain free of the *hongi's* visits. The upper chief was charged with keeping the pole in good condition, and, to the end of inspiring the people, they were told that it was an amulet for the village, the latter to their great satisfaction.[45]

For de Bruyn Kops, the natives' "satisfaction" indexed their almost instinctive affinity for their "civilized" Dutch rulers. The despotic Tidorans, by contrast, only enjoyed the appearance of Papuan loyalty; Papuan chiefs, de Bruyn Kops notes, only put on their yellow costumes and acted like leaders when they learned that the *hongi* was close at hand. But certain details in the passage indicate that the Papuans' enthusiasm for the Dutch may well have rested on equally shaky grounds. The people were "inspired" because they took the escutcheon for an "amulet"—called a *korwar* in this region—the temporary container of a vaguely ancestral form of power.[46] If nineteenth-century accounts are correct, when amulets ceased to work, the Papuans simply cast them into the sea.[47] The details de Bruyn

---

[44] "The disposition of the Papuans is, in a word, bad; they are crude in their manners, cruel to one another, treacherous with foreigners and traders, little subordinated to their own chiefs and more than frank with Europeans. Most writers on New Guinea are agreed on this point; also the work of the famous naturalist, Wallace, who no one should deny a proper look, describes the Papuan in very unfavorable terms." See P. J. B. C. Robide van der Aa, *Reizen naar Nederlandsch Nieuw-Guinea ondernomen op last der Regeering van Nederlandsch-Indie in de jaren 1871, 1872, 1875-1876* ('S-Gravenhage: Martinus Nijhoff, 1879), p. 131.

[45] See G. F. de Bruyn Kops, "Bijdrage tot de kennis der Noord-en Oostkusten van Nieuw Guinea," *Natuurkundig Tijdschrift voor Nederlandsch Indië* 1 (1850): 195.

[46] See Danilyn Rutherford, "The Bible Meets the Idol: Writing and Conversion in Biak, Irian Jaya, Indonesia," *Words and Things: The Anthropology of Christianity*, ed. Fenella Cannell (Durham: Duke University Press, under review).

[47] See Thomas P. van Baaren, *Korwars and Korwar Style: Art and Ancestor Worship in North-West New Guinea* (The Hague: Mouton, 1968); and Rutherford, "The Bible Meets the Idol."

Kops paints into this happy scene belie his wider message: the Papuans' "attachment" to the Dutch may not have been so solid after all.

In arguing that the Papuans' submission to the Tidorans was no more than a façade, colonial observers raised the question of whether the Papuans' submission to the Dutch might not be equally superficial. Needless to say, this question was made all the more pressing by the fact that Dutch expeditions of the period traveled with the *hongi* in tow. Clearly, one could read the signs of Dutch sovereignty—including not only the escutcheons, but also the Papuans' words and gestures—in multiple ways. An account of an 1858 Dutch expedition to Humbolt Bay ends with a long description of the joy with which the Tobati welcomed the raising of a Dutch flag over one of their "temples." At the flag's unfurling, "a cry of amazement and pleasure arose from the gathered crowd."[48] The Tobati were eager for the Dutch officers to return and found a post—an observation that the report's author presents with remarkable confidence, given that no one on the expedition knew the local language. Still, the report contains hints that the natives could be promiscuous in their affections. When the ship first arrived in Humbolt Bay, canoes soon surrounded the vessel, carrying natives whose necklaces reminded the Dutch visitors of the collars worn by French Legionnaires. Among the Papuans' "screams," one word was discernable—"*Moseu*"—interpreted by the travelers as "*Monsieur*"—a sign that the French had gotten to this bay first.[49] The casual way that Tidoran titles circulated among the Papuans—and were accepted from visiting traders—would have left Dutch officials somewhat uneasy. Other Europeans just as easily could have raised their flag on Papuan territory. The Papuans may well have been equally "satisfied" by *any* European bearing gifts.

In fact, the most unlikely of characters did serve as agents of the Dutch colonial state. Much like Furnivall's appropriately named Mr. Gouger, the merchant whom Mr. Maingy appointed as Police Superintendent, Magistrate, and Judge, these characters brought their own interests to the job.[50] The missionaries were particularly inclined to view local happenings through their own distinctive lenses, as we learn in the 1873 Memorandum of Transfer penned by F. Schenck, an outgoing Resident of Ternate. Word reached Ternate in 1872 that a pair of Italian naturalists would soon be visiting New Guinea.[51] At first, the government called on the Resident to lend the visitors his support. But in May 1873, the Resident received a secret missive warning him to watch the naturalists carefully, in

---

[48] See Commissie voor Nieuw-Guinea, *Nieuw Guinea: Ethnographisch en Natuurkundig Onderzocht en Beschreven in 1858*, published by the Koninklijk Instituut voor Taal-, Land- en Volkenkunde van Nederlandsch Indie (Amsterdam: Frederik Muller, 1862), p. 100.

[49] Ibid., p. 86. This is not to say that the escutcheons never served their purpose. Another officer reported in the 1870s that the escutcheon had served its purpose on Roon, where the crew of an English ship, in search of water, had fled when they saw the Dutch coat of arms. See Robide van der Aa, *Reizen naar Nederlandsch Nieuw-Guinea*, p. 93.

[50] "Mr. Maingy thought it would be unnecessary to enhance this salary, as it would suffice 'to grant him the privilege of trading.' Mr. Gouger must have found business profitable when, as Superintendent of Police, he could arrest those who owed him money and then, as Judge and Magistrate, choose whether to proceed them in his own court, civilly or criminally, having in either case good reason to expect a favorable judgement." See Furnivall, *The Fashioning of Leviathan*, p. 23.

[51] See Jeroen A. Overweel, ed., *Topics Relating to Netherlands New Guinea: In Ternate Residency Memoranda of Transfer and other assorted documents*, Irian Jaya Source Materials No. 13 (Leiden: DSALCUL/IRIS, 1995), pp. 58-59.

connection with the Italian government's purported plan to establish a penal colony somewhere in the Netherlands Indies.[52] Woelders, the missionary serving in the area where Beccari and Albertis launched their investigations, responded to the conflicting instructions with skepticism. He quickly developed his own reading of the Italians' objectives: they were not simply spies, they were Jesuits, which in his mind was even worse! Convinced that the Italians were distributing rosaries to the Papuans, Woelders railed against the government's tolerance in a letter reproduced in the Resident's report.

> . . . we Hollanders show such liberality with strangers, not least towards "other thinkers" [i.e. Catholics] who may one day lead us to regret it . . . the Jesuits, notwithstanding a centuries long history that warns us against it . . . we cannot bear to have men surprise us with such Satanic wiles and all faults and errors of description without apprising others of the danger.[53]

While the Resident notes that Woelders wrote "as a missionary," he appreciated the information; it was only through Woelders that he had learned that the Italians had come and gone.

In addition to the missionaries, visiting foreign nationals played a role in governing New Guinea, as another anecdote from Schenk's Memorandum makes clear. Rumors of the murder of crew members from an English pearl-fishing vessel reached Ternate by way of four Papuan heads, who had met the foreigners in Sorong, on the western tip of the Bird's Head.[54] A further report from a Tidoran vassal on one of the Raja Ampat islands filled in the details. Having refused the King of Salawatti's help, the English captain had sent two sloops to Poeloe Jaar, a lonely off-shore island, where the crew met some local people and communicated with gestures that they wanted them to go pearl diving. The local people obliged, then waited on shore until the crew was busy opening shells, at which point they set upon the men and killed them. The captain learned of the incident in Salawatti. After resolving the matter, the captain sailed on, leaving behind three letters: one for the first warship to pass through the area, one for the Prussian Consul General in Hamburg, and a third for the Sultan of Tidore, which thanked him for the King of Salawatti's assistance. In fact, the captain had forced the King of Salawatti to accompany him to the interior near Poeloe Jaar, where the hastily assembled "*hongi*" caught three suspects, including one in possession of rifles belonging to the dead Englishmen. The search party took the culprits back to the scene of the crime, where the captain ordered the King of Salawatti to pronounce judgement. The Englishmen then shot one of the culprits and hung his body from a tree as a warning. The captain left the other prisoners in Salawatti, having urged the King to execute them as well.

The King of Salawatti was understandably quite uneasy about his role in the expedition, given that the ban on *hongi* expeditions was then in force. Still, the Resident was grateful. "Be that as it may, through this hongi expedition, lawful or not, but in any case compelled with a pistol on the chest and thus excusable, they took the law into their own hands, but at the same time bringing a good end to a

---

[52] Ibid., p. 59.
[53] Ibid.
[54] Ibid., pp. 50-54.

thorny affair."⁵⁵ The English captain's actions met the requirements of "common sense" in this place where Dutch officials were more worried about angering foreigners than the niceties of judicial process. Still, the little drama made it clear that Dutch officials were far from possessing a monopoly on "legitimate" force.

By the end of the nineteenth century, this dispersal of official authority was beginning to grate. In 1903, a Dutch writer traveling with a team of naturalists met a headman on the off-shore island of Biak, who was convinced that he had an official appointment from the government on the basis of a letter "that had nothing to do with that and contained the simplest matters."⁵⁶ Although this observer found the Papuans' "familiar" relations with their European visitors amusing—and even heartening—the officers dispatched to bring New Guinea under an orderly administration at the turn of the century had a far less sanguine view of this state of affairs.⁵⁷ While earlier writers were clearly interested in the reactions of the Papuans, their requirements were modest: they asked only that the residents of particular, well-frequented trading stops be willing and able to express their awareness of Dutch sovereignty. Now the goal was to "enlighten" the Papuans. Where nineteenth-century officials confronted the fear of being observed—and replaced—by foreign interlopers, early twentieth-century officials faced the specter of appearing to the natives as the bearers of an alien, distinctly "unenlightened" power.

The writings of Lt. W. K. H. Feuilletau de Bruyn, the officer who "pacified" the island of Biak in 1915, bear evidence of this danger.⁵⁸ Feuilletau de Bruyn's campaign on Biak was part of a broader effort to bring Papuan "criminals" to justice. Instead of exacting collective retribution, the new generation of officials apprehended individuals and sent them to jail. The new policy was no doubt one factor in the mass conversion of coastal Papuans to Christianity. With the government holding them responsible for paying taxes and serving jail terms, the Papuans had good reasons for inviting native evangelists to settle in their villages: they benefited from their fluency in Malay, the Indies' administrative tongue.⁵⁹

---

⁵⁵ Ibid., p. 54.

⁵⁶ The encounter called to mind another headman who had "a receipt from a photographer as a letter of appointment. The letterhead of the receipt was printed with several medals that the man had won at exhibitions, but these stamp-like marks gave the thing its cachet." See H. A. Lorentz, *Eenige maanden onder de Papoea's*, privately published edition dedicated to Prof. Dr. C. E. A. Wichmann, Leader of the New Guinea Expedition of 1903, p. 195.

⁵⁷ "People once admonished us that we associated with them too familiarly and permitted them liberties that were not in fact proper. I believe that these persons are very mistaken and have more in mind the intercourse between Europeans and Malays or Javans. One must not forget that the Papuans feel entirely free and independent and can live very well without us. Indeed, the only thing in which our government can be noticed consists of the fact that the *korano* is given a Dutch flag and a black jacket with gold lace. He thus understands that at the arrival of a ship the bearer of the pretty jacket gets a double portion of the gifts in the form of tobacco and beads." Ibid., pp. 31-32.

⁵⁸ Feuilletau de Bruyn's Military Memorandum of Transfer, which was later published as a book-length monograph, was obviously written with a scholarly audience in mind. See Feuilletau de Bruyn, *Schouten en Padaido-eilanden, Mededeelingen Encyclopaedisch Bureau* 21 (Batavia: Javaasche Boekhandel, 1920).

⁵⁹ See W. K. H. Feuilletau de Bruyn, Militaire Memorie der Schouten-eilanden, August 31, 1916, Nummer Toegang 10-25, Stuk 183, Nienhuis Collectie van de Department van Bevolkszaken Hollandia Rapportenarchief (The Hague: Algemeene Rijksarchief, 1916), p. 244. According to

After a Biak warrior killed one of the Ambonese "teachers" (Malay: *guru*) serving on the island, the government intervened.

Feuilletau de Bruyn's goal in Biak was not merely to track down the subject; it was to institute a form of authority different from that exercised by the Tidorans. With people at such a low level of development, he noted, one achieved more through "justice tempered with mercy" than with a "mailed fist."[60] Nevertheless, in Feuilletau de Bruyn's description of the military campaign, unexpected moments of identification emerge. In a chapter of his Military Memorandum of Transfer on native warfare, he explains how Biak raiders would land their canoes some distance from an enemy village, so they could approach the waterfront houses from the rear. Almost in passing, the Lieutenant admits that he and his troops deployed the same method "with much success."[61] Feuilletau de Bruyn comes close to admitting that the detachment's surprise attacks recalled a long history of punitive raids. In order to compel the perpetrators to surrender, Feuilletau de Bruyn and his men took hostages, some of whom ended up at the government post in Manokwari. It was all the lieutenant could do to convince the locals that their loved ones had not been taken as slaves. As he notes later in the report, it was relatively easy to collect taxes on the island. "Through the levying that Tidore in earlier days imposed, people are used to the idea that taxes are levied by foreigners *in order to prevent the punishment people know they would get, which the population (incorrectly) thought we would do as well*" [the italicized section is crossed out].[62] The fact that Feuilletau de Bruyn felt compelled to eliminate the second half of the sentence in the published version of the text indicates the officer's vague cognizance of his predicament. Leading a detachment that resembled a Biak war party, calling to mind the Tidoran *hongi*, Feuilletau de Bruyn reproduced the "old" order on Biak through his very efforts to impose something new.

Registered subtly in the writings of officials like Feuilletau de Bruyn, this local perspective, which placed the "civilizing mission" in an unexpected light, became even clearer in mission documents of the period. Although missionaries like Friedrich Hartweg, a German who served in Biak during the mid-1920s, should have been grateful to the government for suppressing native raiding parties and heathen feasts, the effects of the new policies did not always meet the brothers' expectations. On the one hand, the native administrators who replaced Feuilletau de Bruyn failed to enforce the new regulations.

> We have a so-called prohibition against dance feasts. And it is naturally not followed. We have a prohibition on palm wine tapping, and that is good, but it is also only on paper. They took Marisan, the notorious raiding party leader, to Ternate [to prison]—and he escaped. They took a pair or so of pirates (murderers) to Manokwari [the government seat]—and they escaped. They have brought three murderers of village heads to the same place—they have escaped. Several years ago, those who incited unrest in North Biak were sent to

---

Feuilletau de Bruyn, the general practice on Biak was for disputants to "buy" an interpreter to represent them in legal proceedings. Matters went badly for those who did not.

[60] See Feuilletau de Bruyn, Militaire Memorie, p. 264.

[61] Ibid., p. 259.

[62] Ibid., p. 360.

Manokwari—each getting eight to ten years—and they all escaped. Can you imagine the impression this makes on the Papuan?[63]

A missionary, Hartweg noted, somewhat disingenuously, should avoid interfering in government affairs. But the Papuans themselves did not draw sharp distinctions between evangelists and government officers—they were all "pastors" (Malay: *pandita*), in their eyes—and government policy had a direct effect on Hartweg's work. The enforcement of the head tax had made it impossible for the missionary to carry out his duties without regular infusions of cash. "No Papuan is of a mind, now that he has to pay taxes and pay them quickly or be hauled away with truncheons and ropes, to work without receiving pay."[64] Due to a financial mix-up, Hartweg had become deeply in debt, not only to the Chinese traders living near the mission post, but also to the Papuans his predecessor had employed.

You know how a few Papuans can be worse than a blood sucker, but almost sixty Papuans have a claim to the 100 guilders [owed by Hartweg's predecessor, Brother Agter, who was evacuated due to poor health]. They can talk you to death . . . [65]

Hartweg had to answer to mission society leaders in the Netherlands, whom he accused, in a particularly ill-tempered letter, of taking him to be "a monarchist or a Bolshevik" after they took issue with his criticisms of the government.[66] But he also had to answer to local interlocutors, as his letters make clear. We can only guess what was at stake for Hartweg's Papuan interlocutors in their interactions with the missionary, but it seems safe to suppose it was not his recognition.[67] Hartweg's letters are tragic, to the extent that we identify with his predicament, but comic, to the degree that within them, we sense how the potential for ridicule made itself felt.

CONCLUSION

The ridiculous is the consequence of colonial intervention in settings where a systematic lack of shared understandings prevails. Such settings are not in any

---

[63] See Friedrich Hartweg, Letter to the Board of September 23, 1926, UZV K31, D12 (Oegstgeest, the Netherlands: Archives of the Hendrik Kraemer Institute). Hartweg did not mention this, but it seems clear that the Papuans' impression of the government's actions was further complicated by the fate of those who did serve out their jail terms—they often returned as Malay-speaking village chiefs.

[64] See Friedrich Hartweg, Letter to the Board of February 7, 1927, UZV K31, D 12 (Oegstgeest, the Netherlands: Archives of the Hendrik Kraemer Institute).

[65] Ibid.

[66] Hartweg's relationship with his superiors only worsened with time. The death of his two-year-old daughter in a dysentery epidemic that Hartweg's family lacked the money to flee was a particularly difficult blow. He left Biak abruptly, and we hear little of him in official mission histories, even if North Biaks in the early 1990s still remembered his visits to their communities.

[67] Elsewhere, I have argued that the mission post appeared to Biaks as a dangerous and alluring site to acquire the treasured media through which local persons and social groups were produced. See Rutherford, *Raiding the Land of the Foreigners* (Princeton: Princeton University Press, 2002).

simple sense the product of isolation. Elsewhere, I have explored how a tendency to fetishize the foreign served to reproduce a mismatch between Biak perspectives and outsiders' points of view.[68] Juxtaposed in the accounts produced by officials and missionaries, one finds evidence that the Papuans have embraced Dutch authority—and the authority of the Lord—and evidence that they have turned their interactions with these outsiders to very different ends. But in this essay, following Furnivall's lead, I have approached this gap in understanding from a different angle, to shed light on the forces that fueled Dutch imperialism in this enormous, "neglected" land.

In assessing these forces, one should not underestimate the impact on Dutch officials of serving in this difficult corner of the Indies. In 1884, A. Haga, a Resident of Ternate, ended his two-volume history of New Guinea on a despondent note: "Sovereignty brings heavy duties and great responsibilities and only over the course of an extended time will any great changes in conditions be foreseen."[69] Rather than governing New Guinea in this unbearably ridiculous fashion, some administrators suggested that the Netherlands should simply sell the territory off. But others, like Feuilletau de Bruyn, did not despair. In the 1930s, Feuilletau de Bruyn joined with former Residents of Ternate, Governors of the Moluccas, and right-wing Dutch politicians in calling for a renewed policy in New Guinea, in part as a way of opening the territory to Indo-European migration.[70] In essays published in *Tijdschrift Nieuw Guinea*, a journal he edited for several years, Feuilletau de Bruyn backed the idea of imposing a penal sanction in New Guinea, which would provide jail terms to coolies who broke their contracts, and of limiting the Papuan's rights to land.[71] Feuilletau de Bruyn's draconian proposals were never adopted. But the publications and institutions of the period set the stage for the Netherlands' retention of New Guinea by providing a justification for separating the territory from the rest of the colonial state.[72]

Arend Lijphart has suggested that the Netherlands' decision to cling to western New Guinea when Indonesia gained independence was a symptom of the "trauma of decolonization."[73] Operating at a deficit, the Dutch experiment in postwar New Guinea could be read as an effort to compensate for the Indies' sudden loss through the salvation of this long "neglected" land. A memoir recounting the

---

[68] Ibid.

[69] See Haga, *Nederlandsch Nieuw-Guinea en de Papoesche eilanden*, vol. 2, p. 435.

[70] See Rutherford, "Trekking to New Guinea: Dutch Colonial Fantasies of a Virgin Land 1900-1940," in *Domesticating the Empire: Race, Gender and Family Life in French and Dutch Colonialism*, ed. Frances Gouda and Julia Clancy-Smith (Charlottesville: University of Virginia Press, 1998).

[71] See Feuilletau de Bruyn, "Economische ontwikkelingsmogelijkheiden van Noord-Nieuw-Guinea in het bijzonder door kolonisatie van Europeanen en Indo Europeanen," *Koloniale Studiën* 17 (1933): 514-39; Feuilletau de Bruyn, "De bevolking van Biak en het kolonisatievraagstuk van Noord Nieuw-Guinea," *Tijdschrift Nieuw Guinea* 1 (1-6) (1936-37): 169-77.

[72] This decade also saw the founding of the New Guinea Studiekring, an organization chaired by van Sandick, a former governor of the Moluccas, and the publication of the first edition of a three-volume compendium on New Guinea. See W. C. Klein, *Nieuw-Guinee*, 3 vols. (Amsterdam: J. H. de Bussy, 1937).

[73] See Arend Lijphart, *The Trauma of Decolonization: The Dutch and West New Guinea* (New Haven: Yale University Press, 1966).

adventures of a minor official on Biak during the 1950s suggests the quixotic nature of this project.[74] Several chapters in the slim volume are devoted to the tension between the "pseudo-perfectionism" of high-ranking officers in the air-conditioned seat of government in Hollandia, and the "imperfections" their subordinates faced on the ground.[75] Van den Berg's recollections sometimes call to mind Furnivall's account of Leviathan's antics.[76] But van den Berg uses humor to defend what he calls the "New Guinea dream."[77] In a chapter entitled, simply, "Colonialism?" he sets straight a rumor that Biak was home to colonial extremists, by recounting how an incident in which an employer chained a Papuan worker to a flagpole was simply an innocent practical joke.[78] But if we follow Furnivall, it becomes clear that absurdity is no stranger to the violent exercise of colonial power.

Biaks have made their own jokes about the colonial experience. One I recorded described a suspect pursued by Feuilletau de Bruyn and his soldiers, who hid from the detachment by climbing a tree. When the Dutch officials were distributing tobacco to a group relaxing below, the suspect could not contain his excitement. "Hey!" he shouted to the startled soldiers. "I get some, too!" And so the poor man took his place in the long line of prisoners, bound by barbed wire wrapped around their necks. This story turns on the tension between colonialism's horizontal and vertical dimensions, but from the perspective of those who bore the brunt of their society's "reform."[79] Furnivall may claim that the colonial state does not have a sense of humor, yet he knew that law and comedy, like law and violence, go together. By assigning *The Fashioning of Leviathan* to his fortunate students, Ben Anderson taught them to approach imperialism from within the Leviathan—where the ridiculous becomes a social fact.

---

[74] See G. W. H. van den Berg, *Baalen Droefheid: Biak-Nederlands Nieuw-Guinea sche(r)tsenderwijs* (The Hague: Moesson, 1981). The title is a neologism playing on the name of a famous governor of Netherlands New Guinea that roughly glosses "Bales of Sorrow." See pp. 7-9.

[75] Ibid., pp. 57-59; 91-93.

[76] At one point, he describes how drivers who wanted a license had to pass a test that entailed identifying the entire repertoire of traffic symbols, even though the island had only one, unofficial, sign. Ibid., pp. 81-83.

[77] Ibid., p. 134.

[78] Ibid., pp. 122-26.

[79] Feuilletau de Bruyn notes that "tobacco" was the "small change" of Biak's "economy"—it is the desire for this that fixes the poor victim in the soldiers' gaze.

A New Regime of Order: The Origin of Modern Surveillance Politics in Indonesia

Takashi Shiraishi

Modern popular politics came to the Indies in the early 1910s with the rise of the *pergerakan* (movement). It was expressed in such forms as newspapers and journals, rallies and meetings, trade unions and strikes, associations and parties, novels, songs, theaters, and revolts. Modern surveillance politics followed in the late 1910s, its arrival marked by the establishment in 1919 of the Algemeene Recherche Dienst (ARD, General Investigation Service) in the attorney general's office (*hoofdparket*). Its reach expanded more widely over the empire and penetrated more deeply into the native world in the 1920s with the creation of a regional intelligence apparatus in each residency. Indonesians called this political intelligence the PID (Politieke Inlichtingendienst, Political Intelligence Service). This was not its official name, though its local manifestations—city, regional, and local intelligence units—were often called political intelligence or political investigation (*politieke inlichtingen*, *politieke recherche*).

The PID grew up with the Indonesian Communist Party (PKI, Partai Komunis Indonesia) as its first enemy. Its tradition—its mentality, its thinking, its way of seeing the native world, and its mode of operations—was shaped by this history. It carried this tradition with it to create a state of normalcy after it destroyed its Communist enemy. It was an answer on the part of the Dutch Indies state to the rise of modern Indonesian popular politics. It constituted—along with prisons and the internment camps, a relatively small modern police force (34,000 strong in 1930) and a small colonial army (37,000 strong in 1930)—a new regime of order which was imposed on the population of sixty million (in 1930) captured in a vast archipelagic empire in the 1930s, the time Indonesians called *zaman normal* (age of normalcy).[1] As such it signified the coming of age of modern surveillance politics in the Indies, the legacy of which was strongly felt in Indonesia until very recently. How, then, did this machine evolve? What were its mechanics? What mentality and thinking informed the machine? How did it work and with what consequences?

---

[1] *Indisch Verslag 1931: II, Statistisch Jaaroverzicht van Nederlandsch-Indie over het Jaar 1930* (Batavia: Landsdrukkerij, 1931), pp. 14, 405-06.

THE COMING OF MODERN POLICING

The history of the Indies police is as old as Dutch colonialism. As virtually all writing on the Dutch Indies/Indonesian police history tells us, the first police officer in the Indies was Jan Steijns van Antwerpen, whom Jan Pieterszoon Coen appointed as *baljuw*, officer of justice and head of police, when he took Jakatra from the Bantenese king and founded Batavia in 1620.[2] But we do not need to go back to the VOC (Vereenigde Oost-Indische Compagnie, the United [Dutch] East India Company) prehistory of the Indies state to understand the modern police that came into being in the early twentieth century. The foundation of the modern police was laid in the early nineteenth century, when the bankrupt VOC was transformed into a state under the Napoleon-appointed old Jacobin governor general, Herman Willem Daendels (1808-1811) and his successor British liberal governor general, Thomas Stamford Raffles (1811-1816).

Daendels did away with the government of Java's North East Coast and divided the area into five prefectures. He organized a corps of *djajangsekar*, native light dragoons, in each prefecture as an instrument of power for the prefect. *Djajangsekar* were later organized in Cirebon and Banten, too, when their sultanates were reduced to residencies under Raffles. Thus started the tradition of para-military armed police to maintain quiet and order in Java's countryside.[3]

Raffles's contribution was greater. He discovered, in Muntinghe's words, "the ancient institution of village administration which had existed since before the times of the Mohammedan domination along the entire coast of Java." In his regulation of February 11, 1814, Raffles made the village headman responsible for policing in his own village and required him to organize a regular night watch for maintaining order, preventing crimes, and arresting criminals. Raffles also divided the territory into areas (residencies), each area into districts (regencies), and each district into divisions headed by a division officer. In each division, the regulation stipulated, a police station was to be established with several subordinate officials called *mantri* and other police officers. With the promulgation of this regulation in February 1814, Raffles laid on paper the foundation of the two most enduring Dutch Indies/Indonesian police institutions: the village police (*desapolitie*) and the administrative police (*bestuurspolitie*).[4]

When the Dutch returned to the Indies in 1818, their government inherited these police institutions. In 1819, however, Governor General G. A. Baron van der

---

[2] See, for instance, A. Neijtzell de Wilde, "De Nederlandsch-Indische Politie," in *Koloniaal Tijdschrift* 13 (1924): 115; Abdulkadir Widjojoatmodjo, *Riwajat Kepolisen di Hindia Ollanda dengan Ringkas: Lezing dengan hadlirat j.m. toen Resident Prijangan Tengah dalam Congres Inlandsche Politie Bond ke-tiga di Bandoeng pada boelan April 1927 tanggal 17* (Semarang: Typ Khouw Beng Wan, 1927), p. 5; "Uit de Voorgeschiedenis der Politie," in *Vereeniging van Hoogere Politie-Ambtenaren, 1916-1936: Jubileum-Nummer van de Nederlandsch-Indische Politiegids bij Gelegenheid van het 20 Jarig Bestaan van de Vereeniging* (Batavia: n.p., 1936), p. 17; P. Dekker, *De Politie in Nederlandsch-Indie: Hare Beknopte Geschiedenis, Haar Taak, Bevoedheid, Organisatie en Optreden* (Soekaboemi: Drukkerij "Insulinde," Tweede Druk, 1938), p. 3.

[3] Dekker, *De Politie*, p. 35; See also Heather Sutherland, *The Making of a Bureaucratic Elite* (Singapore: Heinemann Educational Books, Asian Studies Association of Australia Southeast Asia Publications Series, no. 2, 1979), pp. 7-8.

[4] Dekker, *De Politie*, pp. 37-38; Sutherland, *Making of a Bureaucratic Elite*, pp. 8-9.

Capellen made yet another institutional innovation. Through two regulations on criminal justice and on the administration of police and criminal justice, he made the attorney general (*procureur generaal*) central head of justice and police and made the Resident regional head of the administrative police. But the Residents were not under the attorney general, and though he had his own regional representatives, these officers of justice possessed fewer powers than the Residents. Thus started a dualism. The attorney general and the officers of justice, in effect, became responsible for European justice and police, while the Residents were in charge of native justice and police. This dualism survived into the twentieth century.[5]

This regime remained in force throughout the nineteenth century with minor modifications. In the years from the 1870s to the 1890s, *djajangsekar*, *pradjoerit* (literally, soldiers), and other para-military armed police forces, which had been part of the colonial army and led by non-commissioned army officers, were phased out and replaced by a corps of police agents. This corps was organized out of police *oppassers* (*opas/upas*, messengers, attendants, policemen) of the administrative police, attached to Dutch and native administrative officials—Residents, assistant Residents, *schouten* (sheriffs, chiefs of administrative police in major urban centers), regents, *patih* (regents' chief deputies), district heads (*wedana*), and subdistrict heads (assistant *wedana*). In Java's three urban centers of Batavia, Semarang, and Surabaya, this police organization was placed under the authority of the assistant Resident for police, while in the rest of the empire its police agents were attached, like previous police *oppassers*, to administrative officials. This police force was made responsible for prison and treasury guard duties and for transportation of prisoners and government money, as well as for maintaining order and carrying out normal police duties.[6]

The establishment of the corps of police agents marked the beginning of professional police (*beroepspolitie*) in the Indies, the fourth type of Indies police, along with armed police, village police, and administrative police. In the early twentieth century, however, the combined force of administrative and professional police remained small. In 1907-1908, it was about 9,500 men strong, including police agents in charge of guarding prisons, transporting prisoners, and policing forests and salt and opium monopolies, and was led by about seven hundred police *mantri*. According to the estimate of A. Neijtzell de Wilde, who served as a member of the welfare commission studying the police situation in those days, at least four thousand more police agents and *oppassers* were needed for the 25,000 villages in Java and Madura.[7]

The government also became concerned about police corruption, as was pointed out in many studies on the police about that time. In the early twentieth century, as in the previous century, administrative officials from Residents and regents down to police *mantri* and *oppassers* relied heavily on "henchmen and spies," variously called *palang* (literally, junction), *weri* (spy), *jagabaya* (police), and *jago*

---

[5] Dekker, De Politie, p. 39.

[6] Ibid., pp. 40-44.

[7] Neijtzell de Wilde, "De Nederlandsch-Indische Politie," pp. 119-23. According to Neijtzell de Wilde, each Resident and regent was allocated four *oppassers* in 1907-1908; assistant Residents were allocated three; *patih* one; *wedana* four; assistant *wedana* two; and police *mantri* two. Ibid., p. 119.

(literally, fighting cock). These networks of administrative and police officials and their henchmen and spies formed a twilight zone linking the official state sphere and Java's village world. James Rush describes this twilight zone thus:

> Jagabaya distinguished themselves from ordinary villagers by their supravillage experience and an aptitude for intrigue . . . Their metier was crime, its perpetration and detection, and their services were for hire. Thus they frequently appear alongside other local functionaries as village police (*kapetengan*), appointed by headmen to protect villages from banditry and arson, and as detectives and "secret police" in the service of headmen, *priyayi* officials, and Dutch administrators . . . The social environment of the *jagabaya* was much broader than that of the ordinary villager. *Jagabaya* gathered in opium and gambling dens and consorted among the fringe elements of Javanese society: dancing girls, prostitutes and pimps, traveling show folk, magicians and con-men, brigands, fences, and thieves. It was their familiarity with these elements and their equal familiarity with the village world that made them such valuable resources. *Jagabaya* were, therefore, enlisted in the service of not only the native and Dutch authorities, but also a variety of other individuals and groups whose interests penetrated the village world.[8]

In the nineteenth century, Dutch administrative officials were part of this twilight zone and the government had to live with it to maintain *rust en orde* and to raise revenues. In the early twentieth century, however, when "progress" and "promotion of native welfare" became watchwords for the new Ethical era, the government could no longer afford to tolerate police corruption, and police reform became a major political issue of the day. In 1904 the government commissioned Assistant Resident L. R. Priester to study police reform in Java's three major urban centers, Batavia, Semarang, and Surabaya, and he experimented with reform measures in Semarang, creating a police organization, led by a professional police chief and chief commissioner of police, which was autonomous of the administrative officials in its everyday operation.

Two years later, W. Boekhoudt was commissioned to study police reform in Java and Madura outside the three major urban centers. Not surprisingly, his major concern was the "penetration" of underworld networks of *guru weri* ("spy masters," adepts of magical lore) and their disciples among local administrative and police officials. In his 1907 report he therefore argued for the centralization, institutional autonomy, and professional leadership of the police under the chief commissioner of police, and for the retention of administrative police under the Resident, while

---

[8] James R. Rush, "Social Control and Influence in Nineteenth Century Indonesia: Opium Farms and the Chinese of Java," *Indonesia* 35 (April 1983): 59. Also see his *Opium to Java: Revenue Farming and Chinese Enterprise in Colonial Indonesia, 1860-1910* (Ithaca: Cornell University Press, 1990); Onghokham, "The Inscrutable and the Paranoid: An Investigation into the Sources of the Brotoningrat Affair," in *Southeast Asian Transitions: Approaches through Social History*, ed. Ruth T. McVey (New Haven: Yale University Press, 1978); Neijtzell de Wilde, "De Nederlandsch-Indisch Politie," p. 122; "Nogmaals Politiespionnen," in *De Nederlandsch-Indische Politiegids*, January 1932, no. 7, pp. 51-53; "Uit de Desa II: Spion," in *De Nederlandsch-Indische Politiegids*, December 1934, no. 12, pp. 283-93; *Onderzoek naar de Mindere Welvaart der Inlandsche Bevolking op Java en Madoera: VIIIb. Overzicht van de Uitkomsten der Gewestelijke Onderzoekingen naar 't Recht en de Politie en daaruit gemaakte Gevolgtrekkingen. Deel II. Slotbeschouwingen* (Batavia: Ruygrok, 1912).

suggesting surveillance of rural supravillage underworld figures, from *guru weri* (also called *guru ngelmu* and *guru kadigdayan*) and hermits (such as *pendito, begawan, ajar*) down to gold and silver smiths, heads of dancing girls (*kepala tandak*), brothel owners (*germo*) and so on.[9]

The first major police reorganization was introduced in 1911 on the basis of these studies. The most important of these reforms was the organization of the city police (*stadspolitie*) in Batavia, Semarang, and Surabaya, led by professional police officers (*vakman*). The Batavia city police force (including Meester Cornelis) was six hundred men strong, while the combined Semarang and Surabaya police force was 675 men strong. City police were organized in several other municipalities—Medan, Bandung, Yogyakarta, Surakarta, Malang, and Makassar—in 1914.

In the 1910 plan to strengthen the central police leadership, the government also decided to appoint a second advocate general for police leadership, who would be under the attorney general, and an inspector of police for police management, under the director of internal administration. But the budget for these measures was not approved by the Dutch parliament, making it a major issue for police reform in the 1910s.[10]

In the next year, 1912, an armed police force (*gewapende politie*) was established out of the remaining *pradjoerit* and other local para-military police units. Each region (*gewest*, i.e., residency) received one division and each regency (*afdeeling*) a platoon-size detachment. Each division was commanded by a captain seconded from the colonial army, and the entire armed police was placed under the department of internal administration. Its force strength, initially five thousand, reached ten thousand men in a few years.[11] It should also be mentioned that the police school was opened in 1914 for training police commissioners (*commissarissen*) and inspectors (*opzieners*) to mark the completion of the police reform planned in the early 1910s.[12]

By the time the police reorganization was completed in 1914, however, its shortcomings had become apparent to the government in Buitenzorg and the ministry of colonies in The Hague. One can see why if one recalls its timing. All the studies on which the reform was based had been carried out in the first decade of the twentieth century, the last major study being W. Boekhoudt's, which was completed in 1907. This meant that the reform had not anticipated the rise of the *pergerakan*, the movement, as represented by the Sarekat Islam (SI, Islamic Union), which started in early 1912 and whose enormous expansion, like a "flood," in 1912-1914, was accompanied in many places by street fighting, disturbances,

---

[9] W. Boekhoudt, *Rapport Reorganisatie van het Politiewezen op Java en Madoera (Uitgezonderd de Vostenlanden, de Particuliere Landerijen en de Hoofdplaatsen Batavia, Semarang en Soerabaja), 1906-07* (Batavia: Landsdrukkerij, 1908), pp. 6-9 and 18-19. For a succinct explanation of Priester's and Boekhoudt's studies, see Dekker, *De Politie*, pp. 47-54.

[10] Dekker, *De Politie*, pp. 55-60; Neijtzell de Wilde, "De Nederlandsch-Indische Politie," pp. 124-25. In 1911 the force strength of the entire police in Java and Madura (i.e., city, professional, and administrative police combined) was about eleven thousand men. Neijtzell de Wilde, "De Nederlandsch-Indische Politie," p. 125.

[11] A. Hoorweg, "Gewapende Politie," in *Vereeniging van Hoogere Politie-Ambtenaren 1916-1936*, pp. 41-44.

[12] "De Opleidingsschool van het Personeel der Politie," in ibid., pp. 49-50.

boycotts, beatings, killings, an "improper" attitude toward officials, and other acts of "undermining" state authorities.

Boekhoudt, for instance, had written in 1907 that "national feeling seems not to exist among the Javanese, at least it is fast asleep." In his view, disturbances among Javanese derived from "Pan-Islamism" and/or "fanaticism [*dweepzucht*] for the restoration of a Javanese kingdom," but they were local and did not constitute a threat to the state. *Ratu adil* (just king) movements, which could be easily dealt with in the police courts under legislation forbidding the holding of meetings without permission, did not have any deep political significance anyway. More worrisome, he said, was Pan-Islamism, especially international networks of *tarekat* spanning Java, Singapore, and Mecca.[13]

> [But] it does not mean that it [Pan-Islamism] makes me worry about subversion of authority by an internal enemy. There is no reason for that. . . But I fear for the life of officials and private citizens in the interior, who [have to] rely on themselves because of the absence of state protection until [the arrival of] the military force from the nearby [regional] capital to quell the revolt [*oproer*].[14]

Boekhoudt thus argued for the need of a better armed police force and political police to alert administrative officials to potential troubles in their localities.[15] The reorganized police in the early 1910s could adequately handle the problems he had anticipated.

The problem the Sarekat Islam presented to the government, however, was entirely different. It was not, as Governor General A. W. F. Idenburg well understood, that the SI was subversive, though many Dutch and native administrative officials in the field believed it to be. The chief problem was that it was national, not local, in scope. It did not come from Pan-Islamism and/or *ratu adilism*, but was built on Malay language newspapers and rallies (*vergaderingen*) and led by journalists-turned-*pergerakan*-leaders. Idenburg, moreover, did not want to destroy the SI. He understood it as a sure sign of native awakening, and as adviser for native and Arabic affairs, Dr. D. A. Rinkes, put it, he wanted to guide Sarekat Islam "onto the path we hope or at least not objectionable to our authority."[16] The government had to deal with the SI differently from the way in which it dealt with the native disturbances that derived from Pan-Islamism and fanaticism for the restoration of a Javanese kingdom.

To understand the thinking of high-ranking government officials in the Indies and The Hague about police reform in the mid-1910s, it is useful to examine what P. H. Fromberg Sr. had to say about it. A former member of the Supreme Court and foremost expert on modern Chinese popular movements in the Indies, Fromberg was consulted by the minister of colonies about "who should lead the Indies police?" He addressed the question in light of the rise of modern popular politics in the Indies in 1915.

---

[13] Boekhoudt, *Rapport Reorganisatie*, pp. 3-5.

[14] Ibid., p. 5.

[15] Ibid.

[16] Takashi Shiraishi, *An Age in Motion: Popular Radicalism in Java, 1912-1926* (Ithaca: Cornell University Press, 1990), p. 69. For government policy toward the SI in its early days, see pp. 68-69.

In his view, there was no legal ambiguity about the attorney general being the central leader in the matter of policing. The problem was that he was not in a position institutionally to exert his leadership. Fromberg noted that the adviser for native and Arabic affairs was playing an important role in the popular movement in Java and had an enormous knowledge of religious trends and native languages. He also maintained good relations with prominent people in native society, attended SI rallies and conferences, and read native newspapers. No doubt his reports should be valuable for the attorney general in evaluating the situation. But the adviser, Fromberg reminded the minister, belonged to the department of education and religion, and his reports did not reach the attorney general regularly. He noted that this was also the case with the adviser for Chinese affairs whose reports should have been important for the attorney general in evaluating the Chinese situation in the Indies in the wake of the Chinese revolution in 1911. But his reports, too, did not regularly reach the attorney general because they were submitted to the governor general through the director of internal administration and the attorney general was out of its bureaucratic circuit. As a result, Fromberg argued, the attorney general was left without important information about "natives, Indos [Eurasians], anti-government Muslims, Chinese, boycott organizations, rival Chinese *kongsi* [secret societies], ethnic rivalries, etc.," and knew little more than was reported in Dutch-language newspapers. This was the reason, in his view, that the attorney general was unable to provide any central leadership, when for instance he applied the regulation of associations and assemblies to the SI. In the SI's early days, each local chief took his own measures without consulting the attorney general, and this resulted in confusion. One Resident banned even the smallest SI meeting, while another let the SI hold rallies and meetings more liberally. Similar, too, was the confusion in the government's handling of Chinese "agitations" in the wake of the revolution. The Resident of Surabaya gave the Chinese permission to hoist the Chinese national flag after consulting with the attorney general, while the Resident of Batavia banned it after talking with the governor general.[17]

Fromberg concluded, therefore, that "there is practically no chief of police in the Netherlands Indies." But there should be a central leadership for providing the general guidelines and instructions for policing and for maintaining general supervision over the entire police force, because "rebellious movements, racial conflicts, boycott organizations etc., are not normally confined to a municipality, a division or a region." The same argument can be made, Fromberg added, for policing counterfeit money, piracy, and sugar cane burning. Anyway there should be no confusion on the part of the government in the regulation of associations and assemblies, processions and demonstrations, theaters and films and so on.[18] So his conclusion was:

> He [the attorney general] should get to know the reports of the adviser for native affairs, of the officials for Chinese affairs, of the inspectors of the [government] opium monopoly as regards smugglings, political reports and communications [*verslagen en mededeelingen*], of the residents as far as they have to do with security police [*veiligheidspolitie*], crime statistics as needed

---

[17] P. H. Fromberg Sr., "Nota-Fromberg," in Dekker, *De Politie*, pp. 62-64.
[18] Ibid., p. 67.

for the supervision of district and village policing. . . Police authorities (chief commissioners, Residents, and assistant Residents) should be required to put [regulations they issue] on record and send [their written reports] to the attorney general if they affect general police regulations, for instance, regulations concerning the curbing of cattle theft, sugar cane burning, . . .[19]

It was not until late 1919, however, that Governor General J. P. Graaf van Limburg Stirum decided to take measures, initially on an emergency basis, to make the attorney general's office a functioning central source of authority and leadership for the nation's police forces. The reason was simple. In May 1916, as a result of the Great War in Europe, van Limburg Stirum had created a central political intelligence agency, the Politieke Inlichtingendienst, or PID. Its task was to place foreigners and socialists under surveillance and to investigate revolutionary trends in the Indies. It was a small operation headed by W. Muurling, former captain of the general staff of the Indies army, with one officer each stationed in Batavia, Semarang, and Surabaya. But it reported directly to the governor general, and had regular access to the reports the adviser for native affairs, the adviser for Chinese affairs, the Residents, and city police chiefs sent to Buitenzorg. Van Limburg Stirum could rely on the PID for directing the police. With the end of the War, however, there was no longer any official justification for its continuation. Muurling recommended its disbanding in November 1918. In April 1919 it was formally dissolved, and its functions were transferred to military intelligence.[20]

But the internal security situation, seen from the government's perspective, started to deteriorate precisely in these months. There was a massive anti-Chinese riot in late 1918 in Kudus, a major center of *kretek* cigarette production in Central Java, led by Muslim producers and traders. The *pergerakan* also started to revive in late 1918, for the first time since the heady days of the early SI in 1912 and 1913. Its radical wing, represented by the Insulinde and the "red" Semarang SI led by Semaoen, expanded its influence. A series of peasant strikes took place in the Surakartan countryside, led by Hadji Misbach and local Insulinde activists. Strike actions were also mounted in Central and East Java, especially among sugar factory workers who joined the Sugar Factory Workers' Union, PFB (Personeel Fabriek Bond), led by Yogyakartan CSI (Centraal Sarekat Islam) leader Soeryopranoto. In Toli-Toli, Central Sulawesi, a Dutch controleur was killed in June 1919 when he visited the area to enforce corvée duties, after Abdoel Moeis, loyalist CSI leader, made a propaganda tour there and unwittingly sparked popular enthusiasm for the *pergerakan*.[21]

But most important was the incident that took place in West Java in July 1919. In Garut, Hadji Hasan and his family who resisted forced rice delivery were shot

---

[19] Ibid., p. 75. Also see Nijtzell de Wilde, "De Nederlandsch-Indische Politie," p. 151.

[20] For information on the PID, see R. C. Kwantes, *De Ontwikkeling van de Nationalistische Beweging in Nederlandsch-Indie: Eerste Stuk 1917-medio 1923* (The Development of the Nationalist Movement in the Dutch Indies, first volume, 1917–mid-1923) (Groningen: H. D. Tjeenk Willink, 1975), p. 134; Theodore Friend, *The Blue-Eyed Enemy: Japan against the West in Java and Luzon, 1942-1945* (Princeton: Princeton University Press, 1988), p. 35; Mailrapport [hereafter Mr.] 209x/1919, Verbaal [hereafter Vb.] 10-7-19, no. 45, in the Archives of the former Ministry of the Colonies (Algemeene Rijksarchief, The Hague).

[21] For the *pergerakan* in 1919, see Shiraishi, *An Age in Motion*, Chapters 3 and 4.

to death by armed police led by the assistant Resident. Investigating the shooting, the local authorities "unearthed" the existence of a secret SI organization, SI Afdeeling B (B branch), with "subversive" purposes. In a symbolic way, the Afdeeling B affair exposed the contradiction inherent in Ethical thinking, whose basic idea was that the natives could be guided onto the path of progress under Dutch tutelage. It was this idea on which was built the government's policy toward the *pergerakan* as shown in Governor General Idenburg's recognition of the legal status of the SI in 1913. But the Afdeeling B affair demonstrated that Dutch tutelage was a fantasy of Dutch liberals and that the hidden mysterious forces in native society had found new outlets for exerting themselves in the *pergerakan*. This deeply worried the government. All Java's Residents were instructed to investigate the existence of the SI Afdeeling B in their own regions. Dutch newspapers in the Indies went hysterical about native conspiracies. The European community was in panic.[22]

Immediately after the Afdeeling B affair, Advocate General H. V. Monsanto warned the governor general of the movement's "decay," its "getting wild (*verwildering*)," and suggested that a central investigation bureau attached to the attorney general's office and supported by a regional intelligence network should be created to assume the functions the PID had performed in the war years. He argued:

> Many factual materials are there, scattered all over the government bureaus and regional and local chiefs' offices, but they need to be pieced out, brought together, sorted out, and ordered from the policing point of view [. . .] in order to know with more certainty than [we do] now how extensive a revolutionary drive of various associations has become, what influence this [revolutionary drive] has over the population, . . . what dangers of excesses threaten the country, people, and ultimately the authority.[23]

In his opening address to the Volksraad on September 1, 1919, the governor general announced that "where the movement exceeds the bounds it will bite iron."[24] In the same month, he decided to organize a field police force, *veldpolitie*, as an instrument of repression against "local excesses" and create a general investigation service (*algemeene rechercdedienst*) attached to the attorney general's office. As he informed S. J. Hirsch, the chairman of the powerful sugar syndicate, the first task of the general investigation service was to investigate the Afdeeling B affair.[25]

With this decision, the political policing apparatus was finally in place. In the center, the attorney general led and supervised the entire police operation, while the director of internal administration, assisted by the inspectors of general

---

[22] Ibid., pp. 113-14.

[23] "Advocaat-generaal (H. V. Monsanto) aan gouverneur-generaal (Van Limburg Stirum), 25 juli 1919," in Kwantes, *De Ontwikkeling: 1917-medio 1923*, p. 133.

[24] "Redevoering van zijne Excellentie den Gouverneur Generaal bij gelegenheid van het openbaar gehoor op 1 September 1919," *De Indische Gids* 41 (1919), pp. 1438-39.

[25] "1ste gouvernementssecretaris aan voorzitter van het Algemeen syndicaat van suikerfabrikanten in Nederlandsch-Indie (S. J. Hirsch), 5 maart 1920," in Kwantes, *De Ontwikkeling: 1917-medio 1923*, p. 214.

police (*algemeene politie*) and armed police (*gewapende politie*), was made responsible for the central management of the police force. In the regions, regional police chiefs—the chief commissioners of police in Batavia, Semarang, and Surabaya; adjunct chief commissioners of police in Medan, Bandung, Yogyakarta, and Surakarta; and commissioners of police first class in the rest of the colony—were made responsible for leading and managing the general police force, which included the city police force (*stadspolitie*) with its investigation branch (*stadsrecherche*), field police (*veldpolitie*) with their embryonic regional investigation service (*gewestelijke recherche*), administrative police (*bestuurspolitie*) with their local investigation service (*plaatselijke recherche*), and village police (*desapolitie*).[26]

Mechanics of Political Policing

The ARD (General Investigation Service) was established by the government decree of September 24, 1919, with A. E. van der Lely, commissioner of police first class, as its chief and with a budget of ƒ4,680. Its office was located at Waterlooplein Oost No. 1. Van der Lely, who had served as commissioner of police first class in the Batavia city police from 1915 to 1919, moved to the attorney general's office in late November 1919, though he was formally appointed ARD chief on December 27. His day-to-day task was "to gather, order, sort out and link" "the almost constantly arriving stream of official reports and records as well as the daily news reports" which were sent by the regional investigation services, and "to give instructions and order investigations with reference to that information."[27] The ARD was expected to alert the attorney general to problems and advise him regarding directives and information that ought to be provided to the regional investigation service. To assist the ARD chief with his work, two more officers were appointed in July 1920: Mohamad Jatim, previously with the political intelligence section of the Batavia city police, a native ARD officer with the rank of *wedana* (his appointment was announced on July 30, 1920); and B. R. van der Most, previously commissioner of police second class with the Semarang city police, as deputy chief, though his appointment was not formally announced until February 1925.[28]

Along with the ARD, a new post of second advocate general for police was created, with A. Neijtzell de Wilde (whom we met earlier as a leading expert in police reorganization and as an official, since July 1916, in the attorney general's office) as its first incumbent. The advocate general for police was responsible for the daily supervision of the ARD, but the ARD chief reported directly to the attorney general.

Attorney General G. W. Uhlenbeck informed the heads of the regional administration of the creation and mission of the ARD in a secret circular dated

---

[26] See the organizational chart included in Neijtzell de Wilde, "De Nederlandsch-Indische Politie"; Dekker, *De Politie*, pp. 179 and 191.

[27] Attorney general (G. W. Uhlenbeck) to governor general (van Limburg Stirum), March 20, 1920, Mr. 520x/20.

[28] Uittreksel uit het Register der Besluiten van den Gouverneur Generaal van Nederlandsch-Indie, Buitenzorg, May 15, 1920, no. 2x, Mr. 520x/20. Mohamad Jatim was later promoted to the rank of *patih* in August 1927. Van der Most was most likely the chief of the political intelligence section of the Semarang city police from July 1919 to July 1920.

April 16, 1920, where he assured the Residents that this new organization was not meant to form a second body (*instantie*) for the local police leadership or to change daily police practices. He continued:

> But there should be a center informed of the trends and symptoms in Indies society . . . The task of the general leader of police should be to make the local leaders of police follow the governmental principles known to him, to test the regulations proposed or taken by the local police authorities not only and exclusively based on practical considerations but also in terms of legal provisions, and thus to exercise control over the local leaders of police [to make sure that] the police not run the risk of going astray from the legal framework. The task of the central leadership is to provide general [guide] lines.

This power was now vested in the attorney general, he said, and the advocate general for police and the ARD were to assist him in exercising central leadership in policing. He then went on to describe the mechanics:

> a) In the three urban centers in Java [i.e., Batavia, Semarang, and Surabaya] and in several other places there now exists a city investigation service on a more modern basis. Elsewhere investigation personnel are now being very much strengthened. We now intend, starting with Java and Madura, to attach to the heads of the regional administration who are and remain responsible for the daily exercise of police [power] in their area a technical leader of police (one leader for two residencies for the moment) with the rank of at least commissioner of police first class, who, aside from taking care of the training of police personnel and good cooperation between various police units in the designated domains, must be responsible for an effective division and work of the investigation over the regions concerned.
>
> Finally [the technical leader of police] should [be responsible] for giving more support in their investigation to the intelligence [units of administrative police] which for now must remain in the hands of the European and native administration, and where necessary and feasible should establish a regional investigation depot [*gewestelijke recherchedepot*] to provide assistance in the region wherever local investigation [units] are insufficient for [the investigation of] certain cases.
>
> b) The regional investigation service . . . must report to the central leadership of police [i.e., attorney general] information it obtains which may be of interest to him; It [the ARD] has as its special task to gather, order, and sort out what the regional and local investigation [services] track down and what is reported to it by the local service as interesting for the general leader and furthermore to draw attention of the general leader of police to that which can be useful as information for the regional investigation. The ARD therefore forms an integral part of the central police exercise without which a good general leadership would not be possible.[29]

---

[29] Parket van den Procureur Generaal, "Rondschrijven aan de Hoofden van Gewestelijke Bestuur," Weltevreden, April 16, 1920, Mr. 503x/20.

It should be clear from this circular what institutional shape the political policing apparatus was about to take. In the center, there was the attorney general, the central leader of police, assisted by the advocate general for police and the ARD. In major cities, which included not only Batavia, Semarang, and Surabaya, but also Medan, Padang, Palembang, Bandung, Yogyakarta, Surakarta, Malang, Makassar, and several others by 1920, there was a city police force, led by a chief commissioner of police, adjunct chief commissioner of police, or commissioner of police first class. The city police usually consisted of four branches: secretariat or general affairs; investigation [*recherche*] with a photographic and dactylographic studio and a police library; general control over street patrols, uniforms, firearms, book-keeping, and treasury; and traffic police. Each branch was headed by a commissioner of police first class.[30]

The investigation branch (*afdeeling recherche*), also called the city investigation service (*stadsrecherche*, in comparison to the regional investigation service) or central investigation service (*centrale recherche*, to distinguish it from the general investigation service, the ARD) consisted of several sections, each headed by a commissioner of police second class or police *wedana* (i.e., native police officer with the rank of *wedana* [district chief] which was the highest native police rank). These sections were: general administrative affairs, responsible for gathering and processing criminal data, keeping registers and dossiers, compiling statistics, managing special intelligence archives, and storing information on persons and cases not under investigation; criminal investigation (*opsporingsdienst*); moral police (*zedenpolitie*) in charge of prostitution, trade in women, coolie recruitment, gambling, exploitation of children and women, hotel control, etc.; Chinese affairs; surveillance of immigrants and foreigners; opium police; photographic and dactylographic studio; and, most important, political investigation or intelligence (*politieke recherche* or *politieke inlichtingen*). Subsections were normally headed by police assistant *wedana* (native police officer in the rank of assistant *wedana*) or police *mantri*.[31]

Political intelligence, so called officially after 1926, initially formed a section in the investigation branch, but after 1926-1927 became a branch in its own right, often taking on responsibility for policing immigrants and foreigners and in close communication with the Chinese affairs section. Its task, even defined in general terms, was very extensive. It was responsible for control over the exercise of the right of association and assembly; surveillance of rallies (*vergaderingen*); registration and reporting on meetings (*bijeenkomsten*); handling requests to hold rallies open to the public; reporting on rallies and associations; alerting the Resident and the *hoofdparket* to an association which threatened public order; investigation of secret associations (that is, associations without legal status of incorporation); investigation and recommendation for externment and internment; surveillance of the press; issuance of press cards; surveillance of the import of dangerous printed material and other propaganda means; immigration and emigration; surveillance of stations, hotels, ports, and other public places; control over the weapons trade. It was also in charge of investigating any association

---

[30] Dekker, *De Politie*, pp. 197-99.
[31] Ibid., pp. 203-205 and 211-12; Neijtzell de Wilde, "De Nederlandsch-Indische Politie," p. 126.

applying for the legal status of incorporation; of requests for naturalization and equal status with the Europeans; and control over name changes and so on.[32]

The relationship of the city investigation service with the regional and local investigation services differed from one region to another. In one residency, it was headed by its own chief under the chief of city police and separated from the regional investigation service attached to field police and the local investigation units of the administrative police. In another it was combined with the investigation units of administrative police to form a central investigation service. And in yet another residency the central investigation service was combined with the regional investigation depot and led directly by the city police chief who also acted as technical leader of field police.[33]

The organization of the regional (*gewestelijk*, i.e., residency) investigation service was more complicated. It consisted of the local (*plaatselijk*, i.e., regency, district, and sub-district) investigation units nestled in the administrative police, the investigation units attached to field police detachments, and the regional investigation depot led directly by the technical leader of field police. The most important, however, was the regional investigation depot, which, according to the first advocate general for police, Neijtzell de Wilde, was created to serve as the backbone of regional political policing and to assist the work of the field and administrative police.[34]

The field police began to be organized in 1919 and had replaced the armed police by 1922-1923 except in the Moluccas and Menado. Their initial force strength in 1923 was three thousand field police agents, with 780 horses, 2,500 bicycles, and 420 motorcycles, but the force expanded to about ten thousand men in a few years. Each unit, called a detachment or brigade, was on average thirty men strong, and was led by a posthouse commandant or group chief, and these units were stationed in ninety barracks all over the Indies.[35]

Field police agents were recruited from outside the region but from the same linguistic area. Two hundred inspectors and sixty chief agents were recruited from the Netherlands, while many others were recruited from among non-commissioned officers and soldiers of the former German colonial army in Kianchow. Nine army officers were appointed commissioners of police first class to act as regional leaders. In Java, field police were placed under the technical leader responsible for two residencies, and where there was a city police force, its chief doubled as technical leader.[36]

A small intelligence branch was attached to each field police detachment. It was staffed by one or two police *mantri* and several agents, who worked in close

---

[32] For the whole list of the task of the political intelligence section, see Dekker, *De Politie*, pp. 205-206.

[33] Ibid., p. 206.

[34] Neijtzell de Wilde, "De Nederlandsch-Indische Politie," p. 129.

[35] Ibid., p. 227. Hoorweg, "Gewapende Politie," pp. 44-46. Neijtzell de Wilde, "De Nederlandsch-Indische Politie," p. 133.

[36] "De Opleidingsschool," p. 51; "De Veldpolitie," p. 60. The chief commissioners of police in Batavia, Bandung, Semarang, and Surabaya acted as technical leaders for the field police units in Batavia and Banten, Priangan, Semarang, and Surabaya and Madura respectively; the adjunct chief commissioners of police/commissioners of police first class of Yogyakarta, Surakarta, Madiun, Kediri, and Malang served simultaneously as technical leaders of field police for Yogyakarta, Surakarta, Madiun, Kediri, Pasuruan, and Besuki.

communication with local investigation units under European and native administrative officials and with the regional investigation depot under the field police technical leader.[37]

The regional investigation service was responsible both for criminal investigation and political policing. After 1922, however, when the PKI emerged as the leading force in the *pergerakan*, more emphasis was placed on political policing under the direction of the attorney general. The regional investigation depot was expanded. Its agents were sent to local investigation units to head their activities.[38] This shift was so complete, future Batavia police chief P. Dekker wrote, in retrospect, that the regional investigation service had become synonymous with the political intelligence service by the mid-1920s.[39]

The expansion of general police forces (city, field, and administrative police combined, but excluding village and armed police) can be seen in the tables below (p. 64).

Government police statistics do not tell us how many police officers were in charge of political policing. But it is safe to assume that the majority of native police officers with the ranks of *wedana*, assistant *wedana*, police *mantri*, and detective, as well as a substantial number of police agents, were engaged in political policing. (In the principalities of Surakarta and Yogyakarta, where general police forces, as shown in the table, consisted solely of the city and regional investigation service and the field police units, almost half of police agents were with the investigation service.) As the more than six-fold expansion of native detectives (*rechercheurs*) from 1921 to 1925 illustrates, the political policing apparatus was no doubt significantly expanded in these years. Indeed, if we take police *wedana*, assistant *wedana*, *mantri* and detectives as the core of the political policing apparatus, its strength—1,952 men in 1925—was substantially larger than the core membership of the PKI the attorney general deemed it imperative to intern in Digoel in 1927.

Regional distribution, on the other hand, showed a heavy concentration of police forces in Java, especially in the urban centers of Batavia, Bandung, Semarang, and Surabaya and the sugar regions of Pekalongan, Kediri, and Pasuruan (Malang). (Police strength in Surakarta and Yogyakarta was not pronounced, because principality police forces were not included in the statistics. Were they to be included, their force strength should be on the same level as Priangan-Bandung.)

GROWING UP WITH THE INDONESIAN COMMUNIST PARTY

After the creation of the political policing apparatus in the early 1920s, the *hoofdparket*, the attorney general's office with the ARD as its core, soon emerged as the dominant player in bureaucratic politics regarding native policy (at the latest by 1923), and it remained so until the end of the Dutch era in 1942. One main

---

[37] Neijtzell de Wilde, "De Nederlandsch-Indische Politie," pp. 129.

[38] Cornelis Gijsbert Eliza De Jong, *De Organisatie der Politie in Nederlandsch-Indie* [The organization of the police in the Dutch Indies]. *Proefschrift ter verkrijging van den graad van doctor in de rechtsgeleerdheid aan de Rijksuniversiteit te Leiden* (Leiden: "Luctor et Emergo," 1933), p. 46.

[39] Dekker, *De Politie*, p. 230. See also Neijtzell de Wilde, "De Nederlandsch-Indische Politie," pp. 134 and 159; "De Veldpolitie," p. 60.

loser in this new development was the office for native and Arabic affairs. In the first two decades of the twentieth century, this office had been the most important agency for native policy, but in the 1920s it was reduced to such insignificance that a question was raised in the highest circles of the government in the early 1930s whether it should be replaced by two new agencies: a bureau for political affairs under the director of internal administration; and a bureau for Mohammedan religious affairs under the director of education and religion. Part of the reason for this shift was organizational. While the office for native and Arabic affairs was a small-scale operation without any regional offices, the *hoofdparket* was supported by constant streams of reports and records from the Indies-wide political policing apparatus. But the shift signified more than a change in the way the government gathered intelligence on the *pergerakan*, for it was accompanied by an important change in the way the authorities viewed modern native popular politics. To appreciate this point, we need to compare the ARD with the office for native affairs, above all with respect to their different modes of operation, expertise, mentalities, and fantasies.

The office for native and Arabic affairs was established in 1899 with the legendary Dutch Islamologist, Dr. Snouck Hurgronje, as its first adviser (1899-1906), and it was headed subsequently by Dr. G. A. J. Hazeu (1907-1913, 1917-1920), Dr. D. A. Rinkes (1914-1916), E. Gobée (1927-1937), and Dr. G. F. Pijper (1937-1942), all trained in Indology with good command of Arabic and native languages.[40] In 1933, the director of education and religion and noted historian, B. J. O. Schrieke, who had served as deputy adviser in 1917-1920, put its history this way:

> This Office, which has evolved gradually out of the bureau of the adviser for Mohammedan law, acted as government adviser for native and Arabic affairs in a time when the native world was still silent and therefore to fathom the deeper currents in the native society was an issue.
>
> This situation has changed gradually. In the beginning of this century arose the movement, commonly called the "Asiatic awakening," which broke the silence in the native world. Native political associations emerged, and with them a native press, in which the political opinions living [existing] in the upper layer of the native world—which also soon found a sounding board in the Volksraad—openly found expression. Besides, these opinions were remarkably different from those in earlier times: the more good-natured forms in the past gave way to a significant degree to more or less extremist [forms of opinions such as] (communism, extreme nationalism, non-cooperation, etc.).

---

[40] No adviser was appointed from 1920 to 1926, when the office was run by deputy adviser, R. A. Kern (1921-1922, 1924-1926) and E. Gobée (1923). G. A. J. Hazeu (b. 1870) who obtained a doctorate at Leiden University in 1897 was an expert on Javanese language and culture. H. Aqib Suminto, *Politik Islam Hindia Belanda: Het Kantoor voor Inlandsche Zaken* (Batavia: LP3ES, 1985), p. 125; G. W. J. Drewes, "Balai Pustaka and its Antecedents," in *Papers on Indonesian Languages and Literature*, ed. Nigel Phillips and Khaidir Anwar (London: The Indonesian Etymological Project, 1981), p. 101. D. A. Rinkes (b. 1878) obtained a doctorate at Leiden in 1906 and served as deputy adviser for native affairs from 1911 to 1913 and as head of Balai Pustaka from 1917 to 1927. R. A. Kern (b. 1875) studied Indology in Delft in 1893-1995, and later became a lecturer of Sundanese at Leiden in 1927-1942. E. Gobée (b. 1881) studied Indology at Leiden in 1906-1908 and Arabic in 1915 and was consul in Jeddah from 1917 to 1921. G. F. Pijper (b. 1893) obtained a doctorate in Arabic and Islamology in 1924. Suminto, *Politik Islam*, pp. 132, 128, 141, 147.

Under these changed circumstances, other government organs have come to pay attention to the spiritual trends [*geestesstroomingen*] of the native society, aside from the Office for Native Affairs. During the world war the political intelligence service came into being, which is now transferred to the [*hoofd*]*parket*, while the post of government representative for general affairs [to the Volksraad] was created, which official, together with the government representative for the police, handles the general political situation in the Volksraad. Also the Heads of regional administration, responsible as they are for quiet and order in their regions, keep themselves and their subordinate administrative officials informed of the ideas living in the native world. Thus the question may arise whether aside from the organs mentioned—the Internal Administration on the one hand, the two government representatives on the other, and besides the political intelligence service under the leadership of the Attorney General—there still exists a need for yet another body, in this case the Office for Native Affairs.[41]

As Schrieke points out correctly, the office for native and Arabic affairs was created before the rise of the *pergerakan*, when the native world was silent and, in Boekhoudt's words, "national feeling seems not to exist with the Javanese, at least it is fast asleep." This does not mean that the native world was calm and that there were no disturbances, riots, revolts, and rebellions to disrupt the colonial order. The question, rather, was how to make sense of the natives, their mentalities, their thinking, and their society, for during this time, at the turn of the century, there was a deep sense of mystery among the Dutch concerning natives, Chinese, and Arabs.

In the early twentieth century, however, any threat to order seemed to come, as Boekhoudt said, from "Pan-Islamism" and "fanaticism for the restoration of a Javanese kingdom." This fear informed the establishment of the office for native and Arabic affairs. Its founder, Snouck Hurgronje, argued that

> most of *kyais*, *ulama*, and *hajs* were other-worldly, most of whom desired nothing better than to serve Allah in peace, but fanatical *ulama* dedicated to the notions of Pan-Islam had to be watched. The enemy was not Islam as a religion, but Islam as a political doctrine, both in the shape of agitation by local fanatics and in the shape of Pan-Islam, whether or not it was in fact inspired by Islamic rulers abroad, such as the Caliph.[42]

The office was responsible for "fathoming the deeper currents in the native society" and watching local and international subversive networks of Muslim fanatics—religious scholars and teachers (*kyai* and *ulama*), religious schools, *tarekat* leaders, haji, Indies Arabs, and the Kampung Jawi in Mecca.[43] With the target to watch thus defined, it was natural that those who ran the office as

---

[41] "Directeur van onderwijs en eredienst (B. J. O. Schrieke) aan gouverneur generaal (De Jonge), 28 okt. 1933," in Kwantes, *De Ontwikkeling: Aug. 1933-1942*, pp. 95-96.

[42] Ibid.

[43] Harry J. Benda, *The Crescent and the Rising Sun: Indonesian Islam under the Japanese Occupation, 1942-1945* (The Hague: W. van Hoeve, 1958), pp. 23-24. See also Suminto, *Politik Islam*, pp. 52-58, 64-70, 78-97, 99.

advisers and deputy advisers were trained in Islamology and Indology, had expert knowledge of Islam and the Indies, were well-versed in Arabic and local native languages, and maintained good relations with prominent members of the natives and Indies Arab communities.

Its expertise, however, also led to its eventual undoing, for once the *pergerakan* broke the silence and government agencies other than the office for native affairs started to watch the native world, it soon became clear that Islam was a bogy, that there was no international Islamic conspiracy, and that disturbances, revolts, and rebellions derived not from "Pan-Islamism" but from something else. In his defense of the office for native affairs, Schrieke therefore stressed not Islam but a unique contribution the office had made to the government:

> The officials of the Internal Administration can only be local-oriented because of their task; they miss the general overall picture of the phenomena, whose outward expressions they perceive in their own regions . . . The [*hoofd*]*parket* mainly directs its attention to the unearthing of punishable evidences and thus sees the native society with a limited objective. But the phenomena also have to be digested sociologically, purely scientifically, and this is the task given to the Office for Native Affairs—a task which has to be carried out anyway for a good administration. [Besides] it is the tradition, shaped by Dr. Snouck Hurgronje as adviser for Eastern languages and Mohammedan law, that the Office has not only official but also more personal relationships with those who occupy prominent places in the political and religious areas of native society, by which much valuable information is obtained, which can contribute to a better understanding of what is taking place in the native society: information which comes from circles to which the internal administration and the intelligence service can hardly have access. The adviser for native affairs is the trusted man [*vertrouwensman*] from the early days, to whom the more prominent members of native society expressed [their] feelings and opinions (also criticisms of government policy), who normally keep silent with other officials.[44]

Understandably, Schrieke did not say that the adviser for native affairs as the "trusted man" for the native society had long been suspect because of the radicalization of the *pergerakan*. To see why, we only need to recall one major development in the movement in the early 1920s, what Schrieke calls the rise of "more or less extremist forms [of opinions such as] (communism, extreme nationalism, non-cooperation, etc.)."

In proposing the creation of the ARD, Monsanto as advocate general wrote to the governor general that the *pergerakan* was then showing signs of "decay," of "getting wild," in its radicalization, if seen from the government's perspective. Interestingly, however, he did not, and perhaps could not, theorize about this "decay," because though the Islamic bogy had been discredited, a new Communist bogy had not yet arrived on the scene. But the situation soon changed. In less than half a year after the creation of the ARD, the ISDV (Indische Sociaal-Democratische Vereeniging, Indies Social-Democratic Association) was

---

[44] "Directeur van onderwijs en eredienst (B. J. O. Schrieke) aan gouverneur generaal (De Jonge), 28 okt. 1933," pp. 96-97.

Table 1: General Police, in Terms of Ranks

	1921	1925	1928
Europeans	362	1,092	1,346
Commissioners	28	86	110
Inspectors	130	443	611
Chief Agents	194	526	574
Chief Detectives	10	37	51
Natives	18,341	25,704	31,644
Police *Wedana*	-	5	8
Police Assistant *Wedana*	2	29	54
Police *Mantri*	859	1,198	1,495
Posthouse Commandants	72	524	1,353
Detectives	111	720	1,668
Police Agents	17,657	23,223	27,018
Chauffers	2	5	48
Total	18,703	26,796	32,990

Table 2: General Police, in Terms of Regional Distribution

	1921	1925	1928
Banten	408	585	-
Batavia**	1,438	3,079	5,960
Priangan	1,294	1,406	-
Cirebon	514	686	-
Pekalongan	1,054	1,284	1,349
Semarang	1,782	2,752	2,678
Jepara-Rembang	574	1,029	1,047
Kedu-Banyumas	1,005	955	1,004
Surabaya-Bojonegoro	1,334	2,475	2,657
Madiun	574	829	850
Kediri	999	1,480	1,575
Pasuruan (Malang)	1,333	1,588	1,838
Besuki	699	755	839
Madura	748	760	771
Yogyakarta*	208	533	788
Surakarta*	264	628	792
Java & Madura Total	14,226	20,824	22,148
Sumatra's West Coast	554	579	1,432
Sumatra's East Coast	608	661	2,206
The Rest of the Outer Islands	3,315	4,732	7,204
Grand Total	18,703	26,796	32,990

* The police forces of Kasultanan, Pakualaman, Mangkunegaran, and Kasunanan are not included in the statistics.
** Batavia for 1921 and 1925 includes Buitenzorg and Kwawang; Batavia for 1928 means the whole of West Java.
Calculated from: Handelingen VR, 1920, Begrooting 1921, Stuk O, Afdeeling IV, 5, pp. 2-3; Handelingen VR, 1924, Begrooting 1925, Stuk O, Afd. IV, 6, pp. 2-3, and Afd. IV, 7, pp. 2-3; Handelingen VR, 1927, Begrooting 1928, Afdeeling IV, Stuk 13, pp. 1-3.

transformed into the Perserikatan Kommunist di India (PKI), League of Communists in the Indies, with Semaoen as chairman in May 1920. The SI split, which started to spread from the central leadership to the local in October 1920, became definite with the CSI congress in Madiun in February 1923 and the PKI congress in Bandung and Sukabumi in early March 1923. By early 1924, the PKI and red SIs affiliated with it had emerged triumphant in their rivalry with the non-Communist CSI for leadership of the *pergerakan*. This development made the office for native affairs irrelevant for the government's native policy, for its officials simply did not have any access to the PKI and red SI/SRs (Sarekat Rakjat, People's Unions).

The expansion of the regional investigation apparatus, as we have seen, took place in response to this development. More important, however, was the fact that the political policing apparatus found in the PKI and red SI/SR its first enemy. Police officers from the ARD down to local investigation units developed their investigative expertise while policing the PKI and red SIs. They did not need expert knowledge in Indology, Islamology, and native languages for this task. Most of the local police agents were natives anyway, normally operating in their own areas of origin, who relied on spies and informers for intelligence gathering, and accumulated knowledge about local party figures and organizations: identities and personalities of local leaders and activists, their places of residence and possible hideouts, their aliases, their relatives and friends, their meeting places, couriers, identities and places of their sympathizers, and so forth.

These myriad items were constantly fed into the *hoofdparket*. In order to piece out, sort out, order, link, and make sense of these disparate and often contradictory pieces of information, the ARD under van der Lely needed a "theoretical" framework. Thanks to the rise of the PKI, this was found in the fantastic international Communist conspiracy. The ARD saw Moscow's hands everywhere behind the scenes, and it perceived often poorly coordinated and sometimes purely individual, anarchistic terrorist actions as part of a grand Communist plan directed by the Comintern. It thus developed its own expertise for policing internal and international Communist networks: listing the identities and aliases of leading PKI members in the regions and abroad, of those in communication with the Comintern, their possible travel routes, their hideouts, their meeting, staying, and eating places in Singapore, Penang, and Holland, their contacts, their secret codes, and the secret directives the party central committee issued to the branches, as well as their secret mail addresses, the identities of couriers between the party headquarters and branches, and of spies and informers with access to the party leadership. In short, the ARD created its own topographie and biographie, if we use the terms coined by the founding father of modern secret police, Fouche.[45] Nothing demonstrates the steady accumulation of political policing expertise more graphically than the increase in the number of fingerprint slips and identifications (i.e., photographs) stored in general police headquarters. The number of fingerprint slips increased from 19,077 in 1924, 24,605 in 1925, and 29,467 in 1926, to 36,862 in

---

[45] Eric A. Arnold, Jr., *Fouche, Napoleon, and the General Police* (Washington, DC: University Press of America, 1979), p. 154.

1927, while the number of identifications (photographs) grew from 1,469 in 1924, 2,402 in 1925, and 3,030 in 1926, to 3,710 in 1927.[46]

This history shaped the tradition of political policing in the Indies—its expertise, the way it perceived the *pergerakan*, in terms of Communist, extreme nationalist, non-cooperationist, or cooperationist. Its founding fathers were men such as van der Lely, who, convinced of the importance of his work and with quiet pride in his achievement, wrote thus after his retirement in the Netherlands:

> Having played a role behind the scenes, naturally I cannot go into detail on my ten-year experience as Chief of the General Investigation Service and on the nature and priorities of the "finer" detective work the police there have to perform. It will suffice, therefore, to underline that because foreign influences on the currents in the Far East are very remarkable, but mainly underground, the significance of that "finer" detective work should not be underestimated by any means. The modern police perform this task in a capable way . . . [47]

THE NEW REGIME OF ORDER

The political policing apparatus was thus very much established when the revolts took place in late 1926 and early 1927. There was no break in its evolution because of the revolts. Rather it developed along the logic inherent in its original design: favoring more control and leadership of the *hoofdparket* over the regional investigation service, and of the regional investigation service over the local investigation units; streamlining communications between the ARD and the regional investigation service; encouraging regularization and expansion of the regional investigation service; facilitating deeper penetration by the local investigation units into the village sphere. Two points deserve consideration. One is organizational, and is discussed below. The other, which concerns its political effects, will be addressed in the final part of this essay.

Let us start with the *hoofdparket*. Whether revolts took place or not, attorneys general and advocates general changed regularly. From 1926 to 1942, seven officials served as attorney general: D. G. Wolterbeek Muller (1922-1926); H. G. P. Duyfjes (1926-1928); J. K. Onnen (1928-1929); R. J. M. Verheijen (1929-1934); G. Vonk (1934-1938); H. Marcella (1938-1940); and A. S. Block (1940-1942). In contrast, the ARD had only two chiefs, deputy chiefs, and chief native officers in its entire history: A. E. van der Lely (1919-1929) and B. R. van der Most (1929-1942) as ARD chief; van der Most (1920-1929) and H. J. A. Vermijs (1929-1942) as deputy; and Mohamad Jatim (1920-1935) and Raden Hermansaid (1935-1942) as chief native officer.[48] The

---

[46] "The year" means the end of the year. Centraal Kantoor voor de Statistiek in Nederlandsch-Indie, *Statistisch Jaaroverzicht van Nederlandsch-Indie: Jaargang 1925* (Weltevreden: Landsdrukkerij, 1926), p. 172; *Jaargang 1926* (1927), p. 174; *Jaargang 1927* (1928), p. 207.

[47] A. E. van der Lely, "Handhaving der openbare rust, orde en veiligheid," in *De Nederlandsch-Indische Politiegids*, June 1932, no. 1932, pp. 191-93, originally published in *Rijkseenheid* in January 1932.

[48] See *Regeerings Almanak van Nederlandsch Indie* (Weltevreden, 1919-1941). In the regions the continuity of intelligence personnel is less pronounced. The political intelligence branch of the Batavia city police had four native chiefs: Mohamad Jatim (1920-1922), Naipin (1923-1929), Mas Rangga Soetandoko (1929-1940), and Mas Moehammad Jasin Partadiredja (1940-1942). Bandung and Semarang had perhaps three each, Surabaya four. But the political intelligence branch of the Surakartan police had only one, R. Ramelan, in its entire history.

ARD was run in the post-revolt years by those who had personal memories of the revolts. It was suffused with a determination that "such trouble should never happen again," and its vigilance against Indonesian nationalist politics was always tinged with the officers' fantasies about international Communist conspiracies.

In the provinces, the city and regional investigation apparatuses were strengthened. In the countryside, investigation cores (*recherche kernen*, also called special intelligence services, *speciale inlichtingen-dienst*), that had been established as regional investigation depots in the early 1920s, were expanded in the regions of West Java, Pekalongan, Semarang, Kedu-Banyumas, Yogyakarta, Surakarta, Madiun, Surabaya-Bojonegoro, Pasuruan (Malang), and Sumatra's West and East Coast. Smaller investigation cores were established in Kediri, Besuki, Tapanuli, Palembang, Jambi, Benkulen, Lampung, Bangka, Riouw, the Moluccas, and two regions of Borneo. The police school also started a new course for the training of political intelligence staff.[49] And as we can see in Tables 1 and 2, the force strength of the general police increased from 26,796 in 1925 to 32,990 in 1928, while the number of detectives expanded from 720 to 1,668 in the same period.

This expansion of the political policing apparatus took place in 1927. The governor general instructed the attorney general to present his recommendations for the reform of political policing on December 7, 1926. Attorney general Duyfjes in turn sent a secret circular to the heads of regional administrations on December 29, 1926 instructing them to report on the organizational structure of political policing in their respective regions, the number and ranks of intelligence personnel, and their reform plans. In the same circular, Duyfjes also ordered the Residents to instruct their subordinate administrative and police officers to report directly, by telegraph and if possible by telephone, to the *hoofdparket*, bypassing the administrative hierarchy, on anything that might seem of more than local significance.[50]

Another important development, logical in light of the PKI's international connections and the presence of Communist leaders and fugitives abroad, especially in British Malaya, was international police cooperation between the Indies government and the British Straits Settlements government. Informal police cooperation started in July 1926, when the British authorities in Singapore agreed to allow two police agents sent by the ARD to spy on Indies Communists in British Malaya. Pretending to be Communist fugitives from Yogyakarta, they successfully penetrated local networks of Communists from West Sumatra, and reported back to the ARD (before their identities were exposed by Soebakat in September) about the schism that was developing between Tan Malaka, Soebakat, and Djamaloeddin Tamin on the one hand and the PKI central committee led by Sardjono and Boedisoetjitro on the other regarding the PKI's plan for revolution

---

[49] *Mededeelingen der Regeering omtrent enkele onderwerpen van algemeen belang (Mei 1928)*, (Weltevreden: Landsdrukkerij, 1928), pp. 2-3. See also Procureur Generaal (Duyfjes) aan Gouverneur Generaal (de Graeff), Jan. 10, 1927, Mr. 66x/1927.

[50] Iste Gouvernementssecretaris (H.A. Helb) aan Procureur Generaal (Duyfjes), Dec. 7, 1926, Mr. 1225x/1926; Procureur Generaal aan de Hoofden van Gewestelijk Bestuur, Rondschrijven-Spoed-Geheim, Dec. 29, 1927 and Procureur Generaal aan Gouverneur Generaal (de Graeff), Jan. 10, 1927, both in Mr. 66x/1927.

and the visit of Alimin and Musso to Moscow.[51] With the existence of "a propaganda center" of Indies Communists in Singapore thus confirmed, the attorney general suggested establishing an intelligence unit to watch their activities in Singapore.[52] Negotiations took time, however, and it was only after the revolts in West Java that the Straits Settlements police chief gave the Dutch deputy consul general "a strictly personal and confidential report":

> Our policy at the present moment is to prevent any known Javanese communist from landing in Malaya. Unfortunately . . . we are only able to recognize two or three leaders, so that if the blockade is to be made effective it would be necessary for the Government of the Netherlands East Indies to send over unofficially at least two men, one for Singapore and one for Penang, who could board vessels coming from Java and Sumatra, etc., and warn the police of the presence of extremist leaders or well-known communists.[53]

M. Visbeen, assistant commissioner of police for the Batavia city police, was sent to Singapore with two native detectives in early December. He established a close working relationship with Fairburn, the inspector general of the Straits Settlements police force, and Rene Onraet, chief of its criminal investigation department (the future special police). The high point, and ultimate failure, of Visbeen's investigation work in Singapore was the arrest of Alimin and Musso and their subsequent banishment from British Malaya in December 1926. Visbeen was back in Batavia by July 1927, but important personal connections had been established by then and in the subsequent years he emerged as the expert on Indies communists abroad.[54]

On the more formal level, the Indies government had first recognized the need for international police cooperation in late 1924 and asked British India and French Indochina for intelligence exchange on "the colonial propaganda of the Soviet government" in January 1925. The French did not respond, but negotiations between the Indies government and the British Indian government eventually resulted in an agreement in February 1927 on a direct intelligence exchange between the ARD chief and the director of the intelligence bureau of British India.[55]

But this arrangement turned out to be unsatisfactory, because there was no regular exchange of intelligence.[56] When the governor of the Straits Settlements,

---

[51] See Geheim Rapport, Pinang, Sept. 9, 1926, Sept. 13, 1926, Mr. 971x/1926; Geheim Rapport, Sept. 30, 1926, Mr. 1031x/1926.

[52] 1ste Gouvernementssecretaris aan wd. Consul Generaal der Nederlanden te Singapore, Oct. 25, 1926, Mr. 1031x/1926.

[53] wd. Consul Generaal (Kleyn Molekamp) aan Gouverneur Generaal (de Graeff), Singapore, Nov. 25, 1926, Mr. 12x/1927. See also wd. Consul Generaal aan Gouverneur Generaal, Singapore, Nov. 22, 1926, Mr. 12x/1927.

[54] For Visbeen's activities in Singapore, see Mr. 811x/1927, 902x/1927, and 1104x/1927.

[55] See Procureur Generaal (Duyfjes) aan Gouverneur Generaal (de Graeff), July 15, 1926, Mr. 754x/1926; wd. 1ste Gouvernementssecretaris aan Procureur Generaal (Duyfjes), Aug. 3, 1926, Mr. 754x/1926; Viceroy and Governor General of India to Governor General of the Dutch East Indies, Simla, Sept. 26, 1925, Mr. 70x/27; Viceroy and Governor General of India to Governor General of the Dutch East Indies, Delhi, Dec. 28, 1926, Mr. 70x/27; Procureur Generaal (Duyfjes) aan Gouverneur Generaal, Feb. 24, 1927, Mr. 380x/1927.

[56] See Kwantes, *De Ontwikkeling: 1928-Aug. 1933*, p. 486.

Sir Cecil Clementi, visited Batavia in August 1930, Governor General de Graeff again raised and discussed with the British governor "the question of a closer and more direct and more systematical cooperation between our governments with the aim of controlling and preventing communist agitation." They reached an agreement.[57] A month later, in October 1930, Advocate General for Police G. Vonk visited Singapore and worked out an arrangement with the Straits Settlements police for the "systematic" exchange of:

> a. photographs and descriptions of suspected agitators; b. communist manifestos, posters, and handbills, if necessary in photographic reproduction; c. copies of important reports and sentences concerning communist agitation and of important communist correspondence in photographic reproduction; d. information about plans for extremist action in our mutual territories, the latter should be given with all possible diligence.[58]

It was also agreed that this exchange take place directly between the *hoofdparket* and the inspector general of police in Singapore with regard to communist activities and between the Indies adviser for Chinese affairs and the Straits Settlements secretary for Chinese affairs with regard to matters pertaining to Chinese.

Vonk was euphoric when he returned to Batavia. In his report to the governor general, he wrote that he had received for examination "a great number of bundles [of documents] and reports" about "the political policing trends in the Malay peninsula." With Soekarno's PNI (Partai Nasional Indonesia, Indonesia National Party) obviously in mind, Vonk also found "several issues of very secret reports of the British Indian intelligence bureau" useful in understanding the kind of political policing problems "a preponderantly nationalistic rebellious movement" can pose. But his main interest lay in international communism, in the activities of "Semaoen, Darsono, Alimin, Tan Malaka, Moeso, and others," and he was euphoric because Fairburn, the Singapore police chief, responded positively to his request for "the British authorities in Singapore to ask their police organizations elsewhere to cooperate for the promotion of this specifically Netherlands Indies interest."[59]

The British government in Singapore had its own need for an intelligence exchange with the Dutch Indies government. In British Malaya, the Straits Settlements Police Criminal Intelligence Department (CID-SS, renamed Special Branch in 1933) had been in place since 1918 to deal with political affairs, but it was not until after "a Chinese communist-led riot in Singapore" in March 1927 that the government became serious about communist activities and expanded its police organization, in the words of CID chief Onraet, with "better pay, better buildings,

---

[57] "Gouverneur-generaal (De Graeff) aan gouverneur van de Straits Settlements (sir Cecil Clementi), 16 sept. 1930," in ibid., p. 486.

[58] "Gouverneur-generaal (De Graeff) aan gouverneur van de Straits Settlements (sir Cecil Clementi), 16 sept. 1930, in ibid., pp. 486-87. See also Uittreksel uit het Register der Besluiten van den Gouverneur Generaal van Nederlandsch-Indie, Sept. 26, 1930, Mr. 936x/1930; 1ste Gouvernementssecretaris aan Procureur Generaal, Oct. 23, 1930, Mr. 1035x/1930.

[59] "Rapport advocaat-generaal (G. Vonk) over besprekingen met engelse autoriteiten te Singapore van 10-17 okt. 1930, 18 okt. 1930, in Kwantes, *De Ontwikkeling: 1928-Aug. 1933*, pp. 487-88.

more equipment, a training depot worthy of a force over four thousand strong, sufficient money for secret service, expansion of certain departments, and undivided authority for the police in certain Chinese activities hitherto partly controlled by other Government departments."[60] In British Malaya, however, most communists were Chinese, and as Tan Malaka rightly predicted in 1925, Malays were only marginally involved in the communist movement.[61] This was the reason the Indies adviser for Chinese affairs and the Straits Settlements secretary for Chinese affairs were brought into the intelligence exchange. But there is no question the *hoofdparket* benefited a great deal from the reorganization and expansion of the British Malayan political intelligence apparatus, as we can see in the destruction of the PARI's Singaporean base in 1932.

POLITICS OF POLITICAL POLICING

We have now arrived at a point where we can consider the general nature of political policing in the Indies and the kind of politics it brought forth in the post-revolt years. Two points warrant discussion. One is its political effect on the native society. The other is its effect on its client, the Indies government.

As Thamrin so forcefully argued in his Volkraad speeches in the 1930s, police intervention in the *pergerakan* was commonplace and routine in the post-revolt years.[62] PID officers intervened in speeches and sometimes suspended rallies altogether. The police also carried out house searches and arrests, detained and interrogated many, and censored and confiscated daily, weekly, and monthly newspapers and books. But far more important was the fact that the PID was everywhere, or so Indonesians felt. Though sometimes called secret police (*polisi rahasia*), it was not secret at all. Its officers were always present in open public rallies, sitting on their special seats, prominent for everyone to see. They dropped in on offices of political parties, trade unions, and newspaper publishers, schools run by parties and associations, and places frequented by activists. They stood outside places where informal closed meetings were held. They also relied on spies and informers. The police had a huge secret fund for "maintaining a good system of

---

[60] Rene H. Onraet, *Singapore—A Police Background* (London: Dorothy Crisp, 1947), pp. 96-97. Just as the ARD was a culmination of years of police modernization and professionalization, the CID-SS was led from the beginning by professional police officers. Its first chief, V. G. Savi, who spoke Malay, Fukien, Hindustani, and Punjabi, was one of the first "school boys"—graduates of police cadet service for Hongkong and Malaya established in 1903—to fill the post. Onraet, also a "school boy," who obtained an intensive language training in Amoy, was the second CID-SS chief and as such worked closely with Visbeen in hunting down Indies communist fugitives in the early years of formal and informal Anglo-Dutch police cooperation. The Special Branch had twenty-five officers in 1935 and 43 in 1936, and consisted of five sections responsible for Communist, Japanese, security, political (i.e., non-communist political activities), and alien affairs. For the history of the secret police in British Malaya, see also Alun Jones, "Internal Security in British Malaya, 1915-1935" (PhD dissertation, Yale University, 1970).

[61] See Cheah Boon Kheng, *From PKI to the Comintern, 1924-1941: The Apprenticeship of the Malayan Communist Party: Selected Documents and Discussion, Compiled and Edited with Introductions* (Ithaca: Cornell Southeast Asia Program, 1992), pp. 50-51.

[62] "De Interpellatie-Thamrin in zake het verscherpte politioneel optreden in openbare vergaderingen, enz.," in *De Nederlandsch-Indische Politiegids, June 1933*, no. 6, pp. 176-89. *De Politiegids* published Thamrin's interpellation in the Volkraad in its entirety to show the attorney general's rebuttal.

intelligence work, good informers"—ƒ750,000 in 1932, for instance, and ƒ522,000 even in 1936 when the government budget was cut drastically because of the Depression.[63] Spies and informers were not always professional. No doubt there were some professionals, but more often they were activists who sometimes accepted money, sometimes not, and gave pieces of information to PID officers. Needless to say, everyone knew that there were spies and informers among them.

Indonesians were thus aware, and were made aware by the presence of PID officers, that they were being watched even among fellow activists. And they were aware of the risk of being seen, the risk which might eventually lead them to Digoel. The only sure way of avoiding this risk was to stay away from politics and dodge surveillance by the PID. The kind of atmosphere its ubiquitous presence created among Indonesians is best captured in a question Pramoedya Ananta Toer put in the mouth of an innocent small child, Aku (I), when his mother told him that his big brother Hurip had joined a political party.

> How surprised I was to hear that he meddled in politics. According to my understanding politics is police, and everyone in our house was disgusted with anything to do with police.
> "Is father not angry because he has joined the police?" I asked.
> Mother smiled sweetly, hearing my question. Then with simple words [she] explained what politics meant, which was:
> "Those who join political parties are the enemy of the police."
> And I understood a little.[64]

The dialogue is carefully constructed by Pramoedya to tell a story about how a movement started in a small town in the early 1930s. The most important aspect of this excerpt for our purpose, however, is its observation of an intelligent and innocent small boy who acts as a representative for the uneducated, innocent, but intelligent people (*rakyat*), perhaps, and expresses their understanding that "politics" equals "police." It was this effect which kept the great majority of Indonesians away from politics=police, a crucial condition for the creation of a state of normalcy in the Indies in the age of Digoel.

But political policing, with its special way of watching the population, also shaped the way in which the government saw native society. To understand this point, we only need to look at a few paragraphs randomly taken from the ARD's monthly political policing survey (*politieke-politioneel overzicht*). The ARD started to compile the survey in March 1927, in the wake of the revolts, with a very limited circulation. It was sent to the governor general, select department chiefs, the regional administrative heads (thirty-two in total), the minister of colonies, and Dutch diplomatic representatives in Peking, Tokyo, Bangkok, Washington, Cairo, Singapore, Shanghai, Hongkong, Calcutta, Manila, Sydney, Saigon, and Jedda.[65]

---

[63] "Over Geheim Politie-fondsen," *De Nederlandsch-Indische Politiegids*, Sept. 1936, no. 9, pp. 168-70.

[64] Pramoedya Ananta Toer, "Kemudian Lahirlah Dia," *Tjerita Dari Blora* (Jakarta: Balai Pustaka, 1963), p. 96.

[65] Harry A. Poeze, "Voorwoord," in *Politiek-Politioneele Overzichten van Nederlandsch-Indie: Deel I, 1927-1928*, ed. Harry A. Poeze (The Hague: Martinus Nijhoff, 1982), pp. vii-viii.

The survey consists of five sections: the extremist movement, the national and Islamic movement, the Chinese movement, the trade union movement, and "abroad." Let us look at the December 1927 survey for an example. The sixth and ninth paragraphs in the first section, "The Extremist Movement," run as follows:

> In Kisaran (East Coast of Sumatra) arose a new association, Moehammadijah, which calls for communism but has nothing to do with the organization with the same name located in Java. At a rally held on November 17, a certain H. Saleh, who carried on a campaign in 1925 in Benkulen, explained how the people were oppressed by the government. It was decided after that [meeting] to establish an organization which is reportedly denoted with the initials A. W. (whose meaning is not known so far) with the purpose of recruiting "*brani* [brave]" members secretly. The association is said to have a substructure [*onderbouw*] with the name of Djamatoerhamah.
>
> In the village of Tjipanokolan (in the regency of Bandung), there reportedly exists a PKI branch under the leadership of a certain Iskak, which is said to have fifty members already. In the Tasikmadoe plantation (in Surakarta) there exists an association called Soerjo Moeljo, which reportedly wants to buy firearms to offer resistance to the authority and to kill police officers. The leader, called Irosemito, is under arrest.[66]

No longish analysis of these excerpts is needed. The paragraphs tell us very little. The first records the facts that a rally was held in Kisaran on November 17 and that a man called Haji Saleh gave a speech. We can be reasonably sure that this much took place, but can be certain of nothing more. The second paragraph tells us even less. Based on the information there, we can only be sure, perhaps, that there was an association called Soerjo Moerjo in the Tasikmadu plantation and that a man called Irosemito was placed under arrest. But this much can be expected of any intelligence report. More important is the way in which the terrain was being watched. It is clear that only one thing matters in this report. Whether factually correct or not, there seems to be a danger that subversives might be out there, in Kisaran, in a village near Bandung, and in the Tasikmadu plantation. Irosemito was already under arrest. H. Saleh and Iskak might also be picked up soon. If not, H. Saleh's file will become thicker and a new file will be created for Iskak.

What is missing from the record is the sociological and cultural terrain in which those people lived. Try to imagine Kisaran, a small provincial town in Asahan, a four-hour drive even now from Medan, in the middle of rubber plantations and thick forest, back in the late 1920s. Try to visualize a man called Haji Saleh, addressing the audience at a meeting one fine day in November. We do not know where the meeting was held—at a mosque, in a religious school, or a town square?—what he said, who came to the meeting, let alone who he was, what he did in everyday life, what was his upbringing, and so on. But these things did not matter, because the ARD was watching out for subversives, threats to the state, of whatever persuasion and color. The terrain was rendered flat, and on that stage a man called Haji Saleh stood alone as a subversive.

---

[66] Ibid., p. 188.

Let us also take a look at a few paragraphs from the survey's section concerning the National and Islamic Movement. In November 1927, a new national united front, the PPPKI (Permoefakatan Perhimpoenan-Perhimpoenan Politiek Kebangsaan Indonesia, or Forum for Indonesian National Political Associations) was in the making, which naturally drew a lot of attention from the ARD.

> In this report month the federation of political-national-native parties was officially founded, the foundation of which was laid at the recent PSI [Partij Sarekat Islam] congress . . .
>
> At the initiative of Dr. Soekiman it decided to publish its own national newspaper, for which a committee was established—according to *Sin Po* [a Chinese Malay newspaper published in Batavia]—with Parada Harahap and Mr. Sartono as its members. The advisory committee consists of: Mr. Iskaq Tjokrohadisoerjo, chairman, Dr. Samsi Sastrowidagdo, secretary-treasurer, and Dr. Soekiman and Ir. Soekarno, commissioners.
>
> With the establishment of this federation the influence of the (extreme-national[ist]) intellectuals, who are the promoters of this movement (see the September survey), has made a step forward and the plans to attain an *anti-imperialist (national-religious) bloc* discussed in chapter 4 of the secret political note on the PKI and the July survey will become a bit clearer.[67]

Here we are perhaps on a bit firmer ground factually. There is no reason to doubt the factual data reported in the paragraphs, not only because they can be cross-checked with newspaper reports, but also because we know the ARD was intensely interested in the PPPKI and young "intellectuals," as mentioned in these paragraphs, and that the ARD was obsessed with facts in its own way. Yet all the same, all these men and their actions are read from a special political policing perspective, where what matters boils down to a set of practical questions—whether the *hoofdparket* should intervene in the PPPKI and, if yes, when and at what time; whether the *hoofdparket* should arrest these men and if yes, when and for what reasons; and whether the *hoofdparket* should intervene in the publication of the PPPKI organ and, if yes, when and at what time?

The ARD was watching out for subversives. It was as if only subversives and potential subversives inhabited the terrain under its surveillance, for it only saw them and no one and nothing else. The ARD thus provided the government with a map which told the government where to hit and who to eliminate as a threat to *rust en orde*, and, equally important, the government shaped the terrain in light of the map the ARD produced for the purpose of the political policing of the Indies.

Long after the Dutch Indies empire was gone, P. J. A. Idenburg, son of the Ethical governor general A. F. W. Idenburg, who served as secretary of the council of the Netherlands Indies (1926-1934), wrote an article, "The Dutch Answer on Indonesian Nationalism," which inspired Harry J. Benda to write about the Indies state as a *beamtenstaat* in his essay, "The Pattern of Administrative Reforms in

---

[67] Ibid., pp. 189-90.

the Closing Years of Dutch Rule in Indonesia."[68] After explaining how thorough the PID intelligence work was and how its monthly and quarterly reports were distributed by the *hoofdparket*, Idenburg wrote thus in this article:

> One is hard pressed to assess what influence such intelligence reporting, sound in itself, must have had on the policy of the regional and local administrative officials [toward Indonesian nationalism]. Aside from that, there was no regular political information [forthcoming] from the government, which [could] serve as policy guidelines for the administrative heads . . . Those who followed this intelligence reporting can not but recall with appreciation the soundness with which the information was analyzed and the sobriety of elucidation it provided. Nonetheless, the police could not crawl out of their hide: the considerations naturally emanated from a thought world, which was typically police, and when one compares this steady stream of considerations and reports with what the government representative for general affairs stated about government policy in the Volksraad, one can also see clearly that the police intelligence reporting did not—and also could not—make good the real policy of the governor general.[69]

This is an important insight. The government—the government representative for general affairs included—was as much a hostage of its own political policing as the Indies population, for without any other intelligence reporting, the *hoofdparket* with its monthly and quarterly reports provided the government with the only map that guided it in its policy toward the native world.

---

[68] P. J. A. Idenburg, "Het Nederlandse Antwoord op het Indonesisch Nationalisme," *in Balans van Beleid: Terugblik op de Laatste Halve Eeuw van Nederlandsch-Indie*, ed. H. Baudet and I. J. Brugmans (Assen: van Gorcum, 1961), pp. 121-51. Harry J. Benda, "The Pattern of Administrative Reforms in the Closing Years of Dutch Rule in Indonesia," in *Continuity and Change in Southeast Asia: Collected Journal Articles of Harry J. Benda* (New Haven, CT: Yale University Southeast Asia Studies, Monograph Series no. 18, 1972), pp. 236-52. His well-known discussion on *Beamtenstaten*, so prescient given the fact that he originally published this piece in 1966, is largely taken from Idenburg's article (but Idenburg did not use the word, *beamtenstaten*).

[69] Idenburg, "Het Nederlandse Antwoord," p. 149.

THE SPECTER OF COINCIDENCE

John Pemberton

For me, "Southeast Asia" has been an exceptionally good *locus* from which to try to get accustomed to this kind of haunting.

Benedict Anderson

A photograph recalls Netherlands East Indies Governor General A. C. D de Graeff, his long arm stretched forward, hand held palm down, blessing sacrificial offerings prepared for machinery at the Tjolomadoe sugar mill: Central Java, May 21, 1928 (see Figure One, below). De Graeff is presented in the photograph as calm, confident. He is as reassuring that the mill's enormous cogwheels of production will perform smoothly, without accident, profitably, as he himself appears reassured. It is as though he does not see the ghost in the machine, particularly machine Number One.

This ghost does not have a name, or at least her name was no longer known by the time the photograph was taken.[1] She is a spectral presence that appears sometimes as a detached head, vaporously projected and enlarged within the cogwheels of the machinery, sometimes as a well-dressed figure, wholly intact, suspended in mid-air. She is Javanese. She never speaks. She wears a watch. Her sudden appearance threatens to induce distraction that turns fatal. Grasp slips, a machinist is drawn into the cogs, and the sugar for a while runs red. The ghost is said to be as old as the once-modern Dutch milling machines themselves, already well worn in 1928 and still in operation at the close of the twentieth century: remainders of modernity—this ghost and its machinery—become vestiges of antiquity.

---

[1] This information and much of that informing this essay comes through personal communication in and around the Tjolomadoe factory, Kartosuro, Central Java, 1976, 1982–1984, 1996. I am particularly indebted to Pak R. Parmodisastro (b. 1897, senior machinist since 1922), Pak Karya (b. 1900, senior machinist and offerings specialist), and Pak Sujono Wiradisastra (b. 1908, Mangkunagaran representative). I am indebted as well to Pak Hatmokartoyo (village head), Pak Marlan (head of milling stations), Pak Rachmad (senior clerk), Pak Utomo (junior clerk), Pak Budiyanto (engineer), and other workers at the sugar mill.

76   John Pemberton

Figure One

The name of the photographer (who was most likely Dutch, though quite possibly not) is also no longer known, to Javanese at least. The album in which the source of this print is preserved by the Mangkunagaran Palace in Surakarta, Java, notes only: "In Remembrance of the Visit of Netherlands East Indies Governor General JHr. Mr. A. C. D. de Graeff to Surakarta on Monday the 21st of May 1928." What remains in the photograph is the specter of de Graeff poised in a moment when sacrifice is acknowledged. Behind him, also dressed in colonial whites, appears Prince Mangkunagara VII, remembered for his commitment to cultural preservation, a commitment matched only by his devotion to technological innovation. Just eight years earlier, in 1920, the prince had dedicated the cornerstone for the palace's Tirtomarto Reservoir, the epicenter of a massive Javanese waterworks system that rivaled even Dutch accomplishments in hydraulics. The year 1920 also marked the prince's meticulously documented, highly publicized ritual performance as a Javanese groom. The Tirtomarto dedication marked, in fact, the first in a series of calendrically divined postnuptial ceremonial events that wedded the technologically modern to the patently cultural. Such moments of dedication—the opening of the Mangkunagaran's southern territories Wonogiri railway line by means of shadow-puppet performance, the presentation of choreographically reconfigured Javanese dance traditions under the insistent glow of newly installed electric lighting, and so on—are all attended, necessarily, by the camera and take their place in palace albums.

From circa 1900 on, palace archives were increasingly devoted to documenting ritual practice, on the one hand, and, on the other, modern machinery of production. The archived albums reveal, time and time again, a singular obsession with the force of repetition: ritual, habitual, mechanical. Dedication ceremonies such as those noted above, which wedded the technological to the cultural, simply redoubled the attention paid to this force. The 1928 event in the Tjolomadoe sugar factory was no exception. The ritual moment marking the advent of the harvest season coincided exactly with the dedication of the factory's newly renovated and modernized facilities, now supported by a novel skeleton of ironwork. As de Graeff leans forward to bless the offerings just before they are transported by the new conveyor-belt into the geared four-ton rolls of the first milling machine, it is as if the camera is similarly compelled, almost automatically, by such a force—this force of repetition. For the apparatus of the camera is yet again drawn towards a sighting of repetition and enmeshed, momentarily, with the click of its shutter, in precisely the machinery of the modern for which the camera would seem to stand, on its tripod at a distance, as the hallmark. Such enmeshment suggests a point where the critical distance between the camera and its subject might collapse and the machine consume its own mechanism of reproduction. Not uncoincidentally, this photographic instant of shutter-cock timing also indicates a point when the ghost cannot be seen. What remains in the 1928 photograph is the specter of de Graeff suspended, ceremonially buoyant, before machine Number One.

So many worlds—those of farmlands and their villagers; the palace with its numerous kin and servants; the colonial bureaucracy and its administrators with their families and servants; of Dutch engineers and native trainees; Javanese machinists, Chinese chemists, and Indies coolies; railway personnel, security men, and shamanic technicians—coincide in the strange convergence that produces a sugar factory that it feels almost inappropriate to speak of place. Yet, a ghost would seem to desire siting. To the extent that one might attempt to locate a specific place for this vast machine called Tjolomadoe, it would no doubt lie in the very coincidence of such worlds, as ephemeral as that may be. Were one to retrace the various routes of paths out of canefields lined with oxcarts, paved roads with bicycles and personnel, railway lines tracking milled cane to storage and market, they all cross, eventually, the threshold of the mill proper as they pass under the clock that watches over the mill's acutely synchronized operation. There is a precarious sense in which the convergence of routine labors and the geared coupling of the machines themselves reiterates the peculiar logic of coincidence conjoining such worlds. "[W]ithout the strictest punctuality in promises and services the whole structure would break down into inextricable chaos," observed Georg Simmel of modern life in 1903. "If all the clocks and watches in Berlin would suddenly go wrong in different ways, even if only by one hour, all economic life and communication of the city would be disrupted for a long time."[2]

For colonial administrators in Tjolomadoe, one of the primary perceived threats that accompanied this novel synchronization—beyond breakdown, accident, and loss of profit—was the sheer monotony of the thing. Having worked for decades in a Javanese sugar mill from 1902 on, Jan Poll wrote late in his career to correct this commonplace perception: "Life in the sugar business is not as monotonous

---

[2] Georg Simmel, "The Metropolis and Mental Life" in *The Sociology of Georg Simmel*, ed. Kurt H. Wolff (New York: The Free Press, 1950), pp. 412-13.

as it may seem."[3] Poll recalls happily, "one could always play bridge, dance while the gramophone is played, and billiards were soon available. . . . When one loves the Indies one does not need much to be happy there. You can be happy there without champagne. A social club with its own cinema and gramophone is all one needs for conviviality."[4] Pastimes, amusements, and socials also were mechanically engaged and synchronically sensed, with the camera drawn, of course, towards these times as well. In Tjolomadoe, at the virtual center of all such mechanized synchrony, loomed machine Number One.

One particular place, however, appears to give this factory a certain grounding, and that is a gravesite just east of the mill where Nyai Pulungsih is entombed. Through monthly séances, Pulungsih is invoked as the founder of Tjolomadoe, whose farmlands she commanded through inheritance and whose initial crude machinery she procured through a bold exchange, in the early nineteenth century, by hawking all of her jewelry. She is invoked as well as a figure endowed with magical powers, manifested in heirloomed amulets, especially brilliant agate stones whose refracting centers reveal undulating snakes. And she is invoked, finally, as ancestress of kings, the last woman of common birth to be of genealogical significance to the Mangkunagaran royal house.[5] Not only was she a power source for dominant bloodlines, she demonstrated formidable economic prowess. Countering such a force emanating from outside the walls of the palace, as well as the specter of an enterprising woman operating on her own, Mangkunagara IV took over the sugar estate in 1861, secured investments from Dutch financiers, named its factory "Tjolomadoe" (Mountain of Honey), expanded facilities, formalized administrative structures, and inscribed his name as the enlightened founder of this highly profitable sugar business.

It is not surprising, then, that workers employed by the mill have speculated, from at least the 1920s on, that the ghost of machine Number One is intimately associated with, if not identical to, the spirit of Pulungsih: a specter of origins that seeks revenge for a legacy lost—appropriated by Mangkunagara IV and his successors, all men. The fact that this ghost's most commonly sighted companions assume the form of snakes bearing rust-gold stripes—snakes said to vary in length from the size of a thumb to fullblown crowned serpents—recalls as well the amber agates in Pulungsih's paraphernalia of power. But this speculation stops here, for the ghost never speaks. Her name is never revealed.

It is also speculated that the spectral appearances within the milling machinery emanate from (as do many commanding spectral powers in Central Java) Ratu Kidul, spirit consort of kings and legendary empress of Java's southern waters. But again, the ghost in Tjolomadoe never reveals her identity and shows no outward signs of Java's spirit queen—none at all. It is thus further speculated that this specter was once a member of Ratu Kidul's spirit entourage and sought out by Mangkunagara IV as a guardian of the factory, but who then developed a special

---

[3] Jan Poll, "Op een Suikerfabriek," in *Zóó Leven Wij in Indië* (Amsterdam: W. van Hoeve, 1945), p. 154.

[4] Ibid., p. 162.

[5] Pulungsih wedded a Mangkunagaran prince (Suryamijaya, circa 1810) and bore a daughter (Samsiyah) who wedded the future Mangkunagara III (reigned 1835-1853) and bore a daughter (Dunuk) who, in turn, wedded the future Mangkunagara IV (r. 1853-1881) and bore the future Mangkunagara V (r. 1881-1896), father of Mangkunagara VII (r. 1916-1944).

late-nineteenth-century fondness for machinery, parted ways with her commander, and began to operate with powers all her own. This possibility repeats, in turn, the logic of Pulungsih's threatening prowess, of the uncannily undomesticated, of forces moving on their own, operating by uncertain contracts and demanding sacrificial exchange. It, too, necessarily stops short of conclusion, unnamed, silent.

All such speculation concerning Tjolomadoe's origins and the peculiar spirit of the thing was meant to be put to rest, officially, on April 18, 1937. This date marked Mangkunagara VII's unveiling of a stone taken from the palace's southcoast hills and erected at the factory entrance, a stone said to have mysterious powers, a stone sculpted in the likeness of Mangkunagara IV. The monument would act as a sort of formal lodestone, centering the factory squarely within the Mangkunagaran legacy and permanently grounding the mill's unsettled past and untoward encounters. Since its emplacement, every year just before campaign milling begins, the sculpture has been treated in the fashion of a Hindu-Javanese lingga: it is proffered incense and incantation, anointed with consecrated water, ritually cleansed, and circumambulated in silent procession. Not uncoincidentally, a few weeks later in 1937, just after the monument was installed and at a point of peak intensity in milling, the newly ground sugar yet again ran red for a while. Inside Tjolomadoe, Javanese machinists were not at all surprised.

It seemed self-evident to those close to milling machines that the monument, magically endowed or not, had little effect in securing protection from accidents associated with ghost appearances—thrown tie rods, blown boiler heads, sudden irregular grinding of tensed mill rollers, and so on. Even official offerings such as those blessed by de Graeff, in 1928, poised before the camera and machine Number One, were not really all that effective either. "For the well-being of Tjolomadoe, the campaign, the workers, and the machines . . . ," began the invocation as the offering was conveyed towards the black-hole portal of machine Number One on April 18, 1984. The offering consisted of a pair of sugar cane stalks, "finest in the fields," adorned as a bride and groom. The keep-the-wheels-turning sentiment of progress and profit within this campaign prayer on behalf of Tjolomadoe towards the end of the twentieth century was essentially the same as that offered during de Graeff's visit in 1928. Such conveyor-belt offerings and official prayers have been of little concern, however, to those working the milling and boiler stations. The machinists have long had something else in mind.

The ghost in machine Number One was not the only presence uncaptured by the photograph documenting de Graeff's 1928 visit to Tjolomadoe. Embedded within much of the machinery of Tjolomadoe—underneath boilers, at the base of electrical terminals, along rail tracks, in the chained sprockets, ratcheted wheels, and pitched runoff troughs of the milling machines themselves—were heads of water buffalo and cows, decapitated vestiges of sacrifice, whose glassy eyes stared vacantly into the workings of the factory (see Figure Two, below). The dozen or so heads were already present at the moment when the sugarcane offering was blessed. They had been placed in their respective positions so matter-of-factly, without any apparent rites of sacrifice or ceremonial speeches, that it may very well have seemed that they belonged, somehow, to the machines themselves. The camera was not drawn to them in 1928. Its apparatus was characteristically engaged with points dramatizing repetition, whether manifested ritually in moments of dedication, or mechanically in moments of industrial production. The heads had little to do with such points, just as they were entirely indifferent to de Graeff's call for campaign success and harvest productivity.

Figure Two

Javanese machinists working the milling and boiler stations had put the animal heads into position on the eve of the milling season, just before boilers were ignited and cogs slipped into gear. This was done in 1928 just as it had been for years before and would be every year thereafter.[6] For the machinists, the advent of the campaign meant not productivity and prosperity but the heightened possibility of accident and ghostly encounter. They were just as sure to set the heads in place as they were to set steam valves, to grease cogs and chains. While factory administrators would make reference to "harvest-time rituals" and similarly optimistic phrasings of celebration, it was the machinists' own term for events linked with the advent of milling that would prove the most compelling:

---

[6] The sacrificial heads displayed in Figure Two were, in fact, photographed in 1984 when the camera—in the hands of the present author—could no longer resist the apparent ritual attraction of the moment.

tjemb(r)èngan, the noise of machines in operation, a strange sound of metallic rattling.[7]

The severed heads have not displaced the possibility of accident in Tjolomadoe. Instead, they call attention, annually, to that very possibility for those working close to the machines. In this sense, they have never failed. In this sense, too, their presence is not unlike that of the ghosts—whether in the figure of a woman, spectrally projected, or her serpentine consorts—associated with these machines. The peculiar thing about the snakes who appear, occasionally, always one at a time, is that they go through the milling machinery unharmed, completely intact, and then just disappear. A snake appears on a boiler and two hours later the machine stalls, is repaired, then stalls again. The spectral snake's appearance signals breakdown and thus serves, potentially, as a warning to those able to maintain a certain distance, momentarily reflect on the sighting, and, in so doing, recognize the premonition.

In the case of an extraordinarily large snake or crowned serpent, the sudden appearance itself may prove so startling that an accident follows immediately, without any pause whatsoever. This is especially likely to happen when the ghostly appearance is that of the figure associated with machine Number One, the specter unacknowledged by de Graeff. "There she was, floating over the milling rolls, and he was stunned, terrified. Fell fifteen meters down onto that pump rod. Skewered him, ran clean through. Left him just hanging there," recalled a senior machinist in 1984.[8] The accident is almost as automatic as the timing of the pumping rod's arc. Both reflexes—those of the victim and the instrument of death—are mechanized. One is not even certain about what, exactly, has just "left him": the machine, in gear, as its cogs continue to turn, or the ghost, as she vanished, without a second thought.

This lack of certainty derives, in part, from the fact that the ghosts of Tjolomadoe do not speak but simply linger in the factory, silent, disappearing just as quickly as they appear. There is a sense that they once, perhaps, had names and were able to be summoned up with mantras and appeased. But that was a different time. What remains is the space of a spectrality now generalized. Machinists note that the milling machines are old, very old, and were they to be replaced by new equipment, perhaps ghosts would not appear and accidents not occur. The same is said of the factory's oldest railway engine, Loco Number One: "should've been retired years ago."[9] This is not intended as a comment on the condition of Tjolomadoe's machinery, for the same machinists speak with much pride of their smoothly functioning milling stations, and the machines themselves appear in remarkably good shape, well-tuned and polished. Instead, the very antiquity of the machinery recalls a past that should be obsolete but for some reason is not. The space is thus genuinely haunted.

Within this space, even the most intimate of offerings—the carefully positioned heads of sacrificed domestic animals—presented by those closest to the machines appear unusually ominous. They recall danger that is conjured up in order

---

[7] Another reading of *"tjembrèngan"* suggests that the term derives from *tjèngbèng*, a Chinese-Melayu ritual of graveyard purification held during the month of April. Indies natives serving as chemists in sugar mills were characteristically of Chinese descent.

[8] Pak Karyo, personal communication, Tjolomadoe, April 24, 1984.

[9] Pak Parmodisastro, personal communication, Tjolomadoe, April 28, 1984.

to be expelled, yet the precise source of this danger that takes the form of accident is uncertain. Coupled to this uncertainty is a pronounced ambivalence towards the ghosts themselves, for these ghosts can be reassuring indicators of an accident to be avoided and, at the same time, startling signs of an accident already in progress. To tell stories of such accidents and apparitions is to reaffirm one's distance from ghostly effects, to replay the possibility of a timely premonition when a ghost was once sighted and now, safely, recalled. And yet these stories are themselves ephemeral, existing, like ghosts, only in the time of their appearance, in the time that their recollection takes. To place the severed heads of sacrificial substitutes within the machinery of Tjolomadoe replays a similar possibility, anticipating, as it does, an accident yet to be avoided. It is as if one is given a shadow of a chance, known only in due time at the moment when the accidental aspect of accident becomes fortunate or otherwise.

While de Graeff seems not to have been aware of such an offering or the ghostly effects it portends, Dutch personnel closer to the workings of the sugar factory were not uninformed. Jan Poll recalls, for example, "the bleeding water-buffalo heads. . . . One factory may take these things more seriously than another."[10] After dwelling at length on Javanese ritual affairs—particularly communal feasts—Poll concludes: "While it may be true that in many domains we have something to teach the Indonesians and can bring forth their development, in the domain of culture which is natural and inborn, we can take a lesson from them and then come back for a second one."[11] With their finely tuned sensibilities in ritual matters, Javanese know, somehow, something that "we" too should know, but do not. Offerings are read as traces of this privileged knowledge, just as ritual behavior in Java is sensed to be uncannily in touch with something still beyond the grasp of even the most dedicated of the colony's administrators.

Such a perception no doubt sentimentalizes the sense of otherness that authorized a declared need for colonial development, for transmission of the modern. That this perception should arise within what Poll calls "the domain of culture"—something "they" have, from birth—is not surprising. At the same time, Poll appears genuinely drawn to this thing, ritual or otherwise, about which he knows that he knows little. This sort of attraction appears at another moment in his recollections of the sugar factory, but this time wholly outside the domain of culture and within, instead, what one would assume to be the domain of the modern itself.

> I can never express enough admiration for the special qualities I discovered in our Indonesians during my long career in the Indies. I say "discovered" but that in no way means that I really understood. I must confess that I still am not able to understand.
>
> I will elucidate this with a concrete example. When I had been first machinist for a year in a factory new to me and had the opportunity to train my [native] folk, I made the following proposition to the *"toekangs,"* who are their craftsmen. Whoever among you has a son, if you want him to work in the factory, let him line up tomorrow at such and such hour.[12]

---

[10] Poll, "Op een Suikerfabriek," p. 164.

[11] Ibid., p.165.

[12] Ibid., p.152.

Poll goes on to describe how he chose a dozen native boys who looked bright and were around twelve years old, boys who proved extraordinarily quick at picking up the trade: " . . . they became, almost without exception, excellent specialists."[13]

Such a comment again sentimentalizes relations, this time featuring Poll as the source of lessons learned. And again, at the same time, there is the acknowledgment of something highly admired but not understood. It is not the fact that native youths of the Indies become highly skilled machinists that astonishes Poll. Rather, it is the way this skill manifests itself:

> It is not at all clear to me how such a youth later arrives at the science of how a steam engine works, or a motor drive, how they know their lathes, which pinion they must set to turn one or another screw-thread. In less time than I would have needed to make a very complicated calculation, he knew it all and had done his job without error. People pointed out to me that this was purely routine work, well then I take my hat off to such routine, which even knows what to do with a rare screw-thread. People sometimes explained this as intuition, but surely this is intuition which is determined by an understanding![14]

Yet, what could such an understanding be? "I must confess that I still am not able to understand."

The point where the two domains of "special qualities" coincide—ritual on the one hand, mechanical on the other—lies in the realm of repetition. It is the conjunction of the two that so eludes understanding and remains unsettling. It is as if the culture of premodern Java were already somehow in sync with modern skills, and thus the modernist distinction itself, which would separate the modern from the premodern (the here from the there, the inside from the out, the now from the then, and so on) has begun to disappear, and with it the guiding principles of colonial progress. Through this sensation of routine, this sense of repetition which some would say is informed by intuition, the logic of mechanized behavior has begun to assert itself. It informs all the workings underpinning the vast machine of Tjolomadoe, producing potentially uncanny effects.[15] Poll is attracted and drawn towards this unthinkable logic just as automatically as the camera is drawn towards de Graeff, in 1928, as he ritually blessed the offerings conveyed up the ramp of machine Number One.

Nowhere is the extent of Tjolomadoe's reach more evident than on the railway tracks that extend out from the factory. The camera is drawn towards this as well, and it sits so close to the rails that it becomes enmeshed, for an instant, within the machinery it would expose (see Figure Three, below). The positioning of the camera is not simply accidental; it has been repeated obsessively in a history of

---

[13] Ibid.

[14] Ibid.

[15] Here, one recalls Freud's (1919) discussion of automata in relation to uncanny sensations. Recalling Jentsch's (1906) study of the "uncanny," Freud notes as well "the uncanny effect of epileptic fits . . . because these excite in the spectator the impression of automatic, mechanical processes at work behind the ordinary appearance of mental activity." Sigmund Freud, "The 'Uncanny,'" in *Writings on Art and Literature* (Stanford: Stanford University Press, 1997), pp. 201-2.

photographic encounters with the railway that can be tracked from the mid-nineteenth century on. The fact that essentially the same shot might have been achieved from the front of a train (as was often done), or from the back, reiterates this sense of mechanical conjunction between camera and railway. The viewer is drawn in and inhabits this point of conjunction where the space behind the camera coincides with that of the train. It is a precariously empowered viewpoint which is driven by the machinery of locomotion behind it and, at the same time, completely vulnerable to whatever might come down the tracks. It is the point of potential accident.

Figure Three

A second conjunction between camera and railway occurs from within the train as one looks out through the coach window, away from the oncoming tracks. It facilitates a point of view which, in its very denial of any untoward conjunction, appears far more reassuring. Recalling a 1924 visit to the Indies by the Dutch architect H. P. Berlage, Rudolf Mrázek notes, "As the train pulled out of the station, Berlage pulled his window up: 'the aspects are fleeting . . . cinematographic . . . palm groves, *kampongs*, bridges, green sawah rice fields . . . blue and hazy horizon . . . '" "As far as Berlage could see," Mrázek adds, "beyond the window glass and framed by the window frame there lay the *mooi Indie*, 'beautiful Indies,' a late-colonial image often more significant than the colony itself."[16]

---

[16] Rudolf Mrázek, "From Darkness to Light: Optics of Policing in Late-Colonial Netherlands East Indies," in *Figures of Criminality in Indonesia, the Philippines, and Colonial Vietnam*, ed. Vicente L. Rafael (Ithaca: Cornell University Southeast Asia Program, 1999), p. 18.

What passes by in this sequencing of enframed scenes of village cultivation, unfolding in time with the regular rhythms of the rails, is the image of an Indies at marvelous right angles with the modern railroad, yet all the while in sync with it. This was the beautiful Indies, endowed with a pronounced sense of culture, as Poll imagined, natural and inborn, and exhibiting an abundance of harvest-time celebrations of well-being and prosperity. Such was the image projected by de Graeff as he blessed Javanese sugarcane in 1928. The camera could not miss it.

What is repeatedly bypassed by such an image in its compulsive articulation and reproduction of well-being is the very thought of accident. Just as incidental jolts are cushioned by railway shock-absorbers and padded coach interiors, putting out of mind the dangers of machine irregularities and letting the eye drift effortlessly across ricefields and rooflines, so too, similar irregularities remain invisible—out of frame, perhaps—in the photograph of de Graeff. Potential shocks are absorbed, perhaps, by his figure's ritual gesture. This figure's arm extends outwards, as if holding off something at a distance, yet all eyes seem to adopt the viewpoint of the camera here and look reassuredly towards de Graeff himself.

At the unexpected moment when an accident does occur, shock is doubled. For it is not simply the sudden derailment of a locomotive or the suddenly thrown rod of a tensed milling machine that proves so shocking during the moment of accident, but the coincidental shock that comes with the abruptly reawakened memory of forgotten danger, with the uncanny sensation of something known all along, but routinely suppressed. The machine appears to reassert itself. The repercussions of repetition—mechanical, habitual, ritual—return, full force. Even sustained attempts to locate a position for oneself at a distance from such a force become derailed.[17] When confronted with an unnerving coincidence between the almost automatic skills of native machinists and his own logic of studied calculation, Jan Poll articulated this distance—so seemingly critical to the colonial enterprise—in terms of a need "to understand," to truly grasp, fail as he might. Yet, there may be other terms for registering distance.

The machinery of Tjolomadoe is indeed extensive. To locate a position from which one might point at the thing and hold it at a distance, in view, is not easy. The camera placed close to the tracks confronts us with this difficulty. Just as there is a certain convergence between the apparatus of the camera and that of the railway outside the factory, so too one recalls the numerous moments when the milling machines within the walls of the factory proper presented themselves as fitting photographic subjects and drew the camera in. And just as the tracks connect these moments of engagement between the camera and machine, so too one recalls as well a certain convergence between the railroad and the sugar factory. Made up of

---

[17] It is probably no accident that one of only two personal encounters with the uncanny which Freud recorded in "The 'Uncanny,'" should occur on a train: "I was sitting alone in my *wagon-lit* compartment when a more than usually violent jolt of the train swung back the door of the adjoining washing-cabinet, and an elderly gentleman in a dressing-gown and a traveling cap came in. I assumed that in leaving the washing-cabinet, which lay between the two compartments, he had taken the wrong direction and come into my compartment by mistake. Jumping up with the intention of putting him right, I at once realized to my dismay that the intruder was nothing but my own reflection in the looking-glass on the open door. I can still recollect that I thoroughly disliked his appearance." Freud, "The 'Uncanny,'" p. 225. In this instance, "a more than usually violent jolt" produces not accident, but the conditions for an uncanny reemergence of the double itself.

primarily the same mechanical parts and design—steam valves, pressure seals, and contoured plates for boiler units; slip rings, piston rods, and geared cogs for motor drives—and forged from essentially the same materials, these two aspects of the machine that is Tjolomadoe are virtually indistinguishable. The carriage had become inseparable from the road in the singular system that became known as the railway. "The wheels, rails, and carriages are only part of one great machine, on the proper adjustment of which, one to the other, entirely depends the perfect action of the whole," observed C. H. Greenhow in 1846, introducing *An Exposition of the Danger and Deficiencies of the Present Mode of Railway Construction*.[18] The milling stations within the factory are tracked into precisely the same machine. They are inseparable from it. Through a system of conveyor belts, linked rollers, and mechanized chutes, they are bolted to it. With its oversized steam boilers and multiple cog ensembles, the sugar factory is, in effect, a monstrous locomotive, without wheels.

In colonial Java, no doubt the most significant point of coincidence between the railway and factories like Tjolomadoe was their shared reputation as sites known to produce fatal accidents. To the extent that one observes in this pair of sites one great machine, such a coincidence is not surprising. In Tjolomadoe, this coincidence between train and mill marks the moment when the machine makes its most obviously aggressive move by operating entirely on its own, as if moving by its own geared will. Some nights, the factory's oldest steam locomotive has tracked its way out of the mill. There appears to have been no engineer operating the machine, only the remains of a victim discovered near the tracks the next morning. There also appears never to have been a ghost sighted in conjunction with this form of accident, not in the manner that ghosts have appeared within the factory, just as it seems that there has never been any apparent reason for the person who would become the victim to be there at that time. This is the most automatic form of accident, when coincidence feels fated.

The relatively modest offerings placed by machinists near locomotive Number One appear there more frequently than the sacrificial heads that are positioned, by the same machinists, at their milling stations annually on the eve of the campaign. The timing of these more frequent offerings is not coordinated, in any way, with harvest seasons or milling events. It is strictly calendrical and observed every thirty-five days, marking a significant coincidence between five- and seven-day weeks cycling within Javanese systems of divination. Which is to say, the presentation of these offerings acknowledges a cycling of temporalities that intersect like cogwheels, repeatedly marking intervals whose significance is purely coincidental. The very automaticity of the accident here indicates a moment that cannot be distanced, as it produces an accident that occurs on track, without the possibility of momentary deferral. There are no ghostly sightings that might be recognized as premonitions.

Inside Tjolomadoe a possibility of deferral remains. Ghosts occasionally appear within factory machinery as potential signs of an accident yet to occur, yet to be avoided, an accident whose outcome will be known only in the time it takes to happen. Some machinists keep a distance from such appearances and maintain their stations without mishap. Others, so startled by the sight of a ghost, fall

---

[18] In Wolfgang Schivelbusch, *The Railway Journey: The Industrialization of Time and Space in the Nineteenth Century* (Berkeley: The University of California Press, 1986), p. 20.

headlong into this moment of accident already now irreversibly in progress. Fainting, these victims seem to have seen something which they apparently thought they should not.

In their capacity to startle, ghosts resemble photographs, including many of those appearing in the Mangkunagaran palace albums. Like ghosts, photographs bring into view something that has passed away and is not usually seen, something that perhaps should no longer be seen and yet will not stay away. Photographs remain as unintended traces of a ghostliness within the machinery of the modern. It is no accident that in the early days of the camera, such ghostly implications were developed into spirit photography.

A significant difference distinguishes, nevertheless, these two manifestations of spectral projection. The appearance of a ghost, like that which emerges near machine Number One, is momentary, fleeting. Its being does not depend on—much less derive from—its preservation, but just the opposite: a disappearance which is as sudden as its appearance. It is just this sort of passing—this coming to pass—which so eludes photography. Ghosts simply flash past, in a photographic-like instant as if mimicking the camera, and then vanish into the memory of precisely that which cannot be photographed, no matter how ingeniously the camera tries.

The capacity to startle is not the only respect in which ghosts and photographs resemble one another. Both instances of spectral projection appear unusually capable of anticipating their future recalling as markers of that which no longer is. The instantaneous moment of the camera's shutter click becomes extended into the future, prefiguring a reappearance of something that otherwise would have long faded from sight. The appearance of a ghost—itself already a reappearance—similarly exhibits this sense of anticipation which operates every time a sighting occurs. Each appearance prefigures a peculiar certainty of return.

Such a sense of anticipation is particularly compelling in the case of ghosts appearing within modern machinery, like that associated with Tjolomadoe. The ghost in machine Number One is undoubtedly Javanese, yet she is silent. She does not speak. She may have originated from a source outside the factory and then have been drawn in by a fondness for machines at a time in the late nineteenth century when the novel powers of mechanical operation were increasingly sensed. But even this is uncertain. In that uncertainty, her own powers of operation—the regularity of her movements, timed exactly with milling machine operation; the extraction of sacrificial offerings; the generation of breakdown and accident; and the production of victims—have coincided so perfectly with those of machine Number One that the ghost and machine here seem virtually indistinguishable. The fit is precise. It is as if a place for the ghost had already been reserved in the machine. Or, to put it another way, it is as if this ghost, presumably from the Javanese past, were capable of anticipating its future recalling in the machinery of the modern.

Anticipation, here, thus signals a thoroughly unsettling coincidence of perspective, a point where the distinction separating the modern from the premodern vanishes. What emerges in the gap in understanding posed by such a vanishing, is a ghost that appears somehow intrinsic to the machine and, at times, separable from it. This coincidence of perspective recalls, in turn, the unnerving apparent coincidence between Javanese powers of routine and modern European workings of the intellect that so haunted Poll: "I must confess that I still am not able to understand." In both instances of coincidence, a sense of critical distance collapses. What remains is the apparition of repetition.

Anticipation extends, nevertheless, another possibility. When Tjolomadoe machinists encounter a ghost and are able to maintain their distance from this thing in machine Number One, they do so not by removing themselves from their stations—that is, not by backing off as if to gain perspective—but by remaining perfectly still. This is the moment when they know that, in time, an accident will occur and the moment of the accident itself will pass, just as assuredly as the ghost will disappear. This is the moment when anticipation assumes the form of waiting: a marking of time that counters both the startling potential, as well as the very monotony, of the thing in the machine. A possibility of critical distance thus emerges in this moment, but that distance is, in effect, temporalized.

Figure Four

One wonders, then, whether the apparatus of the camera is really capable of registering such a moment, such a temporality. Perhaps the closest the camera has come in its many encounters with Tjolomadoe occurred during the time of the factory's reconstruction just before the dedication ceremonies in 1928. This was a time when neither machines nor sacrificial offerings were in operation. With most of its machinery disassembled and lying in pieces on the factory floor awaiting replacement parts that would be borrowed secondhand from other factories, Tjolomadoe was immobilized. Its space exhibited a strange disarray. It was an out-of-gear time that slipped easily into an extended moment of waiting so marked that the camera would not miss it.

During this time, this kind of time, a photograph recalls the foregrounded figure of an Indies laborer who is seated, resting, waiting perhaps (see Figure Four, above). The man is looking in the same direction as the camera: their attention is drawn together towards the figure of another laborer positioned almost dead center in the photograph, surrounded by scaffolding of factory reconstruction. This other figure stands motionless, waiting, perhaps resting, as he looks directly back into the camera. Viewpoints in this photograph converge and coincide in a manner that is fundamentally different from the point of view represented in the photograph of de Graeff on May 21, 1928, when milling machines were once again engaged, offerings blessed, and the camera looked on reassuringly from the side at its ritual "beautiful Indies" scene. Here, from the viewpoint of waiting, the camera is drawn into a far more precarious position akin to that looking straight down the railway tracks into a moment of convergence and the possibility of accident. The central figure of the other laborer in this photograph looks straight back and attracts the camera towards a point of coincidence with itself, in a moment of potential collision with its own mechanics of operation. The figure does so simply by looking at the camera and standing still, waiting, perfectly motionless, for the click. It is as if, in such a moment of coincidence, one were waiting for the ghost in the machine to appear.

Yet, the ghost is still not exposed. During this time of disassembly when machines are not yet in gear, the ghost should, in fact, not be in the picture. Through the very appropriateness of an absence, then, the ghost becomes all the more tangible here, all the more anticipated in this extended moment of mechanical pause and waiting. And when the ghost reappears, as she did with a vengeance just after the 1928 dedication ceremonies, foreshadowing accidents for that year, she carries with her not a camera, but the instrument of modernity that might most accurately register the moment of her own passing. She carries a watch.

Images of Colonial Cities in Early Indonesian Novels

Tsuyoshi Kato

Introduction

Despite notable exceptions such as Hanoi, Yogyakarta, and Mandalay, many of the cities of Southeast Asia were created by colonial powers or were transformed from forts, port towns, or even villages into modern cities during the colonial period.[1] By the late nineteenth century, they often incorporated European administrative centers, Chinatowns, and sometimes Arab and Indian sections, in addition to quarters of various indigenous populations. They, or at least some parts of them, were thoroughly European in atmosphere by the 1920s and 1930s, as Japanese cartoonist Osano was to find out when accompanying the Japanese troops invading Batavia (Jakarta) in March 1942 (see Figure One, below).[2]

How did local people perceive these colonial cities, which were in many ways so different from the villages and indigenous urban centers of Southeast Asia? What did life in colonial cities suggest to them in terms of hazards as well as possibilities? What sort of mentality was associated with colonial cities? These are the questions I address in this paper about the cities of the Dutch East Indies. For this purpose, I review six early Indonesian novels published between 1919 and 1933, the period when novels written by "native" Indonesians became popular.

---

[1] This is an abridged and translated version of my article in Japanese with significant revision especially in the final section. See Tsuyoshi Kato, "Oranda-ryo Higashi Indo Shokuminchi Toshi-no Shinsho Fukei: Shoki Balai Poestaka Shosetsu-o Tegakari toshite," *Tonan Ajia Kenkyu* (Southeast Asian Studies) 35, 1 (1997): 77-135. Omitted in translation from the Japanese version are the synopses of the six novels discussed in the article. I express my appreciation to the editorial board of *Tonan Ajia Kenkyu* at Kyoto University, which approved the publication of this article in the present form. I gratefully acknowledge the assistance of Noriaki Oshikawa, Mikio Moriyama, Nobuto Yamamoto, and Sumio Fukami in obtaining the copies of most of the materials used in the original article. I also want to thank Donna J. Amoroso for her editorial help.

[2] Saseo Osano, *Jawa Jugun Gafu* (A picture book by a cartoonist who accompanied the troops to Java) (Jakarta: Jawa Shinbun-sha, 1945), n.p.

Figure One
Batavia as Osano saw it after the Japanese invasion in March of 1942

Two of the six novels are at the center of the present analysis. They are *Sitti Noerbaja—Kasih Ta' Sampai* (Sitti Noerbaja—Love not attained) and *Salah Asoehan* (A wrong upbringing).[3] Both were published by Balai Poestaka, the government printing house initially established in 1908 but actively involved in publication starting in the 1920s. They are perhaps the best- and longest-sellers in the history of Indonesian literature, the former registering its twenty-fourth printing, according to the 1994 edition, and the latter its twentieth printing, according to the 1992 edition.[4]

In selecting the remaining four novels, I took care to introduce some variety. Two, like *Sitti Noerbaja* and *Salah Asoehan*, were published by Balai Poestaka: *Kalau Ta' Oentoeng* (If fortune does not favor) was written by a female author (Selasih, nom de plume of Sariamin Ismail), and *Roesmala Dewi (Pertemoean Djawa dan Andalas)* (Roesmala Dewi [Where Java and Sumatra meet]) was co-written by two authors. The remaining two, *Student Hidjo* (Student Green) and *Rasa Merdika—Hikajat Soedjanmo* (The feeling of freedom—The story of Soedjanmo), were published by private publishing houses and written by Javanese authors; with the exception of Hardjosoemarto, author of *Roesmala Dewi*, who was a Javanese, the other authors of the four novels were Minangkabau.[5]

---

[3] Mh. Roesli, *Sitti Noerbaja—Kasih Ta' Sampai* (Weltevreden: Balai Poestaka, 1922); Abdoel Moeis, *Salah Asoehan*, djilid I, djilid II, djilid III (Weltevreden: Balai Poestaka, 1928). The spelling of Indonesian words in this paper basically follows the old type of spelling used during the Dutch period.

[4] Mh. Rusli, *Sitti Noerbaja—Kasih Ta' Sampai*, cetakan keduapuluh empat (Jakarta: Balai Pustaka, 1994); Abdul Muis, *Salah Asuhan*, cetakan keduapuluh (Jakarta: Balai Pustaka, 1992).

[5] Selasih, *Kalau Ta' Oentoeng* (Batavia-C.: Balai Poestaka, 1933); S. Hardjosoemarto dan A. Dt. Madjoindo, *Roesmala Dewi (Pertemoean Djawa dan Andalas)* (Batavia-C.: Balai Poestaka,

These six novels do not represent the full range of diversity found among Indonesian novels and authors of pre-war days, but many did share these characteristics: five of the authors were male; all were of either Minangkabau or Javanese ethnic background; they were civil servants or journalists-cum-political activists by occupation; and probably all had some education in Dutch. One practical consideration in selecting the six novels was the availability to me of their first editions, as there are sometimes discrepancies between the first and later editions. The possibility of examining contemporary illustrations inserted in the novels is another reason I was eager to read first editions.[6]

KOTA AS COLONIAL CITIES

It is striking, or perhaps not so striking, that the main stories of the novels revolve around cities. Villages do appear in some novels, but as exemplified in *Salah Asoehan*, *Kalau Ta' Oentoeng*, and *Rasa Merdika*, they are the places heroes or heroines leave behind at a certain age or to which they return to die toward the end of the novel. Practically no villages are featured in *Sitti Noerbaja*, *Roesmala Dewi*, and *Student Hidjo*. Yet despite the central importance of the city as a stage for the stories' evolution, few passages in the novels actually describe what cities are like. Counting even one-liners, I found altogether about ten such passages in the six novels. One of the longer passages is quoted below. It is from *Sitti Noerbaja*. Noerbaja (Sitti is an honorific title) visits Batavia to see her lover Samsoe (Samsoe'lbahari), from whom she has been separated for some time. One evening they take a stroll in the capital city of the Dutch East Indies:

> After changing clothes, the two went out hand-in-hand to go sightseeing in the city of Betawi [Batavia] in the evening. Samsoe took Noerbaja here and there, riding a horse-carriage and tram around the city. It is impossible to describe how happy Noerbaja was, seeing the beauty of this city.
> "The city of Betawi is truly big and truly lively, full of very large and beautiful houses as well as shops. It rightly deserves to be the capital city [*iboe negeri*] of East Indies," said Noerbaja.
> Satisfied with sight-seeing, the two of them went into a restaurant because their stomachs felt hungry. After eating, Noerbaja was taken by Samsoe to see a circus [*komidi kuda*] which was being held at the time. After that they at long last made their leisurely way back home.[7]

1932); Marco Kartodikromo, *Student Hidjo* (Semarang: Masman & Stroink, 1919); Soemantri, *Rasa Merdika—Hikajat Soedjanmo* (Semarang: Drukkerij VSTP, 1924). I consulted Teeuw in translating the titles of the six novels into English. See A. Teeuw, *Modern Indonesian Literature*, vol. 1, 2nd ed. (The Hague: Martinus Nijhoff, 1979).

[6] One notable example of differences in successive editions is found in the 1922 and 1994 editions of *Sitti Noerbaja*. In addition to some divergencies in paragraphic divisions, words in the first edition which have colonial connotations—Betawi, guilder (or *f*), Hindia, *amtenar* (civil servant), and *Goebernemén*—are replaced by Jakarta, rupiah, Indonesia, *pegawai*, and Pemerintah in the 1994 edition. Illustrations are attached to four of the six novels, that is, *Sitti Noerbaja*, *Kalau Ta' Oentoeng*, *Roesmala Dewi*, and *Rasa Merdika*. The present analysis fails to include novels written by authors with an Islamic education. One famous author of this sort is Hamka (Haji Abdul Malik Karim Amrullah), whose work is briefly discussed in the final section of this essay.

[7] Mh. Roesli, *Sitti Noerbaja*, p. 201.

The urban characteristics that so delight Noerbaja in the above passage—large size, liveliness, busy traffic, numerous shops, and availability of popular culture—can more or less all be gleaned from similar passages describing cities in *Salah Asoehan, Kalau Ta' Oentoeng, Roesmala Dewi,* and *Student Hidjo.*

The Indonesian term used for "city" in the passage above is *kota*.[8] *Kota*, a Sanskrit-derived word, means "fort, fortress, castle, fortified house; fortifications, works," according to a dictionary originally published in 1812, while *negri*, another Sanskrit-derived word, is "a city, town; a country; province, district." Similarly, according to another dictionary initially published around 1900, *kota* signifies "a fortified place, castle, fortress, fort, city or town, place encircled by walls or other fortification" and *negeri* a "city or town, capital city, principal town, country, district, kingdom, state."[9]

Evidently, *kota* used to mean a fort or fortified town, while *negri* or *negeri* had a double meaning in "old Indonesian" of city and country or kingdom, as if to reflect the often synonymous relationship between the name of the kingdom and its capital city in Indonesian history. Yet in the six novels, *negeri* is seldom used to mean "city," with only a few exceptions. One is the apparently customary expression of *iboe negeri* or "capital city," as seen in the quotation above.[10]

It is remarkable that the novels by and large use *kota* consistently in reference to the city of Batavia or local towns and cities. It seems that *kota* had acquired the primary meaning of "urban center" in the Dutch East Indies by the 1910s. This, as far as I know, was patently not the case in British Malaya, where "old Indonesian," or more precisely Malay, was also used. *Kota* has maintained "fort" as its primary meaning in Malaysia up to the present day. In fact, an English-Malay dictionary published as late as the mid-1960s had difficulty coming up with proper Malay words for "city" and "town." Winstedt provides "*bald, butdan, bandar, pekan*" for city or town, but with frequent qualifications or specifications, such as: found only in literature (*bald*), Arabic (*butdan*), seaport (*bandar*), and market (*pekan*).[11] Currently, *bandar*, a Persian-derived word, and *bandar raya* (large *bandar*) are commonly used to mean town and city in Malaysia.

It is difficult to retrace how and when *kota* began to acquire the connotation of urban center in Indonesian. Probably it has to do with the fact that Batavia grew out of a walled fort called Kota. Kota was and has remained the proper name for the *benedenstad*, or lower town, of Batavia since the time when the center of the city moved further south and inland in the early nineteenth century. I speculate

---

[8] The language used in the six novels was called Malay or *Melayu* during the Dutch period, but is referred to here as Indonesian.

[9] William Marsden, *A Dictionary and Grammar of the Malayan Language*, volume one and volume two, with an Introduction by Russell Jones (Singapore: Oxford University Press, 1984 [1812]), volume one, pp. 272, 350; L. Th. Mayer, *Practisch Maleisch-Hollandsch en Hollandsch-Maleisch Handwoordenboek, benevens kort begrip der Maleische woordvorming en spraakleer*, vijfde druk (Semarang: G.C.T. van Dorp, 1906), pp. 150, 180.

[10] It is significant in this connection that the Indonesian translation of Robinson Crusoe was published in 1882 by Government Printing House located in "Negeri Betawi" or the city of Betawi. See A. F. von de Wall, *Hikajat Robinson Crusoe*, tjitakan jang ka-3 (Negeri Betawi: Pertjitakan Goewernemen, 1882).

[11] Richard Winstedt, *An Abridged English-Malay Dictionary*, fourth edition, enlarged (Kuala Lumpur: Marican & Sons, 1965), pp. 68, 397.

that, in due course, "*kota*" in Indonesian, once associated strictly with Kota or the old center of Batavia, took on a new and general meaning, at least implicitly, of Dutch-created or colonial cities, and then of cities and towns in general.

Aficionados of the novels, who could read Indonesian during the Dutch colonial period under consideration, were mostly educated people living in or having the experience of living in urban areas; the authors of these novels also shared similar characteristics.[12] Given these observations, it is perhaps not surprising that we do not see many passages in the six novels referring to the nature of urban cities. I would maintain that literate Indonesians already shared use of the term "*kota*" and similar ideas about its meaning by the time the six novels were written.

Although the novels under consideration do not offer much concrete description of what cities are like, they are replete with images associated with colonial cities. In particular, four themes or topics can be traced through the novels: love and freedom; the question of "I" or "*saja*"; modern education and administration; and clock time and western calendrical dates.

COLONIAL CITIES AS LOCI OF LOVE AND FREEDOM

The common, central theme of the six novels is love in the face of social convention and tradition. Obstacles which get in the way of love are many. In *Sitti Noerbaja*, the differences between the family background of Noerbaja, a rich merchant's daughter, and of Samsoe'lbahari, a son of local aristocracy, create a minor problem. A far more serious obstacle is posed by old, enormously wealthy Datoek Meringgih, a quintessential villain; he wants to force Noerbaja to marry him by financially ruining and making her father indebted to him. In *Salah Asoehan*, it is racial difference which stands between Corrie, a Eurasian and legally European girl, and Hanafi, a native Indonesian boy. The initial difficulty in *Kalau Ta' Oentoeng* is the disparity in social status between Masroel and Rasmani. The underlying problem throughout the novel, however, is Masroel's irresolute nature; he cannot confess his love to Rasmani, express his desire to marry her to his unyielding parents, or reject an unwanted proposal of marriage.[13] In *Roesmala Dewi*, ethnic difference separates Roesmala Dewi, a Minangkabau girl, and Soeparno, a Javanese boy, but they eventually meet again in the city of Soerabaja and marry. *Rasa Merdika*, which starts out having nothing to do with love, eventually shifts its focus there, too. Soedjanmo worries that his engagement in political activism may make him an unsuitable suitor for Soepini in the eyes of her parents; this concern turns out to be unfounded. The novel *Student Hidjo*, which tells stories of multiple cross-racial relations between young Javanese and young Dutch men and women, alone does not recount barriers to love affairs.

Is love fulfilled? *Rasa Merdika* and *Student Hidjo* result in happy endings, while *Salah Asoehan*, *Kalau Ta' Oentoeng*, and *Sitti Noerbaja* do not. In *Roesmala Dewi*, the heroine is forced into an unwanted marriage, fends off the consummation of marriage, and is later reunited with her lover.

---

[12] Nidhi Aeusrivongse, "Fiction as History: A Study of Pre-war Indonesian Novels and Novelists (1920-1942)" (PhD dissertation, the University of Michigan, 1976), pp. 109-112.

[13] Among the heroes of the novels under consideration, Masroel stands out in his irresolute nature. It is noteworthy that the novel was written by a female author.

Teeuw has already pointed out that one of the major themes in early Indonesian novels, especially those written by Minangkabau authors, is love, above all, unfulfilled love due to forced marriage (*kawin paksa*).[14] There is, however, another theme which is closely tied to love or its antithesis, forced marriage, like two sides of one coin. That is freedom or *merdeka* (*merdika*).[15]

What distinguishes the happy ending from the unhappy ending in the six novels is freedom or its lack. Datoek Meringgih, who embodies the wicked power of wealth, stands between Noerbaja and Samsoe'lbahari. The racial barrier of colonial society separates Corrie and Hanafi. Antiquated village thinking on social homogamy blocks the relationship between Masroel and Rasmani. Soeparno and Roesmala Dewi have to suffer because old Minangkabau *adat* (customs and tradition) does not permit inter-ethnic marriage. All these heroes and heroines, save the last couple, see their love affairs end tragically because they cannot liberate themselves from various social circumstances and conventions.

It is difficult to locate the question of freedom within *Student Hidjo*. The story starts in Java, where colonial order prevails. Orderliness is implied by, among other things, the fact that Hidjo, a Javanese boy, is engaged to a Javanese girl, and a Dutch official is in love with a Dutch teacher. However, things become entangled when Hidjo sails to the Netherlands to study. Dutch girls flirt with Hidjo on the ship. In the Netherlands, he becomes romantically involved with a daughter of the Dutch family with whom he boards. In the meantime, the young Dutch official falls in love with Hidjo's fiancée and abandons his schoolteacher girlfriend. The novel ends with the resumption of colonial order, as Hidjo comes back to Java and marries another Javanese girl, his former fiancée marries Hidjo's bride's brother (also Hidjo's school friend), the Dutch official marries Hidjo's former Dutch girlfriend, and the Dutch schoolteacher marries the official's colleague.

In the end, the four couples are married to socially proper partners and living in the same regency in Java, all occupying respectable positions and social strata in colonial society. Thus, on the surface, *Student Hidjo* is not concerned at all with social constraints and taboos attached to cross-racial romances in colonial society. Irrespective of inter-racial amorous interludes, both at the beginning and at the end of the novel, colonial order prevails as if guided by an invisible hand. It appears that despite seemingly wild possibilities offered by imagined freedom or free imagining, colonial order rebounds either by natural law, habit, or force. Or . . . does it really? Perhaps the whole point of *Student Hidjo* is to show that no amount of free imagining can envisage the fulfillment of cross-racial love in colonial society and that colonial order may not be what it appears to be after the intervention of imagined freedom.

One way of attaining freedom and thus fulfilling one's love is suggested by *Rasa Merdika*. Soedjanmo, son of a sub-district head in Java, is not happy with the colonial order in which peasants suffer from poverty and native officials have to kowtow in front of Dutch officials. Unable to suppress his inexplicable craving for freedom, he secretly quits his subservient apprentice job under a *controleur*—a Dutch local administrator and his father's boss—leaves a goodbye letter for his parents, and takes the train in search of freedom, new knowledge, and a new job. He

---

[14] Teeuw, *Modern Indonesian Literature*, volume I, pp. 54-57.

[15] See also Nidhi, "Fiction as History," pp. 74-75.

eventually settles in P city (*kota* P), finds employment at an European trading company, awakes to political activism, meets Soepini, and falls in love with her.

As the ending of *Rasa Merdika* indicates, in these novels the realization of freedom from social constraints and the fulfillment of love are closely associated with cities. Soeparno and Roesmala Dewi experience the triumph of their love in the city of Soerabaja. Hidjo of *Student Hidjo* carries out his liaison with a Dutch girl in the Dutch city of The Hague. Corrie, the (Eurasian) European girl of *Salah Asoehan*, finally marries Hanafi, with dire consequences, in Batavia, thinking that the capital city may provide their interracial marriage with some social leeway. Cities also make it possible for young couples to show their affection in public, for instance as by walking hand-in-hand (Figure 2)[16] or riding a motorcycle together (Figure 3, below).[17]

Figure Two
Noerbaja and Samsoe'lbahari taking a stroll in Batavia

---

[16] Mh. Roesli, *Sitti Noerbaja*, p. 225.

[17] Hardjosoemarto dan Dt. Madjoindo, *Roesmala Dewi*, front cover.

Figure Three
Roesmala Dewi and Soeparno on a motorcycle in Soerabaja

Villages or places of origin for the protagonists of the six novels are connected with parental love and filial piety. This is the case in *Sitti Noerbaja*, *Salah Asoehan*, *Kalau Ta' Oentoeng*, and *Rasa Merdika*. In contrast, cities are associated with the love of young couples. Parents and relatives seldom appear in cities, nor for that matter do young children. The only children we encounter in the cities of these novels are at the house of Roesmala Dewi's relative in Batavia, with whom she boards. *Roesmala Dewi*, *Student Hidjo*, and *Rasa Merdika* end with the fulfillment of love, but none includes the birth of a baby in their happy endings. In *Rasa Merdika*, Soedjanmo's best friends in P city are a young couple named Sastro and Nji Endang, but no child is mentioned as fruit of their union. It is particularly striking that *Roesmala Dewi*, after recounting the marriage of the hero and heroine in Soerabaja, goes on to relate the marriage of Roesmala Dewi's widowed father and Soeparno's widowed mother, who are eventually to live together in Madioen, but remains silent about the birth of the young couple's offspring. Likewise in *Student Hidjo*, there are two Javanese married couples and two Dutch ones in the last section of the novel titled "Two years have passed," but no baby is mentioned for any of the couples.

Not only are cities dissociated from procreation, but also from production in general. Many of the novels' protagonists are office workers, but the narratives center on their off-duty activities, for example, what they do while they are on leave (*verlof* in Dutch or *perlop* in Indonesian). The novels often use such Indonesian words as *pesiar, melantjong,* and *makan angin,* to go for a ride, go sightseeing, and go for a stroll. Their authors are especially partial to the word *pelesir* or *plesir* (pleasure), which derives from the Dutch *plezier*. It is used when Noerbaja and Samsoe'lbahari go hand-in-hand to see a circus, when Corrie and Hanafi ride a bicycle around Batavia every evening, when Hidjo and his Dutch girlfriend go to a theater in The Hague, or when Soedjanmo and Soepini go out on a picnic with Sastro and Nji Endang.

In the novels, cities make up an environment which provides freedom from the parental love and social constraints found in villages or places of origin. Even after Soedjanmo of *Rasa Merdika* discovers freedom and happiness in P city, no further relationship with his parents back in the village is recounted, although he had appeared full of affection for them at the beginning of the novel. It seems as though this part of the story had to remain untold for Soedjanmo to stay free and happy. Cities also provide time away from procreation and production. Irrespective of a happy or tragic ending, the six novels tell stories of protagonists trying to fulfill their love in an urban environment redolent with freedom of many varieties.

ON THE QUESTION OF "I" OR "SAJA"

One literary device common to the six novels is the prevalence of soliloquy or the verbalization of protagonists' mental or emotional processes. After writing a goodbye letter to his parents, Soedjanmo muses in *Rasa Merdika*:

> "How troubled my parents will be after reading this, since their viewpoint is so narrow," he muttered to himself while wiping tears from his cheek. "However, I [*akoe*] also know that parental love often brings unhappiness to the child. It would be such a folly to let it happen, for the parents will not live forever. That is why I [*saja*] will try to believe in my own strength."[18]

Soliloquy makes explicit the protagonists' own worries, thoughts, feelings, desires, and intentions. It is interesting to observe in this connection how often the novels describe scenes like the one above, in which characters write letters. Scenes that portray characters reading books are also common. These are self-reflective and expressive characters who muse to themselves, convey thoughts, feelings, and intentions through letter-writing, and read letters and books in solitude.

Soliloquy is not necessarily a modern invention in the history of Indonesian and Malay literature, but its self-reflective nature seems to be. Consider, for example, *Sejarah Melayu* (Malay annals), an old Malay literary work supposedly compiled in its present form in the early seventeenth century.[19] In general, only highly aristocratic men soliloquize in *Sejarah Melayu*. When so engaged, the protagonist usually speculates on the desires of a counterpart (for instance, the sultan he serves), or tries to decide what to do, or verbalizes the course of an impending action in his mind. Motives or the intentions underlying actions are not contemplated in soliloquy. The length of these soliloquies is only two to three

---

[18] Soemantri, *Rasa Merdika*, pp. 23-24.

[19] W. G. Shellabear, *Sejarah Melayu*, edisi ketiga, cetakan kedua puluh (Petaling Jaya: Fajar Bakti, 1989).

sentences. In contrast, the novels' protagonists, irrespective of social class or gender, muse, worry, or think for several sentences, sometimes several paragraphs. This does not happen in *Sejarah Melayu*.

Another sign of the self-reflective nature of the novels' protagonists is the relatively frequent use of the phrases *"air moeka"* and *"roman moeka"* for the facial expressions that display and reveal the character's inner thoughts and emotions. Their usage is based on the assumption that the novels' characters have individualized and variant inner states which are usually reflected in, though sometimes hidden from, their facial expressions. Moreover, we see no difference between genders or social classes in the use of these phrases in the novels. Men and women, rich and poor, have *air moeka* and *roman moeka*.

I would suggest that *air moeka* and *roman moeka* were relatively new phrases, or at least newly popularized phrases, in Indonesian at the time when these novels were written.[20] We do not encounter *air moeka* or *roman moeka* in *Sejarah Melayu*. Instead, we find *rupa* (form or appearance [such as attire]) and *paras* (face and looks); *rupa* tends to be applied to men and *paras* to women. They are reserved primarily for high aristocrats and their daughters and generally used to emphasize that the *rupa* or *paras* of a character is excessively beautiful (*terlalu baik*). The terms essentially refer to visible physical markers that signify high social status.

The tendency for *air moeka* and *roman moeka* to appear in the six novels coincides with the introduction of a new material culture to the Dutch East Indies (in fact to much of the non-Western world) in the first decades of the twentieth century. Around the period when the six novels were written and published, mirrors, photography, pictorial magazines, theater plays of various kinds, and movies had been introduced or had become popular in the East Indies.

Examples of the new material culture are discernible in the six novels. One illustration in *Sitti Noerbaja* shows the room of the heroine decorated with two framed photographs on the wall (Figure Four, below).[21] In the same novel, Samsoe'lbahari gives Noerbaja a locket containing his picture before their separation. They later exchange pictures. While trying to open the letter from Noerbaja containing news of her forthcoming unwanted marriage to Datoek Meringgih, Samsoe'lbahari experiences an ominous premonition when her picture falls off the wall. When young Corrie of *Salah Asoehan*, still in school in Batavia, returns to Solok in West Sumatra on vacation, she and Hanafi spend time together going through a magazine, looking at pictures and reading *sja'ir* (stories related in verse form) in it. Mirrors also figure when Masroel of *Kalau Ta' Oentoeng*, after spending the night on a bench at the beach, takes a hand-mirror from his pocket and combs his hair before going to the office.

The new material culture, I argue, was instrumental in enhancing Indonesians' self-awareness of facial expression and countenance, and this was especially true of Indonesians in cities inhabited by socially and ethnically divergent populations. Comparatively frequent references in the novels to *air moeka* and *roman moeka*

---

[20] Marsden's dictionary refers to *"ayer muka"* in the meaning of complexion. See Marsden, *A Dictionary and Grammar of the Malayan Language*, volume two, p. 26.

[21] Mh. Roesli, *Sitti Noerbaja*, p. 163.

Figure Four
Noerbaja in despair thinking that Samsoe'lbahari may not love her any more

probably reflect this new awareness as well as the new understanding of human nature that individuals, regardless of social class or gender, have their own volition and emotion.

In what way is the agent to be generalized who soliloquizes, writes letters, reads books alone silently, expresses or conceals emotion on the face, and seeks love and freedom? In other words, what is the first-person, singular pronoun for this agent in the six novels?

Generally speaking, there are three types of personal pronoun for "I" used in the novels: *hamba*, *akoe*, and *saja*. *Hamba* literally means servant or slave. Among the six novels, the one which uses *hamba* the most to signify "I" is *Sitti Noerbaja*. Characters in *Sitti Noerbaja* use *hamba* when they address their superiors in the social hierarchy. The father of Samsoe'lbahari and Datoek Meringgih also use *hamba* while speaking to each other as a sign of mutual deference and humility.

Hamba is seldom encountered in the other five novels as a personal pronoun. When it is used, it appears in exchanges between persons of marked social difference. In *Salah Asoehan*, for example, a male servant uses *hamba* when addressing Hanafi, his master. In *Rasa Merdika*, Soedjanmo's father, a native colonial official, uses *hamba* when talking to his superior, a Dutch official (*controleur*).

Akoe is a very familiar form of "I" in Austronesian languages. It is found in many local languages of Indonesia; it also exists in Tagalog in the Philippines. It is a colloquial and informal "I," commonly used by social superiors when talking to inferiors in the novels. It is also often used among friends and lovers.

The most popular word for "I" in the novels (with the exception of *Sitti Noerbaja*) is *saja*. In *Salah Asoehan*, Hanafi uses *saja* when communicating with his mother and with the Dutch. The Dutch also use *saja* when talking to Hanafi. In general, *saja* predominates in situations further away from villages or families of origin, namely, in cities and offices.[22]

Saja is an abbreviated form of *sahaja* or *sahja*, a Sanskrit-derived word literally meaning, like *hamba*, slave or servant. It can be used as a first-person, singular personal pronoun. According to William Marsden, who spent eight years in Sumatra in the 1770s,

> [W]e must not understand that the person who employs the term regards himself as the slave, or even as the inferior of him to whom he addresses himself, but that it is his intention, by an affectation of humility, to shew [sic] politeness; and accordingly we find it much used by Malays of rank, in conversation with the superior class of Europeans.[23]

In modern usage, *saja* has shed "an affectation of humility," transforming itself into a rather formal, somewhat literary and self-reflective, general-purpose "I," while *hamba* as a personal pronoun has retained a clear connotation of humility and deference to the present day.[24]

It is not clear how and when the transformation of *saja* took place, but I reckon the following two points are important in considering the process of its transformation. The first point concerns how to translate Dutch or other European writings into Indonesian, in particular, how to translate *"ik"* and "I" at a time when print capitalism in the realm of Indonesian publication took off in the Dutch East Indies. The second point concerns increasingly frequent face-to-face encounters, either in official or social circumstances, between Dutch and Indonesians, as colonial bureaucracy, in line with colonial territory, expanded in the Indies from around 1900, and more Dutch officials, entrepreneurs, and their families arrived in the colony. The Dutch then confronted the question of what kind of "I" to use when conversing with natives in Indonesian.

These were not idle questions, for it was not possible, as the case of *hamba* clearly shows, to express "I" in a hierarchically neutral fashion in Indonesian in social interactions before the transformation or invention of *saja*. The Dutch obviously needed an Indonesian word that could convey the meaning of a "democratic" European "I" and, at the same time, could uphold the high status of

---

[22] *Akoe* and *saja* are old spellings of *aku* and *saya*. As far as soliloquy is concerned, both *akoe* and *saja* soliloquize as seen in the quoted passage from *Rasa Merdika* but *hamba* does not. Soliloquy is more frequently associated with *saja* than with *akoe* in the six novels.

[23] Marsden, *A Dictionary and Grammar of the Malayan Language*, volume two, pp. 44-45.

[24] See, for example, Mohammad Zain, *Kamus Moderen Bahasa Indonesia* (Jakarta: Grafica, 1955), pp. 284, 655. Could it be that *hamba*, a Malay word in origin, has had more difficulty in shedding a connotation of humility and deference than the Sanskrit-derived *sahaja*?

colonizers against the colonized. The word evidently chosen was *saja*, the sort of personal pronoun of politeness.

In the Indonesian translation of *Robinson Crusoe* published in the late nineteenth century, Crusoe generally refers to himself as *sahaja* and sometimes, as when talking to a villain, as *akoe*.[25] This translation of *Robinson Crusoe* retains the old spelling for *saja* with a strong connotation of slave or servant. Yet, *saja* seems to have been rid of its old spelling and to have incorporated the meaning of an European "I" by the early twentieth century.

In the early 1900s, Halkema, a government translator and language teacher in Batavia, published the first edition of his Malay-Dutch, Dutch-Malay dictionary.[26] In the short section on Malay [Indonesian] grammar attached to the dictionary, he explains some differences between *akoe*, *hamba*, and *saja*. The wording makes it clear that the explanation is directed to a Dutch readership, above all, to Dutch officials. According to Halkema, Europeans use *akoe* in speaking to ordinary natives. Native rulers, high chieftains, and the like also use this term in relating to common people. When addressing natives of rank and office either by birth or appointment, Europeans speak of themselves as *saja*. In addressing a reigning native ruler, it is appropriate to use *hamba*. However, even in this situation, *saja* is sufficiently polite if the European faces the ruler as a representative of Dutch authority due to his rank or position. Halkema informs his readers that *saja*, originating from *sahaja* (slave), is more common than *hamba* in various Malay regions (Indonesian regions of the Indies). He advises every European to insist that natives, in talking to Europeans, always refer to themselves as *hamba*. Should they use *saja*, they are being daring in their relation with Europeans, which usually implies disdain.[27]

Despite Halkema's explicit advice to fellow Europeans, it is obvious that the colonizers could not control the use of *saja* for very long, if at all. Although it is difficult to document the process of its dissemination, *saja* must have spread among Indonesians through schools, offices, mass media, political gatherings, and Islamic preaching from the beginning of the twentieth century.

Let us look into a case of print mass media. Print capitalism, whether publishing newspapers, magazines, or novels, markets its product to a generalized, anonymous readership whose social positioning cannot be hierarchically defined. This readership is similar to what Benedict Anderson calls "a homogeneous, collective, public (thus equal-before-the-author) 'you'."[28] To see it from the other perspective, print capitalism needs a formal, rather bookish, and hierarchically neutral "I" who can communicate with Anderson's "you." The same observation obviously applies to political gatherings and organs of nationalist organizations. They need a hierarchy-free, "democratic," yet somewhat formal "I" that can

---

[25] von de Wall, *Hikajat Robinson Crusoe*, *passim*. Friday uses *hamba* in addressing Crusoe.

[26] No date of publication is printed in the book but the particular copy (the second printing of the cheap edition) in my possession has "22 November 1912" handwritten on the front cover, most probably indicating the date of purchase. I surmise that its first edition must have been published around the early 1900s.

[27] H. Halkema, *Maleisch-Hollandsch en Hollandsch-Maleisch Handwoordenboek*, 2de goedkoope uitgave (Batavia: G. Kolff, n.d.), p. LXII.

[28] Benedict R. O'G. Anderson, "*Sembah-Sumpah*: The Politics of Language and Javanese Culture," in his *Language and Power: Exploring Political Cultures in Indonesia* (Ithaca: Cornell University Press, 1990), p. 210.

express the common bond and destiny between "I" and the audience or readers. This "I" could not have been *akoe* or *hamba* as these words were used in the Indonesian language.

Another important arena where this kind of "I" was needed is Islamic preaching. According to a story I heard from an old Islamic teacher in Kuantan, Riau in 1991, there had been no Islamic sermon or preaching, even after Friday's noon prayer, in his village before the 1920s. Before that time, an Islamic teacher merely recited Arabic phrases from the Koran, although neither the audience nor he himself understood their meanings well. Islamic sermons and preaching in Indonesian became popular in the village in the early 1930s after those who had studied at modern Islamic schools in West Sumatra, including my informant, returned home. Islamic preaching was called *meleséng* then. It originated from a Dutch word, *lezing* or lecture. *Saja* must have been indispensable in *meleséng*.[29]

Five out of the six novels show that *saja* had attained a solid place in the Indonesian lexicon by the mid-1920s. Furthermore, this *saja* was more democratic than Halkema's *saja*. The latter could face conflicting pressures in writing and speaking. In writing and especially in translating, it was supposed to be an equivalent of European "*ik*" and "I." In speaking, by which he meant Europeans speaking to natives, it was supposed to delineate social distance between the two. In contrast, *saja* for the Indonesians, whether in writing or speaking, was essentially meant to be used between them and to neutralize rather than delineate social distance among themselves. The Dutch intention notwithstanding, the dissemination and democratization of *saja* must have proceeded in the first couple of decades of the twentieth century in the East Indies.

There remains the question of *Sitti Noerbaja*, namely, why this novel alone prefers *hamba* to *saja*. It is not clear why this is the case. Its author, Mh. Roesli, born in 1889, is one of the older, but not the oldest, of the seven authors involved. The historical setting of *Sitti Noerbaja* is the oldest, as its major events take place in the latter half of the 1890s and the story ends in 1908. The novel also frequently resorts to *pantoen* (quatrains), a popular literary genre in old Minangkabau and Malay literature, to express love and longing between Samsoe'lbahari and Noerbaja. It may well be the oldest manuscript among the six, although it is the second oldest in terms of actual publication.

A more interesting question might be why two novels by Javanese authors, the oldest (*Student Hidjo*) and the third oldest (*Rasa Merdika*), were far more partial to *saja* than *hamba* in comparison with *Sitti Noerbaja*. Discussing why Javanese authors, despite their long literary tradition in Javanese, have mostly written in Indonesian in the modern age, Anderson points out how Indonesian allows them to circumvent the power and danger of pseudo-feudal Javanese language.[30] In passing, he also mentions the "problem of pronouns" encountered by a Javanese author when he tries to write in Javanese, not in the classical form of sung poems performed for a courtly audience, but in the printed form to be consumed by an anonymous

---

[29] On the inception of Islamic preaching in Indonesian in West Sumatra in the late 1910s, see Alirman Hamzah, "Syeikh Muhammad Thaib Umar (1874-1920 M)," in *Riwayat Hidup dan Perjuangan 20 Ulama Besar Sumatera Barat* (Padang: Islamic Centre Sumatera Barat, 1981), pp. 86, 94, and Mahmud Yunus, *Sejarah Pendidikan Islam di Indonesia* (Jakarta: Mutiara, 1979), p. 148. The term "*leséng*" is also used in the scene where Hanafi of *Salah Asoehan* lectures his mother about love. See Abdoel Moeis, *Salah Asoehan*, djilid I, p. 72.

[30] Anderson, *Sembah-Sumpah, passim*.

readership.[31] Perhaps, then, Javanese authors may have played an important role in the history of *saja*'s dissemination in early Indonesian novels.[32]

The European "*ik*" and "I" have long historical anchorage in western society and culture. *Saja*, in contrast, had come into existence only in the early twentieth century. Furthermore, *saja* was an "I" in Indonesian, the language of school and office for most Indonesians, not their mother tongues. That is to say, *saja* was still "drifting" and "wild" without being moored yet to any distinct "social map," if I may borrow the expressions of Takashi Shiraishi.[33] In other words, *saja* was still *merdika* or free. *Saja* was also more active than *hamba*, yet more contemplative and self-reflective than *akoe*. We may say that the birth of this *saja* made it easier to imagine an "I" living and seeking the fulfillment of love in a socially amorphous city and concurrently writing and reading stories of "I."

It is not likely, however, that *saja* would drift forever. For it is inevitable that *saja* would eventually be moored to a newly emerging social map as the Indonesian language began to spread, *saja*'s usage became increasingly well established, and colonial rule was consolidated throughout the Dutch East Indies.

MODERN EDUCATION AND ADMINISTRATION: CHARTING THE SPACE OF THE COLONIAL STATE

In the six novels, schools and offices provide backdrop as well as organizational backbone to the progression of the narrative. The novels' protagonists are all educated in modern secular schools, many in Dutch schools. In addition to the generic term "Dutch school" (*sekolah Belanda*), distinct levels of Dutch education or names of particular Dutch schools are mentioned in the novels: HIS (*Hollandsch Inlandsch School* or Dutch Native School), MULO (*Meer Uitgebreide Lagere Onderwijs* or Extended Primary Education), HBS (*Hoogere Burger School* or Citizens High School), STOVIA (*School tot Opleiding van Inlandsche Artsen* or School for Training of Native Doctors), known also as *Sekolah Dokter Djawa* (School for Javanese Doctors), and KWS (*Koningin Wilhelmina*

---

[31] Ibid., p. 210.

[32] Different from the successful invention of "I," the Indonesian language has had difficulty coining a generally acceptable pronoun for "you." *Bapak* (literally father) and *Ibu* (literally mother) which most probably became popular after about 1950 fill this void to some extent as spoken terms of address among the social equals or from social inferiors to superiors. Another interesting modern pronoun in Indonesian is *mereka* which, I suspect, established itself in the meaning of a generalized and inclusive category for "they, them, their" around the late nineteenth or early twentieth century. It used to be expressed as *dia orang* which combines "he, she, it" (*dia*) and "person or persons" (*orang*). Student Hidjo, the oldest of the six novels, uses both *dia orang* and *marika* (sic) or more commonly *marika itoe*. (*Marika itoe* literally means "those persons." See Marsden, *A Dictionary and Grammar of the Malayan Language*, volume one, p. 322.) It is amusing to note that in one place where the author of Student Hidjo describes a gathering of a nationalistic organization attended by bejeweled aristocrats and others, he seems to have felt compelled to explain what he means by "[t]here they in a mutually friendly way showed an abiding sense of brotherhood" ([d]*isinilah marika itoe sama beramah ramahan menoendjoekkan kekalnja bersaudaraän*" and inserted "aristocrats, non-aristocrats, and others" (*bangsawan dan tidak d.l.l.*) in parentheses after "*marika itoe*." See Marco Kartodikromo, *Student Hidjo*, p. 108.

[33] Takashi Shiraishi, "Indoneshia-no Kindai-niokeru 'Watashi'—Kartini's ik and Suwardi's saya ('I' in Modern Indonesia: Kartini's Ik and Soewardi's Saya)," *Tonan Ajia Kenkyu (Southeast Asian Studies)* 34,1 (1996): 16.

School or Queen Wilhelmina School), known also as *Sekolah Opzichter* (School for Surveyors). All these schools but the last were very familiar to Indonesians in the period when the six novels were published.

Except in *Student Hidjo* and *Rasa Merdika*, schools offer future lovers occasions to meet one another. The paths of these boys and girls of different social backgrounds, ethnicities, and races would never have crossed in earlier times. In some of the novels, young boys and girls go to school together every day like brother and sister, a relationship which eventually blossoms into mutual affection. Schools present a new type of social setting, relatively free of old conventions, in which adolescents of both sexes are drawn together almost accidentally, yet fatefully.[34]

The novels' protagonists, as was usually the case for students at Dutch school, often advance from one level of education to the next. Such climbing of the educational ladder generally signals a new phase in the protagonists' life and a turning point in the stories' development. After graduation, they become government officials, teachers, or office workers. There are some merchants among the protagonists' parents, but they themselves, including some women, earn salaries (*makan gaji*).

Related to the protagonists' penchant for seeking salaried occupations, the novels often refer to official rank and position (*pangkat*) in the colonial administrative structure. The father of one of Samsoe'lbahari's friends in *Sitti Noerbaja* is a chief district attorney (*hoofd djaksa*). Under him are an assistant district attorney (*adjoeng djaksa*), police officers (*menteri polisi*), and junior clerks (*djoeroetoelis*). Arriving in Batavia to see Samsoe'lbahari, Noerbaja is met by a bailiff (*schout*) with a summons triggered by Datoek Meringgih's accusation against her of theft. After hearing of the death of Noerbaja, Samsoe'lbahari fails in a suicide attempt, changes his identity, and reemerges as a *Létenan* Mas in the colonial army. After the death of Samsoe'lbahari, the story ends with a scene in which two childhood friends of Noerbaja and Samsoe'lbahari visit their graves. One of them is a medical doctor (*dokter*) and the other a surveyor (*opzichter*).

Hanafi of *Salah Asoehan*, after graduation from a Dutch school, initially works as a clerk (*klerk*) at the office of an Assistant Resident in West Sumatra. He is later promoted to the position of senior clerk (*commies* or *komis*). He submits a letter of petition asking to be transferred to Batavia after Corrie, his love, moves to the capital of the Dutch East Indies upon her father's death in Solok. In Batavia, he works at a record office (*archief*) of the Department of Internal Administration (*Departemen B.B.*) after serving for a while at its regional office (*kantor Gewest*).

Other positions and formal institutions mentioned in the remaining four novels are: apprenticeship junior clerk (*magang djoeroetoelis*), school headmaster (*goeroe kepala*), school inspector (*opziener sekolah*), [three-year] village school (*sekolah negeri* or *sekolah desa*), teacher (*goeroe*), [promotion] examination (*eksamen*), [five-year] government school (*sekolah Goebernemén*), opium officer (*menteri*

---

[34] This remark also applies to encounters between adolescents of the same sex at school. I think the term "friends" (*kawan, teman,* and *sahabat*) must have begun to take a very distinct and familiar meaning after the modern educational institution was established in Indonesia; the special bond between, for instance, two boys in the same school could not always be explained in terms of their being siblings, relatives, or neighbors. Such a bond apparently existed between Hidjo of *Student Hidjo* and the brother of his future bride who went to the same school and between Samsoe'lbahari.

tjandoe), Resident (*Residen*), post office (*kantor pos*), municipal office (*kantor Gemeente*), local Dutch colonial administrator (*controleur*), [Dutch] female teacher (*onderwijzeres*), administrator (*administrateur*), [native] sub-district head (*assisten wedono*), promotion (*promosi*), and office worker (*employee*). Chief or manager, though not a distinctly named position, also appears often in the novels as the Dutch *chef*. The chief is usually in the position of influencing the hiring, transfer, and promotion of the novels' protagonists.

As also happens with modern education, office work entails a high degree of geographical mobility. The exceptional case is Soedjanmo of *Rasa Merdika,* who leaves his parents behind because he itches for freedom. All the other protagonists, after graduation from school, are mobile because of employment, promotion, or transfer in association with office work. Such geographical mobility is irrevocably entwined with turning points in the protagonists' lives; these may or may not lead to a happy ending.

Many names of cities are referred to in the novels in association with the protagonists' geographical mobility: Padang, Betawi, Solok, Semarang, Bandoeng, Solo, Painan, Boekittinggi, Medan, Tandjoeng Pinang, Soerabaja, and Madioen, in addition to the Dutch cities mentioned in *Student Hidjo. Sitti Noerbaja* starts with a scene in which young Noerbaja and Samsoe'lbahari go home from Dutch school, textbooks and atlases in hand. As this indicates, geography was being taught at Dutch and native schools in the late nineteenth century. Such teaching notwithstanding, I doubt very much that Indonesian readers of the six novels, especially Javanese readers in the 1930s, say, knew where Painan, Solok, or Tandjoeng Pinang were located. Yet they must have been comfortable reading the stories of mobile protagonists, some of whom never return to their place of origin. They would have tacitly understood that these cities were all located within the East Indies and could therefore make sense of and relate to the geographical trajectories of the protagonists' lives.

Politically speaking, towns and cities were not randomly distributed on the administrative map of the Dutch East Indies, nor on the cognitive map of those who lived there. They formed a pyramidal hierarchy in correspondence with their administrative position in the colonial state, a pyramid topped by Batavia, which Noerbaja observed, "rightly deserves to be the capital city of East Indies." Likewise, higher-level schools and offices were generally located in higher-order towns or cities, and they formed different yet overlapping pyramidal hierarchies vis-à-vis those of towns and cities. The combination of these hierarchies charted the colonial space of the Indies. And the novels make clear that this space is branded the Dutch East Indies. Besides names of Dutch schools, many other Dutch words and Indonesianized words of Dutch origin are peppered throughout the novels. The cumulative effect of steady terminological exposure to things Dutch made the readers keenly aware of the colonial existence of the Indies within which the novels' stories unfold, even if no Dutch person played a central role in them.

The notion that colonial authority pervades the Dutch East Indies is reflected in the following exchange between Noerbaja and Samsoe'lbahari. It takes place in Batavia, after it becomes clear that Noerbaja has to go back to Padang for police inspection because of Datoek Meringgih's false accusation against her:

After being silent for a while, Sam said very slowly. "What would you say if we just ran away from here to escape from the police?"

"I think it is useless," answered Noerbaja while shaking her head. "Certainly we will eventually fall into the hands of the police at the end. Besides, where should we hide ourselves? Police are all over the place in Java."[35]

Noerbaja's remark is persuasive because the potential exercise of coercive power by the colonial authority via the police is discernible, though intermittently, in the world of the novels. When Noerbaja, Samsoe'lbahari, and two friends go on a picnic to Padang Hill at the beginning of the story, they come to a park at the top of the hill with an arbor and swings. There is a flagpole with the Dutch tri-colors fluttering in the breeze. The park is kept clean by convicts (*orang hoekoeman*) because on Sunday [Dutch] gentlemen and ladies (*toean-toean dan njonja-njonja*) visit it with food and drink for the good of their bodily health. When Roesmala Dewi and her sick father sail from Batavia to Padang for the latter to have a change of air, they see chained convicts (*orang rantai*) on board. They are being sent to the coalmines of Sawahloento in West Sumatra. Chained convicts are also encountered in *Sitti Noerbaja*. When Samsoe'lbahari travels by ship from Batavia to Padang for school vacation, one convict jumps overboard to commit suicide because he cannot bear the fate of fifteen-years' forced labor awaiting him in Sawahloento.

The pyramidal placement of cities, schools, and offices and the coercive application of police force within the colonial hierarchy do not by themselves guarantee the smooth functioning of the colonial state. These elements of the state need to be connected to one another both horizontally and vertically as nodes of colonial rule by roads, railways, steamships, cars, and horse-carriages. The novels' mobile protagonists do indeed travel by train and steamship for school vacation, educational advancement, employment, or transfer. Train stations and ports are often a dramatic stage for separation in the novels.[36]

Other conduits of colonial rule were telegrams and letters. Prior to the scene quoted above, police await Noerbaja's arrival at the port of Tandjoeng Priok in Batavia because of Datoek Meringgih's telegram of accusation sent from Padang. It is above all letters and post offices that predominate in the novels. Hanafi of *Salah Asoehan* marries his uncle's daughter Rapiah after Corrie decides not to reciprocate his love. Afterwards a young Dutch woman working at Solok's post office is one of the few in Dutch society who will socialize with him, on account of his ill treatment of Rapiah. Roesmala Dewi, after amicably dissolving her first marriage, works at a post office in Boekittinggi. Unnamed postmen are featured as well. Young Hanafi and Corrie are embracing and kissing at Hanafi's house when a postman arrives. At the sound of "Mail!" they come to their senses, leaping away from each other.

---

[35] Mh. Roesli, *Sitti Noerbaja*, p. 198.

[36] Journeys of heroes are an important theme in old Minangkabau and Malay epics such as told in *kaba* and *hikajat*. In contrast to these adventure-filled journeys, protagonists' travels in the six novels show early signs of modern routinization of geographical mobility in terms of modes of transportation and motives for mobility.

The post office sends letters of petition for transfer, notices of transfer, newspapers, magazines, and of course private letters. The novels' protagonists often send or receive letters. The most enthusiastic characters in this respect are Rasmani

Figure Five
Rasmani reading a letter from Masroel

and Masroel of *Kalau Ta' Oentoeng*. The front cover of the novel actually shows Rasmani, now a schoolteacher, reading a letter from Masroel (Figure Five, above). In a 1919 advertisement placed by a printer-cum-office supply shop in an Indonesian periodical, letter paper, envelopes, ink, and penholders were all expressed in Dutch or Dutchized words such as *postpapier, enveloppen, inkt,* and *penhouders*.[37] No doubt letter writing for personal purposes must have been a western-influenced and very modern practice in Indonesia in the first few decades of the twentieth century, yet the novels' protagonists write letters frequently. In no small degree, it is because of their letter writing that even mobile and geographically separated protagonists can relate to each other and the stories of their love can be told.

Letters penetrate through social constraints and directly connect one "I" to another. The ultimate form is a registered letter (*soerat aangeteekend*), like the one Hanafi's mother receives from her son in Batavia informing her of his decision to divorce his wife Rapiah. I heard in West Sumatra while carrying out fieldwork

---

[37] The periodical is *Minangkabau Bergerak—Soerat Kabar dan Advertentie* which was published three times a month in Boekittinggi. The advertisement in question was placed by Drukkerij "Merapi" & Co., Fort de Kock in the issue of Tahoen ke I, No. 1, Augustus 2, 1919.

in the early 1970s that Minangkabau parents used to object to their daughters' going to school since they were afraid girls would write love letters once they knew how to read and write. This anecdote, whether well-founded or not, reveals their understanding of the potential for letters to penetrate the shield of social convention. On the other hand, a most effective way to deny the right of participation in colonial society was to put politically dangerous elements on an isolated island without a post office, as suggested by a Dutch official to the Governor General of the Dutch East Indies in 1925.[38]

Nothing better showed the realization of the colonial state than the diffusion of postal service. It signifies that the people of the Indies began to take for granted that letters, be they official letters or love letters, would be delivered from one corner of the colony to another, or even to a foreign country, through the hand of the anonymous third party representing the state, and that the state could be trusted, though not necessarily completely, with the safe delivery and privacy of the correspondence. Postal service was not meant solely for Dutch authority, high government officials, or native aristocrats; it was for the public. Theoretically, anybody in the Dutch East Indies could make use of it in communicating with anybody else in or outside the colony.

Figure Six
New Model Advertisement

---

[38] Takashi Shiraishi, *An Age in Motion: Popular Radicalism in Java, 1912-1926* (Ithaca: Cornell University Press, 1990), p. 311.

In addition to letters, the postal service delivered parceled goods and money orders. Advertisements in the above-mentioned periodical of 1919 show that the mail-order business was very active. Wholesalers and retailers involved in the sale of batik and cloth seem especially to have relied on it to accept orders through the mail. These advertisements often mention that the vendors would accept payment by cash-on-delivery (*rembours*, an Indonesianized word of French origin meaning reimburse) or prepayment (*oewang dikirim dahoeloe*). Although the periodical was published in Boekittinggi, a local town in West Sumatra, it carried the advertisements of three merchants in Pekalongan, Java, two in Padang, and one in the local weaving village of Siloengkang.[39]

The extensive reach of mail-order and mail-delivery of goods in the East Indies can be extrapolated from an extraordinary, self-proclaimed "New Model Advertisement" (*Reclame Model Baroe*) printed in a 1924 issue of *Bintang Hindia*, a bi-weekly magazine published in Batavia; the magazine ran the same advertisement a few more times over the following two months. In the advertisement, all sorts of merchandise are raining down like a shower from planes over the East Indies (Figure Six).[40] Boats and a steamship in the sea below appear ready to pick up the merchandise and deliver it to the various islands.[41] It is ostensibly a new model advertisement because it offers information on so many goods together with their prices without extensive explanation or copywriting save the name of the merchant (M. J. Mohammad) and the general location of his shop (Weltevreden [in Batavia]). Some prices are listed in the unit of twenty (*kodi*), and I would not be surprised if the advertisement was placed by a wholesaler or "department store" owner who wanted to promote an Indies-wide mail-order and mail-delivery service.

Cities, schools, and offices formed the skeleton of the East Indies, while roads, railways, steamships, telegrams, and letters glued them together and at the same time lubricated the working of the colonial state. Money also functioned as both glue and lubricant and at times embodied the state itself, as symbolized, for example, in the silver coin with designs of Queen Wilhelmina and the Royal Crown. The circulation of colonial currency, like the diffusion of postal service, is tantamount to the pervasiveness of Dutch power and presence.

The six novels refer to money often. Hidjo's fiancée's sarong costs forty guilders, and her diamond earrings two thousand guilders. His monthly expenses while studying in the Netherlands are one hundred guilders. Young Hanafi pays one hundred rupiah (guilder) a month to study at a Dutch school in Batavia. Roesmala Dewi and Soeparno each receive a monthly scholarship of twenty-five guilders one

---

[39] The particular issues of the periodical consulted are *Minangkabau Bergerak*, Tahoen ke I, No. 1, Augustus 2, 1919 and No. 4, September 8, 1919. Other advertisements accepting mail-orders found in these issues include one by a merchant in Pariaman of West Sumatra selling vermifuge and another by a Chinese in Batavia selling a picture of naked Siamese twins, reportedly taken in Amsterdam, for 50 cents per picture with an extra 10 cents for postage!

[40] Some of the goods pictured are batik cloths, a sarong, a tennis racket, an iron bed frame, pajamas, a raincoat, an alarm clock, a wristwatch, hats for men and women, a flashlight, men's and women's shoes, a pencil, a gramophone, a briefcase, a woman's blouse, and a soccer ball. Also included are books, such as English-language books, romantic novels with titles such as *A Rose of Batavia* (*Roos van Batavia*) and *A Jasmine of Agam* (*Melati van Agam*), and how-to books titled *Laws of Love* (*Wet Pertjintaan*) and *Models of Love Letters* (*Model Soerat2 Pertjintaan*).

[41] *Bintang Hindia*, Februari 23, 1929, p. 116.

year after entering a school in Batavia. Other than prices and school-related expenses, frequent references are made to salaries (*gadji*). Hanafi's salary, after his transfer to Batavia, is three hundred rupiah a month. Soedjanmo, to his great surprise, receives a monthly salary of 125 guilders at his new job at a trading company in P city. Masroel of *Kalau Ta' Oentoeng* initially works as an apprentice junior clerk at a village office making ten to fifteen rupiah a month, while Rasmani, after becoming a village school teacher, earns 17.50 guilders a month. Later in Medan Masroel gets a job with the monthly salary of one hunded guilders. Bachtiar, the first husband of Roesmala Dewi, works at the office of the Resident in with a monthly salary of twenty rupiah.

Frequent references to money do not mean mammonism. Datoek Meringgih of *Sitti Noerbaja* is one of the richest persons in Padang. Mh. Roesli, the author of the novel, muses:

> ... because of money, what is high becomes low, what is hard becomes soft, what is far becomes near. Isn't the power of money great? Indeed, what could be more powerful than money? This world revolves around money. At the root of everything is money.[42]

However, Datoek Meringgih is accorded no respect in the novel. He is characterized as lowly in class origin, uneducated, old, mean, rude, and lewd.

In cases where the fathers of protagonists are merchants, such as in *Sitti Noerbaja* and *Student Hidjo*, their social status is described as relatively inferior to that of aristocrats or government officials. Wealth itself, especially naked wealth, does not receive favorable evaluation in the novels. It is shown in a positive light when related to rank and position in the colonial bureaucracy, which, in turn, are differentiated according to salary and corresponding degree of power. And, of course, it is education, preferably Dutch education, that paves the way to these high ranks, positions, and salaries. Before Samsoe'lbahari leaves for school in Batavia, he and Noerbaja take a walk together. He is increasingly uncertain about going to Batavia. Noerbaja reassures him: "Why do you worry? Everything is ready. What you have to do now is to leave and then to study after arriving there. Whenever you finish your study, you will certainly get a high position and a high salary. Those of us here can only watch it happen from a distance yet will feel very happy about it."[43]

Wealth—just like the "I", still free and yet to be moored to a new social map—can become "wild" as seen in the behavior of Datoek Meringgih, who tries to force Noerbaja to marry him by ruining her father financially. Yet, in the novels, potentially wild money can evidently be domesticated by being reined to the educational and administrative systems of the colonial state and thereby calibrated according to educational accomplishment and bureaucratic ranks.

---

[42] Mh. Roesli, *Sitti Noerbaja*, p. 8.
[43] Ibid., p. 69.

CLOCK TIME AND WESTERN CALENDRICAL DATES: PUNCTUATING THE TIME OF THE COLONIAL STATE

The six novels frequently refer to clock time, calendrical dates, and other western ways of time-reckoning. For example, protagonists' ages are often specified. Samsoe'lbahari and Noerbaja are respectively 18 and 15 years old at the beginning of the story. Corrie is 19 at the outset, Hidjo and his fiancée 18 and 13, Soedjanmo 18, Masroel and Rasmani 14 and 9, and Soeparno and Roesmala Dewi 15 and 13 years old.

References to calendrical dates are common too. In some cases, day, month, and year are cited. Samsoe'lbahari writes a letter to Noerbaja from Batavia dated August 10, 1896. Noerbaja in turn writes a letter to Samsoe'lbahari dated March 13, 1897, informing him of her impending marriage to Datoek Meringgih. After hearing of Noerbaja's death, Samsoe'lbahari decides to commit suicide and leaves a letter to his father dated July 13, 1897. (Is it a coincidence that the two letters carrying ill tidings are dated the thirteenth of the month?) Hidjo's fiancée writes a letter to her friend (Hidjo's future bride) inviting her to come to Solo to attend a gathering of Sarekat Islam (Indonesia's first nationalistic mass organization) scheduled on March 3, 1913. Roesmala Dewi and Soeparno start their school life together in Batavia on July 1, 1915 and Roesmala Dewi's mother dies at two o'clock in the morning of December 25, 1916.

General awareness of calendrical dates is also deduced from subscription to newspapers by some characters in the novels. Hanafi, after transferring from Solok to Batavia, visits Corrie at her rented pavilion in the evening, always carrying the day's newspapers so they can read them together. Sastro, a friend of Soedjanmo in *Rasa Merdika*, subscribes to a workers' daily which is delivered in the evening by a postman.

As for days of the week, Friday, the special prayer day of Islam, does not receive any distinct mention in the novels. It is Sunday that is special, because there is neither work nor school. In Batavia, Hanafi spends weekday evenings with Corrie, strolling through various parts of the city. On Sunday, they go out to the beach. It is on a Sunday that Noerbaja, Samsoe'lbahari, and their friends picnic on Padang Hill.

Novels and their protagonists are very conscious of clocks and clock time. At the outset of the novel Samsoe'lbahari and Noerbaja are on their way home from school and check the time by a big clock at the Padang telephone office while waiting for a horse carriage sent by Samsoe'lbahari's father. A clock is also seen on the *pendopo* (front veranda) of the Regent of Jarak in *Student Hidjo*. There are also other signs or devices that register time in the novels. Hanafi, after a rendezvous with Corrie, goes back to his boarding house and lies down on the bed; when he hears the steam whistle of the gas company which lights gas lamps in Batavia, he knows it is already five o'clock in the evening. The night before Samsoe'lbahari leaves for Batavia, he and Noerbaja confess their love for each other on the bench in front of Noerbaja's house. Then they hear the sound of *"Neng"* from a guardhouse (*roemah djaga*), informing the public by the strike of a chime that it is already one o'clock in the morning. In Solok, mail is usually delivered at six o'clock in the evening, according to *Salah Asoehan*. On Thursday, the steamship from Batavia arrives in Padang, carrying mail as well as passengers and goods. Mail is sent from Padang to Solok on the same day, causing Thursday mail delivery in Solok to be at a later hour than usual. Every Thursday from the time Hanafi leaves for Batavia, his mother and his wife Rapiah wait for the postman on the veranda with a lamp on, hoping for news from Hanafi.

As the last case exemplifies, the recognition of clock time and calendrical dates is often connected with the schedules of steamships and trains in the novels. In *Salah Asoehan*, a doctor examines Hanafi, who was bitten by a mad dog, and quickly checks the weekly schedule of ships from Padang to Batavia; Hanafi needs immediate medication in Batavia. It so happens that the ship sails on the following day, so Hanafi leaves for Padang on the next day's early-morning train to board the ship to Batavia. At the end of the novel, Corrie has died in Semarang. Hanafi, who came from Batavia to reconcile with Corrie on her deathbed, spends the night beside her grave. In the morning the caretaker of the graveyard invites him to his house for a cup of coffee, since Hanafi, he says, still has some time before the morning train from Semarang leaves for Batavia at seven o'clock. In *Roesmala Dewi* her widowed and sick father, on his way to Padang for a change of air, tells Roesmala Dewi the departure schedule of their ship from Batavia and urges her to get ready for the trip.

Figure Seven
Advertisement for a Watch: "Late again?" "Yes, sir, because I don't have a Cyma watch, while my friends here have one each."

Two important institutions instrumental in spreading the notion of clock-time and calendrical dates are obviously schools and offices. At the beginning of *Sitti Noerbaja*, Noerbaja and Samsoe'lbahari are in the horse carriage coming home from school. Noerbaja has difficulty understanding how long it will be before the two clock hands meet each other again after twelve o'clock. Samsoe'lbahari tries to explain it using a slate and a chalk. We can also see how student life is punctuated by clock time through Samsoe'lbahari's letter to Noerbaja after he enrolls in STOVIA: he goes to bed at ten, gets up at six in the morning, starts classes at eight after breakfast, and generally finishes them at one.

The novels' protagonists, most of whom eventually become office workers, keep regular hours on weekdays. One morning in Soerabaya, Soeparno, on his way to the office, sees a woman who looks like Roesmala Dewi, his separated lover. He wants to make sure of her identity so, on the following morning, waits for her at the same time at the same location, which leads to their reunion. Their reunion in a large city is possible because of the regular commuting schedules and routes of office workers. A description of the trading company where Soedjanmo works in P city also reveals the regularity of work-related time at the office. "'*Teng-Teng* . . .' a wall clock hung at the office has struck twice, telling that it is already two o'clock and giving a sign to those who work at the office that working hours are already over."[44] This sort of connection between office work and clock time is also vividly reflected in the advertisement for a watch as seen in Figure Seven.[45]

Figure Eight
Mosque and Minaret in West Sumatra around the early twentieth century

The above description underlines the importance of the wall clock (*lontjeng*) in implanting the notion of clock time among Indonesians and, for that matter, among us in general. Wall clocks with a pendulum are often featured in the six novels, either at home or at the office, indicating their indispensability in the

---
[44] Soemantri, *Rasa Merdika*, p. 121.
[45] *Pandji Poestaka*, Augustus 19, 1927, n.p.

116 Tsuyoshi Kato

protagonists' reckoning of time. It is not clear whether producing a clock without a pendulum was technically difficult in the first half of the twentieth century or if people at the time simply liked to have a clock with a pendulum which struck every hour and half-hour. In either case, such a self-assertive clock in terms of sound and sight must have aroused people's interest in and deepened their awareness of clock time.

Wall clocks were not machines merely ticking away time. Figure Eight shows a picture of a mosque and its minaret.[46] The picture was taken sometime in the early twentieth century near Boekittinggi, and I am sure the mosque must have been one of the finest built around that time. The minaret is surrounded by about eight wall clocks showing different times! The pictures in Figure Nine show houses built in the 1920s and 1930s. Both houses, which must have been expensive at the time, have clocks carved into the wall under the front gable. Clearly the wall clock, besides telling time, symbolized wealth and modernity too.[47]

Figure Nine
Engraved Clocks as House Decorations

---

[46] *Indonesia: Images from the Past* (Singapore: Times Edition, 1987), p. 74.
[47] The picture on the left was taken in Curup, Bengkulu in August of 1991, the other in Maninjau, West Sumatra in November of 1995.

In contrast to frequent references to clock time and calendrical dates in the six novels, we seldom encounter Islamic time, for example, the time for the five daily prayers. In fact, no protagonists pray at all in the novels. We rarely encounter the fasting month of the Islamic calendar or *boelan poeasa* either; it is mentioned only once in *Sitti Noerbaja* in its connection with school vacation. Stories of the progatonists' lives unfold irreversibly and lineally according to clock time and western calendrical dates.

THE SHIFTING WORLD OF INDONESIAN NOVELS

What would have been the trajectory of ordinary peasant lives in Indonesia in the early twentieth century? If they had been Muslim, their lives would typically have progressed through birth, circumcision, learning to recite the Koran, marriage, tilling the fields, aging, and death, punctuated with life events such as the births, marriages, feuds, and deaths of family members, relatives, and fellow villagers. Each of these events entailed particular social conventions and *adat*.[48]

The six novels basically remain mute about the sort of life events listed above. Instead, the novels are preoccupied with the stories of "I"s who leave behind the conventional and particularistic social map of village or local community in search of love and freedom. Behind freedom and "I" at the center stage of the novels, there stand two themes. The life courses of the heroes are in a large measure narrated in terms of educational progress and careers in the bureaucracy, and they are punctuated by clock time and western calendrical dates. In due course, the protagonists fall in love, leave their native place, and travel to a city, where all four themes of freedom, "I," modern space, and modern time converge.

"I"s who come to live in the amorphous city cannot, after a while, help being moored to the new, more universalistic social map of the city. We catch a glimpse of this process in the following episode from *Kalau Ta' Oentoeng*. Masroel, who has an unhappy married life with Moeslina, is transferred from the small town of Painan to the city of Padang in West Sumatra. One night he bolts out of the house after a fight with his wife and wanders around the city, eventually dozing off on a bench at the beach due to fatigue.

> When he awoke, Masroel was startled since the sun was already up and high. He quickly sat up and took his watch out of his pocket. It was already close to seven o'clock. At seven thirty he would have to be at the office. His head felt heavy but he forced himself to get up to go home because he did not want to be late to the office. It is necessary for him to go home first, isn't it? To Djati [where his house is] and then to Moeara [where his office is]...but he felt dizzy. Is it better to go straight to the office? But what would Moeslina think then? Wouldn't she get agitated, make a fuss, and seek and ask around here and there?[49]
>
> Because he was getting hungry, he asked a passing schoolchild to buy fried bananas from a nearby food stall and ate these for breakfast.

---

[48] For a good description of village life in West Sumatra in the 1910s and 1920s, see Muhamad Radjab, *Semasa Kecil Di Kampung 1913-1928: Autobiografi Seorang Anak Minangkabau*, cetakan kedua (Jakarta: Balai Pustaka, 1974).

[49] Selasih, *Kalau Ta' Oentoeng*, p. 91.

At seven fifteen Masroel got up from the bench and walked towards the office at Moeara. Before reaching a busy section of the city, he went back for a moment to the beach and stood there taking a small mirror from his pocket. Looking at his face and hair [in the mirror], he felt like laughing. No different from a madman or a drunkard.

"Might I have gone to the office in such a state?" Taking out a handkerchief already wet from the last night's dew [while sleeping on the bench], he wiped his face, then combed his hair, smoothed out the wrinkles on his jacket and trousers, straightened the position of his silk *kopiah* [a black cap], and at long last started walking to the office.[50]

Excusing himself from the office for the day seems completely out of the question for Masroel, who carries a watch and a small mirror in his pockets. Peasants in contemporary village society would have put off work in the field for a day if they felt ill, had to be present at a wedding, or needed to attend to personal matters. In *Kalau Ta' Oentoeng*, such personal matters as a headache or quarrel between husband and wife are not regarded as a reason not to go to the office. To all appearances Masroel is already moored to the new social map embodied in the city. Later divorced from Moeslina, Masroel finds a job in Medan and finally communicates to Rasmani his wish to marry her. Then he receives a letter from Rasmani's sister informing him of her grave illness. But Masroel delays his departure until payday and arrives back in the village a day after Rasmani's death. Masroel is indeed firmly anchored to the new social map.

This observation notwithstanding, the six novels do not make explicit the emergence of the new social map, delineated by a new conceptualization of space (education, bureaucracy, and colonial state) and of time (clock time and western calendrical dates), which was influencing the trajectories of the lives of "I"s. They are also largely silent about the nature of this new map: is it the product of colonialism, modernity, or a combination of both? *Salah Asoehan*, for instance, points out how strong are the racial barriers and prejudice pervading even the multi-racial capital city of the Dutch colony. Yet Hanafi at the end of the novel comes to the realization that his suffering has derived, not from colonialism, but from a wrong upbringing (*salah asoehan*), which made him think he could turn his Eastern character into Western by means of Dutch education.

Among the six, only *Rasa Merdika* hints at an answer to the above question. Soedjanmo intentionally rejects the class structure and constraints of the colonial bureaucracy and sets out on a journey in search of freedom. In S city, his first stop on the journey, he sees a horde of Javanese coolies toiling under the sun, many of whom were driven out of their native villages because they lost their rice lands to sugar plantations. S city embodies a glaring contrast between haves and have-nots, a product of capitalism. Soedjanmo eventually gets a job at a trading company in P city and meets Soepini, with whom he shares a similar political outlook with a tinge of socialism. More importantly for the novel, they also believe in the supremacy of "true love" (*ware liefde*) as the basis of matrimony, in which no ownership of one spouse by the other is involved. The novel seems to suggest that Soedjanmo is at long last to savor the feeling of freedom (*rasa merdika*) after having found his true love.

---

[50] Ibid., p. 93.

The illustration of the critical scene in *Rasa Merdika* shows Soedjanmo asking Soepini if she truly means to reciprocate his love (Figure Ten).[51] They sit on a garden bench. Soedjanmo is completely European in his appearance, starting from his well-pomaded hairstyle to the high collar and down to his shoes, while Soepini is very Javanese in her hairstyle and attire, except for her shoes. Unlike the Javanese clerk in Figure 7, who combines Javanese and European elements in his clothing, Soedjanmo cannot be otherwise, as he has deliberately left behind, among other things, Javanese conventions. Yet the question remains, can Soedjanmo be *merdika* or free from the constraints of the new social map, the sort of constraints suggested by Masroel's experience, by dressing like an European and marrying his love? The answer certainly must be no. By equating the quest for freedom with that for true love, the end of *Rasa Merdika* makes Soedjanmo look tame and comfortable in the new social map, no more restless than at the beginning of the novel.

Figure Ten
Soedjanmo trying to confirm Soepini's love toward him

The years between the mid-1910s and early 1930s, when the six novels were most probably written as well as published, correspond roughly to a period of radical nationalism in Indonesian history. We see some reflections of this in three of the novels. Hidjo's fiancée, her girlfriend, and the latter's brother attend a gathering of Sarekat Islam in Solo in 1913. Soedjanmo meets Soepini for the first

---
[51] Soemantri, *Rasa Merdika*, p. 133.

120   Tsuyoshi Kato

time at a political lecture in P city on nationalism and internationalism given by a journalist from S city. Members of Boedi-Oetama, an organization established in Java in 1908 and considered as the forerunner of Indonesia's national awakening, participated in the funeral of Roesmala Dewi's mother in Tandjoeng Pinang in 1916, since Roesmala Dewi's father was a leader of its local branch. Yet the novels' heroes and heroines, all well educated and mostly government employees, seem by and large content with the status quo and not much bent on radicalism.[52]

It is perhaps no accident that the most radical figure in terms of anti-colonialism turns out to be the only significant villain in the six novels, that is, Datoek Meringgih of *Sitti Noerbaja*. Here is the character who is old, lowly in class origin, uneducated, self-employed and self-made, loaded with "wild" money, mean, vengeful, lewd, unlovable, and unloved. In short, he is the complete opposite of what the six novels' heroes are. When the Dutch introduced taxation to West Sumatra in 1908, a historical fact, the fictional Datoek Meringgih leads a peasant rebellion against the Dutch near Padang, in which he duels with Samsoe'lbahari, then Létenan Mas in the colonial army, and both die in the combat. Datoek Meringgih rebels because he anticipates a heavy tax on his wealth and also suspects that the colonial authority is secretly investigating him for his past wrongdoing. Irrespective of his personal motives, Datoek Meringgih embraces radicalism. This does not happen with the other protagonists of the novels. Soedjanmo, dressed completely like an European, employed at an European private company, conversant in Dutch, and attaining true love, that is to say, economically not dependent on the colonial government and equal to Europeans in every respect, alone seems finally set for radical activism after the novel is over. Among the six novels, *Rasa Merdika* is the only one whose author ends the novel's last page by writing "In a different chapter we will meet them [Soedjanmo and Soepini] again..."

It does not make much sense, however, to point out the lack of radicalism in early Indonesian novels, if we think of the tightened colonial supervision over printed materials after the 1900s, called under the law "hate-sowing articles" (*haatzaai-artikelen*).[53] Novels after all are the product of free imagining and thus can be subversive to political order. The emergence of modern novels in Indonesia in the early twentieth century signified the appearance of a relatively large number of potential readers in addition to a free-imagining literate elite that knew how to enjoy this product and could afford to buy it. It is no wonder that one of the reasons for the establishment of Balai Poestaka was to provide native readers with "politically healthy" reading materials.

An important characteristic of early Indonesian novels, I think, is radical imagining, rather than radical activism. Given the socio-historical situation of early twentieth-century Indonesia, consider some of the unthinkable or unusual things that are imagined and told in the six novels. Samsoe'lbahari and Noerbaja exchange vows of unchanging love and embrace and kiss each other, even though

---

[52] Marco Kartodikromo, *Student Hidjo*, pp. 94-102; Soemantri, *Rasa Merdika*, pp. 63-93; Hardjosoemarto dan Dt. Madjoindo, *Roesmala Dewi*, p. 34. Boedi-Oetama was a Java-centric organization and it is rather strange that in *Roesmala Dewi* its branch exists in Tandjoeng Pinang and, moreover, one of its leaders is a Minangkabau.

[53] Hendrik M. J. Maier, "Phew! Europeesche beschaving!: Marco Kartodikromo's *Student Hidjo*," *Tonan Ajia Kenkyu*, 34,1 (1996): 192, 205-206.

she is already married to Datoek Meringgih. Within ten years of his failure to commit suicide, Samsoe'lbahari reemerges as a "Dutch man" named Létenan Mas. The caretaker of the graveyard on Padang Hill where Noerbaja is buried is surprised to see the Dutch man weeping at the grave of a Muslim. Hanafi of *Salah Asoehan* loves Corrie, a [Eurasian] European girl, and after legally becoming Dutch, eventually marries her. Roesmala Dewi fends off the consummation of an unwanted marriage, works out an amicable divorce, and finally happily remarries Soeparno, her love, without any problem. Soedjanmo of *Rasa Merdika* leaves his parents for a rather unclear reason and shows no sign of getting in touch with them again even after settling down in P city. Only in *Kalau Ta' Oentoeng* nothing much unusual is observable, except for Masroel's irresolute nature and Rasmani's steadfast love for him.

Student Hidjo, unremarkable in terms of radical activism, is unrivaled in radical imagining among the six novels. Imagining in it becomes wild after Hidjo's ship leaves Java for the Netherlands.[54] European girls flirt with him on the ship. The minute the ship arrives at Amsterdam, Hidjo finds situations there to be unusual (*loear biasa*), for "starting that moment, Hidjo can give orders to Dutch people, who, when in the Indies, are mostly arrogant." Employees at his hotel are extremely respectful to him, because they think those newly arrived from the Indies, especially Javanese, must all be rich.

A string of unusual and role-reversal-like experiences ensue. Betje, one of the daughters of the Dutch family with whom Hidjo boards, falls in love with him and seduces him; on their first assignation they sit at a theater café, Hidjo yells "Waiter!" and a "Dutch servant" (*djongos Belanda*, an impossible combination of words in colonial Indonesia) answers him "sir"; in the meantime, Walter, a Dutch official in Java, is infatuated with Hidjo's fiancée, abandons his own Dutch fiancée, who is pregnant, but fails in his courtship; back again in Holland, Hidjo comes to the conclusion that Holland does not suit him, decides to return to Java, breaks the news to Betje on their last assignation, and gives her a bankbook containing his savings of one thousand guilders. Two years later, Hidjo is a district attorney (*djaksa*), Walter an Assistant Resident, and Wardjojo, Hidjo's friend, a Regent, all married and living in the regency of Djarak in Java; the positions of the three men are more or less equal in the colonial administrative hierarchy.

Radical imagining involves imagining that what should not or normally will not happen happens. It seems that the novels' authors, together with their heroes, need to journey to a city where the new social map is in the making and where unusual incidents tend to happen in order to nurture and exercise radical and wild imagining. I suspect that is the reason why *Kalau Ta' Oentoeng* falls short in this respect; its author, who stayed a long time in Pekanbaru after studying in Boekittinggi, and her protagonists lack the experience of long-distance migration to a large city. It is also interesting that *Roesmala Dewi*, as well as *Kalau Ta' Oentoeng*, both published in the early 1930s and the newest of the six novels, feature practically no Dutch characters. We come across, if not cross-racial love affairs, at least one or two significant cross-racial encounters involving relatively extensive conversations between the protagonists and Dutch people in the other

---

[54] After all, relatively few natives went to Europe after the beginning of the twentieth century, although many Europeans came to the Dutch East Indies. Thus the idea of making the hero of an Indonesian novel go to Europe must have required a great deal of unconventional imagining.

novels; this simply does not happen in *Roesmala Dewi* or *Kalau Ta' Oentoeng*. Whatever radical imagining the two novels may incorporate, it cannot be about the Dutch-native or the colonizer-colonized relationship.

A cursory reading of some other novels from the 1930s and early 1940s shows that Dutch characters play a relatively minor role in them. *Layar Terkembang* (With sails unfurled), *Belenggu* (Fetters), and *Merantau ke Deli* (Going abroad to Deli) feature more or less no Dutch figures. In *Katak Hendak Jadi Lembu* (A frog wanting to become an ox), the story of an ambitious native civil servant, a certain A. Jansen, a Dutch colonial official, appears several times, though briefly each time, as he is in the position of influencing the civil servant's promotion. It is in *Pertemuan Djodoh* (Meant for each other) that we find rather important encounters between its heroine and Dutch people.[55] It is possible that Indonesian novels in the 1930s were not preoccupied or did not need to be preoccupied any more with the sort of radical imagining exemplified by *Student Hidjo*. Hidjo or Green remains a student until the page before last in the novel. But he too eventually has to graduate and live in reality, even if it is an imagined one.

"I"s in the world of Indonesian novels in the 1930s and early 1940s were most probably increasingly accustomed to the new social map, the one even relatively *merdeka* or free from the physical presence of the Dutch, and absorbed in the question of inter-ethnic or interpersonal relations rather than inter-racial relations.

Hamka, a Muslim writer-cum-journalist, published *Merantau ke Deli* in 1941; it had originally been serialized in a periodical between 1939 and 1940. It tells the story of a Javanese female contract coolie and her eventual companion, both of whom used to work in the plantation belt of Deli in East Sumatra. Deli, the main stage of the novel, was a center of European plantations in Sumatra, but only a single European appears literally fleetingly in the novel. Toward the end, Poniem, the novel's heroine departs for Medan by train after being divorced from her first husband. As she gazes from the train window, she sees in the distance a big master or *tuan besar* in a large sun helmet and short pants putting on airs and ordering coolies around Poniem had once been the mistress of a senior overseer (*mandur besar*) of the plantation where she worked, and at one time confided to a Minankabau merchant who would become her first husband that "although being looked after outside marriage, I am better off living with him [senior overseer] than becoming a *nyai* [the mistress of a European master who was a favorite heroine of novels in Malay written by Chinese and Eurasian authors in the final quarter of the nineteenth century], for he is still one of my own race."

At the end of the novel, when Poniem And her Javanese companion are already married and successful merchants back in Deli, Hamka writes: "They are happy

---

[55] I read the reprints of these novels in my possession. See S. Takdir Alisjahbana, *Lajar Terkembang*, tjetakan IX (Jakarta: Balai Pustaka, 1972 [1937]); Armijn Pane, *Belenggu*, cetakan kesembilan (Jakarta: Dian Rakyat, 1977 [1940]); Hamka, *Merantau ke Deli*, cetakan ketujuh (Jakarta: Bulan Bintang, 1977 [1941]); N. St. Iskandar, *Katak Hendak Jadi Lembu*, cetakan kedelapan (Jakarta: Balai Pustaka, 1990 [1935]); A. Moeis, *Pertemuan Djodoh*, tjetakan kelima (Bukittinggi: Nusantara, 1964 [1932]). Ratna, the heroine of *Pertemuan Djodoh*, meets a European employer, a Dutch couple, and a tribunal judge during the course of the story. It is noteworthy that she retains her pride in her encounter with these people. For example, she rebuffs an advance by her European employer and steadfastly asserts her innocence when wrongly accused in the tribunal of stealing golden accessories from the Dutch couple.

because they have decided to become Deli people for the rest of their lives. They do not think any more of going back to Java which is hard-pressed by over-population. They have already joined a new society, the society of Deli which consists of various ethnic groups coming from every corner of Indonesia in order later to give birth to new offspring, true children of Indonesia." In the meantime, freedom, above all political freedom, had become something to be acted upon, not something to be imagined, radically or otherwise.

HẢI VÂN, *THE STORM*, VIETNAMESE COMMUNISM INTER-WAR IMAGINATION

Peter Zinoman

Among the many reasons that Vũ Trọng Phụng's novel *The Storm* (*Giông Tố*)—first serialized in *Hanoi Newspaper* (*Hà Nội Báo*) during 1936—should be of more than passing interest to scholars of modern Vietnam is the description that it provides of the mysterious communist Hải Vân.[2] Although fictional characters with vaguely radical politics appear occasionally in colonial-era Vietnamese literature, Vũ Trọng Phụng's unambiguous portrayal of Hải Vân as a leading member of the Communist Party is unique.[3] *The Storm* stops short of identifying the Party by name, but Hải Vân's forthright account of training in Moscow at the "Stalin School for Far Eastern Revolutionaries" points clearly to his affiliation

---

[1] Thanks to Christopher Goscha, Nguyen Nguyet Cam, Hue-Tam Ho Tai, Keith Taylor, and Ben Tran for their critical readings of an earlier draft of this essay.

This essay is inspired by three preoccupations threaded throughout Benedict Anderson's work on the history and politics of Southeast Asia. The first is his concern with the historical development of Southeast Asian political thought. The second is his interest in the Southeast Asian novel as a site for historical and political analysis. And third is his insistence that radical political movements in Southeast Asia must be examined in their local contexts and rigorously historicized before they can be fully understood.

[2] Most references to the text in this essay are from a recently republished edition of the novel. Vũ Trọng Phụng, *Giông Tố* (Hanoi: Văn Học, 1996). Passages censored from the republished edition are cited from an original copy of *Hà Nội Báo*, currently available on microfilm at the Vietnam National Library in Hanoi.

[3] Examples of such hazy political radicals include Dũng in Nhất Linh's *Đoạn Tuyệt* (Breaking the ties) (Hanoi: Đời Nay, 1935); Hạc in Khái Hưng's *Gia Đình* (Family) (Hanoi: Đời Nay, 1937); Mạnh in Nguyễn Văn Phúc's *Con Đường Mới* (New road) (Hanoi: Hương Sơn đường, 1939); and Duy in Hoàng Đạo's *Con Đường Sáng* (Bright road) (Hanoi: Đời Nay, 1940). The most distinctly drawn communist character after Hải Vân is the ex-political prisoner Teacher Minh in Vũ Trọng Phụng's *Vỡ Đê* (The dike breaks), originally serialized in *Tương Lai* (The future) starting on September 27, 1936. Unlike Hải Vân, however, there is no indication that Minh is anything but a rank-and-file party member.

the Indochinese Communist Party (ICP).[4] Hải Vân's powerful position within the party hierarchy is underlined by the gravity and international scope of his political work. Not only does he represent the Party at "a Far Eastern Conference for delegates from the Philippines, Australia, Java, and Taiwan," but he assumes primary responsibility for "negotiating a reconciliation between the old Nationalist Party and the new Internationalist Party."[5] Indeed, thoughtful Vietnamese readers have long noted the congruence of Hải Vân's political assignments in the novel with Nguyễn Ái Quốc's globetrotting activism on behalf of the Comintern during the inter-war years.[6]

Even more surprising than Hải Vân's high profile in *The Storm* is the novel's remarkably flattering depiction of him, especially given the colonial state's well-deserved reputation for censorship and anticommunist repression. Hải Vân is brave, worldly, and deeply charismatic, and his "bright eyes" and "knowing smile" inspire a combination of "fear and respect."[7] His magnetic presence is heightened by his delayed appearance—he makes his first entrance over halfway through the novel—and by the author's reluctance to reveal his true identity until the final stages of the narrative. The enigma of Hải Vân is brought into sharper relief by the lush interiority of the novel's other main characters—a feature that marks *The Storm* as one of the earliest examples of Vietnamese modernism.[8] The fact that readers are privy to the internal world of other major characters in the novel, but not that of Hải Vân, enhances the aura of power and mystery that surrounds him.

The open publication of a colonial-era novel in which a dashing communist plays a leading role points to the remarkably liberal character of the public sphere in Indochina during that brief era (1936–38) when the left-leaning Popular Front government held power in France.[9] But Hải Vân's greatest value to historians lies in the light that he sheds on popular Vietnamese attitudes of the day towards communism and local communist activists. This issue merits attention because studies of early Vietnamese communism tend to approach the movement from the inside (by examining the institutional development of the ICP and the lives and ideas of its leaders) while more or less ignoring perceptions of it from without. It is also important because the Party has long fostered a suspiciously monochromatic image of itself over time as an entity that is invariably modern, scientifically oriented, morally virtuous, socially based in the lower classes, and deeply

---

[4] It is well known that hundreds of ICP members trained at the Stalin School during the 1920s and 1930s. The most recent research on this may be found in the excellent study by Sophie Quinn-Judge, *Ho Chi Minh: The Missing Years* (Berkeley: University of California Press, 2003), and William Duiker, *Ho Chi Minh: A Life* (New York: Hyperion, 2000). Duiker makes significant use of new data from the Comintern archives published in Anotoly A. Sokolov, *Komintern I V'ietnam* (Moscow: Iv Ran, 1998).

[5] *Giông Tố*, pp. 369-71.

[6] This theory has never made it into print for reasons that will become clear.

[7] *Giông Tố*, p. 242.

[8] For a treatment of Vũ Trọng Phụng as a modernist writer, see Peter Zinoman, "Vũ Trọng Phụng and the Nature of Vietnamese Modernism," in *Dumb Luck: A Novel by Vũ Trọng Phụng*, ed. Peter Zinoman, trans. Peter Zinoman and Nguyễn Nguyệt Cầm (Ann Arbor: University of Michigan Press, 2002).

[9] For a discussion of the expansion of the public sphere in Indochina during the Popular Front era, see Shawn McHale, "Printing, Power and the Transformation of Vietnamese Culture, 1920-1945" (PhD dissertation, Cornell University, 1995).

nationalistic. The process whereby this vaguely Stalinist cluster of attributes came to embody the transhistorical nature of the Party unfolded in isomorphic relation to the consolidation of communist control over state power in northern Vietnam after 1954.[10] Vũ Trọng Phụng's portrayal of Hải Vân, however, calls into question the historical continuity of the Party's character and reputation by presenting what might be referred to as a pre-Stalinized portrait of the Vietnamese communist leadership. The recovery of this image is significant because of the likelihood that it reflected a widely held view of the movement during the late colonial era and because it dovetails with a fragmentary body of historical evidence about the nature of the ICP during its formative phase of development.

Hải Vân is also of interest because the character has been at the center of an enduring debate over Vũ Trọng Phụng's political legacy. Raging on and off in communist Vietnam throughout the post-colonial era, the debate has pitted conservative cultural officials hostile to Phụng's work against progressive intellectuals who admire and defend it. The dominance of the "conservatives" during the late 1950s triggered a ban on Phụng's writing for over twenty years, while the onset of Đổi Mới (Renovation) in the 1980s set the stage for the "progressives" to engineer its rehabilitation. Needless to say, the fact that most interpretations of Hải Vân have been made within the hot-house context of this debate has distorted efforts to understand the character and to determine what he signifies about Vũ Trọng Phụng's political orientation. Hence, this essay will offer a brief consideration of the arguments about Hải Vân put forward by Vũ Trọng Phụng's supporters and his detractors and conclude by suggesting an alternative reading of the character that is more consistent, I believe, with the precise historical context within which *The Storm* was written.

VŨ TRỌNG PHỤNG AND *THE STORM*

Vũ Trọng Phụng's portrayal of Hải Vân cannot be seen as a comprehensive representation of what was, after all, a diverse body of Vietnamese popular opinion about communism during the 1930s. However, his celebrity and achievements as both a writer and a journalist endow his account with unusual historical significance. Born into modest circumstances in 1912, Phụng burst onto the Vietnamese literary scene during his late teens when he began publishing "realist" short stories in the popular Hanoi daily *Hanoi Noon* (*Hà Thành Ngọ Báo*).[11] His reputation soared soon thereafter with the publication of two book-length works of non-fiction reportage (*phóng sự*)—*The Man Trap* (1933), which illuminated Hanoi's underworld of con-artists and professional gamblers, and *The Industry of Marrying Westerners* (1934), a study of interracial marriage within the colony.[12] Acclaimed already by the middle of the 1930s as "the king of northern reportage" (*vua phóng*

---

[10] For the influence of Stalinism on intellectual life in the Democratic Republic of Vietnam, see Patricia M. Pelley, *Postcolonial Vietnam: New Histories of the National Past* (Durham: Duke University Press, 2002).

[11] The following treatment of Vũ Trọng Phụng's life and work is based on Zinoman, "Vũ Trọng Phụng and the Nature of Vietnamese Modernism."

[12] *Cạm Bẫy Người* (The man trap) (serialized beginning August, 1933 in *Báo Nhật Tân*; reprint, Hanoi: An Nam Xuất Bản Cục, 1934); *Kỹ Nghệ Lấy Tây* (The industry of marrying Westerners) (December, 1934 in *Báo Nhật Tân*; reprint, Hanoi: Phương Đông, 1936).

sự đất Bắc), Phụng continued to write investigative non-fiction throughout the remainder of his career, including influential exposés into the lives of domestic workers (*Household Servants*), actors (*Clown Make-Up*), and prostitutes (*Venereal Disease Clinic*).[13] During the second half of the decade, Phụng turned his attention to long-format fiction and produced no less than four astonishingly original and diverse novels in 1936 and 1937. In addition to *The Storm*, these included *Dumb Luck*—a masterful parody of the rage for modernization among the inter-war Vietnamese elite; *The Dike Breaks*—a realist melodrama about class struggle and the rise of an anti-colonial consciousness during the late colonial era; and *To Be a Whore*—an explicitly Freudian dramatization of the causes of the growth of the commercial sex industry in colonial Hanoi.[14] Phụng also published poetry, plays, reviews, obituaries, and literary translations, as well as a huge amount of daily reporting and political commentary.[15] The vast quantity and extraordinary quality of Phụng's work is more remarkable owing to the fact that he died at the age of twenty-seven from the combined effects of tuberculosis and opium addiction.

Just as his celebrated reputation as a "realist" writer and an investigative reporter enhanced the authority and veracity of his characterization of Hải Vân, Phụng's famously hard-to-define ideological orientation endowed his portrayal of this fictional communist with an aura of political objectivity. A bitter critic of the colonial regime, the indigenous elite, and the injustices of colonial capitalism, Phụng was equally suspicious of the Left and wrote critically about both the domestic and the international communist movements. He reserved his most damning invective, however, for the way in which the confluence of colonialism, capitalism, and indigenous modernization campaigns had undermined traditional gender relations and triggered an abrupt upsurge in promiscuity, divorce, adultery, rape, and sexually transmitted disease. Indeed, his constant carping on these issues led him to idealize elements of the quasi-Confucian, patriarchal traditional order. Just as the incongruous co-existence of Phụng's anti-colonialism, anti-capitalism, cultural conservatism, and skepticism towards indiscriminate modernization and radical political alternatives has left his political orientation resistant to easy categorization, it also strongly discourages reading his portrayal of Hải Vân as an instrument of partisan propaganda.

Phụng's hatred of class privilege and obsessive concern with the relationship between colonial capitalism and the deterioration of sexual morality are clearly reflected in the plot of *The Storm*. The novel opens with the brutal rape of a peasant girl named Thị Mịch by a rich, powerful, and deeply corrupt businessman named Nghị Hách. In the first of many coincidences, it is revealed that Thị Mịch's

---

[13] *Cơm Thầy Cơm Cô* (Household servants) (March, 1936 in *Hà Nội Báo*; reprint, Hanoi: Minh Phương, 1937); *Vẽ Nhọ Bôi Hề* (Clown make-up) (May, 1934 in *Phụ Nữ Thời Đàm*), *Lục Xì* (Venereal disease clinic) (January, 1937 in *Tương Lai*; reprint, Hanoi: Minh Phương, 1937).

[14] *Số Đỏ* (Dumb luck) (October, 1936 in *Hà Nội Báo*; reprint Hanoi: Lê Cường, 1938); *Vỡ Đê* (The dike breaks) (September, 1936 in *Tương Lai*; reprint Hanoi: Minh Đức, 1957); *Làm Đĩ* (To be a whore) (October, 1936 in *Sông Hương*; reprint Hanoi: Mai Lĩnh, 1939).

[15] Much of this work is available in the five-volume anthology: *Vũ Trọng Phụng: Toàn Tập* (Vũ Trọng Phụng: Complete Works) (Hanoi: Hội Nhà Văn, 1999). Some additional work recently rediscovered is now available in two new collections: *Vẽ Nhọ Bôi Hề* (Clown make-up), ed. Lại Nguyên Ân, compiled by Peter Zinoman (Hanoi: Hội Nhà Văn, 2000); and *Chống Nạng Lên Đường* (Leaning on a stick and hitting the road), ed. Lại Nguyên Ân (Hanoi: Hội Nhà Văn, 2001).

fiancé—Long—is employed at a "reformist" school run by Nghị Hách's son—Tú Anh. The first two-thirds of the narrative follow the efforts of these four characters—Thị Mịch (the rape victim), Long (her fiancé), Nghị Hách (the rapist), and Tú Anh (Nghị Hách's son and Long's boss)—to deal with the consequences of the rape. Nghị Hách uses his power and influence to thwart legal proceedings launched against him by Thị Mịch's family. Thị Mịch attempts suicide, discovers that she is pregnant by the rape, breaks off her engagement with Long, and suffers a mental breakdown that results in the perversion of her heretofore innocent personality. Long undergoes a parallel psychological meltdown and tries to recuperate by seducing (or allowing himself to be seduced by) both Thị Mịch and Nghị Hách's frivolous and thoroughly "modern" daughter, Tuyết. Meanwhile, Tú Anh upbraids his father and persuades him to atone for the rape by taking Thị Mịch as a second wife. In the midst of this conventionally plotted but psychologically compelling melodrama, Hải Vân materializes and initiates secret meetings with several of the characters, paying special attention to Nghị Hách. Following a brief period marked by confusion over Hải Vân's true identity, Nghị Hách recognizes him as an old friend whom he had once framed for a crime that he didn't commit. Nghị Hách compounded this act of betrayal by sleeping with Hải Vân's wife, who died, subsequently, in childbirth. The remainder of the narrative dramatizes an elaborate revenge-plot launched by Hải Vân against Nghị Hách. The plot involves Hải Vân laying the groundwork to blackmail Nghị Hách by unmasking his wife's ongoing infidelity and exposing a linked pair of shocking revelations about his family: Tú Anh is actually Hải Vân's son, and Long is, in fact, the son of Nghị Hách. The discovery of Long's true paternity is especially devastating to Nghị Hách as it brings to light several instances of unnatural sexual relations within his family: Nghị Hách's rape of Mịch is revealed as a father's sexual violation of his son's fiancé; the sexual intercourse that transpires between Long and Thị Mịch (after she has married Nghị Hách) is exposed as a case of a son sleeping with his father's wife; and Long's seduction of Tuyết is recast as an incestuous liaison between siblings. Near the end of the narrative, Hải Vân reveals to Tú Anh—newly acknowledged as his son—that he is in fact a communist agent who has engineered the blackmail of Nghị Hách as a means to raise money on behalf of the Party. The novel concludes with Hải Vân bidding adieu to Tú Anh as he sets sail for further adventures in the middle of a violent storm off the coast of Móng Cáy.

HẢI VÂN AND THE IDEOLOGY OF INTER-WAR VIETNAMESE COMMUNISM

As should be apparent, *The Storm* is more family melodrama than novel of ideas, but its penultimate chapter includes a lengthy episode in which Hải Vân expounds at length on his revolutionary ideals and strategies for political action. Since Hải Vân is portrayed as an important ICP official, his musings on these matters provide insight into how the Party's political orientation was understood during the mid 1930s—at least within one influential quarter of the popular imagination. Most striking in this regard are Hải Vân's highly partisan views on nationalism and internationalism. In contrast to official accounts that emphasize the historical compatibility of these impulses within the modern Vietnamese radical tradition, Hải Vân denounces nationalism, dismissing it as an inadequate alternative to the Marxist internationalism of the ICP. As part of a belated paternal inquiry into his son's political beliefs, Hải Vân asks Tú Anh about his "mind" and "heart." Tú Anh assures his father that he too possesses "ideals."

"Nationalist or internationalist," Hải Vân asks.
"Nationalist, Sir," replies Tú Anh.
Hải Vân frowns.
"How stupid of you!"[16]

Hải Vân then explains to his son the various shortcomings of nationalism. "Your ideology of nationalism is both narrow and unachievable," he chides Tú Anh. "To make distinctions based on race is ignorant. You must abandon this ideology and be willing to befriend poor and miserable Frenchmen. The Annamese *nouveau riche* is your true enemy."[17] Hải Vân's insinuation that nationalism is a form of racism is reinforced by his tendency to see it as an easy ally of fascism and militarism:

> The old nationalist group took money from Germany and Japan. This was very stupid. Our nation [*dân tộc mình*] must not escape from its current yoke only to fall into the hands of the German and Japanese imperialists. We must play no part of their genocidal plans.

Along the same lines, he announces: "I will not treat France as an enemy only to allow the secret agents of Japanese militarism to achieve their ambitions of a unified Asia under the slogan 'Asia for the Asiatics.' Such a regime will bring nothing but misery to our people."[18]

Hải Vân's hostility towards fascism is consistent with what is known of the political line adopted by the ICP following the seventh Comintern Congress in 1935.[19] Devised by Stalin and championed by the Bulgarian general secretary of the Comintern, Georgi Dimitrov, the new line reflected fears about the growing threat posed by Hitler to the Soviet Union. It called for communist parties around the world to shelve temporarily their preoccupation with class struggle and opposition to imperialism in order to join with "progressive" forces and governments (even bourgeois or colonial ones) in an alliance against fascism. Since the novel takes place during the early 1930s, Hải Vân's militant anti-fascism is a literary anachronism that clearly reflects the policy of the ICP in 1936—the year that the novel was published.[20]

While Hải Vân's fixation with fascism dovetails with the ICP's embrace of the Dimitrov line, his rejection of nationalism undermines conventional understandings of the significance of this policy-shift within the history of Vietnamese communism. It is commonly argued that the inclusive popular-frontism

---

[16] *Giông Tố*, p. 370.

[17] Ibid.

[18] Ibid.

[19] The standard treatment remains Huynh Kim Khanh, *Vietnamese Communism, 1925-1945* (Ithaca: Cornell University Press, 1982), pp. 189-231.

[20] Fears about the threat to Indochina posed by Japanese militarism, on the other hand, date from the mid-1920s at least. See, for example, Trần Huy Liệu's warnings about Japanese imperialist ambitions in Indochina in *Một Bầu Tâm Sự* (A heartfelt plea) (Saigon: Nam Đồng Thư Xã, 1927).

encouraged by the new policy helped the ICP to win support during the second half of the 1930s by allowing it to emphasize its nationalist roots—a policy seen as both agreeable to "the masses" and consistent with the most deeply felt political aspirations of Party leaders.[21] But Hải Vân's blunt rejection of nationalism suggests that such an ideological move—if it indeed occurred—was not widely recognized at the time. Alternatively, Hải Vân's opposition to nationalism may reflect something of the durability of the Party's commitment to internationalism and class struggle during the era. This view reverses the conventional wisdom that nationalism rather than Marxist internationalism embodied the core ideology of the inter-war ICP. It finds further support in the contrast between Hải Vân's remarkable enthusiasm for the French radical and revolutionary tradition and his apparent indifference to any tradition (real or imagined) of Vietnamese nationalist heroism. As he explains (again somewhat anachronistically) to Tú Anh:

> We can perhaps place our hopes in the Popular France of Rousseau, Danton, Robespierre, and Blum/Moutet! These are figures that can help to relieve our suffering even if they do not have power at this moment. We will not consider France as our exclusive enemy, on the contrary, members of our own race may be seen as enemies—those who live off the fruits of the labors of others, those who oppress the working class ...[22]

HẢI VÂN AND THE CHARACTER OF INTER-WAR VIETNAMESE COMMUNISTS

If Hải Vân's political opinions reveal something about how the ICP's ideological orientation was perceived during the mid-1930s, other elements of his personality shed light on popular Vietnamese attitudes of the day towards the intimate character of communists. Hải Vân's family background, in this respect, is especially instructive. A lengthy flashback reveals that he was born into a clan of rural scholar-gentry that traces its ancestry back to the famous sixteenth-century scholar Nguyễn Bỉnh Khiêm (aka Trạng Trình).[23] Faithful to the scholarly traditions of his family, the young Hải Vân masters Chinese characters and earns a *khóa sinh* degree. He does not accept a position within the still-functioning imperial Vietnamese bureaucracy, however, since "this was the period when rogues took over the administration and sincere and honest men abandoned government service."[24] Hence, Hải Vân is depicted as the frustrated scion of an illustrious scholar-gentry family whose traditional career prospects are undermined by the colonial state's destruction of the imperial bureaucracy. This depiction is consistent with the actual sociological profile of numerous members of the inter-war Party

---

[21] This argument is often made by historians in Vietnam and is put forward, in a more qualified way, in Huỳnh Kim Khánh, *Vietnamese Communism*, pp. 190, 211-18, and William Duiker, *The Rise of Nationalism in Vietnam, 1900-1941* (Ithaca: Cornell University Press, 1976), pp. 234-55.

[22] *Giông Tố*, p. 370.

[23] Ibid., p. 330. For a succinct but informative introduction to Nguyễn Bỉnh Khiêm's life and work, see Nguyễn Hữu Sơn, "Trạng Trình/Nguyễn Bỉnh Khiêm Đời và Thơ" (Trạng Trình/Nguyễn Bỉnh Khiêm, life and poetry), in Nguyễn Hữu Sơn, *Điểm Tựa Phê Bình Văn Học* (Fulcrum of literary criticism) (Hanoi: Lao Động, 2000), pp. 262-74.

[24] *Giông Tố*, p. 330.

leadership as confirmed by a diverse array of scholars including Hy Van Luong, Alexander Woodside, Bernard Fall, and Trinh Van Thao.[25]

Another key element of Hải Vân's biography is his prison experience. As with every important early leader of the ICP, Hải Vân boasts significant time behind bars.[26] "I have been a prisoner for half of my life," he tells Tú Anh with some exaggeration. "One year in our country [nước nhà], three years in Fujian, and five years in Manchuria."[27] That Hải Vân spent the bulk of his prison time abroad is more consistent with the experiences of top Party leaders like Hồ Chí Minh (jailed in Hong Kong and Southern China) than with low-level operatives who tended to be incarcerated within Indochina. However, like all party members who were jailed during the 1930s, Hải Vân looks back on his years in prison as a period during which he mastered theoretical knowledge and practical political skills that enhanced his effectiveness as a professional revolutionary. "Only in prison could I begin to study," he tells Nghị Hách. "I was locked up for one year with an old Chinese man who taught me the secrets of astrology."[28]

As with his prison credentials, Hải Vân's renunciation of family obligations mirrors an orientation commonly associated with the ICP leadership. Indeed, in what has become an influential formulation, historian Huynh Kim Khanh once described the Party's founding fathers as "secular monks."[29] Vũ Trọng Phụng paints a similar picture when he introduces Hải Vân as a "spirited wanderer" (giang hồ khí phách).[30] "I have changed my name and family background," Hải Vân tells Nghị Hách. "I have wiped away all memories of my meaningless old life so that I may live a new life of wandering and adventure."[31] Continuing in this vein, he states that: "I am not devoted to my family although I know that it exists. Rather I want to empathize with all of society, with all of humanity."[32] Hải Vân's stated commitment to "society" (xã hội) and "humanity" (nhân loại) underlines the broad internationalist breadth of his political horizons and the relative insignificance of the "nation" in his thinking. But it also recalls Huynh Kim Khanh's observation about the relative indifference of leading Communists towards traditional family obligations.

While Vũ Trọng Phụng's depiction of Hải Vân as an ICP leader dovetails in important respects with the historical record, it is inconsistent with sanitized accounts of the history of the inter-war communist leadership put forward by the Party after it assumed state-power in 1954. For example, Hải Vân's upper-class

---

[25] Hy Van Luong, "Agrarian Unrest from an Anthropological Perspective: The Case of Vietnam," *Comparative Politics* 17,2 (January 1985): 165-170; Alexander Woodside, *Community and Revolution in Modern Vietnam* (Boston, MA: Houghton Mifflin, 1976), p. 303; Bernard Fall, *The Viet Minh Regime*, Data Paper No. 14 (Ithaca, NY: Cornell Southeast Asia Program Publications, 1954), p. 74; Trinh Van Thao, *Vietnam du Confucianisme au Communisme* (Paris: L'Harmattan, 1990).

[26] For more on this, see Peter Zinoman, *The Colonial Bastille: A History of Imprisonment in Vietnam, 1862-1940* (Berkeley: University of California Press, 2001).

[27] *Giông Tố*, p. 374.

[28] Ibid., p. 333.

[29] Huynh Kim Khanh, *Vietnamese Communism, 1925-1945*, p. 135.

[30] *Giông Tố*, p. 242.

[31] Ibid., p. 277.

[32] Ibid.

family background does not mesh with the Party's spurious claims about the quasi-proletarian pedigree of its founding fathers.[33] His avowal that he mastered fortune telling in jail does not jibe with communist prison memoirs in which incarcerated party members study only Marxism-Leninism.[34] And his rejection of nationalism undermines official claims about the historical compatibility between Vietnamese nationalism and Vietnamese communism. The banning of *The Storm* by the Party during the 1960s and 1970s owes something to the fact that these deviations from the official historical record were seen as a tendentious distortion of the character of the ICP leadership.

Even more objectionable to Party authorities has been the novel's characterization of Hải Vân's instrumental capabilities and spiritual beliefs. Among Hải Vân's most striking characteristics are the abundance and diversity of his skill, talent, and knowledge. He is fluent in Chinese and a master of disguise. He can drive a car and navigate an ocean voyage. He possesses some knowledge of Western medicine and is a skilled hypnotist. He is an able marksman and a formidable martial artist. He even knows how to prepare a decent opium pipe. Hải Vân owes his easy facility in these areas and many others to the curriculum taught at the Stalin School. "Students there are trained in swordsmanship, shooting, diving, swimming, driving cars, flying planes, Western and Japanese martial arts and political subversion," he explains to Tú Anh. "They also learn rhetorical techniques to win over the masses, how to master the arts of disguise and intimidation, and how to run a security organization and an intelligence service."[35]

In addition to those revolutionary skills he acquired at the Stalin School, Hải Vân controls two bodies of esoteric knowledge that are not normally associated with members of the ICP leadership: geomancy (also known as *feng shui* or *phong thủy* in Vietnamese) and fortune telling. Hải Vân first reveals his knowledge of geomancy—the "science of wind and water"—when he warns Nghị Hách that he has chosen an inauspicious location for his gravesite. In the following scene—set entirely at the gravesite—Hải Vân points out the geomantic shortcomings of the original plot and explains the advantages of an alternative locale. In conclusion, he cautions that the former site will guarantee good fortune for Nghị Hách's family only in the short term ("as with Mạc Đăng Dung") while the latter promises to deliver a more enduring prosperity ("like Trịnh Kiểm or Nguyễn Hoàng.")[36] Hải Vân impresses Nghị Hách further by citing corroborating information from ancient geomantic texts and by using highly technical Sino-Vietnamese terminology to make his case. Later in the narrative, Hải Vân's fluency in the equally specialized language of fortune telling inspires a similar degree of awe in both Nghị Hách and his profligate younger son, Vạn Tóc Mai.[37]

---

[33] The best treatment of this is Christoph Giebel, "Tôn Đức Thắng and the Imagined Ancestries of Vietnamese Communism" (PhD dissertation, Cornell University, 1996).

[34] See Peter Zinoman, "Reading Revolutionary Prison Memoirs," in *The Country of Memory: Remaking the Past in Late Socialist Vietnam*, ed. Hue-Tam Ho Tai (Berkeley: University of California Press, 2001), pp. 21-45.

[35] This passage has been cut from more recent editions of the novel, but it may be found in the original serialization. See *Hà Nội Báo*, September 16, 1936.

[36] *Giông Tố*, p. 274.

[37] Ibid., p. 300.

Connected to Hải Vân's expert facility with geomancy and fortune telling is his apparently profound knowledge of the workings of *số mệnh*—a key concept in Sino-Vietnamese popular religion that may be translated crudely as "fate." Hải Vân's speech is infused with the notion that *số mệnh* represents a powerful, determinative force in human affairs that overwhelms individual agency. He even explains the nuances of the concept to other characters, as when he suggests that the invisible hand of *số mệnh* may have predestined Nghị Hách to commit a host of crimes and wicked acts. "Does that mean I do not have to take responsibility for the things that I have done?" Nghị Hách asks. "That is right," replies Hải Vân. "No one really earns or deserves admiration, hatred, love or scorn. Everything is determined by *số mệnh*."[38] Later, Nghị Hách raises suspicions about the sagacious Chinaman who taught Hải Vân fortune telling in prison. "If he was so talented, why was he still jailed?" Nghị Hách asks, "Why couldn't he escape?" "You understand nothing about *số mệnh*," Hải Vân responds. "No one can escape his or her fate. If we can escape from it, then it can not be called our fate."[39] Since Hải Vân spends much of the novel concealing his true feelings and intentions in order to engage the other characters unwittingly in a secret plot against Nghị Hách, it might be argued that his preoccupation with *số mệnh* is one element of a strategic disguise. But evidence to the contrary may be found in the fact that he continues speaking the language of *số mệnh* to Tú Anh *after* he has revealed to him his true identity and provided him with details of his subterfuge. When Tú Anh begs his father not to set sail during the storm brewing in the novel's penultimate chapter, Hải Vân's assures him that his death is not imminent because, as he explains it, "our *số* has not yet reached its final day."[40]

It is not surprising that conservative communist literary critics have reserved special disdain for Hải Vân's geomancy, fortune telling, and preoccupation with *số mệnh*.[41] The suggestion that a top Party official like Hải Vân might follow these practices and beliefs (or even take them seriously enough to master them) contradicts the official image of communist revolutionaries as thoroughly modern men unswervingly dedicated to the bloodless rationality of scientific Marxism-Leninism. Indeed, throughout its history, the Party has classified such elements of the Sino-Vietnamese tradition as "superstitions" (*mê tín dị đoan*) and waged a variety of campaigns to eradicate them.[42] For critics of *The Storm*, Hải Vân's expertise in these discredited forms of knowledge has been interpreted as evidence of Vũ Trọng Phụng's ignorance of the true nature of communism or as an effort on his part willfully to belittle and misrepresent its character.

A final striking characteristic of Hải Vân is his Machiavellian willingness to employ any means to achieve his ends. Virtually everything that Hải Vân does or

---

[38] Ibid., p. 279.

[39] Ibid., p. 334.

[40] Ibid., p. 372.

[41] Even genuinely "progressive" literary critics take issue with Hải Vân's devotion to *số mệnh*. See, for example, Nguyễn Đăng Mạnh's otherwise illuminating and respectful "Introduction" to *Tuyển Tập Vũ Trọng Phụng* (Collected Works of Vũ Trọng Phụng) (Hanoi: Văn Học, 1987), p. 31. Mạnh criticizes this element of Hải Vân's personality as a unhappy reflection of Vũ Trọng Phụng 's own "fatalism" (*chủ nghĩa định mệnh*).

[42] The best treatment of the Party's campaigns against superstition can be found in Shaun Kingsley Malarney, *Culture, Ritual, and Revolution in Vietnam* (Richmond: Curzon, 2002), pp. 79-107.

says during the course of the narrative is part of a clandestine plot to blackmail Nghị Hách on behalf of the Party. The friendly overtures he makes to Long and Vạn Tóc Mai are designed to gather intelligence about divisions within Nghị Hách's family. He stages his own reconciliation with Nghị Hách in order to heighten his capacity to manipulate him. He forces Tú Anh against his wishes to stay behind at the end of the novel so as to enforce the coercive agreement that he has reached with Nghị Hách. The fact that Hải Vân chooses blackmail as a fund-raising instrument in itself underlines his Machiavellian inclinations. But this impression is deepened by his willingness to engage in all manner of conventionally immoral acts in order to keep the plot on track. For instance, he plies Vạn Tóc Mai with opium in order to loosen his tongue and to enlist him in the plot against his own father. He does not act decisively to prevent Long from committing incest with Tuyết, although he is the only character in the novel who knows that they are brother and sister. He makes arrangements to have Nghị Hách's wife—also the mother of his own child—caught committing adultery *in flagrante delicto* and in front of her two sons and husband to boot!

While such measures may be justified as essential for the eventual success of his scheme, Hải Vân also engages in conventionally amoral behavior that adds little to the ultimate achievement of his aims. For example, as his efforts unfold in the opium den to win over Vạn Tóc Mai, Hải Vân takes the opportunity to "smoke five or six opium pipes himself"—an act that must be interpreted as a personal indulgence since there is no indication that it advances his plans.[43] But the most shocking demonstration of his cavalier personal permissiveness occurs when Nghị Hách attempts to cement his renewed friendship with Hải Vân by inviting him to a late-night bacchanal at his mansion. The scene opens as follows:

> When Hải Vân entered the room, Nghị Hách was lying with two young girls. They were extremely beautiful and their clothes were so thin and flimsy that they seemed almost nude. The sweet smell of opium wafted through the air. There was no furniture except for several plush carpets surrounded by dozens of hand-embroidered pillows. Tiger skins and stuffed tiger heads lay on each side of the opium tray. A set of champagne bottles was arranged on a small table. Next to the wall stood a small movie screen that faced a film projector. Miss Kiểm sat on a pillow beside the projector.[44]

Hải Vân is taken to bathe by one of the girls and returns dressed suggestively in a silk kimono. He drinks a toast with Nghị Hách; the lights go dim and, as the scene comes to a close, a pornographic film entitled *Les 32 Caresses* is projected onto the screen.[45] The abrupt ending of the scene confirms that Hải Vân sticks around to watch the blue movie and strongly hints that his recreational program for the remainder of the evening includes opium smoking and perhaps, even, participation in an orgy.

---

[43] *Giông Tố*, p. 308.
[44] Ibid., p. 337.
[45] Ibid., p. 338.

THE DEBATE OVER HẢI VÂN

Although historians have failed to take advantage of the insights into early Vietnamese communism illuminated by an examination of Hải Vân, the character has been at the center of a high-stakes debate in post-colonial Vietnam over Vũ Trọng Phụng's famously enigmatic political orientation. The intensity of this debate has been enhanced by the fact that Vũ Trọng Phụng's premature death in 1939 undermined the "normal" deliberative process by which communist cultural officials have judged late colonial-era writers and their work.[46] When the debate over Vũ Trọng Phụng began in northern Vietnam during the 1950s, the key element of this process was an unabashedly political assessment of the extent to which colonial-era writers had come to sympathize with the communist-led Việt Minh during the August Revolution (1945) and the anti-French Resistance (1946-1954). The work of talented writers who supported the Việt Minh tended to be categorized as "realist" (hiện thực) or "critical realist" (hiện thực phê phán), taught in school, and selectively republished. The work of writers who opposed the Việt Minh, on the other hand, was classified pejoratively as "romanticism" (chủ nghĩa lãng mạn), "naturalism" (chủ nghĩa tự nhiên), "Trotskyism" (chủ nghĩa Tờ-rốt-kít), or "reactionary literature" (văn học phản động) and pulled from circulation. Hence, Phụng's death—six years before the August Revolution—rendered irrelevant the regime's primary instrument for judging his work. This left the writer's reputation more or less up for grabs when communist cultural officials in the early 1950s began the bureaucratic process of determining which writers to include in the regime's modern literary canon.

Vũ Trọng Phụng's ambiguous official standing was unfortunately clarified in 1956 when intellectuals connected to the quasi-dissident literary movement known as Nhân Văn Giai Phẩm (a kind of northern Vietnamese "Hundred Flowers" movement) launched a low-key campaign to commemorate the writer and republish his work.[47] As part of an effort to link Phụng's famous critique of political and economic injustice in colonial Indochina with their own agitation on behalf of a more open society in post-colonial Vietnam, the leaders of Nhân Văn Giai Phẩm also published a collection of testimonials to the writer—provocatively entitled "Vũ Trọng Phụng Is With Us" (Vũ Trọng Phụng Với Chúng Ta).[48] It is no surprise, therefore, that the repression of Nhân Văn Giai Phẩm later in the decade—marked by the jailing of its leaders, the punishment of its followers, and the public denigration of the liberalizing ideals that it gently promoted—sealed Vũ Trọng Phụng's official reputation as a counter-revolutionary. This was followed by the banning of his work for twenty-five years in northern Vietnam, and throughout the country after 1975, until the onset of Renovation in the mid-1980s.

It was in the context of this broader conflict that the debate over Hải Vân initially unfolded. According to the Nhân Văn Giai Phẩm poet Hoàng Cầm, the barely audible opening salvo of the debate occurred during the early 1950s and took

---

[46] I am referring exclusively to prose fiction, as poetry seems to have been subjected to a slightly different critical regime.

[47] For a recent history of Nhân Văn Giai Phẩm, see Kim Ninh, *A World Transformed: The Politics of Culture in Revolutionary Vietnam, 1945-1965* (Ann Arbor: University of Michigan Press, 2002), pp. 121-63.

[48] Đào Duy Anh, Hoàng Cầm, Phan Khôi, Sỹ Ngọc, Nguyễn Mạnh Tường, Văn Tâm, and Trương Tửu, *Vũ Trọng Phụng Với Chúng Ta* (Hanoi: Minh Đức, 1956).

the form of a "whispering campaign" by orthodox cultural critics about the absence of a sufficiently revolutionary "viewpoint" (lập trường) in Vũ Trọng Phụng's work.[49] In 1957, this position was amplified in print by the historian Văn Tân who argued that Vũ Trọng Phụng's "descriptions of communist characters must be considered a failure since they emphasize all sorts of strange behavior and fail to reflect the truth."[50] Turning to the case of Hải Vân, Văn Tân complained that "this secretive old man is more like a hooligan who specializes in kidnapping and blackmail than a revolutionary leader of the masses."[51] To make matters worse, Văn Tân insisted that Vũ Trọng Phụng's portrayal of Hải Vân as "a fortune-teller and a blackmailer" must be understood as a reflection of the writer's "real attitude towards communism."[52]

Phụng's defenders responded immediately. In a book-length study of the writer published that same year, a brilliant twenty-three-year-old scholar and sympathizer with Nhân Văn Giai Phẩm named Văn Tâm (not to be confused with Văn Tân) argued that Phụng's admittedly problematic portrayal of Hải Vân was forgivable because he was writing during a period when the communist movement operated underground and hence "he had not yet been taught clearly about communist morality."[53] Moreover, Văn Tâm pointed out that Hải Vân was still portrayed in the novel as a "virtuous" figure who was "pure, charitable, knowledgeable, brave, wise, resourceful and dashing."[54] Hence, the characterization of Hải Vân signified to Văn Tâm that Vũ Trọng Phụng supported and admired communism, despite suffering from a basic ignorance about its true nature.

A similarly narrow defense was put forward by the famous novelist Nguyên Hồng in an introduction to a new edition of The Storm published in 1958. As did Văn Tâm, Nguyên Hồng accepted the orthodox position that Hải Vân represented "an inaccurate portrayal of a revolutionary character since he is brutal and vague about the consequences of his actions."[55] But again, Hồng excused this as a sin of ignorance rather than malice: "Vũ Trọng Phụng did not grasp the truth of the revolution, did not live the revolutionary struggle, and did not understand the revolutionary road. Because he did not enjoy a firm and intelligent vantage point from which to observe the revolution led by the working class under the scientific light of Marxism-Leninism—his pen could not bring it to life."[56] With this shortcoming dutifully acknowledged, Nguyên Hồng went on to insist that Vũ Trọng Phụng's Hải Vân was nevertheless meant to "idealize" (lý tưởng hóa) and "sensationalize" (siêu thường hóa) the communists, not to belittle them.

---

[49] Interview with Hoàng Cầm. Hanoi, December 22, 1999.

[50] Văn Tân, "Vũ Trọng Phụng Qua Giông Tố, Vỡ Đê Và Số Đỏ" (Vũ Trọng Phụng through The Storm, The Dike Breaks, and Dumb Luck), Văn Sử Địa 29 (June, 1957): 19.

[51] Ibid.

[52] Ibid.

[53] Văn Tâm, Vũ Trọng Phụng: Nhà Văn Hiện Thực (Vũ Trọng Phụng: realist writer) (Hanoi: Kim Đức, 1957), p. 129.

[54] Ibid., p. 130.

[55] Nguyên Hồng, "Vũ Trọng Phụng Và Những Tác Phẩm Của Anh" (Vũ Trọng Phụng and his work), in Vũ Trọng Phụng, Giông Tố (Hanoi: Văn Nghệ, 1956), p. 16.

[56] Ibid.

The hair-splitting clarifications of Phụng's defenders were no match for the crude counter-attack launched by orthodox critics and spearheaded by politburo member Hoàng Văn Hoan—one of the dozen most powerful officials in the new regime. In a remarkably detailed twenty-page essay circulated internally and entitled "Thoughts on the Problem of Vũ Trọng Phụng Within Vietnamese Literature," Hoan ignored Hải Vân's heroic role in the novel and denounced him as "a hooligan," "a swindler," and "an adulterer" who was "uncouth," "cynical," "immoral," "decadent," and "perverse."[57] Reiterating Văn Tân's position that this "distorted view" represented the writer's "true attitude" towards communism, Hoàng Văn Hoan accused Vũ Trọng Phụng of "hating and slandering the revolution through the image of Hải Vân" and of cynically purveying literature that was "degenerate" and "opportunistic." The essay concluded with an awesome barrage of attacks and insinuations, including charges that Phụng was a hooligan, a pornographer, and an agent of the French secret police.

Hoàng Văn Hoan's hysterical denunciation of Vũ Trọng Phụng triggered an immediate ban on the writer's work; it was excised from literary anthologies, eliminated from school textbooks, and pulled from library shelves.[58] Moreover, Hoan's case against Hải Vân set the tone for all critical treatments of the character for over a generation. For example, in his widely used textbook on modern Vietnamese literature published in 1964, the literary critic Vũ Đức Phúc wrote that Vũ Trọng Phụng "pretended to praise revolutionaries through Hải Vân but that this character is, in fact, nothing but a duplicitous hooligan who leads an extremely corrupt private life. He is unlike a real revolutionary in every way and reveals little more than Vũ Trọng Phụng's bourgeois view-point."[59] Needless to say, the unavailability of Phụng's work for almost twenty-five years served to enhance the authority of this characterization, especially among young readers who were unable to compare the novel itself with the book described by its shrill critics.

The pendulum swung back in 1986 when the Renovation policy loosened the Party's grip on intellectual life and permitted a partial reassessment of the regime's cultural and literary canons. Vũ Trọng Phụng's case was taken up immediately by a small group of progressive-minded literary scholars that included Lại Nguyên Ân, Nguyễn Hoành Khung, Nguyễn Đăng Mạnh, Hoàng Thiếu Sơn, and Trần Hữu Tá. Not only did they help secure permission to republish gradually much of Phụng's work, but they put forward a case for his political rehabilitation that included an effort to deal with his famously problematic portrayal of Hải Vân.

---

[57] "Một vài ý kiến về vấn đề tác phẩm Vũ Trọng Phụng trong văn học Việt Nam" (Thoughts on the problem of Vũ Trọng Phụng's work in Vietnamese literature) was first published in 1994 in *Vũ Trọng Phụng--Con Người và Tác Phẩm* (Vũ Trọng Phụng—life and works), ed. Nguyễn Hoành Khung and Lại Nguyên Ân (Hanoi: Hội Nhà Văn, 1994), pp. 219-45.

[58] The events leading up to the ban on Phụng's work are described in numerous accounts. See especially Bùi Huy Phồn, "Nhớ Và Nghĩ Về Vũ Trọng Phụng" (Recalling and reflecting on Vũ Trọng Phụng), in *Báo Người Hà Nội* 79 (July 1, 1988): 3; and Nguyễn Hoành Khung, "Nhìn Lại Và Suy Nghĩ Xung Quanh một 'Vụ án' Văn học" (Reviewing and reconsidering a literary "case"), in *Vũ Trọng Phụng: Tài Năng Và Sự Thật* (Vũ Trọng Phụng : Genius and truth), ed. Lại Nguyên Ân (Hanoi: Văn Học, 1997), pp. 19-52.

[59] Vũ Đức Phúc, *Sơ Thảo Lịch Sử Văn Học Việt Nam, 1930-1945* (Historical sketch of Vietnamese literature, 1930-1945), (Hanoi: Văn Học, 1964), p. 143.

Although the Renovation scholars had not been active in the now legendary intellectual struggles of the 1950s (most were of a slightly later generation), their arguments resemble the narrow and stunningly unsuccessful defense of Hải Vân that the members of Nhân Văn Giai Phẩm had launched decades earlier. This resemblance is clearly apparent in Nguyễn Đăng Mạnh's essay "Re-reading *The Storm*," which opens with the familiar gambit of conceding the "absolute inaccuracy" of Phụng's portrayal of Hải Vân."[60] It then cites the mitigating fact that Vũ Trọng Phụng was "never a member of the Communist Party" as grounds for a partial exoneration. And it concludes by casting the admittedly "false" (*không đúng*) depiction of Hải Vân in a positive light, describing it as a naive but well-intentioned attempt to "idealize, romanticize, and sensationalize" the communist leadership. Mạnh adds several refinements to this tired defense, such as pointing out analogous shortcomings in the pre-Revolutionary verse of the great communist poet Tố Hữu, but his basic argument remains firmly indebted to the rickety case put forward thirty-years earlier by Nhân Văn Giai Phẩm.

HẢI VÂN AND THE POPULAR FRONT

Vietnamese critics tend to view the contest over Hải Vân as a titanic conflict over literature and politics, but what is most remarkable about the debate is its cramped, limited character. Both sides have focused narrowly on what Hải Vân reveals about Vũ Trọng Phụng's attitude towards communism to the exclusion of all other issues. Neither side has entertained the possibility that Hải Vân may not offer a transparent window into Vũ Trọng Phụng's fundamental political identity. And no discussion has taken place about the intellectual validity of the Party's crudely political standards for judging literature. Such limitations are understandable, given the fact that intellectual debate in post-Renovation Vietnam remains subject to the draconian policing of the Party. More surprising, however, has been the durability of a shared assumption that Vũ Trọng Phụng's political commitments should be seen as a static entity that changed little over the course of his life. Whereas Phụng's detractors have seen him as an essentially "anticommunist" writer, his supporters argue that an intense admiration for communism was equally fundamental to his thinking and identity. The essentializing quality of these characterizations reflects the strident, which-side-are-you-on polemics that dominated intellectual life in northern Vietnam during the revolution and war years and that continue to shape critical discourse today. However, a close examination of (1) the historical context in which *The Storm* was written and (2) Hải Vân's strangely incomplete integration into the novel suggests that both sides of the debate may have misconstrued the way in which the character reflects Vũ Trọng Phụng's political thinking. For when these factors are taken into account, the portrayal of Hải Vân appears to convey less about Vũ Trọng Phụng's enduring ideological commitments and more about the giddy but extremely short-lived optimism with which many Vietnamese greeted the electoral victory of the left-leaning Popular Front government in France—a victory that, not incidentally, coincided precisely with the publication of *The Storm*.

Formed through an alliance of Socialists, Radicals, and Communists, the Popular Front government took power during the middle of 1936 and immediately

---

[60] Nguyễn Đăng Mạnh, "Đọc Lại Giông Tố," in *Tạp Chí Văn Học*, February 1990.

transformed the political climate throughout the French Empire.[61] Hopes for a wide-ranging reform of colonial administration soared in Indochina as the new government promised to release political prisoners, relax press censorship, and enact a comprehensive labor code. This atmosphere of hopeful anticipation deepened with the appointment of Marius Moutet, an outspoken critic of colonial repression, to head the Ministry of Colonies. For many Vietnamese who followed the campaign pledges and early policy initiatives of the new government, it appeared that a confluence of international left-wing forces—embodied by the Popular Front—was poised to overturn decades of colonial oppression. The result was an intense rage for Populism and Leftism in the colony during the middle of the year, even among the previously most conservative and elitist elements of the Vietnamese upper-classes. These hopes, however, proved short-lived. By late 1936, the Popular Front had abandoned most of the reforms promised in its colonial platform, and the wave of optimism that had surged through Vietnamese society earlier in the year gave way to widespread disillusion.[62]

It is tempting to view the collective hopes pinned on the Left in the wake of the Popular Front victory as the key historical precondition for Vũ Trọng Phụng's portrayal of Hải Vân as a *deus ex machina* who abruptly materializes and resolves the plot of *The Storm*. This interpretation of the historical context that gave rise to Hải Vân finds additional support in a rarely acknowledged aspect of the structure of the novel.[63] Hải Vân's sudden appearance, two-thirds of the way through *The Storm*, radically reorients the focus of the narrative from the consequences of the rape of Thị Mịch to Hải Vân's vengeful and politically motivated plotting against the wicked capitalist Nghị Hách. There are at least two reasons why this narrative U-turn is remarkable. The first is the absence of even the slightest foreshadowing, during the earlier phase of the narrative, that Hải Vân exists and will soon intervene to turn upside-down the lives of the novel's main characters. The second is the vanishing-act of Thị Mịch, who does not appear in the novel's final eight chapters. The disappearance of Thị Mịch is especially striking since there is reason to believe that Vũ Trọng Phụng had once intended to make her story the centerpiece of the narrative. Beginning with the eleventh chapter of the original serialized version in *Hanoi Newspaper*, her name—*Thị Mịch*—actually displaces *The Storm* on the newspaper's masthead as the title of the novel.[64]

When seen in the light of the novel's jarringly fractured structure and unstable title, the precise timing of the publication of *The Storm*'s serialized chapters

---

[61] The most detailed treatment of the impact of the Popular Front victory on the political climate in Indochina is Daniel Hémery, *Révolutionnaires vietnamiens et pouvoir colonial en Indochine: communists, trotskystes, nationalistes à Saigon de 1932 à 1937* (Paris: Maspero, 1975), pp.277-424.

[62] A useful treatment is *French Colonial Empire and the Popular Front: Hope and Disillusion*, ed. Tony Chafer and Amanda Sackur (London: Macmillan, 1999).

[63] The following reflections on the relationship between the election of the Popular Front and the narrative structure of *The Storm* are anticipated but not fully fleshed out by Thiều Quang in "Vũ Trọng Phụng: Đời Sống và Con Người" (Vũ Trọng Phụng: the man and his life), first published in the Hanoi occasional journal *Tập San Phê Bình—số đặc biệt* (October1957): 23-24.

[64] See the note on the publishing history of the novel in *Vũ Trọng Phụng—Toàn Tập, Tiểu Thuyết: Dứt Tình, Giông Tố, Vỡ Đê* (Vũ Trọng Phụng—the complete works, the novels: *Break up, The storm, The dike breaks*) (Hanoi: Hội Nhà Văn, 1999), p. 147.

raises the real possibility that Vũ Trọng Phụng may have modified the subject of the novel in mid-stream as a direct response to the electoral victory of the Popular Front. Chapters one through ten, which foreground Thị Mịch and provide no inkling that Hải Vân's arrival is imminent, came out between January 2, 1936 and March 18, 1936—months before the election that ushered the Popular Front into power. For reasons that remain obscure, *Hanoi Newspaper* ceased publication of the novel for seven weeks following the appearance of chapter ten, but started up again with chapter eleven three days after the Popular Front's stunning electoral victory on May 3. Chapters eleven through twenty, which continue the narrative flow established in chapters one through ten, came out in May and June—a two-month transition period during which the new administration in Paris was being assembled. As suggested above, the Vietnamese intelligentsia was fixated during this period by a flurry of rumors and reports that the new government planned to reform colonial administration radically.

Given this atmosphere of hopeful anticipation, it is perhaps no coincidence that the official formation of the Popular Front government in July 1936 coincided with the publication of chapter twenty, in which Hải Vân makes his first appearance and launches the narrative in a radically new and politically proactive direction. The remaining ten chapters, in which Hải Vân's story comes to the fore while Thị Mịch's fades away, were published from August to November, in the midst of the continuing euphoria that marked the heady, hopeful first months of the new regime in France. Although the evidence remains circumstantial, the temporal unfolding of the serialization of *The Storm* suggests that the dramatic victory of the Popular Front prompted Vũ Trọng Phụng to insert Hải Vân into a half-finished narrative that had not been initially assembled with his eventual intervention in mind. This justifies a view of Hải Vân as a remarkably literal offspring of the Popular Front victory. Indeed, it is difficult to imagine the appearance of Hải Vân without the relaxation of censorship triggered by the rise of the new government or the temporary onset of a belief among the Vietnamese intelligentsia that a global confluence of Leftist forces was poised to deliver Indochina from its colonial predicament.

A brief perusal of Vũ Trọng Phụng's writing soon after the publication of *The Storm* shows the writer moving away from the utopian Leftist politics embodied by Hải Vân. Although *The Dike Breaks* (1936-37) and an unfinished novella entitled *The Prisoner is Released* (1939) disclose some sympathy for the plight of Leftist political prisoners, other works reject the faddish Leftist-Populism that overcame elite Vietnamese circles in the wake of the Popular Front victory.[65] Indeed, this is the major theme of Phụng's satirical masterwork *Dumb Luck*, which he began serializing in *Hanoi Newspaper* immediately following the conclusion of *The Storm*. More significantly, Phụng published a withering critique of the Moscow show trials in 1937 and a bitter satire of Vietnamese Stalinist discourse in 1938—journalistic pieces (unmediated by the conventions of fiction) that indicate clearly that his flirtation with the Left was short-lived.[66] This fickleness is not

---

[65] *Người Tù Được Tha* (The prisoner is released) was published only after his death.

[66] Vũ Trọng Phụng wrote a three-part article on the Moscow show trials for *Đông Dương Tạp Chí*, issues 20 (September 25, 1937), 21 (October 3, 1937), and 22 (October 10, 1937)) entitled "Nhân Sự Chia Rẽ Của Đệ—Tam Và Đệ—Tứ: Ta Thử Ngó Lại Cuộc Cách Mệnh Cộng Sản ở Nga Từ Lúc Khởi Thủy Cho Đến Ngày Nay" (The schism between the third and fourth international: Reviewing the communist revolution in Russia from its origins to today). On

surprising given his youth, his omnivorous curiosity about the world around him, and the alacrity with which the local and global political situation waxed and waned during the late 1930s.

CONCLUSION

The analysis of Hải Vân presented in this essay sheds light on two important issues within Vietnamese cultural and political history. On the long-vexed question regarding what Hải Vân reveals about Vũ Trọng Phụng's politics, this essay has suggested that the character may not provide a transparent window into the writer's political orientation. Just as the heroic portrayal of Hải Vân in *The Storm* contradicts the claims of conservative critics that the character reflects Vũ Trọng Phụng's essential hostility towards communism, the extraordinary political moment during which Hải Vân was created (coupled with the political thrust of Phụng's subsequent writing) undermines efforts to read the character as an embodiment of the writer's enduring admiration for the Party. Indeed, the extreme historical contingency of Vũ Trọng Phụng's portrayal of Hải Vân exposes the intellectual poverty of the Party's coercive insistence that all modern historical figures must possess a single, clearly defined political "view-point" (*lập trường*).

A second concern of this essay has been to determine what Vũ Trọng Phụng's Hải Vân reveals about popular perceptions of Vietnamese communism during the mid-1930s. Perhaps most striking, given the intensity of the Party's subsequent efforts to naturalize an historic affiliation between Vietnamese communism and Vietnamese nationalism, is the degree to which these forces are seen as mutually antagonistic. Hải Vân's bitter hostility to nationalism is all the more remarkable since it violated the spirit of the new Comintern line (which advocated the formation of nationally based popular fronts). This contradicts a common claim that the role of the Comintern within the history of Vietnamese communism was to pressure a "naturally" nationalist ICP to subdue its true aspirations and begrudgingly embrace an internationalist Marxist project.[67] In *The Storm*, on the other hand, Vietnamese communism is seen as essentially compatible with internationalism, not nationalism.

In addition, the portrayal of Hải Vân clashes with the conventional image of the early Vietnamese communist leadership that emerged with the consolidation of the communist state during the mid-1950s and exhibited a Stalinist preoccupation with modernity, science, moral rectitude, and lower-class origins. In contrast, Vũ Trọng Phụng's portrayal of Hải Vân suggests a Party rooted in the traditional scholar-gentry, animated by quasi-supernatural prowess and prophetic knowledge, and marked by an amoral instrumentalism and an indulgent attitude towards sensual pleasure.

August 4, 1938, he published an article in *Tiểu Thuyết Thứ Năm* entitled "Đả Đảo Tên Tờ-Rốt-Kýt Huỳnh Văn Phương: Lời Hiệu Triệu Của Một Tay Sịt-Ta-Li-Nít" (Down with Trotskyist punk Huỳnh Văn Phương: The slogan of a Stalinist) that satirized the bitter conflict between Vietnamese Stalinists and Trotskyists.

[67] This argument often find supports in indirect evidence, such as the fact that The Comintern once forced the Vietnamese Communist Party to change its name to the (less nationalist) Indochinese Communist party. While suggestive, such evidence is hardly conclusive as the countervailing case of Hải Vân demonstrates.

Of course, the views and disposition of a single fictional character represent an admittedly thin reed on which to hang generalizations about the nature of "public opinion," much less to draw conclusions about what late colonial-era Vietnamese communism was really like. However, there are several reasons why Vũ Trọng Phụng's depiction of Hải Vân may have enjoyed a widespread influence. As the inter-war intelligentsia's most ardent proponent of both "realism" and non-fiction reportage, Vũ Trọng Phụng took pains to ground his fictional writing in insights gained from primary research and first-hand observation.[68] Given the public's familiarity with his working methods, it is reasonable to assume that readers understood Phụng's description of Hải Vân as an indirect product of his journalistic research. Moreover, the fact that Vũ Trọng Phụng never joined the ICP or any political party and authored an array of items and editorials that offered an indiscriminate mix of praise and criticism for the communist movement endows his writing with a measure of political objectivity. Finally, it seems significant that numerous elements of Hải Vân's biography dovetail with what subsequent historical research has confirmed about the inter-war leadership of the ICP.

Given the paucity of dispassionate scholarship about early Vietnamese communism, a definitive assessment of the historical accuracy of Hải Vân is not currently possible. However, the striking discrepancies between Vũ Trọng Phụng's contemporaneous portrayal of Hải Vân and the official view of early Vietnamese communists put forward retrospectively by the Party (and reflexively adopted in much of the secondary scholarship) indicates, at least, that many of the most basic issues within the history of Vietnamese communism have yet to be adequately settled.

---

[68] The relationship between Vũ Trọng Phụng's nonfiction reportage (*phóng sự*) and his novels is explored extensively in Trần Đăng Thao, "Đóng Góp Của Vũ Trọng Phụng Đối Với Lịch Sử Văn Học Việt Nam Hiện Đại, Trong Lĩnh Vực Phóng Sự Và Tiểu Thuyết" (Vũ Trọng Phụng's contribution to modern Vietnamese literature in the area of reportage and novels) (Phó Tiến Sĩ Dissertation, Đại Học Quốc Gia Hà Nội, 1996).

MOVE OVER, MADONNA: LUANG WICHIT WATHAKAN'S *HUANG RAK HAEW LUK*

Thak Chaloemtiarana

Luang Wichit Wathakan's best-selling novel, *Huang Rak Haew Luk* (Sea of love, chasm of death),[1] addresses three major themes: modernity, nationalism, and gender. Prior to the novel's publication in 1949, Luang Wichit was well known both as the architect of modern Thai nationalism and, perhaps equally importantly, as the dramatist who popularized militant feminism. In his plays (1936-1940), upper-class Thai women took up arms to fight alongside their men in wars of liberation.[2] Luang Wichit even made these women instigators of uprisings against foreign enemies who had subjugated the Thai. With *Huang Rak Haew Luk*, however, Luang Wichit went beyond the notion of nationalistic militant feminism to break new ground: common and lower-class women offer a new, exciting, and international model of the modern militant Thai woman.

But before examining this important novel, it is useful to review briefly Luang Wichit's long career as a government official, diplomat, educator, and writer. Born

---

[1] Luang Wichit Wathakan, *Huang Rak Haew Luk* (Sea of love, chasm of death) (Bangkok: Sangsan Press, 1999). In the foreword of the first edition (Phloenchit Press, 1949) written on February 7, 1949, Luang Wichit writes: "I compare a *haew luk* or deep chasm to the *huang rak* or sea of love because everyone is ready to jump into the sea of love even though it is dangerous. Water flows clear in the sea but one can die if one drinks it. Likewise, love entices us to taste and to drink from it. But in fact, to indulge in the sea of love is no different from descending into a deep chasm where a hasty fall will prove deadly. One should descend carefully because once in the chasm and danger rears its head, it is too late to climb out." The novel was originally published in twenty-six installments totaling 3,229 pages. The reprint cited here comes in four volumes and uses finer print totaling 1,461 pages. The entire novel was written in less than five months. The first printing sold an average of 15,026 copies per installment, which translates to about 390,000 books sold. The author boasts that there is insufficient space in the National Library to shelve the number of books sold. Luang Wichit also claims in the preface to the second edition that the novel has been mentioned in parliamentary speeches, university debates, in exhibitions, etc. He claims that because of the novel's popularity the public must surely accept the novel's leading character, Praphimphan, as the exemplar of the modern Thai woman.

[2] See Scott Barme, *Luang Wichit Wathakan and the Creation of a Thai Identity* (Singapore: Institute of Southeast Asian Studies, 1993), especially pp. 119-31.

as Kimliang Watthanaparuda to a poor family in Uthaithani Province in 1898, Luang Wichit received a Buddhist education as a novice, but was only briefly a monk.[3] He exhibited early promise as a writer and thinker as a student at Wat Mahathat in Bangkok when he topped the nation in the fifth-level Parian Pali examinations. Luang Wichit taught himself English and French, a feat that alarmed his superiors because monks were prohibited from learning foreign languages for fear that they would be exposed to insidious foreign ideas. After spending only two months as a monk, he left to join the Ministry of Foreign Affairs in 1918. Two years later, he won through examination a post to the Siamese legation in France. There he continued his law and political science studies, but he was transferred to London before he was able to finish his studies. During his six years in Europe, Luang Wichit became friendly with Pridi and Luang Phibun, the two leaders of the People's Party that overthrew the absolute monarchy in 1932. He also married a French woman with whom he had two children, a fact that is not widely circulated.[4] Prior to 1932, Luang Wichit carefully navigated a career in the bureaucracy and was somewhat neutral and apolitical. He did not join the People's Party, but later became the ideological architect for nation-building, especially in the Phibun and Sarit governments. He took his role as teacher and nation builder seriously: all of his writing, including his plays and his novels, is overtly didactic.[5]

Although he was fascinated by modern ideas, Luang Wichit was able to promote the construction of the modern Thai state by exploiting its past. In spite of accusations that he took many liberties when writing Thai history, it is undeniable

---

[3] For a detailed biography, see Luang Wichit's cremation volume, *Khana Ratthamontri, Wichitwathakan Anusorn*, September 16, 1962. When asked about his own racial background, Luang Wichit denied that he was part Chinese. He insisted that his Chinese first name was a popular convention at the time. This may be plausible because I know of several relatives whose names began with the Chinese "Kim," which means "gold." They, too, deny any ties with the Chinese. Of course, another explanation is that the pressure to be accepted as Thai was so intense that most local-born ethnic Chinese, or those who have lived for generations in Siam, do not want to identify themselves with the Chinese. More recently, of course, ethnic Chinese who are called "Jek" insist that they are not really Chinese "Jin," but a new hybrid of Thai and Chinese that is really "Thai." Is it plausible that Luang Wichit's fixation with race and pure blood lines reflects his own insecurities?

[4] Luang Wichit married his French teacher, with whom he had two children. They were divorced in 1933. This little-known fact may explain his gender bias when it came to the consideration of Thai conversion. Women can become Thai when married to a Thai man, but a foreign male can never become Thai. Barme, *Luang Wichit Wathakan and the Creation of a Thai Identity*, p. 43.

[5] Luang Wichit's first books focused on world history, biographies of great men, Thai history, and self-improvement. He authored forty-nine books that can be classified under this category. Later, during the height of the nation-building campaign in the early 1930s, he turned to writing semi-historical plays which were successful in providing a "foundational" knowledge of popular history for his Thai audience. All in all, he penned about twenty-four plays. Luang Wichit also lectured on law and history at both Chulalongkorn and Thammasat Universities. He prided himself on being an intellectual and academic and published no less than twenty-four volumes of his lecture notes. Incredibly, Luang Wichit also found the time to write *eighty-four* short stories and novels. Most of his novels focused on how people can struggle against all odds and win; for instance, one of his later novels, *Sang Chiwit* (Building a life) (published posthumously in 1971) chronicled the struggle of a peasant girl against the injustices of society. In that novel, Luang Wichit addresses the controversial issue of class exploitation and the urban-rural divide.

that he left a lasting imprint on how Thais view their past and how that view has influenced their self-understanding. Luang Wichit was the ideologue behind the post-1932 nationalism campaign under the Phibun regime. He wrote academic texts, essays, speeches, plays, songs, and official state proclamations that established new values for Thai society. His imaginative mind helped to promote a belief in the primacy of the state, the immutability of the Thai race, the necessity of militarism, and the worship of historical personalities as national heroes and heroines. He was one of the first to insist that the word "Thai" means "to be free" or "independent," and he made sure that only those who were willing to sacrifice their lives for the nation were recognized as Thai heroes and heroines.

Luang Wichit was, however, selective in his choice of examples of the heroic deeds of past kings and the royals—the good royals such as Ramkhamhaeng and Naresuan who fought against foreign enemies to protect Thai independence. He believed that Sukhothai embodied the essence of "Thai," an essence that became diluted and then polluted during the Ayuthaya period when the kings adopted Khmer forms of architecture and rituals. His didactic plays relied on national crises during the wars between Ayuthaya and Burma as settings. Because of his fascination with international politics, he also used his plays not only to promote nationalism, but to highlight other causes as well.[6] He deviated from the example of Prince Damrong, the acknowledged father of Thai history, when he reinterpreted Thai history to include heroic deeds of the common folk. Perhaps most importantly, Luang Wichit concluded that common Thai men *and women* also played important roles in protecting the nation.

As a playwright, Luang Wichit wrote ten plays between 1936 and 1940. His efforts coincided with the intense promotion of Thai nationalism. He emulated Rama VI's attempt to use performance and theater to establish a more cultured

---

[6] Of his twenty-four major plays, the most influential were the nine that he wrote from 1936 to 1940. *Lued Suphan* (1936) promoted Japan's policy of pan-Asianism; *Ratchamanu* (1937) asserted that the Thai and the Khmer were the same people in order to support irredentist claims. *Chaoying Saen Wi* (1938) clearly advocated the idea that the Thai and Shan in Burma should unite to support pan-Thai claims; the play also reflected the playwright's fascination with Nazi Germany's policy of creating a new political entity based on race. *Prachao Krungthon* (1937) asserted that the Thai and Chinese were brothers. Luang Wichit wrote another ten plays between 1947 and 1949 in an attempt to make a living, for he had been forced out of government service immediately after the war. (He had served as the Thai ambassador to Japan during World War II. On his return to Siam he was accused of war crimes, tried in court, and ultimately acquitted, yet lost his position in government despite the acquittal.) He even formed his own theater company in 1947 to perform the ten plays that he wrote during this time. Luang Wichit wrote his last four plays, known as the "*Anuphab*" series, at the request of the nation's prime minister, Phibun, in his last-ditch attempt to revitalize his political leadership (1954-57); these plays lauded the prowess of Thai leaders. Phibun's successor, Sarit Thanarat, reaped the benefits of Wichit's last works as a playwright. For more detail, see Pisanu Sunthraraks, "Luang Wichit Wathakan: Hegemony and Literature," (PhD dissertation, University of Wisconsin-Madison, 1986); Charnwit Kasetsiri, "Latthi Chatniyom, Latthi Thahan/Nationalism and Militarism," in *Chomphon P. kap Kanmuang Thai Samai Mai* (Field Marshal Phibun and modern Thai politics), ed. Charnwit Kasetsiri et al. (Bangkok: Thammasat University Press, 1999), especially pages 389-92; Jiraporn Wiriyasakpan, "Nationalism and the Transformation of Aesthetic Concepts: Theatre in Thailand During the Phibun Period," (PhD Dissertation, Cornell University, 1992). Jiraporn outlines Luang Wichit's role in redefining Thai performances according to Western categories.

citizenry.[7] As a concept, culture or "*watthanatham*" had been only introduced into the Thai discourse on modernity or "*khwam thansamai*" in the 1930s. This discourse was also central to the fascist ideas of state and racial supremacy that were rampant in Europe. The refinement of culture was important to the Thai leadership, who believed that in order to escape the fate of their neighbors the Thai had to be recognized by Western powers as a "civilized/modern" people.[8] Wichit's early writings focused on "great men," mostly Europeans, and how they became prominent, as a way to demonstrate to his Thai readers how they could improve themselves: a civilized nation (*prathet siwilai*) could not be great unless its peoples were civilized. Nevertheless, the discourse of these early plays does not suggest that the Thai should emulate the West, but that certain achievements in science, technology, and culture, even though Western in form, are in fact indicators of modernity and high culture.

Luang Wichit's first play was called *Luk Ratthathammanun* (Children of the constitution). The play was a box-office disaster.[9] Sensing perhaps that his audience was not ready for theater based solely on modern, abstract themes, Luang Wichit subsequently wrote his first semi-historical drama, *Lued Suphan* (The blood of Suphan). The play *Lued Suphan* boldly pairs a Burmese military officer with a local Thai woman as unlikely lovers. Tragically, both are killed during the Burmese occupation of Ayuthaya. The heroic deeds of Duangchan, the play's heroine, also acknowledge the martial spirit of all Thai women. In the play, Duangchan in fact instigates the uprising against the Burmese invaders. Luang Wichit's second play became an instant hit. Ticket sales allowed him to build a theater and to buy sets and musical equipment. Recognizing the importance of culture, Luang Wichit had accepted the directorship of the newly created department of culture. He also founded the School for Performing Arts. It taught

---

[7] See Thamora Fishel, "Romances of the Sixth Reign: Gender, Sexuality, and Siamese Nationalism," in *Genders and Sexualities in Modern Thailand*, ed. Peter A. Jackson and Nerida M. Cook (Chiangmai: Silkworm Books, 1999), pp. 154-67. Fishel demonstrates that the use of plays to promote modern ideas and nationalism can be traced to Rama VI, and demonstrates that nationalistic ideas are promoted through "performance" in Thailand.

[8] See dialogue between Nai Mun and Nai Khong in Thak Chaloemtiarana, ed., *Thai Politics: Extracts and Documents* (Bangkok: Social Science Association of Thailand, 1977), pp. 270-73. The rationale of this dialogue suggests to the national audience that colonial powers are interested in a civilizing mission. Therefore, to escape being subjected to colonialism, the Thai must become civilized in the eyes of the West. To be civilized is to be modern, and the West represents both. Interestingly, one device that Luang Wichit used to show that Thai women were the equal of others was the promotion of a national beauty pageant. The first Miss Siam contest was held in 1936 as part of the Constitution Day celebrations. Contestants came from all over the kingdom, representing their provinces. Provincial beauty queens discard their traditional *chongkrabaen* style dress for the modern *phasin* at the national competition. Thai beauty queens became the model of the sophisticated modern Thai woman. See Suphatra Kohkitsuksakun, *Tamnan Kanprakuad Nangsao Thai* (History of the Thai beauty pageant) (Bangkok: Samnakphim Dokbia, 1993).

[9] During this period, other writers also wrote stories about valor and how citizens made sacrifices to protect the new state that was defined by its constitution. For example, Kulab Saipradit (pseudonym Siburapha) wrote a short story about a recently married young man who died trying to protect the new state from the Boworadet royalist forces that tried to re-establish the authority of the Crown in 1933. See Siburapha, *Lakon Ratthathammanun* (Farewell dear constitution) (Bangkok: Withawat Press, 1979). This short story was first published in *Thoed Ratthathammanun 2476* (Honor the 1933 constitution).

the usual subjects, but included music and theater on top of regular schoolwork. Conveniently, students from the school performed Luang Wichit's plays.[10]

Luang Wichit was also instrumental in influencing Thai historiography: female historical figures became accepted as national heroines. An obvious example is the somewhat controversial credit given to Thao Suranari.[11] He also wrote numerous nationalistic songs played over the radio, even though he did not know much about music. His plays and songs gave special emphasis to the heroism of common people, especially women, and the public readily embraced their ideas as historical truths.

Between 1939 and 1942, at the height of the nationalist campaign, Luang Wichit chaired a committee that drafted the famous State Convention proclamations known as *Ratthaniyom*.[12] These proclamations changed the country's name from "Siam," which was based on Chinese, to the more modern "Thailand," forced the public to salute the flag at 8 am every morning, to dress properly, to eat and exercise properly, and generally to behave as civilized people. The *Ratthaniyom* focused on ways to make Siam a "modern" state, one that must galvanize its citizens for war and colonial resistance. The *Ratthaniyom* campaign was reinforced by Luang Wichit's plays emphasizing the ideal characteristics necessary to build the modern nation. Many of these characteristics—daring and bravery, compassion, love of honor, love of duty, self-control, and perseverance—were, in fact, borrowed from Inazo Nitobe's *Bushido*, the Japanese code of the warrior.[13]

When the popularity of his plays declined in the late 1940s, Luang Wichit turned to writing novels as a way to reach the public.[14] After becoming established

---

[10] Wichitra Rangsiyanon, *Riang Thoy Roy Chiwit Wichitwathakan* (The life of Wichitwathakan) (Bangkok: Sangsan Books, 2000), especially chapters 3 and 4. This book, written by Luang Wichit's daughter, gives an inside look at his life and work habits. In particular, she describes the struggle her father had to go through to find funds to build Siam's first national theater. His first musical play was staged in what could be described as a tent. Its success brought badly needed revenues that helped build a proper theater. Luang Wichit was convinced that Rama VI was right to think that culture would change the Thai people. To find competent actors and musicians, he founded the Performance Arts School.

[11] Thao Suranari was the wife of the deputy governor of Khorat at the time of the Chao Anuwong rebellion in 1827. She was credited with helping to defeat the Laotian forces at the battle of Thung Samrit. Laotian historiography questions the accuracy of the story. For more on this subject see: Charles Keyes, "National Heroine or Local Spirit?," paper presented to the Sixth Annual Conference on Thai Studies, Chiangmai, October 14-17, 1996. Also, Thak Chaloemtiarana, "Towards a More Inclusive National Narrative," in *Luem Khotngao Ko Phao Phaendin* (Forget the past, torch the earth), ed. Kanchanee La-ongsi and Thanet Aphornsuwan (Bangkok: Matichon Press, 2000), pp. 76-82. Chetana Nagavajara argues that in order to promote gender equality in democratic Siam, women's historical status was re-examined. Some scholars contend that Thai women were quite powerful and held high status during the Sukhothai period, where historical evidence shows that the Queen was required to follow the King out to battle. In something of a parody of this ancient practice, Phibun's wife also took to dressing up in a military uniform and was in fact granted a commission. And during the 1940s when the National Culture Council was established, an active Woman's Department was also created. See Chetana Nagavajara, *Comparative Literature from a Thai Perspective* (Bangkok: Chulalongkorn University Press, 1996), pp. 185-87.

[12] For English translations of the Ratthaniyom documents, see Thak, *Thai Politics*, pp. 245-54.

[13] Barme, *Luang Wichit Wathakan and the Creation of a Thai Identity*, p. 87.

[14] Wichitra tells us that after Hollywood movies became popular and displaced live drama performances after the end of World War II, her father turned to writing novels instead. For a

as a novelist with *Morasum Haeng Chiwit* (A stormy life), he wrote his epic novel *Huang Rak Haew Luk*.[15] Here he projects his view of Thai women to a higher level. From being actors on the national and regional stage, Thai women are given new roles as important *international actors*. In this novel, Luang Wichit also blurs the lines of gender by showing how a Thai woman can be like a man and yet retain her femininity. As in his plays glorifying an imagined past, *Huang Rak Haew Luk* allowed the Thai to imagine new categories of roles that they could dream about fulfilling some day.

Such possibilities are suggested by what Benedict Anderson has identified as "unbounded seriality." According to Anderson, parochial and insular thinking could be replaced by new understanding of possible roles to play in real life that are open to the world and universal in application. For example, through exposure to modern print and performance media, people can begin to imagine that it is possible to assume new roles such as a Hollywood or local movie star, a national hero, a national heroine, a gun runner, a guerrilla fighter, a queen, or even a sophisticated international adventuress.[16]

Not surprisingly, Luang Wichit's model of the modern Thai woman differs radically from previous role models. Traditionally, the possibilities for a Thai woman could be said to derive from traditional literary models: Sita in the Indian epic, the *Ramayana/Ramakian*, Nang Wanthong in *Khun Chang Khun Phaen*, or Queen Jamathewi in *Jamathewiwong*. Surely, the idea of a traditional Thai woman as *"pha phab wai"* or a "neatly folded piece of cloth," presumably to be unfolded by whoever becomes her husband, must come from aristocratic ideas based on Hindu Buddhist beliefs embodied, for example, by Sita, Rama's consort in the Thai *Ramakian*. Scott Barme has also argued that the modern model of the Thai woman is found in the proto-feminist discourse around the mystical figure "Nang

---

brief history of Thai cinema, see Dome Sukwong and Sawasdi Suwannapak, *A Century of Thai Cinema*, trans. David Smyth (London: Thames & Hudson, 2001). So why did Luang Wichit finish his writing career as a "lowly" novelist? In the Thai book market, novels are sometimes referred to as *"nangsu aan len"*—"a book to read for fun"—meaning that they are not serious creative literary works. Although his daughter, Wichitra, tells us that Luang Wichit was able to make more money from his novels than from his salary as a Cabinet Minister, she asserts that her father did not write novels just to make money. More importantly, he told her that people should not look down on this lowly form of writing. In fact, as Luang Wichit reportedly told his daughter, novelists remain famous for eternity, unlike academic authors whose texts must undergo constant revisions to remain useful. New academic texts also make older texts obsolete. But writers such as Shakespeare and Molière remain current and are still taught in schools. Luang Wichit believed that the novel is a very potent form of teaching because people are influenced without realizing it. He went on to cite how history has been changed by the use of novels and plays that affected people's thinking and actions. Luang Wichit was convinced that literature is a powerful weapon for social engineering. See Wichitra, *Riang Thoy Roy Chiwit Wichitwathakan*, pp. 40-41.

[15] It should be noted that even though Luang Wichit was most proud of *Huang Rak Haew Luk* because it covered all of his favorite themes, recent scholars have favored his less lengthy novels. For example, the committee that wrote *Nangsu Di 100 Lem* (One hundred good books) (Bangkok: Samnakngan Kongthun Sanapsanun Kanwichai, 1999) did not select Luang Wichit's most famous novel, *Huang Rak Haew Luk*, nor was he cited for his popular plays. Instead, they picked *Sang Chiwit*, a later and much shorter novel by the author. In Pratheep Muannil, *100 Nak Praphan Thai* (One hundred Thai writers) (Bangkok: Suweeriyasan, 1999), Luang Wichit is cited for his voluminous production. Pratheep acknowledges that *Huang Rak Haew Luk* was one of Luang Wichit's most popular novels.

[16] Benedict Anderson, *The Spectre of Comparisons* (London: Verso Press, 1998), Chapter 1.

Noppamas," a fictional character dating back to thirteenth-century Sukhothai. This *"yod ying"* or supreme woman, he concludes, "was said to have possessed a rare combination of qualities: an agreeable disposition, a lustrous golden complexion (to which her name refers), and above all a keen intelligence and an outstanding ability as both a scholar and poet." According to Barme, in 1905 Thainwan, a controversial Thai thinker, became the first Thai intellectual to dare to write about the role of women in modern Siam.[17] Thainwan argued that women should be allowed to get an education equal to men, and that they should be allowed to work and contribute to the economic well-being of the country. He concludes that the modern Thai woman is one who is educated, graceful, civilized, progressive, and Western in orientation. Unfortunately, this view is incomplete.

Although space will not permit any discussion of the relevance of traditional and classic literature in a debate on gender, it may be most helpful to say that the construction of the modern Thai female identity is a contestation and amalgamation of several ideal types and "possibilities" suggested in popular plays, religious beliefs, traditional practices, lived experiences, and works of fiction. Due to its popularity, Luang Wichit's epic *Huang Rak Haew Luk* figures prominently among the mid-twentieth century literary works that focus on gender issues. And although more studies will have to be conducted to fully assess its impact, there can be no doubt that this novel played a major role in helping construct a new and more modern model of Thai feminism.[18]

---

[17] Scott Barme, "Proto-feminist Discourse in Early Twentieth-Century Siam," in *Genders and Sexualities in Modern Thailand*, ed. Jackson and Nerida, pp. 140-42. Luang Wichit also acknowledges a sense of gratitude for the bravery Thianwan displayed by speaking his mind. He wrote a short preface in 1951 for a book about Thianwan by Sangob Suriyin. See Sangob Suriyin, *Thianwan* (Bangkok: Ruansan Press, 2000). (This is the third edition of a book originally published in 1951.) In Scott Barme's most recent book, *Woman, Man, Bangkok* (Oxford: Rowman & Littlefield, 2002), he discusses the national debate regarding the social position of Thai women during the 1920s and beyond in great detail. Keeping this background in mind, we come to understand that Luang Wichit's literary production, especially his focus on women engaged in dangerous activities, must have been tempered by his exposure to the various exciting new "models" of Thai feminism being publicly tested even before the 1940s. For example, in 1931, several years before Luang Wichit wrote his nationalistic plays and novels celebrating Thai feminism, a startling short story entitled "Chon Chori" (The female bandit leader) appeared in the weekly *Suphab Nari* (Genteel Lady). The story portrays a young Thai woman as a notorious gang leader who plans and stages daring robberies. A picture of this masked female bandit (looking like the Lone Ranger), riding a horse and chasing a speeding car, appears on page 200 in Barme's book. Barme asserts that this early novel is an attempt to challenge the traditional role of the Siamese female and to replace this role model with a character who shows few signs of women's supposed weakness. During the same period, the magazine also serialized historic accounts of the exploits of Queen Suriyothai, who died in elephant combat in the sixteenth century, trying to save her husband, who was caught in a war between Ayutthaya and Burma. In 2001, her story was made into a multi-million dollar movie, funded by the Thai royal court. The movie took great liberties with historical accuracy and clearly conveyed the message that Thai women, both good and bad (albeit chiefly members of the aristocracy), played a pivotal role in statecraft and the many deadly struggles for political power. The film *Suriyothai* had its gala showing in the United States in October 2002, with the Thai Queen in attendance.

[18] As gender is a cultural construct, understanding literature can be one avenue that can give us a window into that culture. Literature not only reflects and expresses the features of culture, but it can also contest old values and propose new ones. See Thelma Kintanar, "Notes on Tradition and the Construction of Gender in Southeast Asian Literary Texts" in *Texts and Contexts: Interactions Between Literature and Culture in Southeast Asia*, ed. Luisa J. Mallari-

Observers of Thai society have marveled at how the Thai female can be portrayed as such a multi-faceted being. She is variously described as the *de facto* head of the family, a businesswoman, a sweet caring mother and wife (whose public demeanor downplays her sexuality), a day laborer, a beauty queen, a whore, a masseuse, a murderer, a nun, and so forth. In a recent study, Rachel Harrison argues that the contemporary public image of Thai women has been essentialized, so that Thai womanhood is represented by two opposite models Harrison calls the "Madonna and the Whore": whether a woman is good or bad depends on her relationship to the family as an institution.[19] Of course one problem with dividing things into two is that it slights the undistributed middle. In this case, a glance at Thai tabloids will reveal yet another possibility, one we may call the "Dangerous Woman."

Thai newspapers consistently exploit those who have loved and lost their lives as a result. Many of the headlines and front-page pictures show murder scenes where the victim is a male lover who has been shot. Other times, the reading public is treated to a picture of two lovers dead from gunshot wounds lying naked or semi-naked in bed. Another famous story that has been circulating among Thai males for several decades is the report of a woman who cut off her philandering husband's genitals and fed them to her ducks. The story is still discussed with much nervous humor among young men, but there is also a warning side to that story. Thai women do in fact commit such acts, but theirs seem not to be merely crimes of passion, but crimes calculated to punish. Therefore, not only are Thai women represented as the mysterious exotic beauties found on tourism posters, or as sexual objects advertised in sex tour brochures in Europe and Japan, they are also represented in the popular press as dangerous lovers.

The evidence is clear that Luang Wichit deliberately set out to create this new role for Thai women. In his preface to the second printing of *Huang Rak Haew Luk*, he asserts that the novel's heroine Praphimphan represents the new Thai woman: her imaginary life of love, lust, and murder provides lessons to the reading public

---

Hall (Quezon City: Department of English and Comparative Literature, University of the Philippines, 1999), p. 17. Gender is defined partly by social relations—the Asian woman is traditionally represented as wife, lover, mother, cook, etc. Women are expected to be gentle, nurturing, faithful, pragmatic, and not necessarily romantic.

[19] Rachel Harrison, "The Madonna and the Whore: Self/'Other' Tensions in the Characterization of the Prostitute by Thai Female Authors," in *Genders and Sexualities in Modern Thailand*, ed. Jackson and Nerida, pp. 168-90. To be fair, Harrison focuses mainly on sexuality and the sexual mores of Thai women. Most current research and writing is focused on traditional feminine roles as they relate to the family, the role of women in the economy, and/or the commodification of the female body in the sex trade. Much of the literature on the last topic explains feminism and sex in economic terms. For example: Virada Somsawasdi and Sally Theobald, eds., *Women, Gender Relations and Development in Thai Society* (Chiangmai: Women's Studies Center, Chiangmai University, 1997); Ryan Bishop and Lillian Robinson, *Night Market* (New York: Routledge, 1998); Andrea Whittaker, *Intimate Knowledge* (St. Leonards: Allen and Unwin, 2000); Jeremy Seabrook, *Travels in the Skin Trade* (London: Pluto Press, 1996); Cleo Odzer, *Patpong Sisters* (New York: Arcade Publishing, 1994); *Kankha Ying* (Trade in women), Report of the Thai Women's Foundation, 1997; Suleeman Wongsuphab, *Nang Ngarm Tu Krachok* [The beauty behind the glass case] (Bangkok: Khled Thai Press, 1987). More research is still needed on the effects of the media, popular culture, music, and popular literature on our understandings of what is feminine.

about how women can overcome their adversaries.[20] Indeed, the very structure of the novel divides neatly into three parts, each defined by Praphimphan's age and the setting. The first part is devoted to Praphimphan's early adult life in Siam and her studying and vacationing in Europe. The middle is devoted to Praphimphan's return to Siam, but with a twist: she remains on the periphery, on the Malay border, and, after committing still more crimes, goes into exile in Africa and Arabia. The last part concerns her recovery from insanity, her homecoming, and her death. Each of these three parts, moreover, has its own distinctive themes. What follows is a necessarily brief summary of the way Luang Wichit has interwoven these themes with the three narrative stages of Praphimphan's life.

I

The story of Praphimphan's early adult life prepares her for a future of international adventure and militant feminism. As the dutiful daughter of a retired, minor government employee whose wealth is dwindling fast, Praphimphan first leads a traditional life. She soon shows her independence, however, by secretly learning how to shoot her father's pistol and then, in an attempt to revenge a prank played on her father, challenging Thongthet, the son of a local notable, to a duel. He doesn't accept, but does fall in love with this daring woman, whose female charms and physical beauty will capture the hearts of many men throughout the novel. Amidst her feminine characteristics, Praphimphan also exhibits masculine identification marks—she likes to shoot and to challenge her tormentors to duels, enjoys drinking coffee (not done by Thai women at that time), and does not forgive those who have wronged her. She can be a nurturing woman with her friends, but a vengeful executioner of her enemies.

Refusing Thongthet's suit, she then moves away from home and takes a job in a factory, a job that represents a new opportunity for her generation of women (the same will be true when, later in the novel, she becomes employed as a legal aide). After again duping her father, Thongthet visits her to ask her to marry him. Pretending to fall for him, Praphimphan lures him into her bedroom and shoots him three times. She then convinces the police that he tried to rape her. In a Hobbesian twist, the weaker sex can kill the stronger when the man is blinded by love or lust.

Once more working as a housekeeper, Praphimphan must look after a family friend, Manote, who is recovering his health. While studying herbal medicine with Dr. Gautier, a French doctor in Vietnam, Manote had fallen in love with Waenfa, the lovely daughter of another French doctor and his Laotian wife. Unfortunately for their love affair, Waenfa had ingested so much poison during her father's medical experiments that she could not be his wife. When Manote kisses her anyway, he promptly falls into a coma. Here, Luang Wichit has created a female figure in all senses "poisonous." The story of Manote and Waenfa describes

---

[20] Wichitra tells us that the wives of soldiers stationed at the military camp in Prachinburi routinely ambushed the weekly shipments of the individual volumes that came by rail. To make sure that they would not miss an installment, they would hijack the books before they reached the book stores. Wichitra, *Riang Thoy Roy Chiwit Wichitwathakan*, p. 39. Luang Wichit also tells his readers in the preface of the second edition that he has heard from his many students now stationed as district officers throughout Siam that *Huang Rak Haew Luk* was read by people of all walks of life, from the governor down to the literate farmer.

the tension between love and passion, beauty and poison, modern and traditional medicine, and even Siam and colonialism. Underlining this theme of the novel, Dr. Gautier warns Manote about women: "All women are poisonous... They only differ in the kinds of poison they possess. Some are so poisonous that they kill us; some make us bankrupt; others make us their love slaves who can never be redeemed. Don't forget that the sea of love is the deep chasm of death. If you slip and fall you will not survive."[21] One can equally argue that Waenfa is an expression of a long-standing misogynistic view of women as polluting and negating man's inner strength. The Buddhist *tamnan* story of Queen Jamathewi, written in 1570 and recounting the story of the founding of Lamphun in the eleventh century, is a good case in point. Queen Jamathewi promised to marry a powerful suitor if he succeeded in throwing his spear from a mountaintop into her city. In one version of the story, the queen tricks her suitor into wearing a hat she had given him, smeared with her menstrual blood. The unclean blood drained the prince's power and his spear fell short of its target. Menstrual blood is seen as unclean and debilitating by men even in modern-day Thailand.

Praphimphan promptly extends this theme by telling Manote that she is more dangerous than the poisonous Waenfa because she was willing to kill—and, indeed, she already had killed—a man. It would be easy to kill someone she loves if that person betrays her love, she warns him: "Because I have never loved, love is sacred to me and must be worshipped. Before I admit to loving someone, I must think and rethink carefully. If I utter my love, I want that person to know that this is a grave matter. And the person whose love I accept will be courting danger."[22]

In a concession to tradition, however, Luang Wichit has their respective parents forbid their marriage and arrange a marriage for each of them. Defiantly, the two lovers vow to keep loving each other despite their spouses: status and "face," while still dominant in modern, democratic Siam, can be ignored and subverted. However, Manote becomes Praphimphan's second victim. After luring him into her bedroom while her husband is away, she shoots him for not upholding his end of their bargain.[23]

In a reverie later in the novel, we learn that just before Praphimphan decides to move with her father to live in the southern part of Siam, a backwater, she disguises herself, lures her husband into a dark alley, and executes him with her pistol. By the age of twenty-two, Praphimphan has become a dangerous woman: of the four men who have loved her, she has killed three. She even confesses humorously to her lawyer, Attaphit, one of the four men who is in love with her, that she has learned to be economical and not use more than two shots to kill her latest victim. She had emptied her gun when she shot her lover, Manote.

---

[21] Luang Wichit Wathakan, *Huang Rak Haew Luk*, p. 123.

[22] Ibid., p. 145.

[23] The novel actually begins with a meeting between Praphimphan's husband and her attorney, Atthaphit. The latter is defending her in a case of manslaughter. Praphimphan at first denied that she had indeed planned to murder Manote, who was her lover. And in a twist of logic, Praphimphan says that her real husband was in fact Manote, and that her relationship with her legal husband was an adulterous affair. But even after Atthaphit finds evidence that his client was indeed guilty, instead of pulling out of the case, he continues and wins her acquittal. Instead of condemning her, Atthaphit praises Praphimphan for being true to her love; he declares her to be a "one hearted woman/*phuying chai deaw*," and falls in love with her.

Following the death of Manote, Praphimphan's father tells her that he has received a large sum of money from Thaimchan and instead of staying in the south of Siam, he is taking Praphimphan to Europe to continue her studies.[24] In Singapore, Praphimphan encounters a nineteen-year-old Thai woman, Waewta, who asks to become her servant. Telling Praphimphan her life story, Waewta reveals that she is a poor villager who made a living selling seaweed, and that she, too, has been involved in a murder. Waewta is thus a younger version of Praphimphan. Together, they set off to explore Europe as a pair of kindred souls.[25]

Traditionally, studying in Europe was exclusively the prerogative of Thai men. That tradition continues in the novel, for the women's male friend Songwut accompanies them, but the journey of Praphimphan and Waewta clearly represents modern female emancipation. What this emancipation consists of is rather less clear, however: Luang Wichit is vague about their course of study. It is almost as though the Thai women are in Europe to learn English and see the world as a version of a "finishing school."

Songwut's role is also representative: he shows that the Thai are the equal of Europeans. Far from being unmistakably Thai, he is assumed to be a Persian prince! He is tall, smart, plays tennis well, and is a superb dancer. Most important, he is an accomplished speaker of English. He even has a brief affair with an older woman, a wayward European countess.

Perhaps because this "prince" is so *sympathique*, the countess unburdens herself to him regarding the nature of women, suggesting that pronouncements about gender are universal and not just Thai or European. The countess makes a series of observations about the nature of women and their relationship to men, especially husbands. She says emphatically that women are by nature verbal beings who need to have a good and sympathetic listener. Women do not want to be alone, but to be loved and appreciated. At one point she says, "Women do not want anything more than to be considered human beings. Women do not want equal rights to men. All they ask is to be allowed to have a life and the right to think for themselves."[26] She laments the fact that women are treated like pets and that men think they are only required to provide a woman with a nice house, food, money, and clothing. Women are expected to act like songbirds in a gilded cage and never escape into the wider world to enjoy themselves. But most women end up sacrificing their bodies out of duty to their husbands, which is no different than being raped. Men should not be so cruel, the countess says. Husbands and wives should be friends and equal partners, and it is the duty of husbands to listen to what their wives have to say. If they fail at this duty, wives may seek friendship elsewhere. It is even important

---

[24] In another twist of morality, Praphimphan's financial benefactor is Thiamchan, a woman who was having an affair with Atthaphit. Thiamchan poisoned Atthaphit's wife and tried to pin the crime on Praphimphan. Perhaps recognizing another kindred soul in the ruthless Thiamchan, who murdered for love, Praphimphan destroys evidence that would have incriminated Thiamchan. In fact, she wishes Thiamchan and Atthaphit well as she leaves Bangkok intent upon living a life in the countryside.

[25] Waewta was a village girl who, for dubious reasons, strangled the sick father of her future husband, Khwan. She wanted to help him inherit his father's fortunes that would otherwise have gone to his stepmother. At the time she committed the murder, she had no interest in Khwan and only agreed to marry him many years later after returning from Europe and at the insistence of Praphimphan. Thus, the murder was senseless at the time it was committed.

[26] Luang Wichit Wathakan, *Huang Rak Haew Luk*, p. 563.

to listen to women who are by nature worriers, the countess insists. Men think logically in terms of cause and effect, but women act on instinct, without concern for consequences. Women are not rational beings, but emotional ones. However, it is most important for men to forgive women for behavior that appears to be irrational.[27] Traditional (if not, perhaps, universal) as these assertions are, they have almost nothing to do with the way Praphimphan acts in this novel. They instead serve as a muted counterpoint, implicitly contrasting the traditionally passive role of Thai (and European) women with the far more compelling actions of Praphimphan.

This first part of the novel ends with a transition that frees Songwut from his sworn obligation to Praphimphan. After failing to win Praphimphan, Songwut falls in love with a half-German gypsy, Salome, who is soon given a new Thai name, Khomkham ("sharp and witty"). In short order, she finds a Thai language text in Rome and learns the language. Luang Wichit's Thai readers, of course, had no idea that this would have been preposterous; they presumably believed that Siam must be an important country and that foreigners would want to study Thai. By this device, Luang Wichit raised Thai to the level of French, Spanish, German, and English. By learning the language of her new lover, Khomkham discards her identity as Salome and becomes Thai. Believing that her husband still loves Praphimphan, she runs away, becomes sick and dies. Her "death"—she leaps into a gorge in the mountains—and "resurrection"—once she knows that Songwut loves her, she comes back to life—is symbolic: she dies a gypsy and is reborn a Thai.[28] Later, she even teaches her son Thai, a point the more telling because there is no real need to do so: she has left her Thai husband, has been reunited with her German father, and is living in South Africa. A woman can become Thai, but, as we shall notice later, a man cannot.

II

The middle of the novel concerns Praphimphan's return to Siam to live in a village near the Malay border and, after she commits still more crimes, her exile in Africa and Arabia. While she is living in the south in Waewta's village and learning to become a writer, her father tries to make her marry her first cousin,

---

[27] The countess had an affair with her husband's younger brother, which led to their divorce. During that divorce, she fell prey to her employer's sexual advances. But together with the employer's wife, she plotted his murder, which was ruled a suicide. In spite of her indiscretion and complicity in a murder, the countess pleads innocent. She acted the way she did because she was a woman who needed attention from her husband. This is not the only instance in the novel where a woman is allowed to have affairs just like men. However, the main differences are that they want to be forgiven if caught, and that they are willing and ready to kill any lovers who cross them. The countess also flirted with Songwut, and there is a suggestion that the two had a brief affair. According to Rachel Harrison, falling in love with European countesses is a common experience among *"hua nork"* (forward and outward looking) young men in Thai novels and constitutes a recurring theme. A similar theme appears in M. C. Akatdamkoeng Raphiphat's *Lakhon Haeng Chiwit* (Circus of life), (1929), one of the earliest Thai novels. Personal correspondence with Rachel Harrison, July 26, 2002.

[28] In fact, what her husband witnessed was a mirage. She had already "died," but her spirit was still roaming about. When her husband found her, he only met her spiritual body or *kayathip* that ran up the mountain to commit suicide by jumping into the *haew luk* (chasm of death).

Chuwong, who had recently divorced. Instead of doing so, Praphimphan befriends his ex-wife, Phuangrak. Their friendship highlights the theme of female solidarity, especially among Thai women. For example, when Phuangrak asks Praphimphan when they first meet if she, Phuangrak, can tell her life story, Praphimphan answers, "Thais do not have to stand on ceremony like the *farang* [Westerners], we are friends belonging to the same race and same nation [*phuen ruam chat ruam prathet*]. Also as friends of the same gender [*phuen ruam phet*], we can easily get to know each other."[29] This particular episode displays Luang Wichit's intention of creating gender solidarity among Thai women, and his interest in the potential of this new solidarity to liberate women from a traditional identity tied to the family and to the male; now a woman can, as a separate entity, bond with other females.

Being liberated, however, does not mean that the traditional concern for the family is eliminated. As Songwut had earlier reconciled the estranged countess and count, so here Praphimphan reconciles Phuangrak with her divorced husband. Luang Wichit still believed that the family is important and should be kept together, even in the face of the new tensions created by modernity.[30]

Set off against this reconciliation is the adultery of Waewta, married now to Khwan, a local farmer whose father she had murdered before setting off to study in Europe. Despite being warned by Praphimphan, Waewta begins an affair with Sirisin, a friend of Songwut's who has just returned from Europe, where he had received a doctorate in economics. Six days later, Sirisin is dead, killed by the jealous husband. Reprimanding Khwan for spying on his wife (but not, incidentally, for murdering her lover), Praphimphan reunites Khwan and Waewta, persuading them to promise that they will remain faithful to each other. This is the third time in the novel that a family is kept together or reunited.

Unfortunately, the police suspect correctly that Praphimphan has murdered Khwan's chauffeur, his accomplice in the murder of Sirisin, so Praphimphan must flee Siam yet again. Sailing solo east towards the Nicobar Islands, she encounters a storm, lashes herself to the mast as the winds engulf her small sailboat, and loses consciousness.

When she comes to, she finds herself in a large ship owned and captained by a nationalist, Supharat, a Mon-Malay gun runner from Tavoy, a territory once claimed by Siam. He tells her he saw her in Europe but was unable to introduce himself: he felt that as a British colonial subject he would be shunned by Asians who came from independent countries.[31] Praphimphan, of course, promptly replies that this distinction means nothing to her. In this novel, fellow Asians and

---

[29] Luang Wichit Wathakan, *Huang Rak Haew Luk*, p. 777.

[30] Phuangrak and Chuwong's divorce was the result of a senseless disagreement about how to treat a servant who had helped Chuwong when he was younger. Phuangrak wanted the maid to be more respectful and subservient, but her husband did not agree. It is not that he felt some obligation to show gratitude, but he believed that if "democratic" Siam was to survive, equality and dignity should be accorded to all citizens. If they were not, there was the danger of class warfare. Chuwong explains to his wife that "revolutions and mass unrest where poor people take over the mansions of the rich and kill their owners resulted from minor incidents such as this... All classes of people should be friends." Apparently, there is still some confusion about how to treat people of lower status in the new democratic Siam.

[31] Luang Wichit Wathakan, *Huang Rak Haew Luk*, p. 914.

nationalists figure as natural friends to the Thai, whose country has never been colonized.

When they go ashore in Tavoy after the weapons are unloaded, Praphimphan and Supharat are quickly spotted by the police. Rather than surrender, they return fire as they make their escape by boat. This action resonates with Luang Wichit's earlier plays, in which Thai women take up the sword to fight against foreign oppressors. Here, of course, swords are replaced by pistols, a modern weapon. Although Supharat is a "good" nationalist, he is not Thai, a factor that weighs with Praphimphan when he too falls in love with her. In contrast to Khomkham, a woman who became "Thai" because she and her son learned to speak the language, Supharat can only *act* like a Thai. As a man, he cannot become Thai.[32]

Praphimphan and Supharat make good their escape, landing in Africa, where they are greeted by Songwut and Khomkham, now reunited.[33] After Supharat departs for Lorenzo Marguez, Praphimphan meets a good friend of Songwut, an Arab named Muni (a word similar to the Thai for "sage" or "monk"). He, too, is a nationalist fighting the authorities. After the (predictable) running gun battle, Praphimphan and Muni escape to a hidden valley, where they take control of the tiny kingdom of Senabad. The new queen of this kingdom is none other than Waenfa, the poisonous woman (in a wonderful moment, Waenfa's worthiness is revealed during the coronation ceremony when a poisonous snake bites her, and it dies). Praphimphan, the poisonous woman by choice, and Waenfa, the poisonous woman by nature, soon become good friends.

Praphimphan is in her element in this part of the novel: she not only is still the dangerous *pistolera*, but the power behind the throne. The monarchy is indeed benevolent. The new rulers proceed to find ways to exploit systematically the valley's natural resources such as gold and diamonds. New houses and roads are built for the people. To help with the mining and the extraction of gold and diamonds, Praphimphan brings in Songwut, Khomkham, and her father, who is an expert on diamond mines. They are soon joined by Supharat. Praphimphan also learns that her protégé Waewta has divorced her jealous husband Khwan. She, too, shows up in Senabad. In effect, Praphimphan has her whole "gang" with her for this adventure. Waewta shows up with a writer by the name of Niphon, a man educated in France and England who had heard of Praphimphan and wanted to write about her adventures. No sooner does he meet her than he, too, falls under her spell.

---

[32] Luang Wichit's concept of race is defined as the "blood" of a people, as demonstrated by the title of his most famous play, *Lued Suphan* (Suphan blood). It is the concept of a common blood line that binds people together. He seems to conflate race, ethnicity, and nationality. In this instance, he privileges men who, upon marrying women with "foreign blood," can make them Thai. This conversion appears throughout the novel, both symbolically and in real life. Luang Wichit reinforces this idea by making Praphimphan reject the offers of love from foreigners because they can never become Thai. But she readily accepts other women such as Khomkham, a German gypsy, and Waenfa, a French Laotian, as Thai. See footnote 4.

[33] Luang Wichit describes Africa and African culture positively to correct previous racist sentiments popularized during the height of the Thai nationalism campaign, when African Negroes were posed as the uncivilized "other." The author appears to have over-compensated for these prejudices, however, when he concludes that certain roof forms of Thai royal architecture are not Indian, but really African, in origin. Luang Wichit Wathakan, *Huang Rak Haew Luk* pp. 972-73.

In this section, Luang Wichit's imagination takes flight. He writes about how a new dynasty is formed by Praphimphan and her friends, outlining its rituals, myths, and violence. Judging from the description, it is not clear whether the author, creator of this new state, is a royalist or a democrat. The state is a monarchy in which every one speaks to the queen in the Thai sacred royal language. But Waenfa, the new queen, is not even Thai; she is half-Lao and half-French. By elevating a Lao-Frenchwoman to the throne, and by appointing a queen, not a king, to rule this fictional state, the author challenges conservative racial assumptions and Thai palatine law governing royal succession (limiting it to males). In doing so, he shows marks of progressive thinking. Yet Luang Wichit is not consistently progressive or utopian, for in this section of the novel he also justifies exploitation by the state and its new rulers. He suggests that no new dynasty or regime can function if it does not engage in some sort of plunder to fill its coffers; he also suggests the ruler should keep some of the newfound wealth. Money is needed for government or for the consolidation of a new leadership.

Such pragmatism seems to have been carried out by Thai political leaders like Police General Phao Sriyanon and Field Marshal Sarit Thanarat in the mid 1950s. The former traded in opium, while his rival skimmed money from the Lottery Bureau.[34] Luang Wichit also writes about different forms of succession in this section—usurpation of the throne through force, coup d'etat by a military group, and the assumption of political leadership through the invocation of God's [or gods'] will. Each new dynasty must amass as much wealth as possible, not just for itself, but so that its friends and family members will be sufficiently rich to help the people. In the mythical kingdom of Senabad, Waenfa, the queen, was at first reluctant to do this, but Praphimphan coaxed her into it, arguing that her state—unlike many others—had not enslaved its people, so that everything the queen did to strengthen her own position was for the good of the people. Such ideas reflect the paternalism so common in many of Luang Wichit's political writings.

Luang Wichit also includes international politics in the novel. Implausible as it may seem, Praphimphan and Muni travel to Geneva to a meeting of the League of Nations to lobby for recognition of the small kingdom and its new queen. This attempt fails, of course, because with only three hundred people their principality is much smaller than others such as Luxembourg, Monaco, or Liechtenstein. More importantly, the proposed kingdom is located in the territory of a major colonial power. To make his readers think that Siam was an important international player, Luang Wichit gives the Thai ambassador more international clout than is plausible. But the story highlights the author's fascination with diplomacy and Siam's role in international politics.

Muni eventually convinces Praphimphan to love him, but she cannot agree to marry him: he is not Thai, and, as a male, he could never become Thai. Only the male bloodline is important to the determination of race. The female can be Thai because she will give birth to children who are Thai through the blood of their father (*jus sanguini*). Always the dangerous woman, Praphimphan unintentionally kills Muni while she is asleep: dreaming she was being assaulted by Thongthet,

---

[34] Legitimizing the use of force, Luang Wichit describes how Praphimphan personally trained a small army not only to protect the small kingdom, but to kill her political rivals. For the struggle between Phao and Sarit, see Thak Chaloemtiarana, *Thailand: the Politics of Despotic Paternalism* (Bangkok: Thammasat University Press, 1978), chapter 2.

the first man she ever killed, she takes out her pistol and shoots him in the chest, only to awaken and find that she has mistakenly killed Muni.

This deadly accident is soon followed by the apparition of her father's spirit, a sign to her that he has died, and Praphimphan suffers a nervous breakdown.

III

When Praphimphan returns to consciousness, it is four years later, and she is in Austria. She, too, has been reborn: during her sleep, none other than Dr. Freud has administered a drug to her; she tells him all, and she wakes up cured from her mental agony. Interestingly, her behavior does not alter: a nurse who has been cruel to her is found dead in a bathtub, and the circumstances strongly suggest that Praphimphan drowned her. Our protagonist is also still eager to help others accomplish illegal and even immoral acts that mete out justice to those who have wronged her or those close to her.[35]

She finally decides to marry, but her choice falls not on a virile male like Supharat or Muni but on a struggling writer, Niphon. The pen may well be mightier than the sword, but Niphon's proposal is not even romantic: he wants to be a great writer and make the world recognize the beauty of Thai literature, and since every man must have a good woman behind him, he asks her to be this woman. A good marriage, he says, can be made from the union of two close friends.

Characteristically, Praphimphan responds to Niphon's letter by asking practical questions as well. She wonders why he would want to marry a middle-aged woman, thirty-three years old, a woman who has been with two men, whose name is on the lips of tens and hundreds of thousands of people, and someone who has once lost her mind. She warns Niphon that at age thirty-three it may be difficult for her to give him children, and that perhaps her insanity could be passed on to their children.

Again, in an inversion of conventional right and wrong, the author makes Niphon praise Praphimphan for setting a good example for other women, for representing the model woman. Niphon tells Praphimphan that

> on face value, your life may appear to be difficult and soiled as you say. But if we were to examine it closely, having had two husbands is not that unusual for women. And after your divorce these past ten years, you have preserved your dignity and have not strayed. The other things that you did, even though they were evil, were acts that sought justice for yourself and for others. Your life is a life of struggle worthy of praise. Praphimphan is a name that is on the lips of tens and hundreds of thousands of people. But they do not speak of your name in negative ways. They see Praphimphan as the model woman. Heaven has created you to become a model for all women, an example of how women should face life.[36]

Luang Wichit's aim to present a radical model of the modern Thai woman could scarcely be more explicit.

---

[35] Praphimphan helps her landlord beat up an old Jew who raped his daughter. The badly crippled old man suffered for many years before succumbing to his injuries.

[36] Luang Wichit Wathakan, *Huang Rak Haew Luk*, p. 1271.

After their wedding, Praphimphan allows Niphon to embrace her. She even turns her cheek to let him kiss her and allows him to kiss her passionately on the lips. She feels the "venom of love" (*phit rak*) enter her body and thinks about the venom of death that coursed through Waenfa's veins. Love can be so sweet and so deadly. In the end, succumbing to the occasion, she implores Niphon: "kiss me, make love to me. Your kiss will erase the fact that I have been kissed before. Embrace me tightly so I can forget past embraces. Caress me all over so I can cleanse my body of past blemishes. What remains is my pure self that belongs only to you."[37] What Freud could not do, the writer-lover-husband Niphon can: she is now purified, cleansed by transcendent love.[38]

But, in almost karmic retribution, her husband comes down with incurable tuberculosis, and tragically, their daughter is born deaf. Niphon hangs himself out of grief, and Praphimphan soon sinks into another depression. She laments that the life of a girl or woman is represented by the dismissive saying "*di muan kan*" or "that's all right"—an ostensibly comforting phrase that is really a sign of resignation or acceptance of one's fate. The birth of a deaf daughter was only "*di muan kan*." This remark was what Rama VI said on his deathbed when he was shown his only child. His only words after learning that he had sired a daughter was "*di muan kan*." Such is the traditional fate of girls and of women.

In an effort to find the blossom of the *toey* plant to cure her daughter's deafness, Praphimphan embarks with Waenfa on a "Thelma-and-Louise" adventure. The two women proceed to paddle a small canoe down the Danube on an expedition to search for the elusive plant.[39] There, some men also prospecting for medicinal plants make the mistake of trying to scare them away. Praphimphan promptly shoots two of them in the leg, after which the men tell her where the plant can be found. Their adventurous trip is exhilarating, liberating, and empowering.

When the two women reach Hungary, immigration officers ask about their nationality. Waewta endears herself to Praphimphan when she tells the officers that she is "Thai" and not "Laotian." This assertion reflects the author's pan-Thai aspirations that emerged prior to World War II. It also exposes the author's jingoism: in Luang Wichit's world, being Thai is better than being Laotian, for the Lao are an inferior people and nation. It is interesting that the author asserts that Hungarians consider themselves Asian—expanding the scope of pan-Asianism

---

[37] Ibid., p. 1285.

[38] Luang Wichit arranges to cleanse Praphimphan's hands of "blood" through two devices. The first is through ritual cleansing or *sadok khro*. During the gun battle with the police in one of her adventures, Praphimphan receives a superficial wound in her side. In her mind, this is a good thing because she has shot other people but has never known what it feels like to be shot. After this ritual cleansing, she believes that her luck will become better. The second cleansing involves transcendence through love when she submits to Niphon.

[39] *Thelma and Louise* refers to the 1990s Hollywood film starring Susan Sarandon and Geena Davis that established the female bonding film genre. The *toey* plant, used as a flavoring for dessert, grows along the banks of a river, pond, or lake; the Thai variety does not flower and propagates through a root system. A popular Thai proverb about unfulfilled love compares the hopeless pursuit with attempts to make the *toey* plant blossom. In this section, Praphimphan's unfulfilled love life generates a flawed "flower"—her deaf daughter. However, redemption will come in the form of a European variety of the plant. Once again, modern civilization is represented by Western science and medicine. But the emphasis is not really on the superiority of the white man himself, but on his superior science and technology, which could be mastered by the Thai—in this case, Waenfa, the Laotian-French woman who identifies herself as Thai.

rather dramatically. Luang Wichit describes how happy the immigration officers were to meet the two Thai women who were fellow "Asians."

After discovering the herb and curing her daughter's deafness, Praphimphan decides to return to Siam to make peace with her enemies and to cremate her father—all very Buddhist motivations. She cremates her father, but she fails to placate the nephew of her godparents and his greedy wife. They betray her to the authorities, who come to arrest her for the murder of Khwan's chauffeur. Instead of giving up, or of allowing Khwan to take the blame for the murder, Praphimphan becomes once more the dangerous woman: she sneaks out of her hideout and murders her two tormentors. In the ensuing gun battle, she is taken out in the style of Bonnie and Clyde, with Khwan dead at her side.

So in the end, Praphimphan cannot escape punishment from the law and dies a violent death. But before the final shootout, it is still unclear whether she will surrender or resist. Her fate is finally sealed when she becomes wounded. Praphimphan reacts in an uncharacteristically non-feminine way. She calls out to Khwan, probably loud enough for the police to hear, that as a wounded *"sua"* (literally "tiger," but in this usage it refers to men who are hardened bandits or outlaws) (s)he must fight to the death. Two questions are raised here: "Why must a woman be militant and dangerous in modern society?" and "why is she breaking the law so often and with impunity?"

Given the framework of Thai nationalism and its wars of liberation, Luang Wichit was able to justify the militant feminism incorporated into his nationalistic dramas. In those plays, he portrayed Thai women as wives whose loyalty extended beyond domesticity to serving their husbands in war by fighting alongside them. A popular reference to Thai women that calls them the "rear legs" of an elephant—her male partner provides the "front legs"—evokes images of battle elephants in wartime and the secondary role of women. Nevertheless, Thai historiography, and especially that of Luang Wichit, makes "space" for women in the national narrative. But in *Huang Rak Haew Luk*, the martial characteristic of Thai women takes on a different trajectory. The fact that the protagonist leaves Siam both voluntarily and involuntarily signifies a separation from the state, a liberation of women from traditional roles. Praphimphan, like other Thai heroines before her, fights alongside freedom fighters, but in this case without explicitly defining that fight in the framework of Thai nationalism. The modern Thai woman has become a free agent who can fight for her own causes.

Luang Wichit seems to suggest that in entering modern society women have to be vigilant in protecting themselves, even if it means breaking the law. In the novel, Praphimphan and the other women (and here the author includes Western women to emphasize the universality of their cause) take the law into their own hands to punish predatory men, men who have humiliated them, and men who have not honored their words. Perhaps the author is showing us that modern society lacks the mechanisms to protect women since traditional norms governing gender relations, norms that afforded more respect to women as idealized mothers, sisters, and wives, have eroded.

The author's disdain or distrust of the legal system pervades this novel. From the first episode to the last, Luang Wichit depicts the law in a bad light. The story begins with the revelation that Atthaphit had concealed incriminating evidence that would have convicted Praphimphan for murder. The novel also describes how Songwut, another lawyer, used blackmail against his own client to help his father-in-law win back a diamond mine in South Africa. In another example, Praphimphan advises her landlord not to trust the law and lawyers, but to mete out his own punishment against the man who had raped his daughter. And finally, on her last trip to Siam, Praphimphan accidentally bumps into the district officer, now a provincial governor, who many years ago had led the police to apprehend her for killing Khwan's driver. Instead of informing the police, the governor carries on a friendly chat with Praphimphan and even light-heartedly asks her not to commit murder again. As a man, he, too, admires the dangerous woman. But the law does not make room for personal admiration or judgments of morality. This negative opinion of the legal system is most likely the result of Luang Wichit's own experiences with the courts, specifically his war crimes trial following his service in Japan during World War II.

Therefore, instead of treating Praphimphan like a dangerous criminal finally brought to justice, Luang Wichit, in the novel's eulogy, valorizes her as a woman of the people, a compassionate woman who was dealt a bad hand. Recalling Niphon's characterization of Praphimphan as the model woman, Atthaphit's eulogy embeds within the novel itself the unbounded seriality of the dangerous woman:

> Praphimphan belongs to you. She served you and the public by being the exemplar of a person who struggled with life. Her fight began when she took her first step and she fought until her last breath. Praphimphan is not a mean-spirited woman. In fact, she is a person with a good heart who is always ready to make sacrifices for her friends. She is loyal and grateful to those who helped her, but she is vengeful when she is crossed. She stood for justice and would not harm anyone who did not strike at her first. Even though the curtain that falls on the drama of her life is black, the color of mourning and grief, her shining name will remain forever on the lips of tens of thousands of people. And if one were to write about her life, it would take thousands of pages to do it justice.[40]

Of course, Luang Wichit has indeed taken over a thousand pages to do her life justice. Praphimphan is the model of the modern Thai female who, while assenting to the traditional view of the female as one who must be protected and forgiven by the male, is also ready to punish those who are unkind to her or who do not keep their promises of love. She values the family, male fidelity, female friendship, and bravery. She is a leader, a world traveler, a freedom fighter, a founder of a nation, a soldier, an obedient daughter, a passionate lover, a wife, a loyal friend, a patron, a feminist, and an executioner. Interweaving the themes of modernity, femininity, violence, and nationalism on an international scale, Luang Wichit Wathakan glorifies in *Huang Rak Haew Luk* a new role for the modern Thai woman. Neither good nor bad, neither Madonna nor whore, hers is a role of nearly boundless possibilities: the Dangerous Woman.

---

[40] Luang Wichit Wathakan, *Huang Rak Haew Luk*, p. 1461.

Foreignness and Vengeance: On Rizal's *El Filibusterismo*

Vicente L. Rafael

The question of the self: "who am I?" not in the sense of "who am I" but who is this "I" that can say "who"? What is the "I" and what becomes of responsibility once the identity of the "I" trembles in secret?

Jacques Derrida[1]

I.

In nearly all of the towns in the Philippines today, one finds monuments to the country's national hero, Jose Rizal (1861-1896). Most of these are smaller variations of the main monument located in Manila. Erected in 1912 under the United States colonial regime, it contains most of the hero's remains and stands close to the site where he was executed by the Spaniards in 1896 for the crime of fomenting a revolution.

What is worth noting about the monument is its foreignness. It was built by the Swiss sculptor Richard Kissling, whose design was chosen in an international competition sponsored by a committee of American colonial officials and Filipino nationalists which included Rizal's older brother.[2] Shipped in pieces from Europe and assembled in the Philippines, the monument depicts Rizal in a winter coat holding a copy of each of his two novels, *Noli me Tangere* (1887) and its sequel, *El Filibusterismo* (1891), both written in Castilian. The monument has since become the focus of official commemorations of Rizal's birth and death as well as the shrine for various civic and religious groups dedicated to preserving his memory.

---

[1] Jacques Derrida, *The Gift of Death*, trans. David Willis (Chicago: University of Chicago Press, 1995), p. 92.

[2] Kissling was actually the runner up. First place went to the Italian sculptor Carlos Napoli, but for a number of reasons he was unable to build the monument. The commission then went to second placer Kissling who also won P100,000. See RJ. C. Baliza, "The Monument in Our Midst," *Starweek*, December 29, 1996, pp. 10-12. My thanks to Ambeth Ocampo for pointing out certain details regarding the Rizal monument as well as facts relating to Rizal's life and work.

Yet the figure of Rizal in this and other monuments remains odd.[3] Attired in nineteenth-century European clothing suitable for winter climates unimaginable in the tropics, he cradles two novels in a language that less than one percent of the population can read, much less write in.[4] One might argue that the incongruity of his memorial is fitting, since during his lifetime Rizal was regarded as unusual, if not out of place, in the Philippines. Colonial authorities suspected him of being a German spy because of his fluency in German and his praise for German schooling. Common folk who had heard of him or seen him perform medical treatments (for he was a doctor) regarded him as a miracle worker, while others saw him, especially after his death, as a Filipino Christ.[5] The revolutionary organization, the Katipunan, took him as their guiding spirit, even if he himself had disavowed their movement, and used his name as their secret password. It was as if his appearance and name provoked everyone in the colony to see in him a range of references which he did not originally intend.

He had what seemed like a remarkable ability to cross geographical borders (by virtue of his frequent travels in and out of the colony) and linguistic differences. (Aside from Tagalog, his mother tongue, he spoke and wrote Spanish fluently and was adept enough in German, French, English, and Italian to translate works in these languages into Spanish and Tagalog. He also knew Greek and Latin, and dabbled in Japanese and Arabic.) In this sense, he could be thought of as a figure of translation. Linking disparate linguistic regions and social groups inside and outside the archipelago, Rizal's image was deemed capable of transmitting messages from outside to those inside the colony and vice versa. The image of Rizal—its reference to external origins and foreign languages—lends it the character of a lingua franca. As with Castilian, which was the language common to *ilustrado* (literally, "enlightened") nationalists who spoke a variety of local languages, Rizal's image seemed capable of crossing linguistic boundaries, and circulating up and down the social hierarchy. In the Philippine colony, then, both

---

[3] See Ambeth Ocampo, *Rizal Without the Overcoat* (Pasig: Anvil Publishing, Inc., 1991), for a series of perspicacious observations on the oddness of Rizal's officially sanctioned visage.

[4] It is interesting to note that the first known monument built to commemorate Rizal shortly after the first anniversary of his death, while the revolution against Spain was still being fought, did not have his figure. It was instead a simple obelisk with "Masonic-tinged abstractions on which only the titles of his two electrifying novels were inscribed—as if to say, Read Them! Then Fight For Your Country's Liberty!" Cited in Benedict Anderson, "Republica, Aura, and Late Nationalist Imaginings," *Qui Parle* 7,1 (1993): 1-21. The quote is on p. 5. The statue on the official monument is modeled after the last known studio photograph Rizal posed for in Madrid around 1891. The seriality of Rizal's monuments is thus based not on an original, but on a photographic reproduction, just as his books were also mechanically reproduced. They are then copies for which there are properly speaking no originals. See Vicente L. Rafael, "Nationalism, Imagery, and Filipino Intelligentsia in the Nineteenth Century," *Critical Inquiry* 16,3 (Spring 1990): 591-611.

[5] Leon Ma. Guerrero, *The First Filipino: A Biography of Jose Rizal* (Manila: National Historical Commission, 1963) is the standard and most lucidly written biography of Rizal. See also W. E. Retana, *Vidas y Escritos del Dr. Jose Rizal* (Madrid:Victoriano Suarez, 1905); Austin Craig, *Life, Lineage, and Labors of Jose Rizal, Philippine Patriot* (Manila: Philippine Education Company, 1913); Reynaldo Ileto, "Rizal and the Underside of Philippine History," in *Moral Order and the Question of Change: Essays on Southeast Asian Thought*, ed. David Wyatt and Alexander Woodside (New Haven: Yale Southeast Asian Program Series, 1982), pp. 274-337; and Marcelino Foronda, *Cults Honoring Rizal* (Manila: R. P. Garcia, 1961).

Castilian and Rizal's image appeared capable of becoming common to all because native to no one.

Put differently, Rizal's monument bears the trace of the foreign origins of the nation: that original aspect of nationalism which owes its genesis to something outside of the nation. That foreignness, however, has been by and large domesticated. His monumentalization seems to be saying that he now belongs to "us"; that "we"—Filipinos, not Spaniards—claim him as our own. "We" heard his message, which was meant only for "us," and we responded by rendering to him the recognition denied by Spanish authorities. His memory is now "our" property.

One then can think of Rizal's monuments as a means of acknowledging his foreignness while simultaneously setting it aside. As with all national monuments, that of Rizal marks his death, bringing "us" who recognize him into a relation with his absence. Yet his death, which is another dimension of his foreignness, no longer need exercise any pressure on the nation's self-conception. If Rizal's strangeness is still palpable in the Philippines today, there is a generalized sense that it has nonetheless been contained, buried, as it were, in the popular assumption that he is the "father" of the nation and, as one of his biographers has put it, the "first Filipino."

In a similar vein, it is rare today for Filipinos to read his novels in their original form. These have long been translated into English and other local vernaculars. In 1957, as part of the so-called Rizal Law, Congress, over the objections of the Catholic Church, required the reading of the novels in English (which is the medium of instruction in schools) among college students, which further dampened interest in the originals. And in recent years, film, operatic, and comic book versions of the novels have tended to displace the novels themselves altogether. The monumentalization of his novels has effected the flattening out of their heterogeneous language and the stereotyping by Filipino readers of the novels' characters as stand-ins for the various political positions opposed or held by its author. In the same vein, the literary nature of his books has been summarily typed as "realist" and "derivative" of Spanish and French models, while their nature as social documents for the late nineteenth century or as quasi-biblical sources of nationalist wisdom has been emphasized by most scholars.

As with Rizal's image, his novels also have foreign origins. The *Noli* and the *Fili*, as they are popularly referred to, were written while Rizal traveled and studied in Europe. The first novel was composed mostly in Paris and published in Berlin in 1887; the second was begun in London, continued in Biarritz, Paris, Brussels, and finally published in Ghent in 1891. While monetary considerations forced Rizal to find the cheapest publisher, there is nonetheless the sense here of nationalist writings emanating from the unlikeliest places beyond the empire, similar to conditions that marked the publication of the primary nationalist newspaper, *La Solidaridad* (published in Barcelona and Madrid from 1889-1895). Both novels were declared subversive by Spanish authorities, their transport and possession criminalized. Rizal and his friends had to arrange for their clandestine delivery to the Philippines. They were smuggled in, usually from Hong Kong, and bribes were routinely paid to customs officials to allow for their entry.[6]

---

[6] See John Schumacher, *The Propaganda Movement, 1880-1895* (Manila: Solidaridad Publishing House, 1973), pp. 82, 235.

The conditions under which the novels were composed and circulated further underlines their strangeness. They were written outside colonial society, addressed to an audience absent from the author's immediate milieu. Their clandestine circulation required the corruption of officials, while their possession, declared a crime, resulted in imprisonment, and their author was himself exiled in the southern Philippines for four years and eventually executed. Thus were the alien origins of the *Noli* and the *Fili* conjoined to the putative criminality of their effects. Indeed, it is this connection of foreignness with criminality that is thematized most persistently in Rizal's second novel. In the discussion that follows, I turn to *El Filibusterismo* to inquire about this link. It is, as we shall see, a novel about messages to which responses, detained by the dead, have long been overdue.[7]

II.

Along with a few other nationalists, Rizal early on entertained the possibility of Philippine separation from Spain as an alternative to political assimilation favored by most of the other *ilustrados*. As early as 1888, he was complaining in several letters that Spain was simply "unwilling to listen."[8] Within months of finishing his second novel in 1891, he left Europe for Hong Kong, then continued on to the Philippines, convinced that the struggle should be waged there. He would follow the train of his words, returning, as it were, to the scene of the crime.

We might ask: what was the manner of this return and the nature of the crime? We get a sense of both in Rizal's dedication of the *Fili*: "To the Memory of the priests Don Mariano Gomez, Don Jose Burgos, and Don Jacinto Zamora," it begins, referring to the three Filipino (i.e., non-peninsular Spaniard) secular priests who were falsely implicated in a local uprising in 1872 and unjustly executed by Spanish authorities.[9] Having earlier criticized the Spanish friars' monopoly over the colony's wealthiest parishes in the 1860s, these three secular priests had also challenged Spanish assumptions about the inferiority of natives and mestizos and the inability of non-Spanish secular priests to run their own parishes. They were thus regarded by *ilustrado* nationalists as their precursors. Representing protonationalist instances of resistance to friar rule, which was regarded as the most repressive aspect of colonial rule, the fates of Fathers Gomez, Burgos, and Zamora also signified assimilationist aspirations gone wrong.

---

[7] I defer a reading of the *Noli* here, and can refer readers to an earlier piece I did, "Language, Gender, and Authority in Rizal's *Noli*," in *RIMA* (Review of Malaysian and Indonesian Affairs) 18 (Winter 1984): 110-40.

[8] Quoted in Schumacher, *Propaganda Movement*, pp. 227, 243. Rizal's frustration with Spain grew from a number of other factors. There were political factors: Spanish intransigence combined with the politically volatile situation in the Spanish parliament where control shifted rapidly between liberals and conservatives between the 1860s and 1890s. Also, Rizal suffered from a series of family tragedies, including the imprisonment of his mother and sister under false charges, the exile of his brother-in-law, father, and brother, and the loss of the family's lands in Calamba, Laguna to the Dominicans. Both novels teem with allusions to these events.

[9] For details surrounding the lives and deaths of Gomez, Burgos and Zamora, see John Schumacher, *Revolutionary Clergy: The Filipino Clergy and the Nationalist Movement, 1850-1903* (Quezon City: Ateneo de Manila University Press, 1981), pp. 1-47.

In recalling their deaths, Rizal commemorates their innocence. He "in no way acknowledges [their] guilt"; instead he holds Spain "culpable for [their] deaths." "Let these pages serve as a belated wreath upon your unknown graves; and may all who . . . attack your memory find their hands soiled with your blood!"[10] Like a gravestone, the book's dedication marks the death of the Filipino fathers. Their execution had made a lasting impression on Rizal when he was a young student in Manila. He wrote to friends later on that had it not been for Gomez, Burgos, and Zamora, he would have been a Jesuit.[11] In their deaths, Rizal hears a message and is compelled to respond. Mourning their deaths leads him not only to mark their "unknown graves," but also to utter a threat: those who attack your memory will be soiled in your blood. They, too, should be made to suffer your fate. The deaths of the Filipino priests instill in Rizal a desire for vindication. The dedication of the *Fili* thus brings together mourning and revenge as two parts of the same reply that he directs to the fathers: those who are dead as well as those who are guilty. Writing thus becomes a practice of gathering and giving back what one has received. In the *Fili*, returning a message means remembering what was said and responding in kind.

But again we might ask: who determines the nature of the message and decides the forms of its return? There is, of course, the author Rizal. Yet in the *Fili*, the author is shadowed by another agent who returns the call of death: the figure of the *filibustero*. In the book's epigraph—what we might think of as its other dedication—Rizal quotes his Austrian friend and nationalist sympathizer Ferdinand Blumentritt, who writes:

> It is easy to suppose that a *filibustero* has bewitched [*hechizado*] in secret the league of friars and reactionaries, so that unconsciously following his inspirations, they favor and foment that politics which has only one end: to extend the ideas of *filibusterismo* all over the country and convince every last Filipino that there exists no other salvation outside of that of the separation from the Motherland.[12]

In Spanish dictionaries, one of the definitions of *filibustero* is that of a pirate, hence a thief. But as one who, we might say in English, "filibusters," s/he is also one who interrupts parliamentary proceedings, smuggling his or her own discourse into the discourses of others. In either case, we can think of the *filibustero* as an intruder, breaking and entering into places where s/he does not properly belong, and doing so by surprise and often in disguise. Small wonder then that, by the later nineteenth century, "*filibustero*" was also glossed as "subversive," in the sense of a disruptive presence, a figure who, by word or deed, suddenly and surreptitiously steals upon the social order. Thus were nationalists referred to by Spanish authorities as *filibusteros*. Their wish to speak and disseminate Castilian as a route to economic and social reform challenged the friar-sanctioned practice of

---

[10] Jose Rizal, *El Filibusterismo* (Ghent: F. Meyer-Van Loo, 1891). I use the facsimile edition published in Manila by the Comision Nacional del Centenario de Jose Rizal, 1961. All references to this book will appear in the text. All translations are mine unless otherwise indicated.

[11] Schumacher, *Propaganda Movement*, p. 29.

[12] Rizal, *El Filibusterismo*, unpaginated.

dissuading the majority of natives from learning the language. The friars, from the beginnings of colonization in the sixteenth century, had administered God's Word in the numerous local vernaculars. They also translated native languages into Castilian for the benefit of the colonial state and their clerical orders. Thus did the friars long enjoy the role of privileged mediators between the metropole and the colony. For Filipino nationalists to seek to spread Castilian to the populace would in effect undercut the mediating authority of the Spanish fathers. In their desire to communicate in Castilian, *ilustrado* nationalists were asking that, rather than regarding them as inferior, the colonial authorities recognize them as the equals of Spaniards. Instead, Spanish authorities prodded by the friars saw nationalists as speaking out of place. Speaking in a language that did not belong to them, they appeared alien to and disruptive of the colonial order.[13]

The political implications that grow out of linguistic disruptions take on a particular inflection in Rizal's citation of Blumentritt. The *filibustero* here is put forth as a kind of sorcerer, a malevolent medium. Later on, Rizal in his preface will refer to the *filibustero* as a "phantom" (*fantasma*) who roams about, haunting the populace. Its presence is thus a secret, so that one may be in contact with a *filibustero* without being aware of it. The power of the *filibustero* lies in his or her ability to make you think what s/he wants you to without your knowledge. Possessed by the thoughts of an other whom you cannot even recognize, you begin to act in ways you did not intend. Thus does the malevolence of the *filibustero* consist of separating you from your own thoughts. And in a colonial context, such a separation can bring you to cut yourself off from the mother country, that is, to mistake separation from Spain for independence.

While the *filibustero* is thought to subvert one's control over one's thoughts and that of the mother country over her sons and daughters, it also insinuates its way to the top of the colonial hierarchy, inserting itself where it does not belong and causing authority to act in ways that go against its interests. The *filibustero* then is a kind of foreign presence who exercises an alienating effect on all those it comes in contact with. Being out of place, it can travel all over the place, promoting the misrecognition of motives and words. For this reason, we can think of the *filibustero*'s foreignness as the force of a transmission that troubles social hierarchy. The *filibustero* possesses the power of translation—the capacity to cross boundaries and put diverse groups in contact with one another—but translation in the service of something outside of colonial society.

What is the "outside" that the *filibustero* works for? Independence, perhaps? Rizal himself remained uncertain. Until the end of his life, he never explicitly favored a final break with Spain, even though he considered political assimilation to be doomed. We can think of the *Fili* as the site within which he rehearsed this ambivalence at the foundation of nationalist sentiments. The novel is a record of hesitations and anxieties raised by the failure of assimilation giving rise to the specters of separation. The figure of the *filibustero* was its medium for

---

[13] For a more detailed discussion of the linguistic hierarchy that informed colonial rule and the challenges to it by Filipino nationalists, see Vicente L. Rafael, "Translation and Revenge: Castilian and the Origins of Nationalism in the Philippines," in *The Places of History: Regionalism Revisited in Latin America*, ed. Doris Somer (Durham: Duke University Press, 1999), pp. 214-35. For a history of translation in the conversion of the native populace, see Vicente L. Rafael, *Contracting Colonialism: Translation and Christian Conversion in Tagalog Society Under Early Spanish Rule* (Durham: Duke University Press, 1993).

tracking and trafficking in the emergence, spread, and containment of such anxieties. It is this fundamentally unsettling nature of the *filibustero* as both medium and message that infects, as it were, both the author and his characters. I try to trace the spread of this infection below.

III.

Most commentaries I know of on the *El Filibusterismo* rank it as an "inferior" because less polished work when compared to Rizal's first novel, *Noli me Tangere*. The *Fili* lacks, for these commentators, the narrative coherence and cheerful humor of its predecessor, putting in their place polemic pronouncements and sarcastic laughter.[14] In writings about nationalism and Rizal, the *Fili* is quickly passed over, its complications largely ignored.

One of the most notable complications is the absence of a single narrative line. The novel is loosely woven around two plots, from which several others emerge. One concerns the attempts, ultimately foiled, of an association of university students to establish a self-supporting academy for the teaching of Castilian in Manila, autonomous from friar control. The other plot deals with the story of Simoun, a mysterious jeweler of unknown origins who, having ingratiated himself with the Governor General, the friars, and local officials, uses his wealth to spread corruption in the colony, hoping thereby to intensify the general misery and hasten a popular uprising. There is an important twist to this story: Simoun is actually Crisostomo Ibarra, the protagonist of the first novel, who was thought to be dead. Persecuted in the earlier novel for his reformist ideals and his love for Maria Clara, the illegitimate daughter of the Franciscan priest Damaso and a devout native woman who had been unable to conceive with her feckless Chinese mestizo husband, he flees the country. In the *Fili*, Ibarra returns years later, disguised as Simoun the wealthy merchant, intent on rescuing Maria Clara from her seclusion in the convent and orchestrating a revolt to wreak revenge on all those he deems responsible for ruining his future.

Both plots end in failure. The students' petition for a Spanish academy is denied. They are subsequently blamed for the mysterious appearance of posters deemed "subversive" at the university. Many are rounded up and imprisoned, and though they are all eventually released, they also retreat into an embittered cynicism. At least one of them, Basilio, is drawn into Simoun's plot. However, Simoun's plans also unravel. He discovers that Maria Clara has died and his plans for instigating an uprising are discovered by colonial authorities. He flees to the rural retreat of Padre Florentino, an older Filipino priest from the generation of Gomez, Burgos, and Zamora. In the end, nothing is resolved. Simoun dies of his wounds and disappointment, and Rizal, speaking through Padre Florentino, launches on what by then was a familiar polemic about the necessity of education, virtuous intentions, and sacrifice in confronting oppression and injustice. The novel is remarkably inconclusive. Its plots do not add up to a political program—in fact

---

[14] See Guerrero, *First Filipino*, pp. 271-85, and Schumacher, *Propaganda Movement*, pp. 235-43, as these are typical of the commentaries on the *Fili*. See also Resil Mojares, *Origins and Rise of the Filipino Novel: A Generic Study of the Novel until 1940* (Manila: University of the Philippines Press, 1983), pp. 137-50. An important exception to this trend, however, is Caroline S. Hau, *Necessary Fictions: Philippine Literature and the Nation, 1946–1980* (Quezon City: Ateneo de Manila University Press, 2000), pp. 48-93.

such a program is studiously avoided. Rather, disillusionment takes on almost baroque proportions. What remains in the end is the author's voice speaking through Padre Florentino, asking the "youth" to come forth and sacrifice themselves for the nation. And after hurling a valuable cache of jewels into the ocean, Padre Florentino then addresses those same jewels—which had been owned by Simoun, who used them for corrupting officials and buying weapons for his uprising—commending them to the care of "Nature" for use in more noble purposes in the future.

What interests me are precisely the ways by which this open-endedness and negativity produce a space for the emergence of an authorial voice addressing an absent audience. In between the twisting and twinning of these plots, Rizal constructs a series of scenes around particular characters. Many of these have only the most tenuous connections to the narratives. Instead, they bear out another kind of emplotment. In these scenes, Rizal obsessively details the recurrence and effects of the foreign detached from its origins in hierarchy. What emerges in these foreign encounters is a certain politics, one colored by anticipation, shame and resentment, that envisions a response through translation. It is my contention that the receipt of the foreign, its recognition and its return, is precisely what marks the domestication of nationalism as specifically "Filipino." Additionally, the failure of recognition and the deferral of the return are built into such a politics, one whose translation requires a voice whose appearance seems new. Such would be the voice of the author.

Where and how do we come to see the emergence of the foreign? How does it call for as well as evade translation and domestication? And what are the consequences of such an event for understanding the linguistic basis of nationalism?

One place to see the emergence of the foreign and its domestication is in the classroom. Rizal writes at length about education in his political essays. For Rizal, education is the key to reformulating social relations. It places youth in the position of receiving and realizing a future. Through education, the future comes across as a promise, hence a kind of performative utterance directed at the youth. But what blocks this speech from reaching its destination, as we saw, are the friars who controlled the educational institutions in the colony. In a chapter entitled "La Clase de Fisica" (The physics class),[15] the novel shows how this blockage is produced. Rizal describes the conditions at the colony's Dominican University in the following way:

> No one went to class in order to learn but only to avoid getting marked absent. The class is reduced to reciting lessons from memory, reading the book and once in a while, answering one or other trivial, abstract, profound, cunning, enigmatic questions. True, there was no shortage of little sermons [*sermonitas*]—they were always the same—about humility, submission, respect for the religious....[16]

In class, one's main concern was to avoid being marked absent. Yet one's presence amounted to little since it entailed the mechanical recitation of texts and the occasional answer to questions as trivial as they were abstract. Education was a

---

[15] Rizal, *El Filibusterismo*, pp. 98-108.
[16] Ibid., p. 89.

matter of hearing what one has already heard before, such as the *sermonitas* on submission and humility, just as it required the repetition of formulaic answers to predictable demands. Nothing truly new was allowed to emerge, and in this sense the classroom was an extension of the church. Hence, for example, the scientific instruments in the physics laboratory were never used by the students and were taken out only on rare occasions to impress important visitors, "like the Holy Sacrament to the prostrated faithful: look at me but do not touch."[17] The students themselves were "used" in a similar manner, for to memorize and repeat the words of a textbook is to turn oneself into a vessel for the passage of the words of authority. One is not expected to make these words one's own, but rather to submit to their force and bear them back to their source as the friar stands by and measures one's fidelity. Such schooling did not lead to a future but to the perpetuation of familiar forms of servility. It was meant to maintain students in their stupidity.

Yet, what made the classroom different from the church was that students were required to recite individually. They could not receive a grade and pass the course, Rizal writes, until they had been recognized (*ser conocido*) and called upon by the professor. By recognizing the student, the professor acknowledges that he sees in that youth a capacity to speak up. At the same time, that capacity constitutes a potential for disruption. In speaking up, the student might also talk back; in repeating the textbook, he might make a mistake and thus utter something uncalled for and unexpected. Such possibilities make the classroom a volatile arena for the reiteration of authority, a place for the potential exposure of authority's limits.

In the physics class, Rizal describes the professor, Padre Millon, as one who "was not of the common run." He knew his physics, but the demands of colonial education required that he assume his role in the ritual of the classroom. Having called the roll, he begins calling on students to recite the day's lesson "word for word." Rizal describes their response:

> The phonographs [*los fonografos*] played, some well, others bad; others stuttered and were prompted. He who recited without a mistake earned a good mark, while he who committed more than three mistakes a bad one.[18]

Used as a medium of instruction, Castilian here has a curious role. In speaking like "phonographs," students mechanically reproduce the lesson. They respond in a language that is wholly exterior to them. Castilian thus comes across not as a means of self-expression but of self-evacuation. One who recites Castilian phonographically demonstrates, among other things, that this language has no place in one's mind. One speaks it without knowing what one is saying, so that it seems to be merely passing through one's body. Drained of intelligibility and detached from intentionality, Castilian thus becomes truly foreign to the students. In speaking it, they become mediums for the reproduction of its foreignness.

One's capacity to reproduce Castilian earns one a mark. One's presence is noted down, and one is left alone by the friar as he moves on to call another student. Each student's grade signifies his submission to the demand for repetition. However, repetition signifies not only the students' acknowledgment of the professor's

---

[17] Ibid., p. 90.
[18] Ibid., p. 92.

authority; it also conveys their distance from his language. For speaking Castilian in this context requires its separation from the rest of one's thoughts. That is, it entails the recognition of the foreign as foreign, as that which belongs to someone else and over which one does not have a proper claim. In speaking up to authority, one acknowledges the sheer passage of the latter's language through oneself. One thus confronts Castilian as the inappropriable: the materialization of an alien presence that periodically assails one and which one periodically is required to fend off. When called to recite, one speaks Castilian in order to put it out of mind in the hope of sending it back where it came from.

However, these recitations are never smooth. Both students and professors find themselves in the midst of other signs which can at times interrupt the circulation of the language of authority. Rizal's interest lies precisely in recording the static against which these signals take place. Amid the tedium of recitations, the friar-professor scans the faces of his students, looking to catch someone unprepared, "wanting to startle him" (*quiso asustarle*). He spies on a "fat boy with a sleepy face and hair stiff and hard like the bristles of a brush, yawning almost to the point of dislocating his jaw, stretching himself, extending his arms as if he were on his bed." The professor zeroes in on the unsuspecting student:

> "*Oy!* you [*tu*], sleepy head, *aba!* What! And lazy, too! Maybe [*seguro*] you don't know the lesson, *ja?!*" Padre Millon not only addressed all the students informally [*tuteaba*] like a good friar, but also spoke to them in the language of the marketplace [*lengua de tienda*].... The interpolation, instead of offending the class, amused them and many laughed: this was something that happened routinely. Nevertheless, the sleepy head did not laugh; he rose up with a jump, rubbed his eyes, and like a steam engine gyrating a phonograph, began to recite....[19]

The boredom of one student triggers the interest of the professor. The latter sees in the former an opportunity to break the monotony of the class. It works. He surprises the student, much to the delight of his classmates, provoking laughter. What is worth noting here is the mode of the friar's speech. He not only speaks down to the students, addressing them individually as *tu* rather than with the more respectful *usted*. More significantly, he speaks to the class in *lengua de tienda*, the language of the marketplace, or what has also been referred to as *español de la cocina*, kitchen Spanish.[20] Consisting of an unstable mix of Castilian and Tagalog, it is a language spoken to and at the lower end of the social hierarchy. In addressing his students in this language, the friar momentarily disrupts the ritual of recitation and turns the classroom into another place, closer to the market than the church.

Hearing this linguistic disruption, one which was a matter of daily routine, the other students laugh. In their laughter, they find themselves occupying a

---

[19] Ibid.

[20] See Ferdinand Blumentritt, "Pag-Diwata Barantes," vol. II, *La Solidaridad*, facsimile edition (Quezon City: University of the Philippines Press, 1973), p. 366. Other kinds of pidgin Spanish existed in the Philippines at this time, including Chavacano, which is still widely spoken among residents of the town of Ternate in Cavite, near where the Spanish shipyards used to be, and in parts of Zamboanga province on the western coast of Mindanao. The contemporary descendent of *lengua de tienda* is, of course, Taglish.

different position. No longer are they anxious and expectant targets. Rather, they become spectators to a comical encounter. Thus are they momentarily released from the grip of Castilian. Instead, they come to share as audiences in another language that belongs neither to them nor to the friar: the *lengua de tienda*.

Their identification with one another, however, finds its locus in the body of the fat boy. Interrupted from his reverie, he bursts out in a convulsive repetition of the lessons like a "steam engine gyrating a phonograph." Startled, he takes shelter in repeating what he does not understand. As if wielding an amulet, he repeats the lesson, hoping to protect himself from further intrusions. But rather than fend off authority, his response sets him up for another ambush. "'*Para, para, para!*' the professor interrupted. 'Jesus! what a rattle!'" The professor then proceeds to ask the student a question about the day's lesson on the nature of mirrors that is not mentioned in the textbook. Uncomprehending, the student tries once again to recite the text. And again he finds himself interrupted by the friar, "inserting *cosas* [what], and *abas* at every moment," while mocking his appearance. Rather than receive a mark for his submission, the student is marked as the object of derision in the language of the market and the laughter of the other students.

Throughout this exchange, the professor's authority comes less from speaking Castilian than from interrupting its flow. He dominates the production of surprise, thereby controlling not only the circulation of Castilian, but also its possible deviations. Herein lies the importance of "market Spanish." Through the *lengua de tienda*, he alerts students to the fact that he is able to hear in Castilian the outbreak of another form of speech. He knows what they are aware of but cannot say: that Castilian can be spoken in ways that evade linguistic authority. He thus communicates the miscommunication intrinsic to colonial sociality and thereby shows himself capable of anticipating the semantic crisis built into the economy of colonial communication.

The students in their laughter also come to recognize their professor's authority. However, it is not in this instance an authority that derives from the language of God or the state, but one that comes from the ability to overhear and transmit the intermittent and interruptive language from below. They see in their professor one who can draw from other sources the means with which to communicate in ways that evade the language of the textbook. Mixing linguistic registers, he appears to mimic those at the periphery of the linguistic hierarchy. Thanks to the friar, Castilian appears to give way, becoming another language that makes possible a momentary joining of his interests with those of his students.

That joining of interests, however, is as evanescent as it is transitory. More significant, it relies on the targeting of an other who can barely speak and cannot laugh. Such is the fate of the fat boy who is finally reduced to saying, in response to a long-winded question that ends with, "what do you say?": "I? Nothing!" (*Yo? Nada!*) When he does speak in a Castilian other than that of the textbook, it is to say that "I" am "nothing." The boy speaks Castilian and finds himself unrecognizable even to himself. Compelled to answer in a foreign language, he finds himself converted into one who is utterly foreign. The professor and his students are thoroughly complicitous in the interruption of Castilian by sharing a language from below. But the result is not the end of hierarchy, only its reconfiguration at the expense of a designated alien. Interrupting the possibility of interruptions, the friar and his students are led to discover and domesticate the foreign residing in their midst, which includes both the Castilian of the lesson and the embodiment of its failure to be correctly returned in the fat boy.

Rizal, however, raises a third possibility. Rather than repeat the language of authority or disrupt its demand in order to reformulate hierarchy, one can say "no" to both. In such a case, conflict would replace subservience. Rather than scapegoating, there would be confrontation; in place of laughter, revenge. This third possibility is played out when Padre Millon calls on another student, the felicitously named Placido Penitente.[21] The friar catches Placido trying to prompt another student who was being grilled. Seeing the native student's embarrassment (*verguenza*, shame, a word that also refers to the private parts of an individual), the professor relishes the thought of further humiliating him. He attacks Placido with a barrage of tendentious questions meant to confuse him and, as usual, amuse the other students. Indiscriminately mixing registers, the priest punctuates his questions with Latinisms and phrases from the *lengua de tienda*, repeatedly punning on Placido's name and forcing him to stutter and commit several errors while reciting. Throughout, the student finds himself the object of the professor's assaults and the class's laughter.

However, something unexpected happens. Turning to his record book to grade the student, the friar discovers that Placido had been marked absent for the day. He had come in late, just after his name had been called on the roll. Officially, he was not there. Yet, not only was he being given a grade; he is also told by the friar that he has fifteen absences and is one short of failing the class. Placido takes exception, for he knows that he's only been absent three times and tells the friar so in impeccable Castilian. The priest replies once again in Spanish pidgin, "*Jusito, jusito, senolia! . . . si te descuidas una mas, sulung! Apuera de la fuerta!*"[22] this time with a Chinese accent that gives a sharper edge to his mockery of the student's protestations. He tells him that he multiplies each absence by five to make up for all the times he does not call the roll. Hearing this, Placido is outraged. He is doubly misrecognized, taken as a mere *indio* incapable of speaking Castilian even when he does, and as a fool incapable of telling the difference between his absence and presence. It is at this point that Placido's embarrassment is converted into anger. Cutting off the friar at mid-sentence, he says,

> "Enough, father, enough! Your Reverence can mark me for mistakes as much as he wants, but he does not have the right to insult me. Your Reverence can stay with the class, but I cannot stand it any longer."

And without taking leave, he left.

The class was shocked [*aterrada*]. Similar acts of indignity [*acto de dignidad*] were almost never seen. Who would have thought that Placido Penitente . . . ? The professor, surprised, bit his lips and watched him leave, moving his head with a menacing motion. With a trembling voice, he then began a sermon on the usual themes, though with much more forcefulness . . . about the increasing arrogance, the innate ingratitude, the vanity, the

---

[21] Rizal, *El Filibusterismo*, pp. 95-99.

[22] Roughly translated, "Enough, enough, *señorito* [i.e., little master], any more discussions and you're out of here, out of the door!" The friar here not only parodies Chinese pronunciations of Spanish, he also mimics the Tagalog tendency to confuse "f" for "p" as when he tendentiously mispronounces *afuera* as *apuera* and *puerta* as *fuerta*.

excessive pride which the demon of darkness had infused in the youth, the little education, the lack of courtesy, etc., etc., etc.[23]

Rizal imagines a moment when the *indio* speaks up not in order to confirm authority in its place but to reject it altogether. Placido tells the Spanish father "enough!" in the latter's language. Addressing the friar as "your reverence" (V.R.), he discovers in Castilian a place from which to separate his interests from those on top. Castilian allows him to fashion an "I" that can say "I can't stand it any more," an "I" that can get across to and, more important, surpass hierarchy. Through Castilian, the "I" appears as one who, in saying "no" to the father, can begin to imagine taking the latter's place. Placido in Castilian interrupts the friar, till then the master of interruption, thereby ceasing to reproduce the latter's interests. Instead, he converts Castilian into his own language, seeming to possess and contain its alien force.

It is the sudden appearance of this mastery that shocks (*aterrar*) the rest of the students. They hear Placido and understand what he says. Yet, they can no longer recognize him. "Who would have thought that Placido Penitente . . . ?" It is as if the students sense in Placido a communicative force that, in responding directly to authority, overtakes its demands. He thus comes across as someone other than who he was supposed to be. Refusing the father, he also separates himself from the rest of the class. He manages to return the surprises of the friar with a surprise of his own: he leaves. But in leaving, he takes on the risk of failure and shows that risk to be an element of his speech.

Where the other students speak Castilian in order to put it out of mind, Placido turns Castilian into a language for stating his own mind. In this way, he becomes a new kind of figure, one who is "rarely seen." Like the startling qualities of the *ilustrado* nationalists, Placido's newness appears strange to those who see it. The friar can only respond with stunned silence, then with a mechanical sermon, the usual harangue whose tediousness Rizal signals with "etc., etc., etc." The friar finds himself in the place of the fat student, retreating behind the repetition of words that everyone has already heard. It is as if he finds himself confronted with a different kind of foreignness, one that is not available to the usual modes of domestication. While it speaks in the language of authority, it exceeds hierarchy as if it were addressing another location.

What is this other location? How else might one come to discover it? What sort of recognition flows out of this other locus of address? In the case of Placido Penitente, the discovery of this address begins with a sense of embarrassment that is converted into anger through the misappropriation of Castilian, both on the friar's and his own part. But what of those who cannot speak Castilian, or at least cannot do so in the ways that might skirt around or past hierarchy? How are they to be recognized? And by whom?

To address these questions, I want to turn to one of the chapters in the *Fili* concerning the story of Juli, a young native woman whose entire family has suffered in the hands of the colonial authorities.[24] Her father, Cabesang Tales, is a farmer whose lands are unjustly confiscated by the friars and their native lackeys. He is subsequently kidnapped by local bandits, a situation that forces Juli to place

---

[23] Rizal, *El Filibusterismo*, p. 98.
[24] Ibid., pp. 227-35.

herself in the domestic service of an older wealthy woman in town in order to pay his ransom. Juli's fiancé is the student Basilio, who is arrested by Spanish authorities on charges of putting up subversive posters at the university. She is compelled to seek the aid of the parish priest, Padre Camorra, popularly known in town as *si cabayo*, or horse, for his "frolicsome" ways with women. Juli is terrified at the prospect of having to submit to his advances, even as she is desperate to seek his intercession to free Basilio from jail. She is thus overwhelmed by guilt. She would be guilty of giving up her honor should she submit to the friar, and guilty if she does not, since it would mean abandoning any hope of helping Basilio. Either she must sacrifice her beloved to keep her virtue, or sacrifice her virtue to save her beloved.

Her predicament unfolds through a series of dreams, "now mournful, now bloody . . . " In these dreams, "complaints and laments would pierce her ears."

> She imagined hearing shots, seeing her father, her father who had done so much for her . . . hunted like an animal because she had hesitated to save him. And her father's figure was transformed and she recognized Basilio, dying and looking at her reproachfully . . . blood issuing forth from his mouth and she would hear Basilio say to her: "Save me! Save me! You alone can save me!" Then a burst of laughter would resound, she would turn her eyes and would see her father looking at her with eyes full of reproach. And Juli would awaken and sit up on her mat, would draw her hand over her forehead and pull back her hair; cold sweat, like the sweat of death, would dampen her.[25]

In her dreams, Juli is assailed by voices and stares from her father and her fiancé, each meshing into the other. In the absence of these two men, their dream images occupy Juli's mind, insisting that they be heard and attended to. She has no control over their return and cannot find the means to meet their demands. Here, guilt is associated with the sense of being filled with voices and images from beyond one's waking life. Such presences convey a single message: "Save me!" Unable to keep from hearing the message, Juli is nonetheless unable to reply. Guilt arises from this failure to stop listening and the inability to fashion an answer; the guilty person is burdened with a sense of obligations unmet and losses unmourned. In Juli's case, it is this failure to return what has been given to her that keeps returning, lodging itself inside, like an alien presence that she cannot get rid of. She is held hostage to the recurring presence of absent fathers. The only other alternative—consorting with the Spanish father—is really no alternative at all, since it amounts to incurring further guilt. To undo one crime, she must commit another.

What might have saved her from this spiraling guilt would have been the intervention of a third term coming between her and her ghostly fathers. It would have been a figure who might have spoken on her behalf, fending off the fathers' demands and effectively absolving her of her debts. Without this third term, debts can only pile up, pushing one to do what one shouldn't, triggering more guilt, and so on around the circle. In Juli's story, the only resolution turns out to be suicide. Entering the priest's quarters, she is "filled with terror . . . she saw death before

---

[25] Ibid., pp. 232-33.

her."²⁶ Before the priest can advance on her, she plunges out of the convent's window, to her death. Unable to domesticate the spectral presences of her fathers and unable to speak past the expectant friar, Juli kills herself. Hearing of her death, the people of the town can do no more than murmur their dismay, "dar[ing] not to mention names." They too, it would seem, are unable to respond adequately to her death. For this reason, they become complicitous in her demise and become infected with her guilt.

In hearing the story of Juli, everyone seems implicated. Her own personal guilt may have been absolved by her death, but the wider guilt that plagued her is passed on to those who hear of her fate. Rizal, in retelling this tale, takes on her guilt and distributes it to his readers. Just as Juli was overcome by the insistence of a message she could not answer, so we the readers are placed by Rizal in the midst of a loss we cannot account for. When a person is troubled by this guilt, there are at least two possibilities. One might, as in Juli's case, feel blocked and be driven to suicide, symbolic or otherwise. But one might also take a different route: that of repaying debts by way of revenge. In doing so, one would constitute oneself as an agent of recognition, as one who receives and registers messages of distress by virtue of one's proximity to another address: that of death. It is this route of revenge, chosen by other characters in the novel, that I want to consider in the following section.²⁷

---

²⁶ Ibid., p. 235.

²⁷ The other possibility in this story, of course, is that Juli could have struck back, taking it upon herself to seek vengence from colonial authority. Instead, she turns against herself. It is in this way that she can come across as a victim whose "innocence" comes to haunt the teller and the one who listens to her story.

Something else is also at stake in Juli's story, however, and this has to do with the gendering of revenge. Among Rizal's women characters, there is in fact one—Doña Victorina—who seeks to exact satisfaction from a Spaniard who has done her wrong. While Doña Victorina had a more prominent role in the first novel, in the *Fili* she makes only the briefest of appearances, mostly in the first chapter, where she is on a boat looking for her crippled Spanish husband who had deserted her after fifteen years of marriage. Rizal, *El Filibusterismo*, pp. 3-4. Victorina is depicted by Rizal as a native dedicated to denying her nativeness. She tries to speak Castilian—and does so badly—by repressing her knowledge of Tagalog; she dresses in what she takes to be European clothing; dyes her hair blonde and cakes her face with cosmetics. She is in this sense someone in disguise, out to seek vengeance from an errant Spanish husband. But rather than approximate the character of male *ilustrados*, Victorina comes across as their parodic double, one who fails to recognize that others fail to recognize her for what she takes herself to be, namely a "Spaniard." Neither native nor Spaniard, she is described by Rizal as a "renegade Filipina who dyes her hair blonde" and whose appearance eludes the racial categories of nineteenth-century ethnologists. Her scandalous appearance might have made her, like the *ilustrados*, into a *filibustero*. Yet, she is merely avoided by the other passengers on the ship, regarded with bemused indifference by colonial authorities and with agitated annoyance by the author. Rather than leading to disruption and conflict, her presence seems to lead only to embarrassment, thus to a sense of shame among those, especially male *ilustrados*, who see her. She is a figure of mis-translation, unable to see herself as such, a foreign presence oblivious to her foreignness. Literalizing for herself the desire for otherness and the linguistic and phallic authority that such desire promises, Victorina construes herself as an agent of revenge. In so doing, she disfigures the self-regard of male *ilustrados* which casts men as the rightful authors of such plots. And for this, she is punished with indifference and marginalized by the author. In this comedic vignette about Doña Victorina, Rizal consolidates what he had already laid out in the *Noli* and in other political writings: namely, the secondary place of women relative to men in nationalism's articulation.

IV.

As we had earlier seen in the dedication of the *Fili*, the question of revenge is linked to the imperative to mourn the dead. The author styles himself as the agent of this double duty. In writing, he pays tribute to the memory of dead fathers and sends a message to those he deems responsible for putting them to death. He faces two ways. In doing so, he also finds himself speaking from two places. As an author, he stands outside of his text, marking the threshold of its fictional reach. But he also exists as a voice who, in addressing his readers and characters, exists inside the text. His identity as the singular author from whom the novel originates is contingent on the dispersal of his presence and the dissemination of his voice throughout other voices and figures in the book.

We might think of Rizal then as a double agent: his role as an author a function of his shifting positions in the stories he tells. We can see this doubleness refracted in the language of the novel itself. Though written in Castilian, the *Fili* is remarkably heteroglossic, full of regional slang, idiomatic expressions, Latinisms, bits of untranslated French, German, and Tagalog, and broken up by the occasional appearance of *lengua de tienda* and Chinese-inflected Spanish. Just as the author's position is split and unstable, so are the languages in which he finds himself writing. Mixing identities and linguistic registers, Rizal as "Rizal" is a figure in the historical emplotment of Filipino nationalism as much as he is a figure whose presence haunts the *Fili*; an author as much as a fictional character: not one or the other, but both/and. He thus remains eccentric relative to any particular identity and at a remove from any one position. His historical specificity lies in his unspecifiability.

In his doubleness, it is tempting for the reader to see Rizal approximating the situation of the *filibustero*, for in the novel the *filibustero* is a figure of corruption as well as critique. It stands astride the tasks of mourning and revenge, translating the demands of one into the force of the other. Yet, as we shall see, the figure of the *filibustero* is precisely what Rizal must conjure up in order to renounce, and in renouncing clarify his status as the author of this text, a status far from settled in the unsettled conditions of the late nineteenth century.

In the novel, the figure of the *filibustero* looms most ominously in the character of the jeweler Simoun. Central to Simoun's identity is his mysterious appearance. He speaks with a "strange accent, a mixture of English and South American . . . dressed in English fashion . . . his long hair, completely white in contrast to the black beard . . . which indicated a mestizo origin." Always he wears "a pair of enormous blue-tinted glasses which completely covered his eyes and part of his cheeks, giving him the appearance of a blind man or one with a defective vision."[28] Wherever he appears in the colony, people take notice. His unknown origins are

---

In this connection, see also Rizal's famous letter to the women of Malolos in 1889 who, like the male students in the novel, sought permission to establish a school that would teach Spanish to the women of their town, and were subsequently turned down. "Sa Mga Kababayang Dalaga Sa Malolos," in Jose Rizal, *Escritos Politicos y Historicos* (Manila: National Historical Commission, 1961), pp. 55-65. It is instructive that he would write this letter in Tagalog, one of the very few he wrote in this language, as if speaking down to them, despite the fact that the women themselves had written their petition in Castilian.

[28] Rizal, *El Filibusterismo*, pp. 5-6.

the regular subject of gossip and speculation. He is alternately referred to as a "Yankee" because of the time he had spent traveling in North America, as an "American mulatto," an "Anglo-Indian," or a "mestizo," and the mysteriousness of his origins is compounded by his "strange [Castilian] accent" and his ability to speak Tagalog and English. What's more, because of his reputed access to both the friar orders and to the Governor General, he acquires such nicknames as the "brown cardinal" and the "black eminence."[29] While Simoun is thought to originate outside of the colonial order, he is nonetheless able to traverse the various levels of colonial society and move up and down the linguistic hierarchy.

His powerful connections, cultivated by his wealth, enable him to circulate within colonial society. Money allows him to cross geographical and social distances without having to be absorbed by any locality or social group. In this sense, money augments his mysteriousness, drawing others to speculate further on what lies beneath his appearance. Such speculations suggest that the figure of Simoun is generally perceived as something more than what he appears to be in personal encounters. He compels others to read him as a sign of and for something else—secret arrangements, unaccountable events, unexpected possibilities, hidden conspiracies—which escape detection.

Simoun's mysteriousness, however, is a disguise. Early on in the novel, the student Basilio, while walking through a cemetery, sees Simoun without his glasses and, much to his surprise, realizes that he is, in fact, Crisostomo Ibarra, the *ilustrado* protagonist of Rizal's first novel. Ibarra as Simoun has come back to exact vengeance from the colonial authorities he holds responsible for destroying his life. Thanks to the machinations of the friars, in particular, Ibarra's father had been thrown in prison, where he eventually died. His body was then dumped in the river by local gravediggers, never to be found. Ibarra's fiancée and the focus of his future happiness, Maria Clara, was taken away from him and sequestered in a convent. And his name was ruined by being associated with a revolt he did not even know of. Hounded as a *filibustero* for seeking to introduce educational reforms, he barely managed to escape from the colonial police, who thought they had shot and killed him as he floated down a river. This flight concluded his story in the earlier novel.

As Simoun, Ibarra returns. Long thought to be dead, he comes back to life, but now as a disguised presence. Whereas Ibarra had in the past sought to use Castilian as a way of securing for himself a place in a reformed order, now as Simoun he seeks to use money to blast that order apart. He explains himself to the stunned Basilio:

> Yes, I am he who [was here] thirteen years ago.... Victim of a vicious system, I have wandered throughout the world, working night and day in order to amass a fortune and carry out my plan. Today I have returned in order to destroy this system, precipitate its corruption, hurl it into the abyss ... even if I have to spill torrents of tears and blood ...
>
> Summoned by the vices of those who govern, I have returned to these islands, and under the cloak of a merchant, I have traversed the towns. With my gold I have opened the way ... and since corruption sets in gradually, I have incited greed, I have favored it, the injustices and abuses have

---

[29] Ibid., p. 44.

multiplied; I have fomented crime, and acts of cruelty in order to accustom people to the prospect of death. . . . I have instigated ambitions to impoverish the treasury; and this being insufficient to lead to a popular uprising, I have wounded the people in their most sensitive fibers . . .[30]

Revealing his secret to Basilio, Ibarra implies that, underneath his disguise, he has not changed. The "I" that announces its return in order to mourn its losses is the same "I" that has wandered the world and now brings with it a plot to exact revenge. "Simoun" is a fiction, a ruse that allows Ibarra to circulate in the colony. As such, it is a second, malleable identity within which to conceal an unchanging one. The strangeness of "Simoun" is thus recognizable to Basilio and the reader as that which refers to Ibarra, carrying out the latter's plans, acting on his behalf, serving to collect what is owed to him. Here, disguise seems to conceal one's identity only in order to consolidate one's claims on the world and one's certainty about oneself.

Money plays a crucial role in "Simoun's" plans. Through money, he—or they, that is, Ibarra and his double, Simoun—is able to incite greed and spread corruption. Simoun is thus not really a merchant, since his interests lie not in the conversion of money to capital and the accumulation of surplus value. Rather, he seeks to harness money into an instrument of his will. It is as if, at the end of each transaction, he does not expect to receive more money but rather to produce more misery. Contrary to Marx's capitalist, who sweats money from every pore, Rizal's fake merchant exudes money in order to sow crime and incite popular uprisings. Like disguise, then, money is an object whose foreignness is here readily transparent and whose disruptive effects are meant to be calculable and knowable in advance, at least from Ibarra's perspective. Money and disguise encapsulate a set of prior wishes and are made to serve the self-same identity. Behind "Simoun" there stands Ibarra; behind money, Ibarra's plan. Thus can Ibarra imagine himself as the author of his plot, the one who holds its secret and determines its unfolding.

Thinking of himself at the origin of his appearances and his plot, Ibarra, speaking through Simoun, depicts his return as a response to a summons issued by "the vices of those who govern." Arriving at the scene of the crime, he sees that neither the victim nor the perpetrator can be helped. Both are so corrupt and so weakened that only through more corruption can they be saved. What might seem like a paradoxical notion takes on a certain force when Simoun declares to Basilio, "I am the Judge [*Yo soy el Juez*] come to punish a system by availing myself of its own crimes . . ."[31] Ibarra as Simoun thus sets himself up as a third term that intervenes and adjudicates matters between colonizer and colonized. He speaks beyond the law and thereby becomes a law unto himself. As judge, he regards himself as the locus of all address and the source of recognition. His achievement is possible because he is also the author of a plot whose elements take him as their privileged referent. As judge and author, Ibarra-Simoun surpasses and subordinates all others in colonial society.

Revenge here entails a particular kind of fantasy. It gives rise to a particular scenario about one's place in relation to others. It entails the idealization of the self as one who was once misrecognized and made to suffer for it, but who now

---

[30] Ibid., pp. 46-47.
[31] Ibid., p. 49.

returns with new powers, in particular the ability to control one's appearances. It is a self capable of distinguishing and disentangling itself from the misperceptions of others. Hence, though one may look and sound foreign, underneath those surfaces one is in control of one's identity. In effect, taking vengeance is simultaneous with putting the foreign in its "proper" place, a place outside of oneself; by this action, one makes it clear that "foreignness" is a mere disguise and thus an instrument with which to carry out one's will.

We see this fantasy at work in Simoun's emphatic dismissal of assimilationist politics. Addressing Basilio in proper Castilian, he mocks the students' efforts to encourage Filipinos to learn the language. For Simoun, such a project is doomed. The friars and the government will never allow it, and the people will never take to it, since it is a foreign language incapable of expressing their native sentiments. At most, Castilian will become the language of a privileged few, thereby aggravating the separation of educated Filipinos from the people. Indeed, the students' advocacy of Castilian amounts to the betrayal of their mother tongue,[32] while their wish for hispanization is like the desire of "the slave who asks only for a little rag with which to wrap his chains so these would make less noise and not bruise the skin . . . ," according to Simoun.[33] He urges them to reject such "slavish thoughts" and instead to think "independently," which means that "neither in rights, nor customs, nor language should the Spaniard be considered here as being in his own home or thought of by people as a fellow citizen, but always as an invader, a foreigner, and sooner or later, you will be free."[34]

For Simoun, then, freedom lies not in identifying with the colonizer, even as equals, but in separating oneself from him. One needs to forget about Castilian and remember only that Spain is a foreign presence that belongs elsewhere. One who gains this perspective need no longer look towards Spain for reforms. Rather, one can in one's own language constitute oneself as an agent of change and recognition.

We can think of revenge then as a relationship of reciprocity whereby one returns what one has received wrongfully back to where one imagines it came from.[35] To take vengeance is to communicate something about Castilian: that it came as a result of an invasion; that it does not belong here; and that it should therefore be returned to its original owners. Only then can "we" regain our proper place at "home." This separatist logic assumes that the domestication of the self occurs simultaneously with the containment of the foreign, its relocation as that which is external and distant. One who speaks Castilian in this case no longer need feel burdened by the stirrings of that which it cannot possess. The economy of revenge allows one to think of assuming the place of the other as the privileged agency of translation and recognition. Rid of this foreignness, the "I" can be free from the need to seek the other's recognition even as it continues to speak in the latter's language. In this way, revenge entertains scenarios of authorship as the basis of authority, exclusion as the basis of freedom. Dissolving one kind of hierarchy, it promotes the desire for another to take its place.

---

[32] Ibid., pp. 47-48.

[33] Ibid., p. 53.

[34] Ibid., p. 49.

[35] For this formulation of revenge, I am indebted to James T. Siegel, *Fetish, Recognition, Revolution* (Princeton: Princeton University Press, 1997), pp. 169-70.

In Simoun's scenario, revenge is associated with a violent uprising that arrives as the culmination of widespread misery and indiscriminate deaths. Basilio, for example, eventually chooses to join Simoun's plot when he learns of Juli's death. Vengeance takes a violent form because it entails responding to a prior violence. It is as if one who takes vengeance speaks in the place of the dead, as the dead's representative. And given the semiotic logic of revenge, to represent the dead is not only a matter of speaking in their place, but speaking as if one came from the dead. This intimacy with the dead is, of course, the position of Simoun, who speaks for Ibarra come back to life, and of Ibarra, who, like Rizal, speaks for his dead father. Thus can one see revenge as a form of mourning, in that the dead are given a proper place in the world, while, at the same time, the foreign is returned back to where it came from. Violence imaged as the flow of blood links the two, serving as a kind of lingua franca that enables one to commemorate the absence of the dead while absenting the foreigner from one's midst. In this way does the phantasm of revenge seek to domesticate nationalism as that which now refers back "here," to the "Filipinos" in the Philippines, where the genealogies of the living can be traced to the unmourned dead, rather than as a force that translates and transmits Filipino demands for reform outward to the rest of the world.

In the *Fili*, however, revenge ultimately fails to deliver on its promise. All of Simoun's plans unravel. He is betrayed by Basilio, who could not reconcile himself to the use of violence. But even before this entanglement with Basilio, Simoun is detained by Rizal himself. Alone in his room on the eve of the uprising, Simoun's reveries about the revolt he has planned are "suddenly interrupted":

> A voice was asking in the interior of his conscience if he, Simoun, was not also part of the garbage of the cursed city, perhaps its most malignant ferment. And like the dead who are to rise at the sound of the oracular trumpet, a thousand bloody phantoms, desperate shadows of murdered men, violated women, others wrenched from their families . . . now arose to echo the mysterious question. For the first time in his criminal career since starting in Havana . . . something rebelled inside of him and protested against his actions. Simoun closed his eyes . . . he refused to look into his conscience and became afraid . . .
>
> "No, I cannot turn back," he exclaimed, wiping away the sweat from his forehead. "The work has gone far and its success will justify me. . . . If I had behaved like you [*vosotros*], I would have succumbed. . . . Fire and steel to the cancer, chastisement to vice, and if the instrument be bad then destroy it afterwards! . . . The end justifies the means. . ."
>
> And with his brain swirling he went to bed and tried to go to sleep.[36]

Revenge holds out the promise of domesticating the alien in both its forms: as the dead whose ghostly returns intrude on the living, and as the colonizer whose language assails and drives one into shame, guilt, and submission. But what domesticates revenge? If vengeance is the exchange of violence for violence, does it not, like guilt, risk spiraling out of control? Can the language of blood call into existence a response other than more of the same? If not, can revenge do any more than increase the frequency of ghostly returns? Rather than lead to domestication

---

[36] Rizal, *El Filibusterismo*, pp. 145-47.

of nationalism, revenge in this case would lead to keeping the foreign in circulation, forcing one to dwell amid its incessant returns.

Perhaps seeing this possibility, Rizal intervenes. He addresses Simoun by way of the latter's conscience. Breaking and entering into his thoughts along with a chorus of ghostly voices, this interior voice mimics the sound of God at the Last Judgement. One might say that the author appears in disguise. His is a voice that emanates from within his character's head, yet confronts him like the sound of voices from the edge of the grave. Speaking from a posthumous perspective, the author situates himself as a foreigner residing within his characters. He periodically interrupts their speech to confront them as a fearsome presence communicating from beyond the colonial order, yet understandable only within its linguistic confines. Thus the author's voice is like a second language. Its sudden emergence from within one's own language compels one to reframe one's thoughts. Simoun is asked by this second voice: aren't you also guilty? That is, it forces him to reformulate his thoughts in response. The second voice holds the first accountable and so contains the latter's speech in both senses of the term. Under the cover of a fictional voice, the author subordinates all other fictional voices, enframing all other plots. The foreign returns in its most intimate yet most impersonal form.

In seeking revenge, Simoun disguised as a foreigner sought to exceed and thereby take the place of the law. But Rizal as the second voice seeks to surpass revenge and put it back in its place: as a criminal act subject to a higher law. Simoun tries to talk back to the author, seeking to separate himself from his characterization. Refusing Rizal's intervention, he imagines himself at the origin of hierarchy, not subject to it, a source of terror, not its recipient. But he falters, his "brain swirling." With his plans already doomed, he finds himself in the grip of authorship's interruptive arrival.

What did it mean to be an author in Rizal's time? In the absence of any scholarship on the sociology of authorship in nineteenth-century Philippine colonial society, we can only speculate.[37] We might start with the question of Rizal's name. According to his own accounting, this was a name that did not originally belong to him nor did it come down from his father. His father's name was Francisco Mercado and his mother's Teodoro Alonso. "Rizal" was added by a provincial governor, "a friend of the family," as a second surname in order to distinguish Rizal's family from the other Mercados in the country to whom they bore no relation.[38] It is difficult to ascertain whether this addition may have followed from the 1848 decree of Governor General Claveria requiring all colonial subjects to take on Spanish surnames in the interest of regularizing the collection of taxes. Hence, even those who already had Spanish surnames, like Rizal's family, were given new names to distinguish them from others with similar names, rendering them more visible to the state. It should not come as a surprise that the members of Rizal's family continued to refer to themselves by the father's original name, Mercado, and the mother by her father's name, Alonso, thinking that they owed neither allegiance to nor affiliation with the second name, Rizal. "Rizal" was then a supplementary formation, something that came from outside the

---

[37] By the same token, literary critics tend to regard Rizal's novels as "realist" without explaining what counts as "real" in his time. See the books cited earlier by Mojares, Guerrero, and Schumacher.

[38] See Guerrero, *First Filipino*, pp. 18-19.

family, rather than a name that was handed down from the father's or mother's line.

Not until 1872, the year of the Cavite revolt that resulted in the execution of the three Filipino secular priests, Gomez, Burgos and Zamora, did the name "Rizal" take on a new significance. In a letter to his Austrian friend, Blumentritt, Rizal recalls how his older brother, Paciano, enrolled him at the Jesuit-run secondary school, Ateneo in Manila, under this second name. Paciano had been associated with one of the martyred priests, Jose Burgos, and it was out of a desire to protect the younger Jose that he had him enrolled under another name. "My family never paid much attention [to our second surname]," Rizal writes more than a decade later, "but now I had to use it, thus giving me the appearance of an illegitimate child!"[39] Rizal sees in the history of his name the convergence of a set of contingencies—the act of a colonial official following a state decree, the shadowy but no less tragic events of 1872, the predicament of his older brother—all of which give him the appearance of something other than who he was supposed to be. His surname functions not as a way of linking him to his father and family, but precisely as a way of obscuring such a link. "Rizal" offered Jose a disguise. The second name concealed the first and thus allowed him to pass through the suspicious gaze of colonial and clerical authority.

The secondary name, however, comes to take on a primary importance out of proportion to its intended function. Jose as "Rizal" soon distinguishes himself in poetry-writing contests, impressing his professors with his facility with Castilian and other foreign languages. In Europe, he signs his name to a series of political essays critical of the colonial order and challenging Spanish historical accounts of pre-colonial Philippine societies. Though he occasionally uses pseudonyms, everyone, *ilustrados* and Spanish authorities alike, knows exactly who these names refer to. And his two novels not only bear this name but also the phrase "Es propiedad del Autor," "the property of the author," at a time when copyright laws in both Spain and the Philippines were yet to be codified. Indeed, by 1891, the year Rizal finished the *Fili*, this second name had become so well known that, as he writes to another friend, "All my family now carry the name Rizal instead of Mercado because the name Rizal means persecution! Good! I too want to join them and be worthy of this family name. . ." His mother had previously been harassed and arrested by the colonial police because, among other things, "she did not identify herself as Realonda de Rizal but simply as Teodora Alonso! But she has always called herself Teodora Alonso!"[40]

Rizal's name thus came to signal a certain notoriety, and his family, having been forced to take it on, were subjected to persecution. Originally meant to conceal his identity, his second name became that through which he was widely known. For this reason, what was meant to save him from suffering now became the means with which to harm and ruin others. As his foremost biographer, Leon Maria Guerrero, wrote, "He must have felt utterly alone, surrounded though he was by his family, for he alone must bear the responsibility for their ruin; because of him they had been driven from their homes in his name."[41] Racked by guilt, Rizal returned to

---

[39] Cited in ibid., p. 38.
[40] Both cited in ibid., pp. 297 and 298 respectively.
[41] Ibid., p. 299.

the Philippines. His return was a response to the distress caused by his name, one which he had used to author a series of texts.

Authorship in this instance brings to Rizal recognition that leads to ruination. He feels himself responsible for his family's fate. The "illegitimate child" now assumes the focal point of the family's identity, at least from the point of view of the colonial authorities. His name takes on a patronymic significance, as that through which his family comes to have a public identity and be rendered targets of colonial pressure. His name reverses the family genealogy. It is now through the youngest son that the family comes to be known. In taking responsibility, Rizal stands as the author of this reversal, one whose effects are linked to criminal acts of subverting authority and reversing hierarchy.

The colonial state thus invested the name "Rizal" with a certain communicative power, seeing in it the medium through which passed challenges to its authority. They recognized in his name far more than Rizal himself had ever intended. In his trial, colonial prosecutors claimed that his name had been used as a "rallying cry" by the revolutionary organization, the Katipunan, to enlist the support of Filipinos and indios, of the wealthy and the poor alike.[42] Indeed, what Guerrero refers to as the "magical power" of Rizal's name was used by the members of the Katipunan as a secret password.[43] The name "Rizal" in this sense worked like a second language, crossing the line between the upper and lower levels of colonial hierarchy, while bringing the disparate groups of each level in touch with one another. It was a watchword through which one came into contact with something new and unexpected.

During his trial, Rizal repeatedly objected to the state's accusations and lamented the rampant misappropriation of his name. "I gave no permission for the use of my name," he wrote in response to the charges that it had served to instigate the revolution, "and the wrong done to me is beyond description."[44] It was as if Rizal found himself confused with Simoun as the author of a separatist conspiracy, caught within a phantasm of revenge he had sought to control. He condemns the revolution as a "ridiculous and barbarous uprising, plotted behind my back. . . . I abominate the crimes for which it is responsible, and I will have nothing to do with it."[45] While he felt some responsibility for the ruination of his family, he could not be held responsible for the catastrophe he thought was about to befall the colony. "How am I to blame for the use of my name by others when I neither knew of it nor could stop it?"[46] Against the misreadings of his name by those above and those below, Rizal claimed innocence. "I am not guilty either of organizing a revolutionary society, or taking part in such societies, or of participating in the rebellion."[47]

In claiming innocence, Rizal disavows responsibility for the uses to which his name had been put outside the domestic circle of his family. The colonial state sought to attribute the upheavals of 1896 to a singular author. Rizal for his part

---

[42] Horacio de la Costa, ed., *The Trial of Rizal* (Quezon City: Ateneo de Manila University Press, 1961), p. 106.

[43] Rizal, *El Filibusterismo*, p. 382.

[44] Guerrero, *First Filipino*, p. 421.

[45] Horacio de la Costa, *The Trial of Rizal*, p. 103.

[46] Guerrero, *First Filipino*, p. 425.

[47] Horacio de la Costa, *The Trial of Rizal*, p. 134.

could not or refused to recognize these events as anything but "barbaric" and "criminal." Revolution appeared to him as the failure to sublimate revenge. For him, it involved the emergence of a kind of speech from below that was not properly traceable to his thoughts and which eluded his ability to translate. For as we have seen in the *Fili*, authorship of the sort Rizal practiced is about the rehearsal and subsequent containment of shame, guilt, and revenge. In his God-like interventions within his characters' speech, he had sought to transform such affects of identification into a discourse of responsibility constituted by "education," "virtue," and "sacrifice." Nationalist authorship, "properly conceived," was a matter of identifying with and domesticating the force of translation, thereby displacing the hegemony of the Spanish friar. As the various scenes of the *Fili* show, the corruption of authority is imagined by Rizal to give rise to an interruptive voice that re-forms relations of inequality. Translation thus brings with it the desire for hierarchy, not its elimination. Insofar as nationalist authorship concerns the designation of the foreign as an ominous but potentially domesticatable element of oneself, as that which one can recognize and so control, it mirrors the logic of Christian conversion in its colonizing context. In both, there exists the wish for communicative transparency: that all messages, whether intended or not, have the same address, and that figures such as the missionary or the author serve as indispensable relays for their transmission.

However, Rizal's life, especially his trial, reveals something of the unexpected and unaccountable consequences of this wish for authorship. Just as evangelization resulted in conversions and translations beyond the reach and outside the expectations of Spanish missionaries—resulting, for example, in the emergence of "folk Catholicism," or figures such as the *filibustero*, or even "Rizal"—so nationalist authorship sparked readings that it could not anticipate, much less control. For rather than leading to the domestication of desires and languages that had been out of place, nationalist authorship tended in fact to spur them in uncharted and, at times, revolutionary directions.

In all cases, Castilian played a key role, keeping a sense of the foreign—that is, that which escaped assimilation either into the colonial or the national—in circulation, available for all kinds of use and misuse. The history of conversion made Castilian over into a medium for transmitting a fantasy about direct communication and unlimited transmissions across socio-geographical divides. The name "Rizal," by the late nineteenth century, thus retained and kept in circulation the sense of the foreign which even he himself could not recognize and account for at the point when Castilian was denied to the rest of the colony's subjects. Proclaiming in his trial that "I am innocent" meant that "I" did not intend to commit a crime which nevertheless bears his signature. His innocence then implies his guilt, the culpability he incurred in ignoring the effects that a second, foreign name would have on those who felt its force.

THE QUESTION OF FOREIGNERS: BAI REN'S *NANYANG PIAOLIUJI* AND THE RE/MAKING OF CHINESE AND PHILIPPINE NATIONNESS[1]

Caroline S. Hau

The years that followed the death of Mao Zedong and the fall of the Gang of Four witnessed the veritable flowering of literary production in the Chinese mainland. During the late seventies and early eighties, artists and writers drew inspiration from three main wellsprings of literary creation: namely, the traumas inflicted by the Cultural Revolution, which produced a body of works known as "scar literature" (*shanghen wenxue*); the impulse to reflect on the recent past and present and their problems, expressed in the so-called "literature of exposure"; and the return of the repressed personal, namely romantic and sexual love and the concerns of the private sphere.[2] Writers also engaged in technical innovation and experimentation, deploying psychological description, as well as paying close attention to problems of narrativity and expression.

These three wellsprings of literary creation had ideological and political significance in that they served to shore up Deng Xiaoping's faction within the Communist Party and its economic and structural reforms. These works did more than criticize the excesses of the Cultural Revolution. By focusing on subjectivity and desire, they also heralded the renaissance of the literary modernism that had

---

[1] I thank Patricio N. Abinales, Filomeno V. Aguilar, Takeshi Hamashita, Deborah Homsher, Audrey Kahin, R. Kwan Laurel, James T. Siegel, Takashi Shiraishi, and Kasian Tejapira for their comments and encouragement. I especially thank Benedict Anderson for the gift of his friendship.

[2] For discussions of the post-Mao literary scene, see the essays in Jeffrey C. Kinkley, ed., *After Mao: Chinese Literature and Society, 1978-1981* (Cambridge, MA: Harvard University Press, 1985); Michael S. Duke, *Blooming and Contending: Chinese Literature in the Post-Mao Era* (Bloomington: University of Indiana Press, 1985); and Perry Link, *The Uses of Literature: Life in the Socialist Chinese Literary System* (New Jersey: Princeton University Press, 2000).

first flourished during the May Fourth movement.[3] In fact, the culture debate of the 1980s hinged on a thoroughgoing critique of Maoist cultural policy, and marked the intellectuals' attempt to carve a semiautonomous space for literary production away from party control.[4] Not surprisingly, the issue of subjectivity (*zhuti xing*) was central to the culture debate, with Chinese theorist Liu Zaifu calling for the recuperation of "humanist" values and the formulation of a "literary subjectivity" that was aimed specifically at challenging the dominant trend in Marxist criticism which had tended to privilege the idea of "collective identity" at the expense of a nuanced analysis of the human subject.[5]

On the face of it, Chinese writer Bai Ren's 1983 novel, *Nanyang[6] Piaoliuji* (Adrift in the Southern Ocean) would seem to fit in the general trend in post-Mao literary production. Though Bai Ren focuses neither on the traumas of the Cultural Revolution, nor on contemporary abuses and injustices, nor on the strictly personal politics of desire, he takes as his topic the overseas Chinese who, upon returning to their "Motherland," found themselves identified as one of the "seven categories of sinister people" (along with landlords, rich peasants, counter-revolutionaries, bad elements, rightists, and enemy agents) during the Cultural Revolution for their allegedly "reactionary" and "bourgeois capitalist" character.[7] Bai Ren himself was a victim of the Cultural Revolution: his 1957 patriotic spoken drama *Bing Lin Cheng Xia* (Soldiers facing the city wall), first staged in 1962 and subsequently seen three times and praised by Premier Zhou Enlai, was one of the works singled out for criticism by Jiang Qing and Lin Biao at the beginning of the Cultural Revolution, and the writer was sent to Gansu and Hunan for ten years of hard labor.[8]

In light of the recognition given by the Deng administration to the overseas Chinese potential economic contribution to the Four Modernizations program,[9] Bai

---

[3] Liu Kang, "Subjectivity, Marxism, and Cultural Theory in China," in *Politics, Ideology, and Literary Discourse in Modern China*, ed. Liu Kang and Xiaobing Tang (Durham: Duke University Press, 1993), p. 24.

[4] Ibid., p. 31. See also Douwe Fokkema, "Creativity and Politics," in *The Cambridge History of China*, vol. 15, ed. Roderick MacFarquhar and John K. Fairbank (Cambridge: Cambridge University Press, 1991), pp. 611-14.

[5] Liu, "Subjectivity, Marxism, and Cultural Theory in China," pp. 12, 43-47.

[6] Nanyang, translated as "Southern Ocean," refers to territories in Southeast Asia that are traversed through the South China Sea. Writes Wang Gungwu, ". . . [A]reas of special concern of Nanyang Chinese have been key coastal strips of mainland Southeast Asia and most of the islands of the Philippines and Indonesia." Wang Gungwu, "A Short History of the Nanyang Chinese," in his *Community and Nation: China, Southeast Asia and Australia* (New South Wales: Asian Studies Association of Australia, and Allen and Unwin, 1992), p. 11.

[7] Theresa Chong Cariño, *China and the Overseas Chinese in Southeast Asia* (Quezon City: New Day Publishers, 1985), p. 44.

[8] Interview with Bai Ren, Beijing, People's Republic of China, September 25, 2001. See also Gong Zhong, "Huaqiao, Zhanshi, Zuojia: Fang Bai Ren" (Huaqiao, warrior, writer: Interview with Bai Ren), *Beijing Dangdai* (n.d.), pp. 207-8.

[9] Wang Gungwu has argued for the need to distinguish between Southeast Asian Chinese investments and investments from Hong Kong and Taiwan in his historical overview of the issue in "The Southeast Asian Chinese and the Development of China," in *Southeast Asian Chinese and China: The Politico-Economic Dimension*, ed. Leo Suryadinata (Singapore: Times Academic Press, 1995), pp. 12-30. For a discussion of, and statistics on, Philippine-Chinese investments in China, see Theresa Chong Cariño's "The Ethnic Chinese, the Philippine Economy and China" in the same book, pp. 216-29; and Leo Suryadinata, "China's Economic

Ren's[10] semi-autobiographical account[11] of a young boy's sojourn[12] and adventures in the Philippines in the mid-1930s may be read as an attempt to redress the negative image of and discrimination against the overseas Chinese during the Maoist years. Bai's novel reinforces Chinese Communist Party leading official Hua Guofeng's official rehabilitation of the "Overseas Chinese" (*huaqiao*) through his statement regarding the positive role played by returned overseas Chinese in "building the Motherland" at the Fifth National People's Congress in February 1978.[13] In *Nanyang Piaoliuji*, Bai Ren speaks of the need to correct the mainland Chinese erroneous conceptions about the overseas Chinese:

> Many of our compatriots in the Mainland believe that the *huaqiao*[14] are all capitalists. Even the relatives in our hometown [*Tangshan*; *Tengsua* in Minnan

---

Modernization and the Ethnic Chinese in ASEAN: A Preliminary Study," also in the same book, p. 208.

[10] Bai (White) Ren (Knife's edge) is the *nom de plume* of novelist, dramatist, and poet Wang Jisheng (who also uses the pen name Wang Song). Born Wang Nian Song in Yongningzhen, Jinjiang, Fujian on October 12, 1918, Bai Ren left for the Philippines in 1933. In the Philippines, he stayed in Iloilo (La Paz), Negros Occidental (Fábrica), Cebu, and Manila. In Manila, he studied at Tiong Se Academy and Philippine Cultural High School, the latter while working part-time as a newspaper boy. Bai Ren returned to China in 1937 and continued his studies at Jimei High School in Fujian. He proceeded to Yenan after graduation and for eight years fought the Japanese at Shantung as a combatant. He participated in several major battles during the Civil War in the late 1940s, including the Liaoshi-Shenyang (Mukden) campaign in 1948. His writing career, spanning the years between 1936 and 1996, has resulted in thirty books which collectively add up to four million words.

[11] The autobiographical elements of *Nanyang* are summarized in detail in Sun Ailing, "Huaqiao Ticai Xiaoshuo de Wenxueteshe" (Characteristics of the Huaqiao novel), *Lun Guiqiao Zuojia Xiaoshuo* (On the novels of returned overseas Chinese) (Singapore: Xinjiapo Yunnan Yuanyashe, 1996), pp. 231-38; and in Wei Jun, "Zai Manchang de Daolushang Qianjin: Ji Juzuojia Bai Ren" (Moving ahead in the long journey: On Bai Ren the dramatist), Photostat copy, n.d., pp. 86-87. See the Afterword of *Nanyang Piaoliuji*, p. 292, for Bai Ren's brief discussion of his use of the first-person narrative. Like his protagonist, Bai Ren had worked as an apprentice in a dry-goods store, and after a period of wandering, during which he was rescued from drowning by a Filipina, he became a working student involved in the anti-Japanese movement. Shortly after his 1983 Philippine visit, Bai Ren wrote a book of essays on the Philippines, *Yongbudiaoxiedehua* (Eternally unwithering flower) (Beijing: Zhongguo Huaqiao Chubangongsi, 1990). Bai Ren has also written two other stories set in the Philippines: "Wo de Feilubin Jiemei A!" (Ah, my Filipino sisters!) *Shijie Ribao* (August 8, 1982): 5, and (August 10, 1982): 5; and "Manila zhi Ai" (Manila love), Photostat manuscript, pp. 107-14.

[12] See Wang Gungwu's dissection of the word "sojourner" in his "Sojourning: The Chinese Experience in Southeast Asia," in *Sojourners and Settlers: Histories of Southeast Asia and the Chinese*, ed. Anthony Reid (New South Wales: Allen and Unwin and Asian Studies Association of Australia, 1996), pp. 1-14.

[13] Cariño, *China and the Overseas Chinese*, p. 53.

[14] For an account of the etymology and usage of the term *huaqiao*, see Wang Gungwu, "The Origins of Hua-Ch'iao," *Community and Nation*, pp. 1-10. *Huaqiao*, for most of its hundred-year history, connoted enforced migration or exile, with semantic overlays of official protection extended to Chinese abroad as well as self-conscious patriotism among the Chinese abroad, expressed as a "cultural" commitment to "remaining Chinese or restoring one's 'Chineseness'" (p. 7). Wang, though, notes that "[w]hile the term retains the surface meaning of 'sojourner,' its extended use had created a serious ambiguity, by covering as it did settlers who were foreign subjects" (p. 9).

Hokkien[15]] look upon the *fanke* [the Hokkien term denoting *lannang*, "our people," who had left China to make a living in a foreign land; literally, visitors or guests in a foreign land[16]] as landlords and feel that going abroad is the path to prosperity. They do not understand the truth about the *huaqiao*. Of course, there are *huaqiao* capitalists, but they are few in number. Eighty to ninety percent of the *huaqiao* are laborers, and a majority of them are small-time vendors, storekeepers, workers, and peasants. They scrimp on food and other necessities in order to save money and return home and support their families.[17]

But while Deng's reformist platform placed a premium on the technical and economic prowess of the overseas Chinese[18]—that is, on the same "reactionary," "capitalist" attributes that had hitherto branded the overseas Chinese as sinister characters in the eyes of the Chinese state—on the ideological plane, the rehabilitation of the overseas Chinese proceeded along a markedly distinct, if not actually opposing, line of argument, which tended to elide the identification of the overseas Chinese with bourgeois capitalism in favor of calling attention to the facticity of overseas Chinese labor. In fact, numerous articles in the Chinese media, the influential *Renmin Ribao* (People's Daily) among them, had sought to correct the "erroneous" conception of the overseas Chinese as capitalists by arguing that the majority of them were laborers who were also oppressed by "imperialists, colonialists, and monopoly capitalists."[19]

This seemingly countervailing impulse to valorize the contribution of overseas Chinese capital investment to national development while stressing the constitutive role of Chinese labor in the making of the Chinese national community deeply informs Bai Ren's narrative project. The general tenor of post-Maoist

---

[15] "Hokkien" is the term used by Philippine Chinese to denote the Philippine-Chinese lingua franca *Minnanhua*.

[16] The historian William Henry Scott, citing the Boxer Codex (1590), has argued that *sangley*, the term which the Spaniards used for "Chinese" from the sixteenth to the early nineteenth centuries, before it was replaced by *chino* in the late nineteenth century, derives from the Chinese words *changlai* (*shonglai* in Hokkien), meaning "regularly come." "Frequently coming" *sangleyes* were called *langlang*, probably derived from *lannang*, but also meaning pirate or corsair. William Henry Scott, *Barangay: Sixteenth-Century Philippine Culture and Society* (Quezon City: Ateneo de Manila University Press, 1994), pp. 190, 279.

[17] Bai Ren, *Nanyang Piaoliuji* (Guangzhou: Huacheng Chubanshe, 1983), p. 112. All quotations in this essay are from this edition. The novel was first serialized in Hong Kong's *Wenjiang Bao* in 1983 and was shortly thereafter published under the title *Nanyang Liulanger* (Orphan wanderer of the Southern Ocean) (Hong Kong: South China Press, 1983). The novel was also serialized in the Manila-based newspaper, *Shijie Ribao* from December 25, 1983 to, roughly, the summer of 1984. Unfortunately, the *Shijie Ribao* publishers began microfilming their newspaper issues for archival purposes only in the mid-1990s; consequently, with very few exceptions, the issues prior to 1990 are now unavailable, and I have been unable to verify the exact date of the newspaper issue containing the final installment of the novel. The 1984 estimate was provided by Bai Ren in his letter to me dated December 30, 2000.

[18] Suryadinata, "China's Economic Modernization and the Ethnic Chinese in ASEAN," pp. 193-207.

[19] Liao Chengzhi, "A Critique of the Reactionary Fallacies of the 'Gang of Four' about the So-called 'Overseas Relations,'" *Renmin Ribao*, (January 4, 1978), translated in *FBIS* (January 5, 1978): E12. See also "Attention Must Be Paid to Overseas Chinese Affairs," *Beijing Review*, no. 3 (January 20, 1978): 14-15. Cited in Cariño, *China and the Overseas Chinese*, p. 56.

cultural production is embodied in the anguished line from army writer Bai Hua's screenplay, *Kulian* (Bitter love), in which a young daughter tells her dying father, "You loved your country but your country didn't love you."[20] Written at a time when the question of whether the cat is black or white has ceased to matter as long as it catches the mouse, Bai Ren's novel appears to harken anachronistically back to the idealism and patriotism of a revolutionary past that is now in danger of being erased from popular memory. Bai Ren's best-known works (*Bing Lin Cheng Xia* and his first novel, 1951's *Zhan Dou Dao Mingtien*)[21] deal with the high noon of Chinese nationalism during the anti-Japanese struggle from 1937 to 1945; indeed, in *Nanyang Piaoliuji*, the protagonist A Song ends his eventful stay in the Philippines on the eve of the outbreak of the Sino-Japanese war, and sails back to China to join the resistance movement.

Yet Bai Ren's *Bildungsroman* narrative, with its focus on the sentimental education of a young, laboring *huaqiao* and its posing of the fraught question of the wandering self within the framework—both conceptual and experiential—of the nation, is, as I will argue in this essay, a reconfiguration of Hu Feng's theory of the "subjective fighting spirit." Formulated, in fact, during the Sino-Japanese war (the same period covered by most of Bai Ren's longer works), the theory of the subjective fighting spirit sought to cement the link between individual consciousness and social revolution by positing the idea of revolutionary resistance at the level of subjective, lived experience. This theory of the revolutionary subject had subsequently been neglected or suppressed by later Chinese literary critics' emphasis on the preeminence of "collectivism" as a mode of revolutionary struggle and national liberation.[22] Already subjected to reductive simplification by dominant Chinese literary criticism during the Mao years, this revolutionary subjectivity, which traces its intellectual lineage to the patriotic anti-imperialism

---

[20] For an extended analysis of *Kulian*, see Duke, *Blooming and Contending*, pp. 123-48. The central character of the "film-poem" is a patriotic overseas Chinese artist named Ling Chenguang who turns his back on his American success in 1949 in order to return to China. Persecuted during the Cultural Revolution, he lives long enough to see the fall of the Gang of Four. Against his wishes, his daughter elects to leave China upon marrying an overseas Chinese. Another important character in *Kulian*, the overseas Chinese poet Xie Qiushan, loses his wife Yun Ying during the upheavals of the 1960s.

[21] *Bai Ren Wenji* Bianweihui, "*Bai Ren Wenji* Chuban ji Zengsong, Zhengding Shuoming" [*Bai Ren's Collected Works*: Information on Publication, Dissemination, and Subscriptions] October 1, 2000, p. 1.

[22] Hu Feng, "Zhi shen zai wei minzhu de douzheng limian" (Situating ourselves in the struggle for democracy), *Hu Feng Pinglun Ji* (Hu Feng's collected critical essays), vol. 3 (Beijing: Renmin Wenxue, 1984), p. 17. A short discussion of literary critic Hu Feng's career and concept of subjectivity can be found in Kirk A. Denton, *The Problematic of Self in Modern Chinese Literature: Hu Feng and Lu Ling* (Stanford: Stanford University Press, 1998), especially pp. 73-116. Born in Hubei in 1902, Hu Feng (1902-85) became a prominent leftist critic in the 1930s and 40s, but was purged (along with two hundred other writers and intellectuals branded as members of the *Hu Feng Fangemingjituan* or "Hu Feng Counterrevolutionary Clique") in 1955 for allegedly promoting an "idealist literature grounded in a bourgeois worldview and thus [posing] a threat to a Marxist materialist ideology" (Denton, *The Problematic of Self*, p. 2). As a result, "[t]he Hu Feng group of writers were effectively erased from modern Chinese literary history, and views of literature stressing the dynamic, creative role for the writer were suppressed" (ibid., p. 3). Denton argues that the concept of the subjective fighting spirit "was an oft-repeated catchword in Hu Feng's sustained attack on Marxist dogmatism and its literary manifestations, 'mechanical determinism' and 'formulism,' and marked an attempt to find a place for individual subjectivity within a Marxist framework" (p. 96).

of the May Fourth enlightenment, is also ironically in the process of being banished to the fringes of historical and popular memory by the kind of liberal-humanist individualism currently being articulated in Chinese literary criticism in consonance with a post-Maoist China undergoing massive economic reorientation along capitalist lines.

Bai Ren's novel memorializes a popular, anti-colonial nationalism that is coursed through the prism of subjectivity. *Nanyang* limns the concept of revolutionary subjectivity by asking, not the post-Maoist question of how one's country came to betray one's love for it, but the forgotten popular-nationalist question of how it is that one came to love one's country in the first place. And it asks this question by considering the situation of those to whom love of country does not come "naturally," that is, those who spent their formative years elsewhere, outside China. But what place, if any, does Bai's delineation of revolutionary subjectivity through a narrative of the *huaqiao's* involvement in the anti-Japanese struggle have in the post-Maoist era of political cynicism and economic decentralization, an era marked by the importation of "postmodern" cultural theory alongside the critical denunciation of Marxist literary orthodoxy? How do we read a novel that has been shaped by media efforts to stress the working-class character and revolutionary contribution of the overseas Chinese simultaneously alongside the seemingly contradictory public policy espousal of capital accumulation ("To Get Rich is Good") and valorizing of overseas Chinese capital investment in the mainland?

These questions cannot be answered without any reference to the Philippines, the setting of Bai Ren's novel, and to questions of "Chineseness," national identification, and belonging that are also salient and equally fraught features of the *huaqiao's* experiential involvement in Southeast Asia. Bai Ren's relative invisibility in Philippine arts and letters has restricted the reception of his novel to a small, Chinese-speaking circle within the Philippines. Yet his realistic depiction of life among the *huaqiao* in the Philippines is one of the rare full-length treatments of that subject to have appeared in print, and constitutes an invaluable source for scholars and students of Philippine studies, and more generally of Southeast Asian studies.

This essay takes up historian Wang Gungwu's call to give overseas Chinese responses to nationalism a place in the recent history of Southeast Asia[23] by looking into the hidden history of the Chinese Left in the Philippines and its role in the making of "national" communities in both China and the Philippines. It is about the political salience of a revolutionary *huaqiao* nationalism that has been marginalized from most histories of the Chinese in the Philippines. It argues that the 1983 Bai Ren novel *Nanyang Piaoliuji*'s depiction of the development of a young Chinese sojourner's patriotic consciousness forces us to question and rethink our commonsensical notions of nationness and national belonging.

This essay delineates Bai Ren's novelistic treatment of the politics of memory and the mutual determination of the constructed terms "China" and the "Philippines" in the subjective constitution of the *huaqiao*. Its primary focus is on the ways in which the novel worked through the idea of a *huaqiao Bildung* (education, also culture) at a specific conjuncture in Chinese and Philippine history through notions of work, pedagogy, and experience. But it also sets out to

---

[23] Wang, "The Limits of Nanyang Chinese Nationalism, 1912-1937," p. 54.

interrogate not just the "borders" of patriotic love, experience, and memory, but of scholarly inquiry as well, which—given its restrictive reliance on the given boundedness of the nation-state and the discourse of citizenship as units of analysis[24]—has tended to elide the crucial delineation by *huaqiao Bildung* of the constitutive relationship between Chinese and Filipino nationalisms. The arguments presented in the following sections attempt to broaden the discussion of both Chinese and Filipino nationness, and of nationalism in general, by showing how the making (and remaking) of national communities depends in part on a historically situated, constitutive experience of the "outside" and of "foreignness," a potentially radical openness to the foreign other that is often ignored, if not repressed by articulations of Chinese and Philippine, as well as Philippine-Chinese, identity politics which favor the assertion of an unnecessarily monolithic and exclusionary national identity.

PLOT SUMMARY

Nanyang Piaoliuji is the story of A Song, a fourteen-year-old Hokkien boy from an impoverished family in Jinjiang, Fujian Province, China and of his four-year sojourn as a shopkeeper's apprentice, a Robinson Crusoe-*manqué*, a newspaper boy, a student, and an activist in various parts of the Philippines from early spring of 1932 to early winter of 1936.

Having borrowed money to purchase, on a ten-year installment arrangement with a professional middleman, a two-hundred-*yuan* alien certificate of registration (*dazi* in Mandarin, or *toa-di* in Hokkien[25]) that entitles him to reside in the Philippines, A Song's family entrusts him to an uncle. At the entry port of M—,[26] they are met by A Song's "paper father" and a Chinese agent in charge of

---

[24] Liren Zheng has criticized the propensity of studies on overseas Chinese nationalism to resort to an "academic loyalty test, which tends to identify overseas Chinese nationalists as either loyal to China or loyal to the countries where they resided." Such a "dichotomous approach... ignores an important fact that at the time there was a new 'imagined community' called overseas Chinese society emerging between China and local nation-states." See his "Overseas Chinese Nationalism in British Malaya 1894-1941," (PhD dissertation, Cornell University, Ithaca, New York, USA, 1997), pp. 3-4.

[25] Bai Ren still has the original landing certificate issued by the Philippine Bureau of Customs describing him as the son of a merchant and entitled by law to remain in the country under the provisions of Section 7 of Act no. 702 of the Philippine Commission. The text of this landing certificate is reproduced in Sun Ailing, "Huaqiao Ticai Xiaoshuo de Wenxueteshe," pp. 231-32. "Obtaining access to a visa to immigrate to the Philippines required one to show kinship to a merchant already present. For some men, this meant purchase of the *teng-ki-toa-li*, or alien certificate of registration. Other men had relatives to claim them. Still other men (and some young women) were adopted by childless Chinese; Filipinos did not adopt Chinese... The *teng-ki-toa-li* system, which was only a kinship on paper, did not constitute adoption; many men never met their supposed 'certificate parents.' But *teng-ki-toa-li* 'brothers,' entering the country as sons of the same man, though perhaps not mutually related, would sometimes develop close personal ties if they were employed together by their sponsor. Some strong lifetime brotherhoods between Iloilo Chinese leaders were created because of this propinquity in immigration histories." John T. Omohundro, *Chinese Merchant Families in Iloilo: Commerce and Kin in a Central Philippine City* (Quezon City: Ateneo de Manila University Press, 1981), pp. 22-23.

[26] All the towns and cities in the novel are referred to only by their initials. M—most likely refers to the capital city of Manila.

facilitating the processing of A Song's documents. Under the name Li Xin, son of the merchant Li Zaixing, A Song with his official papers in hand moves south after a week's stay in the capital, and takes up his apprenticeship in a dry-goods store in L—.

Although A Song's father and brother also operate a shop in the same town, A Song is apprenticed to another shopkeeper to learn the rules of the trade, as was the custom among the Philippine Chinese in the prewar years. As an apprentice, A Song starts at the bottom of the work ladder of responsibility as a janitor and gofer: not yet assigned the privilege of dealing directly with customers by his seniors, he is responsible for sweeping the floor, tying the store awning to the wooden pole, arranging the rice piles on display, cooking rice for the meals, chopping wood and building the fire, and grinding corn and mixing it with molasses. A Song earns praise from his employer for his honesty and industry. But among the store employees and *compañeros* (partners), A Song forms his closest attachment with one of the store workers, the strapping *mestizo* (mixed blood) Chen Shan, whose tragic love affair with the beautiful *mestiza* dancer Yisha, whom he had rescued from rapists but who married a landed spendthrift at her aunt's behest, forms an important subplot of the novel.

The store at which A Song is an apprentice falls victim to the Depression that hits the Philippines in the early thirties. Bad business is compounded by a strong typhoon which floods the store. The owner, a shrewd but illiterate man, decides to return to *Tangshan*, the proverbial term for the Chinese homeland, and leaves his store to his two sons. A Song is quickly disillusioned with the first son, a wastrel who spent all his years of idleness in Manila and, now in charge of the ailing business, resorts to all manner of quick-profit chicanery, including cheating the customers and stealing electricity. The younger brother, who befriends A Song, works as an apprentice at someone else's store.

Despite the hard work and his own dim prospects for advancement in his profession, A Song is able to find the time to learn boxing under Chen Shan (Tan Sua) and to indulge his love of reading. Among the books he is reading, Daniel Defoe's *Robinson Crusoe* will later prove to be of immediate relevance to his own experience. The store is soon forced to close down, and its employees, cast adrift to survive in the rough waters of the economic Depression, go their own way. Chen Shan decides to try his luck in S— as a professional boxer. A Song decides to seek out his uncle for a job (*toulu*, or *taolo* in Hokkien) or, alternatively, go to D— to join his father and brother. The family business, precarious enough to begin with, is utterly destroyed when a fire burns down the store. Father and brother both make their way back to the capital in order to find a way to go back to China. A Song's brother later decides not to go back to China; he renews his love affair with the Chinese *mestiza* Bili, whom he marries after a year.

A Song, alone again, decides to look for Chen Shan in S— and, at the pier, is befriended by Niuniu, a Filipina dressed in men's clothes. A Song is conscripted to work in a boat in exchange for free passage. Only later does he find out that his co-workers are engaged in smuggling. Niuniu, who has developed a fondness for "Pepe," as she christens him, helps A Song escape when the boat stops at an island for its rendezvous. Now a veritable Robinson Crusoe, A Song survives on his wits for three days before he is found by a tribe of friendly indigenous people. The tribal elder, Mohani, invites A Song to stay with them, and, after a few days, helps A Song find his way to the city of S—.

In S—, he encounters a much aged and embittered Chen Shan, deliberately crippled by a vehicular accident at the instigation of a Portuguese-Arab gangster who had asked him to lose a match. Chen advises A Song to pursue his studies at a *huaqiao* high school in M—. A Song, back in the capital, becomes a part-time student, working his way through school as a newspaper delivery boy. Encouraged by his teachers, a number of whom were dissident patriots who had taken refuge in the Philippines after being hounded by the Europeans for their progressive politics and publishing activities in China, A Song takes up writing and immerses himself in the anti-Japanese student movement. He also falls in love with A Hong, a classmate who is also active in the movement. Coming from a well-to-do and conservative Christian family, A Hong is under great pressure to forego seeing her newspaper-boy and part-time student boyfriend, who has been branded a "radical." The two quarrel when A Hong offers to pay for A Song's education. A Song gives up his work as a newspaper boy and turns to full-time studying and writing. After reading a long letter from A Hong, who is torn between her loyalty to her family and her love for A Song, A Song abandons his dream of returning to China with A Hong.

A chance encounter allows him to renew his friendship with a married Niuniu. Trapped in a loveless marriage to the captain of the smuggling ship, Niuniu finds herself falling in love with A Song. A Song faces some difficulties at school and is forced to withdraw from it at the instigation of Huang Xiuzi, a Guomindang sympathizer who was also instrumental in alerting A Hong's parents to her love affair with A Song. A Song transfers to the Nanyang High School as events in China take their inevitable course toward war with Japan. Although A Song is fond of Niuniu, he explains to her his inability to reciprocate her love, owing to his commitment to the anti-Japanese cause. In the meantime, Chen Shan tells A Song that he has exacted retribution from the gangster who had engineered his motor accident, and, with the money he is given by his maternal uncle, is set to leave for Hong Kong. Chen Shan gives A Song enough money for the latter to book himself a passage to North China to join the anti-Japanese resistance effort on the eve of the Sino-Japanese war. As the boat leaves the harbor in late 1936, A Song sees Niuniu waving goodbye.

HUAQIAO BILDUNGSROMAN

Part romance, part adventure story, part travel narrative (*youji*), *Nanyang Piaoliuji* is Bai Ren's own fictionalized *Bildungsroman* detailing in general terms his brief sojourn from 1933 to 1937 in the Philippines. The *Bildungsroman*, literally a "novel of education," charts a character's formative years and intellectual, spiritual, or sentimental education. By focusing on the travails and adventures of a young person, in *Nanyang*'s case an adolescent boy, the *Bildungsroman* highlights youth as the "essence" of modernity, sharing in "the formlessness of the epoch, its protean elusiveness."[27] Preeminent among the characteristics of modernity are mobility and interiority,[28] the themes of wandering and exploration of both the world and oneself, and the potential metamorphoses inherent in this restlessness.

---

[27] Franco Moretti, *The Way of the World: The* Bildungsroman *in European Culture*, new edition, trans. Albert Sbragia (London: Verso, 2000), p. 5.
[28] Ibid., p. 4.

Bai Ren was one of the young Philippine *huaqiao* who left the Philippines to join the anti-Japanese war effort in China.[29] Although he did not join the Communist Party until 1939, two years after he went back to China,[30] his close association with left-leaning intellectuals and Chinese activists based in the Philippines had already aroused the suspicions of and invited persecution from those in the Philippine-Chinese community who had close ties with the rival Guomindang group.

It is not just the autobiographical elements of the story, but the first-person narrative of *Nanyang Piaoliuji* itself that foregrounds the construction of individual subjectivity, thereby enabling Bai Ren to work through the question "How is it that one comes to love one's country?" in a far more detailed way than has been attempted elsewhere in Philippine-Chinese fiction. How does *one*, an individual, come to have an emotional investment in what is essentially an abstraction, "China," an attachment that encompasses yet also supersedes one's identification with the place of one's birth?

The development of individual, patriotic consciousness is not simply the subject of the novel; it is arguably a performative effect of the text. That is, the text not only writes about the formation of the individual by revealing the mechanisms underlying this formation, the text itself contributes to, in fact enables, this very formation. This is because, as Lydia Liu has pointed out in her study of the literature of the May Fourth movement, the first-person narrative creates a split subject which involves the doubling of the "self"—the "self is both the narrating I (subject of enunciation) and the narrated I (subject of utterance)."[31] The subject that comes into being *in* the text is also the subject that writes itself into being *through* the text. *Nanyang* is as much about how A Song represents himself as it is about A Song himself; by foregrounding the narrative act and the writing that enables it, the novel problematizes rather than takes for granted the politics of representation that underwrites the novelistic project.

Indeed, a heightened awareness of the power and politics of representation is very much evident in the novel. Its protagonist, A Song, is a prolific writer and a

---

[29] Huang Zisheng and He Sibing, *Feilubin Huaqiao Shi* (History of the Philippine *huaqiao*) (Guangzhou: Guangdong Gaotejiaoyu Chubanshe, 1987), p. 441. Huang and He name about twenty returned overseas Chinese from the Philippines. Lin Bin provides an invaluable summary of the activities of various leftist organizations (including labor organizations, anti-Japanese patriotic organizations, and a group of *huaqiao* students who left for China and were subsequently trained at Yenan) during the years leading up to the outbreak of the Second World War in her "Zhongguo Xinwenxue Heshizoujin Feilubin de Jikao" (When did China's new literature enter the Philippines?: An examination), *Shijie Ribao* (February 17, 2001): 15. She notes the important role played by May Fourth literary exponents who went to the Philippines (Du Ai, Liang Shangyuan, Huang Wei, among others) in disseminating reading materials, including revolutionary literature such as Mao Zedong's works, that were newly published in China. Especially noteworthy is Lin's mention of the participation of *huaqiao* women in the anti-Japanese movement among the Chinese in the Philippines. A brief account of Bai Ren's post-Philippine career and popular reception of his works (especially of his spoken dramas) is also recounted in Wang Zhenhan, "Bai Ren zai Guxiang" (Bai Ren in the homeland), *Shijie Ribao* (October 10, 1999): 25.

[30] Wei Jun, "Zai Manchang de Daolushang Qianjin," p. 87.

[31] Lydia H. Liu, "Narratives of Modern Selfhood: First-Person Fiction in May Fourth Literature," in *Politics, Ideology, and Literary Discourse in Modern China*, p. 106.

voracious reader whose commerce with the written word is constitutive of his patriotism. A Song renders his acquisition of culture in quasi-biological terms:

> I was like a hungry child, greedily devouring cultural foodstuffs. Good or bad, I wolfed down everything. The culture that I was to acquire in later years was most likely the result of my reading during this time.[32]

A Song "greedily devour[s] cultural foodstuffs," each new piece of reading material feeding his imagination with tales of China and its people, including its heroes and martyrs. The protagonists of the classic Qing novel of manners, *Hong Lou Meng* (A dream of red mansions) even invade his dreams. *Nanyang* highlights the crucial role played by print, by books and magazines and journals, in constructing the "plight" of China and deploying the rhetoric of "national salvation" and revolutionary activism by narrating Japanese activities in that country and disseminating nationalist interpretations of China's recent history. As newspaper boy, A Song literally participates in the dissemination of the printed word, even as he participates in its literal production when he begins contributing articles and stories to one of the Chinese newspapers.

The written word exercises a fascination for A Song, not least because the worlds it conjures up help shape his perceptions of social reality. Its utopian content enables A Song to note the discrepancy between the way things are and the way things ought to be. At the same time, the apparent transparency of the written word coexists alongside its maddeningly elusive "depth," its promise of "hidden" meaning that can only be excavated by repeated acts of (re)reading and by the sharpening of insight that can only come with the reader's growing maturity. Raised on a steady diet of classics and popular works such as *Qi Xia Wu Yi, Xi You Ji, Feng Shen Bang, Shi Gong An,* and *Peng Gong An*, a studiously receptive A Song finds himself unable fully to digest the import of "difficult" works such as Lu Xun's masterpieces, *Kuangren Riji, Kong Yi Ji,* and *A Q Zhengzhuan*. These half-digested stories await supplementation by years of formal education, an account of which occupies nearly half of the novel's narrative.

If A Song's relationship to China is mediated by the text, the Chinese in the Philippines among whom A Song finds himself also have a discursively mediated relationship with China, owing to the visibility of institutions such as schools and print media in *huaqiao* daily life. Education was a cornerstone of the socialization of the *huaqiao* as Chinese patriot, yet the very form it takes, and the relative distancing of this educational process from the China it was crucial in mediating (notwithstanding periodic trips back and forth from China by those who could afford it), served to qualify the nature of the Nanyang nationalism it was supposed to foster and make it different from mainland Chinese nationalism. The kind of "long-distance nationalism"[33] of the overseas Chinese was mediated by overseas

---

[32] Bai, *Nanyang Piaoliuji*, p. 94.

[33] I borrow the term, with important qualifications, from Benedict Anderson, who expounds on the concept in Chapter Three of his *Spectres of Comparison: Nationalism, Southeast Asia and the World* (London: Verso, 1998), pp. 58-74. Anderson's term is used to describe a later phenomenon of self-chosen exile (as opposed to forced exile for economic and political reasons, as in the case of A Song and his activist mentors) on the heels of accelerated capitalist globalization and is used to remark a "serious politics that is at the same time radically unaccountable" (p. 74).

Chinese institutions, networks, and organizations. Moreover, as Wang Gungwu has pointed out:

> Separation from China meant that the nationalism being kept alive among younger generations of Nanyang Chinese was more abstract and cerebral, taught, as it were, through textbooks in the modern Chinese schools and subtly worded articles in local Chinese newspapers and magazines but cut off from where the action was. It was a nationalism held in reserve while the settled Chinese learned to emulate their fathers in profiting from the colonial network and laissez-faire capitalism of the 1920's and 1930's.[34]

The textual mediation of the Nanyang Chinese relationship to China renders the kind of nationalism instilled through the written word open to modification and revision on the basis of the exigencies attending specific events and developments in the Philippines, and the social location of the Chinese within these islands. Among the important sources of qualification are class and educational divides within the so-called "Chinese community" and the varying political orientations of its members, with young, unmarried, working-class men being more inclined to sympathize with the leftist cause.[35]

The transformative influence of education is inscribed in the very logic of *Nanyang Piaoliuji* as an exemplary *Bildungsroman*. The idea of formation that the *Bildungsroman* stresses also presupposes the human capacity for shaping oneself in accordance with an ideal or a set of values. This, after all, is the fundamental premise of education involving not just the mind but the body. What is ironic, though, about this process of self-formation is that A Song's growing sense of revolutionary idealism and the disciplining of his body in preparation for the coming hardship, self-sacrifice, and even abjuration of happiness are eerily mirrored, if not prefigured, by the asceticism and renunciation of pleasure and material comfort in which the small-time merchants were schooled in the Depression-era Philippines of the 1930s. A Song's boss Mr. Hong speaks of his small dry-goods retail business as a product of long years of sweat and labor (the actual term is "a lifetime's heartblood," *ishengdexinxie*). Thus, even though A Song repudiates his putative socialization into the merchant class, and makes much of its oftentimes exploitative practices and its values, his arduous apprenticeship comes to serve him in good stead as the lessons of hard work and discipline imbibed in the course of his socialization as a merchant are channeled into his subsequent career as an activist.

In this respect, the merchant himself is the doppelgänger, the dark double rather than the complete antithesis of the patriotic activist. In the Philippines, the Sino-Japanese war provided the historic occasion for the fusion of merchant

---

[34] Wang Gungwu, "The Limits of Nanyang Chinese Nationalism, 1912-1937," pp. 53-54. Zheng Liren argues against the idea that Chinese nationalism was "taught" to, and calculated and controlled by, China's nationalists, and espouses instead the idea that overseas Chinese nationalism was relatively self-sufficient, growing and developing out of the specific historical and experiential conditions of the overseas Chinese communities throughout Nanyang. In some cases, overseas Chinese nationalists even came into antagonistic conflict with mainland Chinese nationalists over questions of the latter's criticism of the former's "independent attitude." Zheng, "Overseas Chinese Nationalism in British Malaya," pp. 6-9.

[35] Zheng, "Overseas Chinese Nationalism in British Malaya," p. 54.

and patriot, as the merchant also became a patriot who contributed the largest average sum per capita among all Chinese communities in Southeast Asia to helping the war effort in China.[36] But if the merchant's notion of work is inseparable from the demands of asceticism and sacrifice, he is at one and the same time a figure for exploitation because of his identification with money, and the suspicion he attracts, in Filipino public discourse, as a citizen without a country.[37] Not surprisingly, A Song's disillusionment with the materialistic society into which he is thrown expresses itself in terms of his renunciation and repudiation of the chosen profession of his father and brother, the profession for which his family had sacrificed so much and spent so much to ensure his preparation. Yet A Song's own emergent patriotism is precisely enabled—therefore inherently "contaminated"—by "merchant values" of self-abnegation and asceticism that have come to be associated with "Chineseness" in Southeast Asia. In this sense A Song is partly, and unavoidably, indebted to the very system against which he rebels.

In A Song, the conflicting demands of capital and labor and the resulting predicaments generated by the contradiction between capital and labor, with which the Chinese in the Philippines have had to contend, are played out. Nowhere is the contradiction more evident than in A Song's legal status as an alien resident in the Philippines. His official status is guaranteed by a piece of paper, the *teng-ki-toa-li* or alien certificate of registration, and it is this document that he is concerned to salvage and keep with him even when he loses everything during his castaway days on an unknown island. A Song's relationship with the Philippine state is codified in terms of a *legal fiction* which rests on the state's misrecognition of A Song's "blood ties" to a Philippine-Chinese merchant. A Song's alien registration certificate officially affirms a fictive "merchant family" genealogy which allowed the entry into the Philippines of young Chinese men who were neither merchants themselves nor sons of the merchant fathers listed in the document. It is true that even without consanguinity to a merchant, many of these "paper sons" were subsequently socialized into the merchant class through the apprenticeship system. It is also true that many of these paper sons' real fathers were themselves merchants, though, owing to the fact that the *teng-ki-toa-li* they acquired were separate and different from those subsequently acquired by their sons, these real fathers had different legal surnames.

But the fact is that the myth of merchant sons belies a social reality that is much more complex, because riven by internal differences, than the popular image created by the legal classification and representation of the Chinese. The Philippine state, a legatee of the American colonial state's application of the U.S. Exclusion Law to the Philippine Chinese, recognizes the Chinese only insofar as

---

[36] Yung Li Yuk-wai, *The Huaqiao Warriors: Chinese Resistance Movement in the Philippines 1942-1945* (Quezon City: Ateneo de Manila University Press, 1996), p. 23. See also Antonio S. Tan, *The Chinese in the Philippines During the Japanese Occupation 1942-1945* (Quezon City: Asian Center, University of the Philippines Press, 1981), pp. 4-5.

[37] This link between the Chinese merchant and money is elaborated in Chapter Three of my *Necessary Fictions: Philippine Literature and the Nation, 1946-1980* (Quezon City: Ateneo de Manila University Press, 2000), pp. 152-65, and in my "'Who Will Save Us from the "Law"?': The Criminal State and the Illegal Alien in Post-1986 Philippines," in *Figures of Criminality in Indonesia, the Philippines, and Colonial Vietnam*, ed. Vicente L. Rafael (Ithaca: Cornell University Southeast Asia Program Publications, 1999), pp. 128-51.

the Chinese are either merchants or can prove that they are sons of Chinese merchants already based in the Philippines. This immigration rule works to strengthen the association of the Chinese with mercantile capital, but it is complemented by a system of naturalization that makes the acquisition of Filipino citizenship by the Chinese merchant so difficult and expensive that few but the moneyed and the most well-connected socially can be naturalized.

Thus, on the one hand, the Philippine immigration laws served to drive the Chinese ever deeper into a merchant niche, while making it extremely difficult for them to be anything but "Chinese" in legal, and arguably socio-cultural, terms. But on the other hand, corruption within the immigration and naturalization department also allowed the Chinese to evade the strictures of the state's onerous legislation. The "new" Chinese who yearly entered the Philippines were either integrated into the Chinese community's predominantly mercantile middle-class social fabric or, as in the case of A Song and his co-workers at the grocery store, were nominally absorbed but in reality socialized as urban laborers in all but name. These latter—consisting of unmarried men who lived out most of their lives in the company of their co-workers or other fellow workers—formed the Chinese community's underbelly of nominal merchants who, if categorized by socio-economic standing and lifestyle, would be classed as lumpenproletariat.

As men who worked for merchants, or men who pooled their scarce, hard-earned resources to form *kongsi* partnerships in small businesses, but who often as not ended up neither owning shares in the business nor being properly compensated for their labor as "store-minders," these nominal merchants were particularly visible during the Depression years. With small business after small business failing in the wake of the stock market crash in the late 1920s, the Chinese merchant's status became even more pronouncedly fluid and precarious as numerous Chinese flitted between socio-economic boundaries. While sympathetic in his treatment of the Chinese merchant, *Nanyang*'s A Song is ambivalent about the mercantile capitalist ethos. A Song is privy to his employer's eldest son Yaohua's desperate resort to dirty tactics such as bribing the electricity-meter reader and cheating the customers. He hears enough of the latter's oft-quoted philosophy ("have money, have virtue!," "*youchien jiuyoude!*") to form a decidedly pessimistic view of the society, and to realize that he himself is unable to stomach the sordid, exploitative practices that seem intrinsic to the act of buying-and-selling:

> Hong Yaohua's underhanded practices threw a black shadow on my young soul, leaving a deep and lasting impression. Even now, as I recall the past, the scenes remain fresh and vivid in my mind. Although the majority of the *huaqiao* were upright and law-abiding merchants, my young boss's double-dealing tricks played no small role in engendering my subsequent unwillingness to learn the trade [*chansheng buzuomaimai de juexin*].[38]

As an apprentice, A Song sees society from the vantage point of someone who occupies the lowest rung of the socio-economic ladder. *Nanyang*, in fact, lays bare the deep economic, political, and social divisions and tensions that belie the seeming homogeneity of the prosperous, predominantly Minnan Hokkien-speaking

---

[38] Bai, *Nanyang Piaoliuji*, p. 90.

"Chinese community" in the Philippines. These divisions and tensions would become especially apparent during the period leading up to World War II. The ambiguous, often indecisive stance taken toward the world events during the 1930s by prominent Chinese community leaders like Dee C. Chuan and Alfonso Z. Sycip, who sought to protect their interests, both social and economic, provoked harsh criticism from those who favored a less equivocal stand on the political issues affecting the Nanyang Chinese and China.

These conflicts are especially highlighted by the subplot dealing with A Song's love affair with his classmate A Hong. A Hong is active in the anti-Japanese student movement in their school, but she is also subject to pressure from her prominent Protestant family to truncate her involvement with an indigent newspaper boy (and a known troublemaker to boot, according to one of his teachers) and entertain, instead, the suit of the relatively more acceptable Dr. Chen (Tan). A Hong writes A Song a long letter—a veritable *cri de coeur*—which laments the "over-protectiveness" of her parents, yet A Hong cannot finally bring herself, for the sake of her love for A Song, to sever completely her ties with her family.

A Hong's dilemma points to a real gap that separates the Nanyang Chinese bachelors, mainly indigents, from the prosperous Nanyang Chinese who settled down in Nanyang and who, as in the case of A Hong's father, not only have a stake in their adopted country through their business interests, but who have children whom they expect to inherit and reproduce their socio-economic standing. An embittered A Song writes:

> In *huaqiao* society, human relations are governed by the capitalist ethos and bound by feudalistic thinking, which denigrates the poor and idolizes the rich. In matters of marriage, people are expected to marry within their class.[39]

A Hong's family background bears out the complex nature of the "assimilation" process, in which Chineseness and the espousal of a specifically China-centered nationalism cannot but be recontextualized and renegotiated to accommodate the exigencies of everyday life in Southeast Asia. Wang Gungwu argues that

> [b]oth nationalists and the advocates of assimilation among Nanyang Chinese were always the articulate minority at opposite ends of the spectrum while the majority who said little considered the relative strengths of China and the local governments while they carefully erected defences to ensure the survival of their communities.[40]

WORK AS PEDAGOGY

The war in China was without doubt the key political event that cut through the class, educational, and political divisions within the Nanyang Chinese community. It stoked the fires of patriotic fervor among the Nanyang Chinese and served as the most powerful emotive bonding element among members of the community. Yet Wang Gungwu remains convinced that Nanyang Chinese nationalism was overall a "conditional, peripheral, dependent nationalism which

---

[39] Ibid., p. 220.
[40] Wang Gungwu, "The Limits of Nanyang Chinese Nationalism," p. 53.

had no capacity to generate itself because it depended on China to continue to take an interest in them and on expatriate Chinese to continue to prepare later generations to be nationalistic."[41] Argues Wang:

> The quality of nationalism for the few Nanyang Chinese who were attracted to it at the beginning of the century seems to have been determined not so much by a passionate self-discovery because they were strangers being discriminated against in a foreign land or because they found new perspectives in the modern world away from home, but much more by the skillful persuasion of the educated Chinese from China who were able to explain and confirm the sources of all their grievances—a kind of "taught nationalism."[42]

Wang's argument is persuasive, but it glosses over the fact that the process of "self-discovery" is not solely conditioned by the *huaqiao*'s experience of discrimination in the host country. More important, it ignores the complex nature and condition of nationalist pedagogy in the Nanyang territories. Pedagogy is never a one-way process, a simple matter of overseas Chinese passively subjected to "skillful persuasion" by an active cadre of educated Chinese from China. It is true, of course, as shown in *Nanyang*, that good and committed educators did play an important role in teaching students about Chinese history and in encouraging students to organize or participate in the anti-Japanese movement.[43] A Song specifically mentions two teachers, Zhuang *laoshi* (teacher) and Tong *laoshi*, who spurred his growing consciousness of, and his responses to, the imperatives of anti-Japanese resistance and Chinese national salvation. Tong *laoshi* was one of the first people to encourage A Song to publish his articles and stories in the local Chinese daily.

Yet the act of teaching never entails the presupposition of a *tabula rasa* on the part of even the most compliant student. A Song's receptiveness to the ideas and lessons of his teachers is not even conditioned primarily by the authority and persuasiveness of his teachers, as teachers. After all, for every revolutionary Zhuang, there is also a reactionary like Xie *laoshi* who sees fit to foist his own view of Chinese history on his students. A Song's predisposition to respond positively to a very specific version of nationalist pedagogy is rooted in his social location (working class, from an impoverished family) and, most important, in the specificity of his own "educational" experience in the Philippines.

This educational experience is elaborated throughout the novel. In fact, there is a close-knit relationship among the three major episodes, each chronicling an

---

[41] Ibid.

[42] Ibid., p. 42. Interestingly enough, Bai Ren's novel contains no account of A Song's personal experience of discrimination at the hands of Filipinos. Except for the sojourn on a small island, A Song spends most of his time in various Chinatowns in the Philippines. His "Chinese" consciousness is more likely to have been a product of a more generalized discursive construction of the "Intsik" as any or all "Chinese in the Philippines," a construction that may, though it does not necessarily, entail racial discrimination.

[43] Lin Bin, "Zhongguo Xinwenxue Heshizoujin Feilubin de Jikao," p. 15. "More important in its long-term effects was the spread of modern education to the Nanyang Chinese. . . . The young Nanyang Chinese were told that being in the Nanyang was itself a patriotic act but only if they could use their stay there to help China. Thus before long the most effective political activity became inextricably bound with the modern schools and many of the political leaders were the school teachers." Wang, "A Short History of the Nanyang Chinese," p. 33.

aspect of A Song's education, that are recounted in *Nanyang*. The first episode centers on A Song's experience as a shopkeeper's apprentice. The second recounts A Song's brief career as a self-proclaimed Robinson Crusoe on a remote island. The third covers the rest of his stay in the Philippines as a working student. Each of these episodes plays an integral, cumulative role in A Song's sentimental and political education as a committed revolutionary.

As already discussed above, A Song's two-year apprenticeship educates him in the ways of the ruthless, materialistic and atomistic world of commerce, even as his stint of hard physical labor as a merchant's apprentice forms the unwitting yet ineluctable basis of his education in self-discipline, which prepares him for the self-discipline and self-sacrifice warranted by his later decision to join the war effort.

The world is A Song's classroom. He learns about China and Chinese history from acquaintances and friends alike. Casual conversation with a veteran *fanke* yields invaluable information and history lessons on the origins of the word *fanke*, which originally referred to foreign sojourners in China during the Song and Yuan dynasties and subsequently came to be applied to the Hokkien *lannang* who went abroad—a term that encapsulates the becoming-foreign of "our people." A chance encounter with an old *huaqiao* aboard the ship bound for Manila, for example, leads to a short but useful lesson on *huaqiao* history, illustrated with stories of *huaqiao* persecution in the Dutch East Indies as well as *huaqiao* resistance in Singapore. A Song also learns about the local history of *Tengsua* through another old *huaqiao* who regales him with stories of Arabs and Persians who aided the Mongols in putting down peasant rebellions in Quanzhou during the closing years of the Yuan dynasty. Furthermore, A Song learns about Chinese elsewhere in Southeast Asia and in America, and about the need for the *fanke*, as the old *huaqiao* tells A Song, to know their own history in light of their general invisibility in official Chinese and foreign discourses. A key lesson is conveyed by the old *huaqiao* in the following words:

> At present, *huaqiao* can be found residing in ninety-one countries in the world. They rely on their wisdom and hard labor to make important contributions to the societies in which they live.[44]

These conversations would be repeated and amplified not just in the classroom much later, but in the Afterword of the novel itself.

The second episode, which has A Song living like Robinson Crusoe on an island off the coast of Negros before he is rescued by a tribe of indigenous people, further catalyzes A Song's growing activist consciousness. Robinson Crusoe is both an apt and an ironic literary figure for A Song to compare himself with, considering the fact that Defoe's character is the embodiment of the entrepreneurial ethos A Song is unwilling to school himself to live by. A Song draws on the obvious parallels between his experience and Crusoe's forcibly self-sufficient existence on a deserted island. There are other marked similarities between A Song's sojourn in the Philippines and Crusoe's on his island—both these protagonists are country boys rather than city-bred sophisticates; both are disobedient sons who refuse to take the paths their fathers expect them to take; both grow and mature by the

---

[44] Bai, *Nanyang Piaoliuji*, p. 111. The idea is repeated in the Afterword, p. 292.

expedient of trying to survive; both learn about the meaninglessness of worldly goods; and both emerge stronger from their experiences. The crucial difference, however, lies in the fact that Crusoe views his mastery of himself as an indispensable condition of his mastery of his surroundings (i.e., the island), whereas A Song makes no other claim beyond that of having further attained a measure of self-mastery and discipline amidst his surroundings.

The Crusoe episode, part of which A Song spends with his Filipino friend Niuniu, may seem out of place in a novel that is unremittingly realistic in its depiction of life in various parts of the Philippines, but it serves a crucial function in further materializing A Song's patriotic predisposition. The days that A Song spends scrounging for food, battling monkeys and snakes, and later interacting with the kindly indigenous people are remarkable for the fact that it is during this brief period that A Song's memories of his childhood and hometown assume their crystalline form as vivid recollections and, more importantly, as episodic narratives. It is during this time that A Song first learns to tell stories (not least to himself) about—to *narrate*—his Chinese past. In this seemingly desolate corner of the Philippines, A Song recovers fragments of his childhood while learning to reflect, in a sustained and methodical way, on his all-too-brief sojourn in the land of his birth.

If patriotic consciousness is stoked by the narrative investment of meaning in one's childhood memories and one's place of birth, what is interesting about this process of narrating self-discovery is that it is made possible only by what A Song actually sees and does on the Philippine island, and by a group of indigenous people with whom he interacts during his sojourn. The sight of the indigenous people's boats cresting the waves like arrows conjures up in A Song a vivid picture of the Chinese dragonboats during a rowing contest in May. A cactus plant, which Niuniu mistakes for a tomato, triggers A Song's memory of having eaten one. A Song draws on his childhood experience of having captured snakes to do the same thing on the island, and of dealing with snakebites.

The snakes serve as a mnemonic device for a complex chain of interconnected recollections: of A Song's father cooking a snake dish and passing it off as an eel; of his mother, dying when A Song was eight years old; of his father leaving Luzon to live in *Tengsua* for a while; of his own childish pranks, his habit of trapping snakes and keeping them in his desk drawer in the classroom. This last memory sparks an elaborately detailed account of a long-ago lesson on Mencius (*Mengzi*) during which A Song prompted his seatmate Shitou during the latter's class recitation, and got Shitou into real trouble when the boy was later asked by the teacher to recite the same text in front of the class. Subsequently beaten by the teacher for his bad performance, Shitou learns that Hongcai, a female classmate, had snitched on him by informing the teacher of A Song's prompting. An enraged Shitou then tells A Song to put a snake in Hongcai's desk drawer; for this piece of mischief, A Song got twenty raps on his hand.

His encounters and interactions with objects and creatures and people on this Philippine island precisely enable A Song's sense of his past to take shape in his memory, not just as hauntingly vivid fragments, but as full-fledged meaningful stories with a beginning, middle, and end. The Philippines is something more than our commonsensical idea of the *medium* which serves as a self-effacing vehicle for conveying pre-existing ideas about the nation and the self. It is at once the site of, the means for, and the very substance of, the transmutation of A Song's patriotism.

A Song's first-ever sight of two whales in the Negros waters gives flesh and substance to his grandmother's tale of shipwrecked fishermen taking refuge on a small island which turns out to be the back of a whale. Moreover, A Song's survival skills are not only honed by invaluable lessons from the past. His more recent past serves him equally well: Niuniu teaches him how to swim, and he puts his knowledge of the Filipino technique for opening coconut shells to good use to obtain the necessary foodstuffs to see him through until his rescue.

What follows from this instance is even more suggestive, as A Song gets an inkling of the first and only real freedom he will ever enjoy as he lies on the grass, fanned by the sea breeze, and lulled into reverie and sleep by the song of the ocean and the floating sky. Here, he forgets his worries and cares as, immersed in a dream-logged sleep, memories of *Tengsua* and Luzon flow into each other and wash over him. In this dreaming state, he sees the fabled Mt. Bao Ta of his homeland and Chen Shan knocking out his opponent in the boxing ring and the Filipino women gathering at the store front. He hears the strumming of guitars and the *harana* (serenade), and finally, he sees Niuniu swimming in the sea. These images intermingle in his dream, and act as a Lotos-like anodyne that enables him temporarily to forget that he is alone on the island.

A Song's rescue by a group of indigenous people (*heiren*) caps this specific segment of his education. The tribal leader Mohani invites him to stay on with his people, but while A Song warms to the hospitality and friendliness of the indigenous people (and gives Mohani's people his hunting knife as a token of his appreciation), he finds himself inadvertently heartsick for the *huaqiao* society about which he had so recently formed such a negative impression, even as his interaction with the indigenous people becomes an invaluable lesson in hospitality, friendship, mutual trust, and indebtedness.

It is tempting to think of A Song's brief adventure as a kind of palimpsest on which A Song discerns the traces of his Chinese past while writing his experiences in the Philippines. The resulting document of his subjectivity does, indeed, bear traces of earlier writing, but these traces have been altered retrospectively by A Song's act of recounting his Philippine experience. The Robinson Crusoe episode is a miniaturized account of sojourning housed within the general narrative of A Song's adventures in a foreign land in which he comes to "discover" his Chineseness. Yet it, like the overarching narrative of *Nanyang*, also serves to defamiliarize A Song's experience of the originary *Tengsua*, his homeland. A Song's first-hand experiences in the Philippines subtly reshape his memories: they intensify, if not substantiate, the past in ways that alter—no, *create*—the meaning and significance of the past for A Song. This is the first time that A Song is able to think back to "his" childhood, the first occasion in which the past becomes narratable as a retrievable past, both object and subject of narration. And this is so only through the inspiriting power of the material culture of A Song's Philippine sojourn.

The A Song who eventually undertakes to get a formal education is no *tabula rasa*, but an individual whose *educability*,[45] whose capacity and amenability to being educated, has been conditioned by years of "learning" outside the walls of the classroom. A Song is, in a very important sense, educated as well as educable by the

---

[45] For a discussion of the educability of the individual as a *sine qua non* of nationalist pedagogy, see Chapter One of my *Necessary Fictions*, pp. 15-47.

time he enters the classroom, having been "prepped" for it by the labor and experience of the past two years in the Philippines.

Experience and work are important forms of pedagogy, not least because the former, in keeping with the older definition of "experience,"[46] is a form of experimentation in which the subject of the experiment—the knowledge being "gathered" and processed—is the observing and reflecting individual herself and the past and present events in her life. These lessons not only reinforce the individual's sociality by linking her to the world, to other people, to "nature." They serve as grounds for reasoning and analysis, for developing the individual's self-awareness.[47] At the same time, experience also indexes affects and dispositions which exceed the representational logic of analytical reason. Experience, too, may entail a loss of innocence that offers epistemic access to a more "truthful" view of the current milieu. Best of all, although experience is almost always coded as personal and subjective, the fact that it is essentially a work of writing entailing a "subjective witness"[48] lends it a textual quality that enables it to be "shared" with other subjects.

The fact of labor, which in A Song's case has not led to the pursuit of profit, is the defining element of A Song's sense of self:

> These four years in Nanyang, I have depended on my own effort and sweat to survive and get an education. Self-sufficiency is my only principle. I am proud of myself, and I look down on spoiled brats.[49]

Labor also has important implications for redefining A Song's relationship with his family. For one thing, it ends up testing the intimate, "natural" bonds that link A Song to his family. The apprenticeship system ensured that A Song would spend most of his time away from his father and brother, and would acquire his most basic grounding in trade and social interaction with Philippine society not from his kin, but from his co-workers, from members of a larger, because suprafamilial, network of connections. Moreover, A Song's most intimate ties are forged not with his brother, but with the boxer Chen Shan, and with the second son of his employer, with chance acquaintances such as Niuniu, and later, with his classmates, his teachers, and A Hong. A Song himself, as the events in his life make painfully clear, has for the most part had to rely on his own judgment and on the kind advice of other people, his family having enough problems of their own to deal with. *Nanyang* ends not with A Song's reunion with his family, but with his radical decision to move to Northern China, beyond the ambit of the kinship network as he knows it.

Hardship and deprivation for A Song are necessary adjuncts of the imperative to survive in the harsh world during bad times. His story is a test case which bears out the truism that what makes one suffer can only make one better, the truism that hardship only tempers the individual and spurs him toward "maturity." As argued above, it is through work itself that A Song comes to yearn for things other than

---

[46] Raymond Williams, *Keywords: A Vocabulary of Culture and Society* (London: Fontana Press, 1988), pp. 126-29.

[47] Cf. Moretti, *The Way of the World*, p. 29.

[48] Williams, *Keywords*, p. 128.

[49] Bai, *Nanyang Piaoliuji*, pp. 220-21.

thoughts of survival, to pin his hope on the power of the word and the value of commitment to a higher ideal.

> My mind was brimming with new things: full of thoughts about my calamity-ridden homeland, yearning for love, and thirsty for a life of freedom.[50]

Through the activity of work, A Song constructs his world and himself in the process. The formative years of hard labor that sculpt his body, define his personality and his perspective, and in crucial ways inform his decisions regarding his own future, all point to the ceaseless self-experimentation through which A Song finds himself always in the process of becoming something—or someone—else. The inherent malleability and educability of the self predispose A Song to being receptive to the relentless onslaught of ideas and perspectives around him. The fact that the subsequent frothing of ideas would necessitate major rethinking and reinvention of A Song's goals in life and his experiences of the world and events unfolding before him would not have been alarmingly overwhelming to A Song; indeed, he would most certainly have anticipated, if not welcomed, the prospect.

TESTING THE LIMITS OF CHINESE/PHILIPPINE NATIONALISM

Yet for all that *Nanyang* is about A Song's self-formation and political socialization, about his education in accordance to patriotic ideals of self-sacrifice and revolutionary activism, this process of self-formation is fraught with unresolved issues. Foremost among them is the question of the "boundaries" of loyalty drawn by exclusivist notions and practices typical of prevailing official nationalism. A Song's story reveals the constitutive role played by his Philippine experience in conditioning—in fact, *materializing*—his patriotic love for China, but it is precisely the constitutive determination of "Chinese" nationalism by the *huaqiao's* experience of—and experience within—another nation—that is, the grounding of A Song's Chinese nationalism in his intimate experience of an other (foreign) place—which is often elided if not actively suppressed in the official nationalist discourses of both China and the Philippines. In the process, A Song's story is vulnerable to being read in simplistic terms as a clearcut illustration of Chinese nationalism, leaving no room for serious consideration of the politically salient role and transformative potential of his Philippine sojourn in informing either his own "Chinese" nationalism or the Filipinos' nationalist experience. This kind of misreading springs from the assumption that the relationship between the *huaqiao* and China is transparent, that is, self-evidently given and natural, rather than mediated in a complex way by the *huaqiao's* experience in Southeast Asia.

Perhaps the disappearance of A Song from the text of Philippine literary history may be attributed to his decision to leave the Philippines to join the resistance struggle in China. Where nationalism is primarily coded as loyalty to, and identification with, the country of one's birth, A Song's departure from the Philippines lends itself to being read, even within the framework of a specifically Chinese-Filipino identity politics, as an example of the "first-generation"[51]

---

[50] Ibid., p. 246.

[51] This periodizing impulse, which draws on sociological and anthropological categories to characterize the style and substance of overseas Chinese cultural production, is used to

Chinese deliberate disengagement from the Philippines which, in turn, betrays the *huaqiao*'s exclusive orientation toward China and is contrasted with the second- or third-generation *huaren*'s Philippine-centered orientation. *Nanyang* would, by this definition, occupy a marginal place in Philippine-Chinese literature as the writing of a Chinese who did not settle permanently in the Philippines, even as it already occupies a relatively marginal place in mainland Chinese literature as the work of one of the relatively small number of returned overseas Chinese in China (notwithstanding Bai Ren's authorial reputation, which rests on a corpus of critically acclaimed patriotic fiction and drama dealing with the anti-Japanese struggle in China).

The marginalization of *Nanyang* is most emphatically underscored by its relative obscurity within the Philippine literary scene. In spite of the fact that the novel offers one of the most sustained and complex treatments of the nature and vicissitudes of sojourning ever attempted in overseas Chinese writing, *Nanyang* has not been translated into Filipino or English.[52] Even if *Nanyang* were to be fed into the Philippine literary mainstream, critics would be hard pressed to assimilate the novel into the multi-tiered structure (first-generation, second-generation, third-generation writing) that is increasingly being used to characterize Chinese-Filipino literary production.[53] *Nanyang* is neither the story of a *huaqiao* ("Philippine Chinese") who stayed in the Philippines but who remained involved in the local affairs of his hometown in *Tengsua* and retained emotional ties to China, nor is it the story of second-generation children of *huaqiao* ("Filipino Chinese") grappling with their conflicted identities, and even less is it the story of third-generation *huayi*, descendants of the overseas Chinese in the Philippines ("Chinese Filipinos") who proclaim themselves Filipinos comfortable with or curious about their "Chinese heritage."

Yet *Nanyang* resists the barometric impulse, typical of certain influential formulations of Chinese-Filipino literature, to use questions of political allegiance and orientation as critical gauges to determine the inclusion of a given text in, or conversely its exclusion from, the canon of Chinese-Filipino literature. For one

---

highlight conceptual "differences" among "first-generation," "second-generation," and "third-generation" Chinese. This influential formulation of the "Chinese question" informs much of the writings, written in English, dealing with Chinese-Philippine literature. See, for example, Teresita Ang See, "Social Change: Impact on Chinese-Philippine Literature," in her *The Chinese in the Philippines: Problems and Perspectives* (Manila: Kaisa Para sa Kaunlaran, 1990), pp. 68-83; Lily Rose Tope, "The Chinese Margin in Philippine Literature," in *Philippine Post-Colonial Studies: Essays on Language and Literature*, ed. Priscelina Patajo-Legasto and Cristina Pantoja-Hidalgo (Quezon City: Department of English and Comparative Literature, University of the Philippines at Diliman, and University of the Philippines Press, 1993), pp. 73-81; and Charlson Ong, "A Bridge Too Far (Thoughts on Chinese-Filipino Writing)," *Philippines Free Press* (May 14, 1994): 31-32.

[52] In fact, although there are efforts to translate literary works in English and Filipino into Chinese, few if any of the major works by *huaqiao* in Chinese are ever translated into English or Filipino. The notable exception is Joaquin Sy's translation of Chinese-Philippine poetry and of Liang Shang Wan and Cai Jian Hua's 1996 book, *Wha Chi Memoirs* (Manila: Kaisa Para sa Kaunlaran, Inc., 1998).

[53] A heuristic breakdown of the different identity options that were historically and are currently available to the ethnic Chinese in the Philippines can be found in Edgar Wickberg, "Anti-Sinicism and Chinese Identity Options in the Philippines," in *Essential Outsiders: Chinese and Jews in the Modern Transformation of Southeast Asia and Central Europe*, ed. Daniel Chirot and Anthony Reid (Seattle: University of Washington Press, 1997), pp. 153-83.

thing, A Song's decision to leave the Philippines is not conditioned by his *disregard* for the Philippines, but by the pressing demand for action created by the exigencies of historical timing. He reached the decision to depart for China because of the outbreak of the Sino-Japanese War and at a time when the Philippines had not yet declared war on Japan. It was also at a time when the incipient political independence of the Philippines, newly a commonwealth "under American tutelage," appeared dubious in light of the behind-the-scenes machinations to delay the "granting" of political independence to the Philippines by the same high officials who had based their careers on advocacy of Philippine independence. A Song would have had no way of predicting the Philippines' involvement in the world war, in view of the American isolationist policy in the mid- to late thirties. Furthermore, as argued in this essay, it is not true that A Song remained "purely" Chinese when he was in the Philippines, and even less true that he "reverted" to being Chinese after his sojourn in the Philippines.

Even as *Nanyang* resists easy categorization by conventional scholarly treatments of Chinese-Filipino literature, it presents a case against its being considered merely as an example of "regional literature" in mainland China since its setting and plot invoke an audience that is neither strictly mainland Chinese nor even Southern Fujianese. What is remarkable about Bai Ren's novel is the clarity with which it manages to depict the historically determined "alchemy" that turns an immigrant merchant-wannabe into a Chinese nationalist. This alchemy, as argued above, involves a judicious mixing of things Chinese and Philippine, such that the "Chineseness" that is its product challenges deep-seated and widely held notions of the purity and fixity of both "Chinese" and "Filipino" culture.[54]

This mixing evinces itself on the level of language in the text, which is replete with languages other than standard Putonghua: there are Hokkien terms which will be unfamiliar to those who do not speak Minnanhua, which is further characterized by the use of Philippine-Chinese expressions (*huanke* for the *huaqiao*, *tuadi* for the residence certificate, *tsut si a* for *mestizo*, *taoke* for employer, *sengdi* for business, for instance); and there are Chinese-character phonetic transcriptions of Philippine languages (*anim, pito, kamatis, kilo, boy, sarong*), English ("boxing"; the words "ultimatum," "Asia," "OK," King Kong, and "bye-bye" appear in their original romanized form in the text), and Spanish (*chiquito, toma*). Although Bai Ren is careful to provide parenthetical translations of these verbal transcriptions, there are some words that remain untranslated, as when Chen Shan at one point lets loose the invective *putangina*.

---

[54] One would be tempted to use the word "hybrid" here to describe the inflection of Chinese nationalism by *huaqiao* material culture and experience, but hybridity as a postcolonial term is freighted with theoretical assumptions that I wish to avoid. For one thing, its original articulation by Homi K. Bhabha draws on the structural agency of language as a model for psychosocial relations obtaining in colonial space. See his "Signs Taken for Wonders: Questions of Ambivalence and Authority Under a Tree Outside Delhi, May 1817," in *The Location of Culture* (London and New York: Routledge, 1994), pp. 102-22, 264-65. Stripped of its historical valence, this term lends itself to being appropriated in patently ahistorical ways to shore up uncritical celebrations of hybridized Filipino culture. Posited as an explicit challenge to ethnocentric chauvinism rooted in the infrangible "purity" of a given culture, hybridity ends up, ironically, becoming essentialized as *the* fundamental cultural attribute of the countries in the Southeast Asian region.

The novel itself does not always mark the moments when A Song and other characters switch languages, when they go from speaking Cebuano to Minnan Hokkien to Putonghua to English to Tagalog. A Song and Chen Shan talk in Hokkien liberally mixed with Tagalog words and, in Chen Shan's case, curses. A Song and A Hong's intellectual arguments appear to be conducted in Putonghua rather than Minnanhua. The unambiguous exceptions are when A Song speaks to Filipinos. The text indicates that Niuniu converses with A Song in *zhongbudetuhua* or "the native language of the central part" (most probably Cebuano) of the Philippines, while Mohani is conversant in several central Philippine languages. A Song describes himself as a fast learner, and presumably able to pick up languages in the street and the market; he and most other characters in his autobiography speak and narrate in a Putonghua riddled with terms and expressions from other languages.

The effect of the mixing of languages from both inside and outside Chinese Putonghua is to defamiliarize Chinese Putonghua, strip it of its transparency by raising issues of readability, translation, and readership. *Nanyang* was written for a general Chinese-speaking audience, but it also has a special if not poignant resonance for the Philippine-Chinese "insiders" who see the familiar dialectal variations of Chinese and the equally familiar multilingual codes circulating within the Philippines suddenly wrenched from the context of ordinary life and rendered literally visible through their representation in writing. In addition, Bai Ren writes within a multiplicity of languages, and the effect of such an assumption of multiplicity is to problematize the politics of translation. Translating from one language to another cannot any longer be thought of as a bridge linking two distinct languages, because the very act of translation already changes both languages by changing the language into which the "other" language is supposed to be rendered intelligible.[55] Standard Putonghua must now deal not just with the incursion of Jinjiang and Philippine-Chinese Hokkien, but with the appearance within itself of Tagalog, Cebuano, Spanish, and English, in the same way that Philippine-Chinese Hokkien (*gunggong* being the latest) itself evinces the presence of the Filipino lingua franca with its liberal doses of English and Spanish.

A Song translates Hokkien, Tagalog, English, and Spanish into Chinese and vice versa, and every time he does so, he can no longer go back to being the person he was before he entered translation. The A Song who embarks on the task of translation is transformed into an-other A Song who is both Chinese and something else, Filipino as well. A Song becomes "Chinese" only because he has also become "Filipino"—because his Chineseness, far from being an impermeable totality, is always incomplete and partial and therefore open to the experience of being something other than Chinese. This double translation of apparently indisputable and ineluctable cultural differences exposes the constructed nature of these differences and their constitutive openness to the "outside," to other "cultures" or "nations."

This constitutive openness of nationness to the foreign "outside" is not without its own tensions, because nationalism often operates on a set of assumptions (citizenship and allegiance) which tend to stress the singularity of a given nation and the relative cohesion and impermeability of national identity. As it happens,

---

[55] Naoki Sakai, *Translation and Subjectivity: On "Japan" and Cultural Nationalism* (Minneapolis: University of Minnesota Press, 1997), pp. 12-15.

the idea that to be Chinese also admits of the possibility of being other-than-Chinese can be a source of deep uneasiness in a world that operates on the basis of the assumed boundedness and integrity of "national" (if not "cultural") totalities. That the act of movement across borders can have political significance, that it can even create political possibilities for action and change for both countries concerned, can be disturbing and is liable to be interpreted as a threat to the social.

In China, returned overseas Chinese were persecuted for bearing the mark of difference from other Chinese, for having been "contaminated" by their years of living outside China, for being harbingers of alien and alienating capital and bourgeois values which supposedly posed obstacles in the path of national, socialist reconstruction. Communist cadres from Fujian and Guangzhou were particularly vulnerable to censure during the Cultural Revolution, while relatives of overseas Chinese were stripped of their privileges[56] and returned overseas Chinese were discriminated against in the workplace.[57] Bai Ren states in the Afterword that his life in the China to which he had chosen to return remains full of hardship and suffering; the "golden years" of his youth loom large in his imagination precisely because life in the years after has not been easy (*buyi*), the path being extremely bumpy (*daolu kanke*). At best, this indicates that the sacrifices demanded of her patriots apparently did not stop upon China's attainment of national liberation. At worst, his reticence about the exact nature of his suffering underscores all the more the betrayal of patriots like him by elements within the state claiming to speak in the name of the Chinese people.

In the Philippines, the fraught association of Chinese with merchant capital, and much later, with finance capital, engendered state legislation during the Commonwealth and post-war years aimed at curbing the perceived Chinese dominance of the economy. At the same time, state legislation also sought to contain the Chinese "chimerical nationality" through its citizenship laws which, albeit relaxed during the Marcos era through the Mass Naturalization Act, continue nevertheless to foreground the thorny questions of the Chinese identification with money and their ever-doubtful allegiance to the Philippines.[58]

Furthermore, the anti-Left tenor of state policy for much of the post-war period would have also ensured that had Bai Ren stayed on in the Philippines, he would most certainly have been hounded for being a "Communist" or a Communist sympathizer under the Magsaysay, Garcia, Macapagal, Marcos, Aquino, Ramos, Estrada, and most recently the Arroyo, administrations. He would have had to answer to accusations of having allegedly acted to create a Fifth Column among the

---

[56] Special treatment had originally been extended to relatives and dependents of overseas Chinese and included exemption from forced manual labor, and access to special educational facilities and to remittances from overseas and greater rations of consumer goods. See Cariño, *China and the Overseas Chinese*, p. 3.

[57] Interview with "Yisheng" (pseudonym of a returned overseas Chinese from the Philippines), Manila, February 22, 2001.

[58] "Chimerical nationality" is from Karl Marx's "On the Jewish Question," *The Marx-Engels Reader*, ed. Robert C. Tucker, second edition (New York: W. W. Norton and Company, 1978), pp. 26-52. One example of persistent public questioning of the ethnic Chinese allegiance and orientation can be found in Philippine National Artist F. Sionil José's incendiary articles, "Chinese Mischief," *Philippine Star* (February 21, 1999): L-20; "In a war with China, would our local ethnic Chinese be loyal to the Philippines?" *Philippine Star* (February 28, 1999): L-14; and "Stanley Ho and Some Anti-Filipino Chinese," *Philippine Daily Inquirer* (February 6, 2000): 7.

Chinese in the Philippines (as in the case of *Chinese Commercial News* publishers Quintin and Rizal Yuyitung), and his patriotic fervor would still have been derided even by third-generation Chinese Filipinos who simplistically equate emotional attachment to China with political disloyalty to the Philippines. A tragic consequence of this anti-Communist stance has been the silencing, whether forcible or voluntary, of the history of the Chinese Left from accounts of everyday life among the Chinese in the Philippines.

Yet *Nanyang* offers a much more nuanced, and perhaps far more unsettling, picture of the politics of "belonging" and "national identification" and its potentially radical implications for interrogating and redefining nationness. It suggests that, given the right historical opportunity (afforded, in this instance, by the anti-Japanese resistance struggle in Asia) and given the right ideological leanings (in this case, the Left's advocacy of internationalist solidarity against imperialist oppression), one can be patriotically Chinese yet still stake a claim on Philippine national belonging. For not only does A Song owe his "Chineseness" to the specific mediation of his Philippine experience (which includes his stint as merchant apprentice, and his mentors: his lover A Hong, his Filipino friends like Niuniu, and the tribal chief Mohani, among others), his love for China can only be expressed in a form that admits the salience of his love for the second homeland, the Philippines. In the years during which A Song taught himself and was taught by his Chinese compatriots to "remember" a faraway and abstract China in the here-and-now of the Philippines and to contribute his part to the Chinese nationalist cause within the Philippine arena, A Song's "Chinese nationalism" became something other than "Chinese."

One telling instance of the inflection of Chinese patriotic expression by Philippine experience can be seen in the account of A Song's growing involvement in the anti-Japanese resistance movement. A Song's idealism is fired up by, even as it stokes, his romantic involvement with A Hong. Romantic love and patriotic love are, for a time at least, intimately connected in a relation of mutual incitement. In a most revealing scene, the two conduct their courtship in the Luneta, in which they express their love for each other by singing patriotic songs. But what is most telling about this scene is that they do not only sing songs in Chinese—they also warble in English and in "the local language" (*bendihua*). Here, languages and meanings meet and mingle in the common expression of deep-seated emotion.

This Philippine-inflected Chineseness has radical implications insofar as it verifies the oft-repeated but ill-understood generalization that some of the most noted first-generation Chinese nationalists (notably Sun Yat-sen, the founder of the 1911 Chinese Republic, and himself a *huaqiao*) were those who had been exposed to the markedly "foreign" outside. More important, it substantiates Sun Yat-sen's statement that the *huaqiao* were historically the "mothers of revolution" (*gemingzhimu*).[59] At stake is nothing less than a rethinking of nationness and the constitution of the national subject as unitary self.

---

[59] Overseas Chinese based in the Philippines and Vietnam played an important role in sustaining for more than fifty years the anti-Manchu resistance in Southern China during the seventeenth century. Writes Wang Gungwu, "In the Philippines, Cheng Ch'eng-kung [Ming loyalist and anti-Manchu resistance leader Koxinga] received more active support. So important were the revenues from the Philippines, it is said, that the Spanish massacre of the Chinese there in 1622 was a great blow to him and one of the reasons for Cheng Ch'eng-kung's early death." Wang Gungwu, "A Short History of the Nanyang Chinese," pp. 19-20.

Yet even *Nanyang* itself stops short of exploring the full implications of this unsettling of the national self. This truncated move may owe something to the masculinist strain of thinking that dominates the discourse of self-discipline which informs notions of the revolutionary self. There is, curiously, very little close-up, let alone positive, representation of Filipino males in the novel, A Song's narrative being anchored in his social relations with his male Chinese mentors, with the female A Hong, and with a succession of Filipinas who are mainly *mestizas*, and who save his life. This absence of Filipino males, beyond the caricatured "badboys" who harass A Song's Filipina friends, appears to fit in the novelistic project of substantiating a disciplined Chinese revolutionary body—the physical development of the body becoming a literal marker of the growth of political consciousness—that is masculine and desirable,[60] and contrasted with the self-gratifying, unruly, and repulsive "machismo" of Filipino "badboys." This essentialist fantasy creates a "Chinese" male gaze, a traveling Eye/I that self-consciously seeks to occupy the position of the Filipino male in the admiring glance of the Filipina (or more accurately, the Chinese *mestiza* who straddles the Philippine and Chinese cultures), a substitutive or metaphorical strategy that is reinforced by the literary conventions of various colonial travel narratives.[61]

Moreover, the idea of the disciplined revolutionary body often constructs the female gender as the "other" of the male activist, as a domesticating force which vitiates the revolutionary's commitment by its association with carefree pleasures (romantic love) and the claims generated by "its" marital and familial demands. True to the logic of this masculinized revolutionary ethos, A Song's love affairs, especially the one involving A Hong, can only ever end tragically. A Song's relationships with the Filipinas in the novel are telling in another, historical sense. Despite his avid appreciation of her beauty and charm, A Song elects not to reciprocate the love of his best friend Niuniu, and, at one point, even turns down the request of Mohani's daughter that he stay on with the indigenous people and marry her. A Song's repudiation of the love offered by the Filipinas he comes into contact with points to the revolutionary *huaqiao*'s conscious refusal to follow the historical trajectory taken by other male *huaqiao* who, owing to the relatively few Chinese female immigrants in the early years of the century, have had to deal intimately with "local" women, falling in love with and marrying them, and

---

[60] In keeping with the concept of *Bildung*, *Nanyang* charts its protagonist's intellectual development through his physical growth over time. The most telling instance in the novel is the one in which A Song catches a glimpse of his "new self" in the mirror by the staircase of his lodgings and admires the reflected image of "a beautiful young man" (*piaoliang de shaonian*). What follows is a catalogue of idealized features: shiny hair, fair skin, large eyes, regular nose, rosy cheeks, and perfectly shaped mouth, features far removed from those of the callow, skinny child who first arrived in the Philippines barely two years ago (Bai, *Nanyang*, p. 102). Here, the labor-induced flowering of A Song's physical beauty serves as an outward manifestation of his inner self-transformation into a productive and passionate patriot-revolutionary. For a discussion of the reorientation of the modern, politicized body along masculinist lines through ascetic renunciation of feminized sexual desire, domesticity, and consumerism in Chinese literature since the May 4th Movement, see Xiaobing Tang, "*Shanghai, Spring 1930*: Engendering the Revolutionary Body," in his *Chinese Modern: The Heroic and the Quotidian* (Durham: Duke University Press, 2000), pp. 97-130.

[61] For a discussion of the traveling Eye/I, and the *mestizo* character of the colonized hero(ine)s of European sentimental literature, see Mary Louise Pratt, *Imperial Eyes: Travel Writing and Transculturation* (London: Routledge, 1992), p. 86-107, especially 100-101, and Chapter Two of my *Necessary Fictions*, pp. 48-93.

raising sons and daughters who, along with the father himself, may not ever "return" to *Tengsua*.[62] To love, for A Song, is to risk staying on in the Philippines and being unable to go back to one's homeland.

There is, in these accounts of A Song's serially truncated loves, an element of masculinist, even orientalist fantasy, which is evident in the parallel love stories of Chen Shan and A Song's elder brother. Both men fall in love with Filipino women whom they first met when they saved the latter from attempted rape by unsavory characters. *Nanyang* paints an idealized picture of the Chinese working-class males, the beauty of whose bodies attracts the interest of Filipinas. In contrast with A Song's brother, whose love story ends happily in marriage, Chen Shan and A Song both renounce their desires by opting to leave the country.

However, the "male" gaze of the committed Chinese patriot, concerned as it is with standing in for the Filipino male, cannot securely define itself as "Chinese." The novel's delineation of Niuniu's formative influence on A Song blunts the orientalist fantasy shaped by the novel's use of travel-narrative conventions as exemplified by *Robinson Crusoe* while unsettling the asymmetrical relationship between *huaqiao* male and Filipino male. The androgynous Niuniu, first seen in boy's clothing and mistaken for a boy by A Song, shows herself to be A Song's ally and equal, and the relation that they forge, at least in the interim before A Song returns to the hierarchically determined *huaqiao* society and Niuniu begins to desire A Song as a man, is less one of inequality which often obtains between men and women than one of parity and reciprocity between two people whose gender is for the moment indeterminate. It is the beautiful and ebullient Niuniu, one of the best delineated characters in the novel, who sees A Song off at the pier on his voyage back to China, Niuniu who makes the effort to see a Chinese play and expresses her appreciation of Chinese culture, Niuniu who saves A Song from certain death in the hands of the smugglers, Niuniu who teaches A Song how to swim. Niuniu is an important catalyst of A Song's self-transformation. It is this platonic but intense friendship between two equals—rather than a romantic love involving an idealized Chinese man and a pliant and admiring Filipino woman—that Bai offers as an alternative, given his equation of sexual desire with the vitiation of patriotic love.

Moreover, the Chinese patriots whom Bai Ren undertakes to memorialize in his novel did not leave the Philippines without transforming Philippine life as well. Patriotic *huaqiao* who stayed on in the Philippines organized guerrilla units to fight the Japanese. Luis Taruc has written of the role of the famous Chinese leftist Wha-Chi guerrillas in aiding the Huk struggle against the Japanese in this often-quoted passage from his book *Born of the People*:

> The presence of Squadron 48 [Hua Zhi] among the peasants shattered an old and disreputable custom, that of treating Chinese people insultingly, and in general using them as the scapegoat in the blind reaction of Filipinos to evils that lie much deeper in our society. The members of Squadron 48 became much beloved by the people of Central Luzon, who often went out of their way to give them special consideration in billeting, feeding, and assistance.[63]

---

[62] I thank Benedict Anderson for reminding me of the "tropicalization and mestizaje" trajectory of the *huaqiao*.

[63] Luis Taruc, *Born of the People* (New York: International Publisher, 1953), p. 76.

Taruc's second book, however, paints a less rosy picture of the Wha-Chi:

> When the Japanese war broke out, four of their [Chinese Communist] high-ranking officials joined us in the field. Two of them claimed to have already been given training, one in politics, the other in guerrilla warfare, on the Chinese mainland. They were attached to our Politburo as advisers and acted as liaison officers between ourselves and their own anti-Japanese resistance movement.
>
> Their advice was often resisted by Vicente Lava, who was then our general secretary, and by myself. It seemed to us that their advice was always related to Chinese mainland activities rather than Philippine interests.
>
> First they advised us to attack the Japanese relentlessly. Although we did so, we suspected that their motives were chauvinistic, that their main concern was with the battle then going on in China. It seemed to us that they viewed our struggle only as a diversionary action.
>
> When our fight resulted in a fierce Japanese counter-attack, and we suffered heavy casualties, they switched to a defensive strategy, urging us to hide our guns and return to our barrios. They sent most of the members of their own organization home to China. They called this policy "retreat for defense." But the Filipinos in the field refused to put it into action. We had great respect for the Chinese comrades. But when we realized the extent of their chauvinism and self-interest, our respect quickly diminished.[64]

Taruc's account, which castigates the Chinese Communists for being concerned only with China's affairs, ironically reveals his and Lava's own understandable but nevertheless problematic assumption of the infrangibility—the self-contained "inviolability" and, therefore, either-or logic—of Philippine nationalism vis-à-vis other nationalisms. The strong pull of nation-centered thinking on both sides may have sparked tension and mistrust on the part of the Filipino guerrillas, with the result that their willingness to heed the Chinese advice was strongly tempered by their suspicion of the Chinese "chauvinism and self-interest."

Yet the Chinese Communists' "self-centered" practice of sending their comrades back to China actually has a far more mundane explanation than Taruc is willing to grant it—the fact is that these cadres were highly skilled training officers who were also needed in China as much as they were in the Philippines. Socialist commitment to forging international solidarity and mobilizing resistance against Japanese aggression meant that it was not unusual for experienced cadres to have to uproot themselves frequently and move from one place to another, as the need to help train people in guerrilla warfare arose in different places—something that Taruc appears not to have considered. Moreover, Liang Shang Wan and Cai Jian Hua's memoirs offer a much more detailed account of the day-to-day cooperation between Hukbalahap and Wha-Chi guerrillas, an account that, despite its taking an "outsider" or "foreigner" position in its depiction of the anti-Japanese struggle in

---

[64] Luis Taruc, *He Who Rides the Tiger: The Story of an Asian Guerrilla Leader* (New York: Praeger, 1967), pp. 33-34.

the Philippines, points to a number of important collaborative efforts among Chinese and Filipinos in engaging the enemy forces.[65]

In spite of Taruc's mistrust of the Chinese Communist guerrillas' China-centered "chauvinism and self-interest," the role of these guerrillas in the anti-Japanese resistance effort in the Philippines in terms of their participation in the training of Philippine guerrillas cannot be so easily discounted nor quantified, even if they differed with the Filipino guerrillas not just on questions of tactics and strategy but on more fundamental issues such as national allegiance.[66] Furthermore, this contribution to Philippine nationalist struggle was made by Chinese Communists, many of whom did not remain in the Philippines after the war. Their contribution is no less significant just because they decided to go back to China.

And for all that the Chinese guerrillas seemed China-oriented, Taruc's notion of infrangible nationalism does not quite limn the complexity of the Chinese response to the war against the Japanese in the Philippines. The Chinese guerrillas' solidarity with the Filipino resistance struggle can be explained by the fact that Chinese and Filipinos alike were fighting a common enemy. Yet what might account for the fact that after the war, the China-centered guerrillas felt that they had a sufficient stake in Philippine affairs to participate in a mass demonstration on September 23, 1945, at the height of the collaborationism issue in the Philippines, to protest Manuel Roxas's candidacy for president?[67] Prominent Chinese resistance leaders Huang Jie and Li Yongxiao, who headed a contingent of nearly one thousand Chinese leftists, were roundly criticized by Filipino newspapers, as in this editorial which appeared in the *Manila Post*:

> The Chinese can advance no justification for butting into the Philippine collaborationism question, or into any of our other domestic affairs, for that matter. In passing judgment on our congress, the Chinese have stepped over the heads of the Filipino people who had elected their people to congress, the Filipino people who are the only legitimate critics of the officials they have willed into office. Chinese resistance leaders should have directed its trades [sic] against the Nanking puppets and against his [sic] fellow men here in the Philippines who had voluntarily given aid, comfort, and sustenance to the Japanese during the occupation.[68]

By telling the Chinese guerrillas to mind "their" own business and direct their protest action only to issues involving the Chinese community exclusively, the *Manila Post* not only refused to acknowledge the place of Chinese activism in the Filipino struggle against the Japanese; it repudiated the claim made on the Philippines by Chinese guerrillas who risked their lives and saw their comrades die fighting the Japanese *on* Philippine, not Chinese, soil. What is significant about the leftist Chinese guerrillas' action is that even though they did involve themselves in the collaborationism question within the Chinese community, they

---

[65] Liang Shangwan and Cai Jian Hua, *Hua Zhi Huiyilu* (Wha Chi memoirs) (Hong Kong: Bada Chubanshe, 1996), pp. 10-13.

[66] The training provided by the Wha Chi, renamed "Wang Chai," is immortalized in Ninotchka Rosca's novel *State of War* (New York: W. W. Norton and Company, 1988), pp. 289-92.

[67] Yung Li, *The Huaqiao Warriors*, p. 170.

[68] Ibid.

also came to see the necessity of extending their political action beyond the confines of China or even Chinatown by attempting to speak to the Philippine state in a gesture of solidarity with Filipino nationalists who had the right and the obligation to make the state listen and respond to their anti-collaborationist position.

The Chinese guerrillas' action is a signal moment that marks, not so much a shift in the guerrillas' political "position" from being China-centered to Philippine-centered, as a *modulation* from one position to another within a single political continuum. Where the concept of a shift tends to imply a one-way movement from here to there across a distance, however short that distance may be, modulation not only denotes the exertion of a modifying influence on a given entity such as the state, but stresses the potential transmutability of one form or condition (the so-called "China-centered" orientation) into another ("Philippine-centered" orientation) and vice versa. The idea of a shift begins from an assumption of separation often coded in terms of space, of differentiation, that of modulation from an assumption of intimate connection and potential interchangeability, coded in terms of time, of co-incidence. The historical times were such that, in fighting against a common enemy, a "Chinese nationalist" could also be considered a Filipino nationalist without having to give up his Chinese nationalism. One did not have to choose between being *either* a Chinese nationalist *or* a Filipino nationalist; *one could, precisely in being a Chinese nationalist, be a "Filipino" nationalist as well.*

It is true that the Chinese guerrillas did not think of themselves as "dual" nationalists. Their political action derived from, and articulated, a discourse of emancipation which stressed international cooperation and solidarity among leftist groups and forces all over the world. But more than simply a case of international solidarity, the Chinese guerrillas' political action in the Philippines opened itself to the possibility of being articulated as an instance of Filipino nationalist action without necessarily precluding their loyalty and commitment to China.

This kind of *huaqiao* nationalism is a Chinese revolutionary nationalism which, although it promoted political loyalty to the Chinese state, was not necessarily chauvinistic. Instead, it contributed to the development of indigenous nationalism and, later, communism and socialism in Southeast Asia.[69] Whereas some of these overseas Chinese came to identify with the nationalist movements in Southeast Asia (as in the case of Thailand), others identified with the international struggle against imperialist exploitation (as in the case of Indonesia). This progressive, revolutionary form of Chinese nationalism seeks to immunize itself against—yet is also irreducibly transduced by—forms of reified "Chineseness," identified specifically with money, and with merchant "virtues" of asceticism and self-discipline, that were fostered by colonial regimes through census classifications and ethnic/racial policies, and subsequently calcified in everyday life through the historical conflation of "the Chinese" with mercantile capital. The contamination of *huaqiao* revolutionary nationalism by "Chinese" money thus renders the Chinese patriot particularly vulnerable to the exclusionary

---

[69] This point is elaborated in Pheng Cheah's excellent essay, "Chinese Cosmopolitanism in Two Senses and Postcolonial National Memory," in *Cosmopolitan Geographies: New Locations in Literature and Culture*, ed. Vinay Dharwadker (New York: Routledge, 2001), pp. 133-69.

impulses of Southeast Asian indigenous nationalism, which looks upon the Chinese not simply as politically, culturally and emotionally China-oriented "aliens," but as economically powerful ones as well who threaten the political and cultural integrity of the nation.

But what is important about Chinese participation in the mass demonstration against collaborationism is that it posits a conception of nationalist politics in which commonsensical questions of citizenship and allegiance, while not immaterial, are superseded by a higher moral and no less nationalist claim based on the unconditional *gift* of the guerrilla fighters' (self-) sacrifice and the *national indebtedness* occasioned by their act of gift-giving to the Filipino nation at a specific moment in both countries' histories. This gift of self-sacrifice forges an irrevocable bond of solidarity between Chinese guerrillas and "the Filipino people" out of the exigencies of war and requires us to imagine the unimaginable. It substantiates the popular saying that *huaqiao* were not only the "mothers of the revolution" (*gemingzhimu*) but also, as argued in the novel, made "important contributions," by dint of their "wisdom and hard labor," to the societies all over the world in which they live.[70]

Nanyang demands that we learn to imagine how leftist Chinese nationalists can be part of the history of the Philippine national liberation struggle even when they do not claim to be Filipinos. It asks us to recover and embrace, in the words of scholar Pheng Cheah, a disavowed "revolutionary Chinese cosmopolitanism"[71] that played a role in making Philippine history. Finally, it gives political significance to the historic movement across borders of Chinese people who, in the name of international solidarity, aided Filipino nationalists in fighting for national liberation from the Japanese during the 1940s, and in so doing, *changed the terms of their own as well as their allies' notions of nationalism.*

This double or dual nationalism,[72] however, is not a permanent condition, nor even a stable or easily realized one, because it arises only within the context of specific political action enabled by a particular confluence of historico-political contexts. As Thai scholar Kasian Tejapira remarks in his study of the transmutation of Chinese nationalism into Thai nationalism:

> [The fact that t]he emergence of Thai radical nationalism among the *lookjin* communists during the Second World War was ushered in by the other parallel radical nationalism of the Chinese immigrants attests to the intimate complicity and inter-national nature of popular, anti-state nationalisms. Translation thus serves much more than a merely informational function since it transposes concepts, values and beliefs from one national imagination to the formation of another. Given a favorable historic moment when a window of

---

[70] Bai, *Nanyang Piaoliuji*, p. 111.

[71] Ibid.

[72] It may be instructive to recall that Jose Rizal himself can be considered a "dual nationalist" in that he did not find it contradictory to call himself a "Filipino" and a "Spaniard," declaring loyalty to a Spain that he was at great pains in differentiating from the Spanish friars and other colonial evils. I owe Prof. Filomeno V. Aguilar a debt of gratitude for pointing this out.

political opportunity swings open, one can see the beauty of comparisons and fall in love with a nation just for the love of another.[73]

Double nationalism is thus especially vulnerable to erasure by time and forgetfulness of the people on whose behalf the dual-nationalist revolutionaries undertook political action and made self- sacrifices.

Posing the unimaginable question of the Chinese foreigner's "nationalist" contribution to the making of the Philippine nation, in turn, raises an even deeper issue with regard to the limits of taking for granted the use of the nation-state as an analytical and conceptual unit. This is not to argue that the nation-state, or nationalism, is obsolete. Far from it: this essay argues that these concepts remain salient forces and have important socio-political, economic, and cultural implications in everyday life, and no amount of talk about capitalist globalization can afford to discount the importance of the nation even in the new world order. The continuing salience of nationness renders it all the more necessary for scholars to foster a more rigorous study of the concept of nationness, and to take into account experiential forms, such as those depicted in Bai Ren's novel, which test the limits of both Chinese and Philippine nationalism in ways that highlight the making and unmaking of both the Chinese and Philippine social through the material flow of bodies and labor which (re)define the experience of nationness in both countries.

Nanyang shows that the *Bildung* as process is not so much about the successful formation of an individual in accordance with an ideal as it is about how this very formation is dependent on the necessary short-circuiting of the process brought about by the chance or accidental connections which end up reformulating the ideal. *Nanyang* shows how one's experience of one's homeland is shaped by the vicissitudes of one's engagement with the "second homeland" (*dierguxiang*) in which one spends the golden years of childhood and adolescence (*huangjinshidai*).

The "Philippines" that A Song reconstructs from memory is as "phantasmatic" as the abstract "China" he conjures up, and as contingent and provisional. A Song's narrative rendering of the Philippines is markedly replete with silences, gaps, and omissions. There is talk of Dutch persecution of the Chinese in Indonesia, for example, but A Song appears not to have known of the Spanish massacres of the Chinese in the Philippines. The lacunae in A Song's historical knowledge point up the selectiveness and inherent "corruptibility" of memory.

This same historical memory—though fraught and riddled with lacunae—constitutes an imperative that animates Bai Ren's project of recuperating the *huaqiao* experience. Haunted in China by his memories of the Philippines,[74] Bai Ren undertook the difficult task of excavating a buried revolutionary past, of reconstructing a *huaqiao* activism that has disappeared from Chinese official memory, an activism that has also been expunged from Filipino official memory and exists only as a trace, a series of untranslated (if not untold) stories about laboring Chinese, in the Chinese-Filipino memory. *Nanyang* recounts the difficult

---

[73] Kasian Tejapira, *Commodifying Marxism: The Formation of Modern Thai Radical Culture, 1927-1958* (Kyoto, Japan and Victoria, Australia: Kyoto University Press and Trans Pacific Press, 2001), p. 191.

[74] In his Afterword, Bai Ren states that his memories of his youthful experiences in the Philippines loom ever clearer in his mind, appearing unbidden "in front of [his] eyes" (*bushi zai yanmianxian*) and impelling him to set them down in writing. Bai, *Nanyang Piaoliuji*, p. 292.

labor attending the *huaqiao*'s becoming-Chinese by showing how this process took the form of a necessary (though often disavowed) detour that entailed the possibility of the *huaqiao*'s becoming-Filipino. The sojourning *huaqiao* male is constitutively Filipinized through the fact of labor that attends his becoming-Chinese. This experiential detour can serve as a potential corrective to the "chimerical nationality" often attributed to the Chinese, whose ethnicity has been historically conflated with capital; in effect, labor returns as the principal repressed element of Chinese-Philippine history.

The questions *Nanyang* raises are numerous and certainly difficult to answer, but they are questions that need to be posed here and now, in the hope that they may lead to a rethinking of the basic assumptions that inform the theory and practice of nationalism. If one's experience of nationness bears the ineluctable traces of other "nations," other loyalties, what does it mean to claim that one "belongs" to any given nation? What does it mean to immerse oneself in a "collectivity," to call oneself one of the "people" when this "national self" is not unitary, but rather irreducibly marked by something "foreign"? Can one have a claim to a nation other than her own? And can this claim be recognized by the people of that other nation even if the person, a *fanke* who is also a *sangley*, a regular visitor and a frequent guest in a foreign land, whose constantly arriving presence poses the "intolerable question"[75] that destabilizes the conceptual foundations of our notions of Filipino nationness, does not or chooses not to lay any claim? Indeed, can the much-vaunted particularism and exclusivity of nationalist theory and practice be interrogated in such a way as to render nationalism more hospitable to forms of solidarity which may not be based on "political loyalty" or citizenship, and to the difficult question of what it means for a foreigner to be "at home" in a land that she may not even choose to call her own?

---

[75] See Jacques Derrida's deconstructive reading of Plato's dialogues in Jacques Derrida and Anne Dufourmantelle, *Of Hospitality*, trans. Rachel Bowlby (Stanford: Stanford University Press, 2000), p. 11. In his discussion of Socrates' defense of himself against accusations charging him with sophistry, Derrida writes suggestively: "He [Socrates] declares that he is 'foreign' to the language of the courts, to the tribune of the tribunals: he doesn't know how to speak this courtroom language, this legal rhetoric of accusation, defense, and pleading; he doesn't have the skill, he is *like* a foreigner. (Among the serious problems we are dealing with here is that of the foreigner who, inept at speaking the language, always risks being without defense before the law of the country that welcomes or expels him; the foreigner is first of all foreign to the legal language in which the duty of hospitality is formulated, the right to asylum, its limits, norms, policing, etc. He has to ask for hospitality in a language which by definition is not his own, the one imposed on him by the master of the house, the host, the king, the lord, the authorities, the nation, the State, the father, etc. This personage imposes on him translation into the host's own language, and that's the first act of violence. That is where the question of hospitality begins: must we ask the foreigners to understand us, to speak our language, in all the sense of this term, in all its possible extensions, before being able and so as to be able to welcome him into our country? If he was already speaking our language, with all that that implies, if we already shared everything that is shared with a language, would the foreigner still be a foreigner and could we speak of asylum and hospitality with regard to him?)" (pp. 15, 17)

THE MARGINALIZATION OF THE INDIANS IN MALAYSIA: CONTESTING EXPLANATIONS AND THE SEARCH FOR ALTERNATIVES[*]

Francis Loh Kok Wah

INTRODUCTION

Large-scale migration of Tamil Indian males to Malaya began in the late nineteenth century, reaching a peak in the 1910s and 1920s, the so-called "rubber boom" years, when rubber estates were being rapidly developed and tens of thousands of laborers were required each year. British control of the Indian subcontinent as well as of the Malay peninsula facilitated the recruitment of indentured laborers for these estates from the impoverished southern Indian agricultural sector. Indians were also recruited for the development of the infrastructure—the building of roads, railways, telecommunications, and ports and for the laying of power and water supply lines—which was spurred on by the rubber boom. Still others, such as the Punjabis, were recruited as members of the police force, while the better-educated Sri Lankan Tamils were brought in to administer the lower reaches of the colonial bureaucracy and occasionally, of the estates. Invariably, petty traders, moneylenders, artisans, and teachers also followed, principally to serve these overseas Indian settlements.

Mass migration came to an end in the 1930s as a result of the world economic depression. During the remainder of the decade, more Indian females than males arrived in British Malaya, until the outbreak of the Second World War also put an end to that movement between the two regions. Following the war, depressed economic conditions as well as the exigencies of the postwar political situation—notably the rise of anti-colonialism and the impending end to British

---

[*] This is a revised version of a paper which I presented at the workshop "The Re-Integrative Revolution: Managing Diversity and Identity Politics in the Asia Pacific Region," La Trobe University, Melbourne, 14-17 February 2002, convened by Joel Kahn. I wish to thank Joel Kahn and Yeoh Seng Guan for their comments of my paper. I am especially grateful to Audrey Kahin for helping in my revision.

rule—mass migration to Malaya did not resume, nor did mass emigration back to India. Instead, as a result of the arrival of females particularly during the late 1930s, a more familial demographic pattern emerged, with most Indians putting down roots and choosing to stay on in Malaya. Consequently, permanent migrant settlements could be found in the rubber estates throughout the western coast of peninsular Malaya, in quarters for manual workers provided by the various government departments (the Public Works, Malayan Railway, Penang Port Commission, Telecoms, etc), and in urban enclaves of such major towns as Penang, Kuala Lumpur, Klang, Ipoh, Telok Intan, Melaka, and Seremban. In these rural settlements and urban enclaves, temples and shrines, primary schools, shops and restaurants, as well as Indian social, cultural, and (belatedly) political organizations sprouted.

According to the 1991 Census of Malaysia, 1.39 million persons were registered as ethnic Indians, accounting for 7.9 percent of Malaysia's total population. Most of these resided in peninsular Malaysia, where they constituted 9.5 percent of the total population. Almost 80 percent of all Malaysian Indians identified themselves as Tamils, presumably on the grounds of some familiarity with the language. The remaining 20 percent regarded themselves as Malayalees and Telegus (originating from southern India), as well as smaller groups of Punjabis, Gujeratis, Sindhis, Bengalis, etc. (originating from northern India). Significantly, in 1991 only about 36.2 percent of Indians were registered as living in rural areas,[1] compared with the colonial period, when a majority of Indians were registered there.

Apart from these distinctions in terms of places of origin and languages, residences and occupations, the Indians were further differentiated by religion, caste, class, and political orientation. One of the most informed scholars of the Indians in Malaysia, S. Arasaratnam, has stated:

> Only in the widest possible definition of the term "community" could we call the Malaysian Indians a community. In the political and social context of Malaysia the Indians were pressured to look upon themselves as a community and other ethnic groups did look upon them in that way.[2]

Hence, the term Malaysian Indian tends to overstate the similarities and the sense of community among those who are categorized as such. Nevertheless, there have been no lack of attempts to foster as well as to mobilize, largely for political purposes, these disparate groups of Malaysian Indians as a community in multi-ethnic Malaysia. The major Indian-based political party, the Malaysian Indian Congress (MIC), is at the forefront of such attempts. Indeed, its raison d'être is to represent the Malaysian Indian community.

Ethnic posturing on the part of the MIC is not unique. The other major political parties in Malaysia—the United Malays National Organization (UMNO) and the Malaysian Chinese Association (MCA)—also consider themselves as the

---

[1] *Population and Housing Census of Malaysia 1991* (Kuala Lumpur: Department of Statistics, 1995), p. 53.
[2] S. Arasaratnam, "Indian Society of Malaysia and its Leaders: Trends in Leadership and Ideology among Malaysian Indians 1945-1960." Paper presented at the Eighth Conference International Association of Historians of Asia, Kuala Lumpur, August 25-29, 1980.

representatives of their respective communities. The caveat to ethnic posturing, however, is a consociational arrangement among the leaders of these ethnic-based parties, namely the multi-party Barisan Nasional (BN, previously the Alliance Party) at the apex of Malaysian society, where the necessary compromises are worked out for the implied common good and the maintenance of political stability. Put another way, there is little effort made to promote an imagined Malaysian community among the various ethnic groups. The ordinary people, who are regarded as steeped in primordialism, are encouraged to regard themselves as members of exclusive ethnic communities, notwithstanding official pronouncements and exhortations to promote national unity. It is principally the would-be leaders, who, regarding themselves as possessing more universalistic viewpoints, breach these ethnic boundaries. This process is facilitated via institutionalization of a multi-party ruling coalition whose major components are organized as mono-ethnic political parties.

Such constructions of the nation-state rest on weak foundations and can come unstuck for a number of reasons. First, promoting ethnic group formation and exclusivist identities compromises the fostering of ethnic harmony and political stability, let alone an imagined Malaysian nation. Consequently, occasional outbreaks of ethnic violence have occurred. Second, the BN ruling elites have not been as altruistic as envisaged in consociational theory. Many studies have shown that these would-be leaders have indulged in "money politics" whereby Malaysian politicians and political parties use their positions to further their private business interests. Moreover, in trying to gain electoral support to remain in power and so protect these interests, these would-be leaders have quite unabashedly manipulated ethnic sentiments. This is especially evident during elections. And third, increasing numbers of Malaysians have rejected the BN's formula of institutionalizing political participation along ethnic lines albeit with consociational arrangements among the elites. A search for multi-ethnic alternatives to Malaysia's ethnic polarization has developed, especially evident among younger, educated, middle-class Malaysians.

It is within this context that I discuss the case of the Indians in Malaysia. It is an account not only of the marginalization of the Indians and disillusionment with the two principal Indian organizations, the MIC and the National Union of Plantation Workers (NUPW). It is also about a turn to Hinduism on the one hand and the establishment of trans-ethnic NGOs on the other, as sites of contests and alternative visions to the dominant BN formula. The MIC has also proven capable of re-inventing itself constantly in order to maintain its hegemony over Malaysian Indians.

THE KAMPONG RAWA TEMPLE-MOSQUE DISPUTE IN PENANG, 1998

A dispute involving Hindus and Muslims broke out in Penang in March 1998 and threatened to bring Penang to the brink of serious ethnic violence. Initially it pitted Indian Hindus and Indian Muslims living in Kampong Rawa against one another. Located by Sungai Pinang, the Kampong Rawa neighborhood is a low-lying part of the island which invariably gets flooded every rainy season. It is a working-class area and, apparently, one where Indian youth gangs are active.[3]

According to the authorities and political leaders, the Kampong Rawa dispute occurred as a result of the "close proximity" of the Sri Raja Raja Mathuraiveeran Hindu temple to the Masjid Kampong Rawa. True, they were hardly thirty meters apart, but close proximity, in and of itself, need not have been the cause of the dispute. For the proximity of religious buildings did not seem to have posed a problem to Penang residents in the past. If one takes a stroll down Jalan Pitt, for instance, one comes across the Anglican St George's church, followed by the Kuan Yin temple, then the back entrance to the Sri Mariamman Hindu temple, next the Kapitan Kling mosque and at the end of the road the Acheen Street mosque, which itself backs up to the Khoo Kongsi complex where ancestor worship and religious ceremonies are regularly conducted. Even in Kampong Rawa, both places of worship had been in existence for thirty to forty years. If close proximity was indeed the cause, its significance was recent, for it was only in 1996, after a new mosque replaced the original one, and after the extension of the relatively obscure Hindu shrine into a new temple in late 1997, that proximity became an issue. By all accounts, it was the consecration ceremonies held in December 1997 for the new and enlarged temple that drew attention to the fact that the temple was located so near the mosque.

The first showdown occurred on March 20, 1998, when an estimated 200 to 250 Muslims confronted a group of young Hindu men, who, according to an informant, were members of a local gang that had been ringing the temple bells during the usual Muslim Friday prayers. Apparently, the bells had also been rung during prayer time the previous Friday, and when the Muslims protested, the Hindu youths had given assurances that this would not happen again. Hence Muslims considered the ringing on March 20 as provocative. Stone throwing and verbal abuse followed, but a small group of policemen who had rushed in from the nearby Sungai Pinang police station prevented the Muslims from entering the temple. Four additional truckloads of police belonging to the Federal Reserve Unit (FRU, trained to combat urban riots) joined these policemen. They arrested ninety-four people, mostly Indian Muslims, and cordoned off the temple to prevent further incidents. Rumors of what had transpired hit the streets of Penang that night. Messages via the internet carried postings describing the incident, which were often emotional and misinformed. Contrary to some of the rumors in these reports, the dispute did not result in any deaths, although many people were injured. Neither was any mosque or temple or other property razed to the ground. Fortunately the dispute was brought under control by the authorities within two weeks. According to popular assessment, the authorities had acted responsibly.

In the following days, the Penang state government, the police, and the local temple and mosque committees tried to piece together a compromise, ultimately deciding to relocate the temple across the road in an area where the majority of residents were Indians. The rationale was that the temple had been built and extended without the permission of the local authority and the landowner (a

---

[3] Being resident in Penang, it was convenient for me to conduct fieldwork and interviews in Kampong Rawa and in Penang generally as soon as the dispute broke out. Fortuitously, I had been involved in a socio-economic survey of the Indians in Penang, including in Kampong Rawa, from January to February 1998.

Chinese man), i.e. it was an illegal structure. The chief minister Dr Koh Tzu Koon issued a short press statement to that effect.[4] This was the first official statement on the matter.

Meanwhile, two MIC leaders met with the local temple committee and persuaded them to relocate, an action that would also serve to regularize the status of the temple. The MIC leaders assured the committee that they would have access to the temple to conduct the necessary ceremonies prior to relocation. This promise was not kept, however, for the temple was prematurely sealed up to dome-level and the temple grounds were fenced off, denying the temple officials access. About three hundred Hindus gathered downtown in front of the State government building in Komtar to protest this breach of the agreed arrangements. The police quickly dispersed this "illegal" demonstration but made no arrests. However, the general vicinity of Komtar was cordoned off, causing massive traffic jams. More rumors were fueled.

Subsequently, temple officials were allowed to enter the temple in order to transfer the deities to a temporary shed beside the new site. Once the deities were removed and relocated on the evening of March 26, the original structure, no longer considered a temple, was demolished. The chief minister issued a second short statement that the matter had been resolved "in accordance with the Malaysian spirit."[5]

Ceremonies to install the deities in the new temple lasted several hours and continued into the night. Not only had a huge crowd of Hindus gathered to witness the procession and join in the ceremonies, but Muslims too had congregated around the mosque, apparently to protect it against potential attackers. By this time the crowds included not only Sungai Pinang residents, but outsiders as well. Emotions ran high and the police, who were there to prevent trouble, detained five persons.

However, events took an ugly turn the following day. Through word of mouth, the internet, and the distribution of pamphlets, Muslims were encouraged to show up in force in Kampong Rawa at noon on March 27. Fearing that the Hindus would attack the mosque in retaliation for the demolition and relocation of their temple, one of the pamphlets stated that the Muslims would "help the authorities to prevent mischief by Hindus." Ironically, pamphlets distributed among Hindus also called upon them to show up in full force "to defend their temples and to help the authorities prevent the Muslims from creating mischief." Yet another pamphlet declared that Hindus had "to stand up for these rights in Sungai Pinang, otherwise they would be further eroded elsewhere." In response, the police set up roadblocks on the Penang bridge and the entrance to the ferry terminal to deter potential troublemakers from crossing to the island. The general area surrounding Kampong Rawa was also cordoned off. Nonetheless, whereas the usual Friday prayers attracted some five to six hundred people, an estimated crowd of five to seven thousand people gathered in the Kampong Rawa mosque that Friday. Such a large crowd, inevitably, spilled out of the mosque into the surrounding grounds. The Indian Muslims who constituted a significant percentage of the faithful were now clearly outnumbered by Malay Muslims. A huge crowd of Hindus similarly gathered across the road near the site of the new temple, an Indian working-class area.

---

[4] *The Star*, March 24, 1998.
[5] Ibid., March 27, 1998.

Taunts and stones were thrown, but initially there was no direct clash, as the police had placed themselves strategically between the two groups. But the presence of a helicopter hovering over the area created a sense of emergency. Then suddenly the Muslims broke through the police lines. The police fired tear gas into the crowd and used water cannons to disperse the Muslims, or to force them back into the mosque grounds. The police then charged and began arresting the Muslims. Their search in both areas uncovered several molotov cocktails, *parang* (machetes) and other weapons. Altogether another forty-three people were arrested that day, bringing the total arrested to 137. Most were working class youths, some from outside Penang.

In the late afternoon, the then deputy prime minister, Anwar Ibrahim, arrived. After meeting with the security chiefs, the politicians, and the temple and mosque representatives, he called a press conference, the first opportunity the press had to pose questions to the authorities. Anwar announced that the matter had been settled and blamed outsiders for escalating a small local affair into a security-threatening incident, appealing to all to cooperate with the authorities. He also assured the public that the police would carry out their duties fairly but firmly. Then he persuaded the representatives of the mosque and temple committees to shake hands in front of the cameras. These shots appeared on television that evening as well as in the following day's newspapers. The Inspector General of Police next appeared. After being briefed, he too held a press conference to announce that the matter had been resolved. His remarks, too, appeared in the next day's newspapers.[6]

The restored calm in Kampong Rawa and the reassuring visits of the deputy premier and the police chief notwithstanding, several further cases of violence occurred that March 27 night. A few Hindu shrines and temples were desecrated. One mosque in downtown Georgetown had its windowpanes broken, and several popular Indian Muslim eating stalls were targeted. Mischief was also evident along Jalan Pitt where the glass windows of Indian Muslim jewelry stalls were shattered. Proprietors of shops and restaurants, fearful of attacks, boarded up their premises for a few days. Some direct clashes must have also occurred, for there were verified reports and lots of rumors of people seeking outpatient as well as in-patient treatment in the island's hospitals. There were further arrests early on March 28. Rumors of a curfew proved false. Instead more police arrived and more police check points were set up all over the island. Several other incidents occurred that night and more arrests. But by Sunday, March 29, order was fully restored. Altogether, a total of 185 people were arrested "for rioting, illegal assembly and possession of dangerous weapons." There was no doubt that the state authorities had seized the initiative and regained control over the island.

In the wake of the incident, ill feelings persisted for some time in "Little India," the Indian enclave in an old quarter of Georgetown where generations of Indians, both Hindu and Muslim, have lived alongside each other. Some Muslims who had previously lived and conducted businesses there have since, reportedly, moved out of the predominantly Hindu area of Little India.

---

[6] There is a little irony here. Later that year, after Anwar was sacked as deputy prime minister and detained, the Inspector General was involved in beating up a blindfolded Anwar while the latter was in detention.

Several observers have linked the dispute described above with developments in the Indian sub-continent. They refer to the distribution among Indian Muslims of a video of the 1992 destruction of the Babri Masjid conducted by extremist elements associated with the Hindu Bharatiya Janata Party (BJP), which had then just assumed power in India. If true, this connection between unrest in Malaysia and political developments in India is relatively recent and insidious. There is some evidence to support the theory. For instance, according to a local press report,[7] four men from Penang were detained in India in connection with Hindu-Muslim clashes in Tamilnadu state in February 1998. The four, who were photographed together with nine other "suspected terrorists" from the radical Al-Ummah group, were arrested in Madras hours after several bomb blasts occurred in Coimbatore town. The photograph was published in *Tamil Nesan* (on February 19, 1998), a Tamil-language Malaysian daily. In the aftermath of the Kampong Rawa incident, the police, reportedly, investigated possible connections between the bombings in India and the incident in Penang, the findings of which have never been made public.

Whatever the case, at least in Penang, it must be acknowledged that Hindu-Muslim tensions within the Indian community have been building for many years. In part, they relate to political developments in the Indian sub-continent, which have always been given much coverage in the vernacular press. Additionally, there is a regular flow of Indians, both Hindus and Muslims, to and from India. Due to difficulties in acquiring Malaysian citizenship, a fair proportion of these Indian permanent residents in Malaysia remain Indian nationals. This group of transient Penang Indians, and indeed, the majority of Indians in Penang (and in Malaysia generally), are working class and face various types of insecurity related to their employment, housing, educational opportunities for their children, etc. In such an environment, frustrations have grown and tensions developed between Indian Hindus and Indian Muslims. The latter, also referred to as Jawi Peranakan in Penang, have for decades associated closely with local Malays, often intermarrying and even joining UMNO. It is well known among Penangites that a few UMNO branches in Georgetown whose members are overwhelmingly Indian Muslims conduct their meetings in Tamil, not Malay. Consequently, their children, due to intermarriage and schooling in Malay-medium national schools, have acquired a better proficiency of Malay, and on occasion have obtained *bumiputera* (literally "sons of the soil" or indigenous people) status and privileges therein under the auspices of the New Economic Program (NEP). Understandably, some measure of jealousy and animosity has arisen among Hindu Indians who have been denied such privileges despite their poverty. Such feelings possibly contributed to the Kampong Rawa clash.

Generally poor, unable to compete effectively in the Penang market (which is dominated by the Chinese who also constitute the majority population in Penang island), and neglected by the government and the MIC, large groups of poor Indians have become increasingly marginalized. The frustrations of these Penang Indians, both Hindus and Muslims, lie at the root of tensions in "Little India," and help explain the attraction of radical communal politics in India and violent outbursts such as the Kampong Rawa incident. Obviously, the Barisan Nasional's formula for maintaining unity and stability has been coming unstuck, not least because of divisions and tensions among Indians themselves, especially those who find

---

[7] *The Sun*, April 1, 1998.

themselves marginalized. Such intra-Indian tensions also belie the notion of ethnic-based primordial communities.

MARGINALIZATION

The marginalization of Indians in Malaysia is not a new issue. Over the years many academics and journalists have highlighted the problem in both the socio-economic and political spheres.[8] The Malaysian government's latest overall economic development plan, the Second Outline Perspective Plan (OPP2), 1991-2000, also acknowledges the problem:

> The socio-economic position of the Indians (as well as those of certain groups within the Bumiputera community such as the Orang Asli and indigenous groups in Sabah and Sarawak) has lagged behind and the progress achieved by these communities has not been in tandem with the achievements of the other communities. [T]hey have not been given adequate attention in the government's development efforts despite the improvement in levels of income and standards of living for the country as a whole.[9]

However, despite such official awareness, the majority of Indians did not experience much progress during the 1990s, a period of rapid economic growth during which the Malays and Chinese generally prospered. In highlighting the problem of marginalization, I do not suggest that all Indians lagged behind. For a small group of Indians, like their Malay and Chinese counterparts who together constitute the business class, prospered spectacularly, to the extent that intra-ethnic relative poverty—rather than inter-ethnic relative poverty—has become the concern among some researchers.[10] It is therefore the marginalization of poor Indians with which we are concerned. In fact, Samy Vellu, the current MIC leader, has also been very concerned about the plight of the poor Indians and has raised alarms at various meetings, seminars, and especially his party's annual general assemblies.[11] However, Samy Vellu and other MIC leaders tend to present this plight as one involving the entire community, conveniently ignoring the fact that

---

[8] See, for example, Chandra Muzaffar, "Political Marginalisation in Malaysia," in *Indian Communities in Southeast Asia*, ed. K.S. Sandhu and A. Mani (Singapore: Institute of Southeast Asian Studies, 1993), pp. 211-36; D Jeyakumar, "The Indian Poor in Malaysia: Problems and Solutions," in ibid., pp. 405-37; T. Marimuthu, "The Plantation School as an Agent of Social Reproduction," in ibid., pp. 465-83; J. Clad, "The Other Malaysians," *Far Eastern Economic Review* (July 26, 1984): 22-30; S. Jayasankaran, "Tussle in the Plantations," *Malaysian Business* (November 1, 1984): 33-38; M. Jalleh, "Still Awaiting the New Sunrise," *Aliran Monthly* 20, 11/12 (2000): 2-8; S. Ramachandran, *Indian Plantation Labour in Malaysia* (Kuala Lumpur: Institute of Social Analysis, 1994); P. Ramasamy, "Politics of Indian Representation in Malaysia," *Economic and Political Weekly*, November 24, 2001, pp. 4312-18.

[9] *Malaysia, The Second Outline Prospective Plan, 1991-2000* (Kuala Lumpur: Government Printers, 1991), p. 16.

[10] K.S. Jomo, "A Malaysian Middle Class? Some Preliminary Analytical Considerations," in *Rethinking Malaysia*, ed. K.S. Jomo (Kuala Lumpur: Malaysian Social Sciences Association, 1999), pp. 126-48 and pp. 137-38 and SERI, *Socio-Economic Study of the Indian Community in Penang* (Penang: Socio-economic and Environmental Research Institute, 1999). I was a principal researcher in the SERI Study.

[11] See Jalleh, "Still Awaiting the New Sunrise," for a compilation of statements by Samy Vellu.

they and other privileged Indians have actually enriched themselves in recent decades, in spite of the pro-*bumiputera* NEP. Indeed, by harping on the marginalization of Indians as a community, these politicians rationalize their call to the Indians to rally behind the MIC.

The point then is this: marginalization is a class, not an ethnic, issue, although a majority of Indians remain poor. Those employed in the rubber estates still work under a daily-rated wage system, earning an average of 300 to 500 *ringgit* a month in 2002. But a proportion of the Indian poor are also domiciled in the urban areas. This urbanization originally occurred as a result of the "sub-division" or "fragmentation" of the large estates in the 1950s and 1960s, when their European owners, feeling threatened by Malaya's impending independence, began to sell these estates to Malaysians. Since few locals could afford to buy such large estates intact, they were often subdivided; as a result, a majority of their workers were forced to retrench or experienced a drastic reduction in wages, health, and other facilities.[12] A second push to the urban areas occurred beginning in the 1970s, when the estates on the fringes of urban areas were converted into housing projects, industrial estates, commercial complexes, and sometimes golf courses too. This resulted in another round of retrenchment from the estates and further migration to urban areas. According to the Census of Malaysia 1991, some 63.8 percent of the Indian population currently live in urban areas (classified as settlements with more than 10,000 people).[13]

Although rapid industrialization and expansion of the service sector in Penang and the Klang Valley, beginning in the 1970s, created new employment opportunities for the young, only those with skills or adequate years of schooling proved employable. However, poor Indian students attending Tamil primary schools were not performing well. For example, Tamil primary schools in Penang registered the lowest passing rate in the Standard Six examinations in 1996-97,[14] while in 1999, all the students from the twenty-two Tamil primary schools in Selangor who sat for the same examination failed in all subjects.[15]

At any rate, most of these migrants were unable to afford decent urban housing on the basis of their low wages. This was especially true in Penang, where land is scarce and housing and rentals expensive. Hence, most Indians who were displaced ended up in squatter settlements. In Kampong Tin in Perai, opposite Penang island, some stayed in converted shipping containers, while on the island itself in Sungai Tiram, for instance, Indians even made their homes in shelters previously provided for animals. Indians comprised an inequitably large proportion of the squatter population, many of whom were threatened with imminent eviction in 1998 as a result of development activities.[16]

This urbanization of former estate workers, and their problems in securing employment and housing in the new urban environment, constitute the new dimension in Indian marginalization, one that has not been adequately recognized, let alone addressed by the state authorities and other would-be representatives of

---

[12] M. Stenson, *Class, Race and Colonialism in West Malaysia: The Indian Case* (St. Lucia: University of Queensland Press, 1980), p. 20..

[13] Calculated from *Population and Housing Census of Malaysia 1991*, p. 52

[14] SERI, *Socio-economic study*, chapter 6.

[15] *The Sun*, March 12, 2000

[16] SERI, *Socio-economic study*, chapter 7.

the Indians. All too conveniently, their pleas for help have been ignored due to their status as "illegal" squatters.

The economic marginalization of working-class Indians, and their urbanization and social dislocation, have led to serious social problems, including a tendency to violence.[17] This predicament among Indian workers is related to the increasing shortcomings of the two major Indian political organizations, namely the MIC and the NUPW, on which most Indian workers had relied to represent their interests previously, but with which they have become increasingly disillusioned.

THE MALAYSIAN INDIAN CONGRESS

The Malaysian Indian Congress (MIC) was formed in August 1946 to represent the Indian community in Malaysia. Significantly, the MIC's first three presidents were English-speaking non-Tamil professionals, and its limited membership during their tenures was essentially middle-class.[18] It was not until 1955, when V. T. Sambanthan assumed office as MIC's fourth president, that the MIC entered into a coalition with UMNO and the MCA to form the Alliance, a communally-based and conservative multi-ethnic grouping, which has persisted until today under the expanded Barisan Nasional (BN). Under Sambanthan, a south Indian Tamil, the MIC resorted to Tamil communal appeals to develop a mass base. The Tamilization of the MIC continued during the tenures of V. Manikavasagam (the fifth president) and Samy Vellu (the current president), both also Tamils. While Tamilization resulted in popular support for the MIC and facilitated its entry into electoral politics, it also alienated non-Tamils from the organization. Not surprisingly, a certain percentage of middle-class Indians, mostly English-speaking, who did not agree with the communal stance of MIC and its participation in the conservative Alliance coalition, joined other multi-ethnic opposition parties. In the 1970s, however, following the implementation of the New Economic Program (NEP), Manikavasagam and subsequently Samy Vellu recruited English-speaking middle-class south Indians back to the party, although some non-Tamil Indians, alienated by the MIC's Hinduism-related activities, formed small parties like the Punjabi Party of Malaysia and the Malaysian Indian Muslim Congress.

Nevertheless, the MIC claims that it represents the interests of all Indians in Malaysia. Given Malaysia's multi-ethnic complexion and the Indians' minority status, the MIC argues that it is necessary for Indians to be united and represented in the ruling coalition, especially after the introduction of the NEP, for the government's agenda in this program is to improve the socio-economic conditions of the *bumiputera* in general and to promote the creation of a "*bumiputera* industrial and commercial community" in particular.

In response to the NEP, the MIC adopted a two-pronged strategy for protecting Indian interests. First, it tried to persuade the BN government to classify Indians as a separate and distinct group, so that their particular problems as a minority community would be recognized and quotas also allocated for Indians. Unlike the Chinese, the MIC argued, Indians do not have a strong presence in the private sector. The MIC president has claimed that, through his prodding, the Economic

---

[17] For a discussion of disciplinary problems among Indian students and growing violence and crime rates among Indian youths, see ibid., chapters 6 and 8.

[18] Arasaratnam, "Indian Society of Malaysia."

Planning Unit of the Prime Minister's Department has set up a special study team to draw up specific recommendations on how to achieve, initially, some 3 percent equity for Indians.[19] During the 1970s, under Manikavasagam, the MIC also encouraged Indians to get involved in the corporate sector of the economy, but with only limited funds raised, this effort yielded disappointing results.

A second attempt to promote Indian involvement in the corporate sector was made under Samy Vellu's leadership. In the early 1980s, a unit trust along the lines of the Amanah Saham Nasional (which had been set up by the government in 1981 to promote *bumiputera* participation in the share market) was launched. But this scheme too proved unsuccessful.

A more ambitious venture was the setting-up of a modern corporation called Maika Holdings in 1983, which by 1984 boasted a paid-up capital of RM106 million, raised from 66,400 shareholders, principally middle-class and upper-class MIC members. As with similar ventures by the MCA, Maika went on an acquisition drive.[20] By Samy Vellu's own admission, "political power" facilitated Maika's acquisition of interests in the corporatized Malaysian Airlines System, and other privatized entities such as TV3, Malaysian International Shipping Corporation (MISC), Syarikat Telekom Malaysia Berhad (STM), and Edaran Otomobil Nasional Berhad (EON).[21] In effect, Samy Vellu had succeeded in persuading the BN government to treat the Indians separately from the Chinese and to grant a helping hand to Indian businessmen, in this case, to Maika.

A related aspect of these efforts was the MIC's venture into educational projects. Apart from lobbying the government to offer more places for Indians in the public universities, the MIC also set up the Maju Institute of Educational Development (MIED). In turn, MIED launched two technical colleges in the 1990s and a private university in 2001. These tertiary institutions, which largely cater to the middle-class, have been criticized by Indian leaders from inside and outside the MIC. The money spent, the critics argue, should have been redirected towards rehabilitating the Tamil primary schools or providing scholarships to needy students with excellent results to study in existing public universities.

Gomez has persuasively argued that the involvement of the BN political parties in business led to factionalism, as politicians competed for access to these business interests. Such access also fueled patronage networks, which in turn facilitated control of the parties. The MIC was no exception. Soon, allegations were leveled by one group against another that funds had been abused. Beginning in 1988, Maika Holdings itself began registering losses, which MIC president Samy Vellu attributed to the misappropriation of funds by certain party leaders, as well as to poor fiscal management and high operating costs.[22] These problems came to light as a result of the recession in the mid-1980s.

---

[19] *The Star*, Januarty 25, 2002.

[20] E.T. Gomez, "Changing Ownership Patterns, Patronage and the NEP," in *Malaysia: Critical Perspectives: Essays in Honour of Syed Husin Ali* (Petaling Jaya: Malaysian Social Science Association, 1996), pp. 132-54 and pp. 139-40.

[21] Clad, "The Other Malaysians," and E.T. Gomez, *Political Business: Corporate Involvement of Malaysian Political Parties* (Townsville: James Cook University of Northern Queensland, 1995), p. 264.

[22] Gomez, "Changing Ownership Patterns," p. 144.

Maika continued to register losses in the 1990s, as several further financial scandals involving the MIC surfaced, highlighting not only the lack of accountability and transparency in the operations of MIC-related business ventures, but also the factionalism that characterizes the MIC. And to arrest such factionalism, Samy Vellu has resorted to centralization of power.

In the early 1990s, the MIC claimed a membership of 250,000 in about 2,000 branches. Under party rules, the president and other top posts were decided by direct elections involving an estimated fify thousand branch committee members. Traditionally, these party elections have been fiercely contested. But from that time, Samy Vellu strengthened his grip over the MIC. Ostensibly "to reduce politicking" and to "preserve party unity," he revamped the party constitution in order to introduce a so-called "delegates system," approximating that used by UMNO. Under the new system, the party's top posts would no longer be determined by the fifty thousand branch committee members as before, but only by the 1,350 divisional delegates chosen by the branches.[23] As Samy Vellu was the incumbent who controlled the party machinery, this change clearly benefited him. Under the current system, delegates usually elect into office those contestants mentioned on the "president's list," so that many of the principal positions are no longer contested. More than that, under the new party constitution, the president is also empowered to appoint the secretary-general, the treasurer-general, and the various bureau heads, as well the heads of the youth and women's wings, from among the elected committee members of those wings. Another indication of centralization is the vetting of all proposed new branches by the central working committee before approval is granted.

The MIC had succeeded in developing a mass base for itself by resorting to ethnic appeals, just as UMNO and the MCA had done vis-a-vis the Malay and Chinese communities. Apart from recruiting Tamils into the party and helping them to acquire citizenship, the MIC also promoted the use of the Tamil language, called attention to the plight of the Tamil primary schools and their teachers, and supported Tamil culture generally. However, the Tamilization of the party and the formation of a conservative coalition with the ethnic-based UMNO and MCA alienated a group of Indians from the party. With the introduction of the BN's affirmative action policies and in response to the NEP, the MIC, taking its cue from the MCA, began to involve itself in business and educational activities. Promoted ostensibly in the interests of the Indian community, in fact the business and educational projects benefited the minority business and middle classes. But the MIC failed to address the problems of the majority of poor Indians. Increasing factionalism within the MIC, which was only resolved through the president's centralization of powers, led to further disillusionment throughout the middle-class as well as the working class.

THE NATIONAL UNION OF PLANTATION WORKERS

One reason the MIC did not become more involved in the problems of labor was because of the presence of the National Union of Plantation Workers (NUPW). Founded in September 1954, the NUPW was led by Indian trade union leaders active among Indian estate workers, who were independent of the Communist-

---

[23] *The Star*, June 22, 1997.

influenced unions during the immediate post-War period. Indeed, the formation of the NUPW was actively promoted by John Brazier, the colonial trade union advisor, as well as by the Malayan Plantation Industries Employers Association (MPIEA).[24] Perhaps because of the Chinese workers' links to the Communist-led unions, the NUPW focused on recruiting Indian estate workers,[25] but in so doing, it inadvertently entered into a contest with the MIC. Tensions between the two were heightened in the 1960s when Sambanthan launched the National Land Fund Cooperative (NLFC) which was geared towards helping the Indian estate community. The NUPW regarded this initiative, which sought to pool resources to purchase estate land which was then being sub-divided and sold, as a hostile move on the part of the MIC.

Yet the NUPW failed to represent the interests of the estate workers adequately. Of the estimated 250,000 workers employed in the estates in the early 1990s, only 32 percent, principally employed in the larger estates, were unionized. Instead of drawing in the workers from the smaller estates, where conditions were harsher, the NUPW concentrated on those already unionized. Apart from running its businesses, the union officials' other principal work comprised negotiating collective agreements with the Malaysian Agricultural Producers Association (MAPA, the successor to MPIEA) every few years, settling disputes, and collecting union dues. Consequently, conditions in the non-unionized estates actually worsened, since even the small gains achieved from the negotiated collective agreements do not apply in the non-unionized estates.[26]

Four other critical issues characterize the worsening working situation in the estates. First, although productivity levels of the estates have increased,[27] workers' remuneration has not kept pace: real wages have remained constant.

A second problem pertains to housing. Except in a few estates, workers continue to live in quarters or lines provided by the employers. But some of the lines still lack such basic amenities as electricity. Many depend on common standpipes and even common bathroom facilities. Furthermore, upon retirement, workers are obliged to vacate the quarters unless their children are also employed in the estates, which is rarely the case now, since the young prefer to migrate to the urban areas to look for alternative employment. Consequently, elderly former workers and their families face the threat of eviction and homelessness.

A third problem is the re-introduction and increasing use of the "third party contract system" in the estates.[28] Previously utilized mainly to employ Chinese workers who resided elsewhere, currently this system is used to introduce foreign workers into the estate sector, including into unionized estates. Under the scheme, foreign workers are not even entitled to the miniscule benefits and protection won by the NUPW in collective agreements. Additionally, since it is cheaper to employ workers in this manner, jobs are becoming scarce for local workers, unless they are prepared to work under less remunerative conditions. The NUPW has been

---

[24] Ramachandran, *Indian Plantation Labour*, p. 251.

[25] Ibid., pp. 251-52.

[26] Jayasankaran, "Tussle in the Plantations"; P. Ramasamy, *Plantation Labour, Unions, Capital, and the State in Peninsular Malaysia* (Kuala Lumpur: Oxford University Press, 1994).

[27] Jayasankaran, "Tussle in the Plantations"; Jayakumar "The Indian Poor in Malaysia"; and Ramasamy, *Plantation Labour*.

[28] Ramasamy, *Plantation Labour*, p. 288.

unsuccessful in combating this new employment arrangement, which is particularly popular in the smaller and non-unionized estates.

Finally, the NUPW also evolved into a system of patronage. Although delegates met every three years to elect an executive council, in fact P. P. Narayanan, the general secretary from 1954 to 1993, dominated the organization.

Under these circumstances, disillusionment with the NUPW leadership became widespread and union membership progressively declined: from some 124,000 in 1983 to about 65,000 in 1989, accounting for less than 30 percent of the total number of plantation workers.[29] A field survey indicated that 81 percent of the workers polled expressed dissatisfaction with the NUPW's performance and thought that it could have done more for their well-being.[30] Yet another researcher has concluded that the NUPW might be described as "a capitalist union" since it "takes little interest in the welfare of its members... [and] the union's assets worth around $10 million in the mid-1980s have hardly benefited its members who remain one of the poorest segments of Malaysian society. The real beneficiaries ... [were] top union officials."[31]

HINDU REVIVALISM

K. Ramanathan has argued that Islamic revivalism, which began in about the 1980s, has had a "demonstrative effect" on Hinduism. This religion too has experienced its own "revivalism,"[32] principally centered on Hindu temples, worship practices and religious education, with small shrines (like the one in Kampong Rawa) being rebuilt into proper and larger temples through generous public support.

This has been accompanied by a "quest for religious knowledge." Ramanathan notes that among the English-educated middle-class, the periodical *Hinduism Today* is read widely, while other Hindu religious texts in English are also popular. This same group has made efforts to learn the Tamil language in order to understand and appreciate the religious texts and hymns used in worship, and they have pursued the teachings of well-known gurus from India and Malaysia. There has also been a "re-examination of religious tradition" in order to eliminate non-agamic practices which generally characterize village, as opposed to Sanskritic, practices.[33]

I would suggest that there is a class dimension to Hindu revivalism. Among members of the educated middle class, a search has developed for more scriptural knowledge and a turn towards more agamic ways. Conceivably, this search was sparked off by Islamic revivalism, which threatened the identity of the Indian middle class. However, non-agamic practices persist, and indeed, have formed part of the current Hindu revivalism. They constitute the Hinduism of the lower classes,

---

[29] Ramachandran, *Indian Plantation Labour*, p. 294.
[30] Ibid., p. 299.
[31] Ramasamy, *Plantation Labour*, p. 152.
[32] K. Ramanathan, "Hinduism in a Muslim State," *Asian Journal of Political Science* 4,2 (December 1996): 42-62 and 47.
[33] Ibid., pp. 47-48.

which has been influenced by their migration and modernization, as R. Rajoo has noted.[34] Some problems have arisen alongside this revivalism.

The first problem is a technical and legal one. Since colonial times, most temples and shrines had been built without regard to legal ownership of the land upon which they were erected. Most old and even some major temples, built on land belonging to the Telecoms, Malayan Railway, Public Works Department, and alongside government residential quarters housing Indian employees, could be deemed "illegal." The same goes for the vast majority of temples and shrines built on privately owned estates. Regularization of the legal status of the temples, therefore, has become a pressing issue. This situation has caused the Indian public to resort to the MIC since, as it is the representative of Indian interests in government, people anticipate that it would be able to intervene on the community's behalf. Weeks after the Kampong Rawa incident, the MIC, together with the Malaysian Hindu Sangham, called a meeting that was attended by about 450 representatives from Hindu temples and organizations. The upshot of the meeting was formation of a Hindu Religious Co-ordinating Council, set up to conduct a comprehensive survey of the temples to decide their legal status, and, in coordination with the authorities, "determine the regulations that will have to be fulfilled before a temple is built."[35] Significantly, Samy Vellu was to act as patron of the Council.

A second problem is the emerging contest for control of the temples. In accordance with the Societies Act,[36] temple management committees registered themselves and drew up constitutions on their operational procedures, if they had not previously done so. The Act further requires that temples conduct elections for their officials and maintain and submit annual accounts. Although this process has been cumbersome for many temples, it has also had the effect of forcing a major reorganization of both the membership structure and the management of the temples. According to the new rules, any member can seek election to the management committee, thereby freeing positions previously dominated by particular individuals, castes, or groups. Thus, the Hindu temples have been turned into additional arenas for conflict and have become influential cultural-religious organizations and "repositories of honour and power."[37] For while many participate in temple affairs to accumulate merit for personal salvation, others do so to gain social recognition and influence. Not surprisingly, MIC leaders have seized upon such opportunities to gain patronage of the temples, though not without competition from other middle-class Indians.

Yet a third problem relates to the severe shortage of priests, as the demand for more services and instruction has increased. Because there has never been a Brahmin priestly caste in Malaysian Hinduism, temples have traditionally depended on non-Brahmin *pujari* (temple apprentice priests) who specialize in

---

[34] R. Rajoo, "Indian Culture in Malaysia: An Overview," in *Indian Culture and National Culture*, ed. A. Kathirasen (Penang: Penang Indian Cultural and Arts Society, 1984), pp. 39-55.

[35] *The Star*, April 3, 1998.

[36] Under the Act, all formal organizations in the country are required to register themselves with the Registrar of Societies. In 1983, the Act was amended to curb political activities by organizations other than the political parties, after which the provisions of the Act were stringently enforced.

[37] Ramanathan, "Hinduism in a Muslim State," p. 54.

conducting rituals during worship services and ceremonies, but have little or no Sanskritic training.

Ironically, the reorganization of the temple committees, the shortage of priests, and the absence of a scriptural authority, together with increasing disagreements over religious matters more generally, had the unintended consequence of allowing greater latitude for innovation in Malaysian Hinduism, thereby contradicting the rigid separation between the Sanskritic and popular traditions.[38] Previously, working-class individuals without Sanskritic training had been able to assume the status of *pujari*, especially in temples in estates and small towns. Agamization, however, threatens to close even this small door toward social mobility available to lower-class youths. The Hindu Sangham, together with other Hindu organizations, is looking into the possibility of introducing a comprehensive training program for priests lasting four to six years. Meanwhile, the Sangham has also been conducting seminars to instruct the *pujari* and other temple officials on conducting rituals and managing their temples.[39]

These contradictory aspects of Hindu revivalism come together during the annual Thaipusam festival. Held on the first week of the Tamil month of Thai (late January), the festival commemorates the consecration of Lord Murugan (also known as Subramanya) when he is presented with a spear by his mother, the Goddess of Parvathi, to fight demons and ward off evil. Thaipusam, originally a lower-class village temple celebration, has emerged as the most important festival celebrated by Hindus of all classes in Malaysia today. Newspaper accounts of the festival over a twenty-year period (1974-94) indicate that crowd attendance at the Batu Caves in Kuala Lumpur has risen dramatically from 300,000 to 700,000.[40] In January 2002, according to newspaper estimates, more than one million people converged on the Batu Caves, while in Penang an estimated 500,000 made their way to the Waterfall Road temple. Moreover, the major sponsors of the Thaipusam festival are the influential Mariamman temples in Penang and Kuala Lumpur, which are also at the forefront of the movement that advocates adopting agamic forms of worship. Consequently, "the ecstatic rituals of penance...[have] acquired a gloss of respectability often denied to the religious practices of the Little Tradition."[41] Traditional caste distinctions have also been eroded in this environment, though obviously not completely.[42] No longer simply an expression of faith, Thaipusam, more than any other festival or organization, is a celebration and an emblem of the Hindu Indians, of all classes and castes, as an ethnic community, ephemeral though that sense of community might be.

Here then, in Hindu revivalism or simply renewed religious fervor, especially during the specific celebration of Thaipusam, is where yet other Indians have directed their attention in the face of the marginalization and dislocation of the community, and disillusionment with the NUPW and MIC. The low status village festival of poor Indians has now become the emblem and reference point of the

---

[38] S. Ackerman and Raymond Lee, *Heaven in Transition: Non-Muslim Religious Innovation and Ethnic Identity in Malaysia* (Kuala Lumpur: Forum, 1990), p. 91.

[39] *The Star*, June 14, 2001.

[40] Yeoh Seng Guan, "Producing Locality: Space, Houses and Public Culture in a Hindu Festival in Malaysia," *Contributions to Indian Sociology* (n.s.) 35,1 (2001): 33-64 and 56.

[41] Ackerman and Lee, *Heaven in Transition*, p. 93.

[42] Rajoo, "Indian Culture in Malaysia," p. 49.

entire Hindu community in multi-ethnic Malaysia. Ironically, this turn to religion has also allowed the MIC to re-invent itself as a patron of Hindu religious interests. However, such re-drawing of ethnic boundaries, in this case to the exclusion of those Indians who are not Hindus, may yet lead to tensions, even violence, as the discussion of the Kampong Rawa dispute in the first part of this study showed. Another outbreak of ethnic violence between Indian Hindus and Muslim Malays did occur in March 2001, this time in the working-class area of Kampong Medan, in Kuala Lumpur. On this occasion, six people were killed and at least sixty people injured.[43] This latter incident is yet another example of how the construction of exclusivist identities, mixed with considerations of political and socio-economic marginalization, might have contributed to conflict with the "others." It is therefore important to discuss how yet other Indians have sought to address the problem of marginalization from a multi-ethnic standpoint, in an attempt to overcome the exclusive dimensions of identity politics.

THE MIDDLE-CLASS NGOS AND THE SEARCH FOR ALTERNATIVES

Young, educated, middle-class Malaysians of all ethnic groups, frustrated with ethnic polarization, undemocratic rule, economic injustices, and the rise of "money politics," began to search for alternatives during the early 1980s. The search resulted in the formation of non-governmental organizations and their networking with one another, and contributed to considerable political ferment, even within the political parties.[44]

One identifiable group developed among the Indian students in the local universities. Under the auspices of such university clubs as the Tamil Language Society in the University of Malaya and the Indian Cultural Association in Universiti Sains Malaysia, they began to organize discussions and forums to explore social and political issues and to provide voluntary tuition classes to poorer Indian students. After graduation, the students maintained ties to one another and to returnees from overseas universities, and began to be involved in a variety of NGOs, both Indian-based and multi-ethnic.

One of the most influential of these was an Indian-based NGO, the Shri Murugan Centres (SMC) led by Dr. M. Thambirajah, a former University of Malaya lecturer, which was first launched in 1982 and catered particularly to poor Indian youths in the estates and squatter settlements. By 1997, there were an estimated 4,000 SMCs throughout the country providing tuition classes for approximately 20,000 students every weekend. By this time, the SMCs were no longer catering to the poor exclusively. Urban middle-class youths, too, attended the SMCs. The impact of this NGO might be gauged by an incident that occurred in June 1996, when an estimated 200,000 Indian students and parents gathered at the Batu Caves temple outside Kuala Lumpur, in response to a call by the SMC, to pledge to work hard and excel in education. This gathering at the Batu Caves became an annual affair. Currently, an equivalent gathering is also held in the Waterfall Road

---

[43] For details, see "Memorandum to the Prime Minister on the Recent Socio-Economic Centred Ethnic Clashes in Kampung Medan and Its Surrounding Areas off Old Klang Road, Selangor by Group of Concerned Citizens," Kuala Lumpur, March 20, 2001.

[44] Francis Loh, "State-societal Relations in a Rapidly Growing Economy: The Case of Malaysia, 1970-97," in *Economic Liberalisation, Democratisation and Civil Society in the Developing World*, ed. R. Kleinberg and J. Clark (London: Macmillan Press, 2000), pp. 65-87.

Temple in Penang, an event that drew about five thousand students and parents in 1999.[45]

Inevitably, the SMC's success drew the attention of the MIC. Indirect linkages were established between the two organizations, and Thambirajah was invited to sit on the MIC's central working committee. In response to criticisms that he had compromised the SMCs, Thambirajah stated: "a social organization without political support or patronage cannot go far; it cannot expand much. I had to be involved in the MIC to have access to funds and allocations."[46]

Another new NGO was the Centre for Community Studies (CCS), based in Kuala Lumpur, which originally focused its attention on the problems of poor Indians in urban squatter areas. Faced with financial problems, CCS leader Dr. Denison Jayasooria, an England-trained sociologist, entered into an alliance with the MIC and formed the Yayasan Strategik Sosial (YSS). Subsequently, the MIC persuaded the BN government to allocate RM2.7 million for YSS work in thirty-seven locations in Selangor and the Federal Territory.[47] Boasting a large staff as well as part-time MIC volunteers, the YSS now effectively acts as the MIC's new extension into the urban squatter communities, and its efforts will probably enhance the MIC's reputation among the urban Indian poor. But it is also evident that the YSS is no longer concerned with empowering the poor, as originally envisioned.

In contrast to these two welfare and reformist NGOs now associated with the MIC, several other NGOs have remained fiercely independent. Perhaps the best known of these is Alaigal (literally "a wave"). Alaigal is most active in the wider Kinta district, around Ipoh, Perak. The focus of its work is twofold.[48] First, it is committed to helping estate workers gain a fair wage "that is sufficient to meet all the family needs without having to work excessive over-time." Together with NGOs functioning in other parts of the country, it set up the Estate Workers' Support Committee in 1996 and re-launched the campaign for the introduction of a monthly wage scheme that the NUPW had evidently abandoned by the mid-1980s. It produced pamphlets showing not only how unjust the daily-rated wage system was, but also how the industry could easily afford a monthly wage scheme. On this basis, it collected more than 50,000 signatures in support of the campaign. Demonstrations were held, and ultimately the MIC felt pressured to introduce such a scheme. But though the cabinet authorized a study that apparently also supported the demand, it was never made public. A "new" wage scheme has since been introduced. However, Alaigal and even some NUPW leaders have expressed disappointment with the scheme, for the workers' wages are still dependent on the amount of produce they gather daily.

Second, Alaigal also campaigned for the "home ownership scheme," better living conditions for estate workers, as well as just compensation for squatters when evicted by developers. Its eleven-year campaign, conducted in league with former workers of Klebang Estate (outside Ipoh), finally paid off when the developers agreed in November 2000 to pay "just compensation" to the residents. This settlement has been celebrated as "the first time in Malaysia that an estate community has been granted housing lots as compensation for loss of housing caused

---

[45] *The Star*, July 12, 1999.
[46] Ibid., May 25, 1997.
[47] *The Star*, February 5, 2002.
[48] See *Alaigal News*, August 1997.

by a retrenchment exercise." But this victory did not come without sacrifices and suffering. As in the campaign for a monthly wage scheme, here too Alaigal linked up with NGOs working on the same issue elsewhere in Malaysia.[49]

A significant development in this struggle was the rejection of the misnomer *setinggan* (or squatter) in favor of the more appropriate *Peneroka Bandar* (or urban pioneer) since in almost all instances, these pioneers had been the first to appear on the scene to develop urban fringe lands, abandoned agricultural land, disused mining land, or former estate lands. More powerful landowners ultimately claimed these properties, evicting the pioneers despite the fact that their families had often worked the land for several generations. Alaigal prepared and made available a booklet outlining this rationale and the unjustness of the laws, as well as how to conduct a struggle for decent housing and due compensation.[50]

Although Alaigal worked principally among the Indian poor, it argued that in fact all ethnic groups shared their problems. In its cartoon book *Ezuchi* (literally "Awakening"), presented in simple Tamil and through cartoons and targeted at the estate workers, the problems of the workers are identified and then linked to their causes. These included: the archaic wage system; the lack of basic amenities, and the paucity of social services in the estates; the laws which favored the employers and discriminated against the workers; and the weakness of the trade union movement. It then discussed how particular communities of various ethnic groups had struggled in the 1990s to empower themselves and called for the workers to "awaken." Put simply, Alaigal and the other NGOs were recovering the past multi-ethnic socialist alternative.

Ultimately they formed the Partai Sosialis Malaysia (PSM) in 1997. In the wake of the *reformasi* movement, the PSM supported formation of a new opposition coalition, the Barisan Alternatif (BA). In the November 1999 general elections, Dr. Jeyakumar Devaraj, one of Alaigal's stalwarts, also a founding committee member of PSM, challenged MIC president Samy Vellu in the Sungai Siput constituency, just north of Ipoh. Having held the seat since 1978, Samy Vellu was once more successful, but Jeyakumar gave him a good fight, reducing the MIC president's majority from 15,600 to only 5,250 votes. Subsequent court action proved that there were at least 300 persons who were registered as voters in the constituency although they did not reside there.[51] Since the election, Jeyakumar, a physician, has set up a clinic in the constituency while continuing to work among the estate workers and urban pioneers, and he intends to challenge Samy Vellu again in the next elections.

This struggle by Jeyakumar, Alaigal, and the other NGOs on behalf of the working class, their resort to the courts and formal political process as well as mass action, and their multi-ethnic approach to resolving the marginalization of the Indian poor, are diametrically opposed to the unsuccessful attempts by the MIC and NUPW to involve themselves in big business, establish colleges, and appeal to ethnic sentiments. Alaigal and the other NGOs, instead, have recovered the

---

[49] Veerasenan, "Breakthrough in Klebang," *Aliran Monthly* 20,11/12 (2000): 16-17.

[50] Mohd Nasir Hashim, *Peneroka Bandar Menuntut Keadilan* (Kuala Lumpur: Daya Komunikasi, 1994).

[51] Jeyakumar Devaraj, "Sungai Siput: Phantom Voters on the Rolls," in *New Politics in Malaysia*, ed. F. Loh and J. Saravanamuttu (Singapore: Institute of Southeast Asian Studies, forthcoming).

radical tradition that was very much a part of Malaysian political history and which previously involved Malaysians of all ethnic backgrounds, including Indians. That tradition, which had lasted until the 1960s,[52] was almost completely erased by the BN ruling coalition after the Socialist Front, most of whose leaders had been detained, became defunct and the BN's official nationalist narrative began to hold sway. It is to Alaigal's credit, indeed to the credit of many other Malaysian NGOs that have emerged since the 1980s, that the official narrative is increasingly being contested.

CONCLUSION

Elsewhere I have argued that rapid economic growth in the late 1980s and 1990s, which coincided with the replacement of the NEP by the more inclusive but also market-driven National Development Policy (1991-2000), contributed to the emergence of a new discourse of "developmentalism."[53] Focusing on the Malays and Chinese, I argued that a retreat from ethnic politics took place, as UMNO and the BN Chinese parties engaged in business activities and other educational and utilitarian projects. The BN Chinese parties further redefined their roles as the purveyors of development goods and services at the local level. Through privatization and economic deregulation policies, continued state intervention on behalf of the *bumiputera*, and the successful transformation of the BN Chinese parties into extensions of the developmental state, many Malays and Chinese, especially the business and middle classes, prospered. Ethnic tensions between Chinese and Malays also eased. However, this developmentalism set limits on democratization in Malaysia.

This line of analysis requires a caveat. As this study indicates, most Indians did not prosper during the late 1980s and 1990s, not least because, unlike the Chinese, Indians did not have an equivalent stake in the corporate sector to build upon. Neither did the state assume the responsibility of providing for poor Indians when it became clear that the MIC and the NUPW were not doing so. Hence marginalization and social dislocation of poor Indians occurred, and disillusionment with those two principal political organizations was widespread. Thus, developmentalism did not engulf Indians the way it did most Malays and Chinese.

I have argued that this frustration and disillusionment was deflected into renewed religious fervor instead. Coinciding with Islamic revivalism, which middle-class Indians perceived as a threat to Indian identity, there was a Hindu revival. The middle class sponsored various efforts towards the agamization of Hindu religious practices and rituals, but these were somewhat resisted by the lower classes who were more comfortable with their original non-agamic ways. In other words, the direction of Hindu revivalism was contested. Nonetheless, there were incidents of cooperation between the classes of Hindus, as in their common celebration of Thaipusam. No longer simply a religious festival, Thaipusam has

---

[52] See, for instance, Stenson, *Class, Race and Colonialism* and Ramasamy, *Plantation Labour*.

[53] Francis Loh, "Where has (Ethnic) Politics Gone?" in *The Politics of Multiculturalism in Malaysia, Singapore and Indonesia*, ed. R. Hefner (Honolulu: University of Hawai'i Press, 2001), pp. 183-203; idem "Developmentalism and the Limits of Democratic Discourse," in *Democracy in Malaysia: Discourses and Practices*, ed. F. Loh and Khoo Boo Teik (Richmond, Surrey: Curzon, 2002), pp. 19-50.

become a celebration and emblem of Indian ethnicity. Aware of this turn and the potential threat it posed, the MIC has assumed an increasing interest in all things Hindu. However, the redrawing of ethnic boundaries in exclusivist terms, in this case leading to the exclusion of Indians who are not Hindus, possibly contributed to the Kampong Rawa and Kampong Medan incidents. Some new NGOs led by the middle class have also offered alternative explanations and solutions to the Indian predicament, a few seeking to redraw the boundaries of community in trans-ethnic ways. This has led to a breach in the ethnic exclusivist-cum-consociational formula of the BN, but, as our study of the MIC indicates, the ruling elites are equal to the task and are capable of re-inventing themselves in order to maintain their hegemony.

In the situation of Malaysian studies, wherein "primordialism" and "consociationalism" have dominated the analysis of the federation's ethnic politics, Ben Anderson's notion of the nation as imagined, constructed, and modern has encouraged me to look at the problems of ethnic politics and ethnicity generally through new lenses, and to contribute to breaking that original impasse. His discussion of agency, however, has always been contextualized to consider deeper structures, including the state. As I understand it, Anderson's reading of the state incorporated institutions like the military, political parties, and electoral systems; ruling elites and their functionaries; and mechanisms for ideological control, repression, or promoting economic development. These ruling elites have also proved capable of re-inventing themselves, re-constituting the states, and adapting to new ideas. I have also imbibed this notion of the state-qua-state into this and my other writings.

DE-OTHERING JEK COMMUNISTS: REWRITING THAI HISTORY FROM THE VIEWPOINT OF THE ETHNO-IDEOLOGICAL OTHER [1]

Kasian Tejapira

THE DEADLY THAI NATION

In his widely acclaimed and hitherto unsurpassed, penetrating and irreverent analysis of the infamous October 6, 1976 massacre of radical student activists in Thammasat University and subsequent military coup, Ben Anderson succinctly describes the general contours of political culture in modern Siam (better known as Thailand) as follows:

> Thanks in part to their colonized pasts, most Southeast Asian countries have inherited a political vocabulary and rhetoric which is essentially radical-populist, if not leftwing, in character. It is very hard to find anywhere, except perhaps in the Philippines, a calm, self-confident conservative ideology: indeed, since the nineteenth century, conservative culture has been in epistemological shock and on the political defensive, its nationalist credentials deeply suspect. In Siam, mainly because the country escaped direct colonial control, the situation has been, until recently, almost exactly the reverse. The heroes in Thai children's schoolbooks have not been journalists, union leaders, teachers, and politicians who spent years in colonial jails, but above all the "great kings" of the ruling house. In fact, until 1973, it would be hard to imagine a single Thai children's hero who had ever been inside a prison. The prevailing rhetoric had typically been conservative, conformist, and royalist. It was the Left that was always on the defensive, anxious to defend its nationalist credentials against charges of

---

[1] This paper was first prepared for the workshop on "Alternative Histories and Non-Written Sources: New Perspectives from the South," organized by the South-South Exchange Programme for Research on the History of Development (SEPHIS) and Taller de Historia Oral Andina (THOA), in La Paz, Bolivia, May 12-15, 1999. Thanks are due to the Center for Southeast Asian Studies, Kyoto University, for providing the author with the peaceful calm and leisure to write it up.

being "Chinese," Vietnamese," "un-Thai," and "antimonarchy" (this last a clear sign of a successful identification of royal and nationalist symbols). It would even be fair to say that until the repressions of October 6, the taboo on criticism of monarchy as an institution or the monarch as a person was accepted even by those firmly on the Left. ²

While these words were being written, I and about three thousand of my radical student, intellectual, and worker comrades were smarting from the urban blue-tinged white terror in the communist-led maquis around the country and training ourselves ferociously as Maoist rural guerrillas in preparation for the coming showdown with the Thai nation, the one that had tried to kill us, but which we survived.³

---

² Benedict R. O'G. Anderson, "Withdrawal Symptoms," in *The Spectre of Comparisons: Nationalism, Southeast Asia, and the World* (London: Verso, 1998), pp. 161-62. This article first appeared two decades earlier in the *Bulletin of Concerned Asian Scholars* 9,3 (July-Sept. 1977).

³ The October 6, 1976 massacre at Thammasat University, an incident unprecedented in Thai modern history in its violence, savagery, barbarism, and mob participation, was instigated by a trumped-up charge of lèse majesté with regard to the Crown Prince. The charge was brought against student performers who had staged a public mock hanging at Thammasat to protest the brutal extrajudicial hanging of two worker activists by provincial police for putting up posters opposing the return of the deposed military dictator Field Marshal Thanom Kittikachorn. A photograph of the mock hanging under the headline, "Hanging of a Crown Prince lookalike; The whole land is enraged!; The Center [National Student Center of Thailand, the then-leading organ of the radical student movement] tramples on the heart of the Thai nation," was published on the front page of the *Dao Siam* right-wing newspaper, and the allegation was widely and hysterically publicized by the military-controlled radio stations, leading to public anger and outcries against the student movement. The vilification of the student movement by the right-wing press and the state electronic media, as well as the resulting public perception of the movement as a traitorous, un-Thai, arch-anti-monarchical force, were such that the alleged charge was credulously and spontaneously believed not only by rightists but also by the wider public.

Police forces in full combat gear and a maniacal lynch mob then laid siege to Thammasat University and heavily, continuously, and indiscriminately bombarded thousands of unarmed student demonstrators inside with automatic rifles, machine guns, and grenade and rocket launchers. Scores of students were shot, bombed, or beaten to death, some were hanged and burned alive. Most survivors were captured, stripped naked to the waist (women were allowed to keep their bras), and sent to prison. A palace-engineered military coup toppled the elected civilian government later in the evening of that day and led to the establishment of a dictatorial regime under the right-wing extremist, royalist, and arch-anti-communist government of Prime Minister Thanin Kraivichien. It, in turn, was overthrown one year later by a group of opportunistic, reformist military officers.

For the historical background and significance of this incident in the political trajectory of modern Siam, see Benedict Anderson, "Murder and Progress in Modern Siam," in *The Spectre of Comparisons*, pp. 174-91. The above-mentioned front page of *Dao Siam* newspaper is reproduced in Prajuab Amphasawet, *Phlik phaendin: Prawat kanmeuang thai 24 mithunayon 2475 – 14 tulakhom 2516* (Upheaval: A history of Thai politics from 24 June 1932 to 14 October 1973) (Bangkok: Sukkhaphap Jai Press, 2000), p. 548. The media background and public reception of the fateful published photographs of the mock hanging are discussed by Somsak Jeamteerasakul in "Chanuan: Phap lakhorn khwaen kho thi nam pai soo korani 6 tula" (The fuse: The photographs of the staged mock hanging that led to the October 6th incident), in *Prawattisat thi phoeng sang: Ruam botkhwam kiaokab korani 14 tula lae 6 tula* (The invention of history: Collected articles on the October 14th and October 6th incidents) (Bangkok: 6 Tula Ramleuk Press, 2001), pp. 149-54.

THE THAI OFFICIAL NATIONALIST PROJECT

Historically speaking, the official nationalist project of the Thai nation, for the defense of which the above-mentioned young bloods were sacrificed, had two salient dimensions. The first one was *purportedly racialized or ethnicized*, according to which *"Thailand unites the Thai blood and race. A people's state, all parts belong to Thais. . . "*, as its national anthem goes. This imagined nation of pure Thais had from the beginning been positioned by the Thai royal and subsequent military rulers over against *not* the Western colonial powers, *nor* Thailand's colonized and hence actually pacified neighbors, but the Chinese immigrants and their descendants who, as entrepreneurs and coolies, had dominated the modern sector of its economy and urban society since the late nineteenth century.

These so-called "Jews of the Orient," in the menacing words of King Vajiravudh (1910-1925)—the founder of Thai royalist official nationalism[4]—or simply "Jeks" in Thai derogatory popular parlance, were in fact the key agents of economic modernization and political modernity in Siam, or the pioneers of its modern civil society, so to speak. As such, they constituted the only potent domestic socio-economic force that could effectively challenge state authority, as they once did in an organized general strike to protest a capitation tax increase, a strike that paralyzed the capital city for several days in 1910.[5] And yet, their collective entrepreneurial skills and labor force were too precious to the Thai state's modernizing efforts to be simply killed off or expelled. Hence the need to ideologically construct and perpetually invoke their un-Thai ethnicity and status as "settlers" (as against native "owners") in Thailand so as to bluff them into accepting a subservient position in the patron-client relationship with the Thai state authorities. Thus, in its essence, Thai official nationalism was *not racism per se but a racializing or ethnicizing discourse* aimed at establishing and reproducing *unequal power relations between the "Thai" state on the one hand, and "un-Thai" or "never-adequately-or-fully-Thai" capital and society on the other*, on the basis of which state clientelism was practiced and maintained.[6]

The second dimension of the Thai official nationalist project was directly political-ideological and aimed at instilling a conservative and royalist, conformist and obedient pattern of clientelist beliefs and behavior into the general populace at large. Thus, for King Vajiravudh, the *sine qua non* for an authentic Thai national lay not so much in one's ability to speak the Thai language as in one's absolute and unconditional "allegiance to the King of Siam."[7] Prince Damrong, one of King Vajiravudh's uncles, a key architect of the modernization of the Thai absolutist state as well as the acclaimed founding father of Thai national historiography, authoritatively characterized the disposition of the Thai nation in a 1927 lecture as

---

[4] Asvabahu (King Vajiravudh), *Phuak yew haeng booraphathis lae meuang thai jong teun thoed phrom duai lai phra ratchahat khamplae phasa angklis* (The Jews of the Orient and wake up Siam with English translation in the king's handwriting) (Bangkok: King Vajiravudh Memorial Foundation, 1985).

[5] G. William Skinner, *Chinese Society in Thailand: An Analytical History* (Ithaca, NY: Cornell University Press, 1957), pp. 162-65.

[6] For further details, see my "Imagined Uncommunity: The *Lookjin* Middle Class and Thai Official Nationalism," in *Essential Outsiders: Chinese and Jews in the Modern Transformation of Southeast Asia and Central Europe*, ed. Daniel Chirot and Anthony Reid (Seattle and London: University of Washington Press, 1997), pp. 75-98.

[7] Asvabahu (King Vajiravudh), "Khwampenchat doi thaejing" (Real nationhood), in *Pakinnakakhadi* (Miscellanies) (Bangkok: Khlangwitthaya Press, 1975), pp. 241-47.

comprising "Love of National Independence, Toleration, and Power of Assimilation."[8] And later, the militaristic government of Field Marshal Plaek Phibunsongkhram (1938-1944), the Thai Führer, simply decreed in a series of *"Ratthaniyom,"* or "the Cultural Mandates of the State," that "Thailand is a nation of conformists and followers of the leader."[9]

Thus imagined, this nation of sheep plainly disowned and had no place for its "black" fellow countrymen, be they liberal dissenters, democratic activists, or socialist parliamentarians, let alone communist revolutionaries, regardless of their actual race or ethnicity. And since it so happened that the first generation of communists in Siam at that time were all Chinese and Vietnamese immigrants and their descendants,[10] they therefore fell prey to the othering, alienating strategy of the Thai official nationalist project in a double sense, both ethnically and ideologically. Judged according to the ethno-ideology of Thainess, the *jek* communists couldn't possibly be Thai.

THE PLIGHT OF A JEK COMMUNIST

I, of course, happened then to be both a *jek* and *a communist*.

It had not been easy being a *jek student* (or in fact a student of any "un-Thai" ethnic group) in Thai primary and secondary schools during the 1960s and early 1970s, which was the period of an exponential expansion of centralized national education, of rapid and unequal capitalist economic growth under state absolutist developmental planning, and of a political and military alliance with the US against Red China and the Indo-Chinese communist liberation movements.[11] One couldn't really partake in the Thai historical imagination when one was taught in all earnestess that the ethno-genesis of the Thai race had taken place on the Altai mountain range near the northern border of China several millennia back, given the fact that one's father had actually immigrated from Guangdong Province in southern China to Thailand only a few decades earlier.[12] One couldn't surely and comfortably feel part of the Thai nation when one learned from official Thai history textbooks that it must have been one's Chinese great-great grandparents who had driven the great-great grandparents of one's Thai classmates and teachers out of central China all the

---

[8] Prince Damrongrachanuphap, "Laksana kanpokkhrong prathes siam tae boran" (The character of the administration of ancient Siam), Cremation Volume of Mr Dao Buphawes, Rasbamrung Temple, Chon Buri, December 1, 1968, pp. 5-8.

[9] Thaemsuk Numnon, "Meuangthai yuk cheua phoonam" (Thailand in the obey-the-leader age), *Thammasat University Journal* VI,1 (June-September 1976), pp. 144-45.

[10] See my book (based on PhD dissertation), *Commodifying Marxism: The Formation of Modern Thai Radical Culture, 1927-1958* (Kyoto: Kyoto University Press/Melbourne: Trans Pacific Press, 2002), Chapter II.

[11] For further details, see Anderson, "Withdrawal Symptoms," pp. 142-53; and also his "Introduction," to Benedict R. O'G Anderson and Ruchira Mendiones, eds. and trans., *In the Mirror: Literature and Politics in Siam in the American Era* (Bangkok: Éditions Duang Kamol, 1985), esp. pp.19-35.

[12] B. J. Terwiel, "Thai Nationalism and Identity: Popular Themes of the 1930s," in *National Identity and Its Defenders, Thailand, 1939-1989*, ed. Craig J. Reynolds (Clayton, Victoria: Centre of Southeast Asian Studies, Monash University, 1991), pp. 133-54.

way down south to Thailand a thousand years before.[13] As an ethnically predetermined potential "fifth columnist," one became ill at ease and nervous whenever one found government-published anti-Red China propaganda posters posted on school bulletin-boards.

Under these impossible circumstances, one naturally developed *an inbred Thainess Deficiency Syndrome* (or TDS in abbreviation) in a desperate, but vain, doomed and unending attempt to out-Thai the Thais. A person who suffers from TDS typically shows symptoms such as changing one's Chinese clan name into a Thai family name under the persistent urging of one's teachers, trying exceptionally hard to excel in such Thaifying subjects as Thai language and literature, Thai composition and poetry, and hiding or camouflaging one's embarrassing and shameful Chinese accent, language, customs, and parents from fellow schoolmates.[14] And yet, having gone through all these Thaifying rituals, one still couldn't help always feeling like a fake, both inadequate and vulnerable, psycho-culturally rootless, homeless and lost.[15]

AN ALTERNATIVE THAI NATION

Eventually, the Thai state did appear to have managed to create out of its population of designated misfits some kind of Thai nationalists. Nevertheless, the ruse of history taught that these converts turned into nationalists of an unexpected and undesirable kind, as the official nationalist project came home to roost with a vengeance. The radical student and popular movements of the early 1970s provided a kind of home for the "un-Thai" jeks, *khaeks* (i.e. the Thai popular expression for Indians), Laotians, Thais, and so forth. These movements emerged shortly before, and grew tremendously in the aftermath of an unprecedented, spontaneous and massive, bloody popular uprising that overthrew the long-standing, high-handed, and corrupt military dictatorship of Field Marshal Thanom Kittikachorn on October 14, 1973.[16] Through it, together they actively and dedicatedly created a new, alternative imagined Thai national community, one in which the collective ethos of

---

[13] Charnvit Kasetsiri, "From Siam To Thailand: What Is in a Name?," Paper given at the International Conference on Post Colonial Society and Culture in Southeast Asia, Yangon, Myanmar, December 16-18, 1998.

[14] I have diagnosed and dissected the TDS epidemic in "The Miraculous Valorisation of Thainess: The Thai Equivalent of the 'Asian Values' Discourse," Paper prepared for the International Conference on Asian Values, "Asian Values on Trial? Miracle and Failures," organized by the Malaysian Academic Movement (MOVE) and sponsored by the Japan Foundation, at the Grand Seasons Hotel, Kuala Lumpur, November 28-29, 1998.

[15] Quite remarkably, in a long chat I once had with Assoc. Prof. Dr. Chaiwat Satha-Anand, an ethnic-Indian Muslim colleague of mine at Thammasat and the foremost Non-violence Studies scholar in Thailand, it turned out that we had shared the same TDS symptoms in our schooldays. But even more extraordinarily, Dr. Seksan Prasertkul, a former top student leader of the October 14, 1973 popular uprising and the then-Dean of our Faculty, who happened to be sitting nearby, jumped in and remarked that although he himself was a pedigree Thai from a poor fisherman's family in rural central Thailand, he had felt no less alienated in his boyhood from his own official Thai name, the official Thai national education and culture, and the Thai national anthem! Alas, official nationalist Thainess proved to be a sheer state construction whose universal estranging effect cut across ethnic lines and in which even the Thais themselves couldn't feel at home.

[16] For an analysis of the deep socio-economic background and far-reaching cultural political impact of this incident, see Anderson, "Withdrawal Symptoms."

democracy, populism, and egalitarianism replaced the hitherto prevailing authoritarian, élitist, and discriminatory ethno-ideology of Thainess.[17]

However, as this radical popular nationalism was constructed by means of the Marxist-Maoist discourse, with its overriding emphasis on class-related issues, it largely ignored the question of race or ethnicity, which was typically regarded and treated as a secondary, adjunctive matter destined to be automatically resolved and to wither away once the proletariat came to power through a revolution. Thus, despite the fact that a good few activists, especially in the student movement at that time, belonged to the jek and other un-Thai ethnic groups, ethnicity was never seriously raised or debated as a problem in its own right. Thainess, as a key cultural-politically loaded signifier, remained amorphous and unscrutinized and hence, unfortunately, the first ethnicized dimension of the Thai official nationalist project was left unchallenged.

The massive influx of urban radical activists into the communist-led maquis following the October 6, 1976 massacre and coup did not help them come to grips with the cultural politics of ethnic Thainess any better; if anything, it even aggravated the problem. For while the decade-long rural armed struggle of the Communist Party of Thailand (CPT) was in itself a living refutation of the second political-ideological dimension of Thai official nationalism, the party's heavy dependency on Communist China for arms and ammunition, supplies and equipment, sanctuary and training, doctrine and strategy to carry on rural guerrilla warfare and maintain a national political presence had persistently cast doubt on its nationalist credentials and, as a matter of fact, often compromised its self-proclaimed theoretical independence and political autonomy, especially at critical junctures.[18] In addition, the historically determined fact that the significant plurality of top party leaders and senior party cadres was ethnically and/or culturally Chinese, with their ideological and theoretical ears always glued and constantly fine-tuned to Maoist (Radio) Peking, appeared to confirm the newcomers' uneasy, burgeoning suspicion at first hand.[19]

---

[17] The multifarious factors that went into the complex process of radicalization of Thai students and intellectuals of that generation have been best captured in Anderson, "Introduction," *In the Mirror*, pp. 19-35.

[18] For example, the CPT gleefully, if quietly, went along with Communist China when the latter massively attacked Vietnam in February 1979 to "punish" and "teach Vietnam a lesson" for overthrowing the Khmer Rouge, its staunchest ally in the region, two months earlier. Furthermore, the party passively acquiesced at its own expense in a *de facto* anti-Vietnamese strategic alliance which Communist China initiated with the Thai government, its own arch-enemy. As a result, the party estranged its former Indochinese comrades, lost its across-the-border bases and lifeblood supply lines in Laos and Cambodia, and had to "temporarily" close down the Voice of the People of Thailand radio station in southern China, its single most effective broadcasting propaganda organ, when the Thai government demanded it from China. Hence the deafening subsequent accusation that it sold the Thai revolution out to China. See in this regard Benedict Anderson, *Imagined Communities: Reflections on the Origin and Spread of Nationalism* (London: Verso, 1991), pp. 1-2; and also his "Radicalism after Communism," in *The Spectre of Comparisons*, p. 290.

[19] A few minor but very revealing incidents I witnessed firsthand in the CPT-led maquis are worth retelling here.

1) I once took part in a communist youth league study session presided over by a female peasant middle-ranking cadre. The aim of the session was to teach us more about the CPT, in terms of its founding ideological principles, political platform, and organizational structure. Our instructor proceeded to produce out of her bag a neatly printed textbook *in Thai* on which

All these discursive, political and ethno-cultural factors, together with the party's internal "democratic centralist" organizational principles, rigid hierarchical structure, ironclad discipline, and operational culture of secrecy typical of a militant, underground revolutionary movement, made of ethnicity a highly sensitive non-issue that could be represented only in a distorting and refractive light, and thereby effectively foreclosed any open, straightforward, and transparent dealing with it. The situation that thus obtained was an exact mirror image of the Thai ethno-ideological regime in reverse: out there, one could not criticize Thainess because one was un-Thai or never "Thai" enough; in the maquis, one could not question Chineseness for fear of being branded a "Thai" chauvinist or narrow-minded nationalist.

AN ACADEMIC-CUM-CULTURAL POLITICAL AGENDA

To all intents and purposes, the revolutionary movement led by the Communist Party of Thailand collapsed upon itself in the early 1980s as thousands upon thousands of its guerrillas became disillusioned with the party leadership, defected from the maquis, and surrendered their arms to the moderate, reformist, and semi-democratic Thai government *en masse*. I myself left the jungle in April 1981, almost immediately resumed my undergraduate studies at Thammasat University, graduated two and a half years later, became a Thammasat lecturer in political science, and won a scholarship to Cornell in 1985.

Disillusioned and yet unrepentant, I carried my remnant of ideological baggage and theoretical blinkers with me from Thailand in a self-assigned mission to think my way out of the defeat. As a result, most of my Cornell professors had a particularly hard time trying to teach me anything, but a few among them, especially Ben Anderson and Susan Buck-Morse, did not try. No universal truths, general laws, big theories, or ready-made answers were dispensed by them, just questions, a whole lot of tough, unusual, disturbing, mind-boggling questions which haunted me day and night, in and out of class. Gruelingly, clumsily, all too gradually and only semi-self-consciously, I began to grope my way by trial and error out of the intellectual quagmire and political impasse and come up with my own half-baked research questions and cultural political agenda.

---

our course of study would henceforth be based. It turned out that the textbook was in fact a primer on the CPC, i.e. the Communist Party of China, with which she intended, unquestioningly and unthinkingly, to educate us about the Communist Party of Thailand! And so she did.

2) During a dinner in the canteen of the then-CPT Lower Northeastern Regional headquarters situated in Cambodia near its western border with Thailand, I happened to sit close to two senior members of the party regional committee who, initially, ate and chatted with each other and occasionally with me *in Thai*. But when their talk broached a seemingly serious and sensitive topic, they suddenly switched to *Chinese Mandarin*, obviously to prevent me from comprehending it. Although all three of us were ethnically *un-Thais* (two jeks and one ethnic Vietnamese), I couldn't help feeling like a subaltern *Thai* outsider, discriminated against by a restricted "court" (or, perhaps more aptly, "politburo") language, and left the dinner table disconsolately.

3) Some time later, upon learning that I had forgotten most *Chinese Mandarin* I had studied in my boyhood, my female jek party boss (so-called *"jadtang"* or "organizer" in the CPT jargon), the same one mentioned in (1), expressed heartfelt pity for me since Chinese was the language that would have gained me direct access to the wisdom of Chairman Mao and would definitely be of the utmost importance in the near future, so she said.

My agenda was to undermine the deadly cultural infrastructure of the Thai official nation which had made possible and justifiable acts of state terrorism against the people, such as the October 6, 1976 massacre. A Thai nation that would be worth living in must be cultural-politically open to, as well as able to accommodate, the so-branded ethno-ideological un-Thais as rightful and equal members of the nation. The aim was to bequeath to future generations of Thais and un-Thais a land less murderous, where they could live and argue with one another peacefully.

But how did one go about doing so academically?

The provisional answer I improvised was to trace analytically and critically the genealogy (or alternatively, the tradition of invention and reception) of a key signifier in modern Thai cultural politics, namely Thainess, all the while trying to destabilize, denaturalize, or, if one prefers, deconstruct it in the most outrageously irreverent and iconoclastic, most sacrilegiously hilarious and profane manner possible, by making use of basic semiotic concepts and insights. With the sacred and deadly contents of Thainess emptied out and its lid thrown wide open, a semiotic space for contestation was thereby created in which alternative "un-Thai" meanings and referents could come freely into full play as "Thai," including my favorite radical, popular candidates, in a dynamic and open-ended reimagination and reconstruction of a new Thai nation.

DE-ESSENTIALIZING ETHNICITY

I began by tackling ethnicity or the ethnicized notion of Thainess/Chineseness in the Thai official nationalist discourse.

The overall strategy was to detect the subtle and obvious changes this ethnicized-and-ethnicizing couple of signifiers had undergone diachronically from the pre-national period of Siamese history to the national one, and synchronically as it was diversely, variably, and polysemically affected, interpreted, manipulated, and abused by various state and oppositional political actors and economic interests. Initially, I pulled and focused on the pigtail, that most visible and tangible proof of ethnic Chineseness in popular perception and official definition, and proceeded to unravel and problematize it.[20] By invoking the various ambiguous, contextual and situational, disparate and even conflicting meanings respectively given to the pigtail by the Manchu Qing dynasty, the Taiping rebels, the Chinese nationalists, the pre-nationalist Siamese state, the proto-nationalist Thai tax collectors and census takers, a popular commoner Thai poet, and the arch-Thai official nationalist King Vajiravudh, and then playing them off against one another, I showed that the pigtail hadn't necessarily signified Chineseness either in China or Siam and, furthermore, that Chineseness had not necessarily denoted ethnicity.

Pigtail wearers in China could be and had been regarded by different groups of people in different times and under different circumstances as either loyal subjects of the Qing emperor and proud inheritors and custodians of native culture, or, alternately, as invaders and occupiers of, or outsiders and traitors to the Chinese nation, i.e. as either Chinese or non-Chinese. In the same vein, their counterparts in Siam could also be and had variously been categorized by the state authorities as Thai corvée laborers, unassimilated Chinese aliens and tax payers, or unreformed opium addicts of whatever ethnicity. Moreover, there was a distinct possibility that

---

[20] Kasian Tejapira, "Pigtail: A Pre-History of Chineseness in Siam," *Sojourn* 7,1 (1992): 95-122.

some categories of pigtail wearers themselves might not have approved of the pigtail and/or its associated political and cultural identity literally imposed on top of them. Far from naturally and unproblematically indicating ethnicity, the pigtail had been a free-floating, available, and sometimes artificial sign, arbitrarily deployed by the Siamese state to construct and control a transitive, ordered reality called "Chineseness" for administrative, fiscal, political, and cultural purposes, regardless of the ethno-cultural background and self-identification of the people involved. The complex and chaotic historical vistas of the pigtailed non-Chinese, the Chinese without pigtail, false Thais, and fake Chinese that emerged from this portrayal thus belied the presumed essence of ethnic Chineseness.

Next, I directly grappled with Thainess in the official nationalist discourse by zeroing in on some crucial instances in which the ruling élites' arbitrary deployment and manipulation of this seemingly ethnic term for the purposes of ethnicizing non-ethnic ideological and political issues had been particularly stark and revealing. Chief among these instances was their inclusion of the monarchy, the military, and submissive, conformist, clientelist political culture as components in the essence of ethnic Thainess and the Thai nation, and their concomitant exclusion of the earliest generation of jek communists and any form of radical, leftist culture and politics from them. Much the same semiotic maneuver was repeated in the case of "communism," another potent and deadly signifier in Thai cultural politics, to reveal the Thai state's no less arbitrary and ever-changing legal definition and opportunistic application of it to repress all kinds of political dissenters and opponents, regardless of their actual ideological persuasions. In the end, "communism" in Siam had not really signified a distinctive, particular ideology, and anyone who stood in the way of the Thai official nationalist project was in effect designated a "communist."[21]

FROM THE CENTER TO THE MARGINS...

My deconstructive attempt up to that point had been concentrated on *the discourse about the ethno-ideological margins in the center of the Thai state's cultural political power* from the perspective of the jek communist pioneers, the doubly marginalized, as it were, both ethnically and ideologically, with whom I could readily identify and empathize as a latter-day follower. However, given the late Raymond Williams's reminder of "layers of this kind of (hegemonic) alien formation in ourselves, and deep in ourselves,"[22] I then turned my attention to *the discourse of the center in the margins*, i.e. the ways in which the hegemonic ethno-ideology of Thainess *determined* (in the sense of "the setting of limits") the cultural politics of the marginalized and, in turn, the latter's *determination* (in the sense of "the exertion of pressures") radically to subvert and transform it, while at the same time unwittingly and compulsorily internalizing, maintaining, and renewing it in the same process in ever subtler, deeper if modified ways.[23]

---

[21] The discussion in this passage and the following section is based on my book *Commodifying Marxism*, and my "Imagined Uncommunity" article.

[22] Raymond Williams, "You're a Marxist, Aren't You?" *Resources of Hope: Culture, Democracy, Socialism*, ed. Robin Gable (London: Verso, 1989), p. 75.

[23] Raymond Williams, "Determination," in *Marxism and Literature* (Oxford: Oxford University Press, 1985), p. 87. His refreshingly subtle, complex, and revelatory formulation of the well-worn Marxist concept of "determination" there is well worth quoting at length:

Through simulated close surveillance of the largely secretive jek communists and radicals, be it underground or in public, in jail or at large, at home or abroad, accomplished by perusing countless internal party documents and open publications, the legal radical press and published works, government minutes and reports, secret police files, court proceedings, diplomatic intelligence dispatches, and memoirs and interviews of the jek communists and radicals themselves, as well as of their friends and fellow-travelers, rivals and enemies, I painstakingly reconstructed their thirty-year-long ups and downs and persevering attempts to *simultaneously break into and out of "Thainess" at the margins of the Thai polity* in such institutional loci as prisons, party and mass organizations, oppositional print media, local Chinese schools, bookshops, and communities from 1927 to 1958.

I vicariously "watched" them learn to speak, read, and write the Thai language from their Thai conservative-royalist fellow inmates in prison and noticed when one of them in particular asked a member of the latter to coin him a new Thai name to replace his former Chinese one. I "listened" in on the convivial socializing chats, as well as frank and friendly discussions, on ideological and political matters between these two groups of jailed strange bedfellows. I "followed" a couple of jek-communist internationalist volunteers to Yenan, where they helped their Chinese comrades fight the Japanese imperialist invaders, and then back to Thailand, where they proceeded to translate and propagate the Chinese Maoist doctrine they brought home with them into Thai. I "observed" the jek communists put together and put out Thai newspapers, magazines and books, set up and expand party-affiliated radical labor unions, as well as other mass and front organizations, infiltrate schools, universities, Buddhist temples, and literary and journalistic circles, and concentrate their recruitment drive on ethnic "Thai" (read "non-Chinese") workers, students, teachers, monks, writers, journalists, etc. to Thaify their hitherto largely "un-Thai" (read "jek") rank and file. I "witnessed" their ethnicizing naming of the party at its founding congress in an effort to simulate a Thai-ethnicity effect in compensation for a missing reality, and their collective inability to bring themselves to vote a more capable and better qualified tried and tested candidate into the position of Party Secretary at the Second Congress because of his Chinese-accented Thai speech, since that might have compromised the party's bid to reinvent itself as a "Thai" party. In

---

> This is where the full concept of determination is crucial. For in practice determination is never only the setting of limits; it is also the exertion of pressures. As it happens this is also a sense of "determine" in English: to determine or be determined to do something is an act of will and purpose. In a whole social process, these positive determinations, which may be experienced individually but which are always social acts, indeed often specific social formations, have very complex relations with the negative determinations that are experienced as limits. For they are by no means only pressures against the limits, though these are crucially important. They are at least as often pressures derived from the formation and momentum of a given social mode: in effect a compulsion to act in ways that maintain and renew it. They are also, and vitally, pressures exerted by new formations, with their as yet unrealized intentions and demands. "Society" is then never only the "dead husk" which limits social and individual fulfilment. It is always also a constitutive process with very powerful pressures which are both expressed in political, economic, and cultural formations and, to take the full weight of "constitutive," are internalized and become "individual wills." Determination of this whole kind—a complex and interrelated process of limits and pressures—is in the whole social process itself and nowhere else: not in an abstracted "mode of production" nor in an abstracted "psychology."

their all-out exertion to re-ethnicize themselves cultural-politically as "Thai," they could not help playing by at least some of the rules of the Thainess game, being limited by its logic, more or less internalizing it, and thus developing certain typical TDS symptoms as a result. That was the price exacted by, alas, the reproduction of Thainess in the margins.

... AND BACK VIA TRANSLATION ...

Nonetheless, the jek communists' Thaification of radical discourse and movement was finally not in vain. The limits of Thai cultural politics were indeed breached and broadened, and Thainess was substantially changed and radicalized, by their exerted pressures. "Thai Marxism-communism," an ethno-ideological oxymoron and discursive impossibility according to the prevailing discourse of Thai official nationalism, did eventually emerge as a cultural political reality in the 1950s, and its remaining legacy survived the fifteen-year-long brutal repression and wholesale incarceration of its creators and custodians by the absolutist military regime of Field Marshal Sarit Thanarat and Thanom Kittikachorn (1959-1973), to be excavated, reproduced, and recycled as cultural resources of radical hope and resistance against dictatorship and capitalism by latter-day Thai radicals up to the present.

But how did it manage to achieve that feat of radicalization and survival in such extreme adversity?

On the basis of my personal experience and preliminary researches, *translation and rhyming* held the key. Situated at the margins of a national language, translation guards the linguistic border and integrity of a nation-state's "body cultural."[24] Where language is standardized and coinages need to be sanctioned by central authorities, as in modern Thailand, the translation of key foreign political and ideological words becomes a highly politicized and fiercely contested borderland in which the language Border Patrol Police try to screen new translated lexical immigrants, discriminate against radical ones, and declare them *lexicon non grata*, or, failing that, proceed to retranslate (in some cases even pre-translate) them in such a way as to turn them into either quarantined and alien permanent non-residents, or emasculated and tamed, harnessed and domesticated, incorporated and deradicalized, naturalized neuters, while the unauthorized radical translators seek incessantly to smuggle in and procreate their illegitimate lexical brainchild.

In this regard, the modern Thai cultural élite was exceptionally conscious of the politics of translation, as evidenced by the following principle of Thai neologism laid down as early as December 1932 by the late Prince Wan, an Oxford-educated member of the royalty, top diplomat, senior cabinet minister, and the longest-reigning, as well as most prolific, highest authority on Thai official neologism:

---

[24] I derive this apt concept of Prasenjit Duara from Craig J. Reynolds, "Identity, Authenticity, and Reputation in the Postcolonial History of Mainland Southeast Asia," Keynote speech presented at the "International Conference on Post-Colonial Society and Culture in Southeast Asia," Yangon, Myanmar, December 16-18, 1998. Otherwise, the idea in this part is generally inspired by Thongchai Winichakul, *Siam Mapped: A History of the Geo-Body of a Nation* (Honolulu: University of Hawai'i Press, 1994), especially a section entitled "The Border of Thainess," pp. 169-70.

It is the Thai language that will guarantee the security of the Thai nation. This is because if we favor the use of Thai transliterations of Western words about ideas, we may walk too fast. That is we may imitate other people's ideas directly instead of premodifying them to accord with our ideas. But if we use Thai words and hence must coin new ones, we will have to walk deliberately.[25]

Suffice it to point out that among the key Thai cultural political coinages he invented are: *"sangkhom"* (society), *"setthakij"* (economy), *"nayobai"* (policy), *"rabob"* (system), *"raborb"* (regime), *"phatthana"* (development), *"patiwat"* (revolution), *"patiroop"* (reform), *"wiwat"* (evolution), *"kammachip"* (proletariat), *"kradumphi"* (bourgeoisie), *"mualchon"* (masses), *"sangkhomniyom"* (socialism), *"ongkan"* (organization), *"sahaphap"* (union), *"watthanatham"* (culture), *"wiphak"* (critique), *"judyeun"* (standpoint), *"pratya"* (philosophy), *"atthaniyom"* (realism), *"jintaniyom"* (romanticism), etc., inventions so numerous that the Thai radicals and communists simply could not open their mouths without echoing some of the Prince's neologisms! The following are examples of the politics behind some Thai official coinages:

- *Revolution*: Prince Wan's coinage for it in Thai was *Patiwat*, which literally means *turning or rolling back* and hence has a conservative connotation of *restoration*, instead of denoting a radical break with the past, or a progressive and qualitative change of affairs, as in the English original.
- *Communism*: Although Prince Wan did tentatively coin a couple of Thai words for this movement as early as 1934, i.e. *Latthi niyom mualchon* and *Sapsatharananiyom* (literally meaning Massism and Pan-publicism, respectively), the transliterated version *Khommunist* has become universally adopted in both official and popular usages to this day. Sulak Sivaraksa, a conservative royalist intellectual and noted cultural critic, has suggested that the reason for this might be to maintain the alien sound and appearance of the word and the idea, to deny it a legitimate place in the Thai language, to keep it forever as the un-Thai Other at the lexical gate, so to speak. The radical leftists' subsequent feeble attempt to coin a new Thai word for it (such as Naiphi's *Latthi sahachip*, literally meaning Unionism) failed to catch on.
- *Democracy*: The present Thai equivalent of it is *Prachathipatai*. Curiously enough, this coinage of King Rama VI (as early as 1912) initially meant a republic (i.e. a government with no king). The shift in its meaning from "republic" to "democracy" followed a compromise between the People's Party and the Monarchy in the anti-absolutist revolution of 1932, when a constitutional monarchy was chosen in place of a republic, thus allowing for the characterization of the present Thai political system as *"rabob prachathipatai an mi phramahakasat song pen pramuk"* or, if one sticks to the original meaning of *Prachathipatai*, "*Republic with the King as the Head of*

---

[25] Prince Narathipphongpraphan (M. C. Wan Waithayakon Worawan), "Pathakatha reuang siamphak" (A Lecture on Siamese Language), *Chumnum phraniphon khong sassatrajan pholtri phrajaoworawongthoe krommeun narathipphongpraphan* (Selected writings of Professor, Major General, Prince Narathipphongpraphan), ed. Songwit Kaeosri (Bangkok: Bangkok Bank, 1979), p. 416.

State," an oxymoron made possible by the successful taming or metathesis of a foreign-derived radical signifier.

Historically speaking, the Thai radicals and communists were at a disadvantage as far as the politics of translating Marxist-Communist words were concerned. From the 1920s to the mid-1940s, while the ruling élite, state ideologues, and intelligence officials were busy translating and coining these words for the purposes of surveillance and repression of political subversives as well as economic policy debates, the first-generation jek communists were still largely speaking Chinese, organizing and mobilizing the Chinese immigrant communities, and directing their political concerns and activities mainly towards China as good long-distance *huaqiao* nationalists.

It was only after the Second World War that a new generation of radicals and communists, consisting of both Thai-literate jeks and native Thais, saw the necessity of, as well as having the interest and language proficiency to begin, their own independent translation and coinage of Marxist-Communist words in earnest. But by then, the strategic commanding heights in the discursive field had already been occupied by the anti-communists. Here are some examples of the Thai radicals' and communists' attempts at retranslating Marxist-Communist words:

- *Aphiwat*: Dissatisfied with the conservative connotation of *Patiwat*, Pridi Banomyong,[26] himself a one-time democratic socialist revolutionary, coined the word *Aphiwat* instead, which literally denotes super-evolution.
- *Phaessaya*: In place of Prince Wan's rather neutral-sounding and low-key *kradumphi*, Atsani Phonlajan, alias Naiphi or "Specter" in English,[27] a multilingual genius in the Thai language and etymology and probably the most erudite and sophisticated among Thai communist intellectuals, retranslated "the bourgeoisie" as "*phaessaya*," a Sanskrit-derived Thai word which has a wonderful double meaning of a merchant class and/or a prostitute or bitch.
- *Kammakorn*: A pioneering group of ethnic Thai labor union activists and organizers in the 1920s deliberately chose to call their organization and newspaper "*Kammakorn*," a Thai word with a residual meaning of slavery and cruel punishment, as the Thai equivalent of the English word "worker."

---

[26] Pridi Banomyong, 1900-1983, was the top civilian leader and political strategist of the 1932 anti-absolute monarchy, constitutionalist revolution, key architect and minister of the subsequent constitutional regime, head of the underground Free Thai resistance movement against the Japanese occupiers during World War II, one-time prime minister, and the first senior statesman of modern Siam. He went into exile in the aftermath of a right-wing, conservative-royalist military coup in 1947, lived in Communist China for the next two decades, and then moved to Paris, where he stayed until his widely mourned death.

[27] Atsani Phonlajan, 1918-1987, was a self-taught, rebellious, iconoclastic member of the Thai literati and one of the two foremost, versatile, and finest radical Thai poets and literary critics, the other being Jit Poumisak. A lawyer by training and state prosecutor by profession, he was won over to communism by a leading jek Maoist intellectual and went underground to China for theoretical education in the 1950s. Upon the collapse of the communist-led rural armed struggle in the early 1980s, he refused to give himself up to the Thai government, but went over instead to socialist Laos, where he later died of old age a convinced communist revolutionary.

Regarding the word *Kammakorn*, the authorities obviously did not like its negative connotation and have been waging a protracted war against it ever since. For example, the official dictionary of the Ministry of Education published in 1927, and that of the Royal Institute issued in 1950, similarly added an unusual note of caution to the entry specifically to explain that *Kammakorn* was not a slave, as in the English "Laborer (Laboring Class)." In 1956, the then-Police Chief, Police General Phao Sriyanond, bargained with delegates of the radical labor union movement for a change in the Thai rendering of May Day from *"Wan kammakorn"* to *"Wan raeng-ngan"* (or Labor Day) as a precondition for allowing a public celebration on that day. More than thirty years later, the then-Prime Minister of Thailand, General Prem Tinsulanond (1980-1988), pleaded with labor leaders for the same nominal change again at the Government House!

... AND RHYMING MARXISM

And yet, no matter who did the translation or what kind of hidden political agenda he/she originally had in mind, once translated, these Thaified or naturalized Marxist-Communist words had their own indigenous ways of filtering from the margins through the thick of Thai culture to the center. One such route was poetry, or more simply rhyming, whose centrality to Thai traditional culture was likewise attested by two chief representatives of modern Thai poets, one a royalist and the other a communist, in their respective testimonies below:

> Thailand Is a Nation of Rhymers. Siamese Thais are rhymers by habit. There are plenty of poets from the highest to the lowest classes. Some of them are scholars, but many more are illiterates. The scholars who become poets may do so because of their literacy as well as disposition. But the illiterates do so purely on account of their disposition. If we are to publish a collection of all the verses composed by these illiterate rhymers in a year, it will take up a great many volumes.... If one is to estimate what percentage of the population of this country are rhymers, the figure should not be less than that of any other country in the world. We love rhyming so much that we versify not only in our own traditional genres, but also in those of other languages. And once we get hold of them, we do not follow their original version but modify them to suit our ears by adding rhymes, thus making them much more difficult...
>
> No. Mo. So., alias Prince Phitthayalongkorn[28]

> Thai people are rhymers by habit. The sweet-sounding saying of rhymes is almost a commonplace, but its content is another matter.
>
> Intharayut, alias Atsani Phonlajan[29]

The translated Marxist-Communist words were perfectly admissible and convenient candidates for inclusion in Thai poetry for a simple reason: that they were much easier to rhyme with other Thai words than were their original foreign

---

[28] No. Mo. So. (Prince Phitthayalongkorn), *Klon lae nakklon* (Rhymes and rhymers) (Bangkok: Sophonphiphatthanakorn Printing House, 1930), pp. 1-2.

[29] Intharayut (Atsani Phonlajan), "Wannakhadi kao kao" (Old literature), *Aksornsarn*, I,11 (February 1950): 85.

equivalents. For example, according to the first and only Thai rhyming dictionary then available, whereas "socialism" (together with other -isms) has only fifteen Thai words that rhyme with it, its Thai translation, *sangkhomniyom*, has 294 that do.[30]

A particular quality of Thai poetry that makes it an ideal literary genre conducive to an expanded reproduction of Marxist-Communist signifiers is its capacity to say the same thing over and over again lengthily, verbosely, gracefully, powerfully, rhythmically, and rhymingly, thus making it easy to remember and recite or sing. Volumes of beautiful Thai poems have been composed just to say *"Oh, my dear, how much I love you! Do you love me?"* or *"How great the Lord Buddha is!,"* and the like, in a hundred different ways.[31]

Moreover, the practice of composing poetry to convey political ideas had begun in Siam during the late nineteenth and early twentieth centuries. As a result of the impact of Western culture and education, many royal, aristocratic, and even commoner poets had transformed the traditional style and function of Thai poetry from long narratives to short "vehicles of thought," be it liberal, democratic, royalist, or nationalist. In this regard, Thai radical and communist poets later in the century were simply following in their footsteps by turning Thai poetry into a vehicle of Marxist-Communist thought.

In the decade following the Second World War, scores of translated Marxist-Communist signifiers majestically reigned and melodiously rhymed with fellow Thai words in the Thai radicals' and communists' poems. More often than not, they were printed in bold letters or within inverted commas, clearly visible, separate and distinguishable from other non-radical words in the same line, as if to mark themselves off as verbal icons or emblems of the poems' radicalism. In some cases, a reference was given to inform the readers of the source (usually a translated article or essay) from which the original idea of a poem was derived, or the original English equivalent of a translated radical word was provided in a footnote to the poem. In one particular instance, a translator-poet added two Thai words to his translation of a radical English poem that did not appear in the original, namely *"kaona"* (progressive) and *"sajjatham"* (truth). It must have been absolutely clear to him that these two radical signifiers rightfully belonged there.

Thus hundreds of Thai radical poems were composed and published, and consequently thousands of Marxist-Communist signifiers were literally reproduced and displayed on the pages of radical periodicals and books in easily noticeable and memorable forms, owing to the style in which they were printed and fluent rhyming and alliteration. Many lines and stanzas of these poems were subsequently reprinted innumerable times in numerous periodicals and collections, turned into political songs or slogans, written on big posters in labor strikes and mass rallies, or softly, even silently, recited and sung in serene solitude or extreme danger. It was in this manner that Thai poetry helped preserve and pass on Marxism-Communism of the radical signifiers.

---

[30] Laong Misetthi, *Photjananukrom lamdub sara* (Rhyming dictionary) (Bangkok : Rungreuangsan Publisher, 1961), pp. 1218-19, 1236-50.

[31] Suffice it to point out that thirty years earlier, I, then a mere shy and early teenager in a secondary school, had composed a lengthy Thai poem to express my bliss and lament my anguish upon the occasion of my first puppy love. Consisting of a total of two hundred different stanzas, it basically just says: *"Oh, Lady, how beautiful you are! How much I love and long for you! Well, do you love me?"* Alas, as a matter of fact, she didn't even notice me, let alone care to read my poem, but all the same.

And yet, rhyming Marxism did come at a price.

For eventually, the Thai radical poets came up against a dialectical tension inherent in any such attempt, a tension between the theoretical logic of Marxism-Communism and the complex regulations of Thai poetry. The various types of Thai poetry, be it *Khlong, Chand, Kab, Klon,* or *Rai,* are well-known for their highly formalistic and strictly regulated character, called *Chanthalak,* or prosody-characteristics. Their composition has to adhere to a series of complicated patterns, regulations, and requirements with regard to number of syllables, tone, rhythm, and internal and external rhyming ("internal" here means "within a line," while "external" denotes "between lines and stanzas"), which follow a totally different and incompatible logic from that of Marxist-Communist theory.

Consequently, rhymed and Thaified Marxism-Communism couldn't possibly maintain its pristine theoretical integrity and meanings intact across languages and cultures, contexts and media, reproducers and audiences. Especially when the vocabulary was subjected to a further process of mechanical and electronic reproduction, as well as commodification, in an open capitalist cultural market, it became hopelessly open and subject to adulteration, profanation, decontextualization, interpretation, negotiation, revision, resignification, refunctionalization, and de- and re-radicalization *ad infinitum* over which no single authority could have absolute or monopolistic control.

CONCLUSION: RADICALIZING THE NATIONAL SIGNIFIERS

On such a postmodernist-sounding note, one may wonder what's the point of trying to hold onto these free-floating signifiers and use them to imagine and construct a different Thai nation if, to paraphrase Marx and Engels's famous dictum in *The Communist Manifesto,* solid Thainess melts into air and holy Thai Marxism-Communism is hopelessly profaned.[32] As a being-in-the-world (or *dasein,* à la Heidegger) and creature of language and culture, one cannot simply wish away by mere deconstruction a national community and its body cultural, no matter how imagined and phantasmagorical, or distasteful and oppressive, they are. While the signifieds and referents may vary and change, the national signifiers and their accompanying institutions of power are still there and can come back to haunt one at the least expected moments. One thus could not help but always maintain one's presence in the thick of national cultural politics, and be aware of, alert to, and vigilant against any and all maneuvers and counter-maneuvers in the unending war of positions and contestation over the signification of key national signifiers.

It is precisely here, alas, that one could not help transcending one's role as a disinterested cosmopolitan academic and becoming a partisan radical cultural politician or public intellectual in and of a nation for the reason propounded by Ben Anderson at the end of his essay cited from the outset:

---

[32] My conceptual elaboration and empirical substantiation of this thesis appears in Kasian Tejapira, "The Postmodernisation of Thainess," in *Cultural Crisis and Social Memory: Modernity and Identity in Thailand and Laos* (London: Routledge Curzon, 2002), pp. 202-27.

... for modern history shows very clearly that, with the exception of Lenin's Bolshevik party, no revolutionary movement succeeds unless it has won or been conceded the nationalist accolade.[33]

---

[33] Anderson, "Withdrawal Symptoms," p. 173.

Pag-ibig, Pagtatalik at Pakikibaka: Love and Sex inside the Communist Party of the Philippines

Patricio N. Abinales[1]

In April 1977, units of the Communist Party of the Philippines (CPP) and the National Democratic Front (NDF) began receiving copies of a document approved by the Party's executive committee based on the draft written by CPP chairman Jose Ma. Sison. The document, titled "On the Relations of Sexes," outlined the Party's views on heterosexual relationships and provided a set of procedures as to how cadres and activists could strike the proper balance between what the CPP called "sex love" and "class love." The leadership then enjoined cadres to discuss the draft document and to send in their comments.[2]

It took the entire organization six years to discuss the draft, an unusual but perhaps perfectly understandable situation given that the CPP's organizational and military priorities were more focused on expanding the revolution than on taking care of the sexual affairs of its man and woman power. In 1983, however, all deliberations and debates were terminated and the executive committee issued the revision. The new document was re-titled "On Marriage," to underscore Party preferences in regards to the appropriate directions for any heterosexual relationship.[3] It retained the main arguments of the 1977 draft, but also made changes "in certain portions of the [1977] draft based on the suggestions from the

---

[1] The author wishes to thank Audrey Kahin, Donna Amoroso and Carol Hau for their comments, criticisms, and patience. All shortcomings are his alone.

[2] This is quite strange given the "nat-dem" activists were regarded as having a political awareness lower than the Party cadre. This blurring of distinctions, however, suggests that the Executive Committee intended "On Relations of the Sexes" to cover a wider audience.

[3] "Hingil sa Pag-aasawa: Mga Tuntunin sa Pag-aasaw sa Loob ng Partido," Komite Sentral, Partido Komunista ng Pilipinas, Abril 1983. Prof. Neil Garcia of the Department of English, University of the Philippines, alerted me to the fact that the CPP now approves of gay relationships, leading to the formation of the national democratic organization PRO-GAY. There is supposed to be a document formalizing the CPP's endorsement of bisexual and homosexual relationships, but I have yet to read it. I thank Prof. Garcia informing me about these changes in Party regulations.

regions."[4] The document is now officially part of the CPP's regulatory regime, and there is no evidence that Sison, who now controls the Party, intends to get rid of it or amend it to suit current needs. "On Marriage," in short, has become Party law.

This essay is an exploration of the language and content of the 1986 guideline, and the tensions it generates when placed alongside literary writings by cadres that discuss sexual relations. The friction between the CPP's legal and moral impositions (and sanctions) and a surprisingly disparate outlook by some of the Party's literati towards sexuality has engendered a number of interesting contradictions not only within the texts themselves, but also in Party daily life itself. Among these contradictions, three come to mind. First, by the very nature of its revolutionary tradition, the CPP is expected to push for a more liberative praxis of sexuality, especially with respect to women. Yet, instead of addressing this foundational issue, the Party document on sexual relations and marriage directs discussion of female sexuality to directions that contain rather than liberate it.

Likewise, instead of becoming the document of sexual liberation that further marks the progressive and forward-looking temperament of the CPP, the guideline has become the opposite. It has preserved some of the "pre-radical" norms the CPP, a Party of the (radical) Enlightenment, has identified as reflecting the "decadent" bourgeois and "feudal" cultures.[5] The classic example of this ideological regression is the document's treatment of women's virginity. In words that remind one of Catholic Church prohibitions, the Party—in its document, "On Marriage"—has made the preservation of a woman's virginity a vital precondition to marriage. Cadres who lost their virginity were regarded as actual or potential recidivists,[6] and "On Marriage" encourages women who have lost their virginity to get married to their male comrades, especially if the woman becomes pregnant. (Sexually active female cadres also faced the standard penalties of demotion, suspension, or outright expulsion from the movement.)

Finally, instead of blending feminism with Marxism, "On Marriage" tends to exacerbate the contradictions between these two progressive currents. It does not merely patronize women cadres; it also insists that women's issues be subordinate and secondary to the "more fundamental" issue of class. Communism is the superior ideology that trumps feminism. This attempt at social and sexual engineering by the Party leadership was not easily and wholeheartedly accepted by the rank-and-file, and resistance to the message was most apparent in the way literary works by CPP cadres addressed sexual relationships. While in these works sexual relationships are often presented as "side issues" to the "more important" theme of radical resistance or are presented as relationships operating within the larger domain of revolutionary praxis, discussions of sexual ties and sexuality in a number

---

[4] See "Ilang Paliwanag kaugnay sa mga Tuntunin sa Pag-aasawa sa loob ng Partido," Pinagtibay ng Komite Sentral, Partido Komunista ng Pilipinas, Abril 1983. The clarification stated: "Ang kasalukuyang mga tuntunin ang pinal na bersyon ng borador na binalangkas ng KT-KS noong Abril 1977. Binago o dinagdagan ang ilang bahagi ng nasabing borador, ayon sa mga mungkahing mula sa rehiyon." (The following provisions comprise the final version of a draft released by the Executive Committee of the Central Committee in April, 1997. Some changes and additions have been made in certain portions of said draft, based on the recommendations from the regions.) p. 2.

[5] Their pre-radicalism derives from the periods they dominated, i.e., roughly the pre-twentieth century in the West and perhaps up until the 1960s in Asia and the rest of the world.

[6] Mainly female, but could likely include male cadres, too.

of short stories and a Party-approved novel hint at a frequent questioning of Party regulations or, very subtly, disagreements with their perceived inflexibility. Even though these are works of fiction, they can be considered alongside "On Marriage" since they are designed to approximate reality, including that of the Party itself.[7]

LAYING DOWN "THE LINE"

"On Marriage" actually consists of two documents: the first, "Mga Tuntunin sa Pag-aasawa sa Loob ng Partido" (Rules regarding marriage inside the Party), and the appendix "Ilang Paliwanag kaugnay ng mga Tuntunin sa Pag-aasawa sa Loob ng Partido" (Some clarifications in regards to the rules "on marriage" inside the Party), which expands on the first document by giving a detailed question-and-answer presentation on the issues of courtship, marriage, divorce, and disciplinary action.[8]

The document starts with the premise that every member or candidate-member of the Party has the right to fall in love and to court the person he or she is attracted to. This social practice however, is different from any customary infatuation or full rapture because it is a potential or actual love between revolutionaries. Thus:

We recognize that there is love and its basis is personal. But as members or candidate members of the Party, we also voluntarily strive to subsume this love under class love, which means commitment to the revolutionary goals of the Party and the proletariat.	Ipinapalagay na may pag-ibig [sex love], at ito ay may batayang personal. Ngunit bilang mga kasapi o kandidatong kasapi ng Partido, nagkukusa tayong ipailalim ito sa pagmamahal sa kauri [class love] na ang ibig sabihi'y pananalig sa rebolusyonaryong mithiin ng Partido at proletaryado.[9]

The second document expounds on this dichotomy by explaining further why it is necessary that "class love" should dominate "sex love." It has something to do with the latter's tendency to become anarchic, go out of control, and cause harm to lovers and the revolution.

---

[7] Following the CPP premise that proletarian literature must reflect social reality, one can surmise that the stories mirror real sexual relations inside the revolution. See Kris Montanez, *The New Mass Art and Literature and Other Related Essays, 1974-1987* (Manila: Kalikasan Press, 1988), pp. 9-10.

[8] As far as I can recall, only Jose Ma. Sison's *Philippine Society and Revolution* was given similar extra-attention. The CPP's *Basic Mass Course* for new cadres is essentially a question-and-answer kit on *Philippine Society and Revolution*.

[9] "Hinggil sa Pag-aasawa," p. 1. The introduction from the 1977 version was retained.

Anarchism in love results in the violation of the rights of others, irresponsible initiation and dissolution of relationships, and loose morals. This is contrary to our aim to establish a just and progressive society and to our duty to mold proletarian individuals and families who will tirelessly fight to attain this aim. In love, there are discipline and freedom, rights and responsibilities; there are emotional and weighty aspects. In line with this view, we prepared rules so that all members and units of the Party are guided.	Ang anarkismo sa pag-ibig ay nagbubunga ng paglapastangan sa karapatan ng iba, iresponsableng pagpasok at paglabas sa relasyon, at maluwag na moralidad. Ito'y salungat sa layunin nating itatag ang lipunang makatarungan at progresibo at sa tungkulin nating hubugin ang mga tao at pamilyang proletaryado na walang humpay na lalaban para makamit ang layuning ito. Sa pag-ibig, may kalayaan at disiplina, mga karapatan at responsibilidad; may bahaging sa damadamin at bahaging seryoso. Alinsunod sa pananaw na ito, gumawa tayo ng mga tuntunin para magabayan ang lahat ng kasapi at yunit ng Partido.

The appendix also stresses that while falling in love is a "demokratikong karapatan ng bawat kasapi," (the democratic right of each member) it should also not be used as a "sagkaan [ng] malayang pag-pili ng sinuman sa kanyang iibigin at pakakasalan" (an act where some could just choose whom to love as he/she pleases). To make sure that these anarchistic and free-wheeling tendencies can be kept under control, "On Marriage" requires cadres to follow a set of compulsory procedures for falling in love, starting with the proper way of courting.

To initiate a courtship, a member or candidate member must first obtain the explicit permission of the Party unit in charge of his/her task. If the one courted belongs to another Party unit, the suitor's unit must inform the other unit or ask for its permission as long as the courted one agrees. The latter, in turn, must consult with the comrade to be courted. If the courted one refuses, he/she must explain the basis of the refusal.	Para makapangligaw, kailangang kumuha muna ang kasapi o kandidatong kasapi ng tahasang pahintulot ng yunit ng Partido na namamahala sa kanyang gawain. Kung ang liligawan ay kabilang sa ibang yunit ng Partido, ang yunit ng manliligaw ang magpapaabot sa kabilang yunit o hihingi ng pahintulot nito sa panliligaw basta't payag ang liligawan. Kung tumanggi ang nais ligawan, mabuting linawin niya ang batayan ng pagtanggi.

The document explicitly prohibits "competition" among suitors or the acceptance of multiple suitors and does not allow cadres whose marriage annulment or divorce has not yet been recognized or approved by the Party to enter into a new courtship. It enforces stricter rules if one of the parties involved, especially the person to be courted, is not a Party member. Concerning the latter case, "On Marriage" retained a provision in the 1977 draft that gives a cadre-suitor at least six months to convince his/her loved one to become a Party member.[10] With the

---

[10] "Kung ang isang kasapi o kandidatong kasapi ay nais manligaw sa isang di-kasapi, minamabuting may sapat na batayang ang liligawan ay maaaring maging kandidatong kasapi man lang sa loob ng anim na buwan matapos ibigay and pahintulot." (If a member or candidate

New People's Army (NPA), this particular regulation is doubly stringent: one must first fulfill one year's service with an assigned guerrilla unit before being allowed to court or be courted. Finally, the document warns about the pitfalls of the courtship process, principally the possibility that this amorous ritual could divert the attention of those involved from their work, or worse, that an opponent of the revolution who arouses romantic interest could erode and alter the revolutionary standing of a cadre.[11]

Similar regulations apply to cadres who plan to marry. The document refers to the institution of marriage as a "seryosong bagay na dapat mahusay na mapaghandaan ng mga nais magpakasal at ng kinauukulang yunit o mga yunit ng Partido." (Marriage is a serious matter that must be given proper attention and prepartion by the couple and the respective unit or units of the Party.) Couples wishing to marry must seek permission from their respective units, after which all parties will gather to discuss the merits and possible problems of married life. The discussions close with a recommendation to be submitted by each unit to the "higher organs" on whether or not the couple is fit to move to the next stage of their relationship. Once approved, all parties must then prepare for the wedding, and "On Marriage" and its accompanying clarificatory addendum explicitly outline the prerequisites for a successful wedding: an entourage must include, apart from the groom and bride, an officiating Party representative (either a member of the couple's units or someone from the higher organ), witnesses, and sponsors. All members of this cast must be Party members, meaning the wedding, unlike run-of-the-mill nuptials, is exclusive.

Wedding day is vintage revolutionary in form. With one of either the bride's or groom's political officers or a cadre of higher rank presiding, the ceremony starts with the couple giving their *talambuhay* (life story), a substantive overview of the history and politics of their relationship. A round of thorough criticism-self-criticism follows, with the couple as the major target, as well as an open forum where those in attendance can question them about their relationship. Married guests and senior cadres are enjoined to give helpful advice to the soon-to-be-married pair. During the ceremony, the prospective groom and bride will have their shoulders draped by the Party's red flag as they pledge to remain faithful to each other and to use the marriage as a way of strengthening their dedication to the revolutionary cause. They will also vow to rear their children in the revolutionary way, i.e., make them devotees of the revolution early on in their lives. Finally, they will promise to seek the advice of their sponsors, their Party units, and, if need be, the "higher organs" should they encounter problems in their marriage. The ceremony closes with the signing of the marriage contracts by the

---

man lang sa loob ng anim na buwan matapos ibigay and pahintulot." (If a member or candidate member wants to court a non-member, it would be good if the person being courted has enough potential to become a candidate member within six months after permission to court is granted.)

[11] Ang kasapi o kandidatong kasapi ay *hindi pahintulutang lumigaw sa o ligawan ng sinumang may balak na ilayo siya sa rebolusyonaryong gawain* o ng sinumang itinuturing na traydor o sagadsaring kontra-rebolusyonaryo. (italics mine) (A member or candidate member will *not be allowed to court or be courted by someone who has all the intention of taking him/her away from his/her revolutionary work*, a traitor, or an outright counter-revolutionary.)

bridal entourage, a mass singing of revolutionary songs (if security allows it), and a small party.[12]

The CPP is pro-divorce, particularly if or when the marriage becomes an impediment to a couple's revolutionary involvement. Divorce is likewise granted to couples in cases where one of the parties is found to be guilty of infidelity, bigamy, cruelty, or violence as well as willful abandonment by one partner.[13] The Party also allows divorce under extenuating circumstances. For example, when a couple cannot abide by the obligations of the marriage because conditions are unfavorable (for example, if they cannot maintain contact due to counterinsurgency operations or the like), they would be allowed to separate. Usually such a divorce is granted after both parties have been out of touch with each other for five years. Finally, a partner's permanent physical injury can also be used as a basis for divorce. Here "On Marriage" is oddly precise about it: "Kung ang kapansanan ay sa utak at hindi gumagaling, pwedeng ipagkaloob ang diborsyo pagkaraan ng tatlong taon." (If the injury is psychological and shows no signs of healing, divorce can be granted after a three year waiting period.)

To prevent abuse in courtship, marriage, or divorce, "On Marriage" includes an elaborate set of closely supervised disciplinary actions (DA) against erring individuals or couples, and is quite exceptionally harsh on those who use their positions of authority to take advantage of someone who interests them or with whom they are involved. DA is aimed in particular at preventing sexual relations from spinning out of control. At the courtship level, those who do not follow procedures could receive various types of DA. These violations are regarded as indicative of "sexual opportunism" (SO), a broadly defined category of the various sexual and emotional transgressions that the Party must be alert to.

The Party considers sex before marriage to be the most serious of all SOs. As the appendix puts it:

Like sex with a mere acquaintance and sex with different partners, the serious case of sex outside marriage clearly indicates a decadent view of sexual relations, and merits disciplinary action from the minimum penalty of a one-year suspension from Party membership to the maximum of expulsion from the Party.	Ang malubhang kaso ng pakikipagtalik nang hindi kasal tulad ng pakikipagtalik sa hindi man lang kasintahan at sa iba't ibang nagiging kasintahan, ay malinaw na nagpapakita ng bulok na pananaw sa relasyong sekswal, at magagawan ng aksyong pandisiplina na mula sa minimum na isang taong suspension sa pagiging kasapi hanggang sa maksimum na pagtitiwalag sa Partido.

This censorious official opinion applies not only to couples in love, but also their previous relations, and "On Marriage" imposes DA against couples caught in the act, as it were, ranging from suspension as a Party member to outright expulsion.

---

[12] The journalist Ceres Doyo writes about witnessing such a marriage while interviewing the late Antonio Zumel, a prominent Party figure. See "Tony Zumel: journalist, unionist, revolutionary," *Philippine Daily Inquirer*, August 16, 2001.

[13] Like courtship and marriage procedures, divorce procedures are meticulous and tightly supervised. For example, the panel deciding the divorce must consist of members of units not below a Party district committee.

Even cadres who are already engaged to be married, but "could not wait" for sex are not exempt from DA, although because they are in a state of transition, the penalties are comparatively less harsh:

Even if the couple is committed to their relationship, they may still be subjected to disciplinary action if they repeatedly engage in sexual relations in spite of criticisms and reminders from the Party; the disciplinary action though should not affect their standing as members in the Party. The maximum penalty is demotion for those cases where there is clear grave irresponsibility in handling sexual relations and in following decisions and policies of the Party.	Kahit ang magkasintahan ay seryoso sa kanilang relasyon, sila ay maaaring magawaran ng aksyong pandisiplina kapag paulit-ulit na nagtatalik sa kabila ng pagpuna at pagpapaalala ng Partido, bagama't ang aksyong pandisiplina ay hindi dapat makaapekto sa katayuan nila bilang kasapi ng Partido at maari lang umabot sa demosyon sa katungkulan sa mga kaso na may malinaw na may malalang iresponsibilidad sa paghawak sa relasyong sekswal at sa mga desisyo't patakaran ng Partido.

The same DA imposed on SOs becomes more severe and serious once a couple is married. But adulterers and those who use violence or make deadly threats against their partner could face additional penalties—for instance, the victim might be allowed to initiate divorce proceedings—apart from the minimum one-year suspension from the Party or the maximum of expulsion.

Cadre reception of the document was generally positive, especially among women cadres and activists.[14] Yet there were also stirrings of discomfiture. Some urban cadres and activists accepted the document's premise, but remained critical of what they regarded as unwarranted Party interference in their private lives. Others questioned whether a revolutionary Party's responsibility included fashioning an all-encompassing morality for its followers.[15] In the more conservative rural areas, however, the murmurs were few. As the NPA began to recruit more women into its ranks, and as the guerrilla movement started to "establish roots" among what the Party considered to be a relatively conservative peasantry, cadres seemed to feel relieved to have a guideline on sexual conduct in hand. Moreover, young guerrillas were made to understand that the rigors of war demanded that all energies be focused on fighting and organizing. Other "hormonal" urges needed to be suppressed, particularly the sexual ones.[16]

Still, it took six more years before a final version of the guidelines was finished. According to the leadership, this delay was the result of its deliberate effort to conduct as comprehensive a consultation as possible under conditions of war and within an organization so widely dispersed throughout the archipelago. The CPP's 1975 policy of "centralized leadership, decentralized operations" further

---

[14] Interview with Beng, a former CPP cadre who was one of those who pushed for the drafting of a document on sexual relations, January 4, 2002.

[15] Our Party cell was involved in one such discussion during the period. We all bewailed how much the regulations would "cramp our style" when it came to establishing as well as ending sexual relations.

[16] Interview with MG, former NPA guerilla, December 10, 2002.

complicated matters because regional organizations, invoking their right to conceive of plans and procedures based on their local experiences, likewise formulated their own rules on love and marriages.[17]

Once "On Marriage" became law, however, there were problems with its uneven implementation. In the urban areas, cadres took exception to the long list of prohibitions. Party units in the "youth and student sector" were particularly contemptuous of the draft, expressing their resentment by poking fun at the concepts, especially in songs. The song, "Mahirap talagang magmahal ng isang kasama" (How difficult it is to fall in love with a comrade), an adaptation of a song by the pop group Apo Hiking Society, complains of the hassles of romance with a comrade: you can't see him/her because of the countless meetings both of you must attend, the elaborate security arrangements you have to manage, including resorting to aliases, and the pesky "PO" (political officer) who constantly checks your whereabouts. The lyricist even suggests that intra-Party romance can be so frustrating that perhaps a mere "sympathizer" to the revolution would make a better mate. But love is love, and so one has to endure, but precisely because one is "in love," one can also refuse to heed the directive to politicize the relationship.[18]

The seriousness behind the charge of sexual opportunism has also been depreciated by songs that cast the opportunist as a mere playboy, not as the wayward, uncontrollable recidivist that the Party depicts. The song "Buhay ng

---

[17] "Base sa kanilang mga karanasan, nagkusa ang mga panrehiyong organisasyon ng Partido sa paggawa at pagpapairal sa kani-kanilang mga tuntunin" (Based on their experiences, some regional organizations decided to come out with their own versions of the regulations.) In 1975, Amado Guerrero (Jose Ma. Sison) wrote the piece "Specific Characteristics of our People's War," where he outlines the policy of "centralized command, decentralized operations" to adjust to the archipelagic character of the Philippines. See Amado Guerrero, "Specific Characteristics of our People's War," as reprinted in *Philippine Society and Revolution* (Oakland, CA: Association of Filipino Patriots, 1979).

[18] The song, revised by former cadre assigned to the "youth and student sector," goes like this:

Oh, how difficult it is to love a comrade	Mahirap talagang magmahal ng isang kasama
You can't even visit her because she has a meeting.	Hindi mo mabisita 'pagkat may pulong siya
It's difficult, indeed it is.	Mahirap, o mahirap talaga
Perhaps I should just find myself a "sympa,"	Maghanap na lang kaya ng sympa
But every time I see her eyes	Ngunit kapag nakita ko ang kanyang mga mata
I lose sense of my politics!	Nawawala ang aking . . . pulitika!
Just go, attack, come what may . . .	Sige lang, sugod lang, o bahala na
I really don't care if I get criticized.	Bahala na kung magkapunahan pa
Refrain: Dial her phone, never give your real name	Refrain: I-dial mo ang number sa telepono Huwag mong ibigay ang tunay na pangalan mo
But when you get to talk to her on the phone, she'd say to you,	Pag nakausap mo sya, sasabihin sa iyo . . .
"Please call back again, my political officer's here"	Tumawag ka mamaya nanditong P.O. ko . . .
Oh how difficult, how difficult indeed	Mahirap, o mahirap talaga
Oh what a headache, believe me.	O sakit ng ulo maniwala ko
But no matter how much they say,	Ngunit kahit ano pang sabihin nila,
I will never change, I will never change, I will never change.	Hindi pa rin ako magbabago (repeated three times.)

S.O" (The life of a sexual opportunist), which is based on a popular "traditional" song, is illustrative of this impish recharacterization of the sexual opportunist, made more notable by the absence of any citation of the prohibitions outlined by the regulations.

The life of an S.O. is mysterious	Mahiwaga ang buhay ng S.O.
We are uncertain of who he/she is	Kung sino ay hindi natin piho
But I hope we believe	At manalig lagi sana tayo,
Every week there will be a new partner.	Tuwing linggo may kasama siyang bago.
Love is not part of the opportunist's vocabulary	Pag-ibig ay wala sa bokabularyo
For it simply causes too much headache.	At pampasakit lang daw ito ng ulo
Such is the life and joy of someone who has been labeled	Yan ang buhay at ligaya ng isang Nabansagang S.O.
The Sexual Opportunist.[19]	

Those cadres charged with testing the effectiveness of the draft statement were, of course, not happy with these demonstrations of skepticism and even animosity from below. The appendix admitted that some of the more enthusiastic cadres' responses led to a "labis na paggamit sa mga regulasyon kahit sa mga pagkakataong mas kailangan at mas makabubuti ang paghikayat at ang paglilinaw sa mga prinsipyo." (excessive application of the regulations even at times when it was much better to be considerate and to reiterate the principles behind the regulations.) An inquisitorial atmosphere, akin to that found in Catholic girls' or boys' schools where nuns and priests conduct ongoing surveillance, became the norm in unnamed regional organizations of the Party. This excessive vigilance took its toll on cadres, aggravating already difficult conditions created by revolutionary organizing. The issue became serious enough to warrant a warning from the authors of "On Marriage."

Avoid having units and even Party members spend so much time discussing these matters. It is important to explain to the comrades our principles regarding marriage, though this is minor compared to the greater political issues confronting the Party today.	Iwasan lang ang *kumain ng napakalaking panahon ng mga yunit at maging ng mga kasapi ng Partido ang pag-uusap sa mga usaping ito.* Mahalagang linawin sa mga kasama ang mga prinsipyo natin sa pag-aasawa, *pero menor ang gawaing ito kung ihahambing sa malalaking usaping pampulitika na hinaharap ng Partido ngayon.* (italics mine)

---

[19] The author of this naughty song which became popular in the late 1970s was never ascertained.

CONTRADICTIONS

Here, I think, the document's first dilemma arises. By inserting this admonition, the author tacitly acknowledges that sexual relations, an ostensible secondary issue compared to the paramount goal of seizure of power, cannot simply be set aside or wished away. The CPP leadership tries to downplay the complexities of sexual relations, stating that "menor ang gawain ito kung ihahambing sa malalaking usaping pampulitika na hinaharap ng Partido ngayon" (sexual relations are a minor issue compared to the more important political problems the Party faces today). But by issuing "On Marriage" and its accompanying clarification, the Party effectively admits that this "menor na gawain" is not such a trifling problem after all. And in entreating its membership not to spend too much time on love and sexual questions, the Party bosses had conceded, as far back as 1977, that sexuality was as important as organizing political rallies, planning tactical offensives, and entering into tactical coalitions. Moreover, the stern tone of its plea indicates an urgency to resolve sexual questions because such questions have the potential to impede revolutionary progress.

One way that the Party tries to deal with this unstable discrepancy between the popularity of sexuality and its official status as a secondary issue is to show that one can actually mix romance and revolutionary dedication quite well, but only if cadres in love stick closely to revolutionary guidelines. In Dahlia Castillejo's essay "Mula sa *Letter to Chris and Jeng*," the parents explain to their children how their marriage and revolutionary commitment had been equally strengthened through criticism-self-criticism.

> Maybe you would also like to know how your father and mother behaved as members of the district leadership. The highest collective leadership in our area of responsibility then was the District Secretariat, in which both of us were members. During decision-making and other important meetings, we tried to forget temporarily that we were husband and wife so that we could have objective discussions. However, at the beginning your father and I seemed to have opposite personalities, so that sometimes we experienced contradictions. There were times when he was rather slow in making decisions because he was carefully weighing almost everything, while I was impulsive. He would criticize me for this, while there were times when I would criticize his style. However, the occasional contradictions and our honest, open criticism of each other strengthened our unity as comrades and as husband and wife. I do not remember a single night when we did not resolve our differences before we went to sleep.[20]

But the path to resolving this contradiction is fraught with dangers, especially since some revolutionaries, in certain conditions, seem unable to resist love. Evidence of fears or frustrations concerning cadres who are overly engrossed in love and sex are seen in Ruth Firmeza's novel, *Gera*. In this classic novel, Firmeza writes

---

[20] Dahlia Castillejo, "Mula sa *Letter to Chris and Jeng*," in *Muog: Ang Naratibo ng Kanayunan sa Matagalang Digmang Bayan sa Pilipinas* (*Muog: The Narrative from the Countryside during the Protracted Peoples War in the Philippines.*) (Quezon City: University of the Philippines Press, 1998), p. 148.

about how sexual attractions and the discomforts they engender are enduring parts of the daily lives of members of a mobile guerrilla unit.

Bernie passed in front of him, and Ariston noticed the enticing smile of the female comrade. He ended up asking himself: why doesn't he court Bernie instead? But that would be difficult because they belong to different [NPA] units and will most likely rarely see each other.[21]	Dumaan sa kanyang harapan si Bernie. Napansin ni Ariston ang nakabibighaning ngiti ng kasamang dalaga. Natanong tuloy niya ang sarili kung bakit hindi si Bernie ang kanyang ligawan. Pero ni hindi sila nagkasama sa isang yunit o madalas magkakitaan.

There will always be instances when cadres attempt to nurture or revive sexual relations without their unit's knowledge, a potent form of SO, and a dangerous violation of ORS norms, especially since it could affect the fighting ability of the NPA. Such was the case between comrades Vera and Sam, two characters in *Gera*, who once separated with the Party's blessings, but later quietly began seeing each other again. When Sam passed a note to Vera asking that they meet at the river, she reproached him for his boldness, warning that someone might see them and "mapupuna na naman ako." (I will be criticized again.)[22]

It appears that political officers constantly had to admonish their comrades about the distracting effects of love and sexual attraction. In Honorio Barolome de Dios's short story "Dolores," a cadre counsels his comrade that, even as he tried to focus on organizing, his attraction to a potential recruit was obvious. The exposed comrade admits his feelings and voices his concern that he might be DAed if he decides to court this recruit. But the friend merely retorts, "Ah, so let's keep it a secret from the political officers then!" His recommendation is practical, since once the woman has been recruited to the movement—as the courtship can only happen in a context where she and others are being organized by the Party—the problem of the lack of political content would be resolved. In fact, this is what takes place in the story, although the eventual relationship between the cadre and the female recruit would not officially absolve them of their initial violation if judged according to the rules of the CPP leadership.[23]

When reading *Gera* and De Dios's story, one is not only impressed by descriptions of the protracted people's war in the countryside, but also struck by the uneasiness of male and female cadres, united by their shared participation in this guerrilla war, who nurture secrets or express open attraction for one another. Firmeza does not devote more space to these potential and actual dalliances, but by sprinkling episodes involving sexual desires throughout a novel about war, she does show to what extent they impinged on the everyday life of revolutionaries. It is such "distractions" that most concern the authors of "On Marriage." Thus, the appendix repeatedly asserts the pre-eminence of proletarian love over personal love.

---

[21] Ruth Firmeza, *Gera* (Manila: Kilusan sa Paglilinang ng Rebolusyonaryong Panitikan at Sining sa Kanayunan and People's Art, Literature and Education Resource Center, 1991), p. 71.

[22] Firmeza, *Gera*, pp. 24-27.

[23] Honorio Bartolome de Dios, "Dolores," in *Muog*, pp. 260-61, 264.

In general, we subordinate love to proletarian love. This is in accordance with their relationship in the fundamental principle of proletarian revolutionaries: the subordination of personal interests to the interests of the masses.	Sa kabuuan, ating ipinapailalim ang pag-ibig sa pagmamahal sa kauri. Alinsunod ito sa pundamental na paninindigan ng mga proletaryong rebolusyonaryo: ang pagpapailalim ng personal na interes sa interes ng sambayanan.

Furthermore:

The view that personal love is higher than love of class is wrong. This implies the priority of the interests of personal relations over those of the masses. If the view of a comrade is that that which fosters personal relations is of greater value than [that which fosters] the revolution of the Party, then a contradiction between these two interests arises. If eliminating this dangerous idea is not carried out immediately, it may eventually lead to the betrayal of revolutionary aims and principles.	Isang maling ideya ang pangingibabaw ng pag-ibig sa pagmamahal sa kauri. Ang kahulugan nito ay ang pangunguna ng interes ng relasyong personal sa interes ng samabayanan. Kung ganito ang paniniwala ng isang kasama na higit na pinahahalagahan niya ang makabubuti sa relasyong personal kaysa sa makabubuti sa Partido's rebolusyon, magiging magkakasalungat ang interes ng dalawa. Kung hindi maagapan ang pagbaka sa mapanganib na ideyang ito, maari pang humantong ito sa tuluyang pagbitiw sa mga layunin at prinsipyong rebolusyonaryo.

Again, when ORS attempts to resolve the tension between its own strict guidelines and the abiding power of romantic passion, it does so by asserting that cadres in love can strike a proper balance so long as they stick closely to revolutionary guidelines. Thus in a fictional wife's letter to her husband, she is effusive about the link between love and revolution.

> There is only one way now I can make my love for you felt, and that is to persevere in developing our forces, to persevere in the cause which united us in the first place. And yes, how strong I feel when I am reminded of the fact that you are outside in the field gathering up strength into one gigantic force that will one day topple this arrogant enemy. How boldly proud, how utterly defiant I feel![24]

Yet, even these fictional stories that seem to adhere closely to the political line cannot escape the tension between sexuality and revolution. In Bartolome de Dios's story, Dolores's respect for Manuel's political work still could not prevent her from fearing for his life *and* wishing that they lived a "tahimik na buhay. Isang simpleng buhay" (a quiet life, a simple life). The fact that the lovers often discuss this issue in the story suggests that Dolores, even as she accepts Manuel's politics, is not entirely sold on the pre-eminence of revolution over love. Bartolome de Dios ends the story by converting Dolores into a wholehearted supporter of

---

[24] "Letter of a Wife to Her Husband," in *Muog*, p. 62.

Manuel; she holds firm when confronted by military interrogation. This conclusion is properly didactic, but perhaps it suggests that only in times of stress are things settled . . . and settled precariously.[25]

This initial contradiction brings out a number of others, especially when it comes to sex and the role of women in the revolution.

THE QUESTION OF SEX

As stated above, "On Marriage" is unequivocal about the role of copulation inside the revolution—making love is strictly forbidden before marriage. Point 10 in the section on courtship puts the burden on both the individual cadre and his/her unit to prevent pre-marital liaisons: "Hindi dapat magtalik ang magkasintahan. Responsibilidad ng kinauuukulang yunit na alisin ang mga kondisyong nakaeenganyo nito." (Lovers should not engage in sex. It is the responsibility of the concerned Party units to remove all conditions that could lead to premarital sex.)[26] Neither "On Marriage" nor its appendix, however, elaborates on why sex should be limited to married couples. There is no explicit reason offered for the prohibition of extra-marital coitus, and this is one of the surprising elisions of "On Marriage." However, we may be able to find a hint in the Party's attitude towards sex among unmarried cadres.

The Party regards pre-marital sex as especially exploitative of women. According to "On Marriage," imposing a ban on pre-marital coitus is necessary "to preserve a woman's reputation" (kapakanan ng kasamang babae). Judging from such statements, one would surmise that CPP leaders are worried not only about the reputations of female cadres, but also that they might regress into that despised category of "loose women." Hence, if caught, lovers would be penalized according to the rules. In cases where it is shown that the couple truly love each other, they also would be made to marry—especially if the woman gets pregnant.

In cases of pre-marital sex, the welfare of the female comrade should be protected before imposing the corresponding disciplinary action. If there is sufficient basis and those involved are prepared, it would be better for them to get married even if this has not been planned. This is necessary especially if their intimate relationship has resulted in pregnancy.	Sa mga kaso ng pagtatalik ng magkasintahan bago ang kasal, pangalagaan ang kapakanan ng kasamang babae bago ilapat ang kaukulang aksyon pandisiplina. Kung may sapat na batayan at kahandaan na ang mga nasasangkot, kahit wala pa sa taning, mas mabuting ikasal ang magkasintahan. Kailangan ito laluna kapag nagbunga ang pagtatalik.

---

[25] Honorio Barolome de Dios, "Dolores," in *Muog*, p. 263.

[26] The clarification document adds: "Dapat alisin ang mga kondisyong nag-uudyok o makatutukso sa pagtatalik ng mga magkasintahan bago ang kasal. Kailangan din ang gawaing edukasyon tungkol sa kasal at pag-aasawa para maiwasan ang mga kasong ito." (We should remove conditions that encourage or tempt couples to engage in sex before marriage and married life so as to avoid this problem.)

Additionally, if the couple is not yet ready for marriage, the penalties to be imposed may be less harsh, especially if the man and woman promise to refrain from sex in the future:

Avoid severe disciplinary actions for those who engage in pre-marital sex. This case is relatively light and should not be meted disciplinary action if the couple is determined to foster their relationship and if premarital sex does not occur repeatedly.	Iwasan ang napakabigat na mga aksyong pandisiplina sa mga magkasintahang nagtalik bago ang kasal. Relatibong magaan ang kasong ito at di kailangang lapatan ng aksyong pandisiplina kung determinadong magpunyagi sa relasyon ang magkasintahan at kung di paulit-ulit.

Thus the Party leadership strictly instructs its cadres to avoid coitus before marriage, but if a couple has already succumbed to temptation, the Party relaxes its stance and encourages the perpetrators to give serious attention to getting married. And it is here that we encounter additional anomalies.

While the Party adopts this peculiar prescriptive approach to pre-marital sex, it fails to explain why it is a problem. Instead of looking at sex as an inherent part of a relationship, the CPP instead views it as an obstacle to a meaningful relationship. Party bosses seem to presume that sex is not only a reactionary act, but also a physical exploit undertaken by a male cadre to satisfy his lust. Sex, in the mindset of those who wrote "On Marriage" and made it Party law, is not a mutual act of both partners; it is also not an inherent part of proletarian love. This unstated conviction makes the leftist CPP a Filipino conservative movement that is repulsed by the idea of the sex act as representative of individual cupidity.

There is likewise the tacit assumption that a female cadre engages in the sex act either because she has been pressured or simply to satisfy her own lust, and that she is hence uncaring about her *"kapakanan"* (reputation). In the same way that it fails to articulate the reasons for its attitude toward sex in general, the document never really clarifies why preserving a woman cadre's virginity is vital to a proletarian revolutionary relationship. Why does the vanguard value virginity? Why does this historical actor show an unlikely respect for the hymen? "On Marriage" leaves us with this peculiar silence, except for an allusion to the fact that sex can lead to pregnancy. Left with very little official explanation save this reference to the fear of pregnancy, a reader can only speculate that the Party may fear that pre-marital coitus could free a woman from her "inhibitions" and enable her to explore the full meaning of her sexuality. That, in turn, would transform female cadres into "loose women" of a sort that the Party might fear would taint its public image.

In the final analysis, however, even the most stringent of rules cannot prevent people from "making love." Hence, "On Marriage" has to allow some leeway for the errant so that they can amend their ways and make sure that the unauthorized and dangerous liaisons are resolved to the satisfaction of all those involved.

MORE SEX

But even some of the married are wary of these regulations, particularly when it comes to sex. While most of the literary works I surveyed underscore the commitment of married cadres both to each other and to the revolution, not everyone is happy with how the regulations could actually hamper, rather than enhance, wedded sexual intimacy. Zelda Soriano's fascinating short story "Mga Babae sa Kanilang Paghihintay" hints at this discomfort and expresses defiance towards those Party comrades engaged in surveillance of lovers and potential lovers. The defiance is made more emphatic by Soriano's vivid description of a sex act. The whole story is worth retelling:

Nene's eyes fluttered as she caressed the forehead of her youngest. She looked around, searching for the moon through the cracks of their hut. It's eight p.m., she told herself. Nita glanced at her two boys by the door. Her eldest looked dwarfed in his crouched position. She could not help but smile because the second to eldest slept with his legs crossed. She could not leave behind her task because of the masses...	Kumukurap si Nene habang nagmamadaling hinahaplos ni Nita ang noo ng kanyang bunso. Palingalinga siya at hinahagilap sa siwang ng kanilang dampa ang buwan. Alas-otso na, pasya nito sa sarili. Sinulyapan ni Nita ang dalawa pang anak na lalaki na may gawing pintuan. Napunggok nang husto ang kanyang panganay sa pagkakabaluktot. Napangiti siya sa sumunod na panganay dahil nakadekwatro pa ito sa pagutlong. Ang gawain niya ay 'di maiwan para sa sambayanan...
Nene's face was most peaceful. The children are now asleep, Nita convinced herself. Her heart beat faster now. She looked at the moon. Her whole body felt hot. Her eyes scanned the whole house. She caressed her hair gathered by a rubber band and then broke the band, running her fingers through her thick hair towards her shoulders. She stroked her shoulders, slowly down to her breasts. Her nipples hardened. She breathed deeply and sighed.	Payapangpayapa ang mukha ni Nene. Tulog na sila, pangungumbinsi sa sarili ni Nita. Bumibilis ang kabog ng kanyang dibdib. Sinilip niya ang buwan. Nag-iinit ang buo niyang katawan. Ibinaybay ni Nita ang tingin sa kabahayan. Hinaplos niya ang buhok na inipon ng goma sa kanyang likod. Pinatid niya ang goma at saka sinuklay ang daliri ang malagong buhok patungo sa balikat. Hinaplos niya ang balikat, iginapang ang mga palad pababa sa dibdib. Naniningas ang kanyang mga utong. Huminga ng malalim. Napabuntunghininga.
"And when you grow up into a mature individual, will you join the struggle?"	"At kung malaki ka na at may isip na, sasama ka na rin ba sa pakikibaka?"
Nita stood up, walked slowly, tiptoed over her boys, and closed the door. Her whole body shivered as the western wind welcomed it. Her feet groped for slippers. Glancing around, Nita left carefully but quickly for the ricefields.	Tumindig si Nita, marahang humakbang, nilakdangan ang mga anak na lalaki, at saka ipininid ang pinto. Nanginig ang kanyang buong katawan nang salubungin ang hanging kanluranin. Hinagilap ng kanyang mga paa ang tsinelas. Maingat pero mabilis na humakbang si Nita, palingalinga, patakbong lumayo sa dampa, patungo sa sabahan.
"Nita," someone whispered to her right. She squinted to look at the darkness where it came from. The sudden embrace by the man surprised her.	

278 Patricio N. Abinales

"Nita!" the man groaned. He began kissing her slowly on her ears, neck, cheeks, eyes, forehead, nose, and lips. She began to feel the heat in her body again, aching for the man. She embraced him, responding to every kiss.

The man's lips moved from Nita's face down to her neck, shoulders, and then breast. Nita was shaking. Then his hands were all over her back, buttocks, thighs, navel, breasts, head. In a moment, he undressed her. She moaned again. The man undressed and put their clothes on the ground. He then gently laid Nita down. And the shadows moved back and forth, under the dim light of the moon...

On the way back, Nita's footsteps had little strength. She glanced again at the moon. She walked slowly when nearing the hut.

"Comrade Nita?" Nita shivered at the voice which greeted her as she went into the hut. "We're comrades, Ka Nita. You were not here, so we let ourselves in. By the way, is Comrade Nato around?" Nita's skin crawled when hearing her husband's name.[27]

"Nita," may bumulong mula sa kanan. Sinipat ni Nita ang madilim na bahaging iyon. Nagitla siya sa marahas na pagyapos ng lalaki.

"Nita!" Humahalinghing ang lalaki. Hinalikan siya nito sa tenga, sa leeg, sa pisngi, sa mata, sa noo, sa ilong, salabi. Muli siyang nag-init, nanabik. Niyapos din nya ang lalaki, sinagot ang mga halik.

Naglakbay ang mga labi ng lalaki sa mukha ni Nita, sa leeg, balikat, dibdib. Nangangatal siya. Sumunod ay mabilis na gumapang ang mga kamay ng lalaki sa kanyang likod, pwet, hita, puson, dibdib, ulo. Sandali lang ay hinuhubaran na siya nito. Napahalinghing siya. Naghubad ang lalaki at inilatag sa lupa ang damit. Pagkatapos ay marahan nitong inihiga si Nita. At umindayog, umindayog ang mga aninong tinatanglawan ng buwan...Nanlambot ang mga hakbang ni Nita pabalik. Sumulyap siya muli sa buwan. Nagdahandahan siya nang malapit na sa dampa.

"Ka Nita?" Nangatal si Nita sa boses na bumati nang halos papasok na siya sa dampa. "Mga kasam po kami, Ka Nita. Wala po kayo kanina, e, nakituloy na ho kami. Nariyan ho ba si Ka Nato?" Kinalibutan si Nita nang marinig ang pangalan ng asawa.

Soriano's story is unprecedented, and not only because it is (I believe) the first torrid short story ever written by a CPP cadre. The libidinal energy of the story is intensified by the fact that Soriano never tells us who Ka Nita has made love to. Was it her husband, who perhaps broke away from his unit secretly to have this pre-arranged tryst with his wife? Or was it another man, an inamorato she has kept to satisfy a sexual longing her long-absent husband cannot satisfy?[28] The fact that Ka Nita froze in fear when she heard the name of her husband mentioned

---

[27] Zelda Soriano, "Mga Babae sa Kanilang Paghihintay," in *Kung Saan Ako Pupunta* (Manila: n.p. 1993), pp. 30-31.

[28] There is basis in real life for the fear of violating marriage norms. The expulsion of Fr. Conrado Balweg, (the famous priest-turned-guerilla) for example, was not merely because of his ideological disagreements with the Party. The CPP also penalized him for his womanizing, especially when he fathered a child by a woman. This was narrated in Levy Balgos de la Cruz, "Chagun," in *Muog*, pp. 231-34, 237.

Pag-Ibig, Pagtatalik at Pakikibaka 279

suggests that Soriano may want to impress on readers the intense discomfort that cadres or sympathizers undergo because they have to keep their bedside (or in this case, ricefield) liaisons secret for fear of Party criticism and punishment.

The official response to Soriano's piece appears to have been muted, although its exclusion from a collection of CPP literary works suggests that there was opposition to this candid sexual story.[29] When considered along with the Party's expressed concern for the preservation of female cadres' *kapakanan*, discussed above, the dilemma posed by Soriano's story inevitably brings us to a third source of tension: the revolution's attitude towards "The Woman's Question."

THE PARADOX OF WOMEN'S LIBERATION

What makes the CPP one of the more progressive organizations in Philippine society is its recognition of women's oppression by both the political system and by men. Through "On Marriage," the Party recognizes how women occupy a lower status in society, and how many obstacles have been created by the system and by men to prevent their participation in social causes. The CPP vowed that the liberation of women would be part of the social revolution, but added that a real women's movement can only come about if it is connected and embedded into the revolution. The CPP does not condone a distinct women's movement, calling it "sexist" because it accentuates the issues women specifically face as a group at the expense of the "broader" problems confronting the movement.

We are opposed to extreme valuation of the issue of women's liberation and its separation from the overall issue of liberation for the entire nation and oppressed classes. We oppose the "sexist" entry of women into the movement who are fixated about "the war between men and women" and who forget the greater and more important national and class issues. The promotion of the democratic rights of women and the struggle against feudal and bourgeois views regarding them should serve to strongly motivate them in working for the revolution and in unifying the oppressed and enslaved classes so that our class enemies will be dealt the strongest blow.

Tinutulan natin ang labis na pagpapatampok sa usapin ng pagpapalaya ng kababaihan at ang paghihiwalay nito sa pangkalahatang usapin ng pagpapalaya sa buong bansa at sa mga uring pinagsasamantalahan. Tinutulan natin ang 'seksistang' pagdadala sa kilusan ng kababaihan, na nagpapakalulong sa "gyera ng lalaki at babae" at nakakaligtaan ang mas malaki't mahahalagang pambansa at makauring usapin. Ang pagtataguyod sa mga demokratikong karapatan ng kababaihan at ang pagbaka sa mga pyudal at burgis na pananaw sa kanila ay dapat magsilbi sa puspusang pagpapakilos sa kanila sa rebolusyon at sa pagbubuklod ng mga uring pinagsasamantalahan at api para maituon ang pinakamalakas na hambalos sa mga kaaway sa uri.)

---

[29] In *Muog*, only one of Zelda Soriano's stories made it to the collection—the funny and witty "Temyo, Cleo at Banong," which also explores sexual attraction but lacks the lustful intensity of "Mga Babae sa Kanilang Paghihintay." *Muog*, pp. 341-45.

The clarification document proceeds to argue the folly of a separate "sexist" political posture.

...in advancing the women's movement, making a big issue of the difference of women should be avoided, though these could be remedied in the present practice of Party members and the vanguard elements of the masses. This will not be completely solved and changed in the lives of the broadest masses until complete radical changes in the relations of production and in the level of development of the forces of production take place.	. . . sa pagsulong ng kilusan ng kababaihan, dapat iwasan ang pagpapalaki sa usaping tulad ng hatian ng kababaihan, dapat iwasan ang pagpapalaki sa usaping tulad ng hatian sa mga gawaing bahay bagama't mareremedyuhan sa kasalukuyang praktika ng mga kasapi ng Partido at mga sulong na seksyon ng kilusang masa, ay *hindi na ganap na malulutas at hindi pa mababago sa pamumuhay ng malawak na masa, hangga't di nagaganap ang mga radikal na pagbabago sa mga relasyon sa produksyon at antas ng pag-unlad ng mga puwersa sa produksyon.* (italics mine)

The document then reiterates that only through the revolution can women's issues be decisively confronted, and only when a socialist society arises will women's problems be resolved.

The women's movement should be linked closely to the national democratic movement. And the full democratization of the family and the complete liberation of women from the restrictions of household work depend on the victory of the socialist revolution.	Ang kilusan ng kababaihan ay dapat mahigpit na isanib sa buong kilusang pambansa-demokratiko. At ang lubos na demokratisasyon ng pamilya at ang lubos na paglaya ng kababaihan sa mga restriksyon ng gawaing-bahay ay nakasalalay sa tagumpay ng rebolusyong sosyalista.)

The bases for the document's injunction on the woman question are, of course, not new. The Party's insistence that the women's movement be linked to the revolution was first articulated in the early years, when CPP cadres formed the *Malayang Kilusang ng Bagong Kababaihan* (Emancipated Association of New Women, or MAKIBAKA). Within MAKIBAKA, however, women cadres began to challenge this prevalent notion, sparking a healthy exchange between those (generally men) who advocated the subsumption of the women's struggle in the revolution and those (all women) who argued that gender and class revolution ran along parallel and supplementary lines with each other.[30]

---

[30] On this struggle, see Leonora Angeles, "Feminism and Nationalism: The Discourse on the Woman Question and Politics of the Women's Movement in the Philippines" (MA Thesis, University of the Philippines, 1989), pp. 152-56. See also *Maikling Kurso para sa Kababaihan sa Kanayunan*, as quoted by Monico Atienza, *Kilusang Pambansa-Demokratiko sa Wika* (Lunsod Quezon: Unibersidad ng Pilipinas-Sistema Sentro ng Wikang Pilipino, 1992), (The Language Issue and the National Democratic Movement) p. 101. The origins of this view can, of course, be

"On Marriage" suggests that the views of the first group prevailed. Yet, their ascendancy did not mean the woman's question was resolved; on the contrary, the final documents themselves contain internal inconsistencies that raise questions about the extent to which the CPP is serious about the woman's question. Both the rules and their clarification are admittedly protective of women and harsh in assigning punishment when it came to crimes against women. The severity of the penalty against rape or sexual molestation (death), for example, attests to such commitment.[31]

This concern, however, likewise evokes a patronizing attitude that regards women as weak. Judging from "On Marriage," women must be protected from their lovers (when it comes to pre-marital sex) as well as from rapists; they have to be shielded not only from molesters but even cadre husbands who defy the rules to make love to them. The CPP refuses to recognize women cadres as capable of protecting themselves and of valuing their sexuality and their bodies. No wonder then that Nita has to hide her trysts, or, in the case of the women guerrillas in *Gera*, they have to act manly or "Amazon-like," i.e., to hide their bodies, to show they can handle their men. Even then, those who seem to be most masculine can be perplexing to those attracted to them, as evidenced by a guerrilla's plaint about his female comrade in *Gera*, where this same character also complains that women are "mahirap talagang ispelingin" (difficult to figure out).[32]

In reaffirming the secondary status of women's liberation relative to the revolution, and referring to any attempt by women to put gender issues on a par with class war as "sexist," "On Marriage" puts an end to any debate about this issue within and outside the revolution. It also shows the Party's disdain for the attempts by both radical and bourgeois women to fight for their rights, and a disregard for the victories the diverse women's movements in the country had won through the years. Viewed from another angle, the very issuance of the document itself indicates that all is not well within the debate. The Party's pronouncement that class trumps gender, and socialism sits on top of feminism, is negated by the sexual panic that permeates the documents, implying that the debate is not resolved after all.

CONCLUSION

With "On Marriage," the CPP has tried to contain ruptures within its ranks on an issue—sexuality—that refuses to disappear. It appears that this attempt to resolve the issue has spawned more contradictions in the Party's interpretation of sexuality and in the actions of cadres, generating "a multiplicity of discourses" that may yet undermine its moral standing as a party of liberation.[33]

---

traced back to Mao. See "Report on an Investigation of the Peasant Movement in Hunan, March 27, Mao Tse-Tung, "*Selected Works*, vol. 1, 44, as quoted in *Quotations from Chairman Mao Tse Tung* (Peking: Foreign Language Press, 1972), p. 294.

[31] See for example, Gelacio Guillermo's description of the execution of a cadre convicted of a violation against women, which is the main gist of the short story, "Kasama," in *Muog*, p. iii.

[32] Firmeza, *Gera*, pp. 26-27.

[33] Mae Gwendolyn Henderson, "Speaking in Tongues: Dialogics, Dialectics and the Black Woman Writers' Literary Tradition," in *Feminists Theorize the Political*, ed. Judith Butler and Joan W. Scott (New York: Routledge, 1992), p. 149.

The failure of the guidelines to deal with the tensions and anomalies associated with sexuality also ironically makes the Party look and sound like its reactionary antagonist—the Catholic Church. Both institutions create an artificial and socially constructed definition of the sex act, invoking almost the same reason for limiting it to married couples and restricting it among the unmarried—i.e., that the former is legitimate and so endurable, while the latter is illicit and therefore immoral. These parallel doctrines in conservative and radical discourses run counter to the axis most historians map out when illustrating the positive changes associated with the public discussion of sex since the 1960s up to the end of the twentieth century.

For here is the paradox: the Communist Party of the Philippines owes its lineage not merely to the thoughts of Mao Tse-tung and Marx, but to a broader tradition called the Enlightenment. As part of its radical strain, the CPP is, in theory, expected to abide by the liberative features of this "movement," including—I would argue—the expansion and progress of gender and sexual relations. In reality, however, the process of expanding modernity has been uneven and contradictory. It is liberative in certain areas, especially class, but pretty much regressive in others, like gender and sexuality.

"On Marriage" has become just another representation of what the early-twentieth-century feminist Charlotte Gilman called the "androcentric," i.e., it continues to relegate women revolutionaries to a role "of a preposition in relation to man, above him or below him, before him, behind him, beside him, a wholly relative experience."[34] This, in the final analysis, is the main contradiction behind this fascinating but flawed document. While it may have considerably advanced the rights of women within the revolution—especially with respect to courtship and divorce—by regulating sexuality it remains a document permeated with a male bias.

Here is a Philippine radical version of what Angus McLaren calls "sexual panics"—that fear that sex among young unmarried couples, the unauthorized sex by married cadres, or, worse, an affair between a *masa* sympathizer and a guerrilla are debased, corrupt, reactionary and thus have to be prevented.[35] The CPP appears to replicate the warnings of a 1930 Austrian socialist that the country's youth "must be prepared to fight against the sex drive when it challenges the demands of socialist morality."[36] In the long term, one wonders what sexual relationships would look like if ever the CPP should win power and preside over the People's Republic of the Philippines.

---

[34] Charlotte Perkins Gilman, *The Man-Made World; or, Our Androcentric Culture* (New York: Charlton Co., 1911), p. 20.

[35] Angus McLaren, *Twentieth-Century Sexuality: A History* (Oxford: Basil Blackwell, 1999), pp. 9-22, 143-92.

[36] As quoted by McLaren, ibid., p. 40.

THE DIALECTICS OF "EDSA DOS": URBAN SPACE, COLLECTIVE MEMORY, AND THE SPECTACLE OF COMPROMISE

Eva-Lotta E. Hedman[1]

I. INTRODUCTION

During four days in January 2001, a massive show of "People Power" once again ushered in a transfer of executive powers into the hands of a new—and female—president through an extra-constitutional process in the Philippines. Perhaps unsurprisingly, this second round of "People Power" reverberated with a notable nostalgia for the first showdown, in February 1986, between Corazon C. Aquino and Ferdinand E. Marcos. Nonetheless, the inept corruption of popularly elected Joseph "Erap" Ejercito Estrada, and the political maneuvering of vice-president Gloria Macapagal-Arroyo, also suggested a rather different situation from 1986, when the ailing dictator Marcos, propped up by electoral fraud and loyalist troops, confronted the "moral crusade" and popular support of widow-housewife Aquino. Moreover, the campaign to oust Estrada from his presidency in mid-term remained rather more limited—in terms of mobilizational scope and momentum—when compared to the tidal wave of opposition mounting against the Marcos regime in the mid-1980s. Finally, while the manifest drama and courage of the earlier "People Power" response captured the popular imagination far beyond Manila as foreign mass media, government spokesmen, and observer missions expressed their support and admiration in 1986, at the peak of the so-called Second Cold War, there was considerably less international attention and, notably, less enthusiasm generated by the conflict of 2001 in the face of what was widely viewed abroad as an irregular transfer of executive powers in the Philippines. Yet, as suggested by references to the "EDSA Revolution" and "EDSA Dos," the two episodes of "People Power" in 1986 and 2001 were clearly linked in the popular imagination and in

---

[1] Research for this essay was conducted primarily in metropolitan Manila from September 2000-January 2001 with support from the British Academy and the Economic and Social Research Council, U.K. In Manila, research also benefited from contacts with the Institute for Popular Democracy and the Third World Studies Center at the University of the Philippines. As ever, responsibility for any errors of judgement or fact rests with the author alone.

analytical terms by the shared geography of mobilization—on the major highway of Epifanio de los Santos Avenue, commonly known as EDSA.

In the intervening years between "People Power" I and II in the Philippines, the world of course witnessed a number of similarly spectacular displays. In Southeast Asia alone, comparisons have been made with reference to the "failures" of "People Power" in Burma (1988) and Malaysia (1998), and its more celebrated outcomes in Thailand (1992) and Indonesia (1998).[2] In general, the scholarly literature ranges from cursory listings of "cases" of "People Power" in comparative studies on democratization to detailed descriptions of the social composition and political discourse of such campaigns in single-country monographs. In analytical terms, there is a common tendency to privilege voluntarism, agency, and contingency in the existing literature, at the expense of more systematic interrogations into the kinds of structures of power shaping the nature and direction of "the people" as it emerges to lay claim to the nation-state in the parliament of the streets.

While there are several ways to approach these lacunae in the literature, including those promised by a rigorous comparative historical sociology, the return to "People Power" at the very site that first contributed this phenomenon to the broader repertoire and discourse of popular protest provides an especially illuminating perspective. Perhaps not unlike homecomings in general, the second round of "People Power" in the Philippines, or in its local designation, "EDSA Dos," prompts the recognition of something strangely familiar and, notably, this familiarity rendered strange. "EDSA" (Epifanio de los Santos Avenue), initially conceived as a circumferential road to bypass the (old) downtown, but eventually transformed into the heavily clogged main artery of the sprawling metropolis of Manila, once again became an instant moniker for the spectacular drama that cut short one Philippine presidency and launched another.

The significance of EDSA as a center of gravity for such recurring "People Power" episodes is perhaps most readily apparent when considered in light of its rather peculiar place in Metro Manila. First of all, EDSA, or rather the intersection of Epifanio de los Santos Avenue with Ortigas Avenue which emerged as the spectacular site for the unfolding of this "People Power" drama, is nowhere near any symbolic or official seats of political power, whether the presidential residence at Malacañang Palace, the House of Representatives, or the Philippine Senate building. Second, despite recent developments, this part of the metropolis remains at best a second (or, after Binondo, a third) wheel to Makati, the real center of corporate and financial power, as evidenced by the location of the Philippine Stock Exchange, and some 90 percent of the headquarters for the top one thousand corporations, as well as all international banks, in the country.

Moreover, while in hindsight it may seem obvious that the making of "EDSA Dos" came to involve an element of appropriation, and thus to anticipate a return to the scene of the first round in 1986, it is also revealing that, for quite some time, the mounting opposition against Estrada did not seek to lay claim to EDSA. Indeed, it

---

[2] See, for example, Bertil Lintner, *Outrage: Burma's Struggle for Democracy* (Hong Kong: Review Publishing Company, 1989); Farish A. Noor, "Looking for *Reformasi*: The Discursive Dynamics of the Reformasi Movement and Its Prospects as a Political Project," *Indonesia and the Malay World*, 27,77 (March 1999): 5-18; William A. Callahan, *Imagining Democracy: Reading "The Events of May" in Thailand* (Singapore: Institute of Southeast Asian Studies, 1998); and Robin Madrid, "Islamic Students in the Indonesian Student Movement, 1998-1999: Forces for Moderation," *Bulletin of Concerned Asian Scholars*, 31,3 (1999): 17-32.

would be mistaken to underestimate the political difficulties and risks of doing so in view of the putschist origins and subsequent uses of the first "People Power." At the same time, it is probably also the case that the largest complexes of state coercive apparatuses in the metropolis (Camps Aguinaldo and Crame) and the most sacralized of "People Power" monuments in the country (the so-called "EDSA Shrine"), remained of rather limited strategic or symbolic significance in the political landscape and social imaginary of the contemporary Philippines. Despite their relative proximity to the intersection with Ortigas Avenue, for example, the two camps lining EDSA did not seem to loom very large on the mental maps of the gathering crowd. In this regard, it is perhaps not insignificant that the restructuring of the Armed Forces of the Philippines [AFP] in 1992, prompted a certain demilitarization—and demystification—of this urban space as Camp Crame was transformed from military barracks to –an often 'open gates'–national headquarters of the Philippines National Police (PNP). In addition, police and military forces alike were in many ways most conspicuous by their relative absence and notable restraint during the several months of demonstrations prior to "EDSA Dos." Thus, the emergence of "EDSA Dos" in close proximity to these camps and this shrine serves as a suggestive reminder of the kinds of collective forgetting and re-membering at work when history is made to repeat itself, in a fashion.

While located on the very corner of EDSA and Ortigas, the so-called "EDSA Shrine," with its thirty-five-foot bronze and brass Virgin figure towering over a chapel constructed opposite the Robinson Galleria Shopping Mall, probably suffers from much the same general indifference as other official monuments do in the wider social imaginary of people who actually live, work, and commute in this metropolis. Commissioned for the official commemoration of "People Power I" in February 1989, the Virgin statue is situated in such a way that, from a street-level point of view, it remains virtually invisible by virtue of its very height.[3] At the same time, it tends to disappear into the miniaturized city-scape revealed by the kind of roving bird's-eye perspective provided from surrounding "fly-over" highways and the elevated Metropolitan Rail Transit (MRT). Thus, it is perhaps unsurprising that, according to one recent study, not a single person from among five urban poor communities, when asked to identify the "most important places in Metro Manila," mentioned "the People Power monument at the Ortigas Avenue intersection."[4] Of course, official commemorations of "People Power I," with (former) president Aquino and Manila Archbishop Jaime Cardinal Sin in prominent attendance and with broadcast media allowing for the wider circulation of these events as virtual spectacle, have, at least in part, served to celebrate this same site as a "hallowed ground" of sorts. However, there is little evidence to suggest that the EDSA Shrine had already captured the popular imagination by January 2001, whether as a destination for personal pilgrimages (such as those made for decades around the metropolis to attend mass at the churches of Baclaran on Wednesdays, St. Jude's on Thursdays, or Quiapo on Fridays), or as a place invested with larger

---

[3] Artist-sculptor Virginia Ty-Navarro completed the project after a reported sixteen months and P12 million. While this Virgin originally featured "Asian eyes," which Ty-Navarro reportedly refused to alter on request, she has, upon the death of the artist-sculptor, apparently undergone enough of a face job to make her look "more like a popular mestiza movie star." See "A Tribute to Edsa Virgin sculptress," *Philippine Daily Inquirer*, February 25, 2001.

[4] Erhard Berner, *Defending a Place in the City: Localities and the Struggle for Urban Land in Manila* (Quezon City: Ateneo de Manila University Press, 1997), p. 112.

symbolic significance for city or nation in general. (Arguably, the gathering of supporters of the by-then-ousted and jailed Estrada for "People Power III" in April-May 2001 suggests that, post-EDSA Dos, such a designation has entered into a wider social imaginary.)

Indeed, a review of the wave of protest rallies in the months prior to "People Power II" further undermines any a priori assumptions that EDSA figured as a "natural" center of gravity for the mounting political opposition against Estrada. Such protest actions found their way, at various times, to a number of different places in the city, including both the House of Representatives and the Philippine Senate, as well as the private homes of Estrada's political and personal associates.[5] On closer inspection, two alternative protest trajectories, neither of which, significantly, led to EDSA, can be charted time and again during much of this period. In this regard, a discernible pattern emerged, with demonstrators converging, on the one hand, on Mendiola, the dusty, narrow street connecting Manila's old downtown and political battlegrounds with the gates to Malacañang Palace, and, on the other hand, on Ayala, the immaculate wide avenue of Makati, the premier financial and business district of the Philippines. Thus, before examining the events at EDSA, the essay considers these two contrasting—and competing—sites of collective action during the wave of protest that marked the final months of the Estrada presidency.

II. WELCOME TO MENDIOLA

While hardly the first signs of protest against the Estrada presidency, the "Never Again" rally organized for the twenty-eighth anniversary of the (official) declaration of martial law, September 21, 2000, in many ways cracked open the floodgates for the wave of street demonstrations that continued, with some ebbs and flows, until the spectacular endgame at EDSA five months later. By 10 a.m. that day, a growing number of demonstrators had gathered at the otherwise heavily trafficked Welcome Rotunda (or, as announced on the symbolic gateway monument erected in its center, *Mabuhay Lungsod)* on the border of Manila and Quezon Cities. With many supporters arriving in groups by jeepney, a marching formation emerged with routine-like efficiency as if to confirm the presence of veteran organizers and seasoned activists. Indeed, many of the "usual suspects" had turned up—Bagong Alyansang Makabayan (Bayan, New Nationalist Alliance), Gabriela, Kilusang Mayo Uno (KMU, May 1st Movement), and Kilusang Magbubukid ng Pilipinas (KMP, Philippine Peasant Movement)—along with some newly formed groups such as Kalipunan ng Damayang Mahihirap (Kadamay, Task Force Damayan), who protested the lack of government support for the victims of the collapsed dumpsite at Payatas, Manila.

With an octopus effigy of a two-faced Estrada and his cronies in the lead, the demonstrators posed for about a dozen media cameras before starting their long march down España, filing past the University of Santo Tomas (UST) where another assembly was heading in the same direction, continuing along Quezon

---

[5] Senator Miriam Defensor-Santiago's home in Quezon City and the so-called "Boracay Mansion" of presidential (third) "wife" Laarni Enriquez became the targets of such protests. During "All Souls," several cemeteries in metropolitan Manila and elsewhere in the country also became sites for such demonstrations, albeit quite small in scale.

Boulevard and crossing the Pasig River to enter the grounds of Liwasang Bonifacio (formerly Plaza Lawton). With the neo-classical pillars of the imposing Philippine Post Office as background, a motley crew of opposition politicians, priests and nuns, entertainers, and activists took turns on the crowded makeshift stage, flanked by banners and placards, for the next few hours. Meanwhile, people were alternately cheering, milling about, or cooling their feet in the fountain, buying food and drink from the street vendors, or even Che Guevara, Mao, and Lenin t-shirts from the back of a truck. By the late afternoon, a smaller contingent of protesters, perhaps some 1,500 people, marched from Liwasang Bonifacio back across the Pasig and through Quiapo to reach Mendiola, where a large dispatch of policemen, backed up by several fire-trucks and other six-wheelers, blocked further passage in the vicinity of the presidential palace. Although difficult to verify, crowd estimates ranged from the hopeful predictions of organizers, who claimed 30,000 participants, to the following day's media reports, which claimed that, at Liwasang Bonifacio, "the number of protesters peaked only at around 10,000." [6]

On November 14, 2000, declared a "National Day of Protest" by the mounting Estrada opposition, another rally began assembling at Welcome Rotunda in the late morning, headed for Mendiola by way of Liwasang Bonifacio. This time, the protest marchers gathering at Welcome Rotunda were joined by opposition politicians, most prominently Manuel Villar (Rep., Las Piñas), who, in his capacity as Speaker of the House, had sent the impeachment case [against President Estrada] to the Senate before being ousted by a majority vote in Congress only the day before. Having thus joined the parliaments of the street, Villar declared: "It feels better here where I can be the Speaker of the people."[7] In addition to the labor and farmers' organizations, as well as religious groups and NGOs, gathering at Welcome, more than a thousand students also joined, marching from the country's public and private flagship institutions of higher education, University of the Philippines (UP) at Diliman and Ateneo de Manila University (Ateneo).

On this day, more protesters and some politicians also rallied at Liwasang Bonifacio, and many eventually joined in the march to Mendiola. With early arrivals moving down along Mendiola as well as Legarda Streets, and with the rearguard stretching deep down CM Recto and Morayta Streets, this protest counted, at its peak, 80,000 people, according to one estimate.[8] Once again, those who sought to continue onwards found steel fences and police buses blocking the approach to the presidential palace, with so-called anti-riot police standing guard. In the immediate vicinity of Malacañang Palace, more police and barbed wire awaited would-be trespassers (although the government had reportedly issued instructions to exercise maximum tolerance vis-a-vis the political opposition).

---

[6] "Protesters urge Estrada to quit," *Philippine Daily Inquirer*, September 22, 2000.

[7] "Last Quarter Storm: Broad alliance of business, labor, left, NGOs, academe, politicos," *Philippine Daily Inquirer*, November 15, 2000.

[8] This figure was noted by the *Philippine Daily Inquirer*, while rally organizers reportedly estimated "at least 65,000 protesters" in the area around Mendiola. By contrast, official police counts varied from ten thousand (according to PNP Director General Panfilo Lacson) to eighteen thousand (according to Metro Manila Commander General Edgardo Aglipay). See "Last Quarter Storm," *Philippine Daily Inquirer*, November 15, 2000.

Nonetheless, demonstrators proceeded to bring two trucks to the intersection of Mendiola, Recto, and Legarda Streets, where they, under the changing traffic lights, served as a large makeshift stage during [what organizers termed] the *"pamorningan* street party and concert." Surrounded by decrepit three-story buildings, with older local stores and newer fast-food chains opening onto these streets, veteran protest singers and a younger generation of "alternative" performers worked the crowds with the assistance of an impressive sound system, within earshot of the presidential palace guard.

III. CONFETTI ON AYALA

On October 18, 2000, within a week of long-time provincial warlord Luis "Chavit" Singson (Governor, Ilocos Sur) presenting the real smoking gun against the Estrada presidency to the Philippine Congress, Ayala Avenue was transformed by the first of many rallies to assemble in Makati City during the weeks and months before "People Power II."[9] Gathering in the long shadow of the glassed, steel-and-concrete structures towering over this multiple-lane avenue, which cuts a straight line through Makati's international finance and business district, the rally did not start until mid-afternoon, thus facilitating the participation of office workers and their managers. After the National Anthem, the rally featured prayers by Catholic, Protestant, and Muslim clergy, followed by speeches from a string of high-profile Estrada critics from among the business and labor sectors, right- and left-wing organizations, and opposition politicians, including, for the first time, Singson himself. In large part, the program was organized by Lakas ng Bayan (Strength of the Nation) and National Union of Christian Democrats (NUCD), the main political opposition to Estrada's ruling coalition in the Senate and, to a lesser extent, in the House of Representatives. Centered on the large intersection where Ayala Avenue meets Paseo de Roxas, this rally drew an estimated ten thousand supporters—and a shower of confetti from paper shredders on the higher floors of the surrounding office buildings.[10]

After this first protest action in Makati, organizers called on the anti-Estrada opposition to return to Ayala Avenue for weekly rallies. In the weeks to follow, Ayala thus saw an estimated ten thousand people demanding Estrada's resignation on October 25, another rally featuring a mock parade of the president's many "wives" on November 8, and a reported twenty thousand protesters chanting "Erap Resign!" on November 14.[11] An unusual spectacle, billed as a "People Power Lunch," was held at the corner of Ayala Avenue and Paseo de Roxas on November 29. Sponsored in part by the Makati Business Club and "hosted" by socialites from

---

[9] Singson's smoking gun was, of course, his charge that Estrada had received more than P400 million out of the P545 million total *jueteng* (an illegal numbers game) collection nationwide from November 1998 until August 2000, with presidential relatives receiving the rest. See, for example, "Biggest jueteng lord," *Philippine Daily Inquirer*, November 15, 2000.

[10] See, for example, "Rich, poor, left, right attend rally," *Philippine Daily Inquirer*, October 19, 2000.

[11] See, for example, the following articles in the *Philippine Daily Inquirer*: "Pro-, anti-Erap rallies sweep RP," October 26, 2000; and "Last Quarter Storm," November 15, 2000. For reports of the protest action of urban poor and striking workers demanding the resignation of Estrada and all elected officials, a protest that also found its way to Ayala Avenue, see "Makati rally seeks ouster of Erap, Gloria," *Philippine Daily Inquirer*, October 28, 2000.

Forbes Park and other nearby exclusive residential subdivisions (the so-called "villages"), a much-touted symbolic *salo-salo* (sharing of food) awaited the urban and rural poor marchers converging on Makati to demonstrate their opposition to Estrada. Amidst thousands of protesters and not a few media cameras, an ostentatiously simple meal of pork- and chicken *adobo* with rice was thus served at a long table where some bonafide poor people were seated side by side with finger-licking businessmen and smiling socialites in peasant straw-hats.[12]

The anti-Estrada demonstrations briefly sketched above thus provide illuminating examples of a broader and, in some measure, familiar pattern in the contestation, through collective action, of modern citizenship in the nation's foremost city. While the recent opposition to Estrada, not unlike previous rounds of protest against the Marcos dictatorship, at times surfaced in different parts of the metropolis, the demonstrations in Manila and the rallies in Makati described above indicate a certain dialectical movement in the prelude to "People Power" (I and II). That is, the marching on Mendiola in the vicinity of the presidential palace, on the one hand, and the assembling on Ayala Avenue at the heart of the country's premier business district, on the other hand, suggest not merely alternate trajectories, but also, significantly, competing dynamics of popular mobilization.

IV. POLITICAL PROTEST, COLLECTIVE MEMORY, AND PUBLIC SPACE

A closer, if necessarily brief, survey of these distinct urban spaces in Manila and Makati helps to illuminate the peculiar dialectic of popular mobilization against the Estrada presidency. In this regard, Manila's narrow streets and old neighborhoods stand in sharp contrast to the expansive avenues and new architecture of Makati. In addition to the wide gap separating these urban spaces in terms of public infrastructure and private investment, what might be referred to as a deeper structure of feeling also sets Mendiola Street and Ayala Avenue worlds apart in the social imaginary. In this vein, these sites lend themselves to certain (but not other) practices in everyday life, and also, significantly, provide distinct milieus for the mobilization of some (but not any) kind of collective memory, including the appropriation of previous rounds of struggle.[13]

As noted above, the anti-Estrada protests in Manila typically traced a trajectory from Welcome Rotunda, or *Mabuhay Lungsod*, toward Mendiola, with a major rallying point along the way at *Liwasang Bonifacio* (formerly Plaza Lawton). In terms of urban geography, "Welcome" marks the intersection where Quezon Avenue arrives from the center of government agencies and, another jeepney ride or two away, the suburban campuses of UP at Diliman and Ateneo, to meet with España Boulevard, which, in turn, continues in the direction of old Manila. In addition, "Welcome" stands at the crossroads of Mayon Avenue and E. Rodriguez Boulevard, which provide further links to many of the older backstreets and surrounding neighborhoods, where labor-intensive repair shops of various kinds vie for space with *sari-sari* stores and other smaller foodmarts. Moving along España

---

[12] See, for example, the following articles in the *Philippine Daily Inquirer*: "People Power Lunch," November 26, 2000; and "Rally bridges gap between rich, poor," November 30, 2000.

[13] Henri Lefebvre, *The Production of Space*, trans. Donald Nicholson-Smith (Oxford: Blackwell Publishers, 1991). See also the essays in *Yale French Studies: Special Issue on "Everyday Life,"* No. 73 (1987).

Boulevard, usually crowded by jeepney and other (privately owned) "public" transport vehicles, in the direction of the *Liwasang Bonifacio*, these protests also followed a path between Manila's oldest and most populous working-class and urban poor districts, Tondo and Sampaloc.

Continuing the length of España Boulevard, protest rallies reached the University of Santo Tomas (UST), thus approaching Manila's university belt of less prestigious and more crowded colleges, as well as the many vocational schools and technical institutes in this area. Rather than marching directly through the thick of the university belt to Mendiola, these protest rallies regrouped at *Liwasang Bonifacio*, situated across from Binondo and Quiapo at the very heart of old downtown Manila. Formerly known as Plaza Lawton, this site was renamed after the Philippine Revolution's most celebrated working-class hero, Andres Bonifacio, whose statue was erected here in 1963.[14] As suggested by the continued reference to "Lawton" as a destination on jeepney and bus routes, however, this plaza remains perhaps more firmly lodged in the everyday urban social imaginary as a key commuter transit point rather than as an official national commemorative site. In any event, these protest rallies regrouped at *Liwasang Bonifacio* for the final march to Mendiola and, as far as possible, toward Malacañang Palace.

Tracing a route through the areas with the highest combined concentration of student, labor, and urban poor populations not only in Manila, but in the entire metropolis or anywhere else in the Philippines, these demonstrations also provided occasions for the recollection of something other than the practices of everyday life inscribed in this social milieu. That is, this wave of protest actions pointed beyond both the everyday experience (e.g., heavy traffic) and the official commemoration (e.g., historical monuments) that characterize certain urban sites to reveal glimpses of other forms of sociality and politics more deeply embedded in these spaces. In this vein, rallies and marches served in some measure to reconnect the dots on a larger map of prior rounds of struggle, as if recovering, through a kind of spatial reconstruction, what has been referred to elsewhere as "the city of collective memory."[15]

The anti-Estrada rallies described above can be located at three particular points—Welcome, *Liwasang Bonifacio,* and Mendiola—which also correspond to key landmarks of what one observer has referred to as "a fearful geography" of street protests in the late 1960s and early 1970s.[16] Similarly, these points can be identified on the larger map of radical protests against the Marcos regime in the mid-1980s. In this regard, the recent protests at Welcome cannot but invite comparisons with earlier rounds in ways that highlight a certain genealogy of left-wing political activism. To some extent, the Welcome rallies allowed for a kind of ritual celebration of an overall family resemblance and sense of belonging (despite, or perhaps rather because of, all the "collateral damage" due to internal splits and feuding) across several generations of leftist activists. In gathering at

---

[14] The Bonifacio Monument, by Guillermo Tolentino, shows Andres Bonifacio looking out over the plaza, his back turned to the Philippine Post Office Building, itself a monument of sorts to the American colonial period.

[15] M. Christine Boyer, *The City of Collective Memory: Its Historical Imagery and Architectural Entertainments* (Cambridge, MA: MIT Press, 1994).

[16] José F. Lacaba, *Days of Quiet, Nights of Rage: The First Quarter Storm and Other Related Events* (Manila: Asphodel Books, 1986).

Welcome, a new generation of NGO and other political activists thus, in a sense, claimed a certain lineage stretching back, perhaps most proudly, to the first batches of radical students who descended on this site from UP in the late 1960s and early 1970s, and the second wave of activists, the League of Filipino Students, who returned here in the early to mid-1980s.[17] Once a symbolic bridge of sorts between, on the one hand, the emerging politico-cultural Maoist vanguard on UP's privileged suburban frontier and, on the other hand, the growing numbers of activist students, especially young men, from the so-called "diploma mills" in the crowded old downtown, Welcome has served as a space that anchors counter-hegemonic struggles in collective memory, thus suggesting at least the possibility of a partial recall amidst the amnesia of official history.

If Welcome has invited the revisiting of such alternative beginnings, it has been Mendiola that, perhaps without parallel, has pointed to certain counter-hegemonic trajectories and oppositional genealogies in the political history of the metropolis. That is, at Mendiola, what has been referred to elsewhere as the "power of place" has assumed particular significance for the recovery of a politics of protest in this urban landscape.[18] In this regard, it is perhaps no coincidence that Mendiola Bridge emerged as the site of the most direct and, at times, violent confrontations between protesters and government troops in the city during the late pre-martial years. Notably, during the "Battle of Mendiola" on January 30, 1970, student and other radical protesters fought military and police forces for hours over the bridge separating the area surrounding the presidential palace from the heart of downtown where the battle then continued to rage throughout the night.[19] Since then, the "Battle of Mendiola" has left something of an indelible mark on this site in the urban landscape as evidenced by the countless protest actions converging here over the years, including those of the recent anti-Estrada opposition.[20]

In contrast to this particular protest route from Welcome to Mendiola, what may perhaps be referred to as the "place memories" associated with Ayala Avenue of Makati have been of a rather different provenance. On the one hand, the trajectory from Welcome to Mendiola recalls an era in the late 1960s which, at the same time, marked the end of a certain formula for post-war economic growth and prosperity in the wider social imaginary, and the beginning of what emerged as the new dominant "disloyal" opposition, the Communist Party of the Philippines (CPP) and its armed wing, the New People's Army (NPA). On the other hand, the rallies converging on Ayala Avenue hark back to a period in the early 1980s characterized by the exhaustion of the peculiar crony capitalism that evolved under Marcos's long reign and the emergence of a so-called moderate

---

[17] On the 1960s and 1970s, see Lacaba, *Days of Quiet*. On the 1980s, see Aurora Javate-de Dios, Petronilo Bn. Daroy, and Lorna Kalaw-Tirol, eds., *Dictatorship and Revolution: Roots of People Power* (Manila: Conspectus, 1988).

[18] Dolores Hayden, *The Power of Place: Urban Landscapes as Public History* (Cambridge, MA: MIT Press, 1995).

[19] See, especially, Lacaba, *Days of Quiet*.

[20] Note the return of "red rallies" here during the wave of mounting mobilization against Marcos in the mid-1980s. Note also the "Mendiola Massacre" as a key turning point during the early period of post-Marcos restoration (January 1987).

opposition—with the Makati Business Club in the vanguard—against his ailing authoritarian regime.[21]

As noted above, the anti-Estrada protests in Makati focused on Ayala Avenue, which cuts a wide and near-straight passage for about two kilometers from EDSA to Sen. G. Puyat Avenue (still better known by its former name, Buendia). Completed in 1958, the multiple-lane Ayala Avenue was once a runway of the first commercial airport of the Philippines, the Nielson Airport, inaugurated in 1937. Touted as an unparalleled example of private urban planning, albeit with critical political support along the way, Makati was developed into residential and commercial areas according to specific zoning regulations in the post-war period.[22] Following the construction of the Meralco-owned Rockwell Power Plant in Makati after the war, the country's first planned residential subdivisions soon began to appear in the vicinity, starting with the most exclusive of such so-called "villages," Forbes Park, in 1948, and continuing with San Lorenzo (1952), Bel-Air (1954), Urdaneta (1957), San Miguel (1960), Magallanes, and Dasmarinas (1962). Meanwhile, Ayala y Compania, subsequently incorporated as Ayala Securities Corporation, commissioned some of the first buildings to rise along Ayala Avenue from one of the country's (soon-to-be) best-known architects, Leandro V. Locsin, allegedly to "serve as models for those who wanted to put up their own edifices in the area."[23]

Indeed, during this early phase in the development of the country's premier business and financial district, a number of prominent Filipino families and multinational corporations quickly established themselves on Ayala Avenue—including the Rufinos, Sarmientos, Sycip, Gorres, and Velayo, Philippine Airlines, and San Miguel Corporation, as well as B. F. Goodrich, Goodyear, Colgate-Palmolive, Vicks International, and First National City Bank. By the mid-1980s, Makati had come to host the headquarters of some 90 percent of the top one thousand corporations. Only a few years later, moreover, an estimated 90 percent of the growing number of international bank headquarters (and more than half of their Philippine counterparts, too) could be found in Makati. Finally, despite pressure to relocate to the newer Ortigas Complex, trading continues to date on the floors of the imposing Stock Exchange building, along Ayala Avenue, between the intersections with Makati Avenue and Paseo de Roxas.

While Makati's social demographics and local politics reflect marked diversity and complexity due to the presence of urban poor areas (notably populous and thus vote-rich Guadalupe, which received its city charter in 1996), its

---

[21] See, for example, Mark R. Thompson, *The Anti-Marcos Opposition* (New Haven, CT: Yale University Press, 1995); and Eva-Lotta E. Hedman, "Whose Business is it Anyway? Free and Fair Elections in the Philippines," *Public Policy*, 2,3 (July-September 1998): 145-70.

[22] For brief glimpses into the making of Makati, see, for example, "Industry Succeeds in Makati," *Manila Times*, November 16, 1953 (Makati Supplement); "Makati: A Boom Town," *Philippine Graphic*, April 14, 1965, p. 6; and "Private Development of Makati," *Philippines Herald*, April 14, 1967.

[23] Manuel D. Duldulao, *A Vision of Makati—The City* (Manila: Reyes Publishing, Inc., 1996), p. 45. Some of the facts and figures summarized here can be found in this glossy coffee-table publication, which also provides anecdotal evidence of some key family members and their relations with prominent political figures from the days of American colonialism, post-war occupation, and post-colonial "special relations" in the Philippines. The author mentions, for example, Don Enrique Zobel and Manuel Quezon, Joseph R. McMicking (who married Zobel's daughter, Mercedes) and General Douglas MacArthur, the Ayalas and Manuel Roxas.

residential villages and business district remain the most ambitiously realized example to date of privatized and segregated "public space" in the Philippines.[24] As a result, it is perhaps unsurprising that protest rallies held in the heart of Makati's financial and corporate quarters appeared to reflect and reproduce sensibilities—or, perhaps, "geographical imaginations"—quite different from those in Manila described above.[25] That is, despite deliberate efforts by organizers to coordinate anti-Estrada protests across these two realms of the larger metropolis, as well as joining social forces of rich and poor, political elites and activists, within them, the Manila and Makati rallies, upon closer inspection, reveal certain discernible patterns of difference which, in turn, point to more enduring effects of these peculiar urban landscapes upon the mobilization of collective action.

The repertoire of protest showed notable variations from the Mendiola marches to the Ayala assemblies.[26] First of all, compared to the ritualized marching to Mendiola, across a social landscape dotted with the debris of prior rounds of struggle, the Makati rallies provided little in the way of actual movement beyond a few sterile blocks on Ayala Avenue itself. Significantly, there was no attempt to (re)trace anything like an epic journey to arrive at Ayala from the exclusive residential villages and/or the urban poor areas of Makati, which instead remained firmly contained—worlds apart—in the social imaginary. Second, in sharp contrast to the informal sit-ins at Mendiola, where at times thousands of people made themselves at home by crowding together, sharing food, and even sleeping, on the streets, the protest gatherings on Ayala Avenue remained entirely "standing" affairs as if to counteract the dwarfing effect of the surrounding office towers. In this regard, the "People Power Lunch" mentioned above—where, of course, chairs and tables were provided—suggested the notable exception to prove the rule.[27] Third, the prominence of such official symbols as the national anthem and flag in Makati also stood in marked contrast to the old slogans and protest songs which echoed the organized Left's opposition to the Marcos regime, as well as to the newer and more eclectic repertoire of a younger generation, heard and seen during the anti-Estrada demonstrations at Mendiola. While a departure from the official protocol of national anthem and flag, the return of the confetti rallies to Makati also underlined the extent to which such a decidedly "local" innovation in the repertoire of urban protest—with business and financial managers and staff

---

[24] See, for example, Glenda M. Gloria, "Makati: One City, Two Worlds," in *Boss: Five Case Studies of Local Politics in the Philippines,* ed. Jose F. Lacaba (Pasig: Philippine Center for Investigative Journalism, 1995), pp. 65-101. The construction of 'Ayala Alabang' is a more recent example of such privatized segregation on the suburban frontiers of metropolitan Manila, reinforced by road tolls at the highway exits and limited provisions of 'public transport' in the area itself. In this version of a 'total village,' residents enjoy easy access to their own church, school, golf courses, shopping mall, and even a brand new hospital.

[25] See Derek Gregory, *Geographical Imaginations* (Oxford: Blackwell Publishers, 1994).

[26] For an early discussion of protest repertoires, see Charles Tilly, *From Mobilization to Revolution* (Reading, MA: Addison-Wesley, 1978). For a more recent elaboration, see, for example, Sidney Tarrow, *Power in Movement: Social Movements, Collective Action and Politics* (Cambridge: Cambridge University Press, 1994).

[27] In the words of Guillermo Luz, executive director of the Makati Business Club: "Admittedly, this is a very unusual event for business. But we thought it was something worthwhile pursuing because we need to reach out and talk to other people and meet other faces. . . . " *Philippine Daily Inquirer,* November 30, 2000.

using office shredders and windows in the towers lining Ayala Avenue to celebrate, once again, the opposition against a corrupt presidency—remained a phenomenon not quite of the street, but rather of another realm, entrenched high above in the corporate structures looming so large in this social landscape.[28]

As these urban spaces emerged as alternate and competing centers of gravity in the wave of protests against (former) president Estrada during the period from August 2000 to January 2001, the Manila and Makati rallies also highlighted possibilities and limitations associated with the mobilization of the "past in the present crisis."[29] On the one hand, through deliberate efforts on the part of organizers as well as more spontaneous and dispersed forms of remembering, the anti-Estrada opposition drew inspiration from previous rounds of struggle such as the First Quarter Storm of 1970, reincarnated as the "Last Quarter Storm" in Manila thirty years later, and from specific repertoires of protest such as the confetti rallies of Makati in the mid-1980s. Whether marching on Mendiola or rallying at Ayala, the anti-Estrada opposition thus succeeded, at least in some measure due to these kinds of "citations" to prior struggles and protest repertoires, to bring out some of the old guard and to recruit participants among younger generations, as well as to attract support from a broader spectrum of social forces and political coalitions.

On the other hand, the nature and direction of the protests against Estrada also reflected the limits of such attempts at mobilizing and, selectively, appropriating place memories and prior struggles for purposes of building a larger protest movement, whether in Makati or Manila. For example, the spectacle of national socialite Margarita "Tingting" Cojuangco making the rounds at a rally on Ayala Avenue, as if hosting yet another cocktail party, greeting participants and thanking them for coming, could not but underscore that some felt rather more at home in this Makati milieu than did others. As for the Manila rallies, moreover, a corresponding structure of feeling seemed, at least in part, to mitigate against many participants venturing beyond *Liwasang Bonifacio*, or, even for large numbers of those who did take to these narrow streets, settling in for an overnight vigil at a crowded Mendiola.[30]

---

[28] Compared to the older neighborhoods of Manila, with their narrower streets, Makati, with its wide avenues and forbidding entrances to large commercial centers and corporate towers guarded by private security guards, provided little in the way of an informal or moral economy (e.g., food stalls, friendly houses, small alleys) to sustain and protect demonstrators. Indeed, the repertoire of government response also mirrored these contrasts. For example, in lieu of the battle-geared anti-riot police and barbed wire awaiting marchers at Mendiola, Makati protesters were typically greeted by curiously well-groomed police forces in neat uniforms and, on several occasions, with women officers sporting make-up and flowers in the front-row. Of course, the anti-Estrada rallies met with little to no direct repression or even intimidation from agents of state coercive apparatuses compared to that facing the mounting opposition against Marcos in the mid-1980s, especially the so-called red or radical movement.

[29] Reynaldo C. Ileto, "The Past in the Present Crisis," in *The Philippines after Marcos*, ed. R. J. May and Francisco Nemenzo (London: Croon Helm, 1985).

[30] Even among those protesters who, in clusters of fellow workers or students, for example, stayed long into the night at Mendiola, the notion of being at home in the crowd, in the street, seemed to vary a great deal from group to group at different points in time during a particular rally. Indeed, in the course of a given rally, such mood swings could be observed in the enthusiastic response of labor union activists to old protest songs and slogans and, conversely, the responses of university college classmates to other forms of alternative music and dancing

In short, despite claims to past political struggles and victories against a corrupt dictatorship, the powerful sense of classness defining, albeit in very different ways, both Makati and Manila, especially at the heart of Ayala Avenue and Mendiola, served to complicate and undermine the efforts of opposition organizers to mobilize a broad-based, cross-class "People Power" movement against the Estrada presidency.[31] In this regard, it is useful to recall that the peculiar populist appeal that helped gain Estrada, or "Erap," the largest number of presidential votes in Philippine electoral history in May of 1998 also proved difficult to overcome, especially among urban poor supporters, even in the face of the deepening political crisis towards the end of 2000.[32] Thus, a successful opposition movement seemed to require the sublimation of the kind of classness—and latent class conflict—inevitably associated with the Ayala and Mendiola rallies into a more inclusive sense of belonging—and becoming—in city and nation. For reasons that will be examined in the pages to follow, EDSA provided this much-needed third space for the anti-Estrada opposition to gain further momentum, and thus, once again, a synthesis in the kind of mobilizational dialectic sketched above.

V. EDSA: "THE STORY OF THE THIRD"

It was the country's most influential non-politicians, Cory and the Cardinal, who first publicly proclaimed that they would not appear at rallies held anywhere but at EDSA starting on September 21, 2000, the anniversary of the declaration of martial law.[33] At the prayer rallies held at the EDSA Shrine itself in September and October, no crowds gathered outside, Manila Archbishop Jaime Cardinal Sin, the former widowed "housewife" president, and various high-profile politicians, businessmen, socialites, and media personalities could be glimpsed inside the chapel on television broadcasts. By contrast, the November 4 rally at EDSA arguably saw "the biggest throng assembled on that historic

---

thrown into the overall "party" mix by organizers, who, while themselves typically middle-aged and desk-bound, were quite concerned to close such "generational" gaps.

[31] In this regard, the conspicuous absence of Plaza Miranda—once the heart of Manila and, thus arguably, the nation—from the itineraries of the anti-Estrada opposition is noteworthy. The Plaza had recently been subjected to a makeover, finished off with a marble obelisk courtesy of Manila mayor Lito Atienza, but it was perhaps not so much the attempted museification of Plaza Miranda that deterred would-be anti-Estrada demonstrators, but a more pervasive sense of classness, rooted in an old downtown overcrowded with internal migrants, *lumpen* elements, market vendors and churchgoers, and fertile ground for the peculiar populist appeal of "Erap."

[32] While there were few "pro-Erap" rallies, an estimated one million people turned out for the Third National Day of Prayer and Fasting at the Luneta on November 11, 2000. This prayer rally was led by Estrada and leaders of the El Shaddai and Iglesia ni Cristo. See, for example, *Philippine Daily Inquirer*, November 12, 2000. For a discussion of Estrada's peculiar populist appeal, see Eva-Lotta E. Hedman, "The Spectre of Populism in Philippine Politics and Society: *Artista, Masa, Eraption,*" South East Asia Research 9,1 (March 2001): 5-44.

[33] *Philippine Daily Inquirer*, September 21, 2000. As the *jueteng* scandal broke, Manila Archbishop Jaime Cardinal Sin also publicly declared that Estrada had lost "the moral ascendancy to govern," an assessment with which the Catholic Bishops Conference of the Philippines swiftly concurred. *Philippine Daily Inquirer*, October 12 and 14, 2000. For a discussion of morality in Philippine political discourse, see Eric Gutierrez, "Critical Reflections on the Moral Foundations of EDSA 2" (unpublished paper, March 2001).

highway since the 1986 People Power Revolution."[34] Thereafter, on the twenty-third day of the nationally televised and radio-aired presidential impeachment trial, within hours of the fatal senate vote not to suppress crucial evidence on the evening of Tuesday, January 16, 2001, anti-Estrada protesters once again started returning to EDSA, first in a trickle, but soon in growing numbers. While many came and went for only a few hours at a time, a critical mass held vigil until Gloria Macapagal-Arroyo was sworn in as the Philippines' fourteenth president at the foot of the Shrine on Saturday, January 20.[35]

While Epifanio de los Santos Avenue spans from Caloocan in the north to Baclaran in the south, the portion of EDSA that figured as a site of "People Power II" is actually a fairly brief stretch of this major highway, located by Robinson's Galleria, one of the landmark malls that have contributed to the transformation of this sprawling metropolis since the 1990s.[36] In particular, these anti-Estrada demonstrations converged at the otherwise busy intersection of EDSA and Ortigas Avenue, another major thoroughfare which also provides direct access to the Robinson's Galleria mall. Moreover, these rallies increasingly spilled onto the so-called flyovers rising above both EDSA and Ortigas at this intersection, thus presenting participant-observers with an unprecedented balcony experience of the wider spectacle at street level.[37] As a result of yet another recent addition to this urban landscape, the elevated Metropolitan Railway Transit (MRT) trains also offered sweeping panoramic views of these EDSA rallies and, for many of those who decided to join on their way to and/or from work, for example, convenient points of access from nearby stations to the north as well as the south.

While leadership and organization played a significant role in bringing the anti-Estrada opposition to EDSA in such large numbers, as did the cell phone "texting" phenomenon, it is important to appreciate the familiarity and relative ease with which an unusually broad social spectrum of Filipinos had already come to negotiate this peculiar kind of urban space.[38] Hard as one might try, for example, it would be difficult to avoid EDSA, the multiple-lane highway, altogether during even a brief stay in this capital city. Despite such recent additions to the metropolitan road network as "C-5," for example, EDSA has remained the single highway most traveled—and, frequently, congested—by north-south bound

---

[34] Amando Doronila, *Philippine Daily Inquirer*, November 6, 2000. While difficult to verify, the PDI estimated the crowds at EDSA on November 4 at 80-100,000. *Philippine Daily Inquirer*, November 5, 2000.

[35] For a succinct discussion of key events and figures behind the fall of Estrada, see Carl H. Landé, "The Return of 'People Power' in the Philippines," *Journal of Democracy*, 12,2 (April 2001): 92-97, especially.

[36] First baptized "Junio 19" after José Rizal's birthday, but known for years as "Highway 54," EDSA emerged during the construction of new roads and bridges to link what was then the "forests of Diliman" with the towns of Rizal province under Commonwealth President Manuel Quezeon. The longest of these highways, EDSA was renamed much later after Epifanio de los Santos, historian of the Philippine revolution against Spain.

[37] On "flyovers," see Neferti X. M. Tadiar, "Manila's New Metropolitan Form," *differences: A Journal of Feminist Cultural Studies* 5,3 (1993): 154-78, also reprinted in *Discrepant Histories: Translocal Essays on Filipino Cultures*, ed. Vicente L. Rafael (Metro Manila: Anvil Publishing Inc., 1995), pp. 285-313.

[38] On "Generation Text" and the cell-phone phenomenon in the Philippines, see Vicente L. Rafael, "The Call Phone and the Crowd: Messianic Politics in Recent Philippine History" (http://communication.ucsd.edu/people/f_rafael.cellphone.html, posted June 13, 2001).

commuter buses and cars alike, with numerous access points to and from east-west flows of traffic, including the jeepney routes that criss-cross most parts of the city. More recently, the elevated MRT train line has added yet another dimension to this seemingly endless stream of people transported up and down EDSA.

Moreover, as a result of the rapid proliferation of large commercial complexes throughout metropolitan Manila (as well as other parts of the country) during the 1990s, the mall has emerged as a living monument of sorts to contemporary urban Philippine society and culture.[39] Of course, actual consumption at Robinson's Galleria, as well as at many other malls, has necessarily remained confined to more limited strata of the overall population, especially in the upmarket specialty shops and restaurants beyond the food courts and movie theaters. Nonetheless, the practice of "malling"—seeing friends on window-shopping strolls, meeting would-be associates in air-conditioned comfort, taking the family out for a treat, or simply losing oneself in the anonymous crowd—has become perhaps the single most widely shared experience, across distinctions of social class and hierarchy, of urban "public" space in the Philippines today.

Located at the heart of metropolitan Manila's major crossroads and mall belt through which people from all walks of life pass daily, EDSA, the site of these rallies, has thus in many ways retained the open-endedness of what has been referred to elsewhere as "non-places," locations strangely unburdened by the strong sense of classness that inscribes older neighborhoods and newer cityscapes.[40] In this regard, the seemingly endless flow of people who pour into the Robinson's Galleria mall and, eventually, spill back out again onto the EDSA-Ortigas intersection have contributed to the shaping of this urban space as a non-place of sorts, blurring notions of belonging and becoming anchored more firmly at home and at work. In a similar vein, the EDSA rallies also reflected and reproduced this familiar way of being in the mall, as well as this ease of coming and going, without prompting the kinds of anxieties evident in the preoccupation with "rich and poor" at Ayala Avenue or in the undercurrent of class conflict and violence at Mendiola.

Indeed, "People Power II" saw a great deal of milling about not merely near the EDSA Shrine and the major intersection with Ortigas Avenue at street-level, or even, as these rallies grew ever larger, along the flyovers stretching above this space, but also, notably, inside Robinson's Galleria itself. For example, political organizers held meetings at Pizza Hut; a prominent columnist stocked up on cold beers at the supermarket; and many other *rallyistas*, typically in a *barkada* (group of friends), ventured further in search of fast food, coffee, "comfort rooms" (which were hastily closed off), and, in some cases, even a movie at one of the cinemas upstairs in the mall. Having the mall at such close quarters to the large crowds gathering outside also seemed to encourage entire family outings at these rallies, with many parents, perhaps inspired by a sense of history and typically equipped with cameras, bringing even very young children to EDSA. Whether stopping by on their way from work and school, or joining with different groups and coalitions mobilized for this last showdown with the Estrada presidency, or bringing the

---

[39] On the "malling of Manila," see Eva-Lotta E. Hedman, "Malling Manila: Images of a City, Fragments of a Century," in *Philippine Politics and Society in the Twentieth Century: Colonial Legacies, Post-Colonial Trajectories,* Eva-Lotta E. Hedman and John T. Sidel (London: Routledge, 2000), pp. 118-39.

[40] Marc Augé, *Non-places: Introduction to an Anthropology of Supermodernity,* trans. John Howe (London: Verso Press, 1995).

family for a glimpse of history in the making, many of those present at EDSA during these four days in January were, at least in part, sustained by the kind of "R & R" made possible at the mall.

Inasmuch as growing numbers of Filipinos have come to encounter one another as consumers of spectacle, and nowhere more so than at the mall, it is perhaps unsurprising that the rallies at EDSA, compared to those at Ayala and Mendiola, as well as elsewhere in metropolitan Manila, also featured a great deal of commerce and theater alike. These rallies generated unusually brisk business as vendors plied the vast grounds with their many wares, ranging from bottled water and ice cream to cigarettes and *balut* (quail embryo). In addition, a different kind of commerce also flourished as small stalls started appearing under one of the flyovers, offering a wide selection of protest memorabilia and political materials ranging from anti-Estrada T-shirts and "Greatest Hits" music recordings to pocket editions of works by Lenin and Mao. Suggestive evidence of this pervasive sense of "malling" at the EDSA rallies could be glimpsed in brief encounters such as the one between a private-school college graduate, casually browsing and attempting to bargain down the price of a double-CD of so-called "Erap hits," and an increasingly befuddled young "out-of-school" radical-left activist, manning his table in the name of strong political convictions and, inevitably, a concomitant commitment to a "moral economy" of sorts.

At the same time, perhaps more than anywhere else during the wave of anti-Estrada protests, the EDSA rallies provided an unusually hospitable milieu for the spectacular itself, whether in real or virtual time and space. Compared to the kind of political theater staged, for example, by the Concerned Artists of the Philippines (CAP) and veteran director Behn Cervantes as part of other demonstrations in Manila and Makati, at EDSA, the greatest spectacle was somehow the very "scene" of these rallies themselves. As part of that scene, the EDSA rallies also introduced certain innovations in the repertoire of protest such as, for example, the spectacular stunt of *Akbayan* activists in rock-climbing gear descending to unfold large banners from the Ortigas flyover to the cheering crowds below. More generally, the two flyovers at the EDSA-Ortigas intersection were quickly transformed by a veritable advertisement campaign of billboard-sized opposition slogans and "signatures," thus adding not merely a balcony perspective but also yet another level of spectacle to these rallies. While they led participants in prayers and song, seemingly welcome and meaningful to some, if sanctimonious and boring to others, not even the Church hierarchy seemed impervious to this sense of spectacle, as indicated by the example of several Catholic priests, dressed in their traditional sultanas, who occasionally broke out in line-dancing routines at the foot of the EDSA Shrine. Above the steps and makeshift stage of the Shrine, moreover, the anti-Estrada opposition quickly organized an instant headquarters which hosted media events such as the press conference with Philippine superstar Nora "Guy" Aunor, a long-time friend and former lover of "Erap," who went public here at EDSA on Friday, January 19, 2001, with her story of his physical abusiveness in what was widely considered a spectacular coup to win the hearts and minds of the proverbial *masa* and turn them against Estrada.[41] Inasmuch as the media allowed for the wider dissemination of

---

[41] On the Cinderella superstardom of Nora Aunor, see Neferti X. M. Tadiar, "The Noranian Imaginary," in *Geopolitics of the Visible: Essays on Philippine Film Cultures*, ed. Rolando B. Tolentino (Manila: Ateneo de Manila University Press, 2000), pp. 61-76.

"People Power II" as spectacle throughout city and nation, the presence of a number of television crews also had a spectacular effect upon those assembled at EDSA, especially noticeable at night with the crowds visibly coming alive—waving, grinning, jumping, and chanting again—whenever "spotted" by the bright camera lights sweeping these rallies.

VI. IN LIEU OF A CONCLUSION

In contrast with February 1986, observers have noted, "EDSA Dos" as it was quickly labeled in local parlance featured an exclusively civilian leadership, a more decentralized mobilizational process, and a wider social composition of individual participants and coalition blocs alike.[42] Indeed, while the near-simultaneous defections on Friday, January 19, 2001 at EDSA of the chiefs of the Armed Forces, Angelo Reyes, and the Philippine National Police, Panfilo Lacson, as well as Secretary of Defense Orlando Mercado, in many ways spelled the final hours for the Estrada presidency, these moves fell far short of the military involvement at EDSA in 1986, which, after all, started with an aborted coup and, furthermore, was followed by years of putschist adventurism on the part of so-called "reformist" officers. Instead, "EDSA Dos" has been, alternately, criticized (notably in the international media) for adding yet another precedent to the repertoire of extra-constitutional regime transfers, and celebrated (unsurprisingly by many Filipinos stung by such foreign press reports) as evidence of the deepening in Philippine society and politics of the capacity of civil society to act for itself, as it were. In the words of one Filipino commentator, for example, "[v]iewing the process through narrow western constitutional lenses, these accounts fail to see the greater truth about EDSA II: that it was an exercise in direct democracy...."[43]

Whether criticized or celebrated, "EDSA Dos" did of course signal a peculiar departure from constitutionally anchored and otherwise established institutions and processes of political representation in the Philippines. However, it would appear rather mistaken to view, as some have, "Rousseau at work, not John Locke"

---

[42] As noted by Temario Rivera, "the struggle against Estrada brought together an extraordinary political relationship among normally antagonistic groups which saw left-wing and right-wing parties, big business and labour unions, upper and middle classes and the urban poor, Christians and Muslims, Communists and anti-Communists, coming together to topple the administration." Temario Rivera identifies the major political groupings in the anti-Estrada opposition as follows: 1) the left parties with a Marxist heritage, including *Bayan, Sanlakas, Akbayan*, and their affiliate organizations; 2) KOMPIL II, a broad multisectoral formation of several NGOs, people's organizations, church-related groups, labor federations, and the social-democratic Left parties; 3) the Council for Philippine Affairs (COPA), a group of politicians, businesspersons and military contacts, and headed by Jose Cojuangco, former representative and brother of former Pres. Aquino; 4) the *Kangong* Brigade, composed of mostly local government officials led by Governor Jose Lina; 5) the various Christian Churches, both Catholic and Protestant; 6) the business sector led by the Makati Business Club; 7) the Philippine Consultative Assembly, a grouping identified with former Pres. Ramos and Gen. Almonte; and several other more or less autonomous smaller organizations . . . . " Temario Rivera, "The Middle Classes and Democratization in the Philippines: From the Asian Crisis to the Ouster of Estrada" (unpublished paper, February 2001).

[43] Walden Bello, "The Unraveling of a Presidency," *Focus on the Philippines* (an electronic newsletter), posted February 13, 2001, later reprinted in abbreviated form as "Letter from Manila," *The Nation*, February 19, 2001.

in the making of "People Power II."[44] That is, the notion of an unmediated "general will" at work at EDSA, à la Rousseau, is surely much less compelling than the kind of social mediation through spectacle theorized elsewhere and, as suggested in the pages above, perhaps nowhere more acutely felt in the contemporary Philippines than at the mall.[45]

In this regard, it is also useful to consider the transformation of EDSA as urban space in the fifteen-year period between "People Power I and II." In 1986, for example, the EDSA-Ortigas intersection had yet to see the development of Robinson's Galleria, the flyovers, and the MRT, or, for that matter, the rise of corporate and residential towers in the area now named the Ortigas Center. Similarly, further along EDSA, MegaMall and other, up- as well as down-market, commercial complexes in the vicinity had yet to beckon commuters on the smog-filled highway outside. While most accounts of the first "People Power" have stressed the significance of what and who occupied EDSA, this peculiar emptiness—as an urban space in its own right—at the time has attracted much less attention.[46]

However, the return of "People Power" (II) in January of 2001 cannot but underline both the former emptiness and the subsequent filling out of EDSA as urban space. Indeed, propelled by a combination of factors, including a shift in the urban real-estate market and, arguably, the pent-up demand for retail consumption, EDSA in many ways emerged at the forefront of the "malling" phenomenon that has reshaped city landscapes across the Philippines in the course of the 1990s. In this vein, EDSA underwent a marked transformation from what may perhaps be referred to as a mere node, albeit a critical one, in the urban landscape of the mid-1980s to its emergence as a kind of third space, in many ways emblematic of metropolitan Manila in the early twenty-first century.

The emergence of this third space is, of course, in its broad contours, a familiar historical development of the city where, due to what Marx called the "three dramatis personae" of the exchange process, social relations have become both indirect and triangulated. In as much as this notion of the third space rests on the city-as-market, its strong association with the shopping mall in the contemporary Philippines is perhaps unsurprising. In the context of a post-colonial metropolis built upon layers of (Spanish) plaza complexes and (American) highways and subdivisions, moreover, the transformation of EDSA into this third space has also been accompanied by the increasing circulation of another kind of third—a (Philippine) middle class.[47] If many questions remain regarding the relative size,

---

[44] Ibid.

[45] Guy Debord, *The Society of the Spectacle* (New York: Zone Books, 1995).

[46] It was, of course, the aborted coup attempt by so-called rebel soldiers and Marcos's former long-term supporters, Defense Minister Juan Ponce Enrile and Philippine Constabulary Chief General Fidel V. Ramos, and the subsequent calls by Cardinal Sin and others over the Catholic radio station Veritas for civilians to "protect" them, that provided the immediate trigger for "People Power (I)" along the very stretch of EDSA that runs between Camps Aguinaldo and Crame in February of 1986.

[47] See, for example, Michael Pinches, "Entrepreneurship, consumption, ethnicity and national identity in the making of the Philippines' new rich," in *Culture and Privilege in Capitalist Asia*, ed. Michael Pinches (London: Routledge, 1999), pp. 275-301. Compared to the mid-1980s, according to one scholar, "the most common language of social stratification simply distinguished between rich and poor, or *burgis* (bourgeoisie) and *masa* (masses), with only

purchasing power, life world, social imaginary, and, not least, common classification of this middle class, its politics may perhaps be expected to point in the direction of a "third way" of sorts, away from old-style *politicos* and revolutionaries alike.[48]

While "EDSA Dos" thus appeared as an extraordinary spectacle of compromise itself, or, in other words, the ultimate "sign of the Third," it hardly provided a seamless stitching up of the kind of contradictions noted above, between rich and poor, conservatives/moderates, radicals/progressives, and Ayala rallies and Mendiola marches. Indeed, even before the endgame was over at EDSA, a large contingent of political activists, student organizations, union supporters, and other committed progressives broke ranks with the Cardinal and many religious associations, as well as more traditional politicians and their supporters, to embark on a long march down to Mendiola and, ultimately, the presidential palace.[49] Finally, months later, with Estrada behind bars and Macapagal-Arroyo installed in Malacañang, the EDSA Shrine was reportedly "desecrated," Mendiola turned into a battlefield yet again, and the presidential palace eventually attacked by so-called "rioting mobs" of Erap supporters, prompting the declaration of a State of Emergency and leaving some six dead and more than a hundred people injured in the aftermath of Labor Day in the year 2001. As suggested by this fall-out of "EDSA Dos," the travail of Philippine democracy remains a work-in-progress.

But even if Manila's veteran street activists and machine politicians continue to experiment with repeat performances of—or variations on—"EDSA" in years to come, the possibilities for (re)creating "People Power" will remain powerfully shaped by the nature of public space and collective memory in metropolitan Manila. More generally, when examining other instances of "People Power" elsewhere in Southeast Asia and beyond, it is worth remembering—and revising—the old adage: men and women make history, but not in geographical imaginaries of their own making.

---

limited reference to a middle class." Mark Turner, "Imagining the Middle-Class in the Philippines," *Pilipinas* 25 (1995): 87-101.

[48] This turn of phrase, as well as the underlying narrative matrix of the third space, is inspired by Franco Moretti, *Atlas of the European Novel, 1800-1900* (London: Verso, 1998), p. 110.

[49] See, for example, Temario Rivera, "Middle Class Politics: The Philippine Experience," *Journal of Social Science* 45 (September 2000): 1-20.

PILKADES: DEMOCRACY, VILLAGE ELECTIONS, AND PROTEST IN INDONESIA[1]

Douglas Kammen

On June 4, 1998, the governor of Central Java, Maj. Gen. Soewardi, issued a decree instructing district executives to postpone all elections of village heads in the province. The timing of the decree could not have been more peculiar. Two weeks before, on May 21, 1998, President Suharto resigned, ending his thirty-two year rule over Indonesia. Suharto's resignation opened the floodgates of debate over the future of the political system. The most prominent demands included an end to the military's self-appointed dual function (*dwi-fungsi*), free and fair national elections, and that Suharto be tried for corruption and abuse of office. In the context of these broad-based protests and calls for *reformasi* and *demokrasi*, Soewardi's decree appeared to be a step backwards, if not outright anachronistic.

The decision to suspend all village-level elections was prompted by two complementary concerns. First, Soewardi's decree reflected the growing unease over the astonishing level of social unrest, popular protest, and outright violence in Central Java. According to police statistics, between January and July, 1998, there were over 1,300 protests in Central Java alone. More than one-third of these protests were directed at or related to village heads (*kepala desa*).[2] Second, the decree also reflected practical considerations: in Central Java more than 6,250 village elections were scheduled to be held over the next year.[3] The formal logistics of such an electoral exercise included scheduling (at the district level), the formation of electoral committees (at the sub-district level), testing and

---

[1] Earlier versions of this paper were presented at a conference held by the University Historical Research Centre, Yangon University, Rangoon, December 16-18, 1998; the annual meeting of the Association of Asian Studies, held in Boston, March 12, 1999; and the seminar "Dynamics of Local Politics in Indonesia: Change, Challenges and Hopes," sponsored by Lembaga Persemaian Cinta Kemanusiaan (Percik) and the Ford Foundation, Yogyakarta, Indonesia, July 3-7, 2000. I would like to thank Benedict Anderson, Audrey Kahin, Jim Siegel, Made Tony Supriatma, Michael Malley, and Johnly Purba for their comments.

[2] "Di Jateng Demo Pejabat KKN 1.308 Kali," *Kedaulatan Rakyat*, September 26, 1998.

[3] See "Pilkades di Era Reformasi (1): Karena Ditunda, Biaya Suguhan Membengkak," *Suara Merdeka*, November 3, 1998.

selection of candidates to stand for election, campaigning, and finally the actual voting and counting of ballots. On top of this, state officials were concerned about fraud and cheating, the disruptive influence of gambling on the elections, and, of course, security. The huge number of upcoming village elections meant that the levels of protest were likely to intensify.

Soewardi's decree drew an immediate and predictable response—more protest. On June 13, hundreds of candidates for village head (*calon kepala desa*) from Purworejo District demonstrated at the Central Java People's Representative Council (Dewan Perwakilan Rakyat Daerah, DPRD) in Semarang to demand that the governor revoke the recent decree.[4] The reason for this protest, however, was neither simply nor primarily concern about respecting the democratic process. Having purchased the necessary official forms, paid bribes to the selection committee, contributed substantial sums to cover the cost of running the election itself, and spent money on treats (*suguhan*) and outright vote-buying in their communities, these candidates for election from Purworejo were furious because these considerable outlays would be forfeited. Outrage over the decree was not only expressed by the candidates wishing to stand for election. In Semarang, members of the DPRD railed against the governor's decision for being undemocratic. According to one member of the DPRD, "the interests of villagers and candidates for village head must also be considered."[5]

While the decision to postpone village elections was limited to Central Java, protests relating to both the election and legitimacy of village heads were staged throughout the archipelago. In many villages and sub-districts, villagers demanded that "little kings" and "local Suhartos" resign from office (*lengser keprabon*). In turn, local officials vainly attempted to defend themselves, calling on higher ranking officials (and patrons) to maintain the state's administrative machinery. In one such instance, all 306 village heads in Jombang District, East Java, staged a counter-demonstration at the district government office to demand protection against the "reformers."[6]

It would be wrong, however, to conclude that protest over village elections is simply or most fundamentally connected to the so-called *reformasi* movement. Protest over village elections flared up in late 1997, well before students on campuses across Java began to demonstrate against the handling of the economic crisis and Suharto's continued rule. Beginning in mid-1998, villagers did indeed couch their demands in the new language of national politics, calling for an end to "*korupsi, kolusi dan nepotisme*" (corruption, collusion, and nepotism). Nevertheless, that villagers protested at the same time as students and other groups need not mean that their actions were part of a single movement, let alone that one group provided a model for another. Furthermore, while villagers expressed concern about corruption and democracy, it does not follow that they understood (or intended) these concepts to mean the same thing as for students, the urban poor, or the newly disaffected national elite.

The explosion of protest over village elections in 1997–1998 raises a series of questions about collective action and class relations in rural Java. How is it that villagers came to protest around elections rather than some other theme or event?

---

[4] "Pilkades Ditunda, DPRD Jateng Diprotes," *Jawa Pos*, June 14, 1998.

[5] Ibid.

[6] "Unjuk Rasa Marak, 306 Kades Se-Jombang Ancam Mundur," *Jawa Pos*, July 22, 1998.

Why did protest over village elections erupt in late 1997 rather than at some other time? Still more troubling, why were these protests concentrated in some parts of Java while absent elsewhere? Finally, what is the relationship between protest over village elections and the eruption of urban protest demanding Suharto's resignation and national political reform? This chapter seeks to answer these questions.

Governor Soewardi's decision and the response that it elicited also highlighted a central question of the post-Suharto era: how would the rural population participate in a more open electoral process? In searching for answers to these questions, many observers have looked to the 1955 election, generally regarded as the only free and fair election in Indonesian history, for parallels and lessons.[7] I would like to suggest that village elections during the New Order (1965–1998) provide an alternative lens through which to consider the prospects for electoral politics in the post-Suharto era. Indonesia remains a predominantly rural country, and the vast majority of the Indonesian population still lives in village administrative units. Therefore, an examination of village elections over the past decade may provide insight into the meaning of the democratic process in rural Indonesia.

This essay explores the origins and dynamics of protest over village elections in late-New Order Indonesia.[8] It argues that collective action at the village level must be taken seriously on its own merits, and should not be interpreted simply as a distorted image of the national *reformasi* movement. Through an examination of the geographic distribution of village electoral protest, I will argue that this protest is intimately related to control over private as well as collective village resources and the mediation of agrarian class relations by the state. Like much protest, collective action that is directed at the state or channeled through existing political institutions can fruitfully be interpreted as an attempt by one social class to defend itself from other classes. In the case of village elections, this is played out along two dimensions. On the one hand, protest over village elections reflects competition within the village for control over collective resources. This may involve both a defense of communal assets, such as land or forest rights, or attempts by individuals to appropriate these resources for private uses. On the other hand, the position of village head is the point of access for outsiders, and protest over the election of village heads reflects the ongoing struggle between the community and outsider claimants seeking access to village resources.

---

[7] See, for example, the contributions in David Bourchier and John Legge, eds., *Democracy in Indonesia, 1950s and 1990s* (Clayton, Victoria: Centre of Southeast Asian Studies, Monash University, 1994).

[8] It is necessary to underscore the fact that protests directed at village heads and the village administration of course were not confined to the process of elections themselves. I have chosen to limit this study to protests relating to elections for two reasons: first, so as to narrow the universe of cases to a (barely) manageable number and, second, because a study of village elections may help to shed light on the opening of the national electoral system and the meaning of the democratic process to rural Indonesians. A study of protests in 1998–99 against active village heads and public demands that these officials resign or be removed from office would require a somewhat different approach from the one employed here.

FROM PEMILU TO PILKADES

Following the military seizure of power in 1965–66, General Suharto and his associates set about restructuring the political process and consolidating state power. The first steps to simplify the party structure were taken in 1966 when several of the existing parties were forcibly overhauled or liquidated outright. In 1967, the Army declared that its corporatist umbrella organization Golkar (an abbreviation from *golongan karya*, or functional group) would become the regime's electoral machine, though it was carefully defined as not being a political party. Beginning in 1967, the regime pushed through new legislation granting itself the right to appoint representatives to the People's Consultative Assembly (Majelis Permusyawaratan Rakyat, MPR) and the People's Representative Council (Dewan Perwakilan Rakyat, DPR), thus eliminating party control over parliament.[9] Despite the ease with which the military regime emasculated the political parties and monopolized parliamentary seats, it remained uneasy about putting these new arrangements to the test, and the general election scheduled for 1968 was postponed until 1971. The final step in the process of transforming the national political process was taken in 1973 with the forced consolidation of the remaining political parties into two officially recognized parties, the United Development Party (Partai Persatuan Pembangunan, PPP) and the Indonesian Democratic Party (Partai Demokrasi Indonesia, PDI).[10]

In order to prevent the kind of popular political participation that had characterized the Sukarno era, in 1971 the New Order state introduced the concept of the "floating mass" (*massa mengambang*). Rationalized on grounds that the population should not be distracted from the central task of economic development, this concept was cited to explain why political participation was to be limited as far as possible to the ritual act of voting in national elections at five-year intervals. The principle of the "floating mass" was achieved by banning the political parties from activity below the district level (Daerah Tingkat II), except during the brief *kampanye* (campaign) prior to each national election. This ban on party activity at the grassroots level was designed to prevent the already emasculated political parties from developing an organizational base and membership in rural areas.[11] Explicitly defined as *not* a political party, Golkar was not affected by this ban.

Restricting the activities of the political parties in rural areas did not lead to a complete moratorium on political activity in the countryside, however. Just the opposite: by sharply circumscribing the scope of party politics in rural areas and thus preventing the development of a political opposition organized across districts and provinces, the New Order regime could sanction a degree of popular participation in the election of village heads. But the existing regulations on

---

[9] For a view of these developments according to one of the regime's foremost architects, see Ali Moertopo, *Strategi Pembangunan Nasional* (Jakarta: CSIS, 1981), pp. 139-53.

[10] See David Reeve, *Golkar of Indonesia: An Alternative to the Party System* (Singapore: Oxford University Press, 1985).

[11] It was also part of a broader effort to "stabilize" class relations in rural areas. Loekman notes that "within the Ministry of Interior a new department was established—called Direktorat Khusus or Special Directorate—whose job it is to 'protect' the village from outside elements that might disturb the 'harmony' of the village." Loekman Soetrisno, *The Transformation of the Function and Role of the Lurah in Java: A Historical Perspectives* [sic] *1950-1967* (Yogyakarta: Penerbit Aditya Media, 1993), p. 20.

village administration, inherited virtually *in toto* from the Dutch, presented a number of obstacles to the new state. Perhaps the most troubling of these was the appointment of village heads for life.[12] Lifetime appointment resulted not only in entrenched interests, but it also meant that the state faced obstacles in removing uncooperative village heads. Fixed electoral terms were therefore seen as a mechanism allowing for periodic state control over village heads and, by extension, over village politics in general.

In many respects, the use of village elections by the New Order represents a continuation of earlier state practices. During the precolonial period the position of village head was semi-hereditary, though commonly subject to approval by a village council of elders.[13] The position of village head first became elective in parts of Java during the brief British interregnum (1811–1816) in the Indies, a practice that was continued under the Dutch as an inexpensive means of administration.[14] Under the New Order, efforts to amend the laws concerned with local administration were initiated in 1974, but it was not until 1979 that a new law on village government was passed. The law was designed both to standardize and simplify village administration (which varied significantly by region) and to allow the state to penetrate the village more fully and effectively.[15]

Village elections (*pemilihan kepala desa*, commonly abbreviated "pilkades") differ from the national legislative elections (*pemilihan umum*, or "pemilu") in several important respects. Beginning in 1971, national legislative elections were held at regular five-year intervals; electoral competition was between the two political parties (PPP and PDI) and Golkar, not individual candidates, with legislative seats then assigned by each party to loyal members; and legislative members at the national, provincial, and district levels served five-year terms. By contrast, *pilkades* are not held at the same time in each province, district, or even sub-district, but rather are staggered according to the year that the first election was held in a given location; individual candidates stand directly for election without the benefit or mediation of a party or formal organizational structure; and village heads are elected to an eight-year term.[16]

The New Order state retained stringent control over most aspects of the electoral process. First, candidates must meet a host of requirements determined by the state: be aged between twenty-five and sixty years, have a minimum educational attainment, have at least two years of residency in the village, pledge

---

[12] Frans Hüsken, "Village Elections in Central Java: State Control or Local Democracy?" in *Leadership on Java: Gentle Hints, Authoritarian Rule*, ed. Hans Antlov and Sven Cederroth (Surrey: Curzon Press, 1994), p. 125.

[13] Loekman Soetrisno, *Role of the Lurah*, p. xiii.

[14] Hüsken, "Village Elections," p. 120.

[15] The administrative changes contained in Undang Undang No. 5 1979 are discussed in Hans Antlov, *Exemplary Centre, Administrative Periphery: Rural Leadership and the New Order in Java* (Surry: Curzon Press, 1995), pp. 43-44. For the law itself, see A. W. Widjaja, *Pemerintahan Desa dan Administrasi Desa: Menurut Undang-Undang Nomor 5 Tahun 1979 (Sebuah Tinjauan)* (Jakarta: PT RajaGrafindo Persada, 1993).

[16] These differences are discussed succinctly by Suparto Djaja Laksana in "Antara pilkades dan Pemilu," *Angkatan Bersenjata*, November 6, 1990. During the Abdurrahman Wahid presidency, some local officials discussed the possibility of extending the term of village head to ten years. See, for example, "Jabatan Kades 10 Tahun Tidak Rasional," *Suara Merdeka*, March 23, 2000.

allegiance to the state ideology (Pancasila), provide proof of not being related to anyone associated with the banned PKI (Partai Komunis Indonesia, Indonesian Communist Party), and so forth.[17] Second, all potential candidates (*bakal calon kepala desa*) must pass an examination and be approved by a village election committee (*panitia pilkades*). Bribery is commonly acknowledged to be a means of passing this selection process and of preventing rivals from doing so as well. Local officials thus ensure that only approved candidates stand for election and may further orchestrate the competition to guarantee a desired outcome.

Throughout the New Order, village elections served a significant function in integrating the village community into the state apparatus. On the one hand, the exercise of allowing each village to hold an election presented a façade of local sovereignty. While the pool of candidates was vetted (if not arranged) by the state, village elections involved voting directly for individual candidates to the post of village head. Competition was often intense (and remains so today under the new government). On the other hand, village heads not only represented the local community but also served as agents of the state at the grassroots level. All elected village officials were required to join the national Civil Service Association (Korpri) as well as Golkar. This policy clearly deterred interest in the position of village head among candidates who were either hostile to Golkar or who actively supported either of the two "opposition" parties. Village heads were also responsible for the implementation of the large number of state development policies, as well as for maintaining, monitoring, and regulating social and political activity in the village.[18] Perhaps most importantly, as representatives of the state, village heads were entrusted with ensuring the electoral success of Golkar in national elections.

Though passed in 1979, the new law on village government was introduced gradually and unevenly across the archipelago. While elections were held to fill vacancies caused by death, incapacitation, or resignation, during the early 1980s no large-scale effort was made to replace village heads. It was not until 1988, Frans Hüsken explains, "that the government ordered new village elections to be held according to the rules stipulated in the law of 1979."[19] There appear to be two major reasons for this decade-long delay. First, as Hüsken rightly argues, the 1982 oil-price collapse and resulting economic recession severely strained existing state capacities, hindering the adoption of new forms of state activism at the grassroots level. Second, and of greater importance perhaps, the state avoided introducing any new channels of popular participation prior to the quinquennial national electoral exercises and related General Session of the People's Consultative Assembly (Sidang Istimewa Majelis Permusyawaratan Rakyat, SI MPR) that rubber-stamped the (re-)selection of Suharto to additional Presidential terms. As these national elections and the general session were scheduled for 1987 and 1988, respectively, this meant an added delay in implementing the new procedures for the election of village heads.

---

[17] These requirements are discussed in A. W. Widjaja, *Pemerintahan Desa dan Administrasi Desa*, pp. 31-32.

[18] This role is discussed in Frans Hüsken, "Village Elections in Central Java: State Control or Local Democracy?" pp. 121-23.

[19] Ibid., p. 124. In a 1994 publication, Antlov contradicts this, claiming that the reforms were not in fact implemented. See Hans Antlov, *Exemplary Centre, Administrative Periphery*, pp. 182-83.

Following the "sukses" of the national "festival of democracy" (*pesta demokrasi*) in 1987, the Minister of the Interior announced that village elections would be held throughout much of Indonesia over the next several years. In Central Java, for example, between April 1988 and May 1990, 6,465 out of a total of 7,845 villages held elections for the position of village head.[20] Similarly, in East Java 4,909 elections of village heads were held in 1990, with the governor of East Java requesting that all village elections be completed before July 1991 so as not to interfere with the 1992 elections.[21] Similar large-scale electoral exercises were held elsewhere throughout the archipelago, proudly hailed by New Order officials as evidence of democracy.

In launching this massive electoral exercise, the New Order state approached the village administrative unit with a combination of nostalgia, condescension, and fear. This ambivalence is nicely captured by the deputy speaker of the Central Java DPRD who explained: "Democracy in the village is still pure [*murni*], and that's why we need to keep on tending its seeds. It is our collective duty to ensure that this backward village democracy [*demokrasi yang masih tertinggal*] does not disappear."[22] While the village, and by extension the electoral process, is seen as being "pure" (in contrast to the corrupted nature of modern urban life), purity is simultaneously "backwards," thus requiring the paternal guidance of the state to prevent disruption and ensure desired outcomes. Without this guidance, "pure democracy" might vanish into thin air.

Of course, for the state the issue was never that of "cultivating" democracy—pure or otherwise—but rather one of bureaucratic convenience and expedience. On this score, the cyclical differences between *pemilu* and *pilkades* proved especially problematic. Although this first wave of village elections during the 1988–1990 period was held well clear of the national elections, not all villages were involved. Over the next several years, elections continued to be conducted in Java and beyond, though in somewhat smaller numbers. Keenly aware of the potential synergy between village and national affairs, in March 1991, the Director General for General Governance and Autonomous Areas (Dirjen. Pemerintahan Umum dan Otonomi Daerah) Atar Sibero insisted that "all *pilkades* be completed before the 1992 national legislative election."[23] Several weeks later, the Minister for Internal Affairs Gen. (Ret.) Rudini ordered Governors and district executives (*bupati* and *walikota*) to suspend the election of village heads from July 1991 until after the May 1992 legislative election.[24]

Despite these precautions, there are reports from several regions that the village electoral process contributed to mass mobilization in ways that affected participation in and the outcome of the 1992 *pemilu*. For instance, dissatisfaction over village elections in the Wonosobo-Temanggung region of Central Java created resentment that carried over to the *pemilu*, which saw a decrease in Golkar's returns.[25] Similarly, East Java was affected by a wave of protests over village

---

[20] "Sejumlah 6.465 Kepala Desa di Jawa Tengah akan Diganti," *Kompas*, April 8, 1988.

[21] "Pilkades Di Jatim Akan Selesai Akhir Tahun 90," *Suara Pembaruan*, June 23, 1990.

[22] Ibid.

[23] Quoted in "Pilkades Diharapkan Selesai Sebelum Pemilu 1992," *Suara Pembaruan*, March 7, 1991.

[24] "Mendagri: Perintahkan Tunda Pilkades Selama Pemilu," *Kompas*, May 31, 1991.

[25] I would like to thank Made Tony Supriatma for this information.

elections. According to a recent book on grassroots politics: "Protests over village elections flared up between 1990 and 1993 when the Governor of East Java intended for wide-sweeping change in these positions."[26] The authors explain:

> ... during the year prior to the 1992 national election [villagers] often engaged in resistance, such as refusing to vote in elections for village head. Resistance such as this is common in village elections in East Java because villagers feel disadvantaged by the adoption of government policies relating to the political process and the deregulation of agriculture ....[27]

Although localized and relatively minor in character, these disturbances in 1991–1992 highlighted the problems that could arise from synchronicity between *pilkades* and *pemilu*.

With village heads serving an eight-year term, the thousands of villages that held elections between 1988 and 1990 were due to hold their next elections in 1996–1998, thus coinciding with the 1997 national elections and 1998 General Session of the MPR that would select the President. To avert a repeat of the problems faced five years earlier, in July 1996 Governor of Central Java Soewardi postponed village elections until after the 1997 national legislative election and extended the terms of thousands of village heads whose tenure was due to expire over the next year. Legislative members from the PPP and the PDI were incensed, seeing this as an attempt to influence the outcome of the upcoming national legislative election. "They've learned from the previous national election. Last time village elections were held at the same time as the national election, and it turned out that this resulted in a decrease in votes for one of the political parties," one legislator explained, carefully avoiding direct reference to Golkar. Governor Soewardi promptly denied that his decision was politically motivated, explaining "the accusations that the postponement of village-head elections are related to Golkar's strategy to win the national election are not true."[28]

Similar measures were adopted elsewhere in Java. In September 1996, the Deputy Governor of East Java announced: "we prohibit elections for village head until after the 1998 General Session of the People's Consultative Assembly."[29] The reason was not simply that village elections might be disruptive, though this was certainly one consideration. More importantly, however, was that "the current village heads have been appointed as heads of the election committee for the national election (*Ketua Kelompok Panitia Pemungutan Suara*)."[30] In other words, the current village heads were responsible for delivering a Golkar victory. With more than half of the 7,721 village heads in East Java due to complete their terms during this period, the postponement was no idle move.

---

[26] Bagong Suyanto, Muhammad Asfar, and Rudi Pranata, *Gejolak Arus Bawah* (Grassroots discontent) (Jakarta: Pustaka Utama Grafiti, 1994), p. 15.

[27] Ibid., p. x.

[28] "Pilkades Ditunda sampai Usai Pemilu," *Republika*, July 19, 1996. For further debate, see "Penundaan Pilkades Bisa DI-PTUN-kan," *Republika*, July 11, 1996, and "DPRD Jateng Segera Bahas Soal Penundaan Pilkades," *Suara Pembaruan*, July 16, 1996.

[29] "Pemilu, Ribuan Kades Diperpanjang Jabatannya," *Jawa Pos*, September 25, 1996.

[30] Ibid.

In the context of strategies for managing village and national elections that developed over the previous decade, Governor Soewardi's seemingly anachronistic June 1998 decree appears merely as the latest in a long series of postponements. The ironic logic is that village elections must be canceled to ensure the "sukses" of democracy.

MAPPING VILLAGE ELECTORAL PROTEST

The decision to postpone further elections of village heads until after the 1997 *pemilu* created a massive backlog of villages due (or needing) to hold *pilkades*. In contrast to 1992–1993, when village elections were put on hold until after the General Session of the MPR held in March 1993, this backlog was sufficiently serious that it was deemed unwise to delay these elections any longer than absolutely necessary. In Central Java, for example, rather than wait until after the March 1998 meeting of the MPR, the first wave of village elections was initiated in late 1997.[31] The schedule called for 994 elections to be held between October 1997 and March 1998, and then another 4,673 during the 1998/1999 year.[32]

From the outset, these elections were plagued by protest. In all, thirty protests over village elections were recorded between October and December 1997. During the last quarter of 1997, protests clustered in Klaten (eleven cases), the Brebes-Tegal corridor (eight), the Demak-Jepara-Pati-Blora region (six), and Sragen (two).[33] Newspaper headlines told the story: "Without a Quorum, Village Election in Klaten Fails," "Village Election in Planggu Fails Twice," and "During Installation of Village Head, Masses Run Amuk, Burn Cars."[34] The number of protests over village elections increased in early 1998.

The depth and spread of this unrest was largely overshadowed by "national" issues: the deepening of the economic crisis, serious rioting in parts of rural Java, the appearance of elite friction in February, and the subsequent rise of student protest in March. With Suharto's resignation in May, however, the floodgates of "reform" were thrown fully open. Levels of electoral protest further increased as did protests against corrupt local officials and demands that they too, like Suharto, *"lengser keprabon"* (resign from office). These protests continued through year's end and into early 1999, brought to a temporary halt only by the decision to again suspend village elections in April 1999 until the completion of the national election in June.

The study of protest and contentious politics in rural Indonesia is complicated by a dearth of reliable data. State agencies (including the police, the Ministry of Internal Affairs, and provincial governments) rarely release official figures on protest, social disturbances, or riots. Nevertheless, more data are available on rural protest than one might suspect. A search of more than a dozen national and regional newspapers found 410 reported cases of protest related to village elections

---

[31] "Prof Soehardjo SS, SH: Pilkades Lebih Baik Dihapus," *Kedaulatan Rakyat*, October 3, 1997.

[32] Cited in "Pilkades di Jateng Sarat Pelanggaran," *Kedaulatan Rakyat*, November 15, 1997.

[33] During this period there was also one protest in Indramayu, West Java, and one in Bojonegoro, East Java.

[34] See, "Tak Memenuhi Quorum: Pilkades di Klaten Batal," *Kedaulatan Rakyat*, October 23, 1997, and "Dua Kali Pilkades Gagal di Planggu," *Bernas*, October 28, 1997, and "Buntut Pelantikan Kades: Massa Ngamuk, Bakar Mobil," *Kedaulatan Rakyat*, October 26, 1997.

between October 1997, when they first broke out, and the end of March 1999, when village elections were postponed so as not to overlap with the upcoming campaign period and the June national election.[35] While the absolute totals are undoubtedly lower than the actual number of protests, we may take the regional distribution of these cases as a rough, though by no means precise, measure.

It is useful to begin by considering the geographic distribution of protest related to village elections. Of the 410 cases documented over the October 1997–March 1998 period, 97 percent (398) were on Java.[36] Even allowing for possible underreporting in the outer islands, the overwhelming concentration of these cases on Java far exceeds a random distribution. Similarly, on Java itself protest over village elections is neither evenly nor randomly distributed. Two-thirds of these protests occurred in Central Java, 17 percent in West Java, and the remaining 15 percent in East Java. Again, these percentages are neither a function nor a reflection of the total number of villages in each province.

It is necessary to note a geographic anomaly in the data set. As previously noted, village elections in Indonesia have never been held simultaneously throughout the country, or even in a single province, but rather at eight-year intervals calculated from the time of the previous election. After having been put on hold because of the 1997 national elections, village elections were allowed to recommence in late 1997. As had been the case during the previous two decades, elections were held at staggered times. The primary reason for this was concern about potential social unrest and the state's capacity to monitor thousands of elections at the same time. In Central Java, village elections were first initiated in Klaten, Brebes, and Jepara in October-November 1997, with all other districts following over the course of the next fifteen months. Meanwhile, elections were held in seventeen of the twenty-three districts in West Java, and in twenty-four of twenty-nine districts in East Java.[37] In all, elections were held in more than 80 percent of the districts in Java. In other words, the uneven distribution of protest over these elections cannot be accounted for by the uneven scheduling of the elections themselves.

---

[35] For the purposes of this research, I have relied on national newspapers from Jakarta (*Kompas, Suara Pembaruan, Media Indonesia, Angkatan Bersenjata*), as well as regional dailies including *Waspada* (North Sumatra), *Riau Post* (Riau), *Sriwijaya Post* (South Sumatra), *Pikiran Rakyat* (Bandung), *Pantura* (Jakarta and the north coast), *Suara Merdeka* (Semarang), *Kedaulatan Rakyat* and *Bernas* (Yogyakarta), *Surabaya Post* (Surabaya), *Banjarmasin Post* (South Kalimantan), *Bali Post*, and *Kupang Post* (Nusatenggara Timur).

[36] I have also identified an additional 109 cases of protest over village elections for the 1985-1996 period.

[37] In West Java no elections are known to have been held in Pandeglang, Sukabumi, Sumedang, Tasikmalaya, Garut, and Cirebon. In East Java no elections were held in Pacitan, Nganjuk, Lamongan, Blitar, Bondowoso, Situbondo, and Banyuwangi.

Pilkades: *Democracy, Village Elections, and Protest in Indonesia* 313

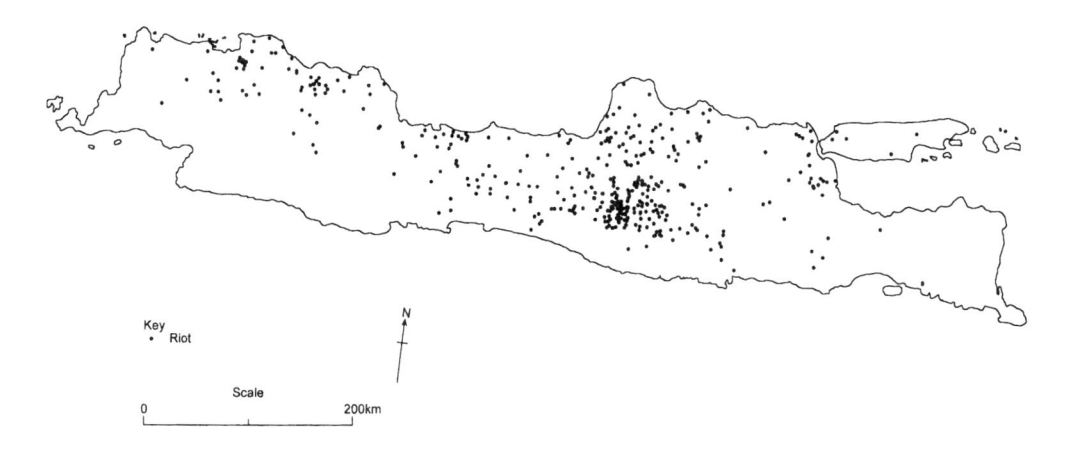

Map One
Village Electoral Protests (1997-1999)

Map Two
Residencies of Java, ca. 1850

A number of observers have assumed that these protests at the village level were part of the national movement demanding *reformasi*. Loekman Soetrisno, for example, writes:

> In June 1998, when *gerakan reformasi* [the reform movement] in the cities subsided with the stepping down of President Suharto, *gerakan reformasi* began to emerge in the countryside. The first targets of this movement were the *kepala desa* [village heads] and their functionaries, particularly those who were known to have actively "collected" votes for Golkar. *Gerakan reformasi* activists in the villages used methods similar to those of their counterparts in the cities . . . They demanded that the *kepala desa* and related officials resign . . . These are new phenomena.[38]

Some of these protests over village elections in fact have involved demands for *reformasi*. In one village in Indramayu, villagers who occupied the district hall carried a poster reading "Peaceful Reformation" (*Reformasi Damai*).[39] At a repeat protest in Kragilan village in Klaten, Central Java, a poster declared: "Mourning the Death of Democracy & the Aspirations of the People of Kragilan."[40] But if one assumes that village electoral protest is part of the national *reformasi* movement and that it represents a call for democratization, it would follow that this protest should be randomly distributed. As we will see, it was not. Furthermore, the wave of protest over village elections began in October–November 1997, well before concerted student protest emerged on university campuses. And though the frequency of protest over village elections increased dramatically during the first half of 1998, this appears to have been more a function of when elections were scheduled than a question of diffusion from urban to rural areas.

More modestly, one might argue that electoral protest is a specific response to corruption—either in the electoral process or on the part of incumbents. Here, too, there are numerous cases in which villagers have protested explicitly against what Indonesian's have come to call KKN (*korupsi, kolusi, nepotisme*). In a village in Pati, Central Java, for example, protesters carried posters reading: "Corruption in Village Elections Upsets the People" (*Kecurangan Pilkades Resahkan Rakyat*).[41] In Tuban, East Java, posters declared, "The selection of the Kembangbilo Village Head is not healthy" and "Don't bribe the people."[42] But KKN is common throughout Indonesia, and there is no reason to suspect that it is any more prevalent or problematic in Kudus or Klaten (both in Central Java) than it is in Lubuklinggau (South Sumatra) or Larantuka (Nusatenggara Timur). Again, appeals to general

---

[38] Loekman Soetrisno, "Current Social and Political Conditions of Rural Indonesia," in *Post-Soeharto Indonesia: Renewal or Chaos?*, ed. Geoff Forrester (New York: St. Martin's Press, 1999), pp. 166-67. Though certainly greater in intensity, protests over village elections are not new phenomena. See footnote 36 for details. See also the excellent volume edited by Sartono Kartodirdjo, *Pesta Demokrasi di Pedesaan: Studi Kasus Pemilihan Kepala Desa di Jawa Tengah dan DIY* (Festival of democracy in the village: Case studies of village-head elections in central Java and Yogyakarta) (Yogyakarta: Penerbit Aditya Media, 1992).

[39] "Ratusan Warga Duduki Pendopo," *Pikiran Rakyat*, July 28, 1998.

[40] The original: "Turut Berduka Cita atas Matinya Demokrasi & Aspirasi Rakyat Kragilan." Quoted in "Lagi, Warga Kragilan Protes Pilkades," *Bernas*, January 8, 1998.

[41] "Warga Wotan Unjuk Rasa ke DPRD, Persoalkan Pilkades," *Suara Merdeka*, January 7, 1998.

[42] "Tuntut Pilkades Diulang, 300 Warga Turun Ke Jalan," *Jawa Pos*, April 30, 1998.

principles or national issues cannot explain the particular distribution of protest over the elections of village heads.

What, then, explains this uneven distribution? Why have villagers in particular areas of Java protested village elections while elsewhere, where the electoral processes and outcomes appear quite similar, there is little or no protest? The answer, I believe, is twofold, involving both (a) how collective resources are allocated and (b) the role of the state in adjudicating class relations in the countryside.

Plotting our (398) cases on a map of Java, we find that these protests are even more highly concentrated than the crude provincial totals suggested. (See Map 1) In West Java, protests related to the election of village heads are concentrated along the northern littoral from Bekasi (immediately to the west of the capital) through Karawang, Subang, Indramayu, Cirebon, Majalengka, and Kuningan, on the border with Central Java. In Central Java protests are spread to the four corners of the province, though there are quite specific clusters: the first concentration is in the Brebes-Tegal area on the north coast; the second clump is seen in the Bagawanta river valley in Purworejo and Wonosobo; and the third and densest concentration is in the eastern third of the province, spreading from Klaten and Wonogiri up to the *pesisir* (north coast) region of Jepara-Pati-Rembang. Finally, in East Java protests appear sporadically throughout the western half of the province, are clustered in the lower Brantas river valley near Surabaya, but are virtually absent in the eastern horseshoe (*tapal kuda*).

This distribution is clearly not random. While these areas are all lowlands, such a purely geographic explanation would fail to account for the lack of protest in many other lowlands of Java (Banten, Banyumas, Madura, Jember, and so on) let alone the vast lowlands in the outer islands. Alternatively, one might suggest that this corresponds to certain cultural zones (the *pesisir* and *Kejawén*, [Java Proper]), but not others (Sunda and the Madurese "horseshoe").[43] Appealing as such a cultural explanation may be, simple correspondence is a far cry from a causal explanation and merely begs the question.

I would like to suggest an alternative explanation that is based on considerations of both agrarian relations and political authority. The distribution of protest over village elections during the October 1997–April 1999 period corresponds nearly perfectly to those areas in which village heads (*kepala desa*) are granted usufruct rights to land (*tanah bengkok*, salary lands) during their eight-year term of office. While the origins of these rights can be traced back to precolonial days, *tanah bengkok* was legally codified under the Dutch in the nineteenth century.[44] For reasons of convenience, economy, and cooptation, under

---

[43] For a map of these regions, see Clifford Geertz, *Agricultural Involution: The Process of Ecological Change in Indonesia* (Berkeley: The University of California Press, 1971), p. 42. In fact, scholars differ over the location of *kejawén*, some seeing it as the broader area of ethnic Javanese culture, others viewing it as "that area which, until the end of the Diponegoro War, was still governed directly by the kingdoms of Surakarta and Yogyakarta...." P. M. Laksono, *Tradition in Javanese Social Structure, Kingdom and Countryside* (Yogyakarta: Gadjah Mada University Press, 1990), p. 4.

[44] The origins of *tanah bengkok* remain unclear. Moertono distinguishes between *lungguh* (appanages) and *tanah bengkok*, and suggests that "the appanage system was an older institution than the *bengkok* system; for the latter system had more the character of a simple remuneration for services rendered, while in the appanage there were traces of administrative rights."

Dutch rule village headmen were "elected from among the villagers and were paid by them: with salary lands and a wide variety of other levies, either in money, produce or labor."[45] Under the Cultivation System (1830–1870), the village head played a central role in the functioning of the complex twenty-one-and-a-half-year leasing system(s) by which communal village lands were made available to Dutch (and some Chinese) estates for growing cash crops.[46] With the introduction of the "Ethical Policy" in the early twentieth century, in much of Java the position of village head was made elective and remuneration provided in the form of salary lands, moves intended to provide an inexpensive means of administration.[47]

The crucial feature is that this reallocation of use-rights for land was carried out by and through the colonial state, of which the village head was the lowest rung. This made it likely that disputes over the use of land would be directed at (or channeled through) the state. In his discussion of early nationalist politics in the Surakarta Residency in the first decades of the twentieth century, Takashi Shiraishi writes: "It was the state to which peasants looked to counter the powerful plantation."[48] Similarly, in his work on the Cirebon Residency during the early twentieth century, Jan Breman explains that the "ultimate mode of protest in accordance with tradition [was] the chance to complain collectively to the highest authority and to seek redress for injustice."[49] This pattern of protest—involving appeals to the state—continued in the postcolonial era.

It is the geographic distribution of these salary lands that concerns us here. Unfortunately, no official data are available on the distribution of *tanah bengkok*. We may, however, rely on a number of secondary sources for information. According to one Indonesian law book, *tanah bengkok* is found in the former Cirebon Residency (*Karesidenan Cirebon*) of West Java, throughout all of Central Java, and in East Java as far east as Pasuruan Residency (*Karesidenan Pasuruan*).[50] This general picture of the geographic distribution of *tanah bengkok* is supported by other sources. Working from 1868 Dutch survey data, Hiroyoshi Kano reports that *tanah bengkok* was found in Cirebon Residency, throughout all residencies in Central Java, and in Madiun, Rembang, Kediri, Surabaya, and Pasuruan Residencies in East Java.[51] Within these areas we can specify the distribution still further: wet-rice

---

Soemarsaid Moertono, *State and Statecraft in Old Java: A Study of the Later Mataram Period, Sixteenth to Nineteenth Century* (Ithaca, NY: Cornell Modern Indonesia Project, 1968), p. 118.

[45] Ibid., p. 121. It appears that the use of elections was introduced unevenly across Java: they were most common in areas where the Cultivation System was put into effect, much less so in the "feudal" *vorstenlanden* (Central Javanese principalities).

[46] Curiously, in his classic work Geertz barely mentions the role of the village headman and only discusses *tanah bengkok* in passing. See also Soemarsaid Moertono, *State and Statecraft in Old Java*, pp. 86, 102, and Loekman Soetrisno, *Role of the Lurah*, p. 6.

[47] Loekman Soetrisno, *Role of the Lurah*, p. 8.

[48] Takashi Shiraishi, *An Age in Motion: Popular Radicalism in Java, 1912-1926* (Ithaca, NY: Cornell University Press, 1990), p. 18.

[49] See Jan Breman, *Control of Land and Labour in Colonial Java: A Case Study of Agrarian Crisis and Reform in the Region of Cirebon during the First Decades of the Twentieth Century* (Holland/USA: Foris Publications, 1983), p. 18.

[50] See *Tanya Jawab Hukum Tanah* (Questions and answers about land law) (Sekretariat Bina Desa/Indhrra, 1975), p. 23.

[51] See Hiroyoshi Kano, "Land Tenure System and the Desa Community in Nineteenth Century Java" (Special Paper No. 5, Institute of Developing Economies, 1977). More recently, Robert

cultivating riverine areas normally have extensive *bengkok* lands (in some areas accounting for up to 30 percent of the village's total communal lands), while upland areas typically have far less.[52]

Following independence, the Indonesian state not only continued these practices, but in fact extended them in certain areas through the reclassification of communal lands. These efforts were staunchly opposed by the PKI, which argued that salary lands were a means of continued class domination in the countryside. Rex Mortimer explains the results of a 1964 party report:

> Concerning village government, the report declared that no fundamental changes had taken place since Dutch colonial times, because the pattern of class domination had remained substantially unaltered, despite the introduction of full adult suffrage for village elections. Village government was still feudal in essence because government officials there had the same economic interests as the landlords.[53]

Over the past three decades, the New Order state made occasional efforts to redress the uneven distribution of *tanah bengkok*. In areas without *tanah bengkok* (or with limited amounts), the state attempted to purchase land or to reclassify communal land to set aside for village officials.[54] Comparing information from the 1860s with their own data on the 1970s, Benjamin White and Gunawan Wiradi found a considerable increase in villages in Priangan (the former residency covering the Sundanese-speaking region of highland West Java) with *tanah bengkok*, though they note that the percentage of villages with this land remains significantly less than elsewhere, as does is the amount of *bengkok* per village.[55] On the other hand, during the 1980s and 1990s there was sporadic discussion about the need to replace *tanah bengkok* with a fixed salary for village heads so as to regularize local government revenue and expenditures and to prevent corruption.[56] For the most part, these efforts were half-hearted, and there are no indications of

---

Hefner has confirmed that *tanah bengkok* is distributed throughout the western half of East Java, adding that "Pasuruan itself is a transitional area. While salary lands [*tanah bengkok*] exist in part of the regency, they are among the smallest in all Java." Robert W. Hefner, *The Political Economy of Mountain Java: An Interpretive History* (Berkeley: University of California Press, 1990), p. 120.

[52] Hefner, *The Political Economy of Mountain Java*, p. 120. Similar estimates are provided in Loekman, *Role of the Lurah*, p. 34.

[53] Rex Mortimer, *Indonesian Communism Under Sukarno: Ideology and Politics, 1959-1965* (Ithaca, NY: Cornell University Press, 1974), p. 306.

[54] For the 1970s, see Loekman Soetrisno, *Role of the Lurah*, p. xv. In Jember, for example, in 1994 the district government allocated funds to purchase additional *tanah bengkok* for villages that were deemed to have too little. Interview, Kantor Pertanahan Nasional, Jember, East Java, April 4, 1999.

[55] Benjamin White and Gunawan Wiradi, "Pola-pola Penguasaan Tanah di DAD Cimanuk Dulu dan Sekarang: Beberapa Catatan Sementara," *Prisma* 9, September 1979, pp. 47-48.

[56] See, for example, "Kades dan Perangkatnya tak akan Terima Bengkok," *Kompas*, August 31, 1988, and "Pilkades Suatu Pesta Rakyat Sejati," *Suara Pembaruan*, November 19, 1990. More recently, local officials have expressed concern that a shift from *tanah bengkok* to a fixed salary, particularly one based on the provincial minimum wage, as proposed by the Governor of Central Java, would lead to increased corruption. For several views, see "Perubahan dari Bengkok ke Gaji Suburkan Korupsi," *Suara Merdeka*, January 6, 1998.

any substantial shift in the regional distribution or allocation of *tanah bengkok* in Java. For present purposes, Kano's data on the geographic spread of *tanah bengkok* are more than adequate.

Map 2 shows that there is an extraordinarily close correspondence between the distribution of *tanah bengkok* and electoral protest during the October 1997–April 1999 period. Electoral protest is found along the north coast of West Java from Bekasi to Kuningan, throughout Central Java, and in the western portion of East Java. The only significant exception to this generalization is the Bogor-Bekasi-Karawang-Subang stretch in West Java (parts of the former residencies of Batavia, Buitenzorg, and Krawang). One also notes the conspicuous absence of protest over village elections in the Yogyakarta region.[57]

The close correlation between *tanah bengkok* and protest over village elections is not coincidental. The often extensive, and therefore lucrative, *tanah bengkok* provides reason for intense electoral competition, and dissatisfaction with the electoral process, or results, in turn may provide the trigger for popular protest. But electoral protest is not simply a question of control over property use. *Tanah bengkok* is distributed in areas characterized by smallholdings (as opposed to plantation economies in Priangan and Pasuruan, or the essentially "feudal" Yogyakarta principalities). It is therefore also necessary to take seriously the nature of collective action according to patterns of land ownership.

ELECTORAL COMPETITION, RESOURCES AND CONFLICT

The Indonesian state—colonial as well as postcolonial—has viewed the issue of village government in essentially economic terms. As far as possible, the state has sought to minimize central expenditures and maximize the village contribution to its own administration. Hence, despite occasional objections, the state continues to rely on *tanah bengkok* to pay the salaries of the village heads and on other village-owned lands (*tanah kas desa*) to pay for the costs of village government. The New Order state applied a similar economic approach to the question of village elections. Despite a formal commitment to defray the costs of holding village elections, these expenses were commonly passed on to the contestants themselves.[58] This was in part a function of inadequate funding, in part too because funds earmarked for village elections never made it to their intended destinations.[59]

Standing for election as village head in Java was (and remains today) extremely expensive. Each prospective candidate (*bakal calon kepala desa*) was required to pass a preliminary test, involving payment of official fees as well as bribes for the district electoral committee. Further payments were commonly necessary to help defray the cost of the election itself. In Brebes, for example, despite a policy stating that the fee was only Rp. 3.5 million, candidates were

---

[57] This remains largely inexplicable, though one suspects that it is a function of Yogya's continued "feudal" political character.

[58] Because law 5 1979 did not specify who was responsible for the costs of village elections, individual provinces subsequently found it necessary to pass their own legislation. In Central Java, for example, Perda [Regional Regulation] No. 7/1983 stipulated that the cost of an election was to be covered by the district government and the village.

[59] See, for example, "Anggaran Pilkades Diminta Segera Cair," *Kompas*, September 4, 1997, and "Biaya Pilkades Ditentukan Kepala Daerah," *Kedaulatan Rakyat*, November 13, 1997.

charged up to Rp. 15 million to stand for election.[60] Further payoffs to the electoral committee were a common means of preventing a particular candidate from competing in the election, or even for ensuring that there was in fact only one candidate allowed to run for office.[61] On the day of the election, candidates and their operatives treated voters to drinks and snacks (*suguhan*) and ran Operation Dawn (Operasi Fajar), an euphemism for vote-buying, involving sums which could range from Rp. 5,000 to Rp. 25,000 per vote.[62] In all, the cost of running for village head could run from Rp. 50-100 million (US$15,000) or more.[63]

For most villagers, of course, outlays of this magnitude were out of the question. The position of village head therefore remained largely the prerogative of land-owning peasants and, more rarely, villagers engaged in business or with connections to the state apparatus. For this reason, it is common for family dynasties to control the position of village head for years. Based on research in Pati, Central Java, Hüsken writes: "In some cases present-day village heads were the fifth or sixth generation in a line dating back to the latter part of the nineteenth century," noting that they consolidated "wealth and power by keeping control over the village administration (which gave also access to the vast salary lands) within the family...."[64]

Under these circumstances, villagers typically viewed village elections in terms of a simple cost-benefit analysis: weighing the considerable expenses required to run for village head against the equally considerable income that might be gained from office. The use-rights to *tanah bengkok* were (and are) the primary incentive. As an article in the *Kompas* daily bluntly explained: "Control over this land [*tanah bengkok*] is the most important reason for villagers to nominate themselves to become village head. In a village with significant *tanah bengkok*, the income from this can make a village head very wealthy."[65] The attraction of *tanah bengkok*—as well as the pervasiveness of official corruption—is captured beautifully in a novel by S. Sinansari Ecip titled *Election Seat*.

> The thought of forty hectares of fertile wet-rice land provided to the village head is a real temptation. With that much wet-rice land, who couldn't buy a car after one year's harvest. And if fertilizer, a tractor, and prime seedlings were used, the harvest could be several times more. Daily office expenses could be covered by donations from villagers....

---

[60] See, "Biaya Pilkades Sudah Disahkan Camat," *Suara Karya*, October 24, 1997.

[61] See, for example, the discussion in "Sering terjadi calon tunggal dalam Pilkades di Purwakarta," *Angkatan Bersenjata*, January 20, 1990.

[62] In the words of a villager in Sleman district, Yogyakarta: "In addition to being a festival of democracy [*pesta demokrasi*], it is also a money party [*pesta uang*] because a smart voter can receive money from all of the contestants." Quoted in "Pjs Kades di Karawang Dikutip Jutaan Rupiah," *Media Indonesia*, January 18, 1996.

[63] For two such estimates, see "Biaya Pendaftaran Pilkades, Rp. 10 Juta," *Suara Karya*, October 20, 1997, and "Persiapan Pilkades diwarnai kasak-kusuk," *Angkatan Bersenjata*, March 9, 1998.

[64] Hüsken, "Village Elections," p. 126. On family dynasties in West Java, see "Pilkades Di Karawang Dinasti Hingga Jampi-jampi," *Suara Karya*, January 16, 1990.

[65] "Mendagri: Jabatan 600 Kades Lowong," *Kompas*, December 16, 1997.

And who could refuse the heartfelt and voluntary donations made by the peasants [*kawula*, the meaning of which is close to "serf"]. Being a village head means being the sole legal power in the area. Being a village head means having economic and political control of the *bengkok* land. People will compete to become the village head.[66]

Tanah bengkok is not the only economic incentive that prompts villagers to run for the position of village head, however. There are at least three other areas in which the village head might profit from his (and less frequently, her)[67] post. First, as the chief administrator, the village head is involved (to varying degrees) in most official development projects and welfare programs.[68] Throughout the New Order it was common, even accepted, practice for officials to siphon off part of these funds for their private use. Second, a wide range of routine village affairs must be approved and relevant documents signed by the village head. This includes all land transactions, rental agreements, issuing building permits, and the registration of marriages and divorces, births and deaths. In each case, it is common practice for the village head to charge a fee, to be determined at his discretion. This may be a source of considerable accumulated income, and equally great displeasure on the part of villagers.[69] Third, and closely related to the second point, the village head is the point of access for outsiders wishing to do business in the village. As such, the village head may serve outside interests by coercing villagers to rent or sell land to developers, by rezoning land for new uses, and even by selling village assets illegally.[70]

There are, in other words, a wide variety of means by which a village head may use his position for economic gain. Given the geographic distribution of protests over village elections, it is necessary to underscore the relative importance of these incentives. Opportunities for corruption and the misuse of village assets are found throughout Indonesia and are in no way specific to Java, let alone to particular regions of Java. They therefore cannot account for the particular spread of protest. The distribution of *tanah bengkok*, on the other hand, corresponds nearly

---

[66] S. Sinansari Ecip, *Kursi Pemilu* (Jakarta: Penerbit Sinar Harapan, 1982), pp. 11-12. The title of the novel is oddly incorrect: "pemilu" is the abbreviation for "national election" (*pemilihan umum*), not village election (*pemilihan kepala desa*, abbreviated "pilkades"). Given that the novel is a thinly disguised account of the national elections, the acronymic slippage is understandable.

[67] In 1996, only 293 of a total of 8,530 village heads in Central Java were women. See, *Potensi Desa Propinsi Jawa Tengah, 1996* (Village resources in Central Java, 1996) (Kantor Statistik Propinsi Jawa Tengah, 1996), p. 77. Similar gender ratios are found in West and East Java.

[68] According to Noer Fauzi, this role increased dramatically following the adoption of the new law on village government in 1979. See Noer Fauzi, "Transformasi Agraria dan Kesejahteraan Kaum Tani," in *Tanah, Rakyat dan Demokrasi* (Land, people, and democracy), ed. Untoro Hariadi and Masruchah (Yogyakarta: Forum LSM-LPSM, 1995), pp. 162-63. Case studies of local leadership are found in Philip Quarles van Ufford, ed., *Kepimpinan Lokal dan Implementasi Program* (Local leadership and program implementation) (Jakarta: Gramedia, 1988).

[69] To provide but one example, villagers in Purwokerto protested the extremely high fee for marriages. See, "Diprotes, Biaya Nikah Rp 400 Ribu," *Suara Merdeka*, September 4, 1998.

[70] The Indonesian press is full of stories of village heads selling village property. Such cases include the sale of village land, of private land belonging to villagers, the village hall, a cemetery, roads, and even bridges.

exactly to those areas in which protests emerged during the October 1997–March 1999 period. We can make sense of this difference by considering the nature of class relations in rural Indonesia.

There is a direct relationship between the amount of *tanah bengkok* and electoral competition. In villages with large and productive salary lands, residents generally show a great interest in village elections and a large number of candidates are involved. Conversely, in areas that do not have *bengkok*, residents are less interested in becoming village head. This problem has been openly discussed by officials and villagers alike. In late 1997, as village elections were allowed to recommence, the Minister of the Interior Yogie S. Memet lamented that "the lack of *tanah bengkok* is the reason people don't want to become village head."[71] In the words of a villager in Wonogiri, Central Java: "Why would anyone want to become village head if the *bengkok* land isn't fertile? It's no longer a secret that it costs millions of rupiah to become village head."[72] Similar statements are heard from villages in Kebumen and Kendal, Ponorogo and Probolinggo.

Tempting as it may appear, it is not possible to use statistical methods to find a precise correlation between *tanah bengkok* and electoral competition, primarily because of the great diversity within individual districts in both the total amount and quality of land. This is neatly illustrated by a 1997 report about elections in twenty-eight villages in Pati district, Central Java: "Officials do not know why there are no candidates for village head in eight villages, but they suspect that it is because these villages do not have sufficient salary land . . . ." The article goes on to explain that in other villages, however, there were large numbers of people applying to run for election: "In Bumiayu village, Wedarijaksa subdistrict, 21 people applied to stand for election. This is understandable because Bumiayu village is prosperous and the salary land is quite extensive."[73] This pattern is repeated throughout Java, and both officials and villagers commonly discuss the connection between *tanah bengkok* and electoral competition.

Interest in the position of village head has varied considerably over time. Officials from various parts of Java have reported that the number of candidates standing for election as village head decreased during the 1990s. This might be so because the size of *bengkok* has decreased,[74] but also because the costs of running for office have increased. There were also more explicitly political reasons for this. As the *reformasi* protests spread in early and mid-1998, village heads came under increasing attack for their corruption and long-standing support of the regime. Despite the potential for personal gain, under these circumstances villagers were often reluctant to take on what was rapidly becoming a thankless job.

Village elections reflect two partially overlapping social cleavages in rural Indonesia. Within the village there are deep divisions between the landed elite, on the one hand, and poor and landless peasants, on the other. A wealthy peasant might mobilize considerable material as well as human resources to win election as

---

[71] See "Mendagri: Sulit Cari Kades Karena Tak Ada Tanah Bengkok," *Suara Karya*, December 16, 1997.

[72] Quoted in "Kurang, Peminat Calon Kades di Wonogiri," *Kompas*, June 24, 1989.

[73] "Belum Ada Pelamar Kades di Delapan Desa," *Kompas*, October 3, 1997.

[74] The problem of insufficient *tanah bengkok* has been exacerbated by the creation of new administrative units, and hence division of village assets, to accommodate the burgeoning population of Java.

village head.[75] In the eyes of poor and landless peasants, this in itself is not problematic. The question is whether the mobilization of resources and (assuming the candidate's successful election) use of office are seen to benefit the poor as well. If so, the village head may receive considerable support from within the community. If the village head is seen to use these resources exclusively to his own advantage, however, poor(er) villagers are more likely to resent him and to mobilize protest.[76]

A second social cleavage in rural Indonesia is seen in the relations between the village community and "outsiders," whether they be state officials or private developers. Insofar as outside actors make claims on village resources, there is likely to be a significant degree of cooperation within the village. This may be the case even when that cooperation first benefits village elites. For maintenance of village assets, even if they remain under the effective control of elites, may be in the (short-term) interest of landless peasants as well. There is an obvious parallel between this argument and Geertz's (now widely rejected) notion of "shared poverty" in rural Java. But while Geertz's argument concerned shared poverty, I am highlighting acquiescence in social stratification insofar as this is understood by villagers to be in defense of the village community or its assets as opposed to outside claimants.[77] The crucial point is that Javanese villages are not characterized exclusively by either cooperation or conflict. Social cleavages in rural Java lie both within the village and between the village and outside parties. The election of village heads highlights both of these cleavages, and it is these divisions that provide the motor for much collective action.

Curiously, in seeking to minimize its expenditures for village administration, the Indonesian state allowed the election of village heads to become extraordinarily "monetized." The most obvious (because officially recognized) prize was *tanah bengkok*, which could make the victor a wealthy person. But competing for the prize was often equally costly, involving outlays of money to officials as well as the villager electorate. Taken together, the resources at stake undoubtedly exceeded what a generous salary would have been by many times. Villagers were therefore confronted with a situation in which a great deal was at stake—in terms of expenses as well as potential gains—under an electoral system characterized by gross biases and rampant corruption.

This mobilization of resources served to highlight tensions among villagers as well as between the village and outside claimants. As protests over village elections emerged in Central Java, state officials expressed concern about these interests. As Major General Mardiyanto, commander of the Diponegoro Regional Command, commented: "We all know that village elections used to be a form of

---

[75] It is important to note a second, parallel, source of resource mobilization connected with village elections: gambling. The considerable sums of money at stake provide yet another reason that dissatisfaction might arise over the results of the election.

[76] One of the best treatments of resistance as well as acquiescence in rural class relations remains James Scott's *Weapons of the Weak: Everyday Forms of Peasant Resistance* (New Haven: Yale University Press, 1985).

[77] This idea was first introduced in Clifford Geertz, "Religious Belief and Economic Behavior in a Central Javanese Town: Some Preliminary Considerations," *Economic Development and Cultural Change* 4,2 (January 1956): 134-58, then repeated in Geertz, *Agricultural Involution*, p. 97. For a summary of his critics see Benjamin White, "'Agricultural Involution' and its Critics: Twenty Years After," *Bulletin of Concerned Asian Scholars* 15,2 (1983): 18-31.

pure democracy, but now they are no longer pure. Now there are all sorts of interests at work."[78] Ironically, these "interests" were in large part the result of the state's own attempt to avoid financial outlays for the electoral process and the salaries of the village heads.

PROTESTING ELECTIONS

In mid-1997, following the completion of the June national elections, provincial officials announced that village elections would recommence beginning in October. Given that thousands of elections had been postponed and thousands more terms were to come due in the next two years, there was pressing need to get this process underway. Despite the high levels of violence during the May campaign and in the immediate aftermath of the June elections, officials did not display any outward concern about village elections. If anything the opposite was true, as officials at the provincial and district levels announced that they would not "drop" candidates and that elections should be held freely and fairly.[79]

From the outset, however, these elections were plagued by disputes and protest. While expressing concern about the process by which candidates were tested and approved to stand for election, as well as the monetization of the elections, officials showed no sign that they viewed these protests as having any bearing on national politics. Nor did officials show any concern that these protests might in some way overflow into other areas or involve other social actors. Villagers, however, took these elections seriously. In Tegal, for instance, protesters carried more than a dozen banners, with slogans reading: "Wipe out the low-class yes-men" (*Basmi penjilat-penjilat kelas kroco*) and "If the candidate for village head is appointed, the earth will shake" (*Calon kades dilantik, dunia gempar*).[80] These suggest that protests were both an attack on higher level officials responsible and a threat that further actions would ensue if the electoral "irregularities" were not mended. Furthermore, it is necessary to underscore the point that these protests cannot be reduced simply to either a defense of democracy or an expression of the high material stakes involved in village elections. The two were inextricably intertwined.

Electoral protest centered on three general issues. The first of these involved villagers' objections to the process by which candidates were selected to stand for office. Those wishing to stand (*bakal calon kepala desa*, or *bacakades*) for office were required to take tests, and only those who passed were allowed to become candidates (*calon kepala desa*, or *cakades*). Forty percent of all protests for which a specific grievance (or set of grievances) can be identified revolved around this selection process. The testing procedure presented ample room for a wide assortment of corrupt practices: the use of fake documents showing educational qualifications, residency, age, or a "clean" [i.e. non-PKI] background; the payment of bribes to local officials; and bias on the part of the electoral committee.

---

[78] Quoted in "Meski kecil, perlu diwaspadai Pilkades," *Angkatan Bersenjata*, December 15, 1997.

[79] See "Pilkades tak Perlu Ujian," *Kedaulatan Rakyat*, July 29, 1997.

[80] Reported in "Ratusan warga datangi bupati dan DPRD, protest Pilkades," *Angkatan Bersenjata*, December 27, 1997.

Villagers were particularly rankled when only one candidate (*calon tunggal*) was allowed to stand for election. This, of course, was frequently the result of bribery on the part of the candidate and/or bias on the part of the election committee to prevent the emergence of competitors. In Probolinggo, East Java, for example, villagers argued that this was "undemocratic" (*kurang demokratis*), and threatened to protest, usually by means of a boycott, if only one candidate was declared eligible to stand for election.[81] Yet this was all too common. The state sought to address the problem of single candidates by stipulating that in such cases the candidate would have to stand against an "empty box" (*bumbung kosong*) or a "blank form" (*blangko kosong*). Should the "empty box" receive more votes than the candidate, a new election would be held.[82]

The second issue that provoked villagers' protests had to do with how the election itself was conducted. Over a third (37 percent) of the cases in the data set fall into this category. Here too there were a myriad irregularities and forms of outright fraud. Fraud might involve individuals voting more than once, more votes being counted than there were eligible voters, participation by those under the minimum age of seventeen, participation by non-residents, vote-buying, intimidation, villagers being prevented from voting, and an assortment of irregularities in the process by which votes were counted. By all appearances "irregularities" were in fact the norm.

Third, often villagers were angered by the outcome of the election itself.[83] Hence, a large number of protests (21 percent of those in the data set) erupted when, or soon after, the results of the election were announced at the village hall. Villagers might protest the victory of a candidate whom they judged to be unacceptable on religious or political grounds, as in Gatak village, Sukoharjo, where the villagers accused the victor's parents of being members of a "banned organization" [i.e. PKI] and of "sponsoring village youths who wished to get drunk."[84] Outrage was particularly strong when a corrupt incumbent was reelected. In Purworejo district, for example, inhabitants of Dewi Village staged a demonstration to protest the victory of Sumarno, whom they accused of having sold village land (*bandha desa*) and engaging in other corrupt practices.[85] Even more egregious was a case in Sugihan village, Sukoharjo, where the newly elected village head had the nerve to sell the *tanah bengkok* before he was even formally

---

[81] "Warga Akan Boikot Calon Tunggal Pilkades; Bupati Hindari Lawan Bumbung Kosong," *Surabaya Post*, April 13, 1998. Given that this was the model of national elections during the New Order, one wonders to what extent villagers understood this as a comment on the national political structure and sign of displeasure with Suharto's rule.

[82] In late 1997, the Central Java legislature debated a new provincial regulation (*Rancangan Peraturan Daerah tentang Tata Cara Pencalonan, Pemilihan, Pengangkatan dan Pemberhentian Kepala Desa*) requiring a minimum of two candidates for each village election. It is not known why this was not approved. Reported in "Bisa Jadi Obat Kasus Pilkades," *Jawa Pos*, December 11, 1997.

[83] It is necessary to note that the large number of cases falling in this category may also be a function of the newspaper reporting, on which this research is based. Journalists may report instances of collective action without noting the particular grievances that gave rise to it.

[84] "Sembilan Kades 'Bermasalah' Temui DPRD," *Suara Merdeka*, November 11, 1998.

[85] Reported in "Baru Terpilih, 3 Kades di Purworejo Diprotes," *Kedaulatan Rakyat*, October 16, 1998.

appointed to his post.[86] Such post-election protests were triggered when one or more of the losing candidates refused to sign the forms acknowledging the results. As the candidate had already mobilized villagers to vote in the election, it was not difficult to encourage his or her supporters to demonstrate against the outcome.

These three sets of grievances were accompanied by three basic repertoires of protest. The first of these repertoires was the boycott. This was a typical response to grievances stemming from the process of testing and approving candidates to stand for election. Such a boycott might take either of two forms. In cases where only a single candidate was standing for office, villagers might make their dissatisfaction known by voting for the empty box or blank ballot. Should "the box" win, a new election would be held. This arrangement represents an attempt by the state to provide an institutional mechanism through which protest might be channeled, thereby lessening the disruptive character of collective action. As the Bupati of Boyolali explained, "If none of the approved candidates is suitable, there's always the blank ballot."[87] This was a common enough occurrence, and, though officially sanctioned, a clear sign of friction between villagers and district officials. Alternatively, villagers who were angered by the testing process or the electoral preparations might simply refuse to participate in the election altogether. Should more than two-thirds of the eligible electorate fail to vote, the election would be declared invalid and another election scheduled in the near future.

The second repertoire of protest was the demonstration in the village itself. Such demonstrations might emerge at any stage of the electoral process. The gathering of hundreds, at times thousands, of angry villagers was invariably accompanied by threats of violence. In Segaran village, Karawang district, for example, one villager commented: "We ask that the Bupati immediately declare that the election is invalid. This can't be put off. If it is, the village head's office might be burned down."[88] These were not idle threats, and more than 70 percent of the electoral demonstrations held in the villages resulted in violence. Forms of violence included fistfights between the supporters of different candidates, destruction of ballot boxes, mass attacks against houses, and not infrequently incineration of the village hall. Violence was sufficiently common that the Bupati of Sukoharjo, Tedjo Suminto, threatened to set up a boxing ring in which villagers could settle their differences after a contentious election: "If these negative excesses [ekses yang kurang baik] continue, I will introduce three steps in village elections. First the announcement of candidates, second the election, and for the third step I'll open an arena for boxing and stone-throwing."[89] But where the Bupati of Sukoharjo could joke about the problem, others took a far less sanguine view of the rising tide of rural violence. Indeed, this violence was one of the primary reasons for Governor Soewardi's decision to postpone further elections in June 1998.

---

[86] See "Belum dilantik, Kades Sugihan jual bengkok," *Solo Pos*, June 24, 1998.

[87] "Tidak memenuhi Kuorum Pilkades Kismoyoso Ditunda," *Suara Merdeka*, April 1, 1998.

[88] Quoted in "Seputar Nusantara," *Media Indonesia*, September 19, 1998.

[89] "Apa Perlu Arena Tinju di Pilkades," *Suara Merdeka*, May 5, 1998.

**Table 1: Issues and Repertoires of Electoral Protest in Java,
October 1997-March 1999** (in number of protests)

	Protest Action				Appeal			
	Boycott		In Village		To Government		Other	
	No.	Viol.	No.	Viol.	No.	Viol.	No.	Viol.
Issue								
Committee corrupt	1	-	3	-	21	2	1	-
Candidate(s) rejected	15	4	11	10	21	2	-	-
Candidate(s) allowed	2	1	3	1	6	-	-	-
Dislike candidates	10	-	1	-	1	-	-	-
Single candidate	3	-	-	-	1	-	1	-
Candidate faked docs.	-	-	1	-	7	-	-	-
Incumbent interferes	-	-	1	1	4	-	1	-
Voting hindered	-	-	3	2	8	-	2	-
Ineligible voters	-	-	4	2	15	2	4	-
Vote buying	-	-	2	1	24	-	2	-
Vote counting	-	-	11	8	23	-	4	-
Intimidation	-	-	2	2	4	-	1	-
Reject winner/outcome	-	-	39	32	22	4	2	-
Unknown	-	-	33	23	58	2	4	-
Total	31	5	114	82	215	12	16	-
Percent	8.1%	1.3%	29.7%	21.4%	56.1%	3.1%	4.1%	-

Viol. = violence during the protest
This includes any collective effort to send letters to the government, appeal to NGOS, or approach the media.

The third repertoire of electoral protest was the "appeal" (*pengaduan*) to a government office outside of the village. Such appeals were most commonly launched at the district seat, though they might also be directed to the subdistrict (*kantor camat*), the police, and even the provincial legislature or governor's office. This tactic was not normally a matter of pressuring officials, though failure to achieve results might lead to this. Rather, appeals typically involved reporting the "wrongdoing" of lower level officials (such as the incumbent village head or the members of the election committee) to their bureaucratic superiors in the hope of official intervention.

Multiple actions during the course of a single election are commonly reported, revealing a natural order to these repertoires of protests. Dissatisfaction during the selection process might lead villagers to mail a letter of protest to the district administration or to demonstrate at the subdistrict office. Whether or not these grievances were addressed, the election would still be held as scheduled. Continued irregularities during the election might prompt a second protest, perhaps violent, in the village. Continued failure to address these grievances might then lead villagers to organize a convoy to the district seat, where they would appeal for intervention and a resolution to the case.

The wave of rural electoral protest that began in late 1997 widened significantly following Suharto's forced resignation in May 1998. Nationwide calls for reform and demands for an end to KKN were echoed at the village level. Some of this was a simple continuation of ongoing protest over abuses committed by village heads, now couched in a new language. But whereas protest over village elections took place in specific areas, reflecting the presence of *tanah bengkok* as a major asset, protest against corrupt officials appeared in a wider geographic area beginning in May 1998. In Tempurejo village, in Magelang district, Central Java, one villager explained: "We recommend that anyone tainted by corruption, collusion and nepotism should have the intelligence and prudence to withdraw immediately."[90] Similar demands were leveled in thousands of villages across the country.

State officials raced to keep pace with the growing demands for reform and calls for an end to corruption. In Bantul, Central Java, one officials announced that changes would be made, but lamely defended his record by explaining that "I never knew about the collection of illegal fees." Villagers enthusiastically greeted the abolition of "money for this and that" (*uang ini-itu*), while at the same time bluntly calling attention to past practices: "It is hoped that now, in the Reform Era, village elections won't involve the kind of funny business that took place in the past."[91] Frequently, however, higher level officials simply shifted the burden of responsibility, claiming that village election committees were levying fees above and beyond those set by the district head.

These official responses provide telling insight into the bureaucratic stranglehold over village economic life that was imposed during the New Order. In Plantaran village, Kendal district, on the north coast of Java, village youths protested forty-six different fees levied by the village head and demanded his resignation.[92] And in Aceh, the Bupati of Pidie hurried to announce the abolition of eleven regional taxes and thirty-three kinds of *retribusi* (including permits for small-scale industry, administration of poultry export, supervision of poultry and livestock export, livestock vaccination, hotel fees, fishing licenses, family identification, the assignment of house numbers, bicycle parking permits, business permits, livestock market licenses, permits for collecting swallows nests, for washing vehicles, for the export of agricultural and industrial produce, cargo, for slaughtering livestock, selling meat, slaughtering poultry, mooring boats, laying cables, etc.).[93]

Although protest might extend from the village to district, and even provincial, offices, these protests were essentially local matters. There is, of course, scattered evidence of outside involvement in some of these protests, particularly on the part of students who had returned to their natal villages. But at no point did villagers organize horizontal organizations that might become a

---

[90] "Dua Perangkat Desa Diminta Mundur," *Suara Merdeka*, May 30, 1998.

[91] "Tak membutuhkan Uang Banyak: Sistem Pilkades di Bantul Diubah," *Kedaulatan Rakyat*, May 30, 1998.

[92] "Terapkan 46 Jenis Pungutan YMT Kades Didemo Warga," *Suara Merdeka*, June 2, 1998.

[93] "Bupati Pidie Hapus 44 Macam Pungutan," *Waspada*, June 2, 1998.

platform on which to lobby for broad structural change. Nor for that matter did students, the urban intelligentsia, or the newly mushrooming political parties demonstrate any real interest in channeling the massive rural ferment and protest into a broader movement. Rather, many viewed the rural uprisings as a threat to middle-class sensibilities and interests. Noted sociologist Loekman Soetrisno's view of village-level protest was typical:

> This must be prevented so that it doesn't turn into a radical or uncontrolled movement. If demonstrations are held against everyone, it will be like it was in the past when people were accused of "being contaminated" [*tidak bersih lingkungan*]. The popular misinterpretation of "demo" [i.e. demonstration] can't be allowed to continue, because it could lead to an anti-reform movement. There's now a tendency for demonstrations to be used as a means of terror.[94]

These protests over village elections cannot be reduced to a question of either the defense of democratic ideals or of material incentives and gain. The two are not only intertwined, but in fact inseparable. Procedural democracy involved mobilizing resources, primary of which was money. Participants' interest in both private gain and the protection of collective assets contributed to the democratic process. The position of village head figured as the crossroads at which the substantial flows of state revenue intersected the equally large flows of the private sector.

CONCLUSION

This essay has argued that the politics of village elections in rural Java are intimately related to access to and control over land. While the general conclusion may come as no surprise, the mechanism through which it is played out appears to be unique to Java. Only in Java were appanage lands characteristic of precolonial Javanese kingdoms consolidated under Dutch colonial rule in the form of salary lands provided to village headmen in lieu of a salary. Furthermore, the extraordinary fertility of wet-rice regions and high population density on Java combined to make land the most valuable of commodities. Taken together, this meant that land was wedded to office and office to land. This was done not in a pattern of large-holdings that might give rise to a class of entrepreneurial plantation owners, nor by granting alienable land rights, but rather in a fragmented and temporally limited system.

The election of village heads in Java highlights two partially overlapping social cleavages. On the one hand, because of the high stakes and equally high costs of running for election, these elections involve serious intra-village conflicts. On the other hand, these elections highlight the ongoing tension between the village as a community and outside claimants, with poor villagers often committed to maintain communal assets, even if that means that they have effectively placed themselves under the control of village elites.

To this we might contrast those areas that do not have *tanah bengkok*. Characterized by less fertile land and larger landholdings, in these areas the state

---

[94] As quoted in "Prof Loekman: Jangan jadi Gerakan Radikal," *Kedaulatan Rakyat*, June 17, 1998.

did not play this periodic, intermediary function of mediating the transfer of land-use rights from peasant communities to private agro-industrialists. In such areas, peasants have less reason to direct their protests against the state. Rather, in Oesthook, Priangan, Banten and elsewhere, peasant protest was aimed directly at the plantation and company owners and commonly took the form of looting and riots, actions directed at the private owners of the means of production. This pattern continued during the New Order. In fact, during the past two years these same areas have been the sites of looting, riots, and other forms of mass violence.

Taken together, the evidence suggests that collective action by peasants in contemporary Java strongly reflects patterns of land use and political authority established during the early colonial period. In areas in which land-use is directly related to local political authority, there is not only greater interest in the electoral process but also a greater likelihood of collective protest. In areas in which communal resources are not assigned to the village head, there appears to be less interest in the democratic process and less likelihood of collective action taking the form of peaceful protest directed at the state.

In light of the above argument, it is useful to return to Governor Soewardi's decree and the concurrent wave of protest in rural Java. In November 1998, the Central Java DPRD announced that the current round of village elections must be finished by March 1999, so as not to overlap with the national election scheduled for May 1999. Of the 7,524 villages in the province, 30 percent had already held their elections; the remaining 70 percent were to be conducted over a sixteen-month period.[95] Given that most villages in Central Java have *tanah bengkok* and that, largely for this reason, the position of village head is highly attractive, high levels of political mobilization and collective action will continue. Furthermore, mobilization and protest arising over these village elections is likely to color the development of party politics and the dynamics of national legislative elections in the future.

One should be wary of equating free electoral competition with fair electoral competition. So long as the costs of village elections are born by the candidates themselves, and so long as vote buying remains a common practice, village elections will remain the preserve of the propertied. In the case of rural Java, this situation is exacerbated by the irony that the state's attempt to avoid fiscal responsibility for democratic institutions (in which it did not itself believe) has resulted in the monetization of the electoral process and the village headship. This is epitomized by the continued centrality of *tanah bengkok*. The prize of electoral victory is land (and secondarily access to state coffers), not political leadership, ideological sway, or influence in policy making. As Barrington Moore Jr. noted long ago in the context of India's post-independence political development, "To democratize the village without altering property relationships is simply absurd."[96]

---

[95] "Mimbar Legislatif: Pilkades Harus Berakhir Maret 1999," *Kedaulatan Rakyat*, November 23, 1998.

[96] Barrington Moore Jr., *Social Origins of Dictatorship and Democracy: Land and Peasant in the Making of the Modern World* (London: Penguin Books, 1966), p. 394.

WHEN SOLDIERS KILL CIVILIANS: BURMA'S CRACKDOWN IN 1988 IN COMPARATIVE PERSPECTIVE[1]

Mary P. Callahan

Why do armies turn their guns on unarmed citizens? How do soldiers—long socialized into roles as protectors of the nation, its mothers and children, and their brethren—hear enemy threats in cries for democratic reform? Under what conditions does popular mobilization constitute a paramount threat to an army?

In this essay, I attempt to answer these questions with regard to Burma. Popular explanations of the military's brutal crackdown on the 1988 pro-democracy uprising and the subsequent reassertion of military political dominance tend to emphasize a particular political pathology that is uniquely endemic to Burma. The army is seen as a politicized institution that never embraced Western-style values of "professionalism." In the view of the outside world, the generals who lead the *tatmadaw* (Burmese for "armed forces") routinely launch brutal campaigns of repression against their own citizens, who occasionally mount heroic and massive attempts to challenge authoritarian rule. Despite the generals' extensive overseas education, training, and service, and despite international pressures—the suspension of most international economic aid, the imposition of an arms embargo, the ban on US visas for senior junta leaders, and the ban on new investment in Burma by US citizens—the military regime has managed to turn the country into a "poster child for a nation destroyed by tyrants," as one American commentator recently noted.[2]

However, when placed in comparative perspective, the characteristics that have been held to explain the Burmese military's harsh response to popular mobilization and political uncertainty are not unique to the *tatmadaw*, and in fact were present in at least one quite comparable case in which a politically powerful

---

[1] The author appreciates the insights of Elizabeth Angell, Vincent Boudreau, Douglas Kammen, Terence Lee, and James Siegel. They read earlier drafts of this essay and offered helpful advice. Any remaining weaknesses are solely the responsibility of the author.

[2] David Rubien, "Aung San Suu Kyi," *Salon.Com*, February 27, 2001, available online at http://www.salon.com/people/bc/2001/02/27/suu_kyi/print.html, accessed April 17, 2001.

military did not use force to halt the demise of an authoritarian regime or to destroy civilian political opposition. In Indonesia, where the military was similarly a pillar of an authoritarian regime for three decades, the army leadership hesitated to deploy troops to defend authoritarianism in the chaotic, waning moments of the Suharto regime in May 1998. The militaries in both Burma (1988) and Indonesia (1998) had similar doctrinal positions delegating to the military responsibility for social, political, and economic stability; both were led by senior officers with vested interests in maintaining the political status quo; both faced widespread urban protests for political reform as well as rural unrest; both had spent years systematically decimating any autonomous opposition that arose in a civil or political society; and both had been the target of international condemnation of their domestic political roles. And yet in Burma, the collapse of the authoritarian regime spurred the army to kill several thousand unarmed civilians in the streets in 1988; and subsequently army leaders constructed a remarkably resilient version of direct military rule. In Indonesia, however, the armed forces leadership wavered at the moment of regime collapse and allowed protestors to force the resignation of the military's supreme benefactor. In the wake of that hesitation, Indonesia's military has remained a major player in the negotiations over political reform, but only one player among many other powerful elites in the struggle for what post-Suharto Indonesia will become.

I argue that the divergent paths taken by these two militaries in chaotic transitional moments can be explained by looking at the variations in the organizational cultures, structures, and practices of the *tatmadaw* and the Indonesian armed forces. In the Burmese case in 1988, a highly mobile, counterinsurgency army confronted pro-democracy protestors whom they came to see as interchangeable with the panoply of insurgent enemies that soldiers had been fighting for forty years. For soldiers, urban protestors—even unarmed nurses, teachers, and Buddhist monks marching in the streets of the capital city—became the functional equivalents of anti-state guerrillas operating in jungle war zones. The army high command injected the norms and tactics of combat into the strategic interaction that accompanies the collapse of authoritarian regimes. In Indonesia, the military was less uniformly poised for the battlefield. Instead it was comprised mostly of territorially based, settled units with comparatively extensive experience in practices of negotiation and compromise with civilian social and economic forces. In fact, when facing regime-threatening popular mobilization, the Indonesian officer corps acted like politicians, while the Burmese officers behaved as war-fighters.

THE 1988 CRACKDOWN IN BURMA

At no point during the Burmese anti-government protests that built to a crescendo in August and September 1988 was a military crackdown a foregone conclusion. In fact, throughout 1988, urban areas were rife with speculation regarding the role the *tatmadaw* would play in the process that many expected would evolve into Burma's democratic revolution. The military's reputation was less tarnished in the early months of the uprising, unlike that of the police, who were responsible for the March deaths of forty-one students who suffocated in a lock-up van. Rumors (*kaw-la-ha-la*) circulated of military units and individual soldiers actively supporting the anti-government forces, pointing to a possible fissure in the faltering regime that many hoped would lead to a democratic opening.

Coming in the wake of the collapse of the twenty-six-year Burma Socialist Program Party (BSPP) government, the 1988 uprising mobilized urban populations in central Burma as never before. The collapse was triggered in September 1987, when a series of demonetization measures devastated the economy and wiped out the savings of most Burmese people. Student demonstrations erupted in Rangoon and continued sporadically into the following year. The police used harsh tactics, including those that led to the deaths of the forty-one students, to put down the demonstrations. Public outcry over these deaths led to further anti-government mobilization of monks, urban professionals, and civil servants, as well as students. As tens of thousands of protestors took to the streets, the BSPP convened an extraordinary party congress in July, during which the long-time dictator Gen. (ret.) Ne Win and other party officials resigned from the party leadership and thereafter named an interim government led by Ne Win's disciple, Brig. Gen. Sein Lwin.[3] A massive outpouring of pro-reform sentiment followed on August 8, 1988, when the numbers on the streets in major urban areas climbed into the hundreds of thousands. The interim government ordered an end to the protests, deployed troops, and sanctioned the massacres of thousands of unarmed demonstrators over the next few days.[4] In a number of cases, protestors fought back, executing police officers and military intelligence operatives and placing their heads on public display.[5] A general strike continued, and with the situation spinning out of control, Sein Lwin resigned on August 12. The old BSPP leadership replaced him with Dr. Maung Maung, a long-time civilian ally of Ne Win's. Over the next month, Dr. Maung Maung made a number of additional political concessions to the protestors (such as ending martial law), but his actions did not silence the cries for reform or heal the increasing paralysis in the country's economy. Finally, on September 18, army leaders took power directly in a coup d'etat. They established the State Law and Order Restoration Council (SLORC) under the chairmanship of the army commander and Ne Win follower Sr. Gen. Saw Maung. Several days of army crackdowns ensued countrywide, resulting in another one thousand deaths in Rangoon and more elsewhere. All told, the year-long crumbling of Burma's socialist authoritarian regime and the accompanying euphoric movement for democracy resulted in a death toll of at least ten thousand people, most of whom were unarmed citizens killed by Burma's soldiers.

In hindsight, this bloody crackdown might appear to be a predictable outcome. Under the previous twenty-six years of BSPP rule, Burma's urban and rural populations in the central regions had developed little or no civil society. There

---

[3] Protestors immediately dubbed Sein Lwin "the Butcher of Rangoon," referring to his involvement in the bloody crackdown on the March 1988 demonstrations, as well as his command of the troops that blew up the Rangoon University Student Union building and killed dozens of students in 1962. As David Steinberg wrote, "The students had wanted Sein Lwin tried, not promoted." From his *Burma: The State of Myanmar* (Washington, DC: Georgetown University Press, 2001), p. 9.

[4] The number of deaths is still unknown. At least three thousand probably died in Rangoon alone, and hundreds (maybe thousands) died in the suppression of protests in other cities following the August 8 demonstrations.

[5] Several months later, army spokesmen claimed that protestors killed more than one hundred people, including thirty members of the armed forces. *The Bangkok Post*, February 4, 1989.

were no organizations with resources, leadership, or followings that could be assembled to mount a serious challenge to the comparatively efficient, bureaucratized, and well-armed military. Absent countervailing forces in Burmese society, officers keen on sustaining their political power would be likely to halt any change that could diminish their clout. However, this explanation raises as many questions as it resolves. If the military was so keen to protect its political power, why did it sit idly by for nearly a year, while the Socialist Party leadership bungled the management of the economic and political crises? Why did the army wait so long to intercede decisively and assert direct political power? Ne Win first offered political concessions—including the call for a transition to a multiparty system—in July, and Dr. Maung Maung pledged even greater concessions that promised the diminution of the military-dominated state's power in August. Why did the army allow these moves?

Two popular explanations of these puzzles have circulated, as activists and scholars have tried over the last decade and a half to make sense of the anti-democratic turn that followed what most hoped would be the onset of Burma's democratic revolution. One explanation focuses on a secret meeting allegedly convened on August 23, 1988 by Ne Win and his colleagues in military intelligence. A few weeks later, a student opposition group circulated a document that is said to have been the plan sketched out in this meeting. It laid out a strategy to defeat the opposition movement by separating the students from the masses, and outlined a plan to "annihilate the student leaders and hardliners."[6] According to the document, while the BSPP leaders would offer some political concessions, military intelligence would use various tactics to stir up violence and chaos, until the masses tired of the violence and turned to the army for protection. While many of the dirty tricks listed in the alleged strategy document were indeed carried out, the document did not surface until several weeks later, which suggests that it may have been a *post facto* forgery. Nonetheless, many anti-military activists still believe that military intelligence was behind the increasing lawlessness and violence of the demonstrations, creating a pretext for political intervention by the military.

A second explanation of the September crackdown centers on the opposition's recruitment of soldiers. Around September 14, eyewitness accounts circulated of young soldiers marching alongside opposition protestors, especially in Rangoon. These early soldier-protestors probably came from Air Force Base 502 at Mingaladon. Over the next couple of days, small groups of navy seamen and army soldiers reportedly appeared in marches elsewhere in the city. At the same time, an opposition leader announced to the world in a BBC interview that 60 percent of the army supported the reform movement.[7] Many observers speculated that this was the last straw for army leaders, who historically have never tolerated dissent in their ranks. Hence, observers speculate that the army, concerned that it had to protect its ranks, carried out the September 18 coup d'etat to end with finality the year of protest.

---

[6] Quoted in Martin Smith, *Burma: Insurgency and the Politics of Ethnicity*, 2nd ed. (London: Zed Press, 1999 [1991]), p. 12.

[7] Tin Oo made this claim in a BBC interview in September 1988. BBC World Service, September 15, 1988, quoted in Smith, *Burma: Insurgency*, p. 457.

Both of these explanations are plausible, but neither of them will be confirmed by evidence until (if) the generals who took power on September 18 open up their hearts, memories, and file cabinets to outside observers. Moreover, both are based on assumptions that the *tatmadaw* was an institution with a direct, indisputable hold on political power in 1988, and that the maintenance of that direct political authority was its defining mission. There is undoubtedly some truth to these propositions. Throughout the Socialist Party era, *tatmadaw* leaders, especially in Rangoon, had fairly extensive influence on BSPP policies and patronage. The military was indeed represented by retired senior officers in the top party positions. However, the junior officers corps and the rank-and-file of the *tatmadaw* nonetheless remained distinct from the party and lived out their daily lives far from the political theatre of Rangoon. In fact, the daily practices of and struggles over political power in the center increasingly became the jurisdiction of only a handful of very senior officers, most of whom retired from the army to become BSPP leaders. The rest of the active-duty armed forces were stationed in remote territory and consumed with the waging of counterinsurgency warfare.

A more accurate explanation of both the crackdown itself and post-crackdown politics requires an examination of the patterns of politics and practices that constituted this military's culture. Since its inception at independence in 1948, the *tatmadaw* has been fighting civil wars that have claimed the lives of at least half a million Burmese, with probably at least fifty thousand soldiers among the dead.[8] The fighting occurred mostly in territory along the borders the country shares with Thailand, Laos, and China. Only at the outset of the internal warfare in the 1940s and on a few rare occasions over the next fifty years did the fighting threaten the capital city or its central environs.

Within a year of independence, the *tatmadaw* had only ten thousand men in uniform, while anti-state armed groups fielded five or more times that many troops. Over the next decade, the besieged elected government authorized a massive expansion of the military, such that by the time of the 1962 coup, there were over 100,000 soldiers in the combined army, navy, and air force. By then, the threats to the capital city and the central region (where most ethnic Burmans[9] reside) had diminished, but the array of anti-state guerrilla forces operating in the border areas had multiplied. In 1962, the coup group moved quickly to put down threats to its new Revolutionary Council. All through the central and border regions, it established dozens of "security and administrative councils" headed by active-duty or retired military officers. A few months after the coup, the Revolutionary Council also set up the Burma Socialist Program Party, which established a geographical and functional hierarchy that ran parallel to the *tatmadaw*'s chain of command. In these early years of the Socialist regime—military leaders rather than BSPP cadres—had ultimate authority over

---

[8] See ibid. (pp. 100-101) for a judicious accounting of the numbers of victims of this civil war.

[9] The majority ethnic group is called "Burman" in English; the Burmans live mainly in the central agricultural valleys and in the southern coastal and delta regions. Although no government has conducted an accurate census of the minority regions since 1931, most government and scholarly sources estimate that the ethnic makeup of the country's 48 million people is as follows: 65 percent Burman, 10 percent Shan, 7 percent Karen, 4 percent Rakhine, 3 percent Chinese, 2 percent Mon, 2 percent Indian, along with small numbers of Assamese and Chin minority peoples. Note that the term "Burmese" usually refers to citizens of the country, and contains no ethnic identification.

day-to-day administrative operations; as Martin Smith notes, local commanders "setting rice quotas or co-opting porters to carry supplies . . . always had the last word."[10]

However, as the party hierarchy gradually became more bureaucratized and articulated across greater functional responsibilities, power over scarce resources, privileges, and profits came to rest in the hands of party officials. They also took charge of preventing the emergence of any rival political parties, unions, student groups, or religious organizations that might challenge the BSPP. While many of these party officials were either serving or retired military officers, they nonetheless had to carry out party activities according to the evolving norms and requirements of the party, rather than imposing military logic on their party duties. As Maung Aung Myoe observed of regional commanders (i.e., very senior military officers) under the Socialist regime, they were chairmen of their regional party committees, but—"their ranking was not in the influential circle. . . [T]hey were subjected to various party committees at the central level, such as party discipline and organizing committees."[11]

Under the Socialist Party regime, the army remained engaged in fighting rebels throughout the country, and underwent a dramatic reorganization into a decentralized, light-infantry-dominated, mobile set of formations designed to carry out counter-guerrilla warfare. From the 1960s through the 1980s, the *tatmadaw* continuously fought small cells of "insurgents," most of whom operated in the territory along Burma's borders. These "enemies" dressed like local civilian populations, knew the territory better than the soldiers in the *tatmadaw* did, and were often indistinguishable from local citizens unlucky enough to be caught in the crossfire. In successive revisions to military strategy and tactics, Burma's military commanders became increasingly inclined to kill anyone suspected of involvement in an insurgency, a proactive response triggered by the fear that they themselves would otherwise be killed by skillfully disguised enemies.[12] Citizens who happened to live in war zones had become enemies of the state.

---

[10] Ibid., p. 200.

[11] Maung Aung Myoe, *The Tatmadaw in Myanmar Since 1988: An Interim Assessment*, Strategic and Defense Studies Centre Working Papers, no. 342, (Canberra: Australian National University, 1999), p. 17.

[12] The annual commanding officers' conferences were the venues for discussions of strategy and tactics. In the conferences held during the 1950s and early 1960s, field officers often complained that the army's harsh tactics were driving local populations into the ranks of the rebel groups; as a result, counterinsurgency doctrine incorporated "hearts-and-minds" psychological warfare tactics to try to win over the support of populations in or near rebel-held areas. However, by 1968, the annual conference arrived at the quite ruthless "Four Cuts" strategy, which remained the dominant counterinsurgency strategy well into the 1980s. The "Four Cuts" approach was to cut off (1) food to the rebels, (2) protection money and other resources that villagers provided rebels, (3) communication between non-rebel villagers and rebels, and (4) the "insurgent's head," which meant to enlist villagers in combat, so as to encircle the rebels. The strategy justified the army's practice of forcing boys and men to serve as porters in areas located near rebel-held territory. The strategy also led the army forcibly to relocate villagers in order to depopulate the landscape near any rebel groups. On the development of strategy and doctrine, see Maung Aung Myoe, *Military Doctrine and Strategy in Myanmar: A Historical Perspective*, Strategic and Defense Studies Centre Working Papers, No. 339 (Canberra: Australian National University, 1999). On the implementation of the Four Cuts strategy, see Hazel Lang, *Fear and Sanctuary: Burmese Refugees in Thailand* (Ithaca: Cornell Southeast Asia Program, 2002).

By the time of the 1988 uprising, this military was a force organized for a defense not against hypothetical external enemies but instead against very concrete threats from citizens who were armed and organized against the state, as well as those unfortunate enough to live in border areas. Officers earned military promotions, perquisites (like overseas training), and medals for their uniforms in a quite standardized process that gave priority first and foremost to success in *combat*, not in party politics.[13] Soldiers and officers lost brothers and friends on battlefields, many located in areas far from their homes and in places where ethnic minority populations looked different, spoke incomprehensible languages, and consequently could never be viewed as anything but potential enemies and killers of the *tatmadaw* brethren. By the late 1980s, the notion that the mostly ethnic minority citizens who resided along Burma's borders were potential enemies held a strong resonance for most ethnic majority Burmans—military and civilian—committed to maintaining the integrity of the Union. Only in 1988, when the map of this strategy was redrawn to make citizens in the center potential enemies as well, did the use of deadly force against the citizenry become subject to scrutiny by Burmese living in the center and by the international community outraged by the crackdowns on popular protests.

Throughout the early months of 1988, the *tatmadaw* was fighting a myriad of different insurgent armies in much of the northern and eastern territory of Burma. Most of these groups neither commented on nor had any connection to the uprising in central Burma until August, when one group—the Burma Communist Party—issued statements in support of the demonstrators and possibly provided minor resources and leadership to some of the protestors. Quite surprisingly, the insurgent groups did not take advantage of the disturbances in central Burma to launch offensives against the *tatmadaw*. In an unusual development, almost no fighting transpired between any insurgents and the *tatmadaw* in the border areas throughout August and September 1988. Hence, as events in Rangoon spiraled increasingly out of control, it became possible for the military leadership to think about pulling back from operational positions in insurgent territory and deploying its combat-seasoned troops to Rangoon. This redeployment is precisely what happened. The high command ordered the 22nd and 33rd Light Infantry Divisions out of combat on the anti-Karen front, and moved them into Rangoon, where they were responsible for some of the most horrific bloodshed. For these soldiers, freshly transferred from counterinsurgency warfare in the border areas against fellow citizens, the nurses, monks, bureaucrats, teachers, students, and housewives on the streets of Rangoon and Mandalay seemed just as dangerous as the nurses, monks, priests, teachers farmers, and housewives that they had fought in the insurgent areas. Whether they spoke Burmese as a first language, or lived in Rangoon or the border areas, civilians had universally become targets of counterinsurgency.[14]

---

[13] I am not suggesting that the BSPP had no influence on promotions or other internal army affairs (such as major decisions over changes in strategy and doctrine). However, more than a dozen retired military officers (in interviews conducted in 1991, 1992, and 1995) reported that a necessary condition for officer promotions and rewards was successful performance in combat; political connections to influential party members might help a particular officer, but only in a handful of cases was anyone promoted who had not been successful in counterinsurgency combat.

[14] I am grateful to James Siegel for suggesting this aspect of the argument to me. E-mail correspondence, January 23, 2002.

THE CRACKDOWN IN COMPARATIVE PERSPECTIVE

The contrasting outcome in Indonesia reinforces this interpretation. Like the demonstrations in Burma in 1988, the popular uprising against the thirty-two-year-old Suharto regime came in the wake of a major economic crisis. By late 1997, Indonesia's economy was in tatters; its currency was valued at an all-time low; the government (on orders from the IMF and World Bank) ended subsidies of important consumer commodities; and urban and rural populations took to the streets to demand reform. Violent riots occurred from December 1997 to February 1998, mostly on Java; these were followed by student protests and assorted other demonstrations that lasted through the resignation of Suharto on May 21, 1998.[15] As the economic chaos and calls for political *reformasi* (reform) spread throughout the year, there was widespread speculation about the military's response to the raging social and political crisis. Many predicted a coup d'etat, and most observers were stunned that the military leadership passively allowed their patron to be dethroned. Why did the Indonesian military not follow the path of the *tatmadaw*?

Looking inside the Indonesian armed forces (then known as Angkatan Bersenjata Republik Indonesia, or ABRI), we find a very different organizational culture, one in which the military no longer viewed all citizens categorically as potential enemies but instead saw them as prospective business partners, allies, and future employers.[16] Moreover, this military had far less regularized and bureaucratized norms and procedures in place, which created a more permeable boundary between military officers and civilian citizens. As a result, while a small number of independently acting combat units did mount a bloody attempt to save the Suharto regime in May 1998, the military-as-an-institution appeared willing to accept a negotiated resolution rather than launch an all-out crackdown. In contrast to the situation in Burma, a quite different matrix of forces created the conditions that produced hesitation and perhaps paralysis among the armed forces as they watched the Suharto regime crumble.

Suharto, who came to power in 1965-1966, consolidated his own central authority by filling key appointments throughout the national and provincial bureaucracies with his followers from the army.[17] Military doctrine enshrined the

---

[15] For analyses of both longer-term and shorter-term reasons for the collapse of the Suharto regime in 1998, see the contributions to Benedict Anderson, ed., *Violence and the State in Suharto's Indonesia* (Ithaca: Cornell Southeast Asia Program, 2001); Donald K. Emmerson, "A Tale of Three Countries," *Journal of Democracy* 10, 4 (October 1999): 35-53; and the contributions to Arief Budiman, Barbara Hatley, and Damien Kingsbury, eds., *Reformasi: Crisis and Change in Indonesia* (Clayton, Australia: Monash Asia Institute, 1999).

[16] Certainly, in the immediate aftermath of the September 30-October 1, 1965, coup attempt by junior officers with links to Communist Party leaders, the armed forces' rhetoric and practices identified citizens as potential communists, and thus enemies of the state. While the New Order iconography and propaganda attempted to keep alive this threat from within, however, there was no serious challenge to the central state during the three-decade New Order regime. In contrast to the attitudes of the Burmese military, which had engaged in violent civil combat year in and year out, the notion of citizens-as-potential-enemies had comparably less resonance among ABRI officers by the 1990s.

[17] Note that for most of the New Order period, the navy and air force were treated with suspicion due to the Sukarnoist sympathies of senior navy and air force officers during the 1960s.

concept of "*dwifungsi*" (literally, "dual function"), which assigned to the military responsibility for social and political development as well as for national security. Under Suharto's "New Order," the military was reorganized into a unified command structure with two distinct wings: operational and territorial. Much like its Burmese counterpart, the Indonesian military's operational forces have carried out brutal counterinsurgency campaigns against separatist and anti-state organizations throughout the New Order and through to today. The army's strategic reserve (KOSTRAD, Komando Strategis Angkatan Darat) and special forces (KOPASSUS, Komando Pasukan Khusus) also have been responsible for systematic torture and killing of regime opponents. However, because of differences between ABRI's territorial structure and the combat-oriented structure of the *tatmadaw*, the experiences of the Burmese and Indonesian militaries have diverged in significant ways. The Indonesian territorial structure—with regional commands subdivided into district and local commands down to the village level—gave the armed forces a presence in social and political affairs throughout the country. As scholar Harold Crouch observed, throughout the New Order, territorial units routinely undertook measures "to prevent political parties, NGOs, trade unions, student organizations, and religious groups from challenging the regime."[18] As the New Order wore on, the military's dealings with these groups eliminated the possibility of using repression and deadly force. Instead many territorial commanders began to incorporate compromise with civilian groups outside of recognized combat zones in a way that was inconceivable in Burma.

Three components of ABRI's evolving organizational culture contributed to the military's move toward conciliation with civilians, and ultimately to its hesitation to deploy force against protesters in the 1990s. First was the practice of *kekaryaan* (secondment of active-duty military personnel to non-military jobs), a system initiated in the 1950s but greatly expanded by Suharto after the establishment of the New Order in 1966. This practice gave Suharto the chance to replace all local and provincial officials with politically reliable military personnel. *Kekaryaan* also allowed Suharto to expand his following of loyalists inside the army by offering lucrative assignments to mid-career and senior officers. *Kekaryaan* peaked in the 1970s, when seconded military personnel served as cabinet ministers, town mayors, village heads, representatives in provincial and district assemblies, directors of government enterprises, and in a variety of more junior positions in these realms. For senior officers on the verge of retirement, these postings gave them opportunities to establish important financial and political connections with local elites who would later ensure supplements to their meager army retirement pensions.[19] However, by the 1990s, Suharto had turned to his family, non-military cronies, and increasingly to Islamic groups to fill these positions, and he offered fewer lucrative political and business opportunities to

---

[18] Harold Crouch, "Wiranto and Habibie: Military-Civilian Relations Since May 1998," in *Reformasi: Crisis and Change*, ed. Budiman et al., p. 145. For an analysis of the patterns of state repression of social forces under Suharto, see Vincent Boudreau, "Diffusing Democracy? People Power in Indonesia and the Philippines," *Bulletin of Concerned Asian Scholars* 31, 4 (1999): 3-18.

[19] Douglas Kammen and Siddharth Chandra, *A Tour of Duty: Changing Patterns of Military Politics in Indonesia in the 1990s* (Ithaca: Cornell Modern Indonesia Project, 1999), pp. 70-77.

senior military officers.[20] What opportunities existed for older military personnel could not be jeopardized by heavy-handed repression.

Second, ABRI's own administrative moves in the 1960s created a large officer corps in the 1990s with diminished prospects for promotion. Douglas Kammen and Siddharth Chandra have shown that the senior officer corps in the 1990s faced declining career opportunities due to the competition engendered by a seven-fold increase in the numbers of cadets admitted to the military academy during the 1960s. Political and organizational constraints prevented expansion of the number of command billets for junior and senior officers, which resulted in intense competition and extremely rapid turnover in command tenures in the 1990s. The *kekaryaan* positions might have provided a safety valve for ambitious officers less likely to earn flag officer ranks than members of earlier academy classes. But since a *kekaryaan* posting was no longer assured as senior officers faced retirement, the military career and post-career prospects of those holding local command positions diminished precipitously in the 1990s. As a result, most officers in territorial units spent the late New Order period fostering good relations with local populations so as to set themselves up for post-retirement incomes in these localities.[21] This experience probably explains why territorial commanders were increasingly open to negotiation rather than the use of force in settling local disturbances in the 1990s, which no doubt further widened the chasm between Suharto's New Order inner circle and ABRI's officer corps.[22]

Third, Suharto's personal control over the system of military appointments had created a divided and nearly paralyzed military by May 1998. In the 1980s and 1990s, he liberally handed out promotions to his relatives, former adjutants, and bodyguards. He appointed them to powerful positions over more senior, experienced candidates. These promotions flouted the traditional military chain of command, a breach which not surprisingly provoked bitterness among those passed over and those committed to merit-based promotions. In the mid-1990s, Suharto played powerful generals off against each other, a ploy that probably created multiple informal chains of command that led only to Suharto. Most significantly, he appointed his former adjutant, Gen. Wiranto, as armed forces commander in February 1998, while naming Wiranto's rival and Suharto's own son-in-law, Lt. Gen. Prabowo Subianto, as commander of the army's strategic reserve.

Hence, by 1998, ABRI had been transformed into a politically ineffectual military that had traded the autonomous political power it held after the 1965-66 political crisis for shares in the spoils of New Order rule. For more than three

---

[20] In 1977, more than 21,000 ABRI personnel were seconded to civilian jobs, with a slow decline over the next two decades (16,000 in 1980, and probably 14,000 in 1992). In 1973, fully one-third of cabinet ministers, two-thirds of provincial governors, and half of ambassadors were active-duty or retired ABRI officers. By 1995, these percentages declined to 24 percent, 40 percent, and 17 percent, respectively. Ian McFarling, *The Dual Function of the Indonesian Armed Forces: Military Politics in Indonesia* (Canberra: Australian Defence Studies Centre, 1996), p. 145; and Robert Lowry, *The Armed Forces of Indonesia*. (Sydney: Allen & Unwin, 1996), p. 188.

[21] The increasing negotiation and compromise among territorial military commanders and civilians was not universal throughout the archipelago and did not seem to influence the activities of the army's operational units. In areas (like Timor and Aceh) where the military was engaged in ongoing combat or effective occupation, local commanders did not hesitate to deploy deadly force against anyone they identified as an enemy of the state.

[22] Kammen and Chandra, *A Tour of Duty*.

decades, Suharto gave many officers and units access to resources and wealth and allowed them to operate with impunity toward the rest of the population, in return for which the military made sure he got reelected every five years. At the same time, Suharto was hardly the patron saint of the military institution, which his manipulations left politically weak and at times incoherent. While most of the middle-ranking and senior officer corps probably considered themselves loyal to their benefactor during the chaos of 1997 and early 1998, there was unquestionably ambivalence and intra-institutional friction over the implications of the New Order bargain. Discipline in the ranks was weak and in many regions non-existent. Soldiers moonlighted as hired thugs, naval ratings as pirates, and officers as smugglers and entrepreneurs. In the countryside, many soldiers lived off the protection money they extorted from local businesses. Suharto had succeeded in weakening the institutional integrity of the armed forces to the degree that they posed no political threat to him. However, when he needed ABRI to rescue him in May 1998, "it had become incapable of decisive action either to save Suharto or to overthrow him."[23]

WHY DO ARMIES KILL UNARMED CITIZENS?

In the early chaotic moments of the collapse of an authoritarian regime, existing institutional arrangements structure the kind of information available to army leaders and the range of possible calculations those leaders are likely to make. When the previously unquestioned leadership of the state falters, the military's institutional culture, norms, and practices do not evaporate overnight. Instead they convey to the institution's leaders expectations about appropriate behavior, as well as about what political and social forces constitute threats to the integrity of the institution and the nation.

Variations in military cultures, organizational practices, and norms are rarely considered relevant to studies of democratization, social movements, and even authoritarian politics.[24] Most scholars and policy analysts treat militaries as undifferentiated organizations that act single-mindedly and uniformly from one country to another. They claim that certain essential characteristics of a military—such as its hierarchically rigid command structure, its monopoly over the legitimate use of force, and its inevitable distrust of civilian political organizations and leaders—render the institution and its leadership universally loath to submit to the inefficiencies, aggravation, and nuisance anticipated in the onset of democratic civilian control. However, in comparing how the Burmese and Indonesian militaries responded to the breakdown of authoritarian regimes, this essay suggests that even militaries that seem most similarly situated may react

---

[23] Editors, "Current Data on the Indonesian Military Elite: January 1, 1998-January 31, 1999," *Indonesia* 67 (April 1999): 138. See also Geoffrey Robinson, "Indonesia: On a New Course?" in *Coercion and Governance: The Declining Political Role of the Military in Asia*, ed. Muthiah Alagappa (Stanford: Stanford University Press, 2001), pp. 226-56.

[24] Noteworthy exceptions include Alfred Stepan, *Rethinking Military Politics: Brazil and the Southern Cone* (Princeton: Princeton University Press, 1988); Felipe Aguero, *Soldiers, Civilians and Democracy: Post-Franco Spain in Comparative Perspective* (Baltimore: Johns Hopkins University Press, 1995); and Jennifer Schirmer, *The Guatemalan Military Project: A Violence Called Democracy* (Philadelphia: University of Pennsylvania Press, 1998). See also Boudreau's analysis of variations in modes of state repression in his "Diffusing Democracy?"

quite differently in comparable transformative political moments. The reason for this variation in response lies in the discrete historical evolution of organizational cultures, routines, and norms particular to each military within each broader political environment.

Moreover, this essay also challenges the literature's unwarranted assumption that a military's only concern is its struggle with potential civilian overseers.[25] In fact, in the chaotic conditions that frequently characterize the waning moments of authoritarian rule and the interim political arrangements that follow, militaries often face a wide range of intra-military problems, frailties, and dilemmas. These result from the same kinds of global forces—as well as discrete local contingencies—that undermine the authoritarian regime. For career officers whose lives, identities, and families have been wrapped up in military service, these concerns about institutional integrity and personal welfare in the midst of an uncertain political environment are as compelling as worries about longer-term processes that might either institutionalize or undermine civilian control. And all of these concerns have their roots in the explicitly political environment that produces different kinds of windows of opportunity for regime change.

In the Burmese case, military leaders never seriously worried about what a liberal democratic future would mean for the status or integrity of the armed forces. Such a consideration was simply unthinkable for a military that had been only marginally involved in the administration of most of Burma's population and resources in the central regions. Focused instead for three decades on holding the Union together by fighting enemies in remote territory, the *tatmadaw* left the politics of compromise and negotiation to the BSPP cadres in the center. When the 1988 uprising occurred, the compromises and accommodations that many hoped would lead to democratic reform were not practices that the military would think of pursuing. Instead, the logic that animated the military's response to popular mobilization was the same logic that had animated its culture for thirty years—that of a particular counterinsurgency strategy. Since the 1960s, citizens had always been potential enemies, and the dwindling of combat with citizens living in the usual zones of insurgency (the border areas) in mid-1988 provided the military leadership the opportunity to bring combat specialists back to the center. The citizens on the streets in central urban areas had become the functional equivalents of the rebels long fought by the *tatmadaw*.

In the Indonesian case, the popular mobilization of 1998 was neither anything new nor terribly threatening to the military. During the New Order, territorial force commanders stationed throughout the archipelago had periodically faced sporadic student, farmer, and labor protests in areas that were not designated as combat zones. Throughout the 1990s, territorial commanders showed increasing hesitation to deploy force to manage such conflicts.[26] As senior officers whose career prospects were uncertain and who would need to make a living in their localities, these territorial commanders could not afford to alienate local elites by arresting and killing their children. At the peak of the hierarchy, the military's leadership had been divided by Suharto's political machinations, aimed at

---

[25] For example, the military's hostility toward civilians is one of the overriding concerns of the contributors to Larry Diamond and Marc F. Plattner, eds., *Civil-Military Relations and Democracy* (Baltimore: Johns Hopkins University Press, 1996).

[26] Boudreau, "Diffusing Democracy?"

allowing no clear rival or heir to emerge. Combined, these experiences of political negotiation and compromise, on the one hand, and paralysis at the top, on the other, yielded a military institution incapable of acting to save its benefactor by halting or killing his challengers.

EPILOGUE: AFTER THE CRISES

In the aftermath of these chaotic moments of regime collapse, the militaries of Burma and Indonesia continued along their diverging trajectories. While the variations in military organizational culture account for the quite different responses of these militaries to authoritarian collapse, structural forces are more likely to explain the even greater divergence in the ways military roles subsequently evolved in the two countries. In Burma, where the BSPP regime collapsed almost as an afterthought to years of economic and bureaucratic deterioration, the new military junta, SLORC, was faced with having to rebuild the economy and the state seemingly from scratch. It did so with the only tools it considered reliable—its military personnel. To assert central control over political and economic affairs throughout the country, the junta undertook a massive expansion of the armed forces. From 1988 to 1996, the *tatmadaw* grew from 186,000 to more than 370,000 soldiers.[27] New army garrisons have been set up in towns and villages throughout the country, while the numbers of naval and air force bases have also increased.[28] The military has expanded its industrial base as well, and set up lucrative military corporate ventures, such as its Myanmar Economic Holdings Corporation and Myanmar Economic Corporation. New military organizations, such as the Office of Strategic Studies, have taken on responsibilities for initiating and coordinating policies that deal with the drug trade, the economy, ethnic minority affairs, and foreign relations. The junta delegated day-to-day administration of the country to its regional commanders. Accordingly, regional commanders have built roads, housing, suburbs, and markets; rearranged urban and rural populations to accommodate tourism and other industries; and expanded surveillance and crowd control capabilities. Along the way, they have amassed enormous wealth and power.

This state rebuilding process brought with it a new geography of military deployment and functional responsibilities. In the aftermath of the bloody end to the 1988 uprising, military leaders correctly calculated that the army lacked the capacity to fight battles in border regions and in Rangoon alike, should an alliance develop between the opposition in central Burma and armed, ethnic-minority rebels beyond the center. Accordingly, Lt. Gen. Khin Nyunt initiated ceasefire negotiations with ethnic rebel groups in 1989. Over the next several years, seventeen of the twenty-one major anti-government forces (with as many as fifty thousand troops) concluded ceasefire agreements with SLORC. In the regions where

---

[27] The junta also spent over $1 billion on 140 new combat aircraft, 30 naval vessels, 170 tanks, 250 armored personnel carriers, as well as rocket launch systems, anti-aircraft artillery, infantry weapons, telecommunications surveillance equipment, and other hardware. Micool Brooke, "The Armed Forces of Myanmar," *Asian Defence Journal*, January 1998, p. 13; and Anthony Davis and Bruce Hawke, "Burma: The Country that Won't Kick the Habit," *Jane's Intelligence Review* (March 1998): 26-31.

[28] Andrew Selth, "The Future of the Burmese Armed Forces," paper prepared for Burma Update Conference, Australian National University, Canberra, August 5-6, 1999, p. 11.

ceasefires were concluded, the junta has deployed the Ministry for the Development of the Border Areas and the National Races (later renamed the "Ministry for the Progress of Border Areas and National Races and Development Affairs") to build roads, Burmese-language schools, hospitals, power plants, telecommunications relay stations, and other institutions aimed at both modernizing and subjugating former rebel-held territory.

In Burma, the gradual two-decade disintegration of the economy and the BSPP left the country with a barely functioning national market and thoroughly rotten administrative apparatus. The ultimate collapse of the BSPP in 1988 gave the military the opportunity to establish an extraordinary degree of army dominance over national affairs. This is not to say that this state- and economy-building process has been smooth and well-executed. In fact, the junta has overextended itself so seriously that it faces unprecedented problems of morale and discipline in its ranks, as well as logistical challenges that it has been utterly incapable of addressing.[29]

In Indonesia, the collapse of Suharto's presidency did not result from a prolonged period of bureaucratic and economic decay such as existed in Burma in the 1970s and 1980s. The economic crisis that was partially responsible for weakening Suharto's hold on power capped off a period of sustained economic boom, not sustained bust as in Burma. The two decades of growth had built durable elite political and economic networks that survived and perhaps flourished in the post-Suharto era. Suharto's successor was his hand-picked vice president, B. J. Habibie. While Habibie did depart remarkably from Suharto in some policy arenas—such as his decision to hold a referendum on the future disposition of East Timor—his regime never challenged the social, economic, and political elites that had risen to prominence in the New Order. Nor did the regimes of Habibie's elected successors, Abdurrahman Wahid (Gus Dur) and Megawati Sukarnoputri.

In the post-Suharto era, the Indonesian military suffered some serious political setbacks, but nonetheless remains one of the surviving and probably flourishing elite institutions that continue to play a major role in national politics. Under Habibie and his successor, President Wahid, the military attempted to seize the mantle of *"reformasi,"* and some senior officers—including Lt. Gens. Bambang Yudhoyono, Agum Gumelar, and Agus Wijojo, and Maj. Gen. Agus Wirahadikusumah—championed the cause of democratization.[30] The armed forces, renamed the Tentara Nasional Indonesia (TNI, Indonesian National Army) in 1999, probably saw democratic tactics as a way to control the agenda and pace for political reform. All of the major political parties and their leaders seemed

---

[29] For more on these issues, see my "Cracks in the Edifice: Military-Society Relations in Burma Since 1988," in *Burma: Strong State/Weak Regime*, ed. Morten Peterson and Emily Rudland (Sydney: Crawford House, 2000), pp. 22-51.

[30] As early as June 1998, Lt. Gen. Bambang Yudhoyono, chief of the army's influential Social and Political Affairs Directorate, published a reform proposal [*ABRI dan Reformasi: Pokok-Pokok Pikiran ABRI Tentang Reformasi Menuju Pencapaian Cita-Cita Nasional* (Jakarta: Mabes ABRI, June 1998)] that declared ABRI's commitment to democratic reforms and called for Indonesia's ratification of international human rights conventions. It also supported limits on presidential powers so that the military could not be misused by an unpopular president seeking to repress opposition. In September 1998, an ABRI seminar held at the armed forces Staff and Command College debated this paper and produced a second paper [*Peran ABRI Abad XXI: Redefinisi, Reposisi dan Reaktualisasi Peran ABRI dalam Kehidupan Bangsa; Makalah Awal Seminar ABRI* (Bandung: Sesko ABRI, September 1998)] outlining the future role of ABRI.

content to let the military dictate its terms for—in Wiranto's words—changing the military's "sociopolitical role in line with the people's maturity" only when Indonesia developed "the strength of our civil society."[31] However, once the door was opened to reform possibilities, popular forces compelled elite political leaders to hasten and broaden the scope of reforms so as to reduce drastically the number of military seats in the parliament and to reject military demands for expanding the institution's emergency powers in 1999.[32]

Undoubtedly the most significant setback for the military's plan to control the *reformasi* agenda was the army's participation in the violence that surrounded the August 30, 1999, referendum on autonomy in East Timor. As the Editors of *Indonesia* argue, the pre- and post-referendum violence proved to be "devastating for the military," which came under intense international condemnation for its role in arming and directing the paramilitaries responsible for the violence. Domestically, the international condemnation dealt the TNI "a humiliating defeat" that appeared to rattle the foundations of the army's own sense of legitimacy and self-definition.[33]

While it is too soon to be certain about how the post-Suharto political struggles will play out, by the time of this writing it is nonetheless clear that the TNI has not simply suffered these political defeats without a fight. Indeed, presidents Habibie and Wahid introduced remarkable reforms that included politically motivated command reshuffles, the removal of Gen. Wiranto from his cabinet position, trials of a small number of lower-ranking military officers accused of human rights violations, the reduction in strength of previously untouchable special forces units, and the removal of the police from the military's chain-of-command. However, the Indonesian armed forces have also reinvigorated and perhaps expanded their role in politics through their alliances with political parties that had existed in the late New Order and have become the major players in post-Suharto politics. In particular, the impeachment of President Wahid and the ascension of Vice President Megawati Sukarnoputri to the presidency could only have been possible with the support of military leaders. Given Megawati's dependence on the military at least at the outset of her presidency, it seems likely

---

[31] "Wiranto Guarded on ABRI's Political Role," *Jakarta Post*, November 12, 1998. The complicity of civilian political elites in the military's attempt to control the reform process is seen earliest in the Ciganjur Declaration of November 11, 1998. Herein, the four major opposition leaders—Abdurrahman Wahid, Megawati Sukarnoputri, Amien Rais, and Hamengkubuwono X (the Sultan of Yogyakarta)—made it clear they would not challenge ABRI's agenda and schedule for political reform. Point Six of the Declaration called for ending the military's dual function, but only very gradually over six years. And the military's political roles were to be phased out "in the framework of realizing a civil society," a message which echoed Wiranto's own warning that *dwifungsi* will end only when the people reach "maturity" within the context of his strengthened civil society; not surprisingly, no one has proposed standards for what this "maturity" or a "realized civil society" would look like. One scholar explains the tentativeness of civilian political leaders: "[T]he leadership of the opposition has tended to be populated by those who feel much more at home with elite-level bargaining and negotiation" than with popular movements, whose agendas threaten elite interests. From Vedi Hadiz, "Contesting Political Change after Suharto," in *Reformasi: Crisis and Change in Indonesia*, ed. Budiman et al., p. 113.

[32] Jose Manuel Tesoro, "Walking on a Tightrope," *Asiaweek*, October 8, 1999.

[33] The Editors, "Changes in Civil-Military Relations Since the Fall of Suharto," *Indonesia* 70 (October 2000): 125-38. See also Robinson's analysis of the impact of the East Timor crisis on evolving civil-military relations, in "Indonesia: On a New Course?" pp. 251-56.

that TNI leaders will regain some control over the reform agenda, particularly with respect to the issue of restructuring civil-military relations in a way that will hinder the establishment of any meaningful civilian oversight and control over military activities in domestic politics.

OTHER SCHOOLS, OTHER PILGRIMAGES, OTHER DREAMS: THE MAKING AND UNMAKING OF *JIHAD* IN SOUTHEAST ASIA

John T. Sidel

INTRODUCTION

In the aftermath of the September 11, 2001 attacks in New York City and Washington, DC, Southeast Asia suddenly reemerged on the maps of global strategic policy-makers and pundits, as a site of conflict, not with World Communism, but with "Islamic Terrorism." Shadowy groups such as Abu Sayyaf of the Philippines and Laskar Jihad of Indonesia soon appeared on official lists of "terrorist organizations" identified by the US government as legitimate targets for legal and/or military action. US Special Forces advisors were promptly dispatched to the island of Basilan, where Philippine government troops were supposedly rooting out remnants of the Abu Sayyaf group, whose members have been linked not only to kidnappings, killings, and bombings in the Philippines, but to plots to assassinate the Pope and the 1993 bombing of the World Trade Center in New York. Meanwhile, US Deputy Defense Secretary Paul Wolfowitz, a leading hawk in the Bush administration and a former ambassador to Jakarta, warned that "going after Al Qaeda in Indonesia is not something that should wait until after Al Qaeda has been uprooted from Afghanistan."[1]

The sense of urgency and importance surrounding this incipient campaign was heightened not only by the inevitable flood of newspaper articles, briefing papers, and Special National Intelligence Estimates "inside the Beltway," but also by events on the ground in Southeast Asia. In Manila, the Macapagal-Arroyo administration pledged its total support to

---

[1] "Of Missiles and Terrorism," *Far Eastern Economic Review*, November 8, 2001, pp. 22-23. See also: "Wawancara Paul Wolfowitz: 'Aksi Teror di Indonesia Disusupi Al-Qaidah,'" *Tempo*, November 19-25, 2001, p. 48.

the "War on Terrorism," even as bombings and armed clashes unfolded in major cities in the Islamicized southern Philippines. Meanwhile, in Jakarta, demonstrations were held outside the US Embassy and threats of bombings and "sweepings" were made against American citizens, while National Intelligence Agency (Badan Intelijen Negara or BIN) chief Lt. Gen. (Ret.) A. M. Hendropriyono lent credence to reports that armed contingents of Al Qaeda activists were training Laskar Jihad forces in Maluku and the Central Sulawesi town of Poso, where inter-religious violence had claimed thousands of lives since 1999.[2]

Finally, after a series of arrests in Malaysia, the Philippines, and Singapore in 2001-2002, an Al Qaeda-linked Islamic terrorist group identified as "Jemaah Islamiyah" was unveiled, so to speak, by security officials in these countries and in Indonesia, where this region-wide network was said to be based. The group's supposed leader, Abu Bakar Ba'asyir, had founded a religious school in Central Java in the early 1970s, spent time in Indonesian prisons for his "extremist" views in the late 1970s and early 1980s, lived in exile in Malaysia for much of the late 1980s and 1990s, and returned at the turn of the century to Indonesia, where he was elected the leader of the Majelis Mujahidin Indonesia, the Assembly of Indonesian Mujahidin.

Thus when a bombing claimed the lives of nearly two hundred foreign tourists at a nightclub in Bali in mid-October 2002, the explosion was immediately attributed to Jemaah Islamiyah and, along with preceding incidents in Yemen and Kenya, included as evidence of a resurgence of Al Qaeda terrorist activity around the world. In response, the Indonesian police detained alleged Jemaah Islamiyah leader Abu Bakar Ba'asyir in connection with a series of earlier alleged offenses and questioned him about his involvement in the bombing. In a few short months, using intelligence reportedly provided by Jemaah Islamiyah members interrogated by the authorities in Singapore, and by an Al Qaeda operative captured by the CIA in Afghanistan, the Indonesian police had made rapid progress in their investigation. By the end of 2002, a series of well publicized arrests had revealed not only the Bali bombers and their accomplices, but a longer trail of Islamic activists and schools stretching across Java, Sumatra, and the Malay Peninsula. In early 2003, as the Abu Sayyaf reemerged to draw a fresh infusion of US Special Forces troops to the southern Philippines, it appeared that a second front in the "War on Terrorism" had been opened in Southeast Asia, with Al Qaeda squaring off against the United States and its local allies.

Thus a picture of extensive Al Qaeda operations in Southeast Asia has come into focus, in journalistic reportage on the region, government press releases, publications, and leaks, and the pseudo-academic writings of self-styled "terrorism experts." Exemplary and influential in this regard is the book *Inside Al Qaeda: Global Network of Terror* by Rohan Gunaratna of the Centre for the Study of Terrorism and Political Violence at the University of St. Andrews in Scotland. Gunaratna, a prominent fixture on

---

[2] See, for example, "A.M. Hendropriyono: 'Kita Harus Bekerja Sama dengan Amerika,'" *Forum Keadilan*, November 19, 2001.

the media and consultancy circuit, writes: "As envisaged by bin Laden, Al Qaeda's influence spread from the Philippines to the rest of South East Asia, where its network is long-standing, well-entrenched and extensive."[3] Using the Philippines as a base, Gunaratna claims, Al Qaeda developed a "well-coordinated regional network" in Indonesia, Malaysia, and Singapore.[4] Zachary Abuza, an American political scientist and occasional television talk-show "terrorism expert," concurs: "Al Qaeda had slowly penetrated the region for more than a decade beginning in 1991, co-opting individuals and groups, establishing independent cells, and finding common cause with local militants."[5]

Viewed through this lens, all roads lead to Kabul, Kandahar, and Peshawar, the central hubs of Al Qaeda's operations since its emergence in the 1990s. After all, leadership roles have been assumed by Southeast Asian veterans of the anti-Soviet struggle of the 1980s, financial and logistical support have been provided by Osama bin Laden, and new recruits have been schooled in terrorist activity in Aghanistan, Pakistan's Northwest Frontier Province, or in camps in the southern Philippines staffed by Al Qaeda trainers. A videotape discovered by US forces at an Al Qaeda facility in Kabul reportedly revealed extensive surveillance of US targets for attack in Singapore.[6] An Al Qaeda operative interrogated—and extensively tortured—by the CIA in Afghanistan likewise provided extensive information about the activities of Abu Bakar Ba'asyir and Jemaah Islamiyah. In the "Global War on Terrorism," such smoking guns may have been carried by Southeast Asians, but they clearly bear the prints of Osama bin Laden and Al Qaeda.

From this perspective, the emergence of "Islamic Terrorism" in Southeast Asia is a phenomenon about which academic specialists on the region have very little if anything to contribute. After all, the prime movers behind the bombings in Bali and the kidnappings in Basilan are said to be found in the far-flung Pashtun badlands of Pakistan and the mountain caves of eastern Afghanistan, and other foot soldiers in this "global network of terror" have been recruited from such distinctly non-Southeast Asian settings as the council estates of North London, the *banlieues* of Paris, and the *förort* of Stockholm, not to mention a long list of Muslim countries in the Middle East. By their very nature, moreover, the identities and activities of the "terrorist cells" in this network are so secretive as to be known—or knowable—only to themselves and the intelligence services of interested governments. Small wonder that the collective response of specialists on Southeast Asia to the "War on Terrorism" in the region has been one of virtual silence and acquiescence, if

---

[3] Rohan Gunaratna, *Inside Al Qaeda: Global Network of Terror* (London: C. Hurst & Company, 2002), p. 175.

[4] Ibid., pp. 185-86. See also: Rohan Gunaratna, "Al-Qaeda's operational ties with allied groups," *Jane's Intelligence Review*, February 1, 2003.

[5] Zachary Abuza, "Tentacles of Terror: Al Qaeda's Southeast Asian Network," *Contemporary Southeast Asia* 24,3 (December 2002): 427-65.

[6] Ministry of Home Affairs, *White Paper: The Jemaah Islamiyah Arrests and the Threat of Terrorism* (Singapore: Ministry of Home Affairs, 2003), pp. 9-14, 26-31.

not nervous embarrassment as to their ignorance and irrelevance in the face of recent events.

Yet if the history of the Vietnam War is any guide, such passivity among Southeast Asia specialists may well prove intellectually and politically irresponsible. For the conventional wisdom on "Islamic Terrorism" in Southeast Asia represents not a consensus among well-informed experts, but rather an official view, promoted by governments in Jakarta, Manila, Singapore, and Washington, and disseminated, without critical comment or question, by journalists and various self-styled "terrorism experts" in universities and so-called think tanks in the region and beyond.[7] Neither excessive cynicism nor elaborate conspiracy theorizing is necessary to raise doubts as to the credibility of the US Central Intelligence Agency, the Singapore Home Affairs Ministry, or the intelligence and security forces of Indonesia and the Philippines as definitive sources of information. "Intelligence" involves not only the collection of information, but also the cultivation of relationships, relationships of power, relationships from which responsible, critical academics should be careful to extricate themselves.

What, then, is to be done? Most obviously, specialists can broaden the range of empirical sources on "Islamic Terrorism" to enrich—and to question—the official view of an Al Qaeda-run network in Southeast Asia that has crystallized and hardened as the conventional wisdom among "respectable" commentators on the region. The mainstream newspapers and magazines of Manila and Jakarta, after all, have provided extensive coverage of this issue over the past few years, with investigative journalists cranking out a number of relevant in-depth reports and books. The magazines, pamphlets, and website postings produced by groups concerned with promoting Islamist causes in Southeast Asia are likewise rich and easily accessible alternative sources of information and interpretation. For the more industrious researcher, moreover, the archives of Amnesty International and other human rights groups are well stocked with documents from the trials of Islamic militants, from Abu Bakar Ba'asyir in the mid-1980s up to the alleged Jemaah Islamiyah activists arrested in Malaysia and Singapore in 2001-2002. Better sources than *The Economist* or *Jane's Defence Weekly* are clearly available, even for those readers unfamiliar with Southeast Asian languages. It is not necessary to rely on third-hand information extracted from captured Al Qaeda operatives kept isolated and mostly naked for weeks on end, deprived of

---

[7] The references cited in Gunaratna and Abuza's footnotes consist almost exclusively of government documents, interviews with members of various security services, and newspaper and magazine articles which are likewise heavily reliant on the very same official sources. With the likes of Gunaratna and Abuza hired as government consultants and cited in the media, a feedback loop of sorts is created, reproduced in publications like *The Economist* and *The Far Eastern Economic Review* and in workshops on "terrorism" in so-called think tanks in Washington, DC, London, and the various capitals of Southeast Asia.

food and sleep, and subjected to room temperatures varying from ten to one hundred degrees Fahrenheit.[8]

Beyond an insistence on empirical depth, moreover, specialists on Southeast Asia might also be expected to assert the primacy—and complexity—of the local conditions, dynamics, and understandings which underpin *jihad* in the region. Such an instinctive response would be entirely understandable in the context of Southeast Asian Studies as a field of intellectual production. After all, from its inception, the very notion of Southeast Asian Studies has been defended and promoted as an indispensable filter or framework for reinterpreting Great Traditions through the prism of "local knowledge." Khmer Hinduism, Javanese Islam, Filipino Catholicism, and Vietnamese (Indonesian, and Thai) Communism have been revealed not as feeble, second-rate imitations, or mere franchise outlets, of Indic Civilization, the Straight Path, Christianity, and the Comintern, but rather as expressions and elaborations of Southeast Asians' distinctive self-understandings and modes of incorporation and indigenization of external sources of inspiration and authority. The Great Tradition glass once deemed half empty has been recast as a Southeast Asian glass more than half full.

In this regard, scholarship on Islam in Southeast Asia is exemplary, whether in its colonial origins or its more recent variants. In his writings on the Islamicized areas of the southern Philippines, for example, the Syrian-born American colonial official Najeeb Saleeby depicted a highly attenuated form of the Muslim faith in Mindanao and the Sulu Archipelago, setting the tone for subsequent work, whether Filipino nationalist writings on "Muslim Filipinos" or American ethnographies of "the Maranao" and "the Taosug" peoples of the South.[9] Meanwhile, in Dutch colonial descriptions of Islam in the Indonesian archipelago, scholars such as Snouck Hurgronje and the members of the *adatrecht* school in Leiden downplayed the currency and credentials of the faith and its representatives in favor of a stress on local customs (*adat*), thus encouraging the codification of local customary laws and promotion of local "cultures," and prefiguring subsquent anthropological reification—and reinforcement—of indigenous "traditions," most notably on Java.[10] In short, whether under colonial or Cold War auspices, the practices and institutions identified with Islam in Southeast Asia have been portrayed largely as integrated elements within the complex tapestries of indigenous cultures, whether Maranao or Taosug, Minangkabau or Javanese.[11]

Recast through this "area studies" lens, what alternative picture of "Islamic Terrorism" comes into focus? The mainstream "area studies" view,

---

[8] On the conditions under which Omar al-Faruq was interrogated at Bagram Air Force Base in Afghanistan, see: Don Van Natta, Jr., "Questioning Terror Suspects in a Dark and Surreal World," *The New York Times*, March 9, 2003.

[9] Najeeb M. Saleeby, *Studies in Moro History, Law, and Religion* (Manila: Bureau of Printing, 1905).

[10] For an early discussion of this history, see: H. Westra, "Custom and Muslim Law in the Netherlands Indies," *Transactions of the Grotius Society* 25 (1939): 151-67.

[11] The classic text in this regard is, of course, Clifford Geertz, *The Religion of Java* (Chicago: University of Chicago Press, 1960).

it appears, might well be perfectly compatible with the Al Qaeda-centered account peddled by the likes of Gunaratna and Abuza, who note, *en passant* and in apparent innocence of the specialist literature, that "the majority of the populations in Southeast Asian societies are secular and tolerant."[12] Only through social dislocation, economic frustration, and psychological confusion amidst the process of rapid urbanization and modernization, indoctrination by Middle Eastern (or immigrant "Arab") preachers, or incorporation into international "terrorist" networks from the days of fighting Soviet troops in Afghanistan, are small oddball groups of Southeast Asians drawn into *jihad*. It is a pathology essentially external to the region.

A more skeptical, and critical, perspective, however, suggests otherwise. After all, even the most casual reader of newspapers in Manila and Jakarta will find an abundance of innuendo and anecdotal evidence suggesting not only duplicity and double-dealing by the Philippine and Indonesian security services in their prosecution of "The War on Terrorism," but also the possibility of their own involvement in the very terrorist activities attributed to Al Qaeda and its local subsidiaries. In this vein, the Abu Sayyaf group operating in Basilan, for example, has been portrayed as engaged not in religious struggle and rebellion against the Philippine government, but in criminal activity and predation, whose possibilities for survival and success depend not on grievances but on "market" opportunities, incentives, and constraints. Such groups as Laskar Jihad in Indonesia have similarly been depicted as creatures of conspiracy, whether as sub-contracted spoilers and bargaining chips for the Suharto family, or as "rent-a-mobs" for disgruntled military officers and politicians eager to destabilize the government in Jakarta. Jemaah Islamiyah has likewise been debunked as the creation—or invention—of the Indonesian, Malaysian, and Singaporean governments who share a common interest in discrediting oppositional forces associated with organized Islam. Not Middle Eastern fundamentalists, but Southeast Asian secularists and Christians, are thus responsible for *jihad* in the region, it would seem.

Yet here too there is a tendency to take the practice and threat of *jihad*—like that of "Communism" in years gone by—both too seriously and not seriously enough. As with the "terrorism experts," *jihad* is viewed as the product of malignant foreign influence and indoctrination, or of malevolent elite conspiracies and manipulable mass followings, which threaten to undermine the multiculturalist, ecumenical foundations of "civic culture" and the uncertain and incomplete processes of consolidating liberal democracies in such countries as the Philippines and Indonesia. As with the "terrorism experts," the content and context of "Islam" are dismissed out of hand as irrelevant, reducible to sinister, pathological symptoms of foreign, "fundamentalist" belief or mere window dressing. The possibility that *jihad* in Southeast Asia, like Osama bin Laden's Al Qaeda organization elsewhere in the world, might reveal something beyond itself is never given serious consideration.

---

[12] Abuza, "Tentacles of Terror," p. 428.

The pages below, by contrast, take this possibility as their essential point of departure. Instead of dismissing—and thereby dispelling—the potential appeal of the call for *jihad* among Southeast Asian Muslims, this essay starts from the contrary premise, of *jihad*'s potential plausibility and legitimacy. Instead of reducing *jihad* to "Islamic fundamentalist" ideas or "rational self-interested" machinations (or some muddled combination thereof), the essay situates such groups as Abu Sayyaf, Laskar Jihad, and Jemaah Islamiyah within the historical context of the institutions, practices, and identities associated with Islam in the Philippines and Indonesia. Instead of viewing Southeast Asian Muslims' connections to the Middle East solely in terms of Afghanistan and Al Qaeda, the essay stresses the historical depth and sociological breadth of transnational networks linking Muslims across the two regions of the Islamic world. Instead of viewing these networks and links as somehow external to Southeast Asia, the essay shows how the long-standing connectedness of Muslims in the region and beyond has run up against other transnational currents and circuitries—those of capitalism, Christianity, and the global system of modern nation-states.

Overall, the aim is to address two inter-related questions: What circumstances have enabled—and constrained—association and mobilization under the sign of "Islam" in Southeast Asia? Why has "terrorism"—or, in the narrow, but now widely popular sense of the term, *jihad*—waged under the banner of Islam in Southeast Asia assumed certain forms at certain times in certain places, but not others? On the one hand, the answers to these questions can only be found through a comparative historical and sociological analysis of Islamic institutions and practices in the Philippines and Indonesia. On the other hand, the essay reveals how *jihad* in Southeast Asia has been shaped not only by Islam, but also by the variegated forms and forces of Christianity, capitalism, and nationalism in the region as well.

THE ABU SAYYAF OF THE SOUTHERN PHILIPPINES

In the case of the Philippines, the most recent and noteworthy manifestations of *jihad* have consisted of the bombing, kidnapping, and extortionary activities of the shadowy Abu Sayyaf ("Father of the Sword") group, whose primary base of operations appears to be located on the island of Basilan in the Sulu Archipelago. Allegedly founded by a Libya-trained Muslim Filipino veteran of the anti-Soviet resistance in Afghanistan, the Abu Sayyaf group first surfaced in the early-mid 1990s in connection with a series of killings and kidnappings of Christian missionaries, nuns, and priests in Basilan and Zamboanga City, a short ferry ride away from the island. In 1995, the group grabbed headlines in the Philippines and beyond in connection with a violent attack on the town of Ipil, Zamboanga del Sur, which emptied the town's bank vaults and store tills and left some fifty residents dead. After a hiatus of five years, the Abu Sayyaf group resurfaced in 2000-2001 with a series of highly publicized kidnappings of Filipino Christians and foreign tourists in the southern Philippines and on the Malaysian resort island of Sipadan, just a brief speedboat ride from the group's hideaways in Basilan and Sulu.[13] Meanwhile, Abu Sayyaf also gained international notoriety as local hosts to Al Qaeda operatives like Ramzi Yousef, who bombed the World Trade Center in 1993, and Khalid Shaikh Mohammed, who allegedly masterminded first an abortive multiple commercial airliner bombing scheme in 1995 and later the successful September 11 attacks on the Twin Towers and the Pentagon in 2001.

Colonial Origins of "Moro" Marginalization in the Philippines

The context and content of the Abu Sayyaf's distinctly predatory brand of *jihad* have been shaped not only by the minority status of Islam in the predominantly Catholic archipelago, but also by the distinctive processes through which capitalist development and national integration began to unfold under Spanish and American colonial auspices. Crucial in this regard was the post-*Reconquista* zeal which animated the Spanish project to stem the spread of Islam in the archipelago, which was well under way by the time of Magellan's ill-fated arrival in Cebu in the early sixteenth century. Colonization meant evangelization, among both the natives of the islands and the "Chinese" immigrants who served as commercial intermediaries in inter-island commerce and the Spanish galleon trade with the Middle Kingdom. The assimilation of this immigrant minority, achieved through intermarriage with native women, conversion to Catholicism, and the baptism and redesignation as *mestizo* (mixed) of the children born to such unions, prefigured the emergence of a commercial class whose "Chinese" ancestry did not stand in the way of its capacity to rule "for itself" and in the name of the Filipino nation. It was thus a class of assimilated Catholic, Chinese *mestizos*—rather than a stigmatized, closed "foreign" minority as in Indonesia—which pioneered the expansion of market circuitries from various port cities into the hinterlands of the archipelago in the nineteenth century. It was also this same class of now self-assuredly Filipino moneylenders, merchants, and landowners who predominated in the national integration of the Philippines through elections in the twentieth century, as municipal mayors, provincial governors, congressmen, senators, and presidents.

Against this backdrop, the marginality of those Filipinos residing in the Islamicized southern areas of the archipelago—now dubbed and demonized as "Moros"—was twofold. First of all, insofar as these areas had remained outside the orbit of Spanish colonial rule, they only belatedly experienced the processes by which the elimination of barriers to "free trade" in the nineteenth century gave rise to a Chinese *mestizo* comprador class for foreign firms in the prosperous port cities in the archipelago. Thus with the incorporation of previously unhispanized areas into the Philippines in the early twentieth century, the path of

---

[13] Mark Turner, "Terrorism and Secession in the Southern Philippines: The Rise of the Abu Sayaff," *Contemporary Southeast Asia* 17,1 (June 1995): 1-19; Marites Danguilan Vitug and Glenda Gloria, *Under The Crescent Moon: Rebellion in Mindanao* (QuezonCity: Ateneo Center for Social Policy and Public Affairs, 2000), pp. 192-245.

internal colonization of Muslim Mindanao and the Sulu Archipelago was opened wide to coconut, corn, and rice millers, moneylenders and bankers, bus, electricity, and shipping companies, and colleges and universities based in Cagayan de Oro, Cebu, Davao, and Manila.

Second, inasmuch as the national integration of the archipelago was achieved through the expansion of colonial democracy "upwards" from small-town mayorships to the Philippine presidency, the delayed onset of this process in the Moro Province and the deferral of its completion until the mid-late 1950s further facilitated internal colonization by non-Muslim interests. Without locally elected congressmen, and with city mayors and provincial governors appointed by Manila, the dispensation of patronage in Muslim Mindanao and the Sulu Archipelago in the first several decades of the twentieth century did not allow local Muslim politicians to accumulate as much wealth and power as did their Christian counterparts elsewhere in the archipelago. Logging concessions, pasture lease agreements, transportation franchises, and titles for large tracts of "public" land fell into the hands of carpetbaggers and their allies from Christian areas of Mindanao, Cebu, Iloilo, and Manila.[14] In short, since before independence, the Muslims in the Philippines have been systematically disadvantaged and subordinated vis-à-vis Christians in the accumulation of cultural, financial, political, and social capital.

Transnational "Islam" and the Sulu Zone

At the same time, the combination of peripherality within the Philippines, on the one hand, and transnational connectedness beyond its borders, on the other, provided the basis for alternative modes of acquiring power and prestige in Muslim Mindanao and the Sulu Archipelago. Manila and other major cities colonized other hinterlands elsewhere in the Philippines, including the "pagan" highlands of the Gran Cordillera mountain range. The entire eastern shelf of the archipelago—stretching from Cagayan Valley in northern Luzon through Quezon Province, the Bicol Peninsula, down to Samar in the Eastern Visayas and the Agusan and Surigao provinces of eastern Mindanao—evolved into an impoverished provider of cheap labor, agricultural commodities, and mineral resources to western centers of capital in the country. It was precisely in these provinces where the Communist Party of the Philippines (CPP) and its New People's Army (NPA) was most successful in its mobilizational efforts against the Marcos regime in the 1970s and early-mid 1980s.

By contrast, the possibilities and patterns of armed mobilization under the banner of Islam in Muslim Mindanao and the Sulu Archipelago were shaped by a uniquely different set of circumstances. Crucial in this regard was the long history and continued reality of the region's close connections with other parts of Southeast Asia, most notably the eastern Malaysian state of Sabah and the Indonesian province of North Sulawesi. As the historian James Warren has shown, the late eighteenth century saw the

---

[14] Patricio N. Abinales, *Making Mindanao: Cotabato and Davao in the Formation of the Philippine Nation-State* (Quezon City: Ateneo de Manila University Press, 2000).

rise of a loosely structured port polity in the southern Philippines, centered on the Sulu Sultanate and extending as far as north Sulawesi and northeastern Borneo. This polity, which Warren memorably dubbed the "Sulu Zone," was based on trade with English merchants eager for marine and jungle products for sale in Chinese ports—and, crucially, on the mobilization of labor to obtain them. Labor for the gathering of tripang, pearl, tortoise shells, and birds' nests was accumulated through "slave-raiding" expeditions in the Hispanized areas of the Philippine archipelago and elsewhere in Southeast Asia which brought thousands of captives annually to Sulu to work as pearl divers and fishermen.[15] Only in the mid-late nineteenth century did the "Forward Movement" of the regime in Manila succeed in forcing the Sulu Sultanate—and the Muslim sultans of central Mindanao—to submit to Spanish authority.[16] Yet as elsewhere in Southeast Asia, the success of the Spanish "Forward Movement" and its consolidation under American auspices created a new Sulu Zone across modern state boundaries, as seen in the reemergence of the dispersed slave-raiders of the Sulu archipelago as bandits, pirates, and smugglers preying on inter-island and international trade.

Even after Philippine independence in the mid-twentieth century, moreover, hundreds of thousands of Filipinos found work in Sabah, on tuna fishing fleets operating off the coast of North Sulawesi, and elsewhere in Indonesia and Malaysia, while smuggling and an officially sanctioned barter trade linked southern Jolo, Zamboanga, and Cotabato City to ports such as Labuan and Manado.[17] In a frontier zone where property rights—titles to agricultural lands, pasture areas, and logging concessions—have remained highly contested and insecure, the extensive illegal flows of goods and labor across international boundaries further strengthened the economic importance of violence, whether asserted in the name of the Philippine state or otherwise.

At the same time, moreover, these linkages between the southern Philippines and the world beyond were reinforced and expanded through the transnational educational pilgrimages and networks associated with Islam. Located at the easternmost fringes of the Muslim world, the institutions and practices associated with the Islamic faith in the southern Philippines by the time of independence in 1946 appear to have been relatively weakly touched or transformed by the religious trends observed in countries where Islam has constituted not only the dominant religion but

---

[15] James Francis Warren, *The Sulu Zone 1768-1898: The Dynamics of External Trade, Slavery, and Ethnicity in the Transformation of a Southeast Asian Maritime State* (Quezon City: New Day Publishers, 1985), p. 53.

[16] Warren, *The Sulu Zone*, pp. 104-25; Reynaldo C. Ileto, *Magindanao 1860-1888: The Career of Datu Uto of Buayan* (Ithaca: Cornell Southeast Asia Program, 1971).

[17] By one 1995 estimate, some 300,000 undocumented Filipinos were working in Sabah and Sarawak. See: Zeus A. Salazar, "The Malay World: Bahasa Melayu in the Philippines," in *The Malayan Connection: Ang Pilipinas sa Dunia Melayu* (Quezon City: Palimbagan ng Lahi, 1998), p. 99.

also a state-supported faith.[18] To this day, Muslim society in Mindanao and the Sulu Archipelago has remained predominantly rural, with levels of literacy and education among the lowest in the Philippines, and thus local institutions of religious learning have achieved only limited success in promoting an understanding of "Islam" as an abstract system of belief.[19] Yet since the 1950s, even as mosques and numbers of pilgrims making the *haj* have multiplied, local Qur'anic schools (*maktab*) and formal Islamic schools (*madari*) have gradually expanded in number and in enrollment, as have Islamic colleges and other higher institutions of religious learning.[20]

Notwithstanding their small numbers and modest credentials, such schools have had an important impact on Muslim society in the southern Philippines. Instead of preparing students for admission into Philippine public high schools or universities, these schools have linked young Muslim students in Mindanao and the Sulu Archipelago to wider Islamic educational networks beyond the archipelago. Over the years, increasing numbers of Muslim students have left the southern Philippines to enroll in Islamic schools and universities in Indonesia and Malaysia, or to avail themselves of opportunities for study in the Middle East, whether at the prestigious Al-Azhar University in Cairo or in lesser known institutions in Pakistan and Saudi Arabia. Not only have such foreign-educated Muslims returned to work as *ustadz* and *ulama* in Mindanao and the Sulu Archipelago, but various foreign Muslim governments, foundations, and groups have provided funding and personnel for the promotion of the faith in the southern Philippines. Thus precisely in the same decades as the Catholic Church in the archipelago experienced a dramatic Filipinization, the institutions and practices associated with Islamic learning and worship became increasingly internationalized in the country.

Jihad

It is thus the combination of these transnational connections with the distinctly American pattern of decentralized democracy that has shaped the possibilities—and limitations—of *jihad* in the southern Philippines. While the early post-war era saw the incorporation of Muslim Mindanao and the Sulu Archipelago into the circuitries of Philippine electoral politics, Marcos's declaration of martial law in 1972, the centralization of law-enforcement in the hands of the Integrated National Police (INP),

---

[18] See: Howard M. Federspiel, "Islam and Muslims in the Southern Territories of the Philippine Islands During the American Colonial Period (1898 to 1946)," *Journal of Southeast Asian Studies* 29,2 (September 1998): 340-56, especially pp. 347-55.

[19] Patricia Horvatich, "Ways of Knowing Islam," *American Ethnologist* 21,4 (1994): 811-26.

[20] For impressions and estimates of these trends, compare: Luis Q. Lacar, Gabino T. Puno, and Nagamura T. Moner, eds., *Madrasah Education in the Philippines and Its Role in National Integration* (Iligan City: MSU-IIT Coordination Center for Research and Development, 1986); "Estimated Number of Madaris (Arabic Schools) as of July 31, 1993," Bureau of Muslims Cultural Affairs, Office on Muslim Affairs, Quezon City, 1993; and Richard Martin, "Resurgent Islam," *Far Eastern Economic Review*, February 17, 1994, pp. 36-37.

Philippine Constabulary (PC), and Armed Forces of the Philippines (AFP), and the awarding of control over the barter trade to the AFP Southern Command (Southcom) engendered considerable local resistance. In the late 1960s, Liberal Party politicians from the predominantly Muslim provinces of Cotabato and Lanao had already begun to sponsor a Muslim Independence Movement (MIM) and to arm and train Muslim guerrilla fighters as a defensive strategy against "an increasingly aggressive national president who was actively strengthening (with money and arms) their Nacionalista Muslim rivals in their home provinces."[21] With the declaration of martial law, moreover, local resistance to Marcos began to coalesce around the Moro National Liberation Front (MNLF).

From its inception, the MNLF drew strength from Islamic and Southeast Asian links stretching far beyond the southern Philippines. As is well known, alongside Manila-educated activists like MNLF Chairman Nur Misuari were dozens of Muslim Filipinos who had studied in Indonesia, Malaysia, and the Middle East, and the MNLF received considerable diplomatic, financial, and logistical backing from foreign sources, ranging from Libya's Qaddafi to Tun Mustapha, the chief minister and political boss of Sabah through the mid-1970s.[22] More generally, over the course of the 1970s and 1980s, the MNLF (and a splinter group, the Moro Islamic Liberation Front or MILF) drew sustenance from the density of remaining cultural, economic, and political linkages across the Sulu Zone. Smuggling and the government-sanctioned barter trade between southern Philippine ports and Labuan provided a regular predatory income for rebel commanders through protection rents, piracy, and shareholder profit, and the thousands of Muslim Filipinos working (illegally) in Malaysian Sabah or on fishing boats in the tuna-rich Indonesian waters off North Sulawesi served as a network for arms, training, and guerrilla recruitment. Knowledgeable observers estimate that many of the MNLF and MILF rank and file spent time as overseas laborers in Sabah. In terms of funding, moreover, Libyan support for the MNLF was matched by Saudi backing for the MILF.

Yet with the revival of competitive electoral politics and the re-decentralization of law enforcement in the late 1980s and early 1990s, the southern Philippines witnessed the domestication and incorporation of many such "Muslim rebels," some of whom had already been demobilized and coopted into local government posts since the Tripoli Agreement between the MNLF and the Marcos government in 1976. Local elections in

---

[21] Thomas M. McKenna, "The Sources of Muslim Separatism in Cotabato," *Pilipinas* 21 (Fall 1993): 11. At the same time, (Christian) Liberal politicians in Central Luzon such as Senator Benigno S. Aquino, Jr. were similarly engaged in collaboration with the revived Communist Party of the Philippines (CPP) and its New People's Army (NPA).

[22] T. J. S. George, *Revolt in Mindanao: The Rise of Islam in Philippine Politics* (Kuala Lumpur: Oxford University Press, 1980); Thomas McKenna, *Muslim Rulers and Rebels: Everyday Politics and Armed Separatism in the Southern Philippines* (Berkeley: University of California Press, 1998), pp. 138-69; Lela G. Noble, "The Moro National Liberation Front in the Philippines," *Pacific Affairs*, 49,3 (1976): 405-24; Samuel K. Tan, *The Internationalization of the Bangsa Moro Struggle* (Quezon City: University of the Philippines Press, 1993).

the late 1980s and 1990s saw the elevation of numerous MNLF and MILF commanders and backers to local government positions, revealing and reinforcing the close linkages between the rival guerrilla groups, on the one hand, and local and national electoral politics, on the other. Local "Muslim rebel" commanders became municipal mayors, provincial governors, and congressmen, and thus developed diverse—and divisive—alliances with (Christian) politicians and businessmen in Manila and elsewhere in the country. The project of unifying the Muslims of the southern Philippines tended to dissolve in the absorptive webs of the country's highly decentralized democracy.

It was thus in the context of both formal peace talks and informal political alliances that the MNLF agreed, in 1996, to cease armed struggle in exchange for government backing of Nur Misuari's bid for the governorship of the Autonomous Region of Muslim Mindanao (ARMM), even as the avowedly more hard-line MILF continued to exercise influence through elected officials in its stronghold in central Mindanao. Subsequent changes of government in Manila trickled down to the ARMM through these byzantine alliances of national politicians and "Muslim rebels," a pattern loosely paralleled among the two main factions of the Communist Party of the Philippines (CPP). Following the Estrada administration's "total war" against the MILF in 2000, new president Gloria Macapagal-Arroyo engineered an abrupt reversal of government policy, as seen in the junking of Misuari as ARMM Governor in 2001 and subsequent efforts to forge a new deal with the MILF.[23]

Yet much as the Spanish "Forward Movement" of the mid-late nineteenth century saw the reemergence of the slave-raiders of the Sulu sultanate as bandits, pirates, and smugglers, so has the post-Marcos reincorporation of Muslim Mindanao and the Sulu Archipelago into the democratic Philippines witnessed new forms of predation and resistance, now under the rubric of *jihad*. Indeed, the shadowy Abu Sayyaf group has surfaced with kidnappings, robberies, and bombings—first in 1994-1996 and again in 2000-2001—precisely in the midst of shifts and squabbles over the terms of trade between Manila politicians and their local MNLF/MILF partners. Moreover, today's Abu Sayyaf group has emerged from among the Samal, Yakan, and Taosug areas of Basilan, Sulu, and the southern Zamboanga Peninsula, in roughly the same arc as their counterparts of the preceding century.[24]

In part, this location must be understood in terms of the decentralized structure of law enforcement in the Philippines, wherein local elected officials enjoy considerable formal and informal influence. It is in this context that market centers and trade routes can be preyed upon from an outside jurisdiction or, better yet, a base of operations spanning several

---

[23] For background, see: Arnold Molina Azurin, *Beyond the Cult of Dissidence in Southern Philippines and Wartorn Zones in the Global Village* (Quezon City: University of the Philippines Press, 1996); Kristin Gaerlan and Mara Stankovitch, eds., *Rebels, Warlords and Ulama: A Reader on Muslim Separatism and the War in Southern Philippines* (Quezon City: Institute for Popular Democracy, 2000).

[24] Jim Warren, "Who Were the Balangingi Samal? Slave Raiding and Ethnogenesis in Nineteenth-Century Sulu," *Journal of Asian Studies* 37,3 (May 1978): 477-90.

jurisdictions. With such a base in Basilan and Sulu and connections beyond, an armed group can "tax" logging concessionaires, bus companies, and plantation owners on Basilan, while using speedboats for kidnappings, killings, and robberies in nearby Zamboanga City, at island tourist resorts off Sabah or Palawan, and along the trade routes connecting the southern Philippines to Sabah, Sulawesi, and Singapore.

In what way should we understand the Abu Sayyaf group to be acting under the banner of Islam in the southern Philippines? Perhaps, as many knowledgeable observers have claimed, the supposedly two-hundred-strong Abu Sayyaf group has been operating in concert with local politicians and policemen,[25] and under a franchise from the Zamboanga City-based Southern Command (Southcom) of the Armed Forces of the Philippines. Whether in the raid on Ipil in 1994 or in the various kidnapping episodes over the years, there have been many indications of military—and police—connivance and coordination with the "Abu Sayyaf," analogous to the involvement of military intelligence in Manila with the kidnapping activities of the allegedly ex-NPA "Red Scorpion Gang" in the early 1990s.[26] In this context, the rubric of "Islamic terrorism" can be used as a flag under which to justify a continued military presence in the southern Philippines, to legitimate violence in the name of the state, and to attract US military assistance, especially in today's "War on Terrorism."

Yet perhaps there is more to the rubric of "Islam" in the southern Philippines than such cynical machinations. Islam, after all, has been a rubric under which "Moros" have established certain kinds of connections beyond the borders of the archipelago and enjoyed avenues for the accumulation of power and prestige not afforded them within the confines of the Philippine nation-state. Thus the bombings of churches and missionary centers, the killings and kidnappings of nuns and priests, and the abductions conducted in Zamboanga City and in various tourist resorts might well have some broader meaning beyond their role in attracting the attention and support of Osama bin Laden and his Al-Qaeda network for the activities of the Abu Sayyaf.

Whether in the form of Christian missionary efforts in Zamboanga, Basilan, and Sulu, tourist resorts catering to foreigners off nearby Sabah and Palawan, or the plantations, logging concessions, and mining operations in these areas run by companies based in Manila, Tokyo, and New York, a new "Forward Movement" is in the making in the old Sulu Zone. Against this backdrop, as MILF and MNLF commanders compete for the favor of Manila politicians and the spoils of local state offices, what better rubric for resisting—or taxing—this Forward Movement, than Abu Sayyaf, "Father of the Sword"? This name, it is said, was imported to the Philippines by returning Muslim Filipino *mujahidin* who had lived and

---

[25] For example, Wahab Akbar, the provincial governor of Basilan, is not only a former MNLF commander and Islamic preacher, but also allegedly one of the founders of the group identified today as Abu Sayyaf.

[26] See, for example, Jose Torres Jr., *Into the Mountain: Hostaged by the Abu Sayyaf* (Quezon City: Claretian Publications, 2001), pp. 145-48.

fought in Afghanistan under the leadership of a certain Abdul Rasul Sayyaf. Sayyaf was reportedly a modest merchant in the main bazaar in Peshawar before he reinvented himself as an anti-Soviet *mujahidin* and won the sponsorship of Pakistani military intelligence and the CIA in the 1980s. Thus the transnational "Islam" under whose banner the Abu Sayyaf group has been operating connotes the power of violence in an insecure border zone, especially violence licensed and subcontracted out by state authorities. Yet linguistic and cultural diversity and the divisiveness, domestication, and parochialism that come with a highly electoralized and decentralized organization of state power have sharply constrained the capacity of this "Islam" to attract, mobilize, and unify the Muslims of the southern Philippines.

LASKAR JIHAD AND JEMAAH ISLAMIYAH IN INDONESIA

Meanwhile, in neighboring Indonesia, *jihad* has assumed a rather different form in recent years, one associated first with the dispatching of armed contingents to areas of inter-religious violence by Laskar Jihad, and then with the bombings attributed to the shadowy group identified as Jemaah Islamiyah. In comparison with the Philippines, the content and context of this *jihad* in Indonesia at the turn of the twenty-first century have been shaped not only by the broader purchase of the Islamic faith in the archipelago, but also by a pattern of class and state formation which has presented very different constraints and opportunities for association and mobilization under the sign of "Islam."

Colonial Rule and "Islam" in the Netherlands East Indies

Despite the extent of Islamization in the Indonesian archipelago by the time of the VOC's arrival in the seventeenth century, the pattern of class and state formation that unfolded under Dutch colonial auspices in the Indies constrained the possibilities for "Islam" in three decisive ways. First of all, the gradual creation of a modern state was achieved through the incorporation, subordination, and bureaucratization of local aristocracies in Java and elsewhere in the archipelago. Unlike in neighboring British Malaya, this process saw the various sultanates of the Indies stripped of authority over religious affairs and encouraged instead to develop local culture—and codify local custom (*adat*)—in ways that reinforced parochial particularisms and reified ethnic divisions among Muslims in the Indies.[27] As Dutch rule spread and deepened in the late nineteenth and early twentieth centuries, moreover, these local aristocrats were retooled into bureaucrats whose entry and ascendancy within the rapidly expanding colonial state spurred the creation of a modern secular school system, out of which many leaders of the Indonesian nationalist movement would eventually emerge. For both the Dutch colonial regime in the era of the "Ethical Policy" and the Indonesian nationalist movement in

---

[27] See, for example, John Pemberton, *On the Subject of "Java"* (Ithaca: Cornell University Press, 1994).

its infancy, secular education and modernization thus came to supplement, if not fully supplant, a set of reinvented "traditions" as the basis for the claim to rule over the archipelago.

Second, under Dutch colonial auspices, the spread and deepening of capitalist market relations in the Indonesian archipelago was pioneered by a comprador business class of decidedly non-Muslim complexion. Thanks to Dutch policies of segregation, the small minority of immigrants from southern China and their offspring were sharply defined as "Chinese" and confined to urban ghettos, with assimilation into local societies (especially on Java) and conversion to Islam strongly discouraged. Spurred on by the establishment of the Cultivation System on Java in the mid-nineteenth century, "Chinese" revenue farmers and merchants expanded their commercial and credit networks deep into the rural hinterlands, firmly establishing themselves as the compradors of the Dutch colonial "plural society." With the abandonment of segregation and the abolition of the revenue farms in the early twentieth century, subsequent generations of immigrants from China and their offspring developed into an Indonesia-wide "Chinese" business class.

Third and finally, the Dutch colonial era saw the emergence of a privileged Christian minority within the ranks of the urban professional classes and the expanding colonial state. In various localities around the archipelago, residual Catholic influences from the early Portuguese era (especially in the eastern islands) and Protestant missionary efforts under Dutch (or occasionally English or German) auspices created pockets of Christian identity centered on missionary schools of various denominations and affiliations. Such schools not only introduced these converts to the Bible and to a distinctly modern notion of ("Great Tradition") religious faith and identity, but also served as transmission belts for the recruitment of colonial civil servants, soldiers, teachers, and professionals. This small but privileged minority of Indonesian Christians was destined to be markedly over-represented in the ranks of the bureaucracy, the Army, the university belt, and the urban middle class.[28] Thus a close connection between Christianity, education, and access to state power was established, in a pattern strikingly reminiscent of the "pillarization" (*verzuiling*) of Dutch society along Protestant and Catholic lines back in the metropole as early as the nineteenth century.

Yet alongside and against the entrenchment of local aristocracies and *adat* chiefs on the one hand, and the growth of new circuitries of modern secular, Christian, and "Chinese" power on the other, the long centuries of Dutch colonial rule also produced new possibilities for identity, association, and mobilization under the sign of "Islam." Muslims had been leaving their villages to visit religious shrines and study in religious boarding schools (*pesantren*) around the Indonesian archipelago for centuries, with small but significant flows of pilgrims and scholars to Mecca on the one hand, and a trickle of Hadrami Arab migrants to Southeast Asia on the other, linking the "periphery" to the "center" of the

---

[28] Gavin W. Jones, "Religion and Education in Indonesia," *Indonesia* 22 (October 1976): 19-56.

Islamic world through the circulation of men, ideas, and texts as well as membership in Sufi brotherhoods (*tarekat*) such as the Naqshbandiyyah.[29] A community of Southeast Asian Muslims—known collectively as the "Jawah"—was well established in Mecca, studying, playing host to Southeast Asian *hajis*, and returning home to the region to impart their wisdom to their co-religionists.[30] These linkages persisted, indeed prospered, under Dutch rule with little interference on the part of the colonial regime.

Yet by the late nineteenth century, economic, political, and technological conditions helped to broaden and deepen the connections between Muslims in the Indonesian archipelago and their co-religionists in the Middle East, where social and intellectual changes were giving rise to new conceptions of "Islam." With the intensification and spread of market relations and modern state circuitries on Java and elsewhere in the Indies came increasing travel, as seen most dramatically in the construction of railroads, thus thickening the flow and widening the arc of religious sojourns and scholarly pursuits across the landscape of Islamic shrines and schools in the Indies and neighboring colonies like British Malaya. With the growth of inter-island trade and travel and the rise of the publishing industry, moreover, the dissemination of books and other publications written in Jawi—i.e. Malay written in Arabic script—greatly strengthened the field of shared communication and consciousness among Muslims in Southeast Asia. Finally, with the opening of the Suez Canal, the invention of the steamboat, and the establishment of Pax Brittanica making sea travel across the Indian Ocean more affordable, rapid, and safe, more and more Muslims from the Indies came to make the *haj* or visit centers of Islamic learning elsewhere in the Middle East, even as larger numbers of migrants from the Hadramaut came to settle in the Indies.

It was against this backdrop that new conceptions of "Islam" came into focus in the Netherlands East Indies, circulating from Cairo and the Hijaz via Singapore, the hub of *haj* travel and Islamic publishing in Southeast Asia. Inspired by Cairene authors ranging from Jamal al-Din al-Afghani and Muhammad 'Abduh to Rashid Rida, and impelled by the widening scope of their own experiences and awareness of the world, some Muslims in the Indies began to think, write, and act in ways that transcended the loose sense of the *bilad al-jawa* ("lands of the Jawa") and the personalistic and particularistic networks of *tarekat* and *pesantren*. They bewailed the divisions and the constraints upon intellectual and social advancement among Muslims which colonial rule, feudalism, and traditional Islamic teaching methods had imposed upon the Islamic world. They embraced "Islam" as a project for the (re)unification and reschooling of the *ummat*.[31]

---

[29] Azyumardi Azra, "The Transmission of Islamic Reformism to Indonesia: Networks of Middle Eastern and Malay-Indonesian 'Ulama' in the Seventeenth and Eighteenth Centuries" (PhD dissertation, Columbia University, 1992).

[30] See: C. Snouck Hurgronje, *Mekka in the Latter Part of the Nineteenth Century* (Leiden: E. J. Brill, 1970), pp. 215-92.

[31] Michael Francis Laffan, *Islamic Nationhood and Colonial Indonesia: The Umma Below the Winds* (London: Routledge/Curzon, 2003).

Signs of these trends were in abundant evidence by the second decade of the twentieth century. The year 1912 saw the founding by Javanese Muslim merchants and scholars of Muhammadiyah, an association devoted to the development of modern schools, known as *madrasah*, which combined new forms of religious instruction with the kind of Western-style schooling that had given Christians such advantages in the Dutch East Indies.[32] Subsequent years witnessed the establishment of other such associations, most notably Al-Irshad and Persatuan Islam (Persis or Islamic Unity) by elements of the Hadrami Arab immigrant merchant community concerned with preserving and promoting both modern educational advancement along the lines pioneered by Christian and Chinese schools in the Indies, and a sense of Islamic identity transcending the borders of the island colony. By the 1920s, the inroads made among Muslims by these associations had inspired religious scholars (*kyai* or *ulama*) affiliated with the established system of rural Islamic boarding schools (*pesantren*) to form Nahdlatul Ulama (Awakening of the Religious Scholars) in defense of "traditional" forms of Islamic learning and worship.

"Islam" and Nationalism in Indonesia

It was also in this context that new forms of identity and association under the rubric of "Islam" came to contribute some of their considerable energies and organizational resources to struggles against Dutch colonial rule. The modernist education promoted by Muhammadiyah fit well within the rubric of the Dutch "Ethical Policy" of the early 1900s and won encouragement and support from the colonial regime, and immigrant "Arab" merchants served as commercial and financial intermediaries for Western firms in the Indies. But the possibility that "Islam" would provide a rubric for anti-colonial resistance was already evident in the so-called Padri movement in West Sumatra in the early 1800s, the Banten revolt of 1888, and the long Aceh War in the final quarter of the nineteenth century.[33] Thus Dutch fear of "Pan-Islamic" movements and conspiracies emanating out of Mecca was a recurring theme in the last century of colonial rule.[34]

Indeed, the much celebrated rise of Indonesian nationalism in the twentieth century was from its inception intimately intertwined with forms of association and mobilization under the banner of "Islam." The first mass movement to mobilize tens, indeed hundreds, of thousands of ordinary people around the Indies, after all, was the Sarekat Islam of the 1910s and early 1920s, whose various activities drew on the associational resources

---

[32] Deliar Noer, *The Modernist Muslim Movement in Indonesia 1900-1942* (Kuala Lumpur: Oxford University Press, 1973).

[33] See, for example, Sartono Kartdirdjo, *The Peasants' Revolt of Banten in 1888* (The Hague: Martinus Nijhoff, 1966); and James T. Siegel, *The Rope of God* (Ann Arbor: University of Michigan Press, 2000).

[34] See: Anthony Reid, "Nineteenth Century Pan-Islam in Indonesia and Malaysia," *Journal of Asian Studies* 6,2 (1967): 267-83; and C. van Dijk, "Colonial fears, 1890-1918: Pan-Islamism and the Germano-Indian Plot," in *Transcending Borders: Arabs, Politics, Trade and Islam in Southeast Asia*, ed. Huub de Jonge and Nico Kaptein (Leiden: KITLV Press, 2002), pp. 53-89.

and solidarities accumulated by Islamic school networks across the archipelago and beyond.[35] While the Sarekat Islam fell prey to internal dissension and later Dutch suppression after the failed rebellions of 1926-27, Islamic networks and associations reemerged in the 1940s to play a crucial role in the Revolusi against the Dutch. Under the Japanese Occupation, a nationwide Council of Indonesian Muslim Associations (Masyumi) was created to help in the administration of occupied Indonesia, and Muslim youths from around Java and beyond were given paramilitary training and organized into armed units of the Hizbullah (Army of God) to confront an anticipated Allied invasion.[36] Thus the school networks, symbols, and solidarities associated with "Islam" were crucial to the anti-Dutch guerrilla struggle during the Revolusi (1945-49), with some of the strongest resistance to the returning colonial regime and its aristocratic collaborators coming from self-consciously Islamic armed groups. In West Java, for example, the guerrilla leader Kartosuwirjo, a protégé of the Sarekat Islam leader H. O. S. Tjokroaminoto and a son-in-law of a prominent Sundanese *kyai*, even proclaimed the formation of the Islamic State of Indonesia (Negara Islam Indonesia) on August 7, 1949.

But this path of mobilization under the banner of Islam ran aground in the face of sociological obstacles to the unification of the Indonesian *ummat* as well as alternative political movements and currents in the archipelago. Under the rubric of a unifying "Islam," after all, considerable diversity and contestation in Muslim associational life, educational networks, and religious practices continued to flourish, with little institutional basis for the centralization and standardization of Islamic authority and orthodoxy. Beyond the broad, pluralistic field of self-consciously Islamic education, association, experience, and consciousness, moreover, alternative solidarities came into being among the population of the Indonesian archipelago. Bureaucratization and commercialization, after all, produced new secular pilgrimages, new school networks, and new publishing circuitries, with the Singapore-centered flow of *jawi* texts eclipsed in the 1910s by newspapers, novels, and pamphlets printed in the cities of the Indies in the romanized Malay which became known as *Bahasa Indonesia*.

The egalitarian, anti-feudal appeal of "Islam," moreover, was soon rivaled by that of the alternative rubric of "Communism," with its own transnational networks, forms of schooling, language and textual production, and blueprints for a post-independence Indonesia. Thus by the late 1910s, the "green" (Islamic) complexion of the Sarekat Islam was complemented—and contested—by the spread of "red" hues, and various stripes of Communism were likewise much in evidence in the affiliations of local guerrilla groups in the Revolusi of the late 1940s. Small wonder that the nationalist leader Sukarno, a graduate of Dutch secular schools, began using the slogan of NASAKOM—Nasionalisme, Agama (Religion), Komunisme—already in the late 1920s to signal the embrace—and

---

[35] Takashi Shiraishi, *An Age in Motion: Popular Radicalism in Java, 1912-1926* (Ithaca: Cornell University Press, 1990).

[36] Harry J. Benda, *The Crescent and the Rising Sun: Indonesian Islam Under the Japanese Occupation 1942-1945* (The Hague: W. van Hoeve, 1958).

domestication—of these two competing transnational networks and currents under the sign of a secular Indonesian nationalism.

Thus the energies and aspirations mobilized behind "Islam" in the Revolusi soon ran up against a very different kind of project, namely the reconstitution of a modern secular state under an Indonesian national banner. The promise of an Islamic state was abandoned in favor of the monotheistic, but multi-faith state ideology Pancasila, and "irregular" Islamic guerrilla leaders were left unrecognized and excluded from the formation of the Indonesian Armed Forces (Tentara Nasional Indonesia) in favor of more "professional" (and in some cases, Dutch trained) officers. Groups led by Kartosuwirjo and other disappointed local guerrilla leaders in South Sulawesi, South Kalimantan, and Aceh continued the armed struggle for a Darul Islam (Home for Islam), but they dwindled into small-scale insurgencies and were fully defeated by the early 1960s.[37]

Meanwhile Masyumi, now reconstituted as a political party, competed in the 1955 elections, but only as one of the "Big Four" parties, each representing a different "current" (*aliran*)—and school network—in a society now defined by deep divisions among its population. Despite its second-place showing, Masyumi was effectively excluded from the fruits of power by an emerging pro-Sukarno coalition including the secular Partai Nasionalis Indonesia, the Partai Komunis Indonesia, and the "traditionalist" Nahdlatul Ulama, entrenched in the Ministry of Religious Affairs since its 1952 breakaway from Masyumi. Deeply disappointed and embittered by this turn of events, elements of the party supported a set of rebellions against Jakarta in the late 1950s, thus precipitating the banning of Masyumi in 1960 and clinching the defeat of "Islam" as a project for the remainder of the Sukarno era.

"Islam" Under the New Order

Yet with the violent elimination of the PKI and the forced retirement of Sukarno in the mid-late 1960s, the possibilities for mobilizing under the banner of "Islam" underwent a series of dramatic changes. University students affiliated with the modernist Himpunan Mahasiswa Islam (HMI) were prominent in anti-PKI and anti-Sukarno demonstrations in Jakarta during this period, and Nahdlatul Ulama played a key role in finessing the transfer of presidential power to Maj. Gen. Suharto and carrying out the anti-communist pogroms in East Java. But the New Order regime that crystallized under Suharto was one in which "Islam" was profoundly marginalized. The Army, which occupied a dominant position within the regime, was led by officers schooled and socialized in a distinctly secular nationalist tradition, with Christians disproportionately well represented and suspicions of organized "Islam" amply established among their ranks. Indeed, Suharto himself had commanded TNI troops responsible for atrocities in the fight against the Darul Islam movement in South Sulawesi in the early 1950s.

---

[37] C. van Dijk, *Rebellion Under the Banner of Islam: The Darul Islam in Indonesia* (The Hague: Martinus Nijhoff, 1981).

Beyond the Armed Forces, moreover, the recruitment and circulation of networks of civilian elites in the New Order regime likewise excluded those associated with Islamic education, association, and aspirations. Initially, the regime incorporated remnants of the local aristocracies which had supported the colonial state under the Dutch and survived and prospered in the post-independence era as the conservative backbone of Sukarno's PNI in many parts of the archipelago. But the exigencies of socio-economic modernization and bureaucratic circulation dictated a pattern of recruitment into—and reproduction of—the political class based not on "blood" but on something dressed up as "merit."

In this regard, the networks of educated Protestants and Catholics enjoyed a privileged position within the Suharto regime. Indeed, the first decades of the New Order saw the rise to unprecedented social and political prominence of members of Indonesia's small Christian minority. From parish schools scattered throughout the archipelago to seminaries to the Protestant and Catholic students' organizations at the most prestigious universities in the country, Indonesian Christians enjoyed a clear head start in the multi-tiered hierarchy of education that fed into the New Order bureaucratic elite, even as their church coffers and business connections were enhanced by the growing numbers of wealthy ethnic-Chinese Protestants and Catholics. Most notoriously, a clique of Catholic activists established a powerful think tank in Jakarta, the Center for Strategic and International Studies (CSIS). Through their positions at Indonesia's top universities, in the military establishment, and CSIS, Christians thus landed themselves and their protégés in the seats of civilian and military power, in the Cabinet, Golkar (the regime's electoral machine), its pseudo-parliamentary bodies, and key media outlets and other business ventures. Even in the late 1980s, the key economic and security portfolios in the Cabinet were in Christian hands.

Besides these influential Christians, a somewhat broader pool of Westernized—and often Dutch-speaking—graduates of Indonesia's leading secular institutions of higher education (and universities in Europe and North America as well) exerted similar forms of influence within the regime and likewise used their patronage and protection to advance the careers and businesses of their former students and other protégés. Yet these cosmopolitan, Western-educated intellectuals, technocrats, and political operators represented a tiny privileged elite in a country where only a small fraction of the population reached the level of tertiary education. Moreover, although most members of these circles were nominally Muslim by faith, very few of them had received a religious education of any kind or participated in Islamic organizations.

Meanwhile, the process of capitalist development in Indonesia also saw the expansion of private non-Muslim wealth and power throughout the archipelago. In the first two decades of the New Order, the overwhelmingly "Chinese" business class was transformed from a collection of small-scale merchants and moneylenders into an interlocking directorate of commercial, financial, and industrial capital. Huge "Chinese" conglomerates emerged, with diverse interests ranging from automobile production to banking, food processing, electronics, household appliances, pharmaceuticals, real-estate, and shipping. In the cities and major towns of the archipelago, the signs of "Chinese" capital loomed increasingly large on the urban landscape: bank outlets, department stores, factories, residential subdivisions, shopping malls, and supermarkets. The names of major "Chinese" capitalists, conglomerates, and commodities—Liem Sioe Liong, BCA, Maspion Group, Indomee—became household words, even as the familiar neighborhood "Chinese" shop was transformed into a local retail outlet for this nationwide, if not properly national, business class.

Into the widening gulf between this narrow ruling class and the broad mass of the Indonesian population stepped the powerful figure of Islam, much as it had done during the late Dutch colonial era, but now without Communism as an alternative pole of ideological and organizational attraction. "Islam," after all, represented a plausible idiom of protest by outsiders against a regime in which foreign and "Chinese" capital, Christians, and graduates of secular institutions of higher education were seen to occupy privileged positions. Signs of this insurgent "Islam" were already in evidence in the election campaigns of 1977 and 1982, with the strong showing by PPP (United Development Party), the sole representative of Islamic political aspirations under the New Order's highly restricted electoral system. By the late 1980s, the regime had largely defanged PPP through a combination of cooptation and repression. But occasional reminders of the popular radical energies associated with an ostensibly unified but unjustly oppressed "Islam"—from the Tanjung Priok and Warsidi massacres of the 1980s to the riots and church burnings of the mid-late 1990s—still inspired considerable fear—and hope.[38]

At the same time, state policies and social trends over the long decades of the Suharto era had worked gradually to propel new generations of Indonesian Muslims socially "upwards" and to help them accumulate the forms of symbolic, cultural, and social capital that facilitated entry into the New Order ruling class. For the Suharto era witnessed not only a dramatic expansion of higher education in Indonesia and a proliferation of all kinds of universities in the country, but also the implementation of numerous policies which furthered the objectification and functionalization of religion, long the project of "modernist" Muslim groups in the country. The anti-communist hysteria of the early Suharto years, for example, drove millions of Indonesians to seek refuge in religious identity, institutions, and faith in the late 1960s to avoid fatal charges of "atheism."[39] New government regulations requiring all citizens to declare their faith, expanding religious classes in state schools, and impeding inter-faith marriages strengthened the public markers and boundaries of religious identities. Thus Indonesian Muslims, in a process observed

---

[38] See: John T. Sidel, "*Islam Fanatik?* PPP and the Limitations of Islamic Populism in Indonesia," in *Populism and Reformism in Southeast Asia: The Threat and Promise of New Politics*, ed. Eva-Lotta E. Hedman and John T. Sidel (New Haven: Yale University Southeast Asia Monograph Series, forthcoming).

[39] Avery Willis, Jr., *Indonesian Revival: Why Two Million Came To Christ* (South Pasadena: William Carey Library, 1977); Robert W. Hefner, "Islamizing Java? Religion and Politics in Rural East Java," *Journal of Asian Studies* 46,3 (August 1987): 533-54.

elsewhere in the Islamic world, increasingly came to understand their religion as "a coherent system of practices and beliefs, rather than merely an unexamined and unexaminable way of life," to think of "knowing Islam" as "a defined set of beliefs *such as those set down in textbook presentations*," and to put Islam "consciously to work for various types of social and political projects."[40]

Indeed, the system of Islamic education in Indonesia grew considerably over the three decades of the New Order. The network of traditional, rural Islamic boarding schools (*pesantren*) expanded dramatically, as did the self-consciously modernist *madrasah*, teachers' academies, religious training schools, and college faculties, and universities associated with Muhammadiyah. At the same time, the State Islamic Institute (Institut Agama Islam Negara or IAIN), first opened by the Ministry of Religious Affairs in 1960, had established fourteen branches around the country by the 1990s, even as the branches of Universitas Islam quadrupled in number during the same period. Meanwhile, mainstream state universities throughout Indonesia saw a marked rise in the numbers of devout Muslim students and the popularity of campus mosques, prayer and religious discussion groups, and Islamic student organizations.[41] By the 1990s, the rising numbers of Indonesians schooled under a distinctly, self-consciously "Islamic" rubric had become a visible feature of urban society.

With the rising number of Muslim professionals, the public sphere of modern, urban middle-class life, for the very first time in Indonesian history, was now also claimed by those who defined themselves as pious Muslims. Indeed, the markers of Islamic piety were now incorporated into the *habitus* of mainstream Indonesian bourgeois propriety and prestige. Wealthy Indonesian Muslims began to avail themselves of luxury pilgrimage tour packages to Mecca,[42] and to enroll in various "institutes," "foundations," "clubs," "intensive courses," and "workshops" in Sufi spirituality and Islamic learning in Jakarta and other major Indonesian cities.[43]

Alongside these rising numbers of self-consciously Muslim professionals were the swelling ranks of what might be termed "professional Muslims," in other words men—and, to a considerably lesser extent, women—who made distinctly modern careers through the promotion of Islam. IAIN graduates filled the growing numbers of posts as instructors in religion in state schools, *madrasah*, and *pesantren*, and joined the expanding ranks of

---

[40] Gregory Starrett, *Putting Islam to Work: Education, Politics, and Religious Transformation in Egypt* (Berkeley: University of California Press, 1998), pp. 9-10. Emphasis added.

[41] See: "Islam Sebagai Baju Zirah di Kalangan Muda," *Tempo*, May 13, 1989, pp. 74-78; and Nurhayati Djamas, "Gerakan Kebangkitan Islam Kaum Muda," in *Gerakan Islam Kontemporer di Indonesia*, ed. Abdul Aziz, Imam Tholkhah, and Soetarman (Jakarta: Pustaka Firdaus, 1989), pp. 207-87.

[42] Moeslim Abdurrahman, "On Hajj Tourism: In Search of Piety and Identity in The New Order Indonesia" (PhD dissertation, University of Illinois at Urbana-Champaign, 2000).

[43] Julia Day Howell, "Sufism and the Indonesian Islamic Revival," *Journal of Asian Studies* 60,3 (August 2001): 718-22.

functionaries in the vast Ministry of Religious Affairs. Books, magazines, pamphlets, and other publications on Islamic affairs proliferated, as did Muslim radio and television talk-shows, promoting the rise of "pop Islam" in the form of pious music stars and preachers (*dai*).[44] Meanwhile, HMI student leaders from elite universities were being recruited in record numbers into the bureaucracy, the business world, and Golkar.

It was to recognize, reinforce, and rechannel these trends that the Ikatan Cendekiawan Muslim Se-Indonesia (ICMI or Association of Indonesian Muslim Intellectuals) was founded under the leadership of Minister of Research and Technology and close Suharto associate B. J. Habibie in the early 1990s. As Minister of Research and Technology since the 1970s, Habibie controlled a sprawling empire of state-owned high-tech enterprises, an enormous state-based patronage empire outside military and technocratic control in the name of high-tech economic nationalism. Through his hold over "strategic industries" and responsibility for infrastructure projects and industrial development schemes, Habibie wielded considerable discretion over government personnel and contracts and built up an enormous clientele of university-educated Muslim *pribumi* ("indigenous") businessmen by granting them privileged access to state loans, contracts, and regulatory breaks. With Suharto's support, Habibie was elevated to the governing body of Golkar and various Habibie protégés won key Cabinet positions and other plum civilian and military posts. Meanwhile, a steady process of ICMI-*isasi* moved forward in Golkar, in the awarding of state contracts, on many university campuses, and beyond. CIDES (Center for Information and Development Studies), an ICMI-affiliated think tank, soon began to compete with the Catholic CSIS, and its daily newspaper *Republika* tried to rival the Catholic-owned *Kompas*. ICMI support and influence soon extended to Islamic publishers, preachers, and pilgrims, into *pesantren, madrasah*, and IAIN, and to figures within both NU and Muhammadiyah. With Habibie at its helm, ICMI incorporated an expanding network of Muslim professionals and "professional Muslims" into the ranks of the national political class.[45]

As this network moved upward within the political class, remaining obstacles to the ascendancy of "Islam" became increasingly palpable. In particular, the accumulation of wealth and power by the Suharto family imposed a ceiling on any further ICMI-ish ambitions for the foreseeable future. Suharto's children, after all, had also won seats on the governing board of Golkar and begun to lobby for their own minions and allies in the Parliament, the Armed Forces, and the Cabinet, and their huge conglomerates continued to capture the juiciest state contracts and monopoly concessions. So long as Suharto was President, his children would remain entrenched at the pinnacle of power, and succession struggles could leave

---

[44] See: "Satria Berdakwah, Raja dari Bawah," *Tempo*, June 20, 1984, pp. 27-30; "Saya Ustad, Bukan Artis," *Tempo*, April 28, 1990, pp. 74-78; "Dai-Dai baru Bak Matahari Terbit," *Tempo*, April 11, 1992, pp. 14-20; and François Raillon, "L'Ordre Nouveau et l'Islam ou l'imbroglio de la foi et de la politique," *Archipel* 30 (1985): 229-61.

[45] Darul Aqsha, Dick van der Meij, and Johan Hendrik Meuleman, *Islam in Indonesia: A Survey of Events and Developments from 1988 to March 1993* (Jakarta: Indonesia-Netherlands Cooperation in Islamic Studies, 1995), pp. 263-76.

state control in the name of their father, rather than in the hands of those who spoke on behalf of Islam.

Viewed against this backdrop, the "Reformasi" campaign that led to the resignation of Suharto in the spring of 1998 was the culmination of a process of self-definition and self-promotion by an ascendant segment of the national political class claiming to represent Indonesian Islam. In the Indonesia of the 1990s, after all, the struggle of "reformist" Muslims was a struggle fought largely through and within the New Order state, as HMI alumni and other affiliates of ICMI asserted their claims to increasing shares of parliamentary seats, Golkar posts, Cabinet ministries, Army commands, and other positions and perks of power. In this struggle, the enemy was not so much Suharto himself but rather the aging dictator's children, whose advantages in the contest over power, wealth, and the impending presidential succession were increasingly experienced—and resented—as a glass ceiling confining the interests and aspirations of an arriviste Muslim segment of the political class. In this context, the riots which swept various provincial towns and cities in 1995-97, and the massive conflagration that hit Jakarta in May 1998, served as powerful reminders of the popular energies which could be mobilized in the name of "Islam." In the end, the call for "Reformasi" was indeed a call by Muslims for the ouster of Suharto, precisely when members of his family were poised to seize control of the Armed Forces, Golkar, and the Cabinet, and, not coincidentally, when ICMI chief Habibie was installed as vice-president.

"Islam" and Democracy in the Post-Suharto Era

Suharto's resignation and Habibie's ascendancy to the Indonesian presidency in late May 1998 thus represented an unprecedented—and long awaited—opportunity for the assumption of state power in Indonesia by those claiming to represent "Islam." During Habibie's twelve months in office, these forces worked assiduously to assert greater control over the Armed Forces and to build a broad coalition of parties that would combine an HMI-dominated Golkar with Muhammadiyah chairman Amien Rais's National Mandate Party (Partai Amanat Nasional or PAN), the Masyumi-style Crescent Moon and Stars Party (Partai Bulan Bintang or PBB), and other allied forces. Such a coalition of parties, it was hoped, would provide a rubric for the retention of power by Habibie and the segment of the political class which claimed to speak for "Islam."

But the contradictions and weaknesses of the position of those claiming to represent "Islam" impeded the effective consolidation of their control over the Indonesian state. After all, these Muslims still comprised only one segment of the political class, as suggested by the complex pattern of alliances and maneuvers—within the regime and in the university belt—which brought it into the driver's seat in May 1998. Whether in the Armed Forces, Golkar, or the Cabinet, modernist Muslims found themselves constrained by the Suharto family's residual influence and by competing clusters of interests and association variously identified with Christian and secular nationalist lineages. The New Order years, after all, had produced not only visible evidence of modernist Muslim upward mobility, but also significant growth in Indonesia's Christian population and in the number of graduates from non-Muslim and secular institutions of higher education. Among themselves, moreover, these modernist Muslims, like their multifarious Protestant counterparts in the Christian world, suffered from the fissiparous tendencies of all post-Reformation religions, and their diverse pieties and purposes were reflected in debilitating political fragmentation and factional strife.

In Indonesian society, moreover, this self-consciously Muslim segment of the political class found its claim to represent Indonesia—or Islam, for that matter—persistently challenged and hotly contested from below. "Islam," after all, was destined to remain an overly ambitious, indeed presumptuous, banner in a nation boasting the single largest Muslim population and the most popular non-governmental Islamic organizations in the world. The elitist pretensions of middle-class modernist Muslims to represent Islam ran up against the reality of the millions of unschooled and underemployed ordinary Indonesians of the faith. Even in the boom years of the early-mid 1990s, when ICMI was expanding its network, thousands of Muslim youths had left the nation's *pesantren, madrasah*, IAIN, and universities for the job market, only to find opportunities for state or private sector employment or upward social mobility strictly limited.

Compared to the upwardly mobile, middle-class modernist Muslim professionals and political operators who traced their roots back to the *madrasah*, the social and political advancement of those hailing from the *pesantren* belt was decidedly more modest.[46] A few steps behind—or below—their *madrasah*-schooled counterparts on the ladder of educational and social hierarchy, such students flocked in record numbers to the expanded network of IAIN and provincial universities, but at elite university campuses the NU-affiliated Pergerakan Mahasiswa Islam Indonesia (PMII or Indonesian Islamic Student Movement) was much more modest in its activities and alumni roster than HMI. With high rates of unemployment for university-educated youth persisting through the boom years of the mid-1990s, it was clear that even those *pesantren* kids who made it as far as college faced an uphill struggle into the new Muslim middle class.[47] Beyond the *pesantren* belt, moreover, where state patronage had made significant inroads by the 1990s, the broad majority of Indonesian Muslims were poor and unlettered, and thus excluded from the kinds of educational experiences and networks that were so crucial for the emergence and ascendancy of the political class which claimed to speak for the *ummat*.

The June 1999 elections constituted an abrupt reversal of the trends that had led to the ascendancy of "Islam," along the lines of the betrayal and disappointment following the Revolusi and the winning of Indonesian independence fifty years earlier. If for decades the path to power in

---

[46] See: Andrée Feillard, *Islam et Armée Dans L'Indonésie Contemporaine: Les Pionniers de la Tradition* (Paris: Editions L'Harmattan, 1995), Chapter 12.

[47] Chris Manning, *Indonesian Labour in Transition: An East Asian Success Story?* (Cambridge: Cambridge University Press, 1998), pp. 177-88.

Indonesia had led from schools to universities to the circuitries of the state, now control over state offices and resources was achieved not through educational networks but through electoral mobilization, in a largely poor and "under-educated" society. Small wonder that the parties which proved most popular were those most inclusive with regard to the extent and form of schooling of the voting public. Most notable in this regard was the Partai Demokrasi Indonesia–Perjuangan (PDI-P or Indonesian Democratic Party of Struggle) led by Megawati Sukarnoputri, the daughter of Indonesia's first president, which captured a plurality of votes in the elections in June 1999. Like her father before her, Megawati represented a secular nationalist tradition, with the PDI-P dominated by non-Muslims (more than one-third of its parliamentary slate) and nominal Muslims with no history of Islamic education or associational affiliation. With Megawati's rise to the vice-presidency in late 1999, her increasing influence under the administration of former NU chairman Abdurrahman Wahid, and her eventual ascendance to the presidency in mid-2001, "Islam" thus experienced a considerable diminution of its previously rising status in the public sphere and claim to state power.

Jihad

It is against this backdrop that the emergence of groups like Laskar Jihad and Jemaah Islamiyah at the turn of the twenty-first century must be understood. Already in mid-late 1998, sudden political liberalization, widespread anti-government protests, and the impending 1999 elections encouraged the Habibie administration and its supporters to expand and experiment with the forms of mobilization in the name of Islam. Elements in the Habibie administration supported the formation of the thuggish Front Pembela Islam (Front for the Defenders of Islam) in Jakarta in 1998 to counter student demonstrations against the government, and various Islamic parties were provided funding and assistance in the 1999 election campaigns.

With Habibie's ouster in 1999 and the diminution of modernist Muslim influence in the state, moreover, the sense of desperation grew. In Jakarta, Habibie's immediate successor, former NU chairman Abdurrahman Wahid, had a long history of defending his "traditionalist" constituency against "modernist" Muslim encroachment by forging alliances with Christians, secular-nationalists, liberal intellectuals, and foreign interests, which were well represented in his cabinet and entourage and his policy preferences. In various parts of the archipelago, moreover, the processes of democratization and decentralization combined with the strong electoral performance of the PDI-P to endanger those forces identified with "Islam."

Nowhere was this more evident than in areas of inter-religious conflict like Maluku and Poso, where Protestants backed the PDI-P against a Muslim vote divided between Golkar and various Islamic parties, even as the PDI-P's leader, vice-president Megawati Sukarnoputri, came to enjoy increasing influence within the Indonesian Armed Forces leadership in Jakarta. Violence against Muslims in Maluku and Poso, after all, was being committed by armed groups of Christians enjoying close links with the PDI-P, financial and logistical support from fellow Christians elsewhere in Indonesia and beyond, as well as the evident protection or collusion of sympathetic elements in the security forces.[48] By mid-2001, moreover, the ascension of Megawati to the presidency brought the secular nationalist/Christian PDI-P into a dominant position in Jakarta, along with senior military officers (both active and retired) with well established records of opposition to the promotion of "Islam." Thus the champions of Islam in Jakarta were understandably keen to help their beleaguered co-religionists in Maluku and Poso, and to protect and promote a stronger sense of religious boundaries in the national arena, where political parties commanding multi-faith constituencies such as Megawati's PDI-P have won millions of votes, dozens of parliamentary seats, and a dangerous level of influence at their expense.

While various Islamic political party leaders thus began to voice support for an organized response to supplement the government's feeble measures to protect Muslims in Maluku, those most visibly and vehemently committed to this struggle were associated with a group formed in January 2000 and known as Laskar Jihad. With their long flowing white robes and goatees, the estimated several thousand members of this saber-wielding group clearly drew inspiration from the Middle East. Indeed, the group's founder was of Hadrami Arab descent, studied in Saudi Arabia, Pakistan, and Yemen, and allegedly spent some time among the *mujahidin* in Afghanistan in the late 1980s.[49]

In fact, Laskar Jihad was a group with deep historical roots in transnational Islamic educational networks and experiences. Many of the *pesantren* and *madrasah* where its leading members had been schooled were established by Islamic associations—Al-Irshad and Persatuan Islam (Islamic Union or Persis)—which were founded in the early twentieth century by Muslims of Hadrami Arab descent and others influenced by the teachings of modernist Islamic scholars in the Middle East. From their inception, these schools placed great emphasis on the study of Arabic and, far more than the more Westernized *madrasah* of Muhammadiyah, prepared their students for higher education in centers of Islamic learning far from the Indonesian archipelago.[50] While the founders and first students were predominantly drawn from among the immigrant Hadrami Arab community in the Indies, by the 1930s the vast majority of students were, by assimilation or ancestry, Indonesians. Yet the fact that these

---

[48] Gerry van Klinken, "The Maluku Wars: Bringing Society Back In," *Indonesia* 71 (April 2001): 1-26; Lorraine V. Aragon, "Communal Violence in Poso, Central Sulawesi: Where People Eat Fish and Fish Eat People," *Indonesia* 72 (October 2001): 45-79; International Crisis Group, *Indonesia: The Search for Peace in Maluku* (Jakarta/Brussels: International Crisis Group, February 2002); Human Rights Watch, *Breakdown: Four Years of Communal Violence in Central Sulawesi* (New York: Human Rights Watch, December 2002).

[49] See: Noorhaidi Hasan, "Faith and Politics: The Rise of the Laskar Jihad in the Era of Transition in Indonesia," *Indonesia* 73 (April 2002): 145-69.

[50] Howard M. Federspiel, *Islam and Ideology in the Emerging Indonesian State: The Persatuan Islam (PERSIS), 1923 to 1957* (Leiden: Brill, 2001).

schools fed into an overseas education network promoted a "sense of separateness" and an "outward orientation, back to the Middle East," encouraging students to understand "that their center was not 'here' in the Indies, but rather 'there' in the heartland of the Arab world."[51] Thus Al-Irshad and Persis activists were understandably ambivalent towards Indonesian nationalism, supporting the struggle against Dutch colonial rule on the one hand, while opposing the construction of a secular nation-state in its stead on the other. Although they contributed their energies to the Revolusi that led to Indonesian independence in 1945-49, many members of these groups were understandably dissatisfied with the place of Islam in the new nation-state and its constitutional democracy and backed the Darul Islam rebellion in areas such as West Java, South Sulawesi, and Aceh in the 1950s and early 1960s.

While Al-Irshad and Persis thus entered the 1960s on the very fringes of Indonesian politics, their enduring transnational linkages combined with the sociological and political trends described in the pages above to allow their networks of schools—and their aspirations for Islam in Indonesia—to survive, grow, and prosper in subsequent decades. Banned for its role in supporting the "regional rebellions," by the 1960s Masyumi could no longer provide an umbrella of state patronage and protection as it had in the early years after independence, and despite their contributions to the anti-communist campaigns of the 1965-66, activists from these circles found themselves utterly marginalized and at times actively persecuted by the seemingly Christian-dominated New Order state. Yet the detention of alleged "Komando Jihad" members in 1977 and the wave of arrests and trials in connection with the Tanjung Priok Incident and related bombings and protests in 1984 must have strengthened the faith of such activists, timed as these events were to coincide with general elections in the first instance and a major PPP congress in the second. With PPP winning in Jakarta and garnering considerable popular support elsewhere in the 1977 elections but then shedding its oppositional stance, Islamic markings, and many of its most prominent backers in 1984, the message seemed clear. Only the repressive tactics of a regime dominated by Catholic generals, Chinese financiers, and secularized, Westernized technocrats could keep at bay the popular forces of "Islam."

Fortified by such hopes and by domestic and foreign sources of funding, Al-Irshad and Persis activists devoted themselves to the crucial task of religious schooling. Their efforts were nurtured by Dewan Dakwah Islamiyah Indonesia (DDII or Indonesian Islamic Preaching Council), an umbrella group founded by former Masyumi leaders in 1967 which drew on donations from Saudi Arabian and other foreign sponsors, as well as from sympathetic Indonesian professionals, businessmen, and government officials. As industrialization and urbanization in the 1970s and 1980s brought millions of Muslim migrants to Jakarta and other major Indonesian cities, Dewan Dakwah Islamiyah Indonesia established hundreds of

---

[51] Natalie Mobini-Kesheh, *The Hadrami Awakening: Community and Identity in the Netherlands East Indies, 1900-1942* (Ithaca: Cornell University Southeast Asia Program, 1999), p. 83.

pesantren and *madrasah* and constructed thousands of mosques. The diversity of origins, ethnicity, and language of this growing new constituency, it was hoped, could be transcended by the universalism of "Islam."

DDII was also especially successful in its *dakwah* activities in the campus mosques of state universities in major Indonesian cities, including such prominent institutions as Institut Teknologi Bandung (ITB), Institut Pertanian Bogor (IPB), Universitas Gadjah Mada (UGM) in Yogyakarta, Universitas Airlangga (Unair) in Surabaya, and Universitas Indonesia (UI) in Jakarta.[52] Thanks to its access to scholarships offered by Saudi-sponsored and other international Islamic organizations, Dewan Dakwah was also able to facilitate study in the Middle East. By the 1990s, moreover, with the demise of the Catholic military intelligence czar Benny Murdani and the rise of Habibie and ICMI, well-connected Dewan Dakwah activists (including some recently released from prison) enjoyed new freedom to preach and to publish, as well as unprecedented access to state patronage and support. Through their inclusion in Habibie's vast patronage empire, such activists extended their influence among government-funded students pursuing post-graduate technological and scientific degrees in Europe and North America, and among the ranks of university lecturers, journalists, publishers, and other "professional Muslims" in Indonesia.

Over the years, the transnational pilgrimages of those schooled under the umbrella of the Al-Irshad, Persis, and DDII networks decisively shaped their understandings of Islam. Beyond the influence of individual Islamic reformist intellectuals from the Middle East, or that of Wahhabist sponsors in Saudi Arabia, the experience of education in countries far from Indonesian shores helped to nurture an understanding of Islam that stressed its most "universal" principles, its appeal as a foundation for supra-national social and spiritual unity, and its potential as a basis for the exercise of power. Some of the graduates of these schools have thus been concerned to "purify" (*memurnikan*) the faith of those accretions of local custom (*adat*)—promoted by the Dutch colonial regime and its successors, sustained by the parochialism and ignorance of the *ummat* and the particularism and opportunism of ill-intentioned intermediaries—which stand in the way of Muslim unity.

Alongside this concern to prevent the localization and fragmentation of Islam in Indonesia there has been an abiding sense of urgency about the defense of the faith against the encroachment of rival transnational forces and forms of identity. After all, the twentieth century saw a significant expansion of the Christian population in Indonesia, as well as increasing inroads by the secularizing circuitries of the capitalist market and the modern nation-state. Thus just as the Persis journal *Pembela Islam* (Defender of Islam) bewailed the weaknesses of Muslims in the face of a

---

[52] Asna Husin, "Philosophical and Sociological Aspects of Da'wah: A Study of Dewan Dakwah Islamiyah Indonesia" (PhD dissertation, Columbia University, 1998), pp. 147-176; "Bermula dari Masjid Salman," *Tempo*, May 13, 1989, pp. 79-81; Abdul Aziz, et al., eds., *Gerakan Islam Kontemporer di Indonesia*.

dynamic Christianity in the 1930s, so did Dewan Dakwah activists rail against the closet secularism of liberal, Western-educated/affiliated Muslim intellectuals in the 1980s and early 1990s. It was thus with ample historical precedent that the spokesmen of Laskar Jihad voiced disappointment with the place of Islam in Indonesia's restored constitutional democracy at the turn of the twenty-first century, and tried to rally Muslims divided by partisan and parochial interests against the predations of Christians and secular nationalists affiliated with Megawati and the PDI-P. It was also in echo of the forced demobilization of irregular Islamic guerrillas at the end of the Revolusi some fifty years earlier that Laskar Jihad found itself losing backing from within the state and facing violent retribution and imprisonment at the hands of the authorities by mid-2001.

These lineages have also been amply apparent in the personage and proclamations of K. H. Abu Bakar Ba'asyir, the elected leader of the Majelis Mujahidin Indonesia and the man accused of inspiring (if not himself operating) the allegedly Al Qaeda-linked "Jemaah Islamiyah" network. Ba'asyir and his followers are said to have plotted terrorist attacks against US targets in the Philippines and Singapore and they stand accused of the Christmas church bombings across the country in December 2000 and the Bali bombing of October 2002.[53] Born in 1938 in Jombang, an East Javanese town well known for its institutions of Islamic schooling, Ba'asyir attended the famous "modern" *pesantren* in Gontor and then went on to Universitas Al-Irsyad, where he studied Islamic jurisprudence. After graduation, he worked with other young Islamic activists under Dewan Dakwah Islamiyah Indonesia to set up two radio stations, whose broadcasts were soon terminated by the government because of their critical and "extremist" content. In the early 1970s, Ba'asyir and his colleagues founded a school, known as Pondok Pesantren Al-Mukmin Ngruki, located first in Solo and then on the outskirts of the city in the regency of Sukoharjo.

There his teachings attracted both a growing stream of Muslim students and the increasing interest and concern of the Indonesian government. Indeed, by the late 1970s Ba'asyir was in prison for his views, and after several years of imprisonment he was able to leave the country for a long period of exile – and continued *dakwah* activity—in Malaysia that ended only with the fall of Suharto.[54] Over the years, moreover, Ba'asyir, his school, its students and alumni have been repeatedly linked by the authorities to various "Islamic terrorist" activities, as seen in the Komando Jihad affair in 1977, the post-Tanjung Priok trials of the mid-1980s, and the massacre of an Islamic community founded by Pesantren Ngruki graduates in Lampung in 1989.[55] Most recently, the authorities have

---

[53] On the Christmas 2000 bombings, see: "Cerita dari Mosaik Bom Natal," *Tempo*, February 25, 2001, pp. 59-80.

[54] See: K. H. Abu Bakar Ba'asyir, *Saya Teroris? (Sebuah "Pledoi")* (Jakarta: Penerbit Republika, 2002), pp. 35-40.

[55] Al Chaidar, *Lampung Bersimbah Darah: Menulusuri Kejahatan "Negara Intelijen" Orde Baru Dalam Peristiwa Jama'ah Warsidi* (Jakarta: Madani Press, 2000).

rounded up countless members of this "Ngruki network" in Indonesia, Malaysia, the Philippines, and Singapore, accusing them of involvement in a variety of terrorist activities and of membership in a "Jemaah Islamiyah" network unheard of since the 1970s.[56]

Whatever his recent "terrorist" activities and affiliations might be, Ba'asyir's origins and aspirations are clearly rooted in a tradition of transnational Islam in Indonesia that dates back many decades. With his former students working as preachers and starting up small *pesantren* across the archipelago and in neighboring Malaysia and the Philippines, and his own children pursuing further Islamic education in Pakistan and Saudi Arabia, Ba'asyir has helped to continue and expand the transnational pattern of pilgrimage, education, and circulation embodied in Al-Irshad and Persis since the early twentieth century. Unlike the *madrasah* founded by the mainstream modernist association Muhammadiyah, which help to prepare Muslim pupils for Indonesian state universities and government employment, Ba'asyir's *pesantren* and the broader network of Al-Irshad, Persis, and now DDII-supported schools open the eyes and minds of their students to horizons that stretch far beyond the shores of the archipelago.

To be sure, the Indonesian state exercises a highly attractive—and absorptive—power for activists like Ba'asyir, whether through the tactical necessity of reaching an "accommodation" of some kind with its intelligence apparatus, or the strategic goal of codifying and implementing Islamic law throughout the country. Indeed, there is abundant evidence of linkages between elements in the Armed Forces and these activist networks over the years, from infiltration and imprisonment in the 1970s and 1980s to close cooperation against the foes of the Suharto and Habibie regimes in the mid-late 1990s, and provision of support to armed Muslim groups in Maluku and Poso at the turn of the century. At the same time, the manifold sinecures in the vast Ministry of Religious Affairs in Jakarta and the provisions of regional autonomy, especially in those regencies where Islamic parties control the local assemblies, have also offered considerable opportunities for the promotion of "Islam" within the rubric of the Indonesian nation-state. Yet the means and ends of this dream transcend the borders of Indonesia, with the nation-state and nationalists viewed as—inherently secular—obstacles and enemies dividing Muslims and thwarting the spread and deepening of a universalist Islam. As Ba'asyir commented acerbically with reference to Sukarno and one of his great heroes: "For me, Kemal Ataturk is not the Father of Turkey, but a traitor to the Islamic community in Turkey."[57]

---

[56] See: International Crisis Group, *Al Qaeda in Southeast Asia: The Case of the "Ngruki Network" in Indonesia* (Jakarta/Brussels: International Crisis Group, August 2002).

[57] "KH Abu Bakar Ba'asyir: 'Hadapi Kaum Sekuler dengan Tegas,'" *Suara Hidayatullah*, February 2001.

CONCLUSION: THE MAKING AND UNMAKING OF *JIHAD* IN SOUTHEAST ASIA

In short, as suggested above, *jihad* in the Philippines and Indonesia today must be understood against a broader historical and sociological canvas, one depicting national and transnational institutions, networks, experiences, and horizons. Overall, the location, timing, and form of the activities of Abu Sayyaf, Laskar Jihad, and Jemaah Islamiyah reflect the very different *national* constraints, opportunities, and imperatives presented by national politics, on the one hand, and the widely varying possibilities of mobilizing armed followers under the banner of Islam, on the other. In the Philippines, where local elections reemerged after the fall of Marcos as the primary path of access to state power, the potential attraction of *jihad* has been weakened by parochialism, partisanship, and competition for patronage among the small, poor, and largely unlettered Muslim minority in the southern periphery of the archipelago. Thus *jihad* has manifested itself through shadowy armed groups engaged in criminal rackets, rather than rallying cries for mass mobilization.

In Indonesia, by contrast, where educational institutions long served as key transmission belts for both social mobilization and access to state power, and where Islamic school networks have grown and prospered in recent decades, the call of *jihad* has been issued in the face of a sudden, sharp decline for "Islam" under conditions of democratization. The call for armed mobilization under the banner of Islam in early 2000 came precisely when and where Muslim communities in Maluku and Central Sulawesi found themselves in violent conflict with well-connected and protected armed Christian groups. The bombings around the country at Christmas 2000 and in a nightclub in the predominantly Hindu PDI-P stronghold of Bali nearly two years later reasserted the ubiquitous spectral power of "Islam," just when its strength and integrity in the parliamentary arena had reached new lows with the cooptation of PPP Chairman Hamzah Haz as Megawati's Vice-President.

Yet, as suggested above, the content and context of the Islam in whose name such forms of *jihad* are waged in the Philippines and Indonesia have also been profoundly *transnational* in nature. This transnational dimension of *jihad* in Southeast Asia is best understood not in terms of an international "Islamic Terrorism" conspiracy under the leadership of Osama bin Laden, nor merely as "blowback"[58] or default option[59] in the wake of the Cold War, nor simply as "sanctified rage"[60] against what has been pithily described as McWorld.[61] In both the Philippines and Indonesia, after all, Islam has long been understood—and experienced—not only as an underlying basis for

---

[58] Chalmers Johnson, *Blowback: The Costs and Consequences of American Empire* (New York: Metropolitan Books, 2000).

[59] Robert Malley, *The Call From Algeria: Third Worldism, Revolution, and the Turn to Islam* (Berkeley: University of California Press, 1996).

[60] V. S. Naipaul, *Among the Believers: An Islamic Journey* (London: Picador, 2001), p. 354.

[61] Benjamin Barber, *Jihad vs. McWorld: How Globalism and Tribalism Are Reshaping the World* (New York: Ballantine Books, 1996).

achieving social unity that transcends national boundaries, but also as a project, inherently incomplete, for unifying Muslims divided by political conspiracies, particularistic practices, and parochial interests and understandings. A project whose further advancement can be experienced first-hand elsewhere in the Islamic world, even in neighboring Malaysia.[62]

From its inception, this project has been defined in no small measure by religious orthodoxy. As scholars have suggested, orthodoxy is best understood not as a disembodied system of belief, but as a relationship of power: "the power to regulate, uphold, require or adjust *correct* practices, and to condemn, exclude, undermine, or replace *incorrect* ones."[63] But relations of orthodoxy, it has been noted, are "a peculiar form of property relation—a relation between people with regard to texts and intellectual technologies—that are potentially more fluid than other sorts of class relations."[64] These relations are contingent both on the sociology of education on the one hand, and the politics of competition between other claimants to knowledge and power. Thus even—indeed, especially—for those Muslim Filipinos and Indonesians who have spent many years in schools closely connected through language, scholarship, and circulation to centers of Islamic learning beyond their national borders, Islam has remained a horizon of sorts, one which now appears to be rapidly receding.

Measured in terms of disappointment with the present or imperative for the future, this horizon has been shaped by other transnational forces as well, most notably those associated with Christianity and the supposedly secular(izing) circuitries of the capitalist market and the modern nation-state. As noted above, it was the impact of first Spanish Catholicism and then American liberalism that condemned Muslims in the Philippine archipelago to minority status, internal colonization, and socio-political fragmentation within a nation-state dominated by Christians. In a similar vein, it was the promotion of *adat* and aristocratic localisms by the Dutch, and the head start enjoyed by graduates of Christian missionary schools and Western secular educational institutions and also by "Chinese" businessmen, that made graduates of Islamic schools feel like such outsiders and late-comers, even in predominantly Muslim Indonesia. The past decade of triumphs for global liberalism in economic, political, and cultural terms have thus been experienced not as the extensions of inclusive, universalistic freedoms, but rather as the intrusions of colonizing, particularistic interests at the expense of "Islam."[65] Small wonder that Osama bin Laden and Al Qaeda inspire a measure of enthrallment, adulation, and emulation among some of their fellow co-religionists in Southeast Asia, and serve as signs of a truly great struggle rather than

---

[62] Michael G. Peletz, *Islamic Modern Religious Courts and Cultural Politics in Malaysia* (Princeton: Princeton University Press, 2002).

[63] Talal Asad, *The Idea of an Anthropology of Islam* (Washington, DC: Georgetown University Center for Contemporary Arab Studies Occasional Paper Series, 1986), p. 15.

[64] Starrett, *Putting Islam to Work*, p. 13.

[65] In terms of "secularism," moreover, see: Talal Asad, *Formations of the Secular: Christianity, Islam, Modernity* (Stanford: Stanford University Press, 2003).

simply sources of support and instructions for identifying targets of terrorist activity in the region.

Thus today, as US-backed Philippine troops besiege Abu Sayyaf camps in Basilan and Sulu and as alleged Jemaah Islamiyah activists face interrogation in jail cells in Jakarta, Manila, and Singapore, it is important to remember that *jihad* in Southeast Asia is overwhelmingly reactive and defensive in nature. Playing late, late "catch-up" in the profane world of modern politics, the purveyors of *jihad* in both the Philippines and Indonesia are in fact waging a rear-guard, losing battle under the banner of "Islam," making desperate, last-gasp efforts to rally—or reawaken—the faithful.[66] With Britney Spears on the radio in the provincial capital of Basilan, and Santa Clauses roaming the shopping malls of Jakarta, bin Laden on the run and bin Bush on the warpath, K. H. Abu Bakar Ba'asyir is surely right to describe *jihad* as a "defensive concept."[67]

---

[66] See: Olivier Roy, *The Failure of Political Islam* (Cambridge: Harvard University Press, 1998); and Gilles Kepel, *Jihad: Expansion et Déclin de l'Islamisme* (Paris: Gallimard, 2000).

[67] "Jihad Konsep Defensif," *Suara Karya*, June 6, 2002.

INTERKOM IN INDONESIA: NOT QUITE AN IMAGINED COMMUNITY

Joshua Barker

INTRODUCTION

Anthropologists have long been concerned with how various forms of mediation help constitute communities. Until recently, however, they have been interested almost exclusively in forms of face-to-face mediation, such as speech, ritual, and exchange. Benedict Anderson's work on the origins of nationalism extends anthropological insights about the role of mediation in community formation to modes of social interaction that transcend face-to-face encounters.[1] He argues that such modern rituals as reading newspapers and novels, memorizing maps in school, and answering census questions both enabled and constrained early nationalist imaginings. He thus provides an example of how to conceptualize the relation between the advent of new forms of *technological* mediation and the formation of human subjectivities and communities.

When Anderson traces the origins of nationalism, he focuses less on signs and their meanings and more on the materialities of sign systems and on the institutions in which these systems are embedded. In this respect, his approach could be compared to that of Friedrich Kittler, whose concept of "discourse networks" combines a Foucaultian understanding of discourse regimes with a McLuhan-like understanding of how media structure the ways in which discourse is transmitted, stored, and retrieved.[2]

If we accept Anderson's argument that the imagined community of the nation has its origins in a very particular discourse network, namely print capitalism, it behooves us to raise the question of what other types of subject and ideas of community emerge in concert with other modern discourse networks that are not based on print. For example: what about such electric media as telephony,

---

[1] Benedict Anderson, *Imagined Communities: Reflections on the Origin and Spread of Nationalism*, rev. ed. (London: Verso, 1991).

[2] Friederich Kittler, *Discourse Networks 1800/1900*, trans. Michael Metteer and Chris Cullens, foreword by David E. Wellbery (Stanford: Stanford University Press, 1990); Michel Foucault, *The Archaeology of Knowledge and the Discourse on Language* (New York: Pantheon, 1972); Marshall McLuhan, *Understanding Media: The Extensions of Man* (New York: Mentor, 1964).

telegraphy, satellite communications, and the Internet? Each of these networks emerged in various locales under quite different sets of political, economic, and cultural circumstances. Why did these networks come to take the shape they did in each given locale? How did the materialities of these networks define—and get re-defined by—imaginings of self, community, and modernity? A study of the complex articulations between these discourse networks on the one hand, and their articulation with non-electric discourse networks on the other, could help to delineate some of the many strands of local modernities.

In this paper I will focus on a very unusual electric discourse network, known as *interkom*. Interkom is unusual in two respects. First, it is a technology that—as far as I know—is completely indigenous to Indonesia. It was invented there and has never been exported beyond Indonesia's borders. Second, unlike the networks mentioned above, which in the Indonesian context have always been organized by the state and thus have structures that are strongly unified and centralized, interkom exists very much outside the networks controlled by the state. For the most part interkom has evolved without any recognition, regulation, or relation to the state at all.

The lack of official recognition might help explain why interkom is largely hidden from the public gaze. A fairly exhaustive search of the archive of a local newspaper in Bandung (*Pikiran Rakyat*), for example, yielded only a handful of references to interkom in the editions published between 1980 and 1990. My ethnographic experience is also telling in this regard. I lived in Indonesia for four years and interviewed communications engineers, experts, and hobbyists for two years before learning that interkom was still in use. While I had heard about interkom from friends who grew up in Yogyakarta, like them I believed it to have been a short-lived fad for kids in the early 1980s and that it had long since disappeared. This misconception was exposed quite by accident. One day I looked out my window in Bandung and saw two men climbing a tree in my front yard. When I asked what they were doing, they explained that they were repairing an interkom line (one of these men became my guide into the netherworld of interkom). As I inquired further and walked around town, I came to realize that interkom lines were strung up to trees and utility poles throughout the city. It seemed that everywhere I went, if I looked up, I would see the string-like cables of interkom networks. My failure to notice this before was not due to any attempts on the part of interkom users to hide the network from observation. In fact, people string up the lines quite openly. The networks are simply overlooked.

In this paper I focus on two main aspects of interkom. The first concerns the evolution of the network itself: the way it has grown and transformed through the years. The second concerns the type of community to which interkom gives shape. The paper is based partly on participant observation—taking part in interkom chat and meetings—and partly on twenty lengthy interviews conducted with interkom users in the northern part of the city of Bandung.

RHIZOMATIC EVOLUTION: FROM *LOKALAN* TO *JALUR LINTAS*

What is interkom? As I encountered it, Interkom is a network of cables linking together tiny food stalls or *warung*, ramshackle city homes, rooms in migrant workers' rooming houses, and farms among rice paddies. Its extension is rhizomatic, stretching from Bandung proper out into rural areas just outside the city limits, following alleyways, roads, and river valleys. Interkom is a local invention, a product of Indonesia's informal economy. In a technical sense, it could be viewed as the homemade analogue of a telephone party line. But in cultural terms, it bears greater resemblance to Citizen Band radio: it is a network where people can chat, listen to music, pass on messages, and exchange information.

When a person is on the interkom line, he or she wears headphones and talks into a microphone. The microphone and headphones are plugged into an interkom set, which usually consists of a gutted amplifier box that has been rewired with new circuits for this purpose. In addition to the headphones, many interkom sets are equipped with a speaker so that others who are not themselves "breaking" (*ngebreak*)—chatting on interkom—at that moment can hear the different sides of the conversation. Many sets are also hooked up to tape decks and radios so that music can be piped into the network for all to hear.

If one asks people who have been involved in interkom since the early 1980s about how the network has changed since that time, they invariably describe its growth as passing through a number of distinct stages. The first lines were used to link together neighboring houses, usually within a single residential compound. They grew relatively quickly to link together a number of different houses within the same *kampung* (neighborhood) or RT (Rukun Tetangga, administrative neighborhood unit). When this process happened in two adjacent *kampung*s, and when the power was sufficient to push further, links were established between the *kampung* networks. In this manner, the larger neighborhood units, known as RW (Rukun Warga), became wired. Up until this point, the evolution occurred in a manner suggesting the growing extension and density of a web. The webs themselves, however, were still quite small: the total extension of such networks, measured as the crow flies, would rarely have exceeded a kilometer or two.

With the higher wattage of the interkom sets in the mid-1990s, however, a different type of line emerged, one that aimed to link together distant points but with a relatively low level of local density. These long-distance lines are known generically as *jalur lintas*: high-speed or traversing lines. With the emergence of *lintas* lines, the old networks that were confined to a neighborhood came to be called *lokalan* or local lines. The longest *lintas* line that was operational during my period of observation (2000-2001) in north Bandung extended for at least seven kilometers. People reported that such lines had on occasion extended even further, connecting to areas outside Bandung that are twenty to twenty-five kilometers away. There were even initiatives to build a Bandung-wide network that would link together all the various parts of the city, although this never materialized.

While this story about the evolution of interkom is a good characterization of an overall developmental trend, it masks many of the complexities of network transformation. The most important of these complexities is the fact that interkom networks do not merely grow by extension and by increasing in density: they actually reproduce through a type of division that resembles mitosis.

People gave three main reasons why users may decide to form a new line. One of the most common reasons was that a given line had simply become too crowded. There are limits to how many people can be talking on a single line and still feel that they can get a word in edgewise. Most people put the ideal number of users on a given line at somewhere between twenty and eighty people (not everyone "breaks" at any given time). When the number of users becomes unmanageable, one will see a tendency for division. Often the name of the new line will reflect its origin: it will be called by the name of the original line, but with the additional specification "two." Thus, for example, a line called Jalur Dalas was divided into Jalur Dalas Satu and Jalur Dalas Dua. Other times, however, or over time, the new line will get its own name. Sometimes the relation between two such lines is expressed in the idiom of kinship: as an older sibling line and a younger sibling line.

A second reason people gave for establishing a new line was to provide a space for a different type of discursive content. This may also be related to the problem of overcrowding, except the solution is not merely to create a new line of the same type, but to create a line dedicated to a particular type of content. This is what happened, for example, when some members of a line called Jalur Selek decided to create a new line called Jalur Musik. As one of the founders of the Music Line described it, they wanted to create a bit of entertainment on the side of the existing line, but in a way that would not bother the members of Jalur Selek who wanted to talk. In other cases, it may not be the content that is being divided up, but the discursive styles. Conversations on interkom can be quite vulgar and coarse, so sometimes members of a line may decide to set up a line that is more polite and refined. People who want to join the new line will have to agree to abide by the discursive conventions. Those who do not abide by the rules risk being disconnected.

A third reason people gave for establishing a new line was to increase the level of privacy. Under these circumstances the new line will have a selected membership. It happens once in a while, for example, that two people who like to spend a lot of time talking to each other will decide to create their own private line that others are not invited to join. In fact, there is a term for this type of line: Jalur Guha or Cave Line.

The initial shape a new line takes depends on the reason for its creation. If the line is established to deal with overcrowding, it is quite likely that it will follow the shape of the original line, at least for a time. The same is generally true if the line is an attempt to create a different venue for different types of content or style, although this will depend on individual members' interest in what the new line has to offer. In the case of a Jalur Guha, in contrast, the line will have quite a different shape and length from that of its parent line.

The fact that there are multiple lines that criss-cross and run in parallel across the landscape means that in any given neighborhood there may be several different lines, some *lokalan* and some *lintas*. What makes any particular one of these lines expand or link up with others varies. Sometimes a line will extend to a new house because someone hears about it from others or tries it out while visiting at someone's house (there is a term for this: *ngeron*). This is what one would expect. What I did not expect, however, is that one of the main reasons people cited for wanting to join a line was what is referred to as *cepretan*. The literal meaning of *cepretan* is "clicking," like the sound of an insect, but here it means cross-talk. The currents that pass over interkom lines are actually quite powerful, and they have a tendency to jump across onto other lines they come close to. (This can cause trouble with the phone provider because interkom signals often jump onto phone lines; when this happens people on the telephone hear interkom conversations in the background.) But when people say *cepretan*, they generally mean cross-talk between interkom lines. Usually the sound is quite faint, but it can be loud enough to render other people's conversation intelligible and to pique one's interest. Such overhearing—made possible by the existence of numerous lines—can thus also cause the lines to grow.

Not all network change leads to network growth. Just as there is a tendency for certain lines to become popular and for these to extend greater and greater distances, gathering more and more users as they grow, so too is there a reverse tendency whereby lines are used less and less. If they are rarely used, there is little incentive to keep them in working order, and people will either intentionally disconnect themselves from the line or simply fail to fix connecting cables when they break. In fact, all four of the lines that I was connected to in 2000 were no longer in operation in 2002. In at least one of these instances, gradual attrition prompted the remaining users to decide *en masse* to dismantle the network so that the cable could be salvaged and put to use in building a new line with a different name and a different geographical extension. Indeed, during the time that those four lines died out, three new lines were born in the same immediate vicinity, gathering together the former users and others in new constellations.

When one takes into consideration the tendency of interkom lines to reproduce and divide, the picture of network evolution becomes far more complex than it appeared at first glance. While one overall trend in the evolution of interkom has thus been toward the development of networks with greater geographic spread and greater densities, processes of division, reproduction, and attrition have mitigated this trend. Rather than the picture of an ever-expanding and increasingly unified network, we are left with a picture of lines growing, connecting to one another, and creating new unities, all the while reproducing, dividing in new ways, and losing pieces here and there.

All of this makes the interkom network seem a lot like segmentary lineage structures. It is as if interkom users have engineered what amounts to a kinship structure—one that did not exist in western Java—within the urban and suburban milieu. There are, however, some crucial differences between interkom lines and lineages. The first difference is that the line that links people is not the link of bloodlines but actual physical cables. So there is no sense in which one's relations to others on the line is determined by birth. Membership in a line is strictly voluntary and can be quite short-lived. The second difference is that these are *lines* not *lineages*. Although some lines may be identified as having sibling-like relations to other lines, people do not see them as being derived from some common ancestor. This means that the lines are seen as extending in space rather than in time. It also means that the lines are fundamentally non-centered, for there are no ancestors with respect to whom measurements of social distance, and thus hierarchy, could be established. Finally, the segmentary lines that constitute interkom are not exclusive. One is not *either* a member of one line *or* the member of another line: one can be a member of multiple lines (this is done by having several lines enter into one's house and by connecting one's interkom set up to the line one wishes to talk on). Thus, the emphasis is on ever-expanding connections rather than on unity, exclusivity, and boundaries. In short, we could say, following Gilles Deleuze and Felix Guatarri, that the structure of interkom differs from that of segmentary lineages in that it is rhizomatic rather than arborescent.[3]

---

[3] Gilles Deleuze and Felix Guatarri. "Introduction: Rhizome," *A Thousand Plateaus: Capitalism and Schizophrenia* (Minneapolis: University of Minnesota Press, 1991), pp. 3-25.

THE LOCALITY OF INTERKOM

While tracing structural transformations in interkom over time sheds light on how the network developed and the types of material constraints that shaped that development, it says little about how interkom relates to other social institutions or what it represents to its users. For a more contextual perspective, it is necessary to look at interkom not as a rhizome that is suspended above other institutions, but one that grows into and out of these institutions in particular ways.

As noted above, early interkom lines emerged in the context of the household and were used to link together different buildings within a residential compound or to link together houses in close proximity. Networks started in a piecemeal fashion as extensions of particular *kampung*-level face-to-face discourse networks. Ibu Karmini, a thirty-four-year-old mother, for example, emphasized that interkom provided a way for her to visit relatives without having to leave the house. So when someone died while she was busy at home, she could pass on the news to her parents via interkom. For her, the early interkom was identified with the types of communicative practices associated with familial ties. For others, early interkom lines represented something a little different: the possibility of a culture of chat that replaced that of *nongkrong*, or hanging out. Rather than hanging out in front of the local *warung*, which was often associated with such costly habits as drinking and gambling, one could hang out and chat on interkom.

Growing out of these *kampung*-level interactions, interkom quickly became a fad. In these early years, some *kampungs* might have as many as twenty or thirty houses on a line (compared to three or four from any given *kampung* nowadays). In many places, interkom was popular enough that communities experimented with turning it into a semi-official communications medium. They did this first at the RT level, then at the RW level, and some communities even tried to wire together whole *kecamatan* (subdistricts). To a certain extent, these initiatives were a function of the times. The early to mid-1980s was a period when the Indonesian government was placing a great deal of emphasis on the importance of neighborhood security.[4] It encouraged RT and RW heads to improve their guardhouses and to work with the local police to organize their neighborhood watches and report the presence of visitors. The government wanted every community to have a guard house with a *kentongan*—a wooden bell that could be struck in particular rhythms to indicate the presence of a threat: one sound for a fire, another for a thief, another for a death.

For a time, users started to imagine interkom as a network that would fulfill the same function as the *kentongan*, but in a high-tech way. A military man, Rahmat, remembered it like this:

> The reason for early [interkom lines] was the need for communication. Communication between the heads of the RW: between RW 1, 2, and 3. At that time security was difficult because telephones were still rare. So we used interkom. So if there was a visitor who wanted to directly report to the RW,

---

[4] Joshua Barker, "State of Fear: Controlling the Criminal Contagion in Suharto's New Order." in *Violence and the State in Suharto's Indonesia*, ed. Benedict R. O'G. Anderson (Ithaca: Southeast Asia Program, 2001), pp. 20-53.

we would let the RW know that if the visitor showed up, there was no need for the signature of the head of the RT.[5]

In north Bandung, Rahmat was active in getting people to build two early lines, one called Jalur Kecamatan (Subdistrict Line), the other Jalur Kantibmas (Security and Order of Society Line). The former line was built in collaboration with the subdistrict office and was used for reporting any gatherings of *kampung* youth, such as for sports meets or concerts. The latter line was linked directly into the local military command (Koramil) and police precinct. As Rahmat explained:

> We connected it to Koramil, so we could pass on information, about crime, delinquent youths, drunkenness, and so on. Yes, cooperation with Koramil back then was very useful. If anyone did something wrong it would be visible.[6]

In the case of Jalur Kantibmas, it was no longer just the face-to-face *kampung* ties associated with families, neighbors, and *nongkrong* communities that were being wired together, but the nested hierarchical ties of local government and local military authority. At least for a brief time, interkom became an additional means for these structures to insinuate themselves deeper into neighborhood life.

In the long run, the experiment with making interkom a tool of the surveillance state was just that: an experiment. Both Jalur Kecamatan and Jalur Kantibmas eventually disappeared, and no similar lines have emerged to replace them. Rather than the state, it was *kampung* culture that ultimately left its imprint on the evolving network. Nowadays, this imprint can be seen in how the network is maintained, in the types of social activities that interkom users engage in, and in the terms in which users imagine the interkom community as it extends further afield, leaving the *kampung*, as such, behind. I will discuss each of these aspects in turn.

The vast majority of interkom lines are run on a very informal basis. An initial group of people, usually not very large, will agree to establish a line and will buy the cable necessary to link together their houses. Once established, the line grows incrementally, from house to house, as others hear about it and want to join up. Each person who joins has to provide the cable necessary to reach the nearest point in the line from his or her particular location. Thus, the line is built out of pieces of cable that are supplied individually or in small groups. Maintenance, however, is a more collective concern, because if the line gets disconnected somewhere in the middle—something that happens quite frequently—it means that large numbers of people will not be able to communicate.

Line maintenance is handled by a number of people called *teknisi* or technicians, who can be called upon when there is a problem. Each *kampung* will have one or two people who act as *teknisi*, usually maintaining more than one line in the area. They do this on a volunteer basis, but may receive some coffee or cigarettes as informal payments from those benefiting from their services.

Occasionally, interkom lines can be organized quite formally. One that I studied had an elected head, a membership fee, rules of use, and small monthly contributions for line maintenance. In essence, it functioned with the same political

---

[5] Personal Interview, Rahmat, October 2000.

[6] Personal Interview, Rahmat, October 2000.

structure as a neighborhood association. The advantage of this system, according to its users, was that any problems with the line were usually fixed within a few hours, as the head supplied any necessary cable and had technicians on call. Furthermore, the quality of sound was good because the cable used throughout the whole line was telephone cable purchased with the money from the membership fees.

Whether organized formally or informally, interkom lines all involve activities and events that resemble the types of things a *kampung* might organize. There are *arisan* (gatherings where women make contributions to a common kitty and take turns winning it) for the women of a particular line, feasts where people gather to eat, and special events like musical festivals and group outings to the beach or to nearby tourist destinations. These events are paid for by those who choose to participate and are often organized to celebrate the anniversary of the formation of the line (HUT, Hari Ulang Tahun, anniversary celebrations). Not all members of a line turn out for these events, but a good number do.

Even as networks extend well beyond the *kampung* sphere, the idiom in which the users imagine the new community continues to be in terms of kinship and *kampung*-like relations.[7] As Dede, a man in his forties, put it:

> Besides communication, [interkom] is for harmonization. Looking for kinship [*persaudaraan*], bringing friends closer together. As we look for kinship, people who we didn't know become people we know. Kinship, really, that is the goal. So every month we gather somewhere to celebrate our friendship. And we have an *arisan*. Yes, basically it is to strengthen the lines of kinship.[8]

Strengthening the lines of kin can be understood in both a metaphorical and a literal sense. People I interviewed often told me that interkom in their area had grown because many residents wished to communicate with relatives who lived some distance away. At the same time, however, people who met on interkom would frequently enter into the types of exchange relations associated with kinship. Whether understood in "literal" or "metaphorical" terms, the important thing was that interkom added to one's circle of relations. Halimah, a thirty-six-year-old grandmother, described types of relations she had on interkom this way:

> It wouldn't be possible to have [interkom] and be enemies ... not possible! Cause you are only friends when you have interkom. That the women on it now have an *arisan*, it's not for nothing. Like when we're finished cooking, we can chat ... Rather than being bored or daydreaming while cleaning, better to chat on the line.[9]

Even though interkom is comprehended within the familiar idiom of kinship and *kampung* relations, it is not reducible to these relations. In fact, what is most

---

[7] In western Java, *kampung* sociality is closely associated with kinship. Most *kampung*s are remembered as having been founded by one family. Although some descendants may have taken up residence elsewhere, and newcomers may numerically predominate, the offspring of the founding family tend to constitute the core of *kampung* social life.

[8] Personal Interview, Dede, November 2000.

[9] Personal Interview, Halimah, December 2000.

fascinating about interkom is the way it allows for the creation of a different kind of world that stands in opposition to everyday life. This opposition is characterized by a sharp distinction between interkom society and face-to-face society. This distinction, borrowed from the older cultures of amateur radio and CB radio, draws a line between the "on-air" (*di udara*) world (sometimes "on-line" or *di jalur*) and "on-land" (*di darat*) world.

Everyone who uses interkom has both an on-land name (*nama darat*) and an on-air name (*nama udara*). On-air names, which may be chosen for oneself or assigned by others, are not all of a given type. Some are Sundanese words with a particular meaning. Some examples of this type were: Seagull, Mr. Open Hand, and Grandpa Swinging Back and Forth. Other names included The Japanese, Scooby-Doo, and Delta, as well as several ordinary Sundanese names. Some people have different on-air names for different lines, while others keep the same name regardless of which line they are on. People who are frequently on-air together eventually learn each other's on-land names. But when invitations are sent out for interkom-related social events, like picnics and anniversary celebrations, they are addressed using people's on-air names. Even in person, people refer to each other by these names.

These on-air names provide a space for people to construct a sense of self that is different from the one they have on-land. Rather than being based on one's familial ties, the place one lives, or one's looks, this sense of self is established largely on the basis of one's discursive style and sound on-air. The types of adjectives people use to describe the voices they like are gentle (*lembut*), sweet and melodious (*merdu*), exquisite (*bagus*), attractive (*menarik*), and enjoyable to the ears (*enak didengar*). People are always experimenting with their voice modulation by speaking in different tones and trying different bass, treble, and reverb settings. Since they cannot hear the output of their own speech, as it sounds on-air, they rely on others to help them find the settings that generate the most attractive sound.

This fascination with the modulated voice as a way to captivate listeners is not restricted to the world of interkom. Local radio personalities achieve stardom on the basis of a particular sound, a fact interkom users are well aware of. Indeed, one user I talked to said that he originally got into interkom because he did not have the background necessary to get a job in radio. This similarity to radio is evident in the term used for someone who likes to act as host on a given interkom network: *penyiar lokalan* (interkom broadcaster). In this sense, interkom represents a kind of amateur version of the radio big leagues, much as home karaoke systems represent an amateur version of singing stardom. Both provide a means to partake in, and to appropriate, the power of modulated voice and to generate a local version of stardom.

The persona one develops on-air does not necessarily carry into interactions on-land. As Ani, an unemployed twenty-six-year-old who lives with her parents, pointed out:

> It's true that when we chat on the line we hear their voice. The voice is great so we figure the person is also great. But then it turns out they are just ordinary .... So voices and people, sometimes they are the same and sometimes they're different.[10]

---

[10] Personal Interview, Ani, December 2000.

According to Iwan, a twenty-eight-year-old civil servant who moonlights at a VCD (Video CD) rental stall in the evenings, it is not just that a person's voice guarantees nothing about his or her other characteristics, but that the sound of a voice on interkom can be quite different from its ordinary sound.

> On air people's vocals are more beautiful because of the influence of modulating technologies. When you meet they aren't that beautiful. Interkom, after all, uses turn control, so you can adjust the bass and treble. You can even give it reverb.[11]

The contrast between people's on-air voice personae and their on-land personae provides the grounds for many humorous stories and some disappointments. A typical story is that of someone who was attracted to the power of an interkom voice and then learned upon meeting the person that he was just a parking attendant. Indeed, within interkom lingo there is actually a word, *kiobok*, which refers to someone who sounds beautiful on air but turns out to be unattractive in person.

The difference between the on-air and on-land worlds is not only marked by a distinction between identities and traits on- and off-air, but also by a difference in discursive style. Everyone I talked to described interkom discourse as being more free (*lebih bebas*) and less subject to the types of constraints that are usually placed on face-to-face interactions. Didin, the forty-two-year-old noodle vendor, described the difference as follows:

> It's different. On the line we joke and chat [but] on land if you meet the person you're rather embarrassed [*malu*]. On the line it is more free, on land it's a little shy if you don't know them that well. After all, on land they have a husband.[12]

This freedom from shyness or shame does not just mean that men and women can interact in ways that would be frowned upon in face-to-face meetings, it also means that they experience a greater freedom from hierarchical discursive patterns. People can get away with teasing and jokes on interkom that would otherwise be considered disrespectful and impolite. Bahrudin, a fifty-three-year-old construction worker, described his own feelings on this:

> On land there are limits. Even when someone is younger than me, there is no way I can say something unpleasant to them on land. It just isn't ethical. But on line I can be burned [by other people] ... they just go on and on. On land it couldn't be that way.[13]

Such freedom, however, does not mean that such considerations are entirely absent. A twenty-nine-year-old man named Tulus said that interkom discourse still has its rules.

---

[11] Personal Interview, Iwan, December 2000.
[12] Personal Interview, Didin, October 2000.
[13] Personal Interview, Bahrudin, December 2000.

> It's the language. The language is different. On-air maybe it is free but there are still rules. You can't say just anything you want to. If you know you're connecting to someone older you talk well, different.[14]

If names, personae, and speech styles found on-air are somewhat discontinuous with those to be found on-land, the discontinuity is driven home by interkom's most popular speech genre, namely, *pojok-memojok* (cornering). Cornering is when two people, usually of the opposite sex, engage in a conversation that involves getting to know each other, flirtation, and intimate banter. It is something quite close to phone sex, but in cornering sexual references are never made explicit, but remain implicit in metaphor, allusion, and innuendo. As a speech genre, cornering is not restricted to interkom; it also exists on CB radio, amateur radio, and the Internet.

On interkom, cornering involves a peculiar mix of intimacy and display. By definition it is a discursive interaction that involves only two people. But as one interkom user pointed out, although only two people are talking, the number listening may be as many as forty. In this sense, cornering is like a dance. Out of a crowd of people, two take the floor and engage in a kind of intimate performance. Then, after a time, they fade back into the darkness of the crowd and another pair emerges to give their performance. On interkom lines in Bandung, this performance is going on almost non-stop day and night.

What is interesting about cornering is that, over the long term, it means most people on a given line come to be paired with a specific partner, referred to either as a *pojokan* (a person with whom one corners) or a *pasangan* (partner). That is, through cornering people establish more or less long-term on-air couples. These couple relationships, along with the friendships and kinship ties that link interkom users, help give a definite but flexible structure to the interkom community. The structure is manifest not in any formal tie, but in ties of loyalty. Edi, a forty-five-year-old laborer in a furniture factory, described such loyalty as follows:

> On some lines there are people who really are loyal. Sometimes when their chatting partner hasn't turned up . . . sometimes they just wait for hours. Sometimes if one wants to shift over to another line one's partner won't allow it.[15]

The twenty-six-year-old Ani also drew attention to the fact that partners can be quite possessive:

> It's like this: on the interkom line each person has a partner. If I talk with someone else it's wrong and people will get angry at me. That's why everyone on the line has a partner, so there are a lot of them.[16]

To appreciate the significance of cornering and coupling on interkom, it is necessary to realize that many of the people involved are—on-land at

---

[14] Personal Interview, Tulus, October 2000.

[15] Personal Interview, Edi, December 2000.

[16] Personal Interview, Ani, December 2000.

least—married and have children. In fact, many of the interviews in which people described the practice of cornering were conducted with both husband and wife present. Yet it appeared not to be a practice that caused any major domestic conflicts. This despite the fact that within the communities where interkom is popular, any hint of on-land infidelity is treated very seriously. This radical divergence is illustrated by the case of a family I know quite well. The husband spent every night until the wee hours cornering on interkom, a situation that provoked only occasional complaints from his wife. But on the one occasion that his wife caught him and a male friend chatting with a single mother—who had nothing to do with interkom—on an empty plot of land next to their house, the wife was completely beside herself, threatening that she would either commit suicide or murder the other woman. While eventually things were sorted out peacefully, the reconciliation took a couple of weeks and ended up involving several families in the *kampung*.

When I asked people about why interkom does not cause such conflicts, the standard response was: because on interkom there are so many people listening. Thus, people expect that nothing too untoward will happen. Furthermore, they explained, everyone knows that interkom is "only for entertainment." As long as it is kept that way, it does not cause any problems. But more than a few people provided a word of caution. Yayah, a thirty-four-year-old housemother, put it most clearly:

> No, [the pairing] is only on interkom. Never bring it down to land ... that would be destruction. No, we all understand this ... If someone jokes with someone else's wife or with someone's husband that's no problem, that's only on line. If that took place on land: bankruptcy.[17]

As long as on-air society can be kept separate from on-land society, things will be just fine. Only if they get mixed-up could things fall apart.[18]

DISCOURSE NETWORKS AND IMAGINED COMMUNITIES

In sum, interkom has a rather peculiar status in relation to older forms of on-land communities. On the one hand, it grows out of these communities and has been heavily shaped by them. In this respect we could say that interkom is "wired" by *kampung* and kin relations. This wiring gives interkom an aura of familiarity, rather than an aura of an alien technology. But at the same time, interkom itself wires these relations and transforms them by extending them outward beyond their usual geographic and social confines. This extension enables the creation of a new field of discursive interactions that are not reducible to face-to-face interactions. The differences between the two are partly due to the various materialities of communication: the differences between seeing people when they speak and only hearing their voices, the differences between modulated electric speech and ordinary speech, the possibility of anonymity, and so forth. The differences are also due to conventions that mark out a special discursive space for interkom, where

---

[17] Personal Interview, Yayah, October 2000.
[18] The situation for unmarried people is more complex, since many people actually use interkom to find spouses.

talk is freer from social constraints and where people can practice the art of cornering and others can listen with envy to the melodious tones of a good performer.

As the dominant speech genre of interkom, cornering helps to pattern interkom social relations into male and female pairs. This flexible structure of pairs departs from other forms of sociality on interkom, which tend to be understood as literal or metaphorical extensions of kin relations into this new domain. In contrast to the latter types of relations, these pairs introduce a form of sociality that could conceivably disrupt the presumed order of face-to-face, on-land family and *kampung* life. Perhaps to guard against this eventuality, interkom users choose to treat interkom as a world unto itself, an on-air world that ought not have any material effect on the on-land world of real families and friendships, except when it acts to strengthen them. The division into on-air and on-land is thus somewhat reminiscent of American conventions that distinguish between television and reality, or reality and virtual reality. But interkom is distinctive because conceptions of self and community—not conceptions of reality—are at stake. Rather than challenge existing conceptions of self and local community, interkom users simply multiply themselves and their communities, using humor and sanctions to negotiate the potential conflicts such multiplication engenders.

One could contrast the sense of community on interkom to the "imagined community" of the nation. That idea of community transcends locality and introduces a type of identity that is fundamentally different from the identities engaged in face-to-face communities, and fundamentally new. In print media and in the *lingua franca* of Melayu, people encountered languages, news events, and personages in a manner that effectively uprooted them from their local contexts and installed them in a more transcendent symbolic and geo-political frame. In identifying themselves with this frame, people came to see themselves as part of a broader community of Indonesians and moderns. In contrast to this, interkom represents a community that is not quite imagined, but also not quite face-to-face. Perhaps we could call it "voice-to-voice" instead of face-to-face. It allows people to move beyond the familiar and safe settings of the household and the *kampung*, but does so in a manner that ensures that the routes back to these local worlds remain open and traversable. The foray into what could have been an unfamiliar world thus becomes an intriguing but relatively unthreatening excursion. It allows one to feel the pleasures and comfort of coming home without actually having left.

This point was impressed upon me by one of the people we interviewed, Dede, a forty-five-year-old who worked in a low-level position in the government body responsible for elections. In relation to interkom, Dede was a colorful figure with a great deal of bravado. When asked about which lines he was connected to, he exclaimed that they were many because the citizens—*warga*—of interkom actively extended their lines to him, since all of them wanted him to join their networks. This, he claimed, was because of his beautiful voice, which had the power to attract the interest of people everywhere. When he was on-air, everyone else would stand by in silence so they could listen. In short, Dede presented himself as the interkom version of a "man of prowess,"[19] someone whose voice had the gravitational pull to attract both listeners and interkom lines. But what was most

---

[19] Oliver W. Wolters, *History, Region, and Culture in Southeast Asian Perspectives*, rev. ed. (Ithaca: Southeast Asia Program, 1999).

interesting about Dede was his on-air names. One of these names spoke to his prowess: Suara Dewa or Voice of Divinity. But his other name was revealing of something else: it was Pak Waas. Waas is a Sundanese word that has a very particular meaning. In his dictionary Jonathan Rigg describes it like this: "Waas" is what is

> . . . said when a pleasurable feeling is caused by seeing someone or something which reminds us of what we ourselves possess, but which, for the moment, is out of our reach. [It is] a happy or pleasing remembrance or emotion regarding something which we do not at the moment see.[20]

"Waas" then is the type of feeling and the type of imagination that I would associate with interkom culture. What is generated as one passes outside of the local is not a fascination with the new and a nostalgic longing for irrecoverable origins, but a pleasurable longing for something that has been transcended but remains within reach. In this respect, the culture of interkom differs from those cultures—like ethnic and national cultures—that have been subjected to control by the state and affected by the dialectics of power. It could have been otherwise. Had the New Order state recognized the usefulness of interkom for initiatives like Jalur Kantibmas, those could have become standardized across the nation and then Indonesia's security state would have been truly wired. But it did not, and interkom users themselves were not terribly interested in that particular path of development. What they were looking for was a form of communication that was relatively free from hierarchy and was "just for fun." Anytime it stopped being fun, all a "breaker" had to do was to pull out his or her cable and disconnect.

---

[20] Jonathan Rigg, *Dictionary of the Sunda Language of Java* (Batavia: Lage, 1862), pp. 524-25. The contemporary usage of waas is not always pleasurable. It can refer, for example, to the feeling one gets when, while looking down from a cliff, one suddenly imagines falling (but does not actually fall).

CONTRIBUTORS

Patricio N. Abinales is associate professor at the Center for Southeast Asian Studies, Kyoto University. He is author of *Making Mindanao: Cotabato and Davao in the Formation of the Philippine Nation-State*.

Mary P. Callahan is an assistant professor in the Jackson School of International Studies at the University of Washington. She is the author of *Making Enemies: War and State-building in Burma* (forthcoming, 2003).

John Pemberton lived in Central Java, off and on, during the years 1971-1984 and studied, most happily, at Cornell University during 1978-1982 and 1985-1989. He now teaches in the Department of Anthropology at Columbia University.

Danilyn Rutherford is Assistant Professor of Anthropology at the University of Chicago and author of *Raiding the Land of the Foreigners: The Limits of the Nation on an Indonesian Frontier*.

Eva-Lotta E. Hedman is a Senior Research Fellow at Queen Elizabeth House, Oxford University. She has formerly held appointments as Millennium Research Fellow at the School of Oriental and African Studies, University of London, and Lecturer in the School of Politics, University of Nottingham.

Audrey R. Kahin is an editor and a historian. She is the author of *Rebellion to Integration: West Sumatra and the Indonesian Polity*.

Tsuyoshi Kato is Professor of Comparative Sociology in the Graduate School of Asian and African Area Studies at Kyoto University, Japan.

Francis Loh Kok Wah is Professor of Politics at Universiti Sains Malaysia, Penang, and secretary of Aliran, a Malaysian NGO devoted to social reform and the defense of human rights.

Charnvit Kasetsiri teaches History and Southeast Asian Studies at Thammasat University, Bangkok, Thailand. In 1963, he received a B.A. in Diplomacy from Thammasat and, in 1972, a Ph.D. in Southeast Asian History from Cornell University. He became Dean of Liberal Arts between 1991-94 and President of his alma mater 1994-95.

Kasian Tejapira teaches political science at Thammasat University in Bangkok, Thailand. He studied at the Department of Government, Cornell University, under Ben Anderson's supervision from 1985 to 1992.

Contributors

Douglas Kammen is a visiting professor at the National University of East Timor. He has taught at the University of Canterbury (NZ) and Hasanuddin University (Makassar).

Takashi Shiraishi serves as professor of Southeast Asian Studies at the Center for Southeast Asian Studies, Kyoto University.

Thak Chaloemtiarana is one of the first graduate students whose committee Ben Anderson chaired. Thak taught political science at Thammasat University until 1981 before returning to Cornell University. Currently, he is a faculty member in the Department of Asian Studies and director of the Southeast Asia Program.

Caroline S. Hau is an associate professor at the Center for Southeast Asian Studies at Kyoto University, Japan. She is the author of *Necessary Fictions: Philippine Literature and the Nation, 1946-1980* and editor of *Intsik: An Anthology of Chinese Filipino Writing*.

Joshua Barker is Assistant Professor in Anthropology at the University of Toronto He has published numerous articles on crime, policing, and technology in Indonesia.

James Siegel is Professor of Anthropology and Asian Studies. He was a colleague of Ben Anderson from the time the latter joined the Cornell faculty.

Vicente L. Rafael is Professor of History at the University of Washington. He is the author of *Contracting Colonialism: Translation and Christian Conversion in Tagalog Society Under Early Spanish Rule*, and *White Love and Other Events in Filipino History*.

John T. Sidel is a Reader in Southeast Asian Politics at the School of Oriental and African Studies, University of London.

Peter Zinoman is Associate Professor of History and Southeast Asian Studies at the University of California, Berkeley. He is the author of *The Colonial Bastille: A History of Imprisonment in Vietnam, 1862-1940* (University of California Press, 2001) and the editor and co-translator of *Dumb Luck: A Novel by Vu Trong Phung* (University of Michigan, 2002).

SOUTHEAST ASIA PROGRAM PUBLICATIONS
Cornell University

Studies on Southeast Asia

Number 35 — *Nationalism and Revolution in Indonesia*, George McTurnan Kahin, intro. Benedict R. O'G. Anderson (reprinted from 1952 edition, Cornell University Press, with permission). 2003. 530 pp. ISBN 0-87727-734-6.

Number 34 — *Golddiggers, Farmers, and Traders in the "Chinese Districts" of West Kalimantan, Indonesia*, Mary Somers Heidhues. 2003. 316 pp. ISBN 0-87727-733-8

Number 33 — *Opusculum de Sectis apud Sinenses et Tunkinenses (A Small Treatise on the Sects among the Chinese and Tonkinese): A Study of Religion in China and North Vietnam in the Eighteenth Century*, Father Adriano de St. Thecla, trans. Olga Dror, with Mariya Berezovska. 2002. 363 pp. ISBN 0-87727-732-X.

Number 32 — *Fear and Sanctuary: Burmese Refugees in Thailand*, Hazel J. Lang. 2002. 204 pp. ISBN 0-87727-731-1.

Number 31 — *Modern Dreams: An Inquiry into Power, Cultural Production, and the Cityscape in Contemporary Urban Penang, Malaysia*, Beng-Lan Goh. 2002. 225 pp. ISBN 0-87727-730-3.

Number 30 — *Violence and the State in Suharto's Indonesia*, ed. Benedict R. O'G. Anderson. 2001. Second printing, 2002. 247 pp. ISBN 0-87727-729-X.

Number 29 — *Studies in Southeast Asian Art: Essays in Honor of Stanley J. O'Connor*, ed. Nora A. Taylor. 2000. 243 pp. Illustrations. ISBN 0-87727-728-1.

Number 28 — *The Hadrami Awakening: Community and Identity in the Netherlands East Indies, 1900-1942*, Natalie Mobini-Kesheh. 1999. 174 pp. ISBN 0-87727-727-3.

Number 27 — *Tales from Djakarta: Caricatures of Circumstances and their Human Beings*, Pramoedya Ananta Toer. 1999. 145 pp. ISBN 0-87727-726-5.

Number 26 — *History, Culture, and Region in Southeast Asian Perspectives*, rev. ed., O. W. Wolters. 1999. 275 pp. ISBN 0-87727-725-7.

Number 25 — *Figures of Criminality in Indonesia, the Philippines, and Colonial Vietnam*, ed. Vicente L. Rafael. 1999. 259 pp. ISBN 0-87727-724-9.

Number 24 — *Paths to Conflagration: Fifty Years of Diplomacy and Warfare in Laos, Thailand, and Vietnam, 1778-1828*, Mayoury Ngaosyvathn and Pheuiphanh Ngaosyvathn. 1998. 268 pp. ISBN 0-87727-723-0.

Number 23 — *Nguyễn Cochinchina: Southern Vietnam in the Seventeenth and Eighteenth Centuries*, Li Tana. 1998. Second printing, 2002. 194 pp. ISBN 0-87727-722-2.

Number 22 — *Young Heroes: The Indonesian Family in Politics*, Saya S. Shiraishi. 1997. 183 pp. ISBN 0-87727-721-4.

Number 21 — *Interpreting Development: Capitalism, Democracy, and the Middle Class in Thailand*, John Girling. 1996. 95 pp. ISBN 0-87727-720-6.

Number 20 — *Making Indonesia*, ed. Daniel S. Lev, Ruth McVey. 1996. 201 pp. ISBN 0-87727-719-2.

Number 19 — *Essays into Vietnamese Pasts*, ed. K. W. Taylor, John K. Whitmore. 1995. 288 pp. ISBN 0-87727-718-4.

Number 18 *In the Land of Lady White Blood: Southern Thailand and the Meaning of History*, Lorraine M. Gesick. 1995. 106 pp. ISBN 0-87727-717-6.

Number 17 *The Vernacular Press and the Emergence of Modern Indonesian Consciousness*, Ahmat Adam. 1995. 220 pp. ISBN 0-87727-716-8.

Number 16 *The Nan Chronicle*, trans., ed. David K. Wyatt. 1994. 158 pp. ISBN 0-87727-715-X.

Number 15 *Selective Judicial Competence: The Cirebon-Priangan Legal Administration, 1680–1792*, Mason C. Hoadley. 1994. 185 pp. ISBN 0-87727-714-1.

Number 14 *Sjahrir: Politics and Exile in Indonesia*, Rudolf Mrázek. 1994. 536 pp. ISBN 0-87727-713-3.

Number 13 *Fair Land Sarawak: Some Recollections of an Expatriate Officer*, Alastair Morrison. 1993. 196 pp. ISBN 0-87727-712-5.

Number 12 *Fields from the Sea: Chinese Junk Trade with Siam during the Late Eighteenth and Early Nineteenth Centuries*, Jennifer Cushman. 1993. 206 pp. ISBN 0-87727-711-7.

Number 11 *Money, Markets, and Trade in Early Southeast Asia: The Development of Indigenous Monetary Systems to AD 1400*, Robert S. Wicks. 1992. 2nd printing 1996. 354 pp., 78 tables, illus., maps. ISBN 0-87727-710-9.

Number 10 *Tai Ahoms and the Stars: Three Ritual Texts to Ward Off Danger*, trans., ed. B. J. Terwiel, Ranoo Wichasin. 1992. 170 pp. ISBN 0-87727-709-5.

Number 9 *Southeast Asian Capitalists*, ed. Ruth McVey. 1992. 2nd printing 1993. 220 pp. ISBN 0-87727-708-7.

Number 8 *The Politics of Colonial Exploitation: Java, the Dutch, and the Cultivation System*, Cornelis Fasseur, ed. R. E. Elson, trans. R. E. Elson, Ary Kraal. 1992. 2nd printing 1994. 266 pp. ISBN 0-87727-707-9.

Number 7 *A Malay Frontier: Unity and Duality in a Sumatran Kingdom*, Jane Drakard. 1990. 215 pp. ISBN 0-87727-706-0.

Number 6 *Trends in Khmer Art*, Jean Boisselier, ed. Natasha Eilenberg, trans. Natasha Eilenberg, Melvin Elliott. 1989. 124 pp., 24 plates. ISBN 0-87727-705-2.

Number 5 *Southeast Asian Ephemeris: Solar and Planetary Positions, A.D. 638–2000*, J. C. Eade. 1989. 175 pp. ISBN 0-87727-704-4.

Number 3 *Thai Radical Discourse: The Real Face of Thai Feudalism Today*, Craig J. Reynolds. 1987. 2nd printing 1994. 186 pp. ISBN 0-87727-702-8.

Number 1 *The Symbolism of the Stupa*, Adrian Snodgrass. 1985. Revised with index, 1988. 3rd printing 1998. 469 pp. ISBN 0-87727-700-1.

SEAP Series

Number 19 *Gender, Household, State: Đổi Mới in Việt Nam*, ed. Jayne Werner and Danièle Bélanger. 2002. 151 pp. ISBN 0-87727-137-2.

Number 18 *Culture and Power in Traditional Siamese Government*, Neil A. Englehart. 2001. 130 pp. ISBN 0-87727-135-6.

Number 17 *Gangsters, Democracy, and the State*, ed. Carl A. Trocki. 1998. Second printing, 2002. 94 pp. ISBN 0-87727-134-8.

Number 16	*Cutting across the Lands: An Annotated Bibliography on Natural Resource Management and Community Development in Indonesia, the Philippines, and Malaysia*, ed. Eveline Ferretti. 1997. 329 pp. ISBN 0-87727-133-X.
Number 15	*The Revolution Falters: The Left in Philippine Politics after 1986*, ed. Patricio N. Abinales. 1996. Second printing, 2002. 182 pp. ISBN 0-87727-132-1.
Number 14	*Being Kammu: My Village, My Life*, Damrong Tayanin. 1994. 138 pp., 22 tables, illus., maps. ISBN 0-87727-130-5.
Number 13	*The American War in Vietnam*, ed. Jayne Werner, David Hunt. 1993. 132 pp. ISBN 0-87727-131-3.
Number 12	*The Political Legacy of Aung San*, ed. Josef Silverstein. Revised edition 1993. 169 pp. ISBN 0-87727-128-3.
Number 10	*Studies on Vietnamese Language and Literature: A Preliminary Bibliography*, Nguyen Dinh Tham. 1992. 227 pp. ISBN 0-87727-127-5.
Number 9	*A Secret Past*, Dokmaisot, trans. Ted Strehlow. 1992. 2nd printing 1997. 72 pp. ISBN 0-87727-126-7.
Number 8	*From PKI to the Comintern, 1924–1941: The Apprenticeship of the Malayan Communist Party*, Cheah Boon Kheng. 1992. 147 pp. ISBN 0-87727-125-9.
Number 7	*Intellectual Property and US Relations with Indonesia, Malaysia, Singapore, and Thailand*, Elisabeth Uphoff. 1991. 67 pp. ISBN 0-87727-124-0.
Number 6	*The Rise and Fall of the Communist Party of Burma (CPB)*, Bertil Lintner. 1990. 124 pp. 26 illus., 14 maps. ISBN 0-87727-123-2.
Number 5	*Japanese Relations with Vietnam: 1951–1987*, Masaya Shiraishi. 1990. 174 pp. ISBN 0-87727-122-4.
Number 3	*Postwar Vietnam: Dilemmas in Socialist Development*, ed. Christine White, David Marr. 1988. 2nd printing 1993. 260 pp. ISBN 0-87727-120-8.
Number 2	*The Dobama Movement in Burma (1930–1938)*, Khin Yi. 1988. 160 pp. ISBN 0-87727-118-6.

Cornell Modern Indonesia Project Publications

Number 75	*A Tour of Duty: Changing Patterns of Military Politics in Indonesia in the 1990s*. Douglas Kammen and Siddharth Chandra. 1999. 99 pp. ISBN 0-87763-049-6.
Number 74	*The Roots of Acehnese Rebellion 1989–1992*, Tim Kell. 1995. 103 pp. ISBN 0-87763-040-2.
Number 73	*"White Book" on the 1992 General Election in Indonesia*, trans. Dwight King. 1994. 72 pp. ISBN 0-87763-039-9.
Number 72	*Popular Indonesian Literature of the Qur'an*, Howard M. Federspiel. 1994. 170 pp. ISBN 0-87763-038-0.
Number 71	*A Javanese Memoir of Sumatra, 1945–1946: Love and Hatred in the Liberation War*, Takao Fusayama. 1993. 150 pp. ISBN 0-87763-037-2.
Number 70	*East Kalimantan: The Decline of a Commercial Aristocracy*, Burhan Magenda. 1991. 120 pp. ISBN 0-87763-036-4.

Number 69   *The Road to Madiun: The Indonesian Communist Uprising of 1948,* Elizabeth Ann Swift. 1989. 120 pp. ISBN 0-87763-035-6.

Number 68   *Intellectuals and Nationalism in Indonesia: A Study of the Following Recruited by Sutan Sjahrir in Occupation Jakarta,* J. D. Legge. 1988. 159 pp. ISBN 0-87763-034-8.

Number 67   *Indonesia Free: A Biography of Mohammad Hatta,* Mavis Rose. 1987. 252 pp. ISBN 0-87763-033-X.

Number 66   *Prisoners at Kota Cane,* Leon Salim, trans. Audrey Kahin. 1986. 112 pp. ISBN 0-87763-032-1.

Number 65   *The Kenpeitai in Java and Sumatra,* trans. Barbara G. Shimer, Guy Hobbs, intro. Theodore Friend. 1986. 80 pp. ISBN 0-87763-031-3.

Number 64   *Suharto and His Generals: Indonesia's Military Politics, 1975–1983,* David Jenkins. 1984. 4th printing 1997. 300 pp. ISBN 0-87763-030-5.

Number 62   *Interpreting Indonesian Politics: Thirteen Contributions to the Debate, 1964–1981,* ed. Benedict Anderson, Audrey Kahin, intro. Daniel S. Lev. 1982. 3rd printing 1991. 172 pp. ISBN 0-87763-028-3.

Number 60   *The Minangkabau Response to Dutch Colonial Rule in the Nineteenth Century,* Elizabeth E. Graves. 1981. 157 pp. ISBN 0-87763-000-3.

Number 59   *Breaking the Chains of Oppression of the Indonesian People: Defense Statement at His Trial on Charges of Insulting the Head of State, Bandung, June 7–10, 1979,* Heri Akhmadi. 1981. 201 pp. ISBN 0-87763-001-1.

Number 57   *Permesta: Half a Rebellion,* Barbara S. Harvey. 1977. 174 pp. ISBN 0-87763-003-8.

Number 55   *Report from Banaran: The Story of the Experiences of a Soldier during the War of Independence,* Maj. Gen. T. B. Simatupang. 1972. 186 pp. ISBN 0-87763-005-4.

Number 52   *A Preliminary Analysis of the October 1 1965, Coup in Indonesia (Prepared in January 1966),* Benedict R. Anderson, Ruth T. McVey, assist. Frederick P. Bunnell. 1971. 3rd printing 1990. 174 pp. ISBN 0-87763-008-9.

Number 51   *The Putera Reports: Problems in Indonesian-Japanese War-Time Cooperation,* Mohammad Hatta, trans., intro. William H. Frederick. 1971. 114 pp. ISBN 0-87763-009-7.

Number 50   *Schools and Politics: The Kaum Muda Movement in West Sumatra (1927–1933),* Taufik Abdullah. 1971. 257 pp. ISBN 0-87763-010-0.

Number 49   *The Foundation of the Partai Muslimin Indonesia,* K. E. Ward. 1970. 75 pp. ISBN 0-87763-011-9.

Number 48   *Nationalism, Islam and Marxism,* Soekarno, intro. Ruth T. McVey. 1970. 2nd printing 1984. 62 pp. ISBN 0-87763-012-7.

Number 43   *State and Statecraft in Old Java: A Study of the Later Mataram Period, 16th to 19th Century,* Soemarsaid Moertono. Revised edition 1981. 180 pp. ISBN 0-87763-017-8.

Number 39   Preliminary Checklist of Indonesian Imprints (1945-1949), John M. Echols. 186 pp. ISBN 0-87763-025-9.

Number 37   *Mythology and the Tolerance of the Javanese,* Benedict R. O'G. Anderson. 2nd edition 1997. 104 pp., 65 illus. ISBN 0-87763-041-0.

Number 25 *The Communist Uprisings of 1926–1927 in Indonesia: Key Documents*, ed., intro. Harry J. Benda, Ruth T. McVey. 1960. 2nd printing 1969. 177 pp. ISBN 0-87763-024-0.

Number 7 *The Soviet View of the Indonesian Revolution,* Ruth T. McVey. 1957. 3rd printing 1969. 90 pp. ISBN 0-87763-018-6.

Number 6 *The Indonesian Elections of 1955,* Herbert Feith. 1957. 2nd printing 1971. 91 pp. ISBN 0-87763-020-8.

Translation Series

Volume 4 *Approaching Suharto's Indonesia from the Margins*, ed. Takashi Shiraishi. 1994. 153 pp. ISBN 0-87727-403-7.

Volume 3 *The Japanese in Colonial Southeast Asia,* ed. Saya Shiraishi, Takashi Shiraishi. 1993. 172 pp. ISBN 0-87727-402-9.

Volume 2 *Indochina in the 1940s and 1950s,* ed. Takashi Shiraishi, Motoo Furuta. 1992. 196 pp. ISBN 0-87727-401-0.

Volume 1 *Reading Southeast Asia,* ed. Takashi Shiraishi. 1990. 188 pp. ISBN 0-87727-400-2.

Language Texts

INDONESIAN

Beginning Indonesian through Self-Instruction, John U. Wolff, Dédé Oetomo, Daniel Fietkiewicz. 3rd revised edition 1992. Vol. 1. 115 pp. ISBN 0-87727-529-7. Vol. 2. 434 pp. ISBN 0-87727-530-0. Vol. 3. 473 pp. ISBN 0-87727-531-9.

Indonesian Readings, John U. Wolff. 1978. 4th printing 1992. 480 pp. ISBN 0-87727-517-3

Indonesian Conversations, John U. Wolff. 1978. 3rd printing 1991. 297 pp. ISBN 0-87727-516-5

Formal Indonesian, John U. Wolff. 2nd revised edition 1986. 446 pp. ISBN 0-87727-515-7

TAGALOG

Pilipino through Self-Instruction, John U. Wolff, Maria Theresa C. Centeno, Der-Hwa V. Rau. 1991. Vol. 1. 342 pp. ISBN 0-87727—525-4. Vol. 2. 378 pp. ISBN 0-87727-526-2. Vol 3. 431 pp. ISBN 0-87727-527-0. Vol. 4. 306 pp. ISBN 0-87727-528-9.

THAI

A. U. A. Language Center Thai Course, J. Marvin Brown. Originally published by the American University Alumni Association Language Center, 1974. Reissued by Cornell Southeast Asia Program, 1991, 1992. Book 1. 267 pp. ISBN 0-87727-506-8. Book 2. 288 pp. ISBN 0-87727-507-6. Book 3. 247 pp. ISBN 0-87727-508-4.

A. U. A. Language Center Thai Course, Reading and Writing Text (mostly reading), 1979. Reissued 1997. 164 pp. ISBN 0-87727-511-4.

A. U. A. Language Center Thai Course, Reading and Writing Workbook (mostly writing), 1979. Reissued 1997. 99 pp. ISBN 0-87727-512-2.

KHMER

Cambodian System of Writing and Beginning Reader, Franklin E. Huffman. Originally published by Yale University Press, 1970. Reissued by Cornell Southeast Asia Program, 4th printing 2002. 365 pp. ISBN 0-300-01314-0.

Modern Spoken Cambodian, Franklin E. Huffman, assist. Charan Promchan, Chhom-Rak Thong Lambert. Originally published by Yale University Press, 1970. Reissued by Cornell Southeast Asia Program, 3rd printing 1991. 451 pp. ISBN 0-300-01316-7.

Intermediate Cambodian Reader, ed. Franklin E. Huffman, assist. Im Proum. Originally published by Yale University Press, 1972. Reissued by Cornell Southeast Asia Program, 1988. 499 pp. ISBN 0-300-01552-6.

Cambodian Literary Reader and Glossary, Franklin E. Huffman, Im Proum. Originally published by Yale University Press, 1977. Reissued by Cornell Southeast Asia Program, 1988. 494 pp. ISBN 0-300-02069-4.

HMONG

White Hmong-English Dictionary, Ernest E. Heimbach. 1969. 8th printing, 2002. 523 pp. ISBN 0-87727-075-9.

VIETNAMESE

Intermediate Spoken Vietnamese, Franklin E. Huffman, Tran Trong Hai. 1980. 3rd printing 1994. ISBN 0-87727-500-9.

* * *

Southeast Asian Studies: Reorientations. Craig J. Reynolds and Ruth McVey. Frank H. Golay Lectures 2 & 3. 70 pp. ISBN 0-87727-301-4.

Javanese Literature in Surakarta Manuscripts, Nancy K. Florida. Vol. 1, *Introduction and Manuscripts of the Karaton Surakarta.* 1993. 410 pp. Frontispiece, illustrations. Hard cover, ISBN 0-87727-602-1, Paperback, ISBN 0-87727-603-X. Vol. 2, *Manuscripts of the Mangkunagaran Palace.* 2000. 576 pp. Frontispiece, illustrations. Paperback, ISBN 0-87727-604-8.

Sbek Thom: Khmer Shadow Theater. Pech Tum Kravel, trans. Sos Kem, ed. Thavro Phim, Sos Kem, Martin Hatch. 1996. 363 pp., 153 photographs. ISBN 0-87727-620-X.

In the Mirror: Literature and Politics in Siam in the American Era, ed. Benedict R. O'G. Anderson, trans. Benedict R. O'G. Anderson, Ruchira Mendiones. 1985. 2nd printing 1991. 303 pp. Paperback. ISBN 974-210-380-1.

To order, please contact:

Cornell University
SEAP Distribution Center
369 Pine Tree Rd.
Ithaca, NY 14850-2819 USA

Online: http://www.einaudi.cornell.edu/southeastasia/publications
Tel: 1-877-865-2432 (Toll free – U.S.)
Fax: (607) 255-7534

E-mail: SEAP-Pubs@cornell.edu
Orders must be prepaid by check or credit card (VISA, MasterCard, Discover).